Creative
Resources
for the
Early Childhood Classroom

Creative
Resources
for the
Early Childhood Classroom
Third Edition

Judy Herr
Yvonne Libby-Larson

Africa • Australia • Canada • Denmark • Japan • Mexico • New Zealand • Philippines
Puerto Rico • Singapore • Spain • United Kingdom • United States

NOTICE TO THE READER

Publisher does not warrant or guarantee any of the products described herein or perform any independent analysis in connection with any of the product information contained herein. Publisher does not assume, and expressly disclaims, any obligation to obtain and include information other than that provided to it by the manufacturer.

The reader is expressly warned to consider and adopt all safety precautions that might be indicated by the activities herein and to avoid all potential hazards. By following the instructions contained herein, the reader willingly assumes all risks in connection with such instructions.

The Publisher makes no representation or warranties of any kind, including but not limited to, the warranties of fitness for particular purpose or merchantability, nor are any such representations implied with respect to the material set forth herein, and the publisher takes no responsibility with respect to such material. The publisher shall not be liable for any special, consequential, or exemplary damages resulting, in whole or part, from the readers' use of, or reliance upon, this material.

COPYRIGHT © 2000
Delmar is a division of Thomson Learning.
The Thomson Learning logo is a registered trademark used herein under license.

Printed in the United States of America

1 2 3 4 5 6 7 8 9 10 XXX 05 04 03 02 01 00 99

Delmar Staff:
Business Unit Director: Susan Simpfenderfer
Executive Editor: Marlene McHugh Pratt
Acquisitions Editor: Erin O'Connor Traylor
Editorial Assistant: Alexis Ferraro
Executive Marketing Manager: Donna Lewis
Executive Production Manager: Wendy Troeger
Production Editor: Sandra Woods
Cover Design: Jay Purcell

For more information, contact:
Delmar, 3 Columbia Circle, PO Box 15015, Albany, NY 12212-0515;
or find us on the World Wide Web at http://www.delmar.com

Asia:
Thomson Learning
60 Albert Street, #15-01
Albert Complex
Singapore 189969
Tel: 65 336 6411
Fax: 65 336 7411

Japan:
Thomson Learning
Palaceside Building 5F
1-1-1 Hitotsubashi, Chiyoda-ku
Tokyo 100 0003 Japan
Tel: 813 5218 6544
Fax: 813 5218 6551

Australia/New Zealand:
Nelson/Thomson Learning
102 Dodds Street
South Melbourne, Victoria 3205
Australia
Tel: 61 39 685 4111
Fax: 61 39 685 4199

UK/Europe/Middle East:
Thomson Learning
Berkshire House
168-173 High Holborn
London
WC1V 7AA United Kingdom
Tel: 44 171 497 1422
Fax: 44 171 497 1426

Thomas Nelson & Sons LTD
Nelson House
Mayfield Road
Walton-on-Thames
KT 12 5PL United Kingdom
Tel: 44 1932 2522111
Fax: 44 1932 246574

Latin America:
Thomson Learning
Seneca, 53
Colonia Polanco
11560 Mexico D.F. Mexico
Tel: 525-281-2906
Fax: 525-281-2656

South Africa:
Thomson Learning
Zonnebloem Building
Constantia Square
526 Sixteenth Road
P.O. Box 2459
Halfway House, 1685
South Africa
Tel: 27 11 805 4819
Fax: 27 11 805 3648

Canada:
Nelson/Thomson Learning
1120 Birchmount Road
Scarborough, Ontario
Canada M1K 5G4
Tel: 416-752-9100
Fax: 416-752-8102

Spain:
Thomson Learning
Calle Magallanes, 25
28015-MADRID
ESPANA
Tel: 34 91 446 33 50
Fax: 34 91 445 62 18

International Headquarters:
Thomson Learning
International Division
290 Harbor Drive, 2nd Floor
Stamford, CT 06902-7477
Tel: 203-969-8700
Fax: 203-969-8751

Library of Congress Cataloging-in-Publication Data
Herr, Judy.
    Creative resources for the early childhood classroom / Judy Herr,
Yvonne Libby-Larson. — 3rd ed.
       p.   cm.
    Includes bibliographical references and index.
    ISBN 0-7668-0543-3
       1. Education, Preschool—Curricula.   2. Unit method of teaching.
    I. Libby-Larson, Yvonne.   II. Title.
    LB1140.4.H47   2000
    372.19—dc21
                       99-14792
                           CIP

CONTENTS

Table of Contents by Subjects

COOKING

FINGERPLAYS

© 2000, Delmar

PREFACE

While reviewing early childhood curriculum resources, it becomes apparent that few books are available using a thematic or unit approach for teaching young children. As a result, our university students, colleagues, and alumni convinced us of the importance of such a book. Likewise, they convinced us of the contribution the book could make to early childhood teachers and, subsequently, the lives of young children.

Before preparing the manuscript, we surveyed hundreds of child care, preschool, and kindergarten teachers. Specifically, we wanted them to share their curriculum problems and concerns. Our response has been to design and write a reference book tailored to their teaching needs using a thematic approach. Each theme or unit contains a flowchart, theme goals, concepts for the children to learn, theme-related vocabulary words, music, fingerplays, science, dramatic play, creative art experiences, sensory, mathematics, cooking experiences, and resources. Additionally, creative ideas for designing child-involvement bulletin boards and parent letters have been included. These resources were identified, by the teachers included in our survey, as being critical components that have been lacking in other curriculum guides.

In addition to the themes included in this book, others can and should be developed for teaching young children. The authors, however, wish to caution the readers that it is the teacher's responsibility to select, plan, and introduce developmentally appropriate themes and learning experiences for his group of children. Specifically, the teacher must tailor the curriculum to meet the individual needs of the children. Consequently, we encourage all teachers to carefully select, adapt, or change any of the activities in this book to meet the needs, abilities, and interests of their group of children to ensure developmental appropriateness. The inside covers of this book should be used as handy references for checking developmental norms.

As you use this guide, you will note that some themes readily lend themselves to particular curriculum areas. As a result, the number of activities listed under each curriculum area will vary from theme to theme.

The detailed Introduction that follows is designed to help teachers use the book most effectively. It includes:

1. A discussion on how to develop the curriculum using a thematic approach;
2. A list of possible themes;
3. Suggestions for writing parent letters;
4. Methods for constructing and evaluating creative involvement bulletin boards; and
5. Criteria for selecting children's books.

What's New in the Third Edition!

1. New Themes and Activities. Over one hundred new activities enrich this third edition. These are spread throughout the book and complement four new themes: ants, containers, eggs, and purple. Each thematic unit begins with a curriculum web. This webbing is designed to inform teachers of the major subconcepts that can be included under each theme. Ideally the teacher will tailor the curriculum to make it developmentally appropriate and meet the needs and interests of her/his children.

2. Revised and Additional Bulletin Boards. The third edition contains some revised as well as four additional bulletin boards.

3. New and Expanded Reference Materials. The sections on books and multimedia which appear at the end of each theme have been carefully researched by Carol Hagness, the Director of the Educational Materials Center, the Pierce Library, University of Wisconsin-Stout.

4. Introduction of Recordings and Songs for Each Thematic Unit. A recording and song section containing music with related concepts has been introduced for each theme where available. Special thanks to Elaine Murphy, Director of Sales and Marketing, Kimbo Educational, for assistance in developing this section. Free catalogs for these materials can be obtained by telephoning 1-800-631-2187, faxing 732-870-3340, or emailing kimboed@aol.com.

Like previous editions, this book would not have been possible without the constant support and encouragement of our families, the center director and laboratory teachers at the Child and Family Study Center, and the early childhood faculty, students, and alumni of the University of Wisconsin-Stout. Our thanks to all of these people and especially to Carla Ahmann, Susan Babler, Mary Babula, Terry Bloomberg, Amanda Branscombe, Margaret Braun, Renee Bruce, Anne Budde, Michele Case, Jill Church, Bruce Cunningham, Jeanette Dianes, Carol Davenport, Jill Davis, Mary DeJardin, Linda DeMoe, Rita Devery, Donna Dixon, Esther Fahm, Lisa Fuerst, Shirley Gebhart, Judy Gifford, Nancy Graese, Barbara Grundleger, Wallace Havens, Betty Herman, Jeffrey Herr, John Herr, Mark Herr, May Herr, Joan Herwig, Priscilla Huffman, Margy Ingram, Paula Iverson, Judy Jax, Angelica Kaiser, Elizabeth (Beth) Kaster, Coro King, Trudy King, Jill Kletstad, Troy Larson, Beth Libby, Janet Maffet, Janet Massa, Nancy McCarthy, Julie Meyers, Betty Misselt, Teresa Mitchell, Kathy Mueller, Robin Muza, Paula Noll, Kristi Olson, Sue Paulson, Mary Pugmire, Kelli Railton, Lori Register, Linda Reiten, Kathy Schaeffer, Mary Selkey, Cheryl Smith, Sue Smith, Amy Sprengler, Barbara Suihkonen, Terri Swim, Terri Tedford, Judy Teske, Sue Unger, Penny Warner, Ed Wenzel, Eileen Zenk and Karen Zimmerman.

We are also grateful to our reviewers:

Audrey Beard, Ed.D.
Albany State University
Albany, GA

Peggy DeMuth
College of Sequoias
Visalia, CA

Judy Patchin
Black Hawk College
Geneseo, IL

Lacey Ann Southerland
Georgia State University
Atlanta, GA

Julianne Stermer
Lane Community College
Eugene, OR

Erie Tejada
University of Texas at Brownsville
Brownsville, TX

Debra Tietze
Rockland Community College
Suffern, NY

Our special thanks to the seven individuals whose assistance made this book possible: Carol Hagness, the Director of the Educational Materials Center at the University of Wisconsin-Stout; Elaine Murphy of Kimbo Educational; Tracey Wellington, who shared teacher-made materials; Marty Springer, University of Wisconsin-Stout staff member, who photographed the teacher-made materials; Erin O'Connor Traylor, our Delmar editor who provided continuous encouragement, support and assistance; and finally, our typists Vicki Weber and Debra Hass.

INTRODUCTION

The purpose of this introduction is to explain the process involved in curriculum planning for young children using the thematic, or unit, approach. To support each theme, planning and construction ideas are included for bulletin boards, parent letters, and a wide variety of classroom learning experiences.

children may be inappropriate for another. To develop an appropriate curriculum, knowledge of the typical development of children is needed. For this reason, the inside covers of this book contain such information. Review these developmental norms before selecting a theme or specific activities.

Curriculum Planning

As you use this resource, remember that children learn best when they can control and act upon their environment. Many opportunities should be available for seeing, touching, tasting, learning, and self-expression. Children need hands-on activities and choices. To construct knowledge, children need to actively manipulate their environment. To provide these opportunities, the teacher's primary role is to set the stage by offering many experiences that stimulate the children's senses and curiosity; children learn by doing and play is their work. As a result, it is the authors' intention that this book will be used as a resource. Specifically, the ideas in this book should help you to enrich, organize, and structure the children's environment, providing them an opportunity to make choices among a wide variety of activities that stimulate their natural curiosity. Knowledge of child development and curriculum must be interwoven. To illustrate, play in the classroom should be child-centered and self-initiated. To provide an environment that promotes these types of play, it is the teacher's role to provide unstructured time, space, and materials. Using a theme approach to plan curriculum is one way to ensure that a wide variety of classroom experiences are provided. Successful early childhood programs provide interesting, challenging, and engaging environments. Children need to learn to think, reason, and become decision makers.

It is important that all curricula be adapted to match the developmental needs of children at a particular age or stage of development. An activity that is appropriate for one group of

Theme Planning

A developmentally appropriate curriculum for young children integrates the children's needs, interests, and abilities and focuses on the whole child. Cognitive, social, emotional, and physical development are all included. Before planning curriculum, observe the children's development. Record observations of what you see. At the same time, note the children's interests and listen carefully. Children's conversations provide clues; this information is vital in theme selection. After this, review your observations by discussing them with other staff members. An appropriate curriculum for young children cannot be planned without understanding their development and interests.

There are many methods for planning a curriculum other than using themes. In fact, you may prefer not to use a theme during parts of the year. If this is your choice, you may wish to use the book as a source of ideas, integrating activities and experiences from a variety of the themes outlined in the book.

Planning a curriculum using a theme approach involves several steps. The first step involves selecting a theme that is appropriate for the developmental level and interests of your group of children. Themes based on the children's interests provide intrinsic motivation for exploration and learning. Meaningful experiences are more easily comprehended and remembered. Moreover, curiosity, enjoyment of participation, and self-direction are heightened. After selecting a theme, the next step is developing a flowchart. From the flowchart, goals, conceptual understandings, and vocabulary words can easily be extracted. The final step in curriculum planning is selecting activities based upon the children's stages of development and available resources. While doing this, the covers of this book should be used as a reference to review development characteristics for children of different ages.

To help you understand the theme approach to curriculum development, each step of the process will be discussed. Included are assessing the children's needs, and developing flowcharts, theme goals, concepts, vocabulary, and activities. In addition, suggestions are given for writing parent letters, designing bulletin boards, and selecting children's books.

Assessment

Assessment is important for planning curriculum, identifying special needs children, and communicating a child's progress to parents. Assessment needs to be a continuous process. It involves a process of observing children during activities throughout the day, recording their behaviors, and documenting their work. Assessment involves records and descriptions of what you observe while the behavior is occurring. Logs and journals can be developed. The developmental norms on the inside cover of this text can be used as a check-list of behavior. You can create a profile of the children's individualized progress in developing skills. Your observations should tell what the children like, don't like, have discovered, know, and want to learn.

Samples of the children's work in an individual portfolio collection should be maintained. A portfolio documents the children's progress, achievements, and efforts. Included should be samples of the children's paintings, drawings, storytelling experiences, oral, and written language. Thus, the portfolio will include products and evidence of the children's accomplishments.

By reviewing the assessment materials you can identify the children's developmental needs and interests. This information will be important in selecting a theme that interests the children and selecting developmentally appropriate learning experiences.

Flowcharts/Webbings. The flowchart is a simple way to record all possible subconcepts that relate to the major concept or theme. To illustrate, plan a theme on apples. In the center of a piece of paper, write the word "apple." Then using an encyclopedia as a resource, record the subconcepts that are related. Include origin, parts, colors, tastes, sizes, textures, food preparation, and nutrition. The following flowchart (See Figure I–1) includes these concepts. In

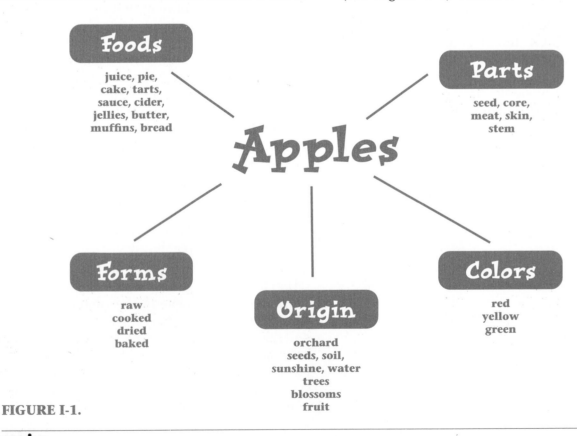

FIGURE I-1.

addition, under each subconcept list content that could be included. For example, apples may be colored green, yellow, or red. By teaching using a thematic approach, we teach children the way environments and humans interconnect. This process helps children make sense out of the human experience.

Theme Goals. Once you have prepared a flowchart webbing, abstracting the theme goals is a simple process. Begin by reviewing the chart. Notice the subheadings listed. For the unit on apples, the subheadings include: foods, parts, forms, and colors. Writing each of these subheadings as a goal is the next step of the process.

Since there were four subheadings, each of these can be included as a goal. In some cases, subheadings may be combined. For example, note the fourth goal listed. It combines several subheadings.

Through participation in the experiences provided by using apples as a curriculum theme, the children may learn:

1. Parts of an apple.
2. Preparation of apples for eating.
3. Apple tastes.
4. Textures, sizes, and colors of apples.
5. The origin of an apple.

Concepts. The concepts must be related to the goal; however, they are more specific. To write the concepts, study the goals. Then prepare sentences that are written in a simple form that children can understand. Examples of concepts for a unit on apples may include:

1. An apple is a fruit.
2. An apple has five parts: seed, core, meat, skin, and stem.
3. Apples grow on trees.
4. A group of apple trees is called an orchard.
5. Bread, pies, puddings, applesauce, dumplings, butter, and jellies can be prepared from apples.
6. Some apples are sweet; others are sour.
7. Apples can be colored green, yellow, or red.
8. Apples can be large or small.
9. Apples may be hard or soft.
10. Apples can be eaten raw.
11. Seeds from an apple can grow into a tree.

Vocabulary. The vocabulary should include new words that you want to informally introduce to the children. Vocabulary words need to be tailored to meet the specific needs of your group of children. The number of vocabulary words will vary, depending upon the theme and the developmental level of the children. For example, it might be assumed that the children know the word sweet, but not tart. So, the definition of the word tart is included. Collectively, the following words could be introduced in this unit: apple, texture, core, blossom, and apple butter. Definitions for these words could include:

1. **apple**—a fruit that is grown on a tree.
2. **texture**—how something feels.
3. **core**—the part of the apple that contains the seeds.
4. **apple blossom**—a flower on the apple tree.
5. **apple butter**—a spread for bread made from apples.

Activities. Now that you have learned how to develop goals related to a theme using a flowchart, you will need to learn how to select developmentally appropriate activities. You will discover that many theme goals can be accomplished by additions to the environment, bulletin boards, field trips, and stories or resource people at large group time. Your major role as an adult, or teacher, is that of a facilitator, planning and preparing the environment to stimulate the child's natural curiosity.

To begin this process, review each goal and determine how it can be introduced in the classroom. For example, if you were going to develop a theme on apples, review the goals. A bulletin board or game could introduce the three colors of apples. The children could also learn these colors through cooking experiences. The third vehicle for teaching the colors of apples would be placing the three colors of apples on a science table.

The five parts of an apple could also be introduced through participation in a tasting or cooking experience, bulletin board, or even discussion on a field trip or at the snack table. Always remember that children need to observe and manipulate the concrete object while engaged in child-initiated or child-directed play that is teacher supported. For that reason, fresh apples could be cut horizontally and placed on the science table with a magnifying glass. Likewise, simultaneously, apple seeds and paper could be available on the art table to construct a collage. Always remember that the best activities for young children are hands-on and open-ended. That is: focus on the process, rather than the product. Children need to learn to think, reason, and become problem solvers. As a teacher, you should take the ideas in this book and use and adapt them for planning and preparing the environment. Always remember that successful early childhood programs provide interesting, challenging, and engaging environments.

Parent Letters

Communication between the child's home and school is important. It builds mutual understanding and cooperation. With the efficiency of modern technology, parent letters are a form of written communication that can be shared on a weekly basis. The most interesting parent letters are written in the active voice. It states the subject did something. To illustrate: "Mark's favorite activities today were playing with blocks and listening to stories on a cassette player."

When writing the parent letter, consider the parent's educational level. Then write the letter in a clear, friendly, concise style. To do this, eliminate all words that are not needed. Limit the length of the letter to a page or two. To assist you with the process, an example of a parent letter is included for each theme.

Parent letters can be divided into three sections. Included should be a general introduction, school activities, and home activities. One way to begin the letter is by introducing new children or staff, or sharing something that happened the previous week. After this, introduce the theme for the coming week by explaining why it was chosen.

The second section of the parent letter could include some of the goals and special activities for the theme. Share with the parents all of the interesting things you will be doing at school throughout the week. By having this information, parents can initiate verbal interaction with their child.

The third section of the parent letter should be related to home activities. Suggest developmentally appropriate activities that the parents can provide in the home. These activities may or may not relate to the theme. Include the words of new songs and fingerplays. This section can also be used to provide parenting information such as the developmental value of specific activities for young children.

Bulletin Boards

Bulletin boards add color, decoration, and interest to the classroom. They also communicate what is happening in the classroom to parents and other visitors. The most effective bulletin boards involve the child. That is, the child will manipulate some pieces of the board. As a result, they are called involvement bulletin boards. Through the concrete experience of interacting with the bulletin board materials, children learn a variety of concepts and skills. Included may be size, shape, color, visual discrimination, eye-hand coordination, etc.

Carefully study the bulletin boards included for each theme in this book. They are simple, containing a replica of objects from the child's immediate environment. Each bulletin board has a purpose. It teaches a skill or concept.

As you prepare the bulletin boards provided in this book, you will become more creative. Gradually, you will combine ideas from several bulletin boards as you develop new themes for curriculum.

An opaque projector is a useful tool for individuals who feel uncomfortable with their drawing skills. Using the opaque projector, you can enlarge images from storybooks, coloring books, greeting cards, wrapping paper, etc. To do this, simply place the image to be copied in the projector. Then tape paper or tagboard on the wall. Turn on the projector. Using a pencil, color marker or crayon, trace the outline of the image onto the paper or tagboard.

Another useful tool for preparing bulletin boards is the overhead projector. Place a clear sheet of acetate on the picture desired for enlargement. This may include figures from a coloring or storybook. Trace around the image using a washable marker designed for transparencies. Project the image onto a wall and follow the same procedures as with the opaque projector.

To make your bulletin board pieces more durable, laminate them. If your center does not have a laminating machine, use clear contact paper. This process works just as well, but it can be more expensive.

Finally, the materials you choose to use on a bulletin board should be safe and durable. Careful attention should be given when selecting attachments. For two-, three- and four-year-old children, adhesive velcro and staples are preferred attachments. **Caution:** Pushpins may be used with older children under *careful supervision.*

Selecting Books

Books for young children need to be selected with care. Before selecting books, once again, refer to the covers and review the typical development for your group of young children. This information can provide a framework for selecting appropriate books.

There are some general guidelines for selecting books. First, children enjoy books that relate to their experiences. They also enjoy action. The words written in the book should be simple, descriptive, and within the child's understanding. The pictures should be large, colorful, and closely represent the actions.

A book that is good for one group of children may be inappropriate for another. You must know the child or group of children for whom the story is being selected. Consider their interests, attention span, and developmental level.

Developmental considerations are important. Two-year-olds enjoy stories about the things they do, know, and enjoy. Commonplace adventure is a preference for three-year-olds. They like to listen to things that could happen to them, including stories about community helpers. Four-year-old children are not as self-centered. These children do not have to be part of every situation that they hear about. Many are ready for short and simple fantasy stories. Five-year-olds like stories that add to their knowledge—that is, books that contain new information.

Curriculum Planning Guide

We hope you find this book to be a valuable guide in planning curriculum. The ideas should help you build curriculum based upon the children's natural interests. The book should also give you ideas so that your program will provide a wide variety of choices for children.

In planning a developmentally valid curriculum, consult the table of contents by subject. It has been prepared to allow you easy selection from all the themes. So pick and choose and make it your own! The contents included are as follows:

—Art
—Cooking
—Dramatic Play
—Features (by Theme)
—Field Trips/Resource People
—Fingerplays
—Group Time
—Large Muscle
—Math
—Rainy Day
—Science
—Sensory
—Songs

Other Sources

Early childhood educators should refer to other Delmar publications when developing appropriate curriculum, including:

1. Ramirez, Gonzalo, Jr. & Ramirez, Jan Lee. *Multiethnic Children's Literature: A Comprehensive Resource Guide.*

2. Dolinar, Kathleen, Boser, Candace, & Holm, Eleanor. *Learning through Play: Curriculum and Activities for the Inclusive Classroom.*

3. Allen, K. Eileen & Marotz, Lynn. *Developmental Profiles: Prebirth to Eight* (3rd ed.).

4. Berns, Roberta M. *Topical Child Development.*

5. Mayesky, Mary. *Creative Activities for Young Children* (6th ed.).

6. Gestwicki, Carol. *Home, School, and Community Relations: A Guide to Working with Parents* (4th ed.).

7. Essa, Eva L. *A Practical Guide to Solving Preschool Behavior Problems* (4th ed.).

8. Sawyer, Walter E. & Jean C. *Integrated Language Arts for Emerging Literacy.*

9. Charlesworth, Rosalind & Lind, Karen K. *Math and Science for Young Children* (3rd ed.).

10. Bentzen, Warren R. *Seeing Young Children: A Guide to Observing and Recording Behavior* (3rd ed.).

11. Davidson, Jane. *Children's Emerging Literacy through Dramatic Play.*

12. Pica, Rae. *Experiences in Movement with Music, Activities, and Theory.*

13. Gestwicki, Carol. *Developmentally Appropriate Practice: Curriculum & Development in Early Education.*

14. Schirrmacher, Robert. *Art and Creative Development for Young Children* (3rd ed.).

15. Click, Phyllis. *Caring for School Age Children* (2nd ed.).

16. Essa, Eva & Penelope Royce Rogers. *Early Childhood Curriculum: From Developmental Model to Application.*

17. Herr, Judy & Terri Swim. *Creative Resources for Infants and Toddlers.*

THEME 1

Colors

black
brown
rust
gray
red

Foods

insects
fruit
plants

Growth Stages

egg
larvae
pupa
adult

Kinds

carpenter
weaver
leaf cutter
fire
cornfield
thief
army

Ants

Roles

queen
worker
soldier
male

Homes

underground,
earthen mounds,
inside trees or
hollow plants

Body Parts

head,
antennas, eyes,
mouth parts,
trunk, six legs,
wings
(males and
young queens)

Importance

eat large number of insects;
food source for birds, frogs,
and other animals

1

Theme Goals

Through participating in the experiences provided by this theme, the children may learn:

1. Kinds of ants.
2. Ant body parts.
3. Colors of ants.
4. Roles of ants.
5. Ant growth stages.
6. Foods ants eat.
7. Ant homes.
8. Importance of ants.

Concepts for the Children to Learn

1. An ant is a small insect.
2. There are many kinds of ants.
3. An ant's body has three main parts.
4. An ant has six legs.
5. Ants can be black, brown, rust, or gray colored.
6. Ants use their mouth parts to grasp food, carry their young, and fight enemies.
7. Ants use their antennas to smell, touch, taste, and hear.
8. Ants build homes in many places.
9. Ants live in groups called colonies.
10. Ants eat other insects, plants, and fruits.
11. The queen ant lays the eggs.
12. Worker ants have many jobs.
13. A soldier ant is a large worker ant.
14. Ants can carry things larger than their bodies.
15. Ants are a food source for birds, frogs, and other animals.

Vocabulary

1. **ant**—a type of small insect.
2. **colony**—a community or group of ants.
3. **queen**—female ant that lays eggs.
4. **workers**—female ants that build the nest, search for food, care for the young, and fight enemies.
5. **soldiers**—largest worker ants.
6. **antennas**—feelers on the head of an insect.
7. **mandibles**—pair of jaws that move from side to side.

Bulletin Board

The purpose of this bulletin board is to promote mathematical skills. Sketch ant hills on heavy construction paper or tagboard. As illustrated, on each ant hill make a dot to represent each ant. Using a felt-tip magic marker, print a numeral on each hill that represents a number of dots. If desired for durability, laminate each ant hill or cover with transparent contact paper. If desired, small rubber or plastic ants may be purchased commercially; otherwise, they can be constructed out of black construction paper.

Parent Letter

Dear Parents,

Another week has quickly come and gone. Before we know it, summer will be here again! Have you noticed the grass getting greener and the birds on the trees? Nature is full of small wonders. This week in school we will be learning about a group of "small wonders." We will find out many things about ants, those small picnic-joining insects! The children will learn about ant body parts, types of ants, foods ants eat, places ants make homes, just to name a few!

AT SCHOOL

Learning experiences planned for this week include:

- finding ants to create an ant farm for the classroom.
- going on a pretend picnic in the dramatic play area—ants included!
- using small plastic ants as game pieces for classroom games.

AT HOME

Try some of these ant activities at home this week:

- Create egg carton ants! Cut a cardboard egg carton into three-cup sections. Paint as desired. Use pipe cleaners or yarn pieces to represent six legs and antennas. Add small pompons, pebbles, or seeds for the eyes, or use purchased craft eyes. Fun!
- Check out books about ants from the library. Some titles to look for:
  Ant Cities by Arthur Dorros
  Two Bad Ants by Chris Van Allsburg
- Take a slow walk around your home or neighborhood with your child and look for ants. Are they all the same size? Color? Can you figure out where their homes are? What do you think they eat?

Have a f-*ant*-astic week!

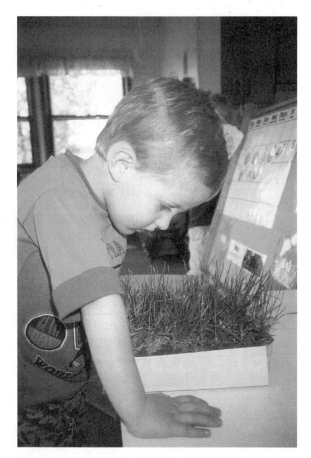

Young children enjoy visually tracking ants crawling through the grass.

Music

1. **"The Ants Go Marching"**
   (Sing to the tune of "When Johnny Comes Marching Home")

   The ants go marching one by one.
   Hurrah, hurrah.
   The ants go marching one by one.
   Hurrah, hurrah.
   The ants go marching one by one.
   The little one stopped to wiggle its thumb.
   They all go marching,
   Marching to escape the rain.

   Continue with:

   The ants go marching two by two.
   The little one stopped to tie its shoe.

   The ants go marching three by three.
   The little one stopped to disagree.

   The ants go marching four by four.
   The little one stopped to shut the door.

   The ants go marching five by five.
   The little one stopped to learn to dive.

   The ants go marching six by six.
   The little one stopped to do some tricks.

   The ants go marching seven by seven.
   The little one stopped to wait for Devon.

   The ants go marching eight by eight.
   The little one stopped to shut the gate.

   The ants go marching nine by nine.
   The little one stopped to walk a line.

   The ants go marching ten by ten.
   The little one stopped to shout, "The End!"

2. **"Six Little Ants"**
   (Sing to the tune of "Six Little Ducks")

   Six little ants that I once knew,
   Black ants, brown ants, gray ants, too.
   But the busiest ants are the workers of the
     bunch.
   They feed the babies with a munch,
     munch, munch.
   Munch, munch, munch. Munch, munch,
     munch.
   They feed the babies with a munch,
     munch, munch.

3. **"Ants"**
   (Sing to the tune of "Mary Had a Little Lamb")

   There's an ant trail underground,
   Underground, underground.
   There's an ant trail underground.
   An ant colony lives down there.

   The job of the queen is to lay the eggs,
   Lay the eggs, lay the eggs.
   The job of the queen is to lay the eggs.
   That's all she has to do.

   The worker ants have many jobs,
   Many jobs, many jobs.
   The worker ants have many jobs,
   They do all the work.

4. **"Little Black Ant"**
   (Sing to the tune of "I'm a Little Teapot")

   I'm a little black ant on the ground.
   I'm so tiny I can hardly be found.
   Look very closely, then you'll see.
   I'm scurrying around—just look at me!

Fingerplays

LITTLE ANTS

One little ant, two little ants,
   (point to a finger for reach number)
Three little ants I see.
Four little ants, five little ants,
Lively as can be.
Six little ants, seven little ants,
Eight in a bowl of glass.
Nine little ants, ten little ants,
Entertain our class.

ANT HILL

Once I saw an ant hill,
   (make fist with one hand)
With no ants about.
So I said, "Dear little ants,
Won't you please come out?"
Then as if the little ants
Had heard my call,
One, two, three, four, five came out.
   (extend fingers one at a time)
And that was all.

CAUGHT AN ANT

One, two, three, four, five,
   (extend a finger for each number)
I caught an ant alive.
Six, seven, eight, nine, ten,
   (extend fingers of other hand)
I let it go again.
Why did I let it go?
   (shrug shoulders)
It bit my finger so.
Which one did it bite?
   (shrug shoulders)
The little one on the right.
   (hold up right pinkie finger)

Sensory

Add to the sensory table:

- Sand and small plastic ants with jars and spoons.
- Playdough, rolling pins, circle cookie cutters (to create ants and ant hills).

Math

Ant Sort

Draw and cut out various-sized ants from different colors of paper. Laminate pieces to make them durable. Children can use the ant pieces for counting activities, as well as for sorting by attributes such as color and size.

Social Studies

Ant Jobs

Ants work together to keep the ant colony alive. Each ant has work to do. Talk about the various roles or jobs that ants have in the colony.

Queen: The queen ant lays thousands and thousands of eggs. There is usually only one queen in a colony.

Workers: Workers are all females. They do the work in the ant city. They find food, store food, and take care of the ant eggs. They will also fight to protect the nest.

New Queens: New queens have wings. They use them to fly away to start new ant colonies. Their wings drop off, and then the queens lay eggs.

Large Muscle

Ant Hill Walk

Cut at least one large ant hill shape out of brown construction paper for each child. Also cut several circles out of white construction paper. Mix up the shapes and tape them to the floor in a circle or trail. Play music and let the children walk, skip, hop, etc. around the shape circle or trail. Stop the music and have each child find an ant hill to stand on. Continue the game as long as there is interest.

Science

1. Ant Farm

If you and the children would like to watch ants close up, try making an ant farm. Begin by sifting soil and/or sand into a clean, clear container that has a lid or cover with holes punched in it. Next, search for some ants. Select ants from the same area so they will likely be from the same colony. Scoop the ants into a separate collecting jar and transfer them to the viewing container. Place a small piece of damp sponge into the container so the ants will have something to drink. Every three days or so use an eyedropper to add a teaspoon of water to the sponge. Put a little food into the jar. Try to see what the ants are eating. Some ants like sweets, some like other insects, and some like seeds. Keep the ant farm in a dark place or cover it with a cloth when the ants are not being viewed. Ants will tend to dig deep tunnels, away from the light. You could also purchase an ant farm for classroom use.

2. Ant Watch

Place a cut piece of fruit or candy outside as ant bait. Check on the food piece periodically with the children to observe if ants have found it. Similarly, cracker or bread crumbs could be placed outside. Children may then be able to watch ants attempt to carry pieces to their nest.

Dramatic Play

Picnic (with ants, of course!)

Provide picnic props such as child-sized picnic table, backpack, tablecloth, picnic basket, cooler, thermos, plastic plates, and silverware. Plastic food items can be added. Have children assist in the preparation of paper ants that can be placed in the picnic area.

Arts and Crafts

1. Ant Prints

Set out several washable black and red ink pads and white paper. To create an ant, have each child press his or her index finger on the ink pad, then make three prints in a row on the paper. Repeat process to make more ants. Provide black and red pens so children can add six legs and antennas.

2. Egg-Carton Ants

Cut cardboard egg cartons into three section pieces. Children can paint their section as desired with "ant color" paints— black, brown, red, gray. When dry, pipe cleaners or yarn pieces can be added to represent six legs and antennas. Eyes can be made from small pompons, pebbles, seeds, or purchased small craft eyes.

3. Clay Ants

Provide clay or playdough for children to create ants. Three small balls or circle shapes can be pushed together to create an ant body. Pipe cleaner pieces can be used for legs and antennas.

Field Trip/ Resource People

Insect Specialist

Contact your local Department of Natural Resources or county 4-H agent to find out if there are any insect specialists in your area that could talk about ants or show examples of types of ants.

Group Time
(games, language)

Ant Partners

Draw and cut out small matching ants from different colors of construction paper. Place the ants in a paper bag and have each child take one. Play music and let the children crawl around the room to find their "ant partners" by matching up their ants. Then have them hold hands with their partners and sit to the side of the group until all have found a partner. Collect the ants and start the game again.

Cooking

1. **Ants on a Log**

   celery sticks
   peanut butter
   raisins

   Spread peanut butter on celery sticks. Place raisins on peanut butter.

2. **Ant Hill Slaw**

   3 carrots, coarsely grated
   3/4 cup raisins
   1/2–3/4 cup mayonnaise
   juice from 1/2 lemon
   dash of salt and pepper

   In a mixing bowl, combine carrots, raisins, and mayonnaise. Add more mayonnaise if needed. Add lemon juice, salt, and pepper. Mix again. Chill in the refrigerator for an hour.

Books

The following books can be used to complement this theme:

Chinery, Michael. (1991). *Ant*. Mahwah, NJ: Troll. (Pbk)

Climo, Shirley. (1995). *The Little Red Ant and the Great Big Crumb: A Mexican Fable*. New York: Clarion Books.

Cole, Joanna. (1996). *The Magic School Bus Gets Ants in Its Pants: A Book About Ants*. New York: Scholastic.

Demuth, Patricia Brennan. (1994). *Those Amazing Ants*. Illus. by S. D. Schindler. New York: Simon & Schuster.

Dorros, Arthur. (1987). *Ant Cities*. Bellevue, WA: Ty Crowell Co.

Fowler, Allan (1998). *Inside an Ant Colony*. Chicago: Children's Press.

Hepworth, Catherine. (1992). *Antics! An Alphabetical Anthology*. New York: G. P. Putnam.

Pinczes, Elinor. (1993). *One Hundred Hungry Ants*. Illus. by Bonnie MacKain. Boston: Houghton Mifflin.

Savage, Stephen. (1995). *Ant*. Illus. by Clive Pritchard. Cincinnati, OH: Thomson Learning.

Multimedia

The following resources can be used to complement this theme:

Ants: Hunters and Gardeners [video]. (1986). National Geographic Society.

The Ants Go Marching [cassette and book]. (1992). Bothell, WA: Wright Group.

"Ants on Parade" on *Songs About Insects, Bugs and Squiggly Things* [compact disc]. (1993). Kimbo Educational.

Magic School Bus Gets Ants in Its Pants [video]. (1997). New York: Distributed by Kidvision.

Scruggs, Joe. *Ants* [compact disc or cassette]. (1994). Shadow Play Records and Video/Educational Graphics Press.

Recording and Song Title

The following recording can be used to complement this theme:

Songs about Insects, Bugs and Squiggly Things—"Ants On Parade"

THEME 2

Foods

juice, pie,
cake, tarts,
sauce, cider,
jellies, butter,
muffins, bread

Parts

seed
core
meat
skin
stem

Apples

Forms

raw
cooked
dried
baked

Origin

orchard
seeds
soil
sunshine
water
trees
blossoms
fruit

Colors

red
yellow
green

Theme Goals

Through participating in the experiences provided by this theme, the children may learn:

1. Parts of an apple.
2. Preparation of apples for eating.
3. Apple tastes.
4. Textures, sizes, and colors of apples.
5. The origin of an apple.

Concepts for the Children to Learn

1. An apple is a fruit.
2. An apple has five parts: seed, core, meat, skin, and stem.
3. Apples grow on trees.
4. A group of apple trees is an orchard.
5. Bread, butter, cakes, pies, pudding, applesauce, dumplings, butter, and jelly can be prepared from apples.
6. Some apples are sweet; others are sour.
7. Apples can be green, yellow, or red.
8. Apples can be large or small.
9. Apples can be hard or soft.
10. Seeds from an apple can grow into a tree.

Vocabulary

1. **apple**—a fruit that is grown on a tree.
2. **texture**—how something feels.
3. **core**—the part of the apple that contains seeds.
4. **apple blossom**—a flower on the apple tree.
5. **apple butter**—a spread for bread made from apples.

Bulletin Board

The purpose of this bulletin board is to develop the mathematical skill of sets, as well as to identify written numerals. Construct red apples. The number will depend upon the developmental level of the children. Laminate the apples. Collect containers for baskets, such as large cottage cheese or pint berry containers. Cover the containers with paper if necessary. Affix numerals on baskets, beginning with the numeral 1. Staple the baskets to the bulletin board. The object is for the children to place the appropriate number of apples in each basket.

Parent Letter

Dear Parents,

Is it true that "an apple a day keeps the doctor away?" I'm not sure, but the children will make many discoveries as we begin a new unit on apples at school. Through active exploration and interaction, they will become more aware of the different flavors of apples, colors of apples, and ways apples can be prepared and eaten.

AT SCHOOL

Some classroom activities for this unit include:

- preparing applesauce for Thursday's snack.
- drying apples in the sun.
- creating apple-shaped sponge prints in the art area.
- visiting the apple orchard! Arrangements have been made for a tour of the apple orchard on Wednesday morning. We will be leaving the center at 10:00 a.m. Feel free to join us.

AT HOME

Apples are a tasty and nutritious food—and most children enjoy eating them. Try a variety of apples for meals or snacks. You might also enjoy preparing caramel apples with your child. A recipe is as follows:

1 pound of vanilla caramels
2 tablespoons of water
dash of salt
6 crisp apples
6 wooden skewers or popsicle sticks

Melt the caramels with water in a microwave oven or double boiler, stirring frequently until smooth. Stir in the salt and stick a wooden skewer or popsicle stick in each apple. Dip the apple into the syrup, turning until the surface of the apple is completely covered.

Cooking is a great way to learn by experience because it involves the whole child—physically, emotionally, socially, and intellectually. It also builds vocabulary and involves amounts, measuring, and fractions, which are mathematical concepts. When a recipe is used, your child will also learn to follow a sequence. Enjoy cooking with your child.

Enjoy an apple with your child today!

Music

1. "If I Had an Apple"
(Sing to the tune of "If I Had a Hammer")

If I had an apple
I'd eat it in the morning,
I'd eat it in the evening,
All over this land.
I'd eat it for breakfast,
I'd eat it for supper,
I'd eat it with all my friends and sisters and
    brothers
All, all over this land.

Source: Chenfield, Mimi Brodsky. *Creative Activities for Young Children.*

2. "Little Apples"
(Sing to the tune of "Ten Little Indians")

One little, two little, three little apples,
Four little, five little, six little apples,
Seven little, eight little, nine little apples,
All fell to the ground.

A variation for older children would be to give each child a number card (with a numeral from 1 through 9). When that number is sung, that child stands up. At the end of the fingerplay all the children fall down.

3. "Apples off My Tree"
(Sing to the tune of "Skip to My Lou")

Pick some apples off my tree,
Pick some apples off my tree,
Pick some apples off my tree,
Pick them all for you and me.

4. "My Apple Tree"
(Sing to the tune of "The Muffin Man")

Did you see my apple tree,
Did you see my apple tree,
Did you see my apple tree,
Full of apples red?

Fingerplays

APPLE TREE

Way up high in the apple tree
    (stretch arm up high)
Two little apples smiled at me.
    (hold up 2 fingers)
I shook that tree as hard as I could
    (make shaking motion)
Down came the apples.
    (make downward motions)
Mmmm—they were good.
    (smile and rub stomach)

PICKING APPLES

Here's a little apple tree.
    (left arm up, fingers spread)
I look up and I can see
    (look at fingers)
Big red apples, ripe and sweet,
    (cup hands to hold apple)
Big red apples, good to eat!
    (raise hands to mouth)
Shake the little apple tree.
    (shake tree with hands)
See the apples fall on me.
    (raise cupped hands and let fall)
Here's a basket, big and round.
    (make circle with arms)
Pick the apples from the ground.
    (pick and put in basket)
Here's an apple I can see.
    (look up to the tree)
I'll reach up. It's ripe and sweet.
    (reach up to upper hand)
That's the apple I will eat!
    (hands to mouth)

AN APPLE

An apple is what I'd like to be.
My shape would be round.
    (fingers in circular shape)
My color would be green.
    (point to something green)
Children could eat me each and every day.
I'm good in tarts and pies and cakes.
    (make these foodshapes)
An apple is good to eat or to bake.
    (make stirring motion)

Applesauce

Help children discover all the wonderful foods prepared from apples.

THE APPLE

Within its polished universe
The apple holds a star.
   (draw design of star with index finger)
A secret constellation
To scatter near and far.
   (point near and far)
Let a knife discover
Where the five points hide.
Split the shiny ruby
And find the star inside.

After introducing the fingerplay the teacher can cut an apple crosswise to find a star.

APPLE TREE

This is the tree
With leaves so green.
   (make leaves with fingers outstretched)
Here are the apples
That hang in between.
   (make fist)
When the wind blows
   (blow)

The apples will fall.
   (falling motion with hand)
Here is the basket to gather them all.
   (use arms to form basket)

Sensory

1. Cut different varieties of apples for a tasting party. This activity can easily be extended. On another day provide the children applesauce, apple pie, apple juice, or apple cider to taste during snack or lunch.

2. Place several different kinds of seeds on the sensory table. In addition, to create interest provide scoops, bowls, and bottles to fill.

Math

1. Cut apple shapes of various sizes from construction paper. Let the children sequence the shapes from smallest to largest.

2. Place a scale and various-sized apples on the math table. The children can experiment by weighing the apples.

Science

1. **Solar Baked Apple Slices**

   Materials: 4 styrofoam cups
   black paper
   scissors
   masking tape
   apple
   knife
   plastic wrap
   rubber bands
   white paper
   foil
   newspaper

   Line 2 cups with black paper. Place 2 equal-sized slices of apple inside each cup. Cover

16

with plastic wrap held by rubber band. With paper and tape make a cone. Place one apple cup into it. Cover the inside of another paper cone with aluminum foil and place second apple cup into it. Place both in a sunny window facing the sun on crumpled newspaper. Which one cooks faster? The apple baked in the aluminum foil.

Source: Sisson, Edith A. *Nature With Children of All Ages*.

2. **Dried Apples**

Peel, core, and cut apples into slices or rings about 1/8 inch thick. Prepare a salt-water solution by mixing a tablespoon of salt in a gallon of water. Place the apples in this solution for several minutes. Remove from the solution. Place the apples in 180-degree oven for 3 to 4 hours or until dry. Turn the apples occasionally.

3. **Oxidation of an Apple**

Cut and core an apple into sections. Dip half the apple into lemon juice and place it on a plate. Place the remaining sections of apple on another plate. What happens to each plate of apples? Discuss the effects of the lemon juice coating which keeps oxygen from the apples. As a result, they do not discolor as rapidly.

4. **Explore an Apple**

Discuss the color, size, and shape of an apple. Then discuss the parts of an apple. Include the skin, stem, core, meat, etc. Feel the apple. Then cut the apple in half. Observe the core and seeds. An apple is a fruit because it contains seeds.

Dramatic Play

Set Up an Apple Stand

Prepare an apple stand by providing the children with bags, plastic apples, cash register, money, stand, and bushels. Encourage buying, selling, and packaging.

Arts and Crafts

1. **Apple Printing**

Cut apple shapes from sponges. Have available individual shallow pans of red, yellow, and green tempera paint. Provide paper. The apple can be used as a painting tool. To illustrate, the children can place an apple half in the paint. After removing the excess paint, the apple can be placed on paper to create a print.

2. **Seed Pictures**

Collect: apple seeds along with other seeds
paper
colors
glue

Each child who chooses to participate should be provided with a small number of seeds. As they are distributed, discuss the seeds' similarities and differences. Provide uninterrupted time for the children to glue seeds onto paper and create pictures.

3. **Shakers**

Collect: appleseeds
paper plates (2 per child)
glue or stapler
color crayons or felt-tip markers

The children can decorate the paper plates with color crayons or felt-tip markers. After this, the seeds can be placed between the two plates. To create the shakers, staple or glue the two plates together by securing the outer edges of the plates. The children can use the shakers as a means of self expression during music or self-directed play.

Field Trips

1. Visit an Apple Orchard

Observe the workers picking, sorting, and/or selling the apples. Call attention to the colors and types of apples.

2. Visit a Grocery Store

Observe all the forms of apples sold in a grocery store. Also, in the produce department, observe the different colors and sizes of apples. To show children differences in weight, take a large apple and place it on a scale. Note the weight. Then take a small apple and repeat the process.

Group Time
(games, language)

1. What Is It?

Collect a variety of fruits such as apples, bananas, and oranges. Begin by placing one fruit in a bag. Choose a child to touch the fruit, describe it, and name it. Repeat with each fruit, discussing the characteristics. During the activity each child should have an opportunity to participate.

2. Transition Activity

The children should stand in a circle. As a record is played, the children pass an apple. When the record stops, the child holding the apple can get up to get a snack, put on outdoor clothes, clean up, etc. Continue until all children have a turn. For older children, more than one apple may be successfully passed at a time.

Cooking

1. Caramel Apple Slices

Prepare the following recipe, which should serve 12 to 14 children.

1 pound caramels
2 tablespoons water
dash of salt
6 crisp apples

Melt caramels with water in the microwave oven or double boiler, stirring frequently until melted. Stir in the salt. Pour the melted caramel over the sliced apples and cool before serving.

2. Applesauce

30 large apples
2 1/2 cups water
1 1/2 cups sugar
1 tablespoon red hots

1. Clean apples by peeling, coring, and cutting into small pieces.
2. Place the apples in a large kettle containing water.
3. Simmer the apples on low heat, stirring occasionally until soft.
4. Add the remaining ingredients.
5. Stir and simmer a few minutes.
6. Cool prior to eating.

3. Persian Apple Dessert

3 medium apples, cut up
2 to 3 tablespoons sugar
2 tablespoons lemon juice
dash of salt

Place half the apples and the remaining ingredients in a blender. Cover and blend until coarsely chopped, about 20 to 30 seconds. Add remaining apples and repeat. Makes 3 servings.

4. Charoses

6 medium apples
1/2 cup raisins
1/2 teaspoon cinnamon
1/2 cup chopped nuts
1/4 cup white grape juice

Chop the peeled or unpeeled apples. Add the remaining ingredients. Mix well and serve.

5. Fruit Leather

2 cups applesauce
vegetable shortening or oil

Preheat oven to 400 degrees. Pour applesauce onto greased shallow pan. Spread to 1/8 inch in thickness. Place pan in oven and lower temperature to 180 degrees. Cook for approximately 3 hours until the leather can be peeled from the pan. Cut with scissors to serve.

6. Dried Apples

5 or 6 apples
2 tablespoons salt
water

Peel, core, and cut apples into slices or rings 1/8 inch thick. Place apple slices in saltwater solution (2 tablespoons per 1 gallon water) for several minutes. Remove from the water. Place in 180-degree oven for 3 to 4 hours until dry. Turn apples occasionally.

Books

The following books can be used to complement this theme:

Aliki. (1991). *The Story of Johnny Appleseed*. New York: Simon & Schuster.

Early, Margaret. (1991). *William Tell*. New York: Harry N. Abrams.

Fisher, Leonard Everett. (1996). *William Tell*. New York: Farrar, Straus & Giroux.

Hall, Zoe. (1996). *The Apple Pie Tree*. Illus. by Shari Halpern. New York: Scholastic.

Hodges, Margaret. (1997). *The True Tale of Johnny Appleseed*. New York: Holiday House.

Lindbergh, Reeve. (1990). *Johnny Appleseed*. Illus. by Kathy Jakobsen. Boston: Little, Brown.

Maestro, Betsy. (1992). *How Do Apples Grow?* New York: HarperCollins.

Marzollo, Jean. (1997). *I Am an Apple*. Illus. by Judith Moffatt. St. Paul, MN: Cartwheel Books. (Pbk)

Micucci, Charles. (1992). *The Life and Times of the Apple*. New York: Orchard Books.

Patent, Dorothy Hinshaw. (1998). *Apple Trees*. Photos by William Munoz. Minneapolis: Lerner Publications.

Priceman, Marjorie. (1994). *How to Make an Apple Pie and See the World*. New York: Knopf.

Rockwell, Anne. (1991). *Apples and Pumpkins*. New York: Simon & Schuster.

Slawson, Michele Benoit. (1994). *Apple Picking Time*. Illus. by Deborah Kogan Ray. New York: Crown Publishers.

Tryon, Leslie. (1993). *Albert's Field Trip*. New York: Simon & Schuster.

Multimedia

The following multimedia products can be used to complement this theme:

Apples [video]. (1996). DeBeck Educational Video.

Kunstler, James Howard. (1992). *Johnny Appleseed* [video]. Told by Garrison Keillor. Rabbit Ears.

Recordings and Song Titles

The following recordings can be used to complement this theme:

Pre-K Hooray—"Apple Pickin'"
Where Is Thumbkin?—"Apples & Bananas"
Songs About Me—"Do You Like Fruit?"

THEME 3

Art

Occupations
artist, weaver, designer, potter, painter, glassblower, cartoonist

Places
art studios, museums, parks, stores, homes, schools, craft shops, historical sites

Tools
paintbrushes, paper, crayons, pencils, paint, chalk, watercolors, markers, needles, scissors, sewing machine, pottery wheel, food

Kinds
folk art
impressionist
modern
child
crafts
romantic

Surfaces
paper, canvas, wood, metal, fabric, yarn, glass, ceramic, plastic, cement

Uses
beauty
decoration
communication
enjoyment

Theme Goals

Through participating in the experiences provided by this theme, the children may learn:

1. The uses of art.
2. Places where works of art can be found.
3. Art tools.
4. Surfaces used for art.
5. Occupations associated with art.
6. Kinds of art.

Concepts for the Children to Learn

1. Art is an expression of feelings and thoughts.
2. Brushes, paints, pencils, felt-tip markers, crayons, chalk, and paper are all art tools.
3. An artist uses art tools to make designs, pictures, or sculptures.
4. Art is a form of communication.
5. A museum has art objects.
6. An art gallery sells art objects.
7. Paper, canvas, and wood can all be painted.
8. We are all artists.
9. Artists create for many reasons—personal enjoyment, gift giving, and career.

Vocabulary

1. **art**—a form of beauty.
2. **crayon**—an art tool made of wax.
3. **paint**—a colored liquid used for decoration.
4. **paintbrush**—a tool for applying paint.
5. **chalk**—a soft stone used for writing or drawing.
6. **artist**—a person who creates art.
7. **gallery**—a place to display works of art.

Bulletin Board

The purpose of this bulletin board is to reinforce color-matching skills. Construct a crayon match bulletin board by drawing 16 crayons on white tagboard. Divide the crayons into pairs. Color each pair of crayons a different color. Include the colors pink, red, blue, yellow, purple, orange, brown, and green. Hang one from each pair on the top of the bulletin board and attach a corresponding colored string from the crayons. Hang the second set of crayons on the lower end of the bulletin board. A pushpin can be added to the bottom set of crayons and the children can match the top crayons to their corresponding match on the bottom of the bulletin board.

Adjust the bulletin board to match the developmental needs and level of the children. For younger children, use fewer color choices. Let the children use the bulletin board during self-directed and self-initiated play periods. Repetition of this activity is important for assimilation, providing it is initiated by the child.

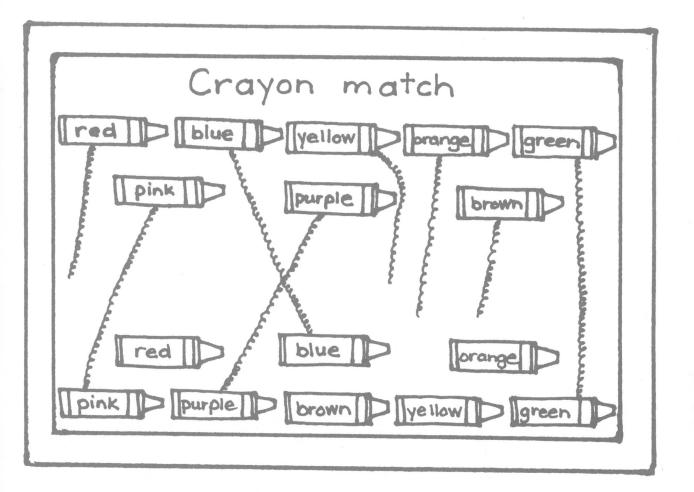

Parent Letter

Dear Parents,

Art is an expressive and aesthetic activity that can be enjoyed throughout life. It is also a curriculum theme that children always enjoy. During our focus on art, the children will be exploring many different types of art tools and supplies. They will also be learning where works of art can be found. Moreover, the art work that they create will be displayed in an outdoor art gallery. You are invited to browse when you pick your child up from the center.

AT SCHOOL

Some of the artistic experiences planned include:

- creating chalk murals on the sidewalk.
- staging an art gallery in the dramatic play area.
- visiting on Tuesday with Bob Jones, a tour guide at the city museum. Mr. Jones will be sharing several art objects with us in our classroom.
- sorting art tools.
- participating in a wide variety of art activities.

AT HOME

You can introduce the concepts of this unit into your home by collecting art tools and exploring them together. A fun art idea is painting on paper using kitchen tools as applicators. Forks, potato mashers, and slotted spoons all work well for this activity. Through this and other art activities your child will be discovering interesting and creative ways for using materials. Art also provides opportunities for experimenting with color.

Have fun looking at art with your child!

24

Fingerplays

CLAY

I stretch it.
  (pulling motion)
I pound it.
  (pounding motion)
I make it firm.
  (pushing motion)
I roll it.
  (rolling motion)
I pinch it.
  (pinching motion)
I make a worm.
  (wiggling motion)

PAINTING

Hands are blue.
  (look at outstretched hands)
Hands are green.
Fingers are red,
In between.
  (wiggle fingers)
Paint on my face.
  (touch face)
Paint on my smock.
  (touch smock)
Paint on my shoes.
  (touch shoes)
Paint on my socks.
  (touch socks)

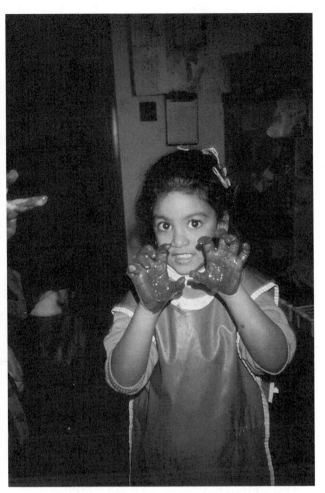

Through art, children can experience new outlets for self-expression.

Music

"Let's Pretend"
(Sing to the tune of "Here We Are Together")

Let's pretend that we are artists,
are artists, are artists.
Let's pretend that we are artists
How happy we'll be.
We'll paint with our brushes,
and draw with our crayons.
Let's pretend that we are artists
How happy we'll be.

Social Studies

The Feel of Color

This activity can be introduced at large group time. Begin by collecting colored construction paper. Individually hold each color up and ask the children how that particular color makes them feel. Adjectives that may be used include: hot, cold, cheerful, warm, sad, tired, happy, clean.

Group Time
(games, language)

Toward the end of the unit, collect all art projects and display them in an art gallery at your center. The children can help hang their own projects and decide where to have the gallery. If weather permits, the art gallery can be set up on the playground using low clotheslines and easels to display the art. If weather does not permit, a gallery can be set up in the classroom or center lobby, using walls and tables to display the art.

Cooking

GRAHAM CRACKER TREAT

Give each child a graham cracker, honey, and a brush to spread the honey. Top with grated cheese, raisins, or coconut.

COOKIE DECORATING

Sugar cookies can be purchased commercially or baked and decorated. Recipes for the cookies and frosting are as follows:

1. **Drop Sugar Cookies**

    2 eggs
    2/3 cup vegetable oil
    2 teaspoons vanilla
    3/4 cup sugar
    2 cups flour
    2 teaspoons baking powder
    1/2 teaspoon salt

    Beat eggs with fork. Stir in oil and vanilla. Blend in sugar until mixture thickens. Add flour, baking powder, and salt. Mix well. Drop dough by teaspoons about 2 inches apart on an ungreased baking sheet. Flatten with the bottom of a plastic glass dipped in sugar. Bake 8 to 10 minutes or until delicate brown. Remove from baking sheet immediately. Makes about 4 dozen cookies that are 2 1/2 inches in diameter.

2. **Favorite Icing**

    1 cup sifted confectioner's sugar
    1/4 teaspoon salt
    1/2 teaspoon vanilla
    1 tablespoon water
    food coloring

    Blend salt, sugar, and vanilla. Add enough water to make frosting easy to spread. Tint with food coloring. Allow children to spread on cookie with spatula or paintbrush.

Science

1. **Art Tools**

    A variety of art tools can be placed on the science table. Included may be brushes, pencils, felt-tip markers, crayons, and chalk. The children can observe, smell, and feel the difference in the tools.

2. **Charcoal**

    Place charcoal pieces and magnifying glasses on the science table.

3. **Rock Writing**

    Provide the children with a variety of soft rocks. The children can experiment drawing on the sidewalks with them.

Dramatic Play

1. **Artist**

    Smocks, easels, and paint tables can be placed in the dramatic play area. The children can use the materials to pretend they are artists.

2. **Art Gallery**

    Mount pictures from magazines on sheets of tagboard. Let the children hang the pictures around the classroom. A cash register and play money for buying and selling the paintings can extend the play.

Arts and Crafts

1. **Frames**

   During the course of this unit, the children can frame, with your assistance, their works of art by mounting them on sheets of colored tagboard and trimming it with a frame-like border. Older children may be able to do this unassisted. Display the works of art in the lobby, classroom—or outdoors, if weather permits.

2. **Experimenting**

   In a unit on art, many kinds of art media need to be explored. Include the following art experiences:

   - markers (both jumbo and skinny)
   - chalk (both wet and dry)
   - charcoal
   - pencils (both colored and lead)
   - crayons (jumbo, regular-sized, and shavings)
   - paint (watercolors, tempera, fingerpaint)
   - paper (colored construction, white, typing, tissue, newsprint, fingerpaint, tagboard)
   - other (tin foil, cotton, glitter, glue and paste, lace, scraps, crepe paper, bags, waxed paper, yarn, and string)
   - tools for painting (marbles, string, fingers, brushes of all sizes, straws, sponges)
   - playdough and clay
   - printing tools (stamps and ink pads, kitchen tools, sponges, potatoes, apples, and carrot ends)
   - seeds

Sensory

Additions to the Sensory Table

1. **Goop**

   Mix together food coloring, 1 cup cornstarch, and 1 cup water in the sensory table. If a larger quantity is desired, double or triple the recipe.

2. **Silly Putty**

   Mix food coloring, 1 cup liquid starch, and 2 cups of glue together. Stir constantly until the ingredients are well mixed. Add more starch as needed.

3. **Wet Sand and Sand Mold Containers**

Large Muscle

1. **Sidewalk Chalk**

   Washable colored chalk can be provided for the children to use outside on the sidewalk. After the activity the designs can be removed with a hose. The children may even enjoy using scrub brushes to remove the design.

2. **Painting**

   Provide large paintbrushes and buckets of water for the children to paint the sidewalks, walls, and fences surrounding your center or school.

3. **Foot Art**

   Prepare a thick tempera paint and pour a small amount in a shallow pan. Roll out long sheets of paper. The children can take off their shoes and socks, step into the tempera paint, and walk or dance across the sheets of paper. Provide buckets with soapy water and towels at the end of the paper for the children to wash their feet. Dry the foot paintings and send them home with the children.

Field Trips/ Resource People

1. Museum

Take a field trip to a museum, if one is available. Observe art objects. Point out and discuss color and form.

2. Art Store

Take a walk to a nearby art store. Observe the many kinds of pencils, markers, crayons, paints, and other art supplies that are available.

3. Resource People

Invite the following people to show the children their artwork.

- painter
- potter
- weaver
- glass blower
- sculptor

Math

1. Counting Cans

Counting cans for this unit can be made from empty soup cans with filed edges. On each can write a numeral. The number prepared will depend upon the developmental needs of the children. Then provide an equal number of the following objects: pencils, pens, markers, paintbrushes, crayons, chalk sticks, sponges, etc. The object is for the children to relate the number of objects to numerals on the can.

2. Measuring Art Tools

Art tools come in all different lengths. Provide a variety of art tools and rulers, or a tape measure that has been taped to the table. The children can measure the objects to find which one is the longest. Make a chart showing the longest tool and continuing to the shortest.

3. Sorting Art Supplies

A large ice cream pail can be used to hold pencils, pens, markers, crayons, glue bottles, etc. that can be sorted into shoeboxes.

Painting Surfaces

There are many types of interesting surfaces that children can successfully use for painting. The list of possibilities are limited only by one's imagination. Included are:

- construction paper
- newsprint (plain/printed)
- tissue paper
- tracing paper
- tin foil
- clear/colored acetate
- wood
- cardboard
- shelf paper
- paper table cloths
- paper place mats
- waxed paper
- boxes
- leather scrap
- sand paper
- paper toweling
- mirror
- plexiglass
- paper bags
- cookie sheets
- meat trays—plastic, cardboard, styrofoam
- table surfaces

Books

The following books can be used to complement this theme:

Anholt, Laurence. (1994). *Camille and the Sunflowers: A Story about Vincent Van Gogh.* Hauppauge, NY: Barron's Educational Series.

Auch, Mary Jane. (1996). *Eggs Mark the Spot.* New York: Holiday House.

Blizzard, Gladys. *Come Look with Me* series. West Palm Beach: Lickle Publishing. *Animals in Art.* (1992); *Enjoying Art with Children.* (1991); *Exploring Landscape Art with Children.* (1992); *World of Play.* (1993).

Catalanotto, Peter. (1995). *The Painter.* New York: Orchard Books.

Cooney, Barbara. (1990). *Hattie and the Wild Waves.* New York: Viking.

Crespi, Francesca. (1995). *A Walk in Monet's Garden: Full Color Pop-Up with Guided Tour.* Boston: Little, Brown.

De Paola, Tomie. (1989). *Art Lesson.* New York: G. P. Putnam.

Dixon, Annabelle. (1990). *Clay.* Photos by Ed Barber. Ada, OK: Garrett.

Dunrea, Olivier. (1995). *The Painter Who Loved Chickens.* New York: Farrar, Straus & Giroux.

Florian, Douglas. (1993). *Painter.* New York: Greenwillow.

Folk Art Counting Book. (1992). Developed by Amy Watson and the Staff of the Abby Aldrich Rockefeller Folk Art Center. New York: Abrams.

Hest, Amy. (1996). *Jamaica Louise James.* Illus. by Sheila White Samton. Cambridge, MA: Candlewick Press.

Hurd, Thacher. (1996). *Art Dog.* New York: HarperCollins.

Jeunesse, Gallimard. (1991). *Colors.* Illus. by P. M. Valet. New York: Scholastic.

Le Tord, Bijou. (1995). *Blue Butterfly: A Story about Claude Monet.* New York: Bantam.

Lynn, Sara. (1993). *Play with Paint.* Minneapolis: Carolrhoda Books.

Micklethwait, Lucy. (1992). *I Spy: An Alphabet in Art.* New York: Greenwillow. *I Spy a Freight Train: Transportation in Art.* (1996); *I Spy a Lion: Animals in Art.* Nashville: Ideals, (1993); *Spot a Cat.* New York: Dorling Kindersley. (1995); *Spot a Dog.* New York: Dorling Kindersley. (1995).

Moon, Nicola. (1997). *Lucy's Picture.* Illus. by Lynn Munsinger. New York: Dial Books.

Porte, Barbara Ann. (1995). *Chickens Chickens.* Illus. by Greg Henry. New York: Orchard Books.

Richardson, Joy. (1993). *Inside the Museum: A Children's Guide to the Metropolitan Museum of Art.* New York: Abrams.

Rockwell, Anne F. (1993). *Mr. Panda's Painting.* New York: Simon & Schuster.

Stanley, Diane. (1994). *The Gentleman and the Kitchen Maid.* Illus. by Dennis Nolan. New York: Dial Books.

Venezia, Mike. (1988–1997). *Getting to Know the World's Greatest Artists* series. Chicago: Children's Press. 23+ titles.

Winter, Jeanette. (1996). *Josefina.* Orlando: Harcourt Brace.

Wolestein, Diane. (1992). *Little Mouse's Painting.* Illus. by Jaryjane Begin. New York: William Morrow.

Yenawine, Philip. (1991). *Colors.* The Museum of Modern Art. New York: Delacorte Press.

Multimedia

The following multimedia products can be used to complement this theme:

I Want to Be an Artist [video]. (1993). Glenview, IL: Crystal Productions.

Kid Pix Studio [CD-ROM]. (1994). Novato, CA: Broderbund.

New Kid Pix [CD-ROM]. (1996). Novato, CA: Broderbund.

Paint, Write and Play [CD-ROM]. (1996). Fremont, CA: Learning Company.

Polisar, Barry Louis. *Barry's Scrapbook: A Window into Art* [video]. (1994). ALA Video/Library Video Network.

Rylant, Cynthia. *All I See* [video]. (1990). Hightstown, NJ: McGraw-Hill Media.

Recordings and Song Titles

The following recordings can be used to complement this theme:

There's Music in the Colors

I Like Myself—"Draw a Circle"

Where Is Thumbkin?—"The Color Song"

Pre-K Hooray—"Color Wheel Dance"

Homemade Games—"Color Square"

Piggyback Sons—"Colors"

Children Love to Sing and Dance (The Learning Station)—"Everything Has a Color"

Let's Visit Lullaby Land—"Colour My World"

Rainbow of Songs—"Primary Colors"

THEME 4

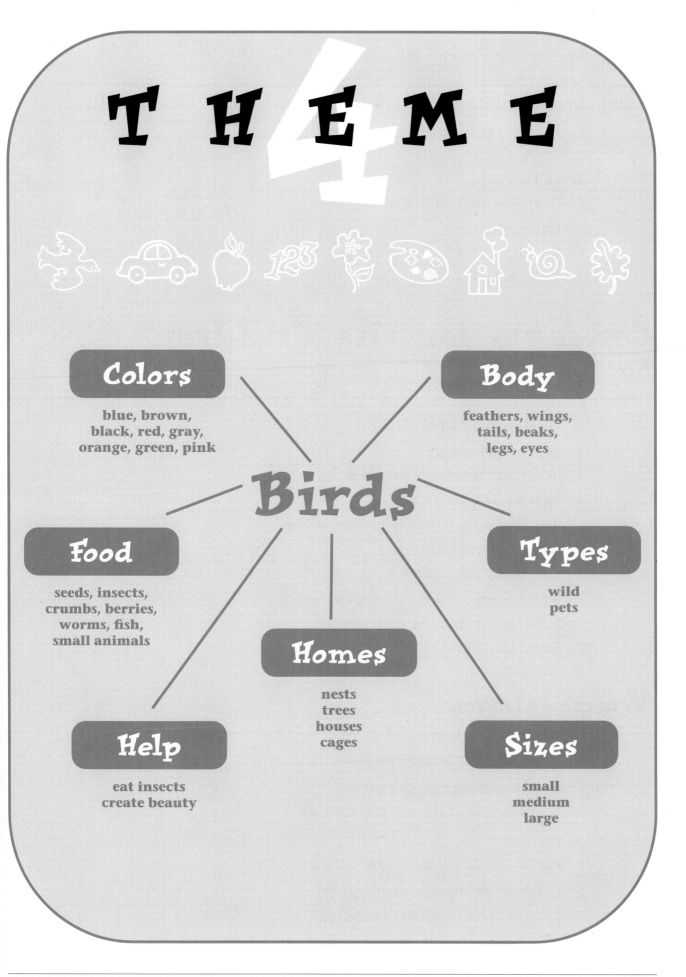

Colors

blue, brown,
black, red, gray,
orange, green, pink

Body

feathers, wings,
tails, beaks,
legs, eyes

Birds

Food

seeds, insects,
crumbs, berries,
worms, fish,
small animals

Types

wild
pets

Homes

nests
trees
houses
cages

Help

eat insects
create beauty

Sizes

small
medium
large

Theme Goals

Through participating in the experiences provided by this theme, the children may learn:

1. The bird's body parts.
2. Types of birds.
3. Bird homes.
4. Foods that birds eat.
5. Ways birds help.
6. Sizes of birds.
7. Colors of birds.

Concepts for the Children to Learn

1. There are many kinds of birds.
2. Birds hatch from eggs.
3. Birds have feathers, wings, and beaks.
4. Most birds fly.
5. Birds live in nests, trees, houses, and cages.
6. Some birds are pets.
7. Many birds make sounds.
8. Birds eat seeds, insects, crumbs, and worms.
9. Some birds eat fish and small animals.
10. Some birds help us by eating insects.

Vocabulary

1. **beak**—the part around a bird's mouth.
2. **bird watching**—watching birds.
3. **bird feeder**—a container for bird food.
4. **feathers**—cover skin of a bird.
5. **hatch**—to come from an egg.
6. **nest**—bed or home prepared by a bird.
7. **perch**—a pole for a bird to stand on.
8. **wing**—movable body part that helps most birds fly.

Bulletin Board

The purpose of this bulletin board is to develop skills in matching. To construct the board, cut ten bird nests out of brown-colored tagboard. Draw a set of dots, beginning with one, on each bird nest. Tack the nest on the bulletin board. Next, construct the same number of birds out of tagboard. Write a numeral on each bird beginning with one. By matching the numeral on each bird to the number of dots on the nests, the children can help each bird find a home. The number of birds and nests on this bulletin board should match the children's developmental needs.

Parent Letter

Dear Parents,

The children will be discussing our "feathered friends"—birds—during our next unit. They will be introduced to birds kept as pets and birds in the wild. In addition, they will discover the unique body parts of birds and the homes in which they live. By participating in class activities, the children will learn that birds are more similar than they are dissimilar.

AT SCHOOL

Some of the activities planned for the unit on birds include:

- observing different types of bird nests with a magnifying glass at the science table.
- visiting with Jodi's pet canary on Wednesday.
- creating collages using birdseed and glue in the art area.
- making bird feeders to hang outdoors in our play yard.
- building bird houses.

AT HOME

Whether you live in the city or country, chances are there are birds nearby. If you have birds in your yard, the following game may be fun to play with your child. Set an egg or kitchen timer for three to five minutes. Then look out the window and see how many birds you can see. For each bird, drop a button in a jar. When the timer goes off, count how many buttons are in the jar. This game will strengthen your child's observation skills and increase his understanding of number concepts. Variations of this game would be to observe for cars, squirrels, or any other object that can be counted.

Happy bird watching!

34

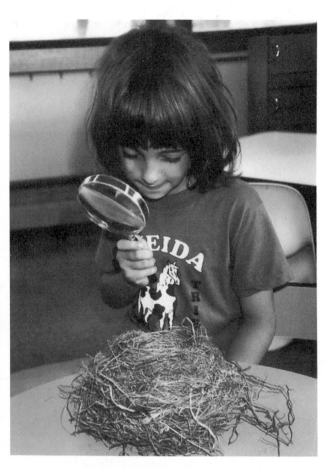

Children enjoy exploring bird habitats.

Music

1. **"Birds"**
    (Sing to the tune of "Here We Go Round the Mulberry Bush")

    The first verse remains the same, with the children walking around in a circle holding hands.

    This is the way we scratch for worms,
      scratch for worms, scratch for worms.
    This is the way we scratch for worms
      so early in the morning.
      (children move foot in a scratching
      motion like a chicken)
    This is the way we peck our food . . .
      (children peck)
    This is the way we sit on our eggs . . .
      (children squat down)
    This is the way we flap our wings . . .
      (bend arms at elbows, and put thumbs
      under armpits, flap)

    This is the way we fly away . . .
      (children can "fly" anywhere they want,
      but return to the circle at the end of the
      verse)

2. **"Pretty Birds"**
    (Sing to the tune of "Ten Little Indians")

    One pretty, two pretty
    Three pretty birdies.
    Four pretty, five pretty,
    Six pretty birdies.
    Seven pretty, eight pretty,
    Nine pretty birdies,
    All sitting in a tree.

Fingerplays

THE DUCK

I waddle when I walk.
  (hold arms and elbows high and twist
  trunk side to side or squat down)
I quack when I walk
  (place palms together and open and close)
And I have webbed toes on my feet.
  (spread fingers wide)
Rain coming down, makes me smile, not
  frown
  (smile)
And I dive for something to eat.
  (put hands together and make diving
  motion)

Source: Hillert, Margaret. (1982). *Action Verse for Early Childhood*. Minneapolis: T.S. Denison and Co. Inc.

THE OWL

There's a wide-eyed owl
  (encircle each eye with thumb and
  forefinger)
With a pointed nose.
  (direct forefingers to a point downside of
  nose)
And two pointed ears
  (extend forefingers up from top of head)
And claws for toes.
  (curve fingers like claws)
He lives high in a tree.
  (point overhead)

When he looks at you
   (point to another child)
He flaps his wings
   (bend elbows and flap arms like wings)
And says "whoo, whoo, whoo."

Source: Hillert, Margaret. (1982). *Action Verse for Early Childhood*. Minneapolis: T.S. Denison and Co. Inc.

HOUSES

Here is a nest for a robin.
   (cup both hands)
Here is a hive for a bee.
   (fists together)
Here is a hole for the bunny;
   (finger and thumb make circle)
And here is a house for me!
   (fingertips together to make roof)

TWO LITTLE BLACKBIRDS

Two little blackbirds sitting on a hill,
   (close fists, extend index fingers)
One named Jack. One named Jill.
   (talk to one finger; talk to other finger)
Fly away Jack. Fly away Jill.
   (toss index fingers over shoulder
   separately)
Come back, Jack. Come back Jill.
   (bring back hands separately with index
   fingers extended)

BIRD FEEDER

Here is the bird feeder. Here are seeds and
  crumbs.
   (left hand out flat, right hand cupped)
Sprinkle them on and see what comes.
   (sprinkling motion with right hand over
   left hand)
One cardinal, one chickadee, one junco,
  one jay,
   (join fingers of right hand and peck at
   the bird feeder once for each bird)
Four of my bird friends are eating today.
   (hold up four fingers of left hand)

IF I WERE A BIRD

If I were a bird, I'd sing a song
And fly about the whole day long.
   (twine thumbs together and move hands
   like wings)

And when the night comes, go to rest,
   (tilt head and close eyes)
Up in my cozy little nest.
   (cup hands together to form nest)

TAP TAP TAP

Tap, tap, tap goes the woodpecker
   (tap with right pointer finger on inside
   of left wrist)
As he pecks a hole in a tree.
   (make hole with pointer finger and
   thumb)
He is making a house with a window
To peep at you and me.
   (hold circle made with finger and thumb
   in front of eye)

STRETCH, STRETCH

Stretch, stretch away up high:
On your tiptoes, reach the sky.
See the bluebirds flying high.
   (wave hands)
Now bend down and touch your toes.
Now sway as the North Wind blows.
Waddle as the gander goes!

Science

1. **Bird Feeders**

Make bird feeders. Suet can be purchased from a butcher shop or meat department of a supermarket. For each feeder, purchase 1/2 pound of suet, a 12" x 12" piece of netting, and birdseed. Begin by rolling the suet in birdseed. Place the seeded suet in the netting. Tie the four corners of the netting together and hang in tree or set outside on window ledge for children to observe.

2. **Grapefruit Cup Feeders**

Place seeds in an empty grapefruit half. If possible, place the feeder in an observable location for the children. Some children may wish to take their feeders home.

3. Science Table

On the science table, provide magnifying glasses and the following items:

- feathers
- eggs
- nests

4. Observing a Bird

Arrange for a caged parakeet to visit the classroom. A parent may volunteer or a pet store may lend a bird for a week. Encourage the children to note the structure of the cage, the beauty of the bird, food eaten, and the behavior of the bird.

Dramatic Play

1. Birdhouse

Construct a large birdhouse out of cardboard. Place in the dramatic play area, allowing the children to imitate birds. Unless adequate room is available, this may be more appropriate for an outdoor activity. Bird accessories such as teacher-made beaks and wings may be supplied to stimulate interest.

2. Bird Nest

Place several hay bales in the corner of a play yard, confining the materials to one area. Let the child rearrange the straw to simulate a bird nest.

3. Hatching

Here is a general idea of what you can say to create the hatching experience with young children. Say, "Close your eyes. Curl up very small; as small as you can. Lie on your side. Think of how dark it is inside your egg. Yes, you're in an egg! You're tiny and curled up and quiet. It's very dark. Very warm. But now, try to wiggle a little—just a little! Remember, your eggshell is all around you. You can wiggle your wingtips a little, and maybe your toes. You can shake your head just a little. Hey! Your beak is touching some-thing. I think your beak is touching the eggshell. Tap the shell gently with your beak. Hear that? Yes, that's you making that noise. Keep tapping. A little harder. Something is happening. The shell has cracked—oh, close your eyes. It's bright out there. Now you can wiggle a little more. The shell is falling away. You can stretch out, stretch to be as long as you can make yourself. Stretch your feet. Stretch your wings. Doesn't that feel good, after being in that little egg? Stretch! You're brand new—can you stand up, slowly? Can you see other new baby birds?"

Arts and Crafts

1. Feather Painting

On the art table, place feathers, thin paper, and paint. Let the children experiment with different paint consistencies and types of feathers. Suggestion: Inexpensive feather dusters from discount stores are a good source of feathers. Individual feathers can be cut off as needed.

2. Birdseed Collages

Birdseed, paper, and white glue are needed for this activity. Apply glue to paper and sprinkle birdseed over the glue. For a variation, use additional types of seeds such as corn and sunflower seeds.

3. Eggshell Collage

Save eggshells and dye them. Crush the dyed shells into small pieces. Using glue, apply the eggshells to paper.

4. Robin Eggs

Cut easel paper into the shape of an egg. Provide light blue paint with sand for speckles.

5. Dying Eggs

Boil an egg for each child. Then let the children paint the eggs with easel brushes. The eggs can be eaten at snack time or taken home.

Sensory

Additions to the Sensory Table

- feathers and sand
- eggshells
- sticks and twigs for nests
- worms and soil
- water, rubber ducks, and other water toys
- birdseed and measuring tools

Field Trips/ Resource People

1. **Pet Store**

   Take a field trip to a pet store. Arrange to have the manager show the children birds and bird cages. Ask the manager how to care for birds.

2. **Bird Sanctuary**

   Take a field trip to a bird sanctuary, nature area, pond, or park. Observe where birds live.

3. **Museum**

   Arrange to visit a nature museum or taxidermy studio to look at stuffed birds. Extend the activity by providing magnifying glasses.

4. **Zoo**

   Visit the bird house. Observe the colors and sizes of birds.

5. **Resource People**

   Invite resource people to visit the classroom. Suggestions include:

   - wildlife management people
   - ornithologists
   - veterinarians
   - bird owners
   - bird watchers
   - pet store owners

Math

1. **Feather Sorting**

   During the self-directed activity period, place a variety of feathers on a table. Encourage the children to sort them according to attributes such as color, size, and/or texture. This activity can be followed with other sorting activities including egg shapes and pictures of birds.

2. **Cracked Eggs**

   Cut tagboard egg shapes. Using scissors, cut the eggs in half making a jagged line. Record a numeral on one side of the egg and corresponding dots on the other side. The number of eggs prepared should reflect the children's developmental level.

Social Studies

1. **Caring for Birds**

   Arrange for a pet canary to visit the classroom. The children can take turns feeding and caring for the bird. Responsibilities include cleaning the cage, providing water and birdseed. Also, a cuttlebone should be inserted in the bars of the cage within reach of the bird's bill. This bone will help keep the bird's bill sharp and clean, providing the bird uses it.

2. **Bird Feeders**

   Purchase birdseed and small paper cups. The children can fill a cup with a small amount of seed. After this, the teacher can attach a small string to the cup for use as a handle. The bird feeders can then be hung in bushes outdoors. If bushes are not available, they can be placed on window sills.

Group Time
(games, language)

1. Little Birds

This is a movement game that allows for activity. To add interest, the teacher may use a tambourine for rhythm. One child can be the mother bird and the remainder of the children can act out the story.

All the little birds are asleep in their nest.
All the little birds are taking a rest.
They do not even twitter, they do not even tweet.
Everything is quiet up and down the street.
Then came the mother bird and tapped them on the head.
They opened up one little eye and this is what was said,
"Come little birdies, it's time to learn to fly,
Come little birdies, fly way up in the sky."
Fly fly, oh fly away, fly, fly, fly
Fly fly, oh fly away, fly away so high.
Fly fly, oh, fly away, birds can fly the best.
Fly fly, oh, fly away, now fly back to your nest.

2. Who Is Inside?

The purpose of this game is to encourage the child to develop listening skills. To prepare for the activity, find a piece of large muscle equipment such as a jungle gym to serve as the bird house. Cover it with a large blanket. To play the game one child looks away from the group or covers his eyes. A second child should go into the bird house. The first child says, "Who is inside?" The second child replies, "I am inside the bird house." Then the first child tries to guess who is in the bird house by recognizing the voice. Other clues may be asked for, if voice alone does not work.

3. Little Red Hen

Tell the story of the Little Red Hen. After they have heard the story, let the children help make bread.

Cooking

1. Egg Salad Sandwiches

eggs
bread
mayonnaise
dry mustard (just a pinch)
salt
pepper

Boil, shell, and mash the eggs, adding enough mayonnaise to provide a consistent texture. Add salt, pepper, and dry mustard to flavor. Spread on the bread.

2. French Bread Recipe

1/2 cup water
2 packages rapid rise yeast
1 tablespoon salt
2 cups lukewarm water
7 to 7 1/2 cups all-purpose flour

Soften the yeast in 1/2 cup lukewarm water. Be careful that the water isn't too warm or the activity of the yeast will be destroyed. Add salt to 2 cups of lukewarm warm water in a large bowl. Gradually, add 2 cups of flour and beat well. Add the softened yeast and gradually add the remaining flour, beating well after each addition. Turn the soft dough out on a lightly floured surface and knead until elastic. Lightly grease a bowl and place the dough into it, turning once to grease surface. Let rise until double. Divide into 2 portions. Bake in a 375-degree oven until light brown, about 35 minutes.

3. Bird's Nest Salad

1 grated carrot
1/2 cup canned Chinese noodles
mayonnaise to moisten
peas or grapes

Have the children grate a carrot. Next have them mix the carrot with 1/2 cup canned Chinese noodles and mayonnaise to moisten. Put a mound of this salad on a plate and push in the middle with a spoon to form a nest. Peas or grapes can be added to the nest to represent bird eggs. The nest could also be set on top of a lettuce leaf. Makes 2 salads.

Source: Warren, Jean. (1982). *Super Snacks*. Alderwood Manor, WA: Warren Publishing.

4. **Egg Foo Young**

12 eggs
1/2 cup finely chopped onion
1/3 cup chopped green pepper
3/4 teaspoon salt
dash of pepper
2 16-ounce cans bean sprouts, drained

Sauce:
2 tablespoons cornstarch
2 teaspoons sugar
2 cubes or 2 teaspoons chicken bouillon
dash of ginger
2 cups of water
3 tablespoons soy sauce

Heat oven to 300 degrees. Beat eggs in a large bowl. Add remaining ingredients, except sauce ingredients; mix well. Heat 2 tablespoons of oil in a large skillet. Drop egg mixture by tablespoons into skillet and fry until golden. Turn and brown other side. Drain on a paper towel. Continue to cook the remaining egg mixture, adding oil to skillet if necessary. Keep warm in 300-degree oven while preparing sauce. Combine the first four sauce ingredients in a saucepan. Add water and soy sauce. Cook until mixture boils and thickens, stirring constantly.

Books

The following books can be used to complement this theme:

Arnosky, Jim. (1992). *Crinkleroot's Guide to Knowing the Birds*. New York: Simon & Schuster.

Arnosky, Jim. (1993). *Crinkleroot's 25 Birds Every Child Should Know*. Minneapolis: Bradbury.

Arnosky, Jim. (1997). *Watching Water Birds*. Washington, D.C.: National Geographic Society.

Bennett, Penelope. (1995). *Town Parrot*. Illus. by Sue Heap. Cambridge, MA: Candlewick Press.

Berger, Bruce. (1995). *A Dazzle of Hummingbirds*. Illus. by John Chellman. Morristown, NJ: Silver Burdett.

Bernhard, Emery. (1994). *Eagles: Lions of the Sky*. Illus. by Durga Bernhard. New York: Holiday House.

Brenner, Barbara and Julia Takaya. (1996). *Chibi: A True Story from Japan*. Illus. by June Otani. New York: Clarion Books.

Cannon, Janell. (1993). *Stellaluna*. Orlando: Harcourt Brace.

Cherry, Lynne. (1997). *Flute's Journey: The Life of a Wood Thrush*. San Diego, CA: Gulliver Books.

Demuth, Patricia. (1994). *Cradles in the Trees: The Story of Bird Nests*. Illus. by Suzanne Barnes. New York: Simon & Schuster.

Ehlert, Louis. (1997). *Cuckoo: A Mexican Folktale*. Orlando: Harcourt Brace.

Esbensen, Barbara Juster. (1991). *Tiger with Wings: The Great Horned Owl*. Illus. by Mary Barrett Brown. New York: Orchard Books.

Ezra, Mark. (1997). *The Frightened Little Owl*. Illus. by Gavin Rowe. New York: Crocodile Books.

Flanagan, Alice K. (1996). *New True Book* series. Chicago: Children's Press. *Desert Birds; Night Birds; Seabirds; Songbirds; Talking Birds*.

Fontanel, Beatrice. (1992). *The Penguin*. Illus. by Valerie Tracqui. Watertown, MA: Charlesbridge Publishers. (Pbk)

Foster, Joanna. (1995). *The Magpies' Nest*. Illus. by Julie Downing. New York: Clarion Books.

Gans, Roma and Paul Mirocha. (1996). *How Do Birds Find Their Way?* New York: HarperCollins.

Gibbons, Gail. (1997). *Gulls—Gulls—Gulls*. New York: Holiday House.

Gibbons, Gail. (1998). *Soaring with the Wind: The Bald Eagle*. New York: William Morrow.

Jenkins, Priscilla Belz. (1995). *Nest Full of Eggs*. Illus. by Lizzy Rockwell. New York: HarperCollins.

Kalbacken, Joan. (1997). *Peacocks and Peahens*. Chicago: Children's Press.

Lewin, Betsy. (1995). *Booby Hatch*. New York: Clarion Books.

Maynard, Thane. (1997). *Ostriches*. Mankato, MN: Child's World.

Mazzola, Frank. (1997). *Counting Is for the Birds*. Watertown, MA: Charlesbridge Publishers.

McMillan, Bruce. (1995). *Nights of the Pufflings*. Boston: Houghton Mifflin.

Morrison, Gordon. (1998). *Bald Eagle*. Boston: Houghton Mifflin.

Neitzel, Shirley. (1997). *The House I'll Build for the Wrens*. New York: Greenwillow Books.

Owens, Mary Beth. (1993). *Counting Cranes*. Boston: Little, Brown.

Parry-Jones, Jemima. (1992). *Amazing Birds of Prey*. Illus. by Mike Dunning. New York: Knopf.

Pfeffer, Wendy. (1996). *Mute Swans*. Morristown, NJ: Silver Burdett Press.

Rau, Dana Meachen. (1995). *Robin at Hickory Street*. Illus. by Joel Snyder. Norwalk, CT: Soundprints/ Smithsonian Institution.

Rockwell, Anne. (1992). *Our Yard Is Full of Birds*. New York: Macmillan.

Royston, Angela. (1992). *Birds*. New York: Aladdin Books.

Savage, Stephen. (1995). *Duck*. Illus. by Steve Lings. Cincinnati, OH: Thomson Learning.

Savage, Stephen. (1995). *Seagull*. Illus. by Andre Boos. Cincinnati, OH: Thomson Learning.

Sill, Cathryn P. (1991). *About Birds: A Guide for Children*. Illus. by John Sill. Atlanta: Peachtree Publishers.

Swinburne, Stephen R. (1996). *Swallows in the Birdhouse*. Illus. by Robin Brickman. Brookfield, CT: Millbrook Press.

Torres, Leyla. (1993). *Subway Sparrow*. New York: Farrar, Straus & Giroux.

Willis, Nancy Carol. (1996). *The Robins in Your Backyard*. Montchanin, DE: Cucumber Island Storytellers.

Multimedia

The following multimedia products can be used to complement this theme:

"Birds and How They Grow" on *Animals and How They Grow* [CD-ROM]. (1993). Washington, D.C.: National Geographic Society.

Eastman, P. D. (1991). *Are You My Mother? Plus Two More P. D. Eastman Classics* [video]. New York: Random House Video.

Flying, Trying, and Honking Around [video]. (1994). Washington, D.C.: National Geographic Kids Video.

Recordings and Song Titles

The following recordings can be used to complement the theme:

Singable Nursery Rhymes—"Mary's Canary," "The Little Bird," "The Robin," "Sing a Song of Sixpence," "Swan"

Six Little Ducks—"Six Little Ducks," "Little White Duck," "Old MacDonald Had a Farm"

THEME 5

Blue

Flowers
iris, lupine,
Texas bluebonnets,
crocus,
colored carnations,
lobelia

Objects
cars, bikes, sky,
paint, blocks,
toy trucks,
magic markers,
crayons

Food
blueberries
grapes
Jello

Symbolic
cold
sad
music
tantrum

Color Mixing
blue + yellow = green
blue + red = purple

Theme Goals

Through participating in the experiences provided by this theme, the children may learn:

1. Blue is the color of many objects.
2. A type of berry is colored blue.
3. Some flowers are colored blue.
4. Blue can be mixed with other colors.

Concepts for the Children to Learn

1. Blue is the name of a color.
2. Mixing blue with yellow makes green.
3. Blue mixed with red makes purple.
4. Some cars and bikes are a blue color.
5. On sunny, clear days the sky is a blue color.
6. Blueberries and grapes are examples of blue-colored foods.
7. There are many shades of blue.
8. An iris can be colored blue.

Vocabulary

1. **blue**—a primary color.
2. **primary colors**—red, yellow, and blue.
3. **tints**—are created by adding white to a color.
4. **hues**—are created by adding black to a color.

Bulletin Board

The purpose of this bulletin board is to develop visual discrimination skills. A blue bulletin board can be constructed by focusing on familiar objects. Draw pictures of many familiar objects on tagboard. Color them various shades of blue. Cut the objects out and laminate. Next, trace the pictures, allowing 1/4-inch borders, on black construction paper. Cut out shadow pieces and hang on the bulletin board. Add a magnet piece to each shadow and picture. The children can match each picture to its corresponding shadow.

Parent Letter

Dear Parents,

Colors! Colors! Colors! Colors are all around us. In our curriculum, we will be focusing our activities on the color blue. The children will learn that blue can be mixed with red to make purple. When the color yellow is mixed with blue, green is created. The children will also become aware that many familiar objects are blue in color. Moreover, they will learn that the color blue has many associations, including sadness, cold, and music.

AT SCHOOL

Some of the learning experiences planned for this unit include:

- singing a song called "Two Little Bluejays."
- looking out our blue windows in the classroom.
- playing in a paint store in the dramatic play area.
- fingerpainting with blue paint.
- eating blueberries for snack.

AT HOME

You can make almost any meal entertaining by occasionally adding a small amount of food coloring to one of your food items. Children often find this amusing. The food coloring adds interest to your food and meal times become fun! Try adding a drop or two to milk, vanilla pudding, mashed potatoes, scrambled eggs, or cottage cheese. Does the color of a food affect its taste? (Try drinking green milk!) You be the judge! To further develop an awareness of color, identify foods that are red, blue, yellow, etc. This improves memory, classification, and receptive and expressive language skills.

Have a great time helping your child discover the color blue!

46

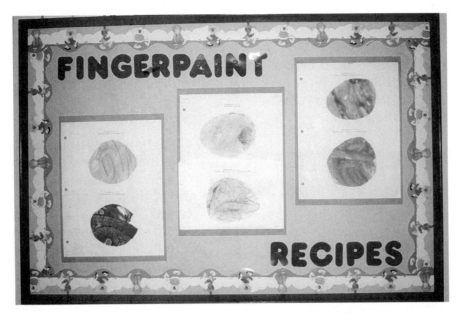

Constructing a bulletin board with items that are blue is one way to learn about colors.

Music

1. **"Two Little Bluejays"**
   (Sing to the tune of "Two Little Blackbirds")

   Two little bluejays
   sitting on a hill
   One named Sue
   One named Bill.

   Fly away Sue
   Fly away Bill.
   Come back Sue
   Come back Bill.

   Two little bluejays
   sitting on a hill
   One named Sue
   One named Bill.

   To add interest, you can substitute names
   after the song has been sung several times.
   The children will enjoy hearing their names.

2. **"Finding Colors"**
   (Sing to the tune of "The Muffin Man")

   Oh, can you find the color blue,
   The color blue, the color blue?
   Oh, can you find the color blue,
   Somewhere in this room?

Science

1. **Just One Drop**

   Each child will need a smock for this activity. Provide a glass of water and blue food coloring. Encourage the children to add a drop of blue food coloring to the water. Watch as the water becomes a light blue. Add a few more drops of food coloring, observing as the blue water turns a darker shade.

2. **Blue Color Paddles**

   Construct blue color paddles out of stiff tagboard and blue overhead transparency sheets. Make a form for the paddle out of tagboard, leaving the inside empty. Put the sheet of blue transparency paper on the back, glue, and trim. The children can hold the paddle up to their eyes and see how the colors have changed.

3. **Blue Windows**

   Place blue-colored cellophane or acetate sheets over some of the windows in the classroom. It is fun to look out the windows and see the blue world.

4. Dying Carnations

Place the stem of a white carnation in a bottle of water with blue food coloring added on the science table. Observe the change of the petal colors.

Dramatic Play

Paint Store

Provide paintbrushes, buckets, and paint sample books. The addition of a cash register, play money, and pads of paper will extend the children's play.

Arts and Crafts

1. Arm Dancing

Provide each child with two blue crayons and a large sheet of paper. Play music encouraging the children to color, using both arms. Because of the structure of this activity, it should be limited to older children.

2. Sponge Painting

Collect sponge pieces, thick blue tempera paint, and sheets of light blue paper. If desired, clothespins can be clipped on the sponges and used as handles. To use as a tool, dip the sponge into blue paint and print on light blue paper.

3. Easel Ideas

- Feature different shades of blue paint at the easel.
- Use blue paint on aluminum foil.
- Add whipped soap flakes to blue paint.
- Add a container of yellow paint to the easel. Allow the children to mix the yellow and blue paints at the easel. This activity can be extended by providing red and blue tempera paint.

4. Fingerpainting

Blue fingerpaint and large sheets of paper should be placed in the art area.

5. Melted Crayon Design

Grate broken blue crayons. Place the shreddings on one square of waxed paper 6 inches x 6 inches. On top of the shreddings, place another 6-inch x 6-inch piece of waxed paper. Cover with a dishtowel or old cloth. Apply heat with a warm iron for about 30 seconds. Let the sheets cool, and the child can trim them with scissors. These melted crayon designs can be used as nice sun catchers on the windows. **Caution:** This activity needs to be closely supervised. Only the teacher should handle the hot iron.

Sensory

Additions to the Sensory Table

1. Water with Blue Food Coloring

2. Blue Goop

Mix together blue food coloring, 1 cup cornstarch, and 1 cup of water.

Large Muscle

1. Painting

Provide a bucket of blue-colored water and large paintbrushes. Encourage the children to paint the sidewalks, building, fence, sandbox, etc.

2. Blue Ribbon Dance

Make blue streamer ribbons by attaching blue crepe paper to unsharpened pencils. Play lively music and encourage the children to move to the music.

Field Trips

1. "Blue" Watching

Walk around your center's neighborhood and observe blue items. Things to look for include cars, bikes, birds, houses, flowers, etc. When you return, have the children dictate a list. Record their responses.

2. Paint Store

Visit a local paint store. Observe all the different shades of blue paint. Look carefully to see if they look similar. Ask the store manager for discarded sample cards. These cards can be added to the materials to use in the art area.

Social Studies

Eye Color

Prepare an eye color chart with the children. Colors on the chart should include blue, brown, and green. Under each category, record the children's names who have that particular eye color. Extend the activity by adding the number of children with each color.

Group Time
(games, language)

1. Bluebird, Bluebird

The children should join hands and stand in a circle. Construct one bluebird necklace out of yarn and construction paper. Choose one child to be the first bluebird. This bluebird weaves in and out of the children's arms while the remainder of the children chant:

"Bluebird, bluebird through my window
Bluebird, bluebird through my window
Bluebird, bluebird through my window
Who will be the next bluebird?"

At this time the child takes off the necklace and hands it to a child he would like to be the next bluebird.

2. I Spy

The teacher says, "I spy something blue that is sitting on the piano bench," or other such statements. The children will look around and try to figure out what the teacher has spied. Older children may enjoy taking turns repeating, "I spy something on the _____."

Cooking

1. Blueberries

Wash and prepare fresh or frozen blueberries for snack. Blueberry muffins are also appropriate for this theme.

2. Blueberry Muffins

2 tablespoons sugar
1 3/4 cups flour
2 1/2 teaspoons baking powder
3/4 teaspoon salt
1 egg
1/2 cup milk
1/3 cup salad oil

Mix all of the ingredients together. Add 2 tablespoons of sugar to 1 cup frozen or fresh blueberries. Mix slightly and gently add to the batter. Bake at 400 degrees for approximately 25 minutes.

3. Cream Cheese and Crackers

Tint cream cheese blue with food coloring and spread on crackers.

4. Cupcakes

Add blue food coloring to a white cake mix. Fill paper cupcake holders with the batter and bake as directed.

Transitions: Dismissal of Children

- colors of clothing/types of clothing/patterns of fabrics (stripes, polka dots, plaid)
- shoes (boots, shoes with buckles, shoes with ties, shoes with velcro, slip-on shoes, jelly shoes) Also, number of eyelets on shoes, number of buckles
- ages in years
- number of brothers/sisters
- hair/eye color
- birthdays in certain months
- name cards
- first letter of names
- last names
- rhyming names
- animal or word that starts with same sound as your name (Tiger-Tom)
- give each child a turn at something while putting rugs away (blowing a bubble, strumming a guitar, hugging puppet)
- play "I Spy" by saying, "I spy someone wearing blue pants and a Mickey Mouse sweatshirt."
- play a quick game of "Simon Says" and then have Simon tell where the children are to go next.

"Two Little Blackbirds"

Two little blackbirds sitting on a hill
One named Jack, one named Jill
Fly away Jack, fly away Jill,
Come back Jack, come back Jill.

Two little blackbirds sitting on a hill,
One named Jack, one named Jill.

"I Have a Very Special Friend"
(Sing to the Tune of "Bingo")

I have a very special friend,
Can you guess his name-o?
J-A-R-E-D, J-A-R-E-D,
J-A-R-E-D,
And Jared is his name-o.

"I'm Looking For Someone"

I'm looking for someone named Kristen,
I'm looking for someone named Kristen,
If there is someone named Kristen here now,
Stand up and take a bow.
(Or, Stand up and go to lunch.)

"Where, Oh, Where Is My Friend"

Where, oh, where is my friend Travis?
Where, oh, where is my friend Travis?
Where, oh, where is my friend Travis?
Please come to the door.

"How Did You Come to School Today?"

How did you come to school today,
How did you come on Monday? (Child responds)
He came in a blue car,
Came in a blue car on Monday.

"One Elephant Went Out to Play"

One elephant went out to play
Upon a spider's web one day.
He had such enormous fun
That he called for another elephant to come.

GROUP DISMISSAL

- hop like a bunny
- walk as quiet as a mouse
- tiptoe
- walk backwards
- count steps as you walk
- have footsteps for group to walk on or a winding trail to follow

"This Train" (Tune: "This Train is Bound for Glory")

This train is bound for the lunchroom,
This train is bound for the lunchroom,
This train is bound for the lunchroom,
Katie, get on board.
Matthew, get on board.
Zachary, get on board.
Afton, get on board.

- Change lunchroom to fit situation.

FILLERS

"One Potato"
One potato, two potato, three potato, four
Five potato, six potato, seven potato, more.

"And One and Two"
And one and two and three
    and four,
And five and six and seven
    and eight.
(Repeat faster)

"Colors Here and There"
Colors here and there,
Colors everywhere.
What's the name of this
    color here?

"This is What I Can Do"
This is what I can do,
Everybody do it, too.
This is what I can do,
Now I pass it on to you.

"A Peanut Sat on a Rail-
    road Track"
A peanut sat on a railroad
    track,
Its heart was all a-flutter.
Engine Nine came down the
    track,
Toot! Toot! Peanut butter!
    apple—applesauce
    banana—banana split
    orange—orange juice

"Lickety Lick"
Lickety lick, lickety lick,
The batter is getting all
    thickety thick.
What shall we bake?

What shall we bake?
A great, big beautiful carrot
    cake.
Change "carrot" to any kind
of cake

"I Clap My Hands"
I clap my hands. (Echo)
I stamp my feet. (Echo)
I turn around. (Echo)
And it's really neat.
    (Echo)
I touch my shoulders.
    (Echo)
I touch my nose. (Echo)
I touch my knees. (Echo)
And that's how it goes.
    (Echo)

Books

The following books can be used to complement this theme:

Bogacki, Tomek and Tomasz Bogacki. (1998). *Story of a Blue Bird.* New York: Farrar, Straus & Giroux.

Burnett, Frances H. (1993). *Land of the Blue Flower.* Illus. by Judith Ann Griffith. Tiburon, CA: H. J. Kramer.

Campilonga, Margaret S. (1996). *Blue Frogs.* Illus. by Carl Lindahl. Circleville, NY: Chicken Soup Press.

Childress, Mark. (1996). *Joshua and the Big Bad Blue Crabs.* Illus. by Mary B. Brown. Boston: Little, Brown.

Davies, Nicola. (1997). *Big Blue Whale.* Illus. by Nick Maland. Cambridge, MA: Candlewick Press.

Demarest, Chris L. (1995). *My Blue Boat.* Orlando: Harcourt Brace.

Hausman, Gerals. (1998). *The Story of Blue Elk.* Illus. by Kristina Rodanas. Boston: Houghton Mifflin.

Inkpen, Mick. (1996). *The Blue Balloon, Vol. 1.* Boston: Little, Brown.

Jensen, Patsy. (1993). *Paul Bunyan and His Blue Ox.* Illus. by Jean Pidgeon. Mahwah, NJ: Troll.

Lewin, Betsy. (1995). *Booby Hatch.* New York: Clarion Books.

Lionni, Leo. (1995). *Little Blue and Little Yellow.* New York: Mulberry Books. (Pbk)

Onyefulu, Ifeoma. (1997). *Chidi Only Likes Blue: An African Book of Colors.* New York: Cobblehill.

Oram, Hiawyn. (1993). *Out of the Blue: Poems about Color.* Illus. by David McKee. New York: Hyperion.

Ostheeren, Ingrid, et al. (1996). *The Blue Monster.* New York: North South Books.

Pulver, Robin. (1994). *Mrs. Toggle's Beautiful Blue Shoe.* Illus. by R. W. Alley. New York: Simon & Schuster.

Whitman, Candaceaut. (1998). *Bring on the Blue.* New York: Abbeville Press.

Woolfitt, Gabrielle. (1992). *Blue (Colors).* Minneapolis: Carolrhoda Books.

Multimedia

The following multimedia products can be used to complement this theme:

"The Big Piece of Blue Corn" on *Tall Tales, Yarns and Whoppers* [video]. (1991). Atlas Video, Inc.

Colors, Shapes, and Counting [video]. Kimbo Educational.

"Look Blue" on *There's Music in the Colors* [cassette]. Kimbo Educational.

Peter's Colors Adventure [CD-ROM]. (1994). Arborescence.

Recordings and Song Titles

The following recordings can be used to complement the theme:

There's Music in the Colors

I Like Myself—"Draw a Circle"

Where is Thumbkin?—"The Color Song"

Pre-K Hooray—"Color Wheel Dance"

Homemade Games—"Color Square"

Piggyback Sons—"Colors"

Children Love to Sing and Dance (The Learning Station)—"Everything Has a Color"

Let's Visit Lullaby Land—"Colour My World"

Rainbow of Songs—"Primary Colors"

T H E M E 6

Flat Breads

taco shells
pita bread
tortilla
lefse

Places Prepared

homes
restaurants
bakeries
supermarkets

Breads

Basic Ingredients

flour
water
milk
yeast
shortening

Yeast Breads

Danish pastries
croissants
rolls
breads
bagels
sweet rolls

Quick Breads

cornbread, biscuits,
coffee cakes, muffins,
popovers, scones,
pancakes, waffles

Theme Goals

Through participating in the experiences provided by this theme, the children may learn:

1. The basic ingredients of bread.
2. Places bread is prepared.
3. Types of yeast bread.
4. Types of flat bread.
5. Types of quick bread.

Concepts for the Children to Learn

1. There are many kinds of breads.
2. Breads are important for good health.
3. Bread is called the staff of life.
4. The basic ingredients used in preparing bread are flour, water and/or milk, and shortening.
5. Bread can be prepared in homes, bakeries, supermarkets, and restaurants.
6. Breads can be large or small in size.
7. Breads can have different flavors.
8. Some breads contain a fruit filling and are called sweet rolls.
9. Breads can be shaped into different forms: round, twisted, and oblong.
10. Breads can be hard or soft.
11. Breads can be part of a meal or snack.

Vocabulary

1. **bread**—a food prepared by mixing flour or grain meal with water or milk and shortening.
2. **crust**—the outside part of the bread.
3. **leaven**—a food that makes the bread dough rise.
4. **flour**—wheat that has been ground to a soft powder.

Bulletin Board

The purpose of this bulletin board is to promote visual discrimination skills and call attention to various types of baked goods. Create this bulletin board by drawing baked goods on a piece of tagboard as illustrated. Pictures from magazines could also be used. If drawn, color and add detail to the bakery items with felt-tip markers, cut out, and laminate. Trace these pieces onto black construction paper. Count out the pieces and attach to the bulletin board. Use map tacks or adhesive magnet pieces for children to match the corresponding baked good to its shadow.

Parent Letter

Dear Parents,

Did you know that bread is one of the most widely eaten foods? It is often called the "staff of life" and it provides a large share of people's energy and protein. Our next curriculum will focus on a theme related to breads. Activities will help your child learn the different types of bread and the ingredients of bread, including the purpose of yeast. Your child will also participate in making bread. Special breads are also used in different cultural ceremonies.

AT SCHOOL

Some of the curriculum activities related to the theme will include:
- Tasting many kinds of breads.
- Sorting and then eating pretzels of various sizes and shapes.
- Baking bread on Thursday and observing the action of yeast.
- Making and selling baked goods in the Bakery Shop located in the dramatic play area.

AT HOME

We encourage you to participate in our celebration of bread. The next time you and your child are in the grocery store, find the bakery or bread department. Point out the different types and sizes of breads. Ask questions to help your child recognize similarities and differences.

Bake breads with your child and create warm family memories. Here is a simple recipe that you may want to try:

ZUCCHINI BREAD

1 1/2 cups all-purpose flour	1/4 cup cooking oil
3/4 cup sugar	1/4 teaspoon nutmeg
1 teaspoon ground cinnamon	1 beaten egg
1/2 teaspoon baking soda	1/4 teaspoon finely shredded lemon peel
1/4 teaspoon salt	1 cup shredded zucchini
1/4 teaspoon baking powder	1/2 cup chopped walnuts

Grease an 8x4x2-inch loaf pan. In a medium bowl mix together flour, sugar, cinnamon, baking powder, and nutmeg. Make a well in the center of the dry mixture and add the zucchini. Stir only until mixture is folded in. Add the chopped walnuts.

Pour batter into the prepared loaf pan. Bake in a preheated oven set at 350 degrees for 55 to 60 minutes. Remove from the oven and cool on a wire rack for 10–12 minutes. Remove the bread from the pan and continue cooling on the wire rack. Wrap when cooled and let sit overnight before slicing.

A variation of this recipe would be to substitute shredded apples for the zucchini.

Enjoy a slice of bread with your child today!

56

It's tasty trying different kinds of bread and pastries.

Music

1. **"If I Had a Bagel"**
   (Sing to the tune "If I Had a Hammer")

   If I had a bagel.
   I'd eat it in the morning,
   I'd eat it in the evening,
   All over this land.
   I'd eat it for breakfast,
   I'd eat it for supper,
   I'd eat it with all my friends and sisters and
     brothers,
   All, all over this land.

2. **"Little Donuts"**
   (Sing to the tune of "Ten Little Indians")

   One little, two little, three little donuts
   Four little, five little, six little donuts
   Seven little, eight little, nine little donuts
   Ten donuts in the bakery shop.

3. **"Let's Pretend"**
   (Sing to the tune of "Here We Are Together")

   Let's pretend that we are bakers,
   Are bakers, are bakers
   Let's pretend that we are bakers,
   As busy as can be.

We'll knead all the dough out
And bake loaves of bread.
Let's pretend that we are bakers
As busy as can be.

Fingerplay

FIVE LITTLE DONUTS

Down around the corner, at the bakery shop
There were five little donuts with sugar on
   top.
   (hold up five fingers)
Along came _____ (child's name), all alone.
And she/he took the biggest one home.

Continue the verses until all the donuts are
gone.

Science

1. **Bread Grains**
   On the science table set out containers of
   grains used to make bread for the children
   to examine. Examples include wheat, corn,
   oats, and rye. Provide magnifying glasses
   for children to explore the grains.

2. Weighing Bread Grains

The property of mass can be explored by providing a balance scale and bread grains at the science table. Scoops and spoons could be available to assist the children.

3. Baking Bread

The process of bread baking is definitely a science activity. The children can observe changes in substances and make predictions about the final outcome. Choose a bread recipe listed under the cooking section of this theme. Prepare a recipe chart for classroom use. Stress cooking safety with the children.

Dramatic Play

1. Bakery

Prepare the housekeeping area to resemble a bakery where the children can pretend to make breads and bake goods to sell to their classmates as customers. Provide the following items: aprons, baker's hats, bowls, mixing spoons, pans, rolling pins, muffin tins, measuring cups, egg cartons, empty bread/ roll mix boxes, oven mitts or hot pads, a cash register, and poster/pictures depicting baked goods.

2. Restaurant

Prepare the housekeeping area as a restaurant. Provide props such as a tablecloth, dishes, cooking utensils, and a cash register with play money. Create menus by cutting pictures from magazines and gluing onto construction paper. Include pictures of different baked goods.

Arts and Crafts

1. Bread Collage

Provide magazines for the children to find and cut out pictures of different types of breads. These pictures can be glued or pasted to a piece of construction paper or a paper plate, creating a bread collage.

2. Playdough

The children can assist in preparing playdough. If the mixture is left uncolored, it will resemble bread dough and have a similar consistency. Place three cups of flour and one cup of salt in a mixing bowl. Add 3/4 cup of water and stir. Keep adding small amounts of water and mix until the dough is workable, but not sticky.

3. Muffin Tin Paint Trays

Fill muffin tins with various colors of paint in the art area for the children to use. Pastry brushes could be used as paint applicators.

4. Biscuit Cutter Prints

Place biscuit cutters and a shallow pan of paint out at the art table. The children can dip the biscuit cutter into the paint. After this, the biscuit cutter can be placed on a piece of construction paper. The children can repeat the process as desired.

5. Bread Sponge Painting

Cut sponges into different shapes and types of bread. Place the sponges and shallow trays of tempera paint on the art table. The children can dip a sponge into the paint and then press it onto a piece of paper to create a bread-shaped print.

Sensory

1. Different types of grains can be placed in the sensory table. Examples include corn, rice, wheat, barley, and oats. Provide pails, scoops, measuring cups, flour sifters, and spoons to encourage active exploration.

2. Place playdough in the sensory table with rolling pins, measuring cups, muffin tins, and plastic knives.

3. Cooking utensils used for preparing baked goods can be placed in the sensory table with soapy water and dish cloths. The children can "wash" the items.

Large Muscle

1. Tricycles

During outdoor play, encourage children to use the tricycles for making bakery deliveries.

2. Bread Trail

Set up a bread trail in the classroom. Tape pictures of the bread creating a trail on the floor. Have the children follow the trail by walking or hopping.

Field Trips

1. Bakery

Arrange a visit to a local bakery. Observe the process of bread and baked goods production. Discuss a baker's job and uniform.

2. Farm

Take a trip to a farm where grains are grown. Notice the equipment and machinery used to plant and harvest the crops.

3. Grocery Store

Tour a grocery store and find the bakery department. The children can look at the many types of breads and ways they are packaged.

Math

1. Favorite Bread Graph

After tasting various types of breads, the children can assist in making a class graph of their favorite types of breads. Across the top of a piece of tagboard, print the caption "Our Favorite Breads." Draw or paste pictures of different types or flavors of breads along the left-hand side of the tagboard.

On the chart, place each child's name or picture next to the picture of his/her favorite bread. The results of the graph can be shared with the children using math vocabulary words such as most, more,

fewer, least, etc. Display the graph for future reference.

2. Muffin Tin Math

Muffin tins can be used for counting and sorting activities based upon the children's developmental level. For example, numerals can be printed in each cup, and the children can place the corresponding set of corn or toy pieces in each cup. Likewise, colored circles can be cut out of construction paper and glued to the bottom of the muffin cups. The children then can place objects of matching colors in the corresponding muffin cups.

3. Pretzel Sort and Count

Provide each child with a cup containing various sizes and shapes of pretzels. Encourage the children to empty the cup onto a clean napkin or plate and sort the pretzels by size or shape. If appropriate, the children can count how many pretzels they have of each shape. Upon completion of the activity, the pretzels can be eaten by the children.

4. Breadstick Seriation

Provide breadsticks or pictures of breadsticks of varying lengths. The children can place the breadsticks in order from shortest to longest.

Social Studies

1. Baker

The occupation of baker can be examined through books and discussion.

2. Sharing Breads

Bake breads or muffins to give to a home for the elderly, the homeless, or some other organization. If possible, take a walk and have the children deliver them.

3. Visitor

Invite people from various cultural backgrounds to bake or share breads originating from their native countries. As a follow-up activity, assist the children in writing thank-you notes.

Group Time
(games, language)

1. Bread-Tasting Party

Bake or purchase various types and flavors of breads. Cut the bread into small pieces and place these samples on paper plates for the children to taste. Discuss the types of breads, textures, flavors, and scents.

2. Yeast Experiment

To demonstrate the effects of yeast, try this experiment. Pour one package of dry yeast, 1/2 cup of sugar, and one cup of warm water into an empty soda bottle. Cover the bottle opening with a balloon and watch it expand.

3. The Little Red Hen

Read the story of *The Little Red Hen* by Paul Galdone. After reading the story several times so that the children are familiar with the content, it can be acted out. Simple props can be provided to assist the children in creative dramatics and recreating the story.

4. Bread Basket Upset

This game is played in a circle formation on chairs or carpet squares. One child is asked to sit in the middle of the circle as the baker. Hand a picture of a different type of bread—bagel, roll, muffin, etc.—to each of the other children. To play the game, the baker calls out the name of a bread. The children holding that particular bread exchange places. The game continues. When the baker calls out, "Bread Basket Upset," all of the children must exchange places, including the baker. The child who is unable to find a place is the new baker.

Cooking

1. Bag Bread

Collect the following ingredients:

3 cups of bread flour
2 packages of fast-rising yeast
1/4 cup sugar
1 1/2 teaspoon salt
1 1/2 cup warm water (125 to 130 degrees)
4 teaspoons vegetable oil

In a gallon-sized heavy plastic ziplock freezer bag place 1 1/2 cups flour, dry yeast, and salt. Close. Let the children mix the ingredients by shaking and working the bag with their fingers to blend the ingredients.

Add the oil and warm water to the ingredients in the bag. Reseal the bag and demonstrate to the children how to mix the ingredients. Gradually add the remaining flour until the mixture forms a stiff ball.

Grease your hands with a solid vegetable oil. Remove the dough from the bag and place on a lightly floured surface. Knead about five minutes. Small air pockets that appear as bubbles will form under the surface of the dough when it has been sufficiently kneaded. When they appear, let the children observe them.

Let the dough rest for 5–10 minutes. Grease two bread pans. Divide the dough in half. Shape into two loaves. Place each loaf in a greased bread pan. Cover with a kitchen towel. Let rise for an hour. Bake at 375 degrees for 25–30 minutes.

2. Pretzels

Collect the following ingredients:

1 teaspoon salt
2 1/2 teaspoons sugar
1 package of fast-rising yeast
1 cup warm water (125 to 130 degrees).
1 tablespoon vegetable oil
1 egg yolk, beaten with 1 tablespoon water
3–3 1/2 cups flour

Combine 1 1/2 cups of flour, the dry yeast, sugar, and salt in a large bowl. Add the warm water and vegetable oil and mix at low speed with an electric mixer for three minutes. Add an additional 1/2 cup flour and beat at high speed for two to three minutes. Stir in the remaining flour to form a soft dough. **Caution:** Use of the electric mixer needs to be carefully supervised.

Lightly flour a surface. Place the soft dough on the floured surface and knead for approximately 10 minutes. Grease a bowl with vegetable oil and place the dough in to rise. Cover with a dish towel for 30–45 minutes.

Punch the air out of the dough and divide into 20 equal pieces. Demonstrate to the children how to roll a piece into a rope 12–14 inches long. Form the rope into a pretzel. Place on a greased baking sheet. Cover again and let rise in a warm place for about 25 minutes.

Brush each of the pretzels with the egg yolk mixture. Preheat the oven to 375 degrees. Bake for 15 minutes and remove from pan. Place on a wire rack to cool.

3. Chappatis

This recipe, which comes from India, serves 6; consequently, it will need to be adjusted to accommodate the number of children who need to be served.

1 1/2 cups of whole wheat flour
1/2 teaspoon salt
2/3 cup warm water
a small amount of cooking oil

Mix the flour and salt together in a bowl. Stir in water a small amount at a time until the mixture forms a ball.

On a floured surface, knead dough for 5–10 minutes, until it is a smooth, sticky ball. Let rise in a covered bowl for 30 minutes.

Cut the dough into six pieces. Roll each piece out into a circle that is about eight inches in diameter.

Lightly oil a frying pan with oil and heat until it smokes. **Caution:** This portion of the activity needs to be carefully supervised to promote a safe environment.

Cook each circle of dough until it is brown and puffy on both sides. The chappatis are more flavorful when eaten warm.

4. Cheesey Puff Bread

3 3/4 cups of bread flour
1 package rapid-rise dry yeast
1 teaspoon salt
1/2 cup milk
2 tablespoons margarine
2 eggs
1 cup grated cheddar cheese
1/2 cup warm water
3 tablespoons sugar

Combine the dry yeast, sugar, salt, and 1 1/2 cups of flour in a large mixing bowl. Heat the milk, water, and margarine on the stove or in the microwave oven until warm to the touch. Add the dry ingredients. Then beat at low speed with an electric mixer. Add 1/2 cup of flour and the eggs. Beat at high speed for 2–3 minutes. Stir in the cheese and enough flour to make a soft dough.

On a lightly floured surface, knead the dough until it is elastic and smooth. Typically this will take 6–10 minutes. Place the dough in a greased bowl and let rise for 15–30 minutes.

Grease the entire inner surface of two 1-lb. coffee cans. Divide the dough into two equal pieces. Place each piece in a can. Cover the top of the can with a piece of aluminum foil. Let the dough rise for 35 minutes.

Bake for 30 minutes in a 375-degree oven. Remove from cans and cool on a wire rack.

Books

The following books can be used to complement this theme:

Barton, Byron. (1993). *The Little Red Hen.* New York: HarperCollins.

Carle, Eric. (1995). *Walter the Baker.* New York: Simon & Schuster.

Curtis, Neil and Peter Greenland. (1992). *How Bread Is Made (I Wonder).* Minneapolis: Lerner Publications.

Czernecky, Stefan et al. (1992). *The Sleeping Bread.* New York: Hyperion.

De Paola, Tomie. (1997). *Antonio the Bread Boy.* New York: G. P. Putnam.

Dooley, Norah. (1995). *Everybody Bakes Bread.* Illus. by Peter J. Thornton. Minneapolis: Carolrhoda Books.

Dragonwagon, Crescent. (1991). *This Is the Bread I Baked for Ned.* Illus. by Isadore Seltzer. New York: Simon & Schuster.

Flanagan, Romie and Alice K. (1998). *Mr. Santizo's Tasty Treats.* Chicago: Children's Press.

Gershator, David et al. (1995). *Bread Is for Eating.* New York: Holt.

Granowsky, Alvin. (1996). *Help Yourself, Little Red Hen! (Another side to the story).* Illus. by Wendy Edelson and Jane K. Manning. Austin, TX: Raintree/Steck Vaughn.

Heath, Amy. (1992). *Sophie's Role.* Illus. by Sheila Hamanaka. New York: Simon & Schuster.

Hoban, Russell. (1993). *Bread and Jam for Frances.* Illus. by Lillian Hoban. New York: HarperCollins.

Hoopes, Lyn Littlefield. (1996). *The Unbeatable Bread.* Illus. by Brad Sneed. New York: Dial Books.

Pellam, David. (1991). *Sam's Sandwich.* New York: Dutton. (flap book)

Wolff, Ferida. (1993). *Seven Loaves of Bread.* Illus. by Katie Keller. New York: William Morrow.

Multimedia

The following multimedia products can be used to complement this theme:

Greg and Steve. "Muffin Man" on *We All Live Together, Volume 2* [compact disc]. Youngheart Records.

"The Muffin Man" on *Toddler Tunes: 26 Classic Songs for Toddlers* [compact disc]. (1995). Franklin, TN: Cedarmont Music; distributed by Benson Music Group.

THEME 7

Parts
handle
bristles

Hair Styles
long
short
thick
thin
no hair

Brushes

Users
all people
barbers
janitors/maids
dentists
artists
painters
animal groomers

Uses
cleaning
grooming/hygiene
painting
cooking

Names
paint brush
scrub brush
toothbrush
hairbrush
clothes brush
vegetable brush
pastry brush
pet brush
powder brush
eyebrow brush
nail brush
picks

Materials
plastic
wood
nylon
hair

Theme Goals

Through participating in the experiences provided by this theme, the children may learn:

1. Parts of a brush.
2. Kinds of brushes.
3. Uses of brushes.
4. Materials used to make brushes.
5. Community helpers who need brushes for their work.

Concepts for the Children to Learn

1. A brush is a tool.
2. Brushes come in many sizes.
3. Brushes have handles.
4. Some brushes are used for cleaning in our homes.
5. Toothbrushes help clean our teeth.
6. Hairbrushes are used for grooming.
7. A pastry brush is used for cooking.
8. Brushes can be made of plastic, wood, or nylon.
9. Some people use brushes while working.

Vocabulary

1. **brush**—a tool made of bristles or wires attached to a handle.
2. **bristle**—a short, stiff hair or thread-like object.
3. **handle**—the part of a brush that is held.
4. **groom**—to clean.
5. **powder brush**—a brush that is used to apply facial powder.
6. **toothbrush**—a small brush used to clean teeth.
7. **vegetable brush**—a stiff brush used to clean vegetables.
8. **dog brush**—a brush used to clean a dog's hair.

Bulletin Board

The purpose of this bulletin board is to promote the development of color identification and matching skills. Construct and paint pallets and brushes out of tagboard. Use a different colored marker to draw paint spots on each pallet and to "paint" the bristles of each brush. Laminate all the pieces. Attach the pallets to the bulletin board. Map tacks, putty, or velcro may be used to place the brushes next to the corresponding color of paint pallet.

Parent Letter

Dear Parents,

Did you ever stop to think about the number and types of brushes we use in a day? Brushes will be the next subject that we will explore. Each one has a different function and helps us do a different job. Through the activities related to the theme, the children will become aware of the many types and uses of brushes. In addition, they will be exposed to materials used in constructing brushes.

AT SCHOOL

Some of the learning experiences this week will include:

- setting up a hair stylist shop in the dramatic play area (and discussing different hair styles and colors).
- "painting" outside with buckets of water and brushes.
- observing teeth being cleaned with electric and hand-held brushes as we visit Dr. Smith's dental office on Thursday morning.
- painting with a variety of brushes at the easel each day.

AT HOME

With your child, go through your home and locate brushes. Examples include: toothbrushes, hairbrushes, paintbrushes, fingernail polish brushes, pastry brushes, and makeup brushes. Compare and sort the various brushes. This will help your child discriminate among weights, colors, sizes, textures, and shapes. The brushes can also be counted to determine which room contains the most and which the least number of brushes, which will promote the understanding of number concepts.

Paint a picture with your child today!

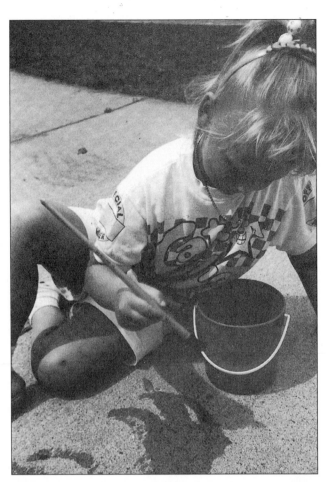

Painting with water-soluble paints on pavement is a creative activity.

BRUSHES IN MY HOME

These brushes in my home
Are simply everywhere.
I use them for my teeth each day,
    (brushing teeth motion)
And also for my hair.
    (hair brushing motion)

We use them in the kitchen sink
    (scrubbing motion)
And in the toilet bowls
    (scrubbing motion)
For putting polish on my shoes
    (touch shoes and rub)
And to waterproof the soles.

Brushes are used to polish the floors
    (polishing motions)
And also paint the wall,
    (painting motion)
To clean the charcoal barbecue,
    (brushing motion)
It's hard to name them all.

MY TOOTHBRUSH

I have a little toothbrush.
    (use pointer for toothbrush)
I hold it very tightly.
    (make tight fist)
I brush my teeth each morning
    (pretend to brush teeth)
And then again at night.

SHINY SHOES

First I loosen mud and dirt,
My shoes I then rub clean.
For shoes in such a dreadful sight,
Never should be seen.

I spread the polish on the shoes.
And then I let it dry.
I brush the shoes until they shine.
And sparkle in my eye.

Music

"Using Brushes"
(Sing to the tune of "Mulberry Bush")

This is the way we brush our teeth,
brush our teeth, brush our teeth.
This is the way we brush our teeth
So early in the morning.

Variations:

⊙ This is the way we brush our hair. . . .

⊙ This is the way we polish our nails. . . .

⊙ This is the way we paint the house. . . .

Act out each verse, and allow the children to make up more verses.

Science

1. Identifying Brushes

Inside the feely box, place various small brushes. The children can reach into the box, feel the object, and try to identify it by name.

2. Exploring Bristles

Add to the science table a variety of brushes and magnifying glasses. Allow the children to observe the bristles up close, noting similarities and differences.

Dramatic Play

1. Hair Stylist

Collect hairspray bottles, brushes, empty shampoo bottles, chairs, mirrors, hair dryers, and curling irons, and place in the dramatic play area. **Caution:** Cut the cords off the electrical appliances.

2. Water Painting

In an outdoors area, provide children with buckets of water and house paintbrushes. They can pretend to "paint" the building, sidewalks, equipment, and fence.

3. Shining Shoes

In the dramatic play area, place clear shoe polish, shoes, brushes, and shining cloths for the children to use to polish shoes.

Arts and Crafts

1. Brush Painting

Place various brushes such as hair, makeup, toothbrushes, and clothes brushes on a table in the art area. In addition, thin tempera paint and paper should be provided. Let the children explore the painting process with a variety of brushes.

2. Easel Ideas

Each day change the type of brushes the children can use while painting at the easel. Variations may include: sponge brushes, discarded toothbrushes, nail polish brushes, vegetable brushes, and makeup brushes.

3. Box House Painting

Place a large cardboard box outside. To decorate it provide smocks, house painting brushes, and tempera paint for the children.

Large Muscle

Sidewalk Brushing

Place buckets of water and paintbrushes for use outdoors on sidewalks, fences, and buildings.

Field Trips/ Resource People

1. The Street Sweeper

Contact the city maintenance department. Invite them to clean the street in front of the center or school for the children to observe.

2. Artist's Studio

Visit a local artist's studio. Observe the various brushes used.

3. Dentist's Office

Visit a dentist's office. Ask the dentist to demonstrate and explain the use of various brushes.

4. Animal Groomer

Invite an animal groomer to school. Ask the groomer to show the equipment, emphasizing the importance of brushes.

Math

1. Sequencing

Collect various-sized paintbrushes. Encourage the children to sequence them by height and width.

2. Weighing Brushes

Place a balance scale and several brushes in the math area. Encourage the children to weigh and balance the brushes.

3. Toothbrush Counting

Collect toothbrushes and cans. Label each can with a numeral. The children can place the corresponding number of brushes into each labeled can. If desired, the toothbrushes can be constructed out of tagboard.

Social Studies

1. Brushes Chart

Design a "Brushes in our Classroom" chart. Encourage the children to find all that are used in the classroom.

2. Helper Chart

Design a helper chart. Include tasks such as sweeping floors, cleaning paintbrushes, putting brushes, and brooms away. This chart can encourage the children to use brushes every day in the classroom.

Group Time
(games, language)

1. Brush Hunt

Hide several brushes in the classroom. Have one child search for the brushes. When he gets close to them, clap loudly. When he is further away, clap quietly.

2. Brush of the Day

At group time each day introduce a new brush. Discuss the shape, color, materials, and uses. Then allow the children to use the brush in the classroom during self-selected play period.

Cooking

1. Cleaning Vegetables

Place several washtubs filled with water in the cooking area. Then provide children with fresh carrots and brushes. Encourage the children to clean the carrots using a vegetable brush. The carrots can be used to make carrot cake, muffins, or can be added to soup.

2. Pretzels

1 1/2 cups warm water
1 envelope yeast
4 cups flour
1 teaspoon salt
1 tablespoon sugar
1 egg
coarse salt (optional)

Mix water, yeast, sugar. Let stand for 5 minutes. Place salt and flour in a bowl. Add the yeast and stir to prepare dough mixture. Shape the dough. Beat egg and apply the egg glaze with a pastry brush. Sprinkle with salt if desired. Bake at 425 degrees for approximately 12 minutes.

Paint Applicators

There are many ways to apply paint. The size and shape of the following applicators produce unique results. While some are recycleable, others are disposable.

RECYCLABLE EXAMPLES

paintbrushes, varying sizes
    and widths
whisk brooms
fingers and hands
tongue depressors or
    popsicle sticks
potato mashers
forks and spoons
toothbrushes
aerosol can lids
cookie cutters
spray bottles
string/yarn
roll-on deodorant
    bottles
squeeze bottles (plastic
    ketchup containers)
marbles and beads
styrofoam shapes
sponges
feet
spools
rollers

**DISPOSABLE APPLICATORS
TO USE WITH PAINT**

twigs and sticks
string/yarn
feathers
pinecones
rocks
cloth
cardboard tubes
straws
leaves
cotton balls
cotton swabs

Books

The following books can be used to complement this theme:

Lillegard, Dee. (1987). *I Can Be a Beautician.* Chicago: Children's Press.

Tripp, Valerie. (1987). *The Penguins Paint.* Chicago: Children's Press.

De Paola, Tomie. (1988). *The Legend of the Indian Paintbrush.* New York: G. P. Putnam.

Hoban, Tara. (1987). *Dots, Spots, Speckles, & Stripes.* New York: Greenwillow.

Small, David. (1985). *Imogene's Antlers.* New York: Crown.

Testa, Fulvio. (1986). *If You Take a Paintbrush: A Book of Colors.* New York: Dial Books.

Quinlan, Patricia. (1992). *Brush Them Bright.* New York: Walt Disney Publishing.

Recordings and Song Titles

The following recordings can be used to complement the theme:

Self Help Skills—"Combing My Hair"
Get Up & Grow—"Brush Your Teeth"

THEME 8

Bubbles

Purpose
bathing
cleaning
playing

Sizes
large
medium
small

Coloring
food coloring

Ingredients
soap
water

Tools for Making
straws
bubble rings
strings
funnels
coat hangers
pipes
berry baskets
six-pack rings

Theme Goals

Through participating in the experiences provided by this theme, the children may learn:

1. Purposes of bubbles.
2. Bubble ingredients.
3. Tools for making bubbles.
4. Colors of bubbles.
5. Bubble shapes.
6. Ways to create bubbles.
7. Sizes of bubbles.

Concepts for the Children to Learn

1. Bubbles are made with soap and water.
2. Bubbles are all around us in foods, baths, water, and drinks.
3. Food coloring can be used to add color to bubbles.
4. Bubbles can be created by blowing or by waving a tool.
5. Bubbles have a skin that holds air inside of them.
6. Straws, bubble rings, strings, funnels, and coat hangers can be used as tools to make bubbles.

Vocabulary

1. **bubble**—a round circle that has a skin and contains air.
2. **bubble skin**—the outside of the bubble that holds the air.
3. **bubble solution**—a mixture of water and liquid soap.
4. **bubble wand**—a tool used to make bubbles.

Bulletin Board

The purpose of this bulletin board is to promote the active exploration of household items that can be used to make bubbles. Collect items such as pipe cleaners, funnels, spools, six-pack rings, berry baskets, and scissors. Construct and label boxes and/or pockets to hold items on the bulletin board. Containers of bubble solution should be placed near the bulletin board for the children to experiment with to make bubbles with household items. Provide towels in the area to encourage the children to assist in wiping up spills.

Parent Letter

Dear Parents,

What do you get when you mix water and soap? Bubbles! The children will make many fascinating discoveries as we focus on a Bubbles theme. Through experiences provided, the children will learn the ingredients used in making bubbles, sizes of bubbles, and tools for making bubbles.

AT SCHOOL

Some of the learning experiences planned to highlight bubble concepts are:

- washing dolls and dishes in the sensory table.
- testing many bubble solution recipes.
- making bubbles with common household items such as plastic berry baskets, funnels, straws, pipe cleaners, spools, and scissors.
- creating prints of bubbles in the art area.

AT HOME

Try the following activities with your child to reinforce bubble concepts at home:

- allow your child to assist in washing dishes after a meal. This experience will give your child a sense of responsibility and promote self-esteem, as well as heighten his/her awareness of the purpose of bubbles for cleaning.
- prepare the following bubble solution with your child, then blow some bubbles! You need one cup of water, two tablespoons of liquid dish soap, and one tablespoon of glycerine (optional). Enjoy!

Have a good time with your child!

74

Catching bubbles outdoors is a good science experience.

Music

1. **"Pop! Goes the Bubble"**
   (Sing to the tune of "Pop! Goes the Weasel")

   Soap and water can be mixed.
   To make a bubble solution.
   Carefully blow,
   Now, watch it go!
   Pop! Goes the bubble!

2. **"Can You Blow a Big Bubble?"**
   (Sing to the tune of "The Muffin Man")

   Can you blow a big bubble?
   A big bubble, a big bubble?
   Can you blow a big bubble,
   With your bubble gum?

3. **"I'm a Little Bubble"**
   (Sing to the tune of "I'm a Little Teapot")

   I'm a little bubble, shiny and round.
   I gently float down to the ground.
   The wind lifts me up and then I drop.
   Down to the dry ground where I pop.

4. **"Ten Little Bubbles"**
   (Sing to the tune of "Ten Little Indians")

   One little, two little, three little bubbles.
   Four little, five little, six little bubbles.
   Seven little, eight little, nine little bubbles.
   Ten bubbles floating to the ground.

5. **"Here's a Bubble"**
   (Sing to the tune of "Frere Jacques")

   Here's a bubble, here's a bubble.
   Big and round; big and round.
   See it floating gently,
   See it floating gently,
   To the ground; to the ground.

Fingerplays

HERE IS A BUBBLE

Here is a bubble
   (make a circle with thumb and index
   finger)
And here's a bubble
   (make a bigger circle with two thumbs
   and index finger)
And here is a great big bubble I see.
   (make a large circle with arms)
Let's count the bubbles we've made.
One, two, three.
   (repeat prior actions)

DRAW A BUBBLE

Draw a bubble, draw a bubble.
Make it very round.
   (make a shape in the air with index
   finger)
Draw a bubble, draw a bubble.
No corners can be found.
   (repeat actions)

Science

1. Bubble Solutions

Encourage the children to assist in preparing the following bubble solutions. (Note: The use of glycerine in preparing the bubble solution is optional. It helps to provide a stronger skin on the bubble, but the solutions can be prepared without this ingredient.)

Recipe #1

1/4 cup liquid dish soap
1/2 cup water
1 teaspoon sugar

Recipe #2: Outdoor Use

3 cups water
2 cups liquid dish soap (Joy detergent)
1/2 cup light corn syrup

Recipe #3

2/3 liquid dish soap
1 gallon of water
1 tablespoon glycerine

2. Bubble Gadgets

Prepare a bubble solution and make some bubbles! Use the following to make great bubbles.

- plastic berry baskets
- pipe cleaners or thin electrical wire shaped into wands
- six-pack holders
- egg poacher trays
- funnels
- children's scissors—hold the blades and dip the finger holders into the bubble solution.
- tin cans—open at both ends.
- paper cups—poke a hole in the bottom of a paper cup. Dip the rim into a bubble solution and blow through the hole.
- plastic straws—use a single straw or tape several together in a bundle.
- straws and string—thread three feet of thin thread through two plastic straws. Tie the string together. Hold the straws and pull them to form a rectangle with the string. Dip into a bubble solution and pull upward. As you move the frame, a bubble will form. Bring the two straws together to close off the bubble. This technique requires practice.
- Hula Hoop—fill a small wading pool with two inches of bubble solution. The Hula Hoop can be used as a giant wand by dipping the hoop in a solution and lifting it up carefully.

3. Wet/Dry

While blowing bubbles with the children try touching a bubble with a dry finger. Repeat using a wet finger. What happens? You will observe that bubbles break when they touch an object that is dry.

4. Bubble Jar

Fill a small plastic bottle half-full of water. Add a few drops of food coloring, if desired. Add baby oil or mineral oil to completely fill the jar. Secure the bottle tightly. Then slowly tilt the bottle from side to side. When this occurs, the liquid in the jar resembles waves. Bubbles can be created by shaking the bottle. Encourage the children to observe these reactions.

5. Air Bubbles in Food

Examine the air bubbles in pieces of bread, Swiss cheese, and carbonated drinks.

6. Bubbling Raisins

Place two or three raisins in a small bottle of sparkling mineral water. Secure the cap and watch the bubbles form as the raisins sink and float.

Dramatic Play

1. Housekeeping

Fill the sink in the dramatic play area with soapy water. Provide dishes, dish cloth, towels, and a dish rack for the children to wash the dishes.

2. Hair Stylist

Set up a hair stylist studio in the dramatic play area. Include props such as a cash register, empty shampoo and hair spray containers, mirrors, brushes, combs, barrettes, curlers, discarded hair dryer and curling irons, towels and smocks. Display pictures of hairstyles and hair products. **Caution:** Cut the electric cords off the hair dryers and curling irons to prevent possible injuries.

Arts and Crafts

1. Bubble Prints

For each bubble-print color desired, mix one part liquid tempera paint with two parts liquid dish soap in a small container. Place a straw in the solution and blow until the bubbles rise above the rim of the container. Remove the straw and place a piece of paper over the bubbles. As the bubbles break, they will leave a print on the paper. (Each child will need a straw for this activity. A pin may be used to poke holes near the top of the straws to prevent the children from accidentally sucking in the paint mixture.)

Variation: Small bubble wands can be dipped into the paint bubble solution and blown so the bubbles will land on a piece of paper, either at the easel or on the ground outdoors.

2. Bubble Gum Wrapper Collages

Collect wrappers from bubble gum to be placed on the art with paper and glue. The children can use these materials to create collages.

3. Bubble Paint Containers

Collect containers that hold commercially prepared bubble solutions. Recycle the containers by using them to hold various colors of paints at the easel or art table.

Sensory

1. Wash Dolls

Fill the sensory table with warm water and add a few tablespoons of dish soap. Provide plastic dolls, washcloths, and towels.

2. Dishwashing

Place plastic dishes and dishcloths in a sensory table filled with warm soapy water. A dish drying rack could be set up nearby or towels could be provided to dry the dishes.

3. Bubble Bath

Purchase or make bubble bath soap to put along with scoops, measuring cups, and pails at the sensory table.

4. Bubble Solution

The sensory table can be used to hold a bubble solution and bubble-making tools.

5. Pumps and Water

Fill the sensory table with water. Add water pumps, turkey basters, and siphons to create air bubbles in the water.

Field Trips/ Resource People

1. Hair Stylist

Visit a hair stylist to watch a customer receive a shampoo.

2. Pet Groomer

Invite a pet groomer to demonstrate giving a dog a bath.

Math

1. Bubble Count

If appropriate, encourage the children to blow a set of bubbles that you specify. For example, if you say the number "three," the children would try to blow three bubbles.

2. Bubble Wand Sort

Collect small commercially manufactured bubble wands and place them in a small basket. These wands can be sorted by size or color. They could also be counted or placed in order by size.

3. Geometric Bubble Shapes

Attach the ends of two straws together with duct tape or paper clips, creating the desired shapes. Six straws will be needed to make a pyramid and 12 to make a cube. The frames can be dipped into bubble solutions and observed.

Group Times
(games, language)

1. What's Missing?—Game

Place several items used to prepare bubbles on a tray. At group time, show and discuss the items. To play the game, cover the tray with a towel and carefully remove one item. Children then identify the missing item. The game can be made more challenging by adding more items to the tray, or by removing more than one item at a time.

2. Bubbles—Creative Dramatics

Guide the children through a creative dramatics activity as they pretend to be bubbles. They can act out being:

- a tiny bubble
- a giant bubble
- a bubble floating on a windy day
- a bubble landing on the grass
- a bubble floating high in the air
- a bubble in a sink
- a bubble in a piece of bread

3. Favorite Bubble Gum Chart

At the top of a piece of tagboard, print the caption "Our Favorite Bubble Gum." Along the left-hand side, glue bubble gum wrappers representing different brands or flavors. Present the chart at group time and ask each child to choose one as his/her favorite. Record the children's names or place their pictures next to the response. If appropriate, count the number of "votes" each brand received and print in on the chart. Display the chart in the classroom and refer to it throughout the unit.

Cooking

1. Bubbly Beverage

6-oz. can frozen orange juice
6-oz. can frozen lemonade
6-oz. can frozen limeade
6-oz. can frozen pineapple juice (optional)
1 liter lemon-lime soda, chilled
1 liter club soda, chilled

Combine ingredients in a punch or large bowl. Stir to blend the ingredients. Serve over ice, if desired.

2. Root Beer

5 gallons cold water
5 lbs. white sugar
3-oz. bottle root beer extract
5 lbs. dry ice

In a large stone crock or plastic container (do not use metal) mix sugar with 1 gallon of water. Add the remainder of the water and root beer extract. Stir. Carefully add the dry ice. After the ice melts, the root beer can be transferred into other containers to store for 2–3 days.

78

© 2000, Delmar

Books

The following books can be used to complement this theme:

Arnold, Tedd. (1995). *No More Water in the Tub*. New York: Dial Books.

Bergen, Stuart. (1996). *Fozzie's Bubble Bath*. Illus. by Rick Brown. New York: Grosset & Dunlap.

Bradbury, Judy. (1997). *Double Bubble Trouble!* Illus. by Cathy Trachok. Hightstown, NJ: McGraw-Hill.

Buxbaum, Susan Kovacs et al. (1992). *Splash! All about Baths*. Boston: Little, Brown.

Cowley, Joy. (1990). *Mrs. Wish-Washy*. Bothell, WA: Wright Group.

Edwards, Frank B. (1998). *Troubles with Bubbles*. Illus. by John Bianchi. Kingston, ON: Bungalo Books. (New Reader Series)

Everett, Louise. (1989). *Bubble Gum in the Sky*. Illus. by Paul Harvey. Mahwah, NJ: Troll. (Pbk)

Goodman, Joan Elizabeth. (1996). *Bernard's Bath*. Illus. by Dominic Catalano. Honesdale, PA: Boyds Mills Press.

Mayer, Mercer. (1997). *Just a Bubble Bath*. Utica, NY: Good Times Publishing.

Noble, Kate. (1994). *Bubble Gum*. Illus. by Rachel Bass. Chicago: Silver Seahorse Press.

O'Connor, Jane. (1997). *Benny's Big Bubble*. Illus. by Tomi De Paola. New York: Price Stern Sloan.

Wood, Audrey. (1991). *King Bidgood's in the Bathtub*. Orlando: Harcourt Brace.

Multimedia

The following multimedia products can be used to complement this theme:

De Paola, Tomie. *The Bubble Factory* [cassette and book]. (1997). New York: Scholastic.

Johnson, Laura. "Be a Bubble" on *Fun Activities for Toddlers* [cassette]. Available from Kimbo Educational.

The Tots and the Lovely Bubbly Surprise [video]. (1997). Troy, MI: Ragdoll Productions; distributed by Anchor Bay Entertainment.

Walcoff, Larry et al. *Bubbles: How Do Insects Walk on Water?* [video]. (1992). Bloomington, IN: Agency for Instructional Technology. (*Science for You* series)

Recordings and Song Titles

The following recordings can be used to complement this theme:

Pop Rock Parachute—"Bubblehouse"
Fun Activities for Toddlers—"Be a Bubble"

THEME 9

Materials

brick, wood,
cement, steel,
glass

Purpose

shelter
storage

Buildings

Parts

basement
rooms
windows
doors
roof
walls
chimney
ceilings
floors
frame

Types

homes, schools, offices,
stores, malls,
hospital/clinic,
police station, fire station,
library, church, bank,
restaurant,
handicapped accessible

Construction Workers

carpenters
electricians
architects
designer/decorator
mason
plumbers

Theme Goals

Through participating in the experiences provided by this theme, the children may learn:

1. Types of buildings.
2. Purposes of buildings.
3. Materials used to make buildings.
4. Parts of a building.

Concepts for the Children to Learn

1. There are many types of buildings: homes, offices, stores, hospitals, malls, etc.
2. Buildings can be made of brick, wood, cement, steel, and glass.
3. Many workers help construct buildings: architects, carpenters, electricians, plumbers, and masons.
4. Buildings can be used for shelter and storage.
5. Most buildings have a roof, walls, windows, and a floor.

Vocabulary

1. **building**—a structure.
2. **mall**—a building containing many stores.
3. **skyscraper**—a very tall building.
4. **carpenter**—a person who builds.
5. **electrician**—a person who wires a building for light, heat, and cooking.
6. **architect**—a person who designs a building.
7. **room**—a part of a building set off by walls.
8. **ceiling**—the top "wall" of a room.
9. **roof**—the top covering of a building.

Bulletin Board

The purpose of this bulletin board is to develop awareness of size as well as visual discrimination skills and hand-eye coordination. Construct house shapes out of tagboard ranging in size from small to large. Color the shapes and laminate. Punch a hole in the top of each house. Trace each house shape on black construction paper and cut out. Hang the shadow pieces on the bulletin board with a pushpin inserted in the top of each. During self-directed and self-initiated play, the children can match each colored house to the corresponding shadow piece by hanging it on the pushpin.

Parent Letter

Dear Parents,

Your home, the library, our school . . . these are all buildings with which your child is familiar. Buildings will be our next theme. Discoveries will be made regarding different kinds and parts of buildings, materials used to construct buildings, and construction workers who erect buildings.

AT SCHOOL

A sampling of the learning experiences include:

- building with various materials—such as boxes and milk cartons.
- working at the woodworking bench to practice hammering, drilling, and sawing.
- weighing and balancing bricks.
- taking a walk to a construction site and observing the building process.
- identifying different types of buildings.

AT HOME

You can reinforce building concepts on your way to and from the center by pointing out any buildings of interest, such as the fire station, police station, hospital, library, shopping mall, and restaurants. Children are naturally curious about why and how things happen. If you pass any construction sites, point out the materials and equipment used, as well as the jobs of the workers. This will help your child develop receptive and expressive language skills as well as stimulate their interest. Concepts of time can also be fostered if you are able to visit the construction site over an extended period of time. You and your child will be able to keep track of progress in the development of the building.

Enjoy your child as you reinforce concepts related to buildings.

Music

"Go In and Out the Window"

Form a circle with the children and hold hands. While holding hands have the children raise their arms up to form windows. Let each child have a turn weaving in and out the windows. Use the following chant as you play.

_____ goes in and out the windows,
In and out the windows,
In and out the windows.
_____ goes in and out the windows,
As we did before.

Fill in child's name in the _____.

Fingerplays

THE CARPENTER'S TOOLS

The carpenter's hammer goes rap, rap, rap
   (make hammering motion with fist)
And his saw goes see, saw, see.
   (make sawing motion with arm and hand)
He planes and hammers and saws
   (make motions for each)
While he builds a building for me.
   (point to yourself)

CARPENTER

This is the way he saws the wood
   (make sawing motion)
Sawing, sawing, sawing.

This is the way she nails a nail
   (make hammering motion)
Nailing, nailing, nailing.

This is the way he paints a building
   (make brushing motion)
Painting, painting, painting.

Together we will build a big house.

MY HOUSE

I'm going to build a little house.
   (draw house with fingers by outlining in the air)
With windows big and bright,
   (spread out arms)
With chimney tall and curling smoke
   (show tall chimney with hands)
Drifting out of sight.
   (shade eyes with hands to look)
In winter when the snowflakes fall
   (use fingers to make the motion of snow falling downward)
Or when I hear a storm,
   (place hand to ear)
I'll go sit in my little house
   (draw house again)
Where I'll be snug and warm.
   (hug self)

Science

1. Building Materials

Collect materials such as wood, brick, cement, metal, and magnifying glasses and place on the science table. Encourage the children to observe the various materials up close.

2. Mixing Cement

Make cement using a small amount of cement and water. Mix materials together in a large plastic ice cream bucket. Allow the children to help. The children can also observe and feel the wet cement.

3. Building Tools

Collect and place various tools such as a hammer, level, wedge, and screwdriver on the science table for the children to examine. Discuss each tool and demonstrate how it is used. Then place the tools in the woodworking area. Provide wood and styrofoam so that the children are encouraged to use the tools as a self-selected activity with close adult supervision.

Dramatic Play

1. Library

Rearrange the dramatic play area to resemble a library. Include books, library cards, book markers, tables, and chairs for the children's use.

2. Buildings

Collect large cardboard boxes from an appliance dealer. The children can construct their own buildings and paint them with tempera paint.

3. Construction Site

Place cardboard boxes, blocks, plastic pipes, wheelbarrows, hard hats, paper, and pencils in the dramatic play area to represent a construction site.

Arts and Crafts

1. Our Home

Provide paper, crayons, and markers for each child to draw his home. Collect all of the drawings and place them in mural fashion on a large piece of paper to create a town. To extend this activity, have the children also draw buildings in the town to extend the mural. (This activity may be limited to kindergarten children or children who have reached the representational stage of art development.)

2. Blueprints

Blueprint paper, pencils, and markers should be placed in the art area. The children will enjoy marking on it. Older children may also enjoy using rulers and straight edges.

3. Building Shapes

Cut out building shapes from easel paper. Place at the easel, allowing children to paint their buildings.

4. Building Collages

Collect magazines with pictures of houses. Encourage children to cut or tear out pictures of buildings. The pictures can be glued on paper to create a mural.

5. Creating Structures

Save half-pint milk cartons. Rinse well and allow the children to paint, color, and decorate the cartons to look like buildings.

Sensory

1. Wet Sand

Fill the sensory table with sand and add water. Provide cups, square plastic containers, bowls, etc., for children to create molds with the sand.

2. Wood Shavings

Place wood shavings in the sensory table.

3. Scented Playdough

Prepare scented playdough and place in the sensory table.

Large Muscle

Workbench

Call attention during group time to the woodworking bench and explain the activities that can occur there. Try to encourage the children to practice pounding nails, sawing, drilling, etc., during self-initiated play.

Field Trips/ Resource People

1. Building Site

Visit a local building site if available. Observe and discuss the people who are working, how buildings look, and safety. Take pictures. When the pictures are developed, post them in the classroom.

2. Neighborhood Walk

Take a walk around the neighborhood. Observe the various kinds of buildings. Talk about the different sizes and colors of the buildings.

3. Library

Visit a library. Observe how books are stored. Read the children a story while there. If possible, allow the children to check out books.

4. Browsing at the Mall

Visit the shopping mall. Talk about the mall being a large building that houses a variety of stores. Visit a few of the stores that may be of special interest to the children. Included may be a toy store, pet store, and a sporting goods store.

5. Resource People

Invite people to visit the classroom, such as:

- construction worker
- carpenter
- electrician
- architect
- decorator/designer
- plumber

Math

1. Weighing Bricks

Set out balance scale and small bricks. The children can weigh and balance the bricks.

2. Wipe-off Windows

Cut out and laminate a variety of buildings with varying numbers of windows. Provide children with grease markers or watercolor markers. Encourage the children to count the number of windows of each building and print the corresponding numeral on the building. The numerals can be wiped off with a damp cloth. (This activity would be most appropriate for kindergarten children.)

3. Blocks

Set out blocks of various shapes including triangles, rectangles, and squares for the children to build with.

Social Studies

1. Buildings in Our Town

Make a chart with the children's names listed vertically on the right-hand side. Across the top of the chart draw buildings or glue pictures of buildings that the children have visited. Suggestions include a theater, supermarket, clinic, museum, post office, fire station, etc. At group time, ask the children what buildings they have visited. Mark the sites for each child.

2. Unusual Buildings

Show pictures of unusual buildings cut from various magazines, travel guides, etc. Allow the children to use their creative thinking by asking them the use of each building. All answers and possibilities should be acknowledged.

3. Occupation Match

Cut out pictures of buildings and the people who work in them. Examples would include: hospital—nurse, fire station—firefighter. Glue these pictures to tagboard and laminate. The children should be encouraged to match each worker to the appropriate building.

Group Time
(games, language)

1. Identifying Buildings

Collect several pictures of buildings that are easily identified such as school, fire station, hospital, home. Talk about each picture. Ask, "How do you know this is a school?" Discuss the function of each building. To help the children, pictures of buildings in their community can be used.

2. Exploring Our Center

Explore your center. Walk around the outside and observe walls, windows, roof, etc. Explore the inside also. Check out the rooms, floor, walls, ceiling, stairs. . . . Colors, materials and size are some things you can discuss with each. Allow the children to help make an "Our Center Has . . ." chart.

Cooking

Sugar Cookies

1 1/2 cups powdered sugar
1 cup margarine or butter
1 egg
1 teaspoon vanilla
2 1/2 cups all-purpose flour
1 teaspoon baking soda
1 teaspoon cream of tartar
granulated sugar

Mix the powdered sugar, margarine, egg, and vanilla together. Stir in the flour, baking soda, and cream of tartar. Chill, to prevent sticking while rolling the dough out. Heat the oven to 375 degrees. Roll out the dough. Cut into squares, triangles, diamonds, rectangles, circles. Sprinkle with sugar. Place on a lightly greased cookie sheet. Bake until lightly brown, about 7 to 8 minutes. Give each child 3 to 5 cookies. Allow them to make buildings with their shapes before eating.

Books

The following books can be used to complement this theme:

Ackerman, Karen. (1995). *The Sleeping Porch*. Illus. by Elizabeth Sayles. New York: William Morrow.

Barton, Byron. (1997). *Machines at Work*. New York: HarperCollins.

Dorros, Arthur. (1992). *This Is My House*. New York: Scholastic.

Gibbons, Gail. (1990). *How a House Is Built*. New York: Holiday House.

Gibbons, Gail. (1986). *Up Goes the Skyscraper!* New York: Macmillan.

Hautzig, David. (1994). *At the Supermarket*. New York: Orchard Books.

Hoban, Tana. (1997). *A Construction Zone*. New York: Greenwillow.

James, Alan. (1989). *Homes on Water*. Minneapolis: Lerner Publications.

Jaspersohn, William. (1994). *My Hometown Library*. Boston: Houghton Mifflin.

Kalman, Bobbie. (1994). *Homes Around the World*. New York: Crabtree Publishing.

McDonald, Megan. (1996). *My House Has Stars*. Illus. by Peter Catalanotto. New York: Orchard Books.

Miller, Marilyn. (1996). *Behind the Scenes at the Shopping Mall*. Illus. by Ingo Fast. Austin, TX: Raintree/Steck Vaughn.

Morris, Ann. (1992). *Houses and Homes*. Photos by Ken Heyman. New York: Lothrop, Lee & Shepard.

Novak, Matt. (1996). *Elmer Blunt's Open House*. New York: Orchard Books. (Pbk)

Richardson, Joy. (1994). *Skyscrapers*. New York: Franklin Watts.

Rounds, Glen. (1995). *Sod Houses on the Great Plains*. New York: Holiday House.

Seltzer, Isadore. (1992). *The House I Live In: At Home in America*. Colchester, CT: Atheneum.

Shelby, Anne. (1996). *The Someday House*. Illus. by Rosanne Litzinger. New York: Orchard Books.

Shemie, Bonnie. (1990). *Houses of Bark*. San Francisco: Children's Book Press.

Yeoman, John. (1995). *The Do-It-Yourself House That Jack Built*. Illus. by Quentin Blake. Colchester, CT: Atheneum.

Multimedia

The following multimedia products can be used to complement this theme:

Building Skyscrapers [video]. (1994). New York: David Alpert Associates, Inc.

Community Construction Kit [CD-ROM]. (1998). Watertown, MA: Tom Snyder Productions.

Dig Hole, Build House [video]. (1994). Gig Harbor, WA: Real World Video.

The Fire Station [video]. (1990). Washington, D.C.: National Geographic Society.

Gryphon Bricks [CD-ROM]. (1996). San Diego, CA: Gryphon Software Corp.

Let's Build a House [video]. (1996). San Diego, CA: Video Connections.

THEME 16

Equipment
tent, camper,
lantern/flashlight,
sleeping bag

Activities
boating,
waterskiing, hiking,
cooking outdoors,
horseback riding,
telling stories,
fishing,
bird watching,
observing wild animals

Camping

Foods
hot dogs
marshmallows
beans
fish

Places
woods,
campgrounds,
parks, lakes,
backyards,
rooftops,
home, school

Transportation
camper, car, pickup truck,
motorcycle, van, canoe,
bicycle, horse

Theme Goals

Through participating in the experiences provided by this theme, the children may learn:

1. Places where people camp.
2. Equipment used for camping.
3. Camping transportation.
4. Camping activities.
5. Foods we eat while camping.

Concepts for the Children to Learn

1. A tent is a shelter used for camping.
2. We can camp in the woods or at a campground.
3. We can also camp in a park, at a lake, or in our backyard.
4. Hot dogs, fish, marshmallows, and beans are all camping foods.
5. A camper can be driven or attached to the back of a car or pickup truck.
6. Lanterns and flashlights are sources of light used for camping.
7. A sleeping bag is a blanket used for camping.
8. Some people camp by a lake to water ski and go boating and fishing.

Vocabulary

1. **backpack**—a zippered bag worn on one's back to carry objects.
2. **recreational vehicle**—a living and sleeping area on wheels.
3. **campfire**—a controlled fire that is made at a campground.
4. **campsite**—a place for tents and campers to park.
5. **camping**—living outdoors in sleeping bags, tents, cabins, or campers.
6. **woods**—an area with many trees.
7. **hiking**—taking a long walk.
8. **sleeping bag**—a zippered blanket.
9. **tent**—a movable shelter made out of material.
10. **lantern**—a covered light used for camping.

Bulletin Board

The purpose of this bulletin board is to develop skills in recognizing colors and color words. Construct several tents out of tagboard as illustrated. Make an identical set out of white tagboard. Color the first set of tents using the primary colors. Print the color names using corresponding colored markers onto the second set of tents. Laminate the materials. Staple the tents with color names to bulletin board. Punch holes in colored tents. Children can attach the tent to a pushpin on the corresponding color word tent.

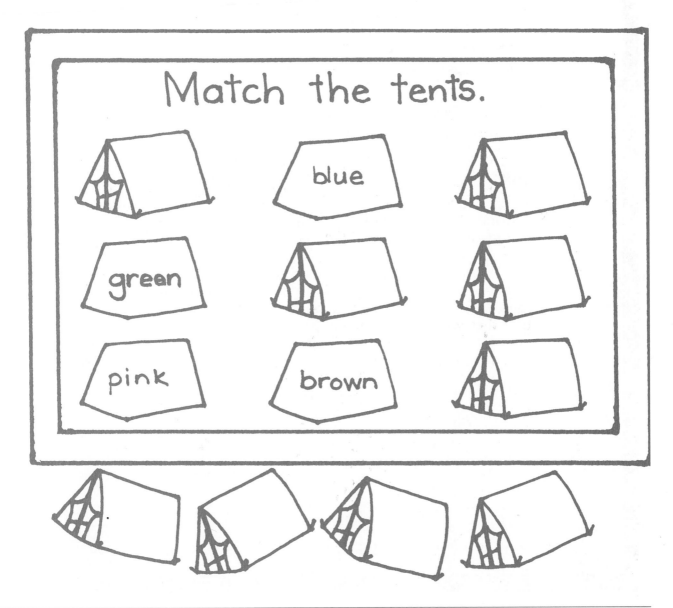

Parent Letter

Dear Parents,

With summer approaching, we will begin focusing on a fun family activity—camping! The children will become aware of items and equipment that are commonly used while camping. From listening to the children's conversations, it sounds as if many have already been camping with their families. It should be fun to hear the camping stories they will share!

AT SCHOOL

Some of the learning experiences planned include:

- setting up the dramatic play area with a tent, sleeping bags, and other camping items.
- singing songs around a pretend campfire.
- going on a "bear hunt" (a rhythmic chant).
- preparing foods that are eaten while camping.
- cleaning up after camping.

AT HOME

Help your child create a tent by draping a sheet over a table. Provide a flashlight and a blanket or sleeping bag and your child will be prepared for hours of indoor camping fun! Through dramatic play experiences children relive and clarify situations and roles. They act out how they see the world and how they view relationships among people.

If you have any photographs or slides of family camping trips, we would be delighted if you would share them with us. Contact me and we can work out a time that would be convenient for you. Thanks!

Plan a camping trip with your child today!

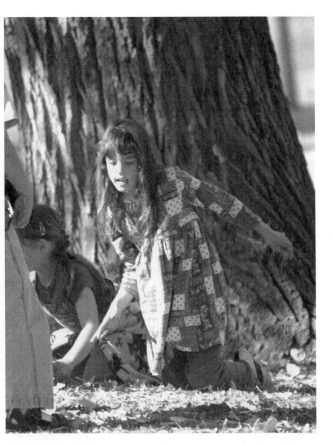

Having a picnic is one of the best things about camping.

Music

1. **"A Camping We Will Go"**
   (Sing to the tune of "The Farmer and the Dell")

   A camping we will go.
   A camping we will go.
   Hi ho we're off to the woods.
   A camping we will go.

   Saba will bring the tent.
   Oh Saba will bring the tent.
   Hi ho we're off to the woods.
   A camping we will go.

   Juan will bring the food.
   Oh Juan will bring the food.
   Hi ho we're off to the woods.
   A camping we will go.

   The names in the song can be changed to children's names.

2. **"Two Little Black Bears"**
   (Sing to the tune of "Two Little Blackbirds")

   Two little black bears sitting on a hill
   One named Jack, one named Jill
   Run away Jack
   Run away Jill
   Come back Jack
   Come back Jill.
   Two little black bears sitting on a hill
   One named Jack, one named Jill.

3. **Campfire Songs**

   Pretend that you are sitting around a campfire. Explain to the children that often people sing their favorite songs around a campfire. Encourage the children to name their favorite songs, and then sing some of them.

Fingerplays

BY THE CAMPFIRE

We sat around the campfire
On a chilly night
   (hug self)
Telling spooky stories
In the pale moonlight
   (look up to the sky)

Then we added some more logs,
To make the fire bright,
And sang some favorite camp songs
Together with all our might.
   (extend arms outward)
And when the fire flickered
and embers began to form.
We snuggled in our sleeping bags all cozy,
   tired, and warm.
   (lie on ground, hug self)

Source: Wilmes, Liz & Dick. *Everyday Circle Times*. Building Block Publications.

FIVE LITTLE BEAR CUBS

Five little bear cubs
Eating an apple core.
One had a sore tummy
And then there were four.

Four little bear cubs
Climbing in a tree.
One fell out
And then there were three.

Three little bear cubs
Playing peek-a-boo.
One was afraid
And then there were two.

Two little bear cubs
Sitting in the sun.
One ran away
And then there was one.

One little bear cub
Sitting all alone.
He saw his mommy
And then he ran home.

Science

1. Scavenger Hunt

While outside, have the children find plants growing, insects crawling, insects flying, a plant growing on a tree, a vine, a flower, bird feathers, a root, a seed, etc.

2. Sink/Float

Collect various pieces of camping equipment. Fill the water table with water and let the children test which objects sink or float. If desired make a chart.

3. Magnifying Glasses

Provide magnifying glasses for looking at objects seen on a camping trip.

Dramatic Play

1. Camping

Collect various types of clothing and camping equipment and place in the dramatic play area or outdoors. Include items such as hiking boots, sweatshirts, raincoats, sleeping bags, backpacks, cooking tools, and a tent.

2. Puppets

Develop a puppet corner in the dramatic play area including various animal puppets that would be seen while camping.

3. Going Fishing

Set up a rocking boat or a large box in the classroom or outdoors. Prepare paper fish with paper clips attached to them. Include a fishing pole made from a wooden dowel and a long string with a magnet attached to the end.

4. Going to the Beach

In the dramatic play area, set up lawn chairs, beach towels, buckets, shovels, sunglasses, etc. Weather permitting, these items could also be placed outdoors.

Arts and Crafts

1. Easel Ideas

- paint with leaves, sticks, flowers, and rocks.
- paint with colors seen in the forest such as brown, green, yellow, and orange.
- cut easel paper into the following shapes: tent, rabbits, chipmunks, and fish.

2. Camping Collage

Collect leaves, pebbles, twigs, pine cones, etc. Provide glue and sturdy tagboard. Encourage the children to create a collage on the tagboard using the materials found while camping.

3. Tackle Box

Make two holes approximately three inches apart in the center of the lid of an egg carton. To form the handle, thread a cord through the holes and tie. Paint the box. In the box, place paper clips for hooks and S-shaped styrofoam pieces for worms.

Sensory

Sensory Table Additions

- leaves
- rocks
- pebbles
- mud and sand
- twigs
- evergreen needles and branches
- water

Large Muscle

1. **Caves**

   Using large packing boxes or barrels placed horizontally on the playground, allow the children to pretend to be wild animals in caves.

2. **"Bear Hunt"**

   This is a chant. Prepare the children by asking them to listen and watch carefully so that they can echo back each phrase and imitate the motions as they accompany the story. Begin by patting your hands on your thighs to make foot-step sounds.

   Let's go on a bear hunt . . . (echo)
   We're going to find a bear . . . (echo)
   I've got my camera . . . (echo)
   Open the door, squeak . . . (echo)
   Walk down the walk . . . (echo)
   Open the gate, creak . . . (echo)
   Walk down the road . . . (echo)
   Coming to a wheat field . . . (echo)
   Can't go under it . . . (echo)
   Can't go over it . . . (echo)
   Have to walk through it . . . (echo)
       (stop patting your thighs and rub your
       hands together to make a swishing
       sound)
   Got through the wheat field . . . (echo)
   Coming to a bridge . . . (echo)
   Can't go under it . . . (echo)
   Can't go around it . . . (echo)
   Have to walk over it . . . (echo)
       (stop patting your thighs and pound
       your fists on your chest)

   Over the bridge . . . (echo)
   Coming to a tree . . . (echo)
   Can't go under it . . . (echo)
   Can't go around it . . . (echo)
   We'll have to climb it . . . (echo)
       (stop patting your thighs and place one
       fist on top of the other in a climbing
       motion)
   All the way to the top . . . (echo)
       (look from one side to the other)
   Do you see a bear . . . ? (echo)
   No (shaking head) . . . (echo)
   We'll have to climb down . . . (echo)
       (place fist under fist to climb down)
   Coming to a river . . . (echo)
   We can't go under it . . . (echo)
   We can't fly over it . . . (echo)
   Can't go around it . . . (echo)
   We'll have to cross it . . . (echo)
   Let's get in the boat . . . (echo)
   And row, row, row . . .
       (all sing "Row, Row, Row Your Boat"
       accompanied with rowing motions)
   We got across the river . . . (echo)
   We're coming to a cave . . . (echo)
   We can't go under it . . . (echo)
   We can't go over it . . . (echo)
   Can't go around it . . . (echo)
   We'll have to go in it . . . (echo)
   Let's tip-toe
       (use fingertips to pat thighs)
       (whisper)
   It's dark inside . . . (echo)
   It's very dark inside . . . (echo)
   I can see two eyes . . . (echo)
   And a big furry body . . . (echo)
   And I feel a wet nose . . . (echo)
       (Yell)
   It's a BEAR . . . RUN . . . (echo)
       (patting hands very quickly)
   Run back to the river,
   Row the boat across the river,
       (rowing motion)
   Run to the tree
   Climb up and climb down
       (do climbing motion)
   Run to the bridge and cross it
       (pat chest)
   Run through the wheat field
       (swish hands together)
   Run up the road

Open the gate . . . it creaks,
  (open gate)
Run up the walk,
Open the door . . . it squeaks,
  (open door)
SLAM IT!
  (clap hands together)

Source: Wirth, Marion, Stassevitch, Verna, Shotwell, Rita, & Stemmler, Patricia. *Musical Games, Fingerplays and Rhythmic Activities for Early Childhood*. Parker Publishing Co. Inc.

Field Trips

1. **Department Store**

   Visit a department store or a sporting goods store where camping tents and other equipment are displayed.

2. **Picnic**

   Pack a picnic lunch or snack and take it to an area campground.

3. **Camper Salesperson**

   Visit a recreational vehicle dealer and tour a large mobile home.

Math

Camping Scavenger Hunt

Before the children go outdoors, instruct them to find things on your playground that you would see while camping. Sort them and count them when they bring them into the classroom (five twigs, three rocks, etc.).

Social Studies

1. **Pictures**

   Collect pictures of different campsites. Share them by displaying them in the classroom at the children's eye level.

2. **Camping Experiences**

   At group time ask if any of the children have been camping. Let them tell the rest of the children what they did while they were camping. Ask where they slept, what they ate, where the bathroom was, etc.

Group Time
(games, language)

1. **What's Missing**

   Have different pieces of camping equipment available to show the children. Include a canteen, portable stove, sleeping bag, cooking tools, lantern, etc. Discuss each item, and then have the children close their eyes. Take one of the objects away and then have the children guess which object is missing.

2. **Camping Safety**

   Discuss camping safety. Include these points:

   ☺ always put out fires before going to sleep.

   ☺ swim in safe areas and with a partner.

   ☺ when walking, or hiking away from your campsite, always have an adult with you.

   ☺ always wear a life jacket in the boat.

3. **Pack the Backpack**

   Bring into the classroom a large backpack. Also have many camping items available such as sweatshirts, flashlights, lanterns, foods, raincoats, etc. The teacher gives the children instructions that they are going to pretend to go on a hike to the beach. What is one thing they will need to bring along? Why? Continue until all of the children have had a chance to contribute.

Cooking

1. **S'Mores**

   Place a large marshmallow on a square graham cracker. Next place a square of sweet chocolate on top of the marshmallow. After this, place the graham cracker on a baking sheet into a 250-degree oven for about 5 minutes or until the chocolate starts to melt. Remove the s'more and press a second graham cracker square on top of the chocolate. Let cool for a few minutes, and serve while still slightly warm.

2. **Venezuela Breakfast Cocoa**

   1/4 cup water
   3 tablespoons cocoa
   2 tablespoons sugar
   2 cups milk
   1 teaspoon vanilla

1. Bring the water to a boil in a saucepan.

2. Stir in the cocoa and sugar until they are blended. Turn the heat very low.

3. Slowly pour the milk into the saucepan with the cocoa mixture. Stir steadily to keep the mixture from burning. Continue cooking the mixture over low heat for about 2 minutes. Do not let it boil or skin will form on the top.

4. When the cocoa is hot, remove it from the stove and stir in the vanilla.

5. Carefully pour the cocoa into the cups. Serve warm.

Source: Touff, Terry, & Ratner, Marilyn. (1974). *Many Hands Cooking*. New York: Thomas Y. Crowell Company.

Books

The following books can be used to complement this theme:

Bauer, Marion Dane. (1995). *When I Go Camping with Grandma*. Illus. by Allen Garns. Morago, CA: Bridgewater Books.

Brillhart, Julie. (1997). *When Daddy Took Us Camping*. Niles, IL: Albert Whitman & Co.

Brown, Mark Tolon. (1984). *Arthur Goes to Camp*. Madison, WI: Demco Media.

Brown, M. K. (1995). *Let's Go Camping with Mr. Sillypants*. New York: Crown Publishers.

Christelow, Eileen. (1998). *Jerome Camps Out*. New York: Clarion Books.

Duffey, Betsy. (1996). *Camp Knock Knock*. Illus. by Fiona Dunbar. New York: Delacorte Press.

Hoff, Syd. (1996). *Danny and the Dinosaur Go to Camp*. New York: HarperCollins.

Howe, James. (1995). *Pinky and Rex and the Double-Dad Weekend*. Illus. by Melissa Sweet. New York: Atheneum.

Kalman, Bobbie D. (1995). *Summer Camp*. New York: Crabtree Publishing.

Locker, Thomas. (1984). *Where the River Begins*. New York: Dial Books.

Rand, Gloria. (1996). *Willie Takes a Hike*. Illus. by Ted Rand. Orlando: Harcourt Brace.

Say, Allen. (1989). *The Lost Lake*. Boston: Houghton Mifflin.

Shaw, Nancy E. (1994). *Sheep Take a Hike*. Illus. by Margot Apple. Boston: Houghton Mifflin.

Tafuri, Nancy. (1987). *Do Not Disturb*. New York: William Morrow.

Wallace, Ian. (1997). *A Winter's Tale*. Washington, D.C.: Groundwood Books.

Williams, Vera B. (1983). *Three Days on a River in a Red Canoe*. New York: Greenwillow.

Multimedia

The following multimedia products can be used to complement this theme:

Barney's Campfire Sing-Along [video]. (1990). Allen, TX: Lyons Group.

Let's Go Camping [video]. (1995). Burlington, VT: Vermont Story Works.

Mercer Mayer's Just Me and My Dad [CD-ROM]. (1996). New York: GT Interactive Software.

Scrapbook Of Teacher-Made Materials

Lacing Cards

Construction Materials:
Construction paper or tagboard, yarn or shoe strings, and a colored felt-tip markers

Related Themes
Fruits and vegetables, Health

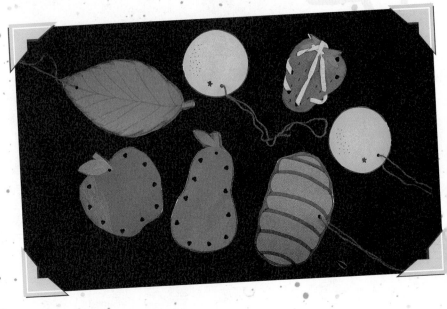

Nursery Rhyme Folder Game

Construction Materials:
File folder, nursery rhyme stickers, circle stickers, and a colored felt-tip marker

Related Themes:
Nursery rhymes, Friends

Color Sorting Card

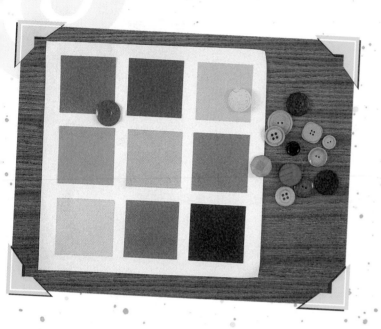

Construction Materials:
A square of white tagboard, colored square of red, blue, yellow, green, orange, purple, pink, brown and black paper, and objects to sort by colors such as buttons, beads, crayons, or chips

Related Themes:
Blue, Red, Yellow, Purple, Clothing

Name Practice Boards

Construction Materials:
Colored construction paper, lined paper, and a black felt-tip marker

Related Themes:
Friends, Communication, Mail Carrier

Peek-a-Boo Cards

Construction Materials:
File folders and magazine pictures

Related Themes:
Birds, Cats, Dogs, Zoo Animals, Pets, Mice, Scissors

Dramatic Play Menus

Construction Materials:
File folder, colored construction paper, and felt-tip markers

Related Themes:
Health, Families, Friends, Occupations

Caramel Apple Math

Construction Materials:
Tongue depressors, brown tagboard, cupcake liners, small circles, and felt-tip markers

Related Themes:
Apples, Numbers, Health, Fruits and Vegetables, Circus

Insect Memory Game

Construction Materials:
Juice can lids or tagboard squares and insect stickers

Related Themes:
Insects and Spiders, Spring, Summer, Camping, Gardens, Water

ACTIVITY 9

Fruit Sort Cards

Construction Materials:
Tagboard squares, fruit stickers or pictures, and black felt-tip markers

Related Themes:
Fruits and Vegetables, Communication, Apples, Health, Numbers, Plants

ACTIVITY 10

Felt Frogs on a Log

Construction Materials:
Log, green felt pieces, craft eggs, polyester filling, and a felt-tip marker

Related Themes:
Water, Camping, Summer, Nursery Rhymes, Creative Movement

ACTIVITY 11

Friendly Frog Masks

Construction Materials:
Green tagboard, black felt-tip marker, and a craft stick

Related Themes:
Nursery Rhymes, Camping, Summer, Creative Movement, Water

ACTIVITY 12

Pepperoni Pizza

Construction Materials:
Cardboard circle, red construction paper, yellow and white yarn, and green felt pieces

Related Themes:
Numbers, Health, Families, Friends, Occupations

ACTIVITY 13

Valentine Number Cards

Construction Materials:
Pink and white construction paper and red tagboard

Related Themes:
Valentine's Day, Shapes, Numbers, Red, Mail Carrier, Communication, Feelings, Friends

Tongue Depressor Puzzles

Construction Materials:
Two tongue depressors for each puzzle and a set of felt-tip markers

Related Themes:
Fruits and Vegetables, Gardens, Breads, Health, Doctors and Nurses, Plants

Snowmen Match

Construction Materials:
Stickers or wrapping figures and tagboard for mounting

Related Themes:
Winter, Clothing, Numbers, Shapes, Hats

"This Old Man" Cue Cards

Construction Materials:
Ten tagboard rectangles and felt-tip markers

Related Themes:
Nursery Rhymes, Music, Communication, Numbers

Animal Home Match

Construction Materials:
Colored felt pieces and felt-tip markers

Related Themes:
Birds, Cats, Dogs, Homes, Friends, Pets

Spring Words Chart

Construction Materials:
Large sheet of colored tagboard, set of colored felt-tip markers, manuscript strips or lined paper, and white construction paper

Related Themes:
Spring, Communication, Flowers, Pets, Clothing, Farm Animals, Water

Pizza Topping Chart

Construction Materials:
Sheet of tagboard, colored construction paper, and a black felt-tip marker

Related Themes:
Occupations, Health, Families, Friends

Our Favorite Ice Cream Graph

Construction Materials:
Large sheet of tagboard, colored construction paper, and felt-tip markers

Related Themes:
Dairy Products, Health, Friends, Summer, Circus, Camping, Numbers

Bakery Dramatic Play Chart

Construction Materials:
Sheet of colored tagboard, construction paper, and felt-tip markers

Related Themes:
Breads, Health, Occupations

"Hush Little Baby" Cue Card

Construction Materials:
Large piece of tagboard and colored felt-tip markers

Related Themes:
Music, Families, Nursery Rhymes

Easter Egg Game Board

Construction Materials:
Tagboard, colored Easter egg stickers, and felt-tip markers

Related Themes:
Eggs, Easter, Friends, Health, Numbers, Shapes

Sensory Bottles

Construction Materials:

Plastic soda bottle with cap, mineral oil, food coloring, and objects such as beads, glitter, dice, or sequins

Related Themes:

Containers, Bubbles, Water, Blue, Red, Yellow, Purple, Creative Movement

Dramatic Play Felt Hamburgers

Construction Materials:

Colored felt pieces, polyester filling, yellow and white pipe cleaners

Related Themes:

Health, Camping, Breads, Occupations, Families, Friends

Beanbag Bear Toss

Construction Materials:
Felt pieces, polyester stuffing, felt-tip markers, and basket or bucket

Related Themes:
Containers, Zoo Animals, Numbers, Circus

Paper Cup Sort Palette

Construction Materials:
Colored tagboard, paper cups, construction paper, crayons or other objects to sort by color

Related Themes:
Art, Blue, Red, Yellow, Purple, Numbers

Felt-Mitten Duck Puppets

Construction Materials:
Colored felt, colored tagboard, and a felt-tip marker

Related Themes:
Birds, Puppets, Communication, Nursery Rhymes, Easter, Farm Animals, Pets, Yellow, Spring

ACTIVITY 29
Caterpillar Sock Puppet

Construction Materials:
   White tube sock and fabric scraps

Related Themes:
   Insects and Spiders, Puppets, Communication,
   Gardens, Nursery Rhymes

ACTIVITY 30
Bookworm Bookstore
Dramatic Play Sign

Construction Materials:
   Green and yellow tagboard, felt-tip
   markers, and string to hang sign

Related Themes:
   Nursery Rhymes, Communication,
   Families, Friends, Occupations

ACTIVITY 31
Fish Pond

Construction Materials:
   Plastic tablecloth, colored tagboard,
   and felt-tip markers

Related Themes:
   Fish, Camping, Sports, Zoo Animals,
   Spring, Summer

Humpty Dumpty

Construction Materials:
Cardboard blocks, white pillowcase, black and pink felt pieces, polyester filling, and a black felt-tip marker

Related Themes:
Eggs, Nursery Rhymes, Communication

Popcorn Toss Game

Construction Materials:
Plastic bucket, tablecloth, and white pom-poms

Related Themes:
Circus, Friends, Families, Health, Garden, Camping

Transportation Mat

Construction Materials:
Plastic tablecloth, set of colored felt-tip markers, and small wheeled toys

Related Themes:
Cars, Trucks, and Buses, Wheels, Occupations

Dramatic Play Traffic Light

Construction Materials:
Colored construction paper, tagboard, and a black felt-tip marker

Related Themes:
Cars, Trucks, and Buses, Wheels, Safety, Communication

St. Patrick's Day Words

Construction Materials:
Sheet of tagboard, manuscript strips or lined paper, St. Patrick's stickers, and a green felt-tip marker

Related Themes:
Spring, Communication

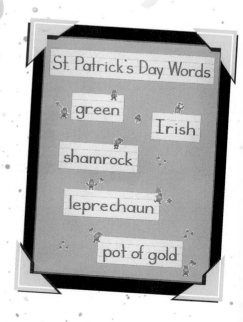

St. Patrick's Day Words

green

Irish

shamrock

leprechaun

pot of gold

THEME 11

Cars, Trucks, and Buses

Uses

moves objects
moves people

Care

wash
wax
vacuum
repair

Sizes

small
medium
large

Inside Parts

horn, steering wheel,
seats, blinkers,
seat belts, radio,
knobs & buttons,
mirrors, clock, motor

Outside Parts

wheels, hood,
headlights, trunk,
mirrors, windows,
doors, windshield
wipers, antenna

Colors

white, black,
blue, green,
yellow, gray

Kinds

TRUCKS	CARS	BUSES
dump	compact, van,	school
fire	stationwagon,	city
pickup	convertible,	tour
tank	police, taxi,	
semi	ambulance	

Safety

speed, seatbelts,
noise, activities,
airbags,
handicapped
accessible,
number of people,
gasoline,
sit until stopped

Theme Goals

Through participating in the experiences provided by this theme, the children may learn:

1. Kinds of cars, trucks, and buses.
2. Care of vehicles.
3. Uses of vehicles.
4. Inside and outside parts of vehicles.
5. Colors and sizes of vehicles.

Concepts for the Children to Learn

1. There are many kinds of cars, trucks, and buses.
2. Trucks and buses are usually bigger than cars.
3. Trucks can be used to haul objects.
4. People use cars, trucks, and buses to move from place to place.
5. Compact cars are small.
6. A license is needed to drive a car, truck, or bus.
7. Cars, trucks, and buses need gas to run.
8. Gas can be obtained at a filling station.
9. Vehicles need to be vacuumed, washed, waxed, and repaired.
10. Headlights, mirrors, and wheels are parts of a car.

Vocabulary

1. **car**—vehicle used for moving people.
2. **truck**—a wheeled vehicle used to move people and big objects.
3. **bus**—a vehicle that carries many people.
4. **driver**—operates the vehicle.
5. **passenger**—the rider.
6. **fuel**—gas, diesel, etc., used to produce power.
7. **gas**—produces power to move a vehicle.
8. **motor**—makes the vehicle move by creating energy.

Bulletin Board

The purpose of the bulletin board is to reinforce color recognition and matching skills, as well as develop one-to-one correspondence concepts. Construct garage shapes out of tagboard. Color each garage a different color and hang on the bulletin board. Hang a pushpin in the center of each garage. Next, construct the same number of cars as garages from tagboard. Color each car a different color to correspond with the colors of the garages. Use a paper punch to make a hole in each car. The children can park each car in its corresponding colored garage.

Parent Letter

Dear Parents,

Cars, trucks, and buses—these are all transportation vehicles that your child sees daily. Because of the children's interest, we are beginning a unit on "Cars, Trucks, and Buses." Through participating in the planned experiences, the children will learn that there are many colors, sizes, and kinds of cars, trucks, and buses. They will also become aware of the occupations associated with the vehicles including taxi drivers, bus drivers, and mechanics.

AT SCHOOL

Some of the activities planned for this unit include:

- painting with small cars at the art table.
- looking at and listening to many books and stories about trucks, buses, and cars.
- setting up a gas station in the dramatic play area.
- visiting with Officer Lewis from the police department, who will show the children his squad car at 10:30 on Thursday.

AT HOME

You can foster the concepts of this unit at home by taking your child with you the next time you need to buy gas for your vehicle. There are many different types of trucks and cars to observe at the filling station. Also, provide soapy water and a sponge and let your child help you wash the family vehicle. Children enjoy taking part in grown-up activities and this helps to build a sense of responsibility and self-esteem.

Enjoy your child as you explore concepts related to cars, trucks, and buses.

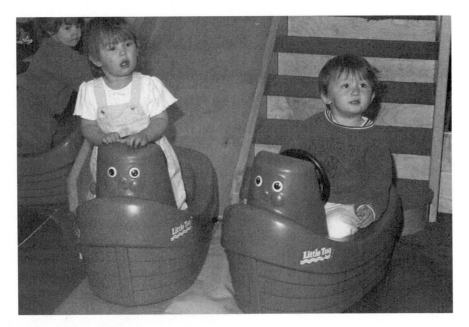

Time to race!

Fingerplays

OUR FAMILY CAR

This is our family car
(make fists as if holding a steering wheel)
The engine purrs like new.
Four wheels and a body,
(hold up four fingers)
It is painted blue.

Dad and Mom use it for business
(hold fists as if holding a steering wheel)
Or to drive us to the store.
We take it on vacation
You couldn't ask for more.
(shake head "no")

In the winter weather
If we should miss the bus,
(make sad face)
We can still get to our school,
In the family car we trust.
(hold fists as if holding a steering wheel)

Source: Wilmes, Liz & Dick. (1983). *Everyday Circle Times*.
Building Block Publishers, Illinois.

WINDSHIELD WIPER

I'm a windshield wiper
(bend arm at elbow with fingers pointing
up)

This is how I go
(move arm to left and right, pivoting at
elbow)
Back and forth, back and forth
(continue back and forth motion)
In the rain and snow.
(continue back and forth motion)

HERE IS A CAR

Here is a car, shiny and bright.
(cup one hand and place on other palm)
This is the windshield that lets in the light.
(hands open, fingertips touching)
Here are wheels that go round and round.
(two fists)
I sit in the back seat and make not a sound.
(sit quietly with hands in lap)

THE CAR RIDE

(Left arm, held out with bent elbow and
open palm, is road; right fist is car.)

"Vroom!" says the engine
(place car on left shoulder)
As the driver starts the car.
(shake car)

"Mmmm," say the windows
As the driver takes it far.
(travel over upper arm)

"Errr," say the tires
As it rounds the final bend,
    (turn at elbow, proceed over forearm)

"Ahhh," says the driver
As his trip comes to an end.
    (stop car on left flattened palm)

SCHOOL BUS

I go to the bus stop each day
    (walk one hand across table)
Where the bus comes to take us away.
    (stop, have other hand wait also)
We stand single file
    (one behind the other)
And walk down the aisle
    (step up imaginary steps onto bus)
When the bus driver talks, we obey.

Science

1. **License Plates**

   Collect license plates from different states and different vehicles and place them on a table for the children to explore.

2. **Feely Box**

   Put transportation toys in a feely box. Include cars, trucks, and buses. Individually let the children feel inside the box and identify the type of toy.

Dramatic Play

1. **Filling Station**

   Provide cardboard boxes for cars and hoses for the gas pumps. Also, make available play money and steering wheels.

2. **Bus**

   Set up a bus situation by lining up chairs in one or two long rows. Provide a steering wheel for the driver. A money bucket and play money can also be provided. If a steering wheel is unavailable, heavy round pizza cardboards can be used to improvise.

3. **Taxi**

   Set up two rows of chairs side by side to represent a taxi. Use a pizza cardboard, or other round object, as the steering wheel. Provide a telephone, dress-up clothes for the passengers, and a hat for the driver. A "TAXI" sign can also be placed by the chairs to invite play.

4. **Fire Truck**

   Contact the local fire chief and ask to use old hoses, fire hats, and fire fighter clothing.

Arts and Crafts

1. **License Plate Rubbings**

   Place paper on top of a license plate. Using the side of a large crayon, rub across the top of the license plate.

2. **Car Painting**

   Provide several small plastic cars, trucks, and large sheets of white paper. Also, have available low, flat pans of thin tempera paint. Encourage the children to take the cars and trucks and roll the wheels in the paint. They can then transfer the car to their own paper and make car or truck tracks on the paper.

3. **Designing Cars**

   Provide the children with large appliance-sized cardboard boxes. To protect the floor surface, place a large sheet of plastic underneath. Provide the children with paint, markers, and collage materials to decorate the boxes as cars. When the cars dry, they can be moved into the block building, dramatic play area, or outdoor area.

4. **Scrapbooks or Collages**

   Provide magazines for children to cut or tear out pictures of cars and trucks to make a collage or small scrapbook.

Sensory

Sensory Table Additions

- cars and trucks with wet sand
- baby oil and water

Large Muscle

1. **"Fill 'er Up"**

   The trikes, wagons, and scooters can be used outside on the playground. A gas pump can be constructed out of an old cardboard box with an attached hose.

2. **Car, Car, Truck**

   Play this simple variation of "Duck, Duck, Goose" by substituting the words, "Car, Car, Truck."

3. **Wash a Car**

   If possible, wash a compact-size car. Provide a hose, sponges, brushes, a bucket, and soapy water. If an actual car is not available, children can wash tricycles, bicycles, scooters, and wagons.

Field Trips/ Resource People

1. **City Bus**

   Take the children for a ride around town on a city bus. When boarding, allow each child to place his own money in the meter. Observe the length of the bus. While inside, watch how the bus driver operates the bus. Also, have a school bus driver visit and tell about the job and the importance of safety on a bus.

2. **Taxi Driver**

   Invite a taxi driver to visit and show the features of the taxi.

3. **Patrol Car**

   Invite a police officer to bring a squad car to the center. The radio, siren, and flashing lights can be demonstrated. Let the children sit in the car.

4. **Fire Truck**

   Invite a local firefighter to bring a fire truck to the center. Let the children climb in the truck and observe the parts.

5. **Semi-truck Driver**

   Invite a semi driver to bring the truck to school. Observe the size, number of wheels, and parts of the cab. Let the children sit in the cab.

6. **Ambulance**

   Invite an ambulance driver to bring the vehicle to school. Let the children inspect the contents.

Math

1. **Cars and Garages**

   Car garages can be constructed out of empty half-pint milk cartons. Collect and carefully wash the milk cartons. Cut out one side and write a numeral starting with one on each carton. Next, collect a corresponding number of small matchbox cars. Attach a strip of paper with a numeral from one to the appropriate number on each car's top. The children can drive each car into the garage with the corresponding numeral.

2. **License Plate Match**

   Construct two sets of identical license plates. Print a pattern of letters or numerals on each set. Mix them up. Children can try to match the pairs.

3. **Car, Truck, or Bus Sequencing**

   Cut out various-sized cars, trucks, or buses and laminate. Children can sequence them from largest to smallest and vice versa.

4. Sorting

Construct cars, trucks, and buses of different colors and laminate. Children can sort according to color.

Social Studies

Discussion on Safety

Have a group discussion on safety when riding in a car. Allow children to come up with suggestions. Write them down on a chart and display in classroom during the unit. The addition of pictures or drawings would be helpful for younger children.

Group Time
(games, language)

1. Thank-You Note

Write a thank-you note to a resource person. Allow children to dictate and sign it.

2. Red Light, Green Light

Select one child to pretend to be a traffic light. The traffic light places his back to children lined up at the other end of the room. When the traffic light says, "Green Light," or holds up green paper, the other children attempt to creep up on the traffic light. At any time the traffic light can say, "Red Light," or hold up a red paper and quickly turn around. Creeping children must freeze. Any child caught moving is sent back to the starting line. Play continues until one child reaches the traffic light. This child becomes the new traffic light.

Cooking

1. Cracker Wheels

For this recipe each child will need:

4 round crackers
1/2 hot dog
1/2 a slice of 4" x 4" cheese

Slice hot dogs and place on a cracker. Place cheese over the top. Place in oven at 350 degrees for 3 to 5 minutes or microwave for 30 seconds. Let cool and eat.

2. Greek Honey Twists

3 eggs, beaten
2 tablespoons vegetable oil
1/2 teaspoon baking powder
1/4 teaspoon salt
1 3/4 to 2 cups all-purpose flour
vegetable oil
1/4 cup honey
1 tablespoon water
ground cinnamon to taste

Mix eggs, 2 tablespoons oil, baking powder, and salt in a large bowl. Gradually stir in enough flour to make a very stiff dough. Knead 5 minutes. Roll half the dough at a time as thin as possible on well-floured surface with a stockinet-covered rolling pin. Cut into wheel shapes. Twist into the shape of the numeral eight. Cover with damp towel to prevent drying.

Heat 2 to 3 inches of oil to 375 degrees. Fry 3 to 5 twists at a time until golden brown, turning once, about 45 seconds on each side. Drain on paper towels. Heat honey and water to boiling; boil 1 minute. Cool slightly. Drizzle over twists; sprinkle with cinnamon. Makes 32 twists.

Source: *Betty Crocker's International Cookbook.* (1980). New York: Random House.

Books

The following books can be used to complement this theme:

Bingham, Caroline. *Mighty Machines* series. New York: Dorling Kindersley. *Big Rig*. Illus. by Mary Ling. (1996); *Fire Truck: And Other Emergency Machines*. (1995); *Monster Machines* (1998); *Race Car* (1996).

Blanchard, Arlene. (1995). *The Dump Truck*. Illus. by Tony Wells. Cambridge, MA: Candlewick Press.

Crews, Donald. (1984). *School Bus*. New York: William Morrow.

Eick, Jean. (1997). *Giant Dump Trucks*. Illus. by Michael Sellner. Minneapolis: Abdo & Daughters.

Gibbons, Gail. (1987). *Fill It Up: All About Service Stations*. New York: Harper-Collins.

Gray, Libba Moore. (1994). *The Little Black Truck*. Illus. by Elizabeth Sayles. New York: Simon & Schuster.

Howland, Naomi. (1994). *ABCDrive!: A Car Trip Alphabet*. New York: Clarion Books.

Katz, Bobbi. (1997). *Truck Talk: Rhymes on Wheels*. St. Paul, MN: Cartwheel Books.

Kirk, Daniel. (1997). *Trash Trucks*. New York: G. P. Putnam.

Oxlade, Chris. (1997). *Car (Take It Apart)*. Morristown, NJ: Silver Burdett.

Mahy, Margaret. (1994). *The Rattlebang Picnic*. Illus. by Steven Kellogg. New York: Dial Books.

Marston, Hope Irvin. (1993). *Big Rigs*. New York: Cobblehill Books.

Patrick, Denise Lewis. (1993). *The Car Washing Street*. Illus. by John Ward. New York: William Morrow.

Radford, Derek. (1997). *Harry at the Garage*. Cambridge, MA: Candlewick Press.

Ready, Dee. (1998). *School Bus Driver*. New York: Capstone.

Richardson, Joy. (1994). *Cars*. New York: Franklin Watts.

Rockwell, Anne F. (1992). *Cars*. New York: Dutton.

Royston, Angela. (1991). *Cars*. Photos by Tim Ridley. New York: Macmillan.

Wilkins, Verna Allette et al. (1993). *Mum Can Fix It*. Lawrenceville, NJ: Red Sea Press.

Multimedia

The following multimedia products can be used to complement this theme:

Big Red [video]. (1993). Mill Valley, CA: Fire Dog Pictures.

Firefighter [CD-ROM]. (1994). New York: Simon & Schuster Interactive.

How a Car is Built [video]. (1995). Think Media.

K.C.'s First Bus Ride [video]. (1994). KidSafety of America.

Murphy, Jane Lawliss. *Cars, Trucks and Trains* [compact disc]. (1997). Long Branch, NJ: Kimbo Educational.

Snowplows at Work [video]. (1994). Truckee, CA: Bill Aaron Productions.

Recordings and Song Titles

The following recordings can be used to complement the theme:

Cars, Trucks and Trains
People in Our Neighborhood—"Motoring"
Car Songs—"Car, Car Song"
Six Little Ducks—"The Wheels on the Bus"
Put Your Finger in the Air—"Car Goes Beep"
Pre-K Hooray—"Stop at the Red Light"

THEME 12

Cats

Body Parts
fur
paws and claws
tail
whiskers
eyes
ears
nose
mouth

Care
food
water
grooming
exercise
shelter
medical

Food
water
cat food

Homes
houses
farms

Types
long-haired
short-haired
different colors

Theme Goals

Through participating in the experiences provided by this theme, the children may learn:

1. Types of cats.

2. Body parts of a cat.

3. Cats need special care.

4. What cats eat, drink, and where they live.

Concepts for the Children to Learn

1. Cats can be black, brown, white, grey, yellow, or calico.

2. Cats use their claws for many things.

3. Cats meow and purr to communicate.

4. Cats have legs, eyes, ears, a mouth, nose, and a tail.

5. Cats have fur on their skin.

6. Cats should be handled carefully and gently.

7. There are many different sizes and types of cats.

8. Cats need food, water, and exercise everyday.

9. Many different people help cats.

10. A kitten is a baby cat.

11. Cats like to play.

Vocabulary

1. **kitten**—a baby cat.

2. **pet**—an animal kept for pleasure.

3. **paw**—the cat's foot.

4. **veterinarian**—an animal doctor.

5. **leash**—a rope, chain, or cord that attaches to a collar.

6. **collar**—a band worn around the cat's neck.

7. **whiskers**—stiff hair growing around the cat's nose, mouth, and eyes.

8. **coat**—hair covering the skin.

Bulletin Board

The purpose of this bulletin board is to promote visual discrimination, pattern matching, and hand-eye coordination skills. Construct cats' bodies and heads out of tagboard, coloring each a different color and fur pattern. Laminate all pieces. Attach cat bodies to the bulletin board. Children then match the heads to the corresponding body.

Cat match

Parent Letter

Dear Parents,

We have many exciting activities planned at school as we begin our study on cats. We will be learning about a cat's body structure, how to care and feed our cats, and different types of cats.

AT SCHOOL

Some of the learning experiences planned include:

- taking a field trip to the veterinarian's office and pet store.
- making a chart of different types of cats.
- setting up a cat grooming area in dramatic play.
- listening to stories about cats.
- looking at pictures of cats.

AT HOME

We will be learning the fingerplay "Two Little Kittens." You may want to try it with your child at home:

Two little kittens found a ball of yarn
    (hold up 2 fingers . . . cup hands together to form a ball)
As they were playing near a barn.
    (bring hands together pointed upward for barn)
One little kitten jumped in the hay,
    (hold up 1 finger . . . make jumping then wiggling motion)
The other little kitten ran away.
    (make running motion with other hand)

Fingerplays and rhymes help children develop language vocabulary and sequencing skills. The actions that often accompany fingerplays develop fine motor development.

Have fun with your child!

What is your favorite breed of cat?

Music

1. **"Two Little Kittens"**
   (Sing to the tune of "Two Little Blackbirds")

   Two little kittens sitting on a hill
   One named Jack, one named Jill
   Run away Jack, run away Jill
   Come back Jack, come back Jill
   Two little kittens sitting on a hill
   One named Jack, one named Jill.

2. **"Kitty"**
   (Sing to the tune of "Bingo")

   I have a cat. She's very shy.
   But she comes when I call Kitty.
   K-I-T-T-Y
   K-I-T-T-Y
   K-I-T-T-Y
   And Kitty is her name-o.

   Variation: Let children think of other names.

Fingerplays

MRS. KITTY'S DINNER

Mrs. Kitty, sleek and fat,
   (put thumb up with fingers folded on
   right hand)
With her kittens four.
   (hold up four fingers on right hand)
Went to sleep upon the mat
   (make a fist)
By the kitchen door.

Mrs. Kitty heard a noise.
Up she jumped in glee.
   (thumb up on right hand)
"Kittens, maybe that's a mouse?
   (all 5 fingers on right hand up)
Let's go and see!"

Creeping, creeping, creeping on.
   (slowly sneaking with 5 fingers on floor)
Silently they stole.
But the little mouse had gone
   (mouse is thumb on left hand)
Back into his hole.

A KITTEN

A kitten is fast asleep under the chair.
  (thumb under hands)
And Sung Jee can't find her.
She's looked everywhere.
  (fingers circling eyes to look)
Under the table
  (peek under one hand)
And under the bed
  (peek under other hand)
She looked in the corner, and then Sung
  Jee said,
"Come Kitty, come Kitty, this milk is for
  you."
  (curve hands for dish)
And out came Kitty calling "mew, mew,
  mew."

THREE CATS

One little cat and two little cats
went out for a romp one day.
  (hold up 1 finger and then 2 fingers with
  other hand)
One little cat and two little cats
make how many cats at play?
  (ask how many that makes)
Three little cats had lots of fun
till growing tired away ran _____?
  (take 1 finger away and ask how many
  ran away)
I really think that he was most unkind to
  the _____ little cats that were left
  behind.
  (ask how many are left)

KITTEN IS HIDING

A kitten is hiding under a chair,
  (hide one thumb in other hand)
I looked and looked for her everywhere.
  (peer about with hand on forehead)
Under the table and under the bed,
  (pretend to look)
I looked in the corner and then I said,
"Come Kitty, come Kitty, I have milk for
  you."
  (cup hands to make dish and extend)
Kitty came running and calling, "Mew,
  mew."
  (run fingers up arm)

TWO LITTLE KITTENS

Two little kittens found a ball of yarn
  (hold up 2 fingers . . . cup hands
  together to form a ball)
As they were playing near a barn.
  (bring hands together pointed upward
  for barn)
One little kitten jumped in the hay,
  (hold up one finger . . . make jumping,
  then wiggling motion)
The other little kitten ran away.
  (make running motion with other hand)

Science

1. Provide a scale and different cat items
   (such as cat toys, collar, food dish, etc.)
   to weigh.

2. During the social studies activity, "Share
   Your Cat," arrange for a cat and a kitten
   to be in the classroom at the same time.
   With the help of parents, weigh the cats
   or kittens and discuss with the children
   the differences.

3. Set out a magnifying glass to observe
   different kinds of dry cat food.

4. Talk about a cat who has claws and one
   that is declawed. Ask various questions
   such as: Why do cats have claws? Why
   are cats declawed? Where do cats go to
   be declawed? etc.

5. Discuss the various parts of a cat's body
   and how they can protect the cat.
   (Examples: fur, whiskers, etc.)

6. Discuss what a cat's body does when it
   feels danger.

Dramatic Play

1. **Cat Grooming**

Provide the children with empty shampoo
and conditioner bottles, brushes, combs,
ribbons, collars, plastic bathtub, towels,
and stuffed animal cats.

2. Veterinarian's Office

Provide various medical supplies such as a stethoscope, bandages, and thermometers along with stuffed cats.

3. Cats!

Let children pretend they are cats by using cat masks or costumes. Also, you may want to try using yarn balls, boxes to curl up in, and empty cat food boxes. Allow the children to act out the story "The Three Little Kitttens" or other cat stories.

4. Circus or Zoo

Lions, cheetas, panthers, leopards, and tigers are also cats. Use large boxes for cages.

Arts and Crafts

1. Kitty Collage

Let children find and cut or tear out pictures of cats from greeting cards and magazines. Children can then paste their cats on pieces of construction paper.

2. Pom Pom Painting

Set out several different colors of tempera paint. Using pom-pom balls, let children create their own designs on construction paper.

3. Cat Mask

Using paper plates or paper bags along with paper scraps, yarn, crayons, scissors, and paint, let the children design cat masks.

4. Paw Prints

Let children pretend they are cats using their hands and paint to make prints.

Large Muscle

1. Bean Bag Toss

Make a cat shape on plywood with holes of different sizes cut out. The children can try from varying distances to throw bean bags through the holes.

2. Yarn Balls

Set up baskets at varying distances from a masking tape line on the floor. Toss yarn balls into the baskets.

3. Cat Pounce

Children pretend to be cats and pounce from one line to another.

4. Climbing Cats

Bring a wooden climber into the classroom or set it up outside. The children can pretend to be cats and climb on the climber.

5. Cat Movements

Write down all the words that describe how cats move. Allow the children to demonstrate the movements. Also, use music in the background.

Field Trips/ Resource People

1. Pet Store

Take a field trip to a pet store. Ask the manager how to care for cats. Observe the different types of cats, cages, collars, leashes, and food.

2. Veterinarian's Office

Take a field trip to a veterinarian's office or animal hospital. Compare the similarities and differences to a doctor's office.

3. Variety Store

Visit a variety store and observe pet accessories.

4. **Resource People**

Invite resource people. Suggestions include:

- ⊚ cat groomer
- ⊚ humane society representative
- ⊚ pet store owner
- ⊚ veterinarian
- ⊚ parents to bring in pet cats

Math

1. **Matching Game**

Have the children match the number of cats on a card to the correct numeral. (Cat stickers work well.)

2. **How Many Paper Clips**

Make several different sizes of cats out of tagboard. Children measure each cat with the paper clips.

3. **Whisker Count**

Make several cat faces with one numeral on each face. Children attach the correct number of whiskers (pipe cleaners, felt, paper strips, etc.) according to the numeral on the cat.

Social Studies

1. **Chart**

Make a chart with the children of different types of cats.

2. **Displays**

Display different pictures of cats around the room.

3. **Share Your Cat**

Invite the children and the parents to bring in a pet cat on specified days. (Have your camera ready! Take pictures and display them on a bulletin board.) Encourage the children to talk about their cat's colors, likes, body, etc.

4. **Cat Safety**

Discuss cat safety with the class. Items that may be discussed include why cats use their claws, what to do if you find a stray cat, the uses of collars and leashes.

Group Time
(games, language)

1. **Copycats**

Have one child be the cat and clap a rhythm for the group. The other children listen and then be the copycats. They clap the same rhythm as the cat did. Another child now becomes the cat and creates a rhythm for the copycats to imitate.

2. **Nice Kitty**

One child is chosen to be the kitty. The rest of the children sit in a circle. As the kitty goes to each child in the circle he pets the kitty and says, "nice kitty," but the kitty makes no reply. Finally, the kitty meows in response to one child. That child must run around the outside of the circle as the kitty chases him. If the child returns to his original place before the kitty can catch him, the child becomes the new kitty. This activity is appropriate for four-, five-, and six-year-old children.

3. **Listen Carefully**

The children should sit in a circle. One child is selected to be the mother cat. After mother cat has left the room, choose several other children to be kittens. All of the children cover their mouths with both hands and the kittens start saying, "meow, meow, meow." When the mother cat returns she should listen carefully to find all of her kittens. When she has found them all, another child should be chosen mother cat and the game can continue.

4. **Farmer in the Dell**

The children can play "Farmer in the Dell."

Cooking

1. **Cheese Cat**

   English muffins
   cheese slices

   Allow the children to cut out a cat face on their own slice of cheese. Put the cheese on top of the English muffin and bake long enough to melt the cheese.

2. **Cat Face**

   1/2 peach (head)
   almonds (ears)
   red hots (eyes)
   raisin (nose)
   stick pretzels (whiskers)

   Create a cat face using the ideas above or a variety of other items.

Books

The following books can be used to complement this theme:

Aylesworth, Jim. (1989). *Mother Halverson's New Cat*. New York: Macmillan.

Brown, Ruth. (1986). *Our Cat Flossie*. New York: E. P. Dutton.

Bryan, Ashley. (1985). *The Cat's Purr*. New York: Atheneum.

Carle, Eric. (1991). *Have You Seen My Cat?* Saxonville, MA: Picture Book Studio Ltd.

Dupont, Marie. (1991). *Your First Kitten*. Neptune City, NJ: TFH Publications.

Ehlert, Lois. (1990). *Feathers for Lunch*. San Diego: Harcourt Brace.

Farjeon, Eleanor. (1990). *Cats Sleep Anywhere*. New York: HarperCollins Children's Books.

Hutchins, Hazel. (1992). *And You Can Be the Cat*. Buffalo, NY: Firefly Books, Ltd.

Kanao, Keiko. (1987). *Kitten Up a Tree*. New York: Alfred A. Knopf.

Kherdian, David, & Hogrogian, Nonny. (1990). *The Cat's Midsummer Jamboree*. New York: Philomel Books.

Kuklin, Susan. (1988). *Taking My Cat to the Vet*. New York: Bradbury Press.

Kunhardt, Edith. (1987). *Kittens, Kittens, Kittens*. New York: Golden Books.

Larrick, Nancy (Ed.). (1988). *Cats Are Cats*. New York: Philomel Books.

Mantegazza, Giovanna. (1992). *The Cat*. Honesdale, PA: Boyds Mills Press.

Martin, Bengt. (1992). *Olaf the Ship's Cat*. Yardley, PA: Checkerboard.

Marzello, Jean. (1990). *Pretend You're a Cat*. New York: Dial Books for Young Readers.

Matthias, Catherine. (1987). *I Love Cats*. Chicago: Children's Press.

McCue, Lisa. (1990). *Kittens Love*. New York: Random House.

Moncure, Jane. (1990). *Caring for My Kitty*. Mankato, MN: Children's World, Inc.

Nottridge, Rhoda. (1990). *Let's Look at Big Cats*. New York: Franklin Watts, Inc.

Parnell, Peter. (1989). *Cats from Away*. New York: Macmillan.

Petty, Kate. (1992). *Baby Animals: Kittens*. Hauppauge, NY: Barron's Educational Series, Inc.

Piers, Helen. (1992). *Taking Care of Your Cat*. Hauppauge, NY: Barron's Educational Series, Inc.

Pittman, Helena C. (1990). *Miss Hindy's Cats*. Minneapolis: Carolrhoda Books.

Polushkin, Maria. (1990). *Here's That Kitten!* New York: Macmillan.

Simon, Seymour. (1991). *Big Cats*. New York: HarperCollins.

Multimedia

The following multimedia products can be used to complement this theme:

Crume, Marion. *I Like Cats* [record].

Carr, Rachel. "Stretch Like a Cat" on *Be a Frog, a Bird, or a Tree* [record].

Sharon, Lois, & Bram. "The Cat Came Back" on *Singing, Swinging* [record].

Seeger, Pete. "My Little Kitty" on *Birds, Beasts, Bugs and Little Fishes* [record].

Kittens, Kids and a Frog [Apple/IBM software (Ages: 6–7)]. Hartley.

Sugar and Snails and Kitty-Cat Tails [Mac/Apple software, PK-2]. Entrex.

Recordings and Song Titles

The following recordings can be used to complement this theme:

I Like Myself—"The Cat and the Mouse"

Animal Walks—"Cat Stretch"

A to Z, the Animals and Me—"Cat Who Clowns Around"

T H ⅓ M E

Colors

red
green
white

Sounds

songs (carols)
bells

Christmas

Foods

cookies
eggnog
candy canes
candy

Symbols

ornaments,
lights, sleigh,
gifts, stockings,
Christmas cards,
candles,
Santa Claus,
star, garland, snow,
elves, wreaths,
religious

Plants

trees
poinsettias
mistletoe
holly

Theme Goals

Through participating in the experiences provided by this theme, the children may learn:

1. Christmas colors.
2. Christmas foods.
3. Christmas plants.
4. Symbols of Christmas.
5. Sounds heard at Christmas.

Concepts for the Children to Learn

1. Red, green, and white are Christmas colors.
2. Christmas cookies and candies are special treats for Christmas.
3. Santa Claus, reindeer, stockings, and Christmas trees are symbols of Christmas.
4. Decorating Christmas trees is a Christmas activity.
5. Christmas ornaments and garlands are hung on Christmas trees.
6. There are special Christmas songs.
7. Bells and Christmas carols are sounds heard at Christmas.
8. Pointsettias, evergreen trees, and mistletoe are Christmas plants.
9. Many people spend Christmas with their families and friends.
10. Some people hang special stockings that are filled with candy and small gifts.
11. Christmas is a time for giving and receiving gifts for some people.
12. Christians believe that Jesus was born on Christmas day.

Vocabulary

1. **Santa Claus**—a jolly man who wears a red suit and symbolizes Christmas.
2. **evergreen tree**—a tree decorated for the Christmas holidays.
3. **wreath**—a decoration made from evergreen branches.
4. **elf**—Santa's helper.
5. **star**—a treetop decoration.
6. **stocking**—a large Christmas sock.
7. **reindeer**—animals used to pull Santa's sleigh.
8. **present**—a gift.
9. **ornament**—decoration for the home or tree.
10. **carol**—a Christmas song.
11. **piñata**—brightly colored papier-mâché figure that is filled with candy and gifts.

122

Bulletin Board

The purpose of this bulletin board is to foster a positive self-concept, as well as name-recognition skills. Construct a stocking out of tagboard for each child in your class. Print the name across the top and punch a hole in the top with a paper punch. Hang a Christmas poster or teacher-made poster in the center of the bulletin board. Next, attach pushpins to the bulletin board, allowing enough room for each stocking to hang on a pin. The children can hang their own stockings on the bulletin board as they arrive each day.

Parent Letter

Dear Parents,

The holiday season is approaching. All we need to do is drive through our neighborhoods to see decorations and busy shoppers everywhere. Holiday songs are heard, and Santa is in the thoughts and sentences of many children. At school we will be participating in many Christmas activities. The children will learn the colors, plants, and symbols that are associated with the Christmas season.

AT SCHOOL

A few of the Christmas learning experiences planned include:

- creating ornaments to decorate the classroom Christmas tree.
- painting with pine boughs at the easel.
- making Christmas cookies.
- designing Christmas cards in the art area.
- practicing songs for our holiday program. Keep your eyes open for a special invitation! The program will be held on December 19th at 3:30. Mark your calendar.

AT HOME

Music and singing are wonderful ways to communicate our feelings, and we often have many feelings this time of year! When singing Christmas carols, encourage traditional songs as well as this new song:

"I'm a Little Pine Tree"
(Sing to the tune of "I'm a Little Teapot")

I'm a little pine tree tall and straight
Here are my branches for you to decorate.   *(extend arms)*
First we'll put the shiny star on top.   *(touch head)*
Just be careful the balls don't drop.   *(clap hands)*
Now be sure to plug in all the lights
So I will look very cheerful and bright.
Then put all the presents under me.
I'm all set for Christmas, as you can see!

REMINDER

Our last day of school will be December 23. School will open again on January 3 of the new year.

Happy holidays to you and yours!

124

Santa Claus and Christmas make winter fun.

Music

1. **"Rudolph the Red-Nosed Reindeer"**
   (traditional)

2. **"Jingle Bells"**
   (traditional)

3. **"The Twelve Days of Christmas"**
   (traditional)

4. **"We Wish You a Merry Christmas"**
   (traditional)

5. **"Peppermint Stick Song"**

   Oh I took a lick of my
      peppermint stick
   And I thought it tasted yummy.
   Oh it used to hang on my
      Christmas tree,
   But I like it better in my tummy.

6. **"S-A-N-T-A"**
   (Sing to the tune of "B-I-N-G-O")

   There was a man on Christmas Day
   And Santa was his name-o.
   S-A-N-T-A
   S-A-N-T-A
   S-A-N-T-A
   And Santa was his name-o.

7. **"Up on the House Top"**
   (traditional)

8. **"Santa Claus is Coming to Town"**
   (traditional)

9. **"Circle Christmas Verse"**

   Two, four, six, eight.
   Santa Claus don't be late;
   Here's my stocking, I can't wait!
   Two, four, six, eight.

10. **"Christmas Chant"**

    With a "hey" and a "Hi" and a "ho-ho-ho,"
    Somebody tickled old Santa Claus' toe.
    Get up ol' Santa, there's work to be done,
    The children must have their holiday fun.
    With a "hey" and a "hi" and a "ho-ho-ho,"
    Santa Claus, Santa Claus,
    GO-GO-GO!

11. **"Santa's in His Shop"**
    (Sing to the tune of "The Farmer in the Dell")

    Santa's in his shop
    Santa's in his shop
    What a scene for Christmas
    Santa's in his shop.

    Other verses:
    Santa takes a drum
    The drum takes a doll
    The doll takes a train
    The train takes a ball
    The ball takes a top
    They're all in the shop
    The top stays in the shop

    Pictures could be constructed for use
    during the singing of each toy.

Fingerplays

SANTA'S WORKSHOP

   Here is Santa's workshop.
      (form peak with both hands)
   Here is Santa Claus.
      (hold up thumb)
   Here are Santa's little elves
      (wiggle fingers)
   Putting toys upon the shelves.

125

HERE IS THE CHIMNEY

Here is the chimney.
    (make fist and tuck in thumb)
Here is the top.
    (cover with hand)
Open it up quick
    (lift hand up)
And out Santa will pop.
    (pop out thumb)

FIVE LITTLE CHRISTMAS COOKIES

(hold up five fingers, take one away as directed by poem)

Five little Christmas cookies on a plate by
    the door,
One was eaten and then there were four.

Four little Christmas cookies, gazing up at me,
One was eaten and then there were three.

Three little Christmas cookies, enough for
    me and you,
One was eaten and then there were two.

Two little Christmas cookies sitting in the
    sun,
One was eaten and then there was one.

One little Christmas cookie, better grab it
    fast,
As you can see, the others surely didn't last.

PRESENTS

See all the presents by the Christmas tree?
    (hand shades eyes)
Some for you,
    (point)
And some for me—
    (point)
Long ones,
    (extend arms)
Tall ones,
    (measure hand up from floor)
Short ones, too.
    (hand to floor—low)
And here is a round one
    (circle with arms)
Wrapped in blue.

Isn't it fun to look and see
    (hand shade eyes)
All of the presents by the Christmas tree?
    (arms open wide)

Science

1. Making Candles

Candles can be made for Christmas gifts. This experience provides an opportunity for the children to see how a substance can change from solid to liquid and back to a solid form. The children can place pieces of paraffin in a tin can that is bent at the top, forming a spout. A red or green crayon piece can be used to add color.

The bottom of the tin cans should be placed in a pan of water and heated on the stove until the paraffin is melted. Meanwhile, the children can prepare small paper cups.

In the bottom of each paper cup mold place a wick. Wicks can be made by tying a piece of string to a paper clip and a pencil. Then lay the pencil horizontally across the cup allowing the string to hang vertically into the cup. When the wax is melted, the teacher should carefully pour the wax into the cup. After the wax hardens, the candles can be used as decorations or presents.
Caution: This activity should be restricted to four- and five-year-old children. Constant supervision of this activity is required for safety.

2. Add to the Science Area:

   ⊚ pine needles and branches with magnifying glasses
   ⊚ pinecones with a balance scale
   ⊚ red, green, and white materials representing different textures

3. Bells

Collect bells of various shapes and sizes. Listen for differences in sounds in relation to the sizes of the bells.

4. Feely Box

A feely box containing Christmas items such as bows, cookie cutters, wrapping paper, non-breakable ornaments, stockings, bells, candles, etc., can be placed on the science table.

Dramatic Play

Gift Wrapping

Collect and place in the dramatic play area empty boxes, scraps of wrapping paper, comic paper, wallpaper books, and scraps. Scissors, tape, bows, and ribbon should also be provided.

Arts and Crafts

1. **Christmas Chains**

   Cut sheets of red, green, and white construction paper into strips. Demonstrate how to form the links. The links can be pasted, taped, or stapled, depending upon the developmental level of the children.

2. **Cookie Cutter Painting**

   Provide Christmas cookie cutters, paper, and shallow pans containing red and green paint. The children can apply the paint to the paper using the cookie cutters as printing tools.

3. **Rudolph**

   Begin the activity by encouraging the children to trace their shoe. This will be used for Rudolph's face. Then the children should trace both of their hands, which will be used as the reindeer's antlers. Finally, cut out a red circle to be used as the reindeer's nose. Have the children paste all the pieces together on a sheet of paper and add facial features.

4. **Designing Wrapping Paper**

   The children can design their own wrapping paper using newsprint, ink stampers, felt-tip colored markers, tempera paint, etc. Glitter can also be glued onto the paper.

5. **Creating Christmas Cards**

   Paper, felt-tip colored markers, and crayons should be available at the art table. Christmas stencils can also be provided.

6. **Pine Bough Painting**

   Collect short pine boughs to use as painting tools. The tools can be placed at the easel or used with a shallow pan of tempera paint at tables.

7. **Candy Cane Marble Painting**

   Cut red construction paper into candy cane shapes. Marble paint with white tempera paint.

8. **Seasonal Stencils**

   Spread glue inside a seasonal stencil. Apply glitter over the glued area.

9. **Glittery Pine Cones**

   Paint pine cones with tempera paint, sprinkle with glitter, and allow the paint to dry. The glittery pine cones can be used for classroom decorations, presents, or taken home.

10. **Paper Wreaths**

    Purchase green muffin tin liners. To make the paper wreaths, cut out a large ring from light tagboard or construction paper for each child in the class. The children can glue the green muffin tin liners to the ring, adding small pieces of red yarn, crayons, or felt-tip marker symbols to represent berries if desired.

11. **Playdough Cookies**

    Using red, green, and white playdough and Christmas cookie cutters, the children can make playdough cookies.

    Favorite Playdough

    Combine and boil until dissolved:

    2 cups water
    1/2 cup salt
    food coloring or tempera

    Mix while very hot:

    2 tablespoons salad oil
    2 tablespoons alum
    2 cups flour

    Knead approximately five minutes until smooth. Store in an airtight covered container.

Sensory

1. **Add to the Sensory Table:**
   - pine branches, needles, and cones
   - scented red and green playdough
   - icicles or snow (if possible) with thermometers
   - water for a sink and float activity; add different Christmas objects such as bells, plastic stars, and cookie cutters
   - Add scents such as peppermint and ginger to water

2. **Holiday Cubes**

   Prepare ice cube trays using water that is colored with red and green food coloring. Freeze. Place in the sensory table.

Field Trips

1. **Christmas Tree Farm**

   Plan a trip to a Christmas tree farm so the children can cut down a Christmas tree. Check your state's licensing requirements regarding the use of fresh Christmas trees and decorations in the center or classroom.

2. **Caroling**

   Plan to go Christmas caroling at a local nursing home or even for another group of children. After caroling, Christmas cookies could be shared.

Math

1. **Christmas Card Sort**

   Place a variety of Christmas cards on a table in the math area. During self-selected or self-initiated periods, the children can sort by color, pictures, size, etc.

2. **Christmas Card Puzzles**

   Collect two sets of identical Christmas cards. Cut the covers off the cards. Cut one of each of the identical sets of cards into puzzle pieces. The matching card can be used as a form for the children to match the pieces on.

Group Time
(games, language)

1. **Find the Christmas Bell**

   For this activity the children should be standing in a circle. One child is given a bell. Then the child should hide, while the remainder of the children cover their eyes. After the child has hidden, he begins to ring the bell, signaling the remainder of the children to listen for the sound and identify where the bell is hidden. Turns should be taken, allowing each child an opportunity to hide and ring the bell.

2. **"Guess What's Inside"**

   Place a familiar object inside a box. Let the children shake, feel, and try to identify the object. After this, open the box and show the children the object. This activity works well in small groups as well as large groups.

Cooking

1. **Candy Canes**

   Prepare the basic sugar dough recipe for cookie cutters. Divide the recipe in half. Add red food coloring to one half of the dough. Show the children how to roll a piece of red dough in a strip about 3 inches long by 1/2 inch wide. Repeat this process using the white dough. Then twist the two strips together, shaping into a candy cane. Bake the cookies in a 350-degree oven for 7 to 10 minutes.

2. Basic Sugar Dough for Cookie Cutters

1/2 cup butter
1 cup sugar
1 egg
1/2 teaspoon salt
2 teaspoons baking powder
2 cups flour
1/2 teaspoon vanilla

Cut into desired shapes. Place on lightly greased baking sheets. Bake 8 minutes at 400 degrees. This recipe makes approximately 3 to 4 dozen cookies.

3. Eggnog

4 eggs
2 teaspoons vanilla
4 tablespoons honey
4 cups milk

Beat all of the ingredients together until light and foamy. Pour into glasses or cups and shake a little nutmeg on the top of the eggnog. This adds color and flavor. The recipe makes one quart. Eggnog should always be served immediately or refrigerated until snack or lunch. It should not be served to children who are allergic to eggs.

Gifts for Parents

Wax Paper Placemats

wax paper that is heavily waxed
crayon shavings
paper designs
dish towel
scissors

Use at least one of the following:
yarn   lace
fabric   dried leaves

Cut the wax paper into 12-inch by 20-inch sheets (2 per mat). Place crayon shavings between the wax paper. Then decorate with other items. Place towel on wax paper and press with warm iron until crayon melts. Fringe the edges.

Popsicle Stick Picture Frames

popsicle sticks (10 per frame)
glue
picture

Make a background of sticks and glue picture in place. Add additional sticks around the edges, front, and back for the frame and for support. For a freestanding frame add more popsicle sticks to both the front and the back at the bottom.

Refrigerator Magnets

small magnets
glue
any type of decoration (paper cut-outs, plaster of paris molds, yarn, styrofoam pieces, buttons, etc.)

Glue the decorations to the magnet.

Service Certificate

paper
crayons
pencils
lace
ribbon

Have the children write and decorate a certificate that states some service they will do for their parents. (Example: This certificate is good for washing the dishes; sweeping the floor; picking up my toys; etc.)

Ornaments

plaster of Paris
any mold
glitter
yarn
straw

Pour the plaster of Paris into the mold. Decorate with glitter and let dry. If so desired, place a straw into the mold and string with yarn or thread.

Refrigerator Clothespin

clothespins
glue
sequins/glitter/beads
small magnet

Let the children put glue on one side of the clothespin. Sprinkle this area with glitter, sequins, or beads. Then assist the child in gluing the magnet to the other side.

Patchwork Flowerpot

precut fabric squares
glue
tins (for glue)
flower pots   (continued)

Gifts for Parents (continued)

Patchwork Flowerpot
(continued)

Let the children soak the fabric squares one at a time in the glue. Press onto the pot in a patchwork design. Let dry overnight.

Snapshot Magnet

snapshot
plastic lid
scissors (preferably pinking
   shears)
glue
magnet

Trace the outline of the lid onto the back of the picture. Cut the picture out and glue it onto the lid. Glue the magnet to the underside of the lid.

Holiday Pin

outline of a heart, wreath,
   etc., cut out of tagboard
glue
sequins, beads, buttons, yarn
purchased backing for a pin

Let the children decorate the cardboard figure with glue and other decorating items. Glue onto purchased backing for a pin.

Flowers with Vase

styrofoam egg carton
pipe cleaner
scissors
glass jar or bottle
liquid starch
colored tissue paper
   (cut into squares)
glue
yarn
paintbrush

Cut individual sections from egg carton and punch a hole in the bottom of each. Insert a pipe cleaner through the hole as a stem. Use the scissors to cut the petals.

For the vase: Using the paintbrush, cover a portion of the jar with liquid starch. Apply the tissue paper squares until the jar is covered. Add another coat of liquid starch. Dip the yarn into the glue and wrap it around the jar. Insert the flower for a decoration.

Pine Cone Ornament

pinecones   glue
paint   glitter
paintbrush   yarn

Paint the pinecones. Then roll the pinecones in the glue and then into a dish filled with glitter. Tie a loop of yarn for hanging.

Paperweights

glass furniture glides
crepe paper
crayons
glue
plaster of Paris
felt piece
scissors

Children decorate a picture and then cut it to fit the glide. Place the picture face down into the recessed part of the glide. Pour plaster of Paris over the top of the picture and let it dry. Glue a felt piece over the plaster.

Rock Paperweight

large rocks
paint

Let the children paint a design on a rock they have chosen and give to their parents as a present.

Soap Balls

1 cup Ivory Snow
   detergent
1/8 cup of water
food coloring
colored nylon netting
ribbon

Add the food coloring to the water and then add the Ivory Snow detergent. Shape the mixture into balls or any shape. Wrap in colored netting and tie with ribbon.

Closet Clove Scenter

orange
cloves
netting
ribbon

Have the children push the pointed ends of the cloves into an orange. Cover the orange completely. Wrap netting around the orange and tie it with the ribbon. These make good closet or dresser drawer scenters.

Handprint Wreath

Colored construction
   paper
scissors
glue
pencil
cardboard/tagboard circle

Let the children trace their hand and cut it out. Glue the palm of the hand to the cardboard circle. Using a pencil, roll the fingertips of the hand until curly.

Bird's Nest

1 can sweetened condensed milk
2 teaspoons vanilla
3 to 4 cups powdered milk
1 cup confectioners' sugar
yellow food coloring

Mix all the ingredients together and add food coloring to tint the mixture to a yellow-brown color. Give each child a portion and let him mold a bird's nest. Chill for 2 hours. If so desired, green tinted coconut may be added for grass and put in the nest. Add small jelly beans for bird's eggs.

Flower Pots

plaster of Paris
1/2-pint milk containers
straws (3 to 4 for each container)
scissors
construction paper
paint
paintbrush
stapler

Cut the cartons in half and use the bottom half. Pour 1 to 3 inches of plaster into the containers. Stick 3 or 4 straws into the plaster and let harden. After plaster has hardened, remove the plaster very carefully from the milk carton. Let the children paint the plaster pot and make flowers from construction paper and staple the flowers to the straws.

Cookie Jar

coffee can with lid or oatmeal box
construction paper
crayons or felt-tip markers
glue
scissors

Cover the can with construction paper and glue to seal. Let the children decorate their cans with crayons or felt-tip markers. For an added gift, make cookies in the classroom to send home in the jars.

Felt Printing

felt
glue
wood block
tempera paint
scissors

Let the children cut the felt pieces into any shape. Glue the shape onto the wood block. Dip into a shallow pan of tempera paint. Print on newspaper to test.

Napkin Holder

paper plates
scissors
yarn
paper punch
crayons
clear shellac

Cut one paper plate in half. Place the inside together and punch holes through the lower half only. Use yarn to lace the plates together. Punch a small hole at the top for hanging. Decorate with crayons or felt-tip markers. Coat with shellac. May be used as a potholder, napkin, or card holder.

Clay Figures

4 cups flour
1 1/2 cup water
1 cup salt paint
paintbrush

Combine flour, water, and salt. Knead for 5 to 10 minutes. Roll and cut dough into figures. (Cookie cutters work well.) Make a hole at the top of the figure. Bake in a 250-degree oven for 2 hours or until hard. When cool, paint to decorate.

Key Holder

8 popsicle sticks
construction paper or a cutout from a greeting card
self-adhesive picture hanger
yarn

Glue five sticks together edge to edge. Cut one 3/4-inch piece of stick and glue it across the 5 sticks. Glue 2 sticks across the top parallel to the 5 sticks. Turn the sticks over. Cut paper or a greeting card to fit between the crossed sticks. Place on the self-adhesive hanger and tie yarn to the top for hanging.

Planter Trivets

7 popsicle sticks
glue

Glue four popsicle sticks into a square, the top two overlapping the bottom ones. Fill in the open space with the remaining three and glue into place.

Pencil Holder

empty soup cans
construction paper or contact paper
crayons or felt-tip markers
glue
scissors

Cover the can with construction or contact paper. Decorate with crayons or markers and use as a pencil holder.

Gifts for Parents (continued)

Plaster Hand Prints

plaster of Paris
1-inch-deep square
    container
paint
paintbrush

Pour plaster of Paris into the container. Have the child place his hand in the plaster to make a mold. Let the mold dry and remove it from the container. Let the child paint the mold and give as a gift with the following poem:

My Hands

Sometimes you get discour-
    aged
Because I am so small
And always have my finger-
    prints
On furniture and walls.

But every day I'm growing
    up
And soon I'll be so tall
That all those little hand-
    prints
Will be hard for you to
    recall.
So here's a little handprint
Just for you to see
Exactly how my fingers
    looked
When I was little me.

Books

The following books can be used to complement this theme:

Ammon, Richard. (1996). *An Amish Christmas*. Illus. by Pamela Patrick. New York: Atheneum.

Barracca, Debra et al. (1994). *A Taxi Dog Christmas*. Illus. by Alan Ayers. New York: Dial Books.

Brett, Jan. (1990). *Christmas Reindeer*. New York: G. P. Putnam.

Brimmer, Larry Dane. *Merry Christmas Old Armadillo*. (1995). Illus. by Dominic Catalano. Honesdale, PA: Boyds Mills Press.

Brown, Margaret Wise. (1996). *On Christmas Eve*. Newly illus. by Nancy Edwards Calder. New York: HarperCollins.

Brown, Margaret Wise. (1994). *A Pussycat's Christmas*. Newly illus. by Anne Mortimer. New York: HarperCollins.

Burningham, John. (1993). *Harvey Shumfenburger's Christmas Present*. Cambridge, MA: Candlewick Press.

Carlstrom, Nancy White (1995). *I Am Christmas*. Illus. by Lori McElrath-Eslick. Grand Rapids, MI: Wm. B. Eerdmans Publishing Co.

Ciavonne, Jean. (1995). *Carlos, Light the Farolito*. Illus. by Donna Clair. New York: Clarion Books.

Davis, Rebecca. (1995). *The 12 Days of Christmas*. Illus. by Linnea Asplind Riley. New York: Simon & Schuster.

Day, Alexandra. (1994). *Carl's Christmas*. Orlando: Harcourt Brace.

De Paola, Tomie. (1994). *Legend of the Poinsettia*. New York: G. P. Putnam.

Fearrington, Ann. (1996). *Christmas Lights*. Boston: Houghton Mifflin.

Francisco, X. Mora. (1993). *La Gran Fiesta*. Port Atkinson, WI: Highsmith Co.

George, William T. (1992). *Christmas at Long Pond*. Illus. by Lindsay Barrett George. New York: Greenwillow.

Hoffman, Mary. (1997). *An Angel Just Like Me*. Illus. by Cornelius Van Wright. New York: Dial Books.

Jordan, Sandra. (1993). *Christmas Tree Farm*. New York: Orchard Books.

Moore, Clement C. (1996). *'Twas the Night B'Fore Christmas: An African-American Version*. Melodye Rosales. New York: Scholastic.

Packard, Mary. *Christmas Kitten*. Illus. by Jenny Williams. San Francisco: Children's Book Press, 1997.

Rahaman, Vashanti. (1996). *O Christmas Tree*. Illus. by Frane Lessac. Honesdale, PA: Boyds Mills Press.

Rylant, Cynthia. (1997). *Silver Packages: An Appalachian Christmas Story*. Illus. by Chris K. Soentpiet. New York: Orchard Books.

Say, Allen. (1991). *Tree of Cranes*. Boston: Houghton Mifflin.

Stevenson, James. (1996). *The Oldest Elf*. New York: William Morrow.

Tompert, Ann. (1994). *A Carol for Christmas*. Illus. by Laura Kelly. New York: Simon & Schuster.

Waldron, Jan L. (1997). *Angel Pig and the Hidden Christmas*. Illus. by David M. McPhail. New York: Dutton.

Multimedia

The following multimedia products can be used to complement this theme:

De Paola, Tomie. *Merry Christmas, Strega Nona* [talking book]. (1991). Read by Celeste Holm. Old Greenwich, CT: Listening Library.

A Multicultural Christmas [video]. (1993). Niles, IL: United Learning.

The Night Before Christmas [CD-ROM]. (1991). Toronto, Ont.: Discis Knowledge Research.

Palmer, Hap. *Holiday Songs and Rhythms* [compact disc]. (1997). Educational Activities.

Raffi. *Raffi's Christmas Album* [cassette]. (1983). Kimbo Educational.

Recordings and Song Titles

The following recordings can be used to complement this theme:

Santa's Sack of Christmas Songs

Holiday Songs for All Occasions—"My Christmas Wish"

Holiday Piggyback Songs—"I've Been Waiting for Christmas," "Where Is Santa?," "Did You Ever See a Reindeer?," "Little Green Tree"

Raffi's Christmas Album

A Children's Christmas (The Learning Station)

Pre-K Hooray—"Christmas in Killarney"

Singing Calendar—"December"

Holiday Action Songs—"Santa Claus Is Coming," "Santa's Helpers," "The Toy Piano," "The Very Little Ball," "The Mechanical Toys," "Tip Toe To Bed"

THEME 14

Circus

Places
tents
wagons
parks
parades

Acts
trapeze
high wire
animal shows
clown
cannon
tumbling
bicycle
juggling

Animals
lions
horses
elephants
tigers
dogs
seals
bears

People
ring master
trapeze artist
tumblers
animal trainer
clowns
high wire walker
grounds crew
makeup artist
costume designer

Theme Goals

Through participating in the experiences provided by this theme, the children may learn:

1. Different circus acts.
2. People who work for a circus.
3. Animals that perform in a circus.
4. Places to watch a circus.

Concepts for the Children to Learn

1. The circus is fun.
2. Many adults and children enjoy the circus.
3. The circus can be performed under a big tent.
4. An animal trainer teaches animals tricks.
5. Circus shows have colorful clowns.
6. Clowns wear makeup.
7. Music is played at the circus.
8. People and animals do special tricks in the circus.
9. Many people work at the circus.

Vocabulary

1. **circus**—traveling show with people and animals.
2. **circus parade**—a march of people and animals at the beginning of the performance.
3. **clowns**—people who wear makeup and dress in silly clothes.
4. **trapeze**—short bar used for swinging.
5. **ringmaster**—person in charge of the circus performance.
6. **makeup**—colored face paint.
7. **stilts**—long sticks a performer stands on to be taller.

Bulletin Board

The purpose of this bulletin board is to develop color recognition and matching skills. Construct eight clown faces with collars out of tagboard. Color each collar a different color using felt-tip markers. Hang these pieces on the bulletin board. Next, construct eight hat pieces out of tagboard. Color each one a different color, to correspond with the colors of the clowns' collars. Punch holes in the hats, and use pushpins to hold the hats above the appropriate clown. The children can match the colored hats to the clown wearing the same-colored collar.

Parent Letter

Dear Parents,

We are starting a unit that will be fun and exciting for everyone—the circus! Developing an awareness of special people and animals enhances an appreciation of others. It also stimulates children's curiosity to learn more about other people and people's jobs. The children will be learning about the many acts and performances of circus people and animals.

AT SCHOOL

Some of the many fun and exciting things we will be doing include:

- listening to the story *Harriet Goes to the Circus* by Betsy and Guilio Maestro.
- dressing up in clown suits and applying makeup in the dramatic play area.
- acting out a small circus of our own.
- making clown face puppets.
- imitating circus clowns.
- looking at books containing circus animals.
- viewing the video *Circus*.

We will have a very special visitor come to our room on Friday—a clown! He will show us how he applies his makeup and will perform for us. You are invited to join us for the fun at 3:00 p.m. to share in this activity.

AT HOME

It has been said that the circus is perhaps the world's oldest form of entertainment. Pictures of circus acts drawn over 3,000 years ago have been discovered on walls of caves. Most children enjoy clowns and dressing up as clowns. Prepare clown makeup with your child by adding a few drops of food coloring to cold cream. Have your child use his fingers or a clean paintbrush to paint his face. This activity will help develop an awareness of colors, as well as help him or her realize that appearances can change but the person remains the same!

Enjoy your child!

138

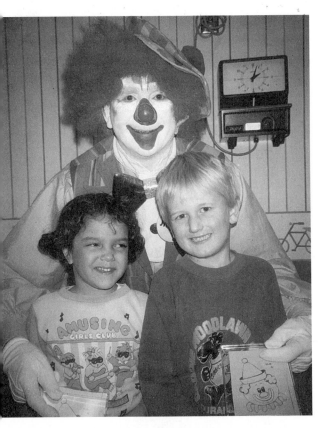

Clowns like to make people laugh.

Music

1. **"Circus"**
(Sing to the tune of "Did You Ever See a Lassie")

Let's pretend that we are clowns, are
  clowns, are clowns.
Let's pretend that we are clowns.
We'll have so much fun.
We'll put on our makeup and make people
  laugh hard.
Let's pretend that we are clowns.
We'll have so much fun.

Let's pretend that we are elephants, are
  elephants, are elephants.
Let's pretend that we are elephants.
We'll have so much fun.
We'll sway back and forth and stand on
  just two legs.
Let's pretend that we are elephants.
We'll have so much fun.

Let's pretend that we are on a trapeze, a
  trapeze, a trapeze.
Let's pretend that we are on a trapeze.
We'll have so much fun.
We'll swing high and swoop low and make
  people shout "oh!"
Let's pretend that we are on a trapeze.
We'll have so much fun!

2. **"The Ringmaster"**
(Sing to tune of "The Farmer and the Dell")

The ringmaster has a circus.
The ringmaster has a circus.
Hi-ho the clowns are here.
The ringmaster has a circus.

The ringmaster takes a clown.
The ringmaster takes a clown.
Hi-ho the clowns are here.
The ringmaster takes a clown.

The clown takes an elephant . . .

Use clowns, elephants, lions, tigers, tightrope walker, trapeze artist, acrobat, etc.

Fingerplays

GOING TO THE CIRCUS

Going to the circus to have a lot of fun.
  (hold closed fist, and raise fingers to indi-
  cate number)
The animals parading one by one.
Now they are walking 2 by 2,
A great big lion and a caribou.
Now they are walking 3 by 3,
The elephants and the chimpanzee.
Now they are walking 4 by 4,
A striped tiger and a big old bear.
Now they are walking 5 by 5,
It makes us laugh when they arrive.

ELEPHANTS

Elephants walk like this and like that.
  (sway body back and forth)
They're terribly big; they're terribly fat.
  (spread arms wide in a circular motion)
They have no hands, they have no toes,
And goodness gracious, what a NOSE!
  (put arms together and sway for
  elephant nose)

FIVE LITTLE CLOWNS

Five little clowns running through the door.
   (hold up one hand, put down one finger
   at each verse)
One fell down and then there were four.
Four little clowns in an apple tree.
One fell out and then there were three.
Three little clowns stirring up some stew.
One fell in and then there were two.
Two little clowns having lots of fun.
One ran away and then there was one.
One little clown left sitting in the sun.
He went home and then there were none!

CIRCUS CLOWN

I'd like to be a circus clown
And make a funny face,
   (make a funny face)
And have all the people laugh at me
As I jump around the place.
   (act silly and jump around)

THE CIRCUS IS COMING

The circus is coming hurray, hurray!
   (clap hands)
The clowns are silly; see them play.
   (make a face)
The animals parade one by one
   (walk fingers on lap)
While clowns juggle balls for fun.
   (pretend to juggle)
The lion growls; the tigers roar,
   (paw in the air)
While the elephant walks on all fours.
   (swing arms like an elephant trunk)
The circus is coming hurray, hurray!
   (clap hands)

Source: Rountree, Barbara, et al. (1981). *Creative Teaching with Puppets*. Alabama: The Learning Line, Inc.

Science

1. Circus Balloons

Cut several pieces of tagboard into circles. If desired, cover the balloons with transparent contact or lamination paper. On each table have three cups of colored water—red, yellow, and blue—with a brush in each cup. The child can mix all or any two colors and see which colors they can create for their circus balloons.

2. Shape the Clown

Cut several large outlines of clowns' heads from tagboard or construction paper and many eyes, hats, ears, noses, ruffles, and bowties. Make a large die with an ear, nose, hat, eye, ruffle, and bow tie. (One on each of the six sides.) The children can take turns rolling the die to construct their clown face. If a child rolls a die with the shape they already have, they must wait for their next turn.

Source: *Teacher-made Games*. (1980). Missouri: Parent-Child Early Education.

3. Seal and Ball Color/Word Match

Cut several seals out of different-colored tagboard. Out of the same colors cut several balls. Write the correct color on each ball. The children match each ball with the word on it to the correct seal.

4. Sizzle Fun

Pour 1 inch of vinegar in a soda or catsup bottle. Put 2 teaspoons of baking soda inside a balloon. Quickly slip the open end of the balloon over the soda bottle. Watch the balloon fill with gas created by the interaction of the vinegar with the baking soda.

5. Texture Clown

Construct a large clown from tagboard. Use different textured materials to create the clown's features. Make two sets. Place the extra set in a box or a bag. The children may pick a piece of textured material from the bag and match it to the identical textured piece used as a clown feature.

6. Make Peanut Butter

Take the shells off fresh peanuts. Blend peanuts in a blender until smooth. Add 1 1/2 to 2 tablespoons of oil per cup of peanuts and blend well. Add 1/2 teaspoon salt per cup if desired. Spread on bread or crackers and eat for snack.

Dramatic Play

1. Clown Makeup

Prepare clown makeup by mixing 1 part facial cream with 1 drop food coloring. Place clown makeup by a large mirror in the dramatic play area. The children apply makeup to their faces. Clown suits can also be provided if available.

2. Circus

Set up a circus in your classroom. Make a circle out of masking tape on the floor. The children can take turns performing in the ring. The addition of Hula Hoops, animal and clown costumes, tickets, and chairs would extend the children's play in this area.

3. Animal Trainers

Each child can bring in their favorite stuffed animals on an assigned day. The children can pretend to be animal trainers for the circus. They may choose to act out different animal performances.

Arts and Crafts

1. Clown Stencils

Cut several clown figures out of tagboard. Place felt-tip markers, crayons, pencils, and stencils on the art table. The children can trace the stencils.

2. Easel Ideas
- clown face-shaped paper
- circus tent-shaped paper

3. Circus Wagons

Collect old cardboard boxes and square food containers. The children can make circus wagons by decorating the boxes. When each child is through making his or her wagon, all of the boxes can be placed together for a circus train.

4. Clown Face Masks

Provide paper plates and felt-tip markers to make paper plate clown masks. Glue the plate to a tongue depressor. The children can use the masks as puppets.

5. Playdough Animals

Prepare playdough by combining:

2 cups flour
1 cup salt
1 cup hot water
2 tablespoons oil
4 teaspoons cream of tartar
food coloring

Mix the ingredients. Then knead the mixture until smooth. This dough may be kept in a plastic bag or covered container. If the dough becomes sticky, add additional flour.

6. Peanut Shell Collages

Provide peanut shells, glue, and paper for the children to create collages.

Sensory

Provide rubber or plastic animal figurines for the children to play with in the water table.

Large Muscle

1. Tightrope Walker

Provide a balance beam and a stick for the children to hold perpendicular to their bodies.

2. Dancing Elephants

Provide each child with a scarf and play music. The children can pretend to be dancing elephants.

3. Bean Bag Toss

Make a large clown or other circus person or animal bean bag toss out of thick cardboard. Cut the eyes, nose, and mouth holes all large enough for the bean bags to go through. For older children, assign each hole a certain number of points and maintain a score chart or card.

4. Can Stilts

Provide large tin cans with prebored holes on sides and thick string or twine for the children to make can stilts. Once completed, the children stand on the cans and walk around the room.

5. Tightrope Transition

As a transition, place a 10-foot line of masking tape on the floor. The children can pretend to tightrope walk over to the next activity.

6. Monkey, Monkey, Clown

Play Duck, Duck, Goose but change the words to Monkey, Monkey, Clown.

These games are most appropriate for older children—four-, five-, six-, and seven-year-olds.

Field Trips/ Resource People

1. Clown Makeup

Invite a clown to demonstrate putting on makeup. Then have the clown put on a small skit and talk about the circus.

2. The Circus

If possible, go to a circus or circus parade in your area.

Math

1. Clown Hat Match

Make sets of matching colored hats. On one set print a numeral. On the matching hats print an identical number of dots. The children match the dots to the numbers.

2. Circus Sorting

Find several pictures of symbols that represent a circus. Also include other pictures. Place all pictures in a pile. The children can sort pictures into two piles. One pile will represent circus objects.

3. Growing Chart

Make a growing chart in the shape of a giraffe. If desired, another animal can be substituted. Record each child's height on the chart at various times during the year.

Social Studies

1. Circus Life

Read *You Think It's Fun to be a Clown!* by David A. Adler. When finished, discuss the lives of circus people.

2. Body Parts

Make a large clown out of tagboard. Make corresponding matching body parts such as arms, legs, ears, shoes, hands, and fingers. The children can match the parts.

Group Time
(games, language)

1. Making a Clown

Give each child a paper and one crayon. Have children draw as you recite this fingerplay:

Draw a circle round and big,
Add a few hairs as a wig.
Make a circle for a nose,

142

Now a smile, broad and wide.
Put an ear on either side.
Add some eyes, but not a frown.
Now you have your very own clown.

This activity should only be used with older children when it is developmentally appropriate and when self-selected during small group time.

Source: Indenbaum, Valerie & Shapiro, Marcia. (1985). *The Everything Book for Teachers of Young Children*. Michigan: Partner Press.

2. Circus Pictures

Place pictures of clowns and circus things around the room at the children's eye level. Introduce the pictures at group time and discuss each picture.

3. Who Took My Nose?

Prepare red circles from construction paper. Seat the children in a circle. Give each child a red circle to tape on their nose. Then, have everyone close their eyes. Tap one child. This child should get up and go to another child and take his nose. When the child returns to his place the teacher claps her hands and all the children open their eyes. The children then try to identify the child who took the nose.

4. Clown Lotto

Adhere clown face stickers, or draw simple clown faces, on several 2-inch × 2-inch pieces of tagboard. Also, prepare lotto boards using the same stickers or drawings. To play, turn all cards face down. Children take turns choosing a card from the table and seeing if it matches a picture on their game boards.

Cooking

1. Clown Snack

Place a pear in the middle of a plate. Sprinkle grated cheese on the pear for hair. Add raisin eyes, a cherry nose, and a raisin mouth. Finally, make a ruffle collar from a lettuce leaf.

2. Cheese Popcorn

1/4 cup butter
1/4 cup dry cheddar cheese
3 cups popped popcorn

Melt butter and grate cheese. Mix together and pour over popcorn. Stir until well coated. Salt to taste if desired.

Source: Warren, Jean. (1982). *Super Snacks*. Alderwood Manor, WA: Warren Publishing House.

Books

The following books can be used to complement this theme:

Bond, Michael. (1992). *Paddington at the Circus*. Illus. by John Lobban. New York: HarperCollins.

Burmingham, John. (1994). *Cannonball Simp*. Cambridge, MA: Candlewick Press.

Chwast, Seymour. (1993). *The Twelve Circus Rings*. Orlando: Harcourt Brace.

De Paola, Tomie. (1992). *Jingle, the Christmas Clown*. New York: G. P. Putnam.

Duncan, Lois. (1993). *The Circus Comes Home: When the Greatest Show on Earth Rode the Rails*. Illus. by Joseph Janney Steinmetz. New York: Doubleday.

Ehlert, Lois. (1992). *Circus*. New York: HarperCollins.

Ernst, Lisa Campbell. (1996). *Ginger Jumps*. Madison, WI: Demco Media.

Johnson, Neil. (1995). *Big-Top Circus*. New York: Dial Books.

McCully, Emily Arnold. (1992). *Mirette on the Highwire*. New York: G. P. Putnam.

Paxton, Tom. (1997). *Engelbert Joins the Circus*. Illus. by Roberta Wilson. New York: William Morrow.

Schumaker, Ward. (1997). *Sing a Song of Circus*. Orlando: Harcourt Brace.

Spier, Peter. (1992). *Peter Spier's Circus*. New York: Delacorte Press.

Vincent, Gabrielle. (1989). *Ernest and Celestine at the Circus*. New York: Greenwillow.

Ziefert, Harriet M. (1992). *Clown Games*. Illus. by Larry Stevens. New York: Viking.

Multimedia

The following multimedia products can be used to complement this theme:

"Circus Baby" by Maud and Miska Petersham on *Max's Chocolate Chicken and Other Stories for Young Children* [video]. (1993). Weston, CT: Children's Circle Home Video; Los Angeles, CA: distributed by Wood Knapp Video.

Circus [video]. (1984). Edited by Steven Rosofsky. Chicago: Encyclopaedia Britannica Educational Corporation.

Do It Yourself Kid's Circus [cassette]. Available from Kimbo Educational.

Hanna, Jack. (1994). *A Day with the Greatest Show on Earth*. Glastonbury, CT: VideoTours.

Rogers, Fred. *Circus Fun* [video]. (1995, ©1987). Beverly Hills, CA: CBS/Fox Video.

Seuss, Dr. *Horton Hatches the Egg/If I Ran the Circus* [video]. (1992). Narrated by Billy Crystal. Random House.

Recordings and Song Titles

The following recordings can be used to complement this theme:

Do It Yourself Kids Circus
Animal Walks—"Animal Parade"

THEME 15

Clothing

Uses
ceremonial
protection
decoration
identification
costumes

Workers
tailor
seamstress
salesperson
laundromat assistant
shoe repair person

Care
wash
dry
mend
press
steam
polish
brush

Equipment
sewing machine,
washing machine,
dryer, washboard,
iron, ironing board,
brushes, steamer,
needle, clothespins,
hangers

Kinds
pants
uniforms
dresses
sweaters
skirts
shirts
shoes
socks
hats
gloves
coats
pajamas
scarves

Theme Goals

Through participating in the experiences provided by this theme, the children may learn:

1. Types of clothing.
2. Clothing workers.
3. Uses of clothing.
4. Care of clothing.
5. Equipment used with clothing.

Concepts for the Children to Learn

1. Clothing is a covering for our body.
2. Pants, dresses, shirts, and sweaters are some of the clothing we wear on our bodies.
3. Shoes, socks, and boots are clothing for our feet.
4. Gloves and mittens are coverings for our hands.
5. Hats and scarves are coverings for our head.
6. Protection, decoration, and identification are uses for clothing.
7. There are many colors and sizes of clothing.
8. A tailor and a seamstress make and mend clothing.
9. Clothing needs to be cleaned.
10. Clothespins and hangers are used to hang clothes.
11. Clothes identify workers.
12. Needle and thread, brushes, and irons are needed to care for clothing.

Vocabulary

1. **clothing**—a covering for the body.
2. **shirt**—clothing that covers the chest and sometimes the arms.
3. **shoes**—clothing for our feet.
4. **skirt**—clothing that hangs from the waist.
5. **hat**—clothing that covers our head.
6. **coat/jacket**—a piece of clothing that is often used for warmth and is worn over other clothing.
7. **clothespin**—a clip used to hang clothes on a clothesline or a hanger.
8. **washing machine**—an appliance used to clean clothes.
9. **dryer**—an appliance that dries clothes.
10. **laundromat**—a place to clean clothes.

Bulletin Board

The purpose of this bulletin board is to develop visual perception and discrimination skills. A "Sort the Clothes" bulletin board can be an addition to the clothing unit. Construct shorts and shirt pieces out of tagboard. The number used will be dependent upon the size of the bulletin board and the development appropriateness of the children. Draw a pattern on a pair of shorts and the same pattern on one of the shirts. Continue, drawing a different pattern for each shorts and shirt set. Hang the shorts on the bulletin board, and hang a pushpin on top of the shorts, so the children can hang the corresponding patterned shirt on top of the shorts.

Sort the clothes.

Parent Letter

Dear Parents,

We will be beginning a unit on clothing. Through participating in this unit, the children will learn about many different kinds of clothing. They will also become aware of the purposes and care of clothing.

AT SCHOOL

Some of the learning experiences planned for this unit include:

- sorting clothes hangers by color.
- going to a laundromat in the dramatic play area.
- making newspaper skirts at the art table.
- washing doll clothes in the sensory table.

We will also be taking a walk to the Corner Laundromat on Tuesday afternoon. We will be looking at the big laundry carts, washers and dryers, and folding tables. If you would like to join us, please contact me. We will be leaving the center at 3:00 p.m.

AT HOME

You can foster the concepts introduced in this unit by encouraging your child to select what he will wear to school each day. To promote independence, begin by placing your child's clothes in a low drawer allowing easy access to the clothing. To make mornings more enjoyable, encourage your child to select clothes at night that can be worn the next day. Find a location to place the clothes. Also, if your child has doll clothes, fill the kitchen sink or a tub with soapy water, and let your child wash the doll clothes. This will help your child learn how to care for clothing.

Have fun exploring clothing concepts.

We take turns washing the clothes.

Fingerplay

DRESS FOR THE WEATHER

If you go without your coat
   (put on coat)
When the wind is damp and chill,
   (hug self)
You could end up in bed, my friend,
   (shake finger)
Feverish, sneezing, and ill.
   (look sick, sneeze)
Wear your boots through snow and mud
   (put on boots)
And during a thunderstorm.
Also wear a waterproof coat and hat
   (put on coat and hat)
To keep yourself dry and warm.

Source: Cromwell, Hibner, & Faitel. (1983). *Finger Frolics.*
Michigan: Partner Press.

Science

Fabric Sink and Float

Provide various kinds of clothing and fabric on the science table along with a large tub of water. The children can test the different types of clothing to see which will sink and which will float. Some clothing articles will sink while other clothing articles float until they become saturated with water. After a test has been made, the clothes can be hung to dry.

Dramatic Play

1. **Clothing Store**

   Place dress-up clothing on hangers and a rack. A cash register, play money, bags, and small shopping carts can also be provided to extend the play.

2. **Party Clothes**

   Provide dressy clothes, jewelry, shoes, hats, and purses.

3. Uniforms

Collect occupational clothing and hats, such as police officer shirts and hats, a firefighter's hat, nurse and doctor lab coats, and artist smocks. High school athletic uniforms can also be provided. After use, store this box so the uniforms are available upon request for other units.

4. Hanging Clothes

String a low clothesline in the classroom or outdoors. Provide clothespins and doll clothes for the children to hang up.

5. Laundromat

Collect two large appliance-sized boxes. Cut a hole in the top of one to represent a washing machine, and cut a front door in the other to represent a dryer. A laundry basket, empty soap box, and play clothing may be welcome additions to extend the play.

Arts and Crafts

1. Dress the Paper Doll

Prepare clothing to fit paper dolls out of construction paper scraps. For younger children, the dolls can be pre-cut. Older children may be able to cut their own dolls if the lines are traced on paper, and a simple pattern is provided.

2. Newspaper Skirts

Depending upon the developmental level of the children, newspaper skirts can be constructed in the classroom. Begin by stapling about 10 sheets of newspaper across at the top. Draw a bold line about two inches from the staples. Then instruct the children to vertically cut from the bottom edge of the paper, all the way up to the bold line, creating strips. String pieces can be attached by stapling to the top of both sides to enable the skirt to be tied in the back.

3. Easel Ideas

- feature clothes-shaped easel paper
- paint using tools created by attaching small sponges to a clothespin

Sensory

1. Washing Clothes

Fill the sensory table with soapy water and let the children wash doll clothing. After being washed, the clothes can be hung on a low clothesline.

2. Add to the Sensory Table

- clothespins

Large Muscle

1. Clothespin Drop

Collect clothespins and a series of jars with mouth openings of varying widths. The children can stand near the jar and drop the clothespins into it. To ensure success, the younger children should be guided to try the jar with the largest opening.

2. Bean Bag Toss

Bean bags can be tossed into empty laundry baskets.

3. Clothes Race

Fill bags with large-sized clothing items. Give a bag to each child. Signal the children to begin dressing up with the clothing. The object is to see how quickly they can put all of the clothes items in the bag over their own clothing. This activity is more appropriate for five-, six-, and seven-year-olds who have better large motor coordination and development.

Field Trips/ Resource People

1. Clothing Store

Visit a children's clothing store. Look at the different colors, sizes, and types of clothing.

2. Tailor/Seamstress

Invite a seamstress to visit your classroom to show the children how they make, mend, and repair clothing. The seamstress can demonstrate tools and share some of the clothing articles they have made.

3. Laundromat

Take a walk to a local laundromat. Observe the facility. Point out the sizes of the different kinds of washing machines and dryers. Explain the use of the laundry carts and folding tables.

Math

1. Clothes Seriation

Provide a basketful of clothes for the children to line up from largest to smallest. Include hats, sweatshirts, shoes, and pants. Use clothing items whose sizes are easily distinguishable.

2. Line 'em Up

Print numerals on clothespins. The children can attach the clothespins on a low clothesline and sequence them in numerical order.

3. Hanger Sort

Colored hangers can be sorted into laundry baskets or on a clothesline by color.

4. Sock Match

Collect many different pairs of socks. Combine in a laundry basket. The children can find the matching pairs and fold them.

Social Studies

1. Weather Clothing

Bring in examples of clothing worn in each of the four seasons. Provide four laundry baskets. Label each basket with a picture representing a sunny hot day, a rainy day, a cold day, and a fall or spring day. Then encourage the children to sort the clothing according to the weather label on the basket.

2. Who Wears It?

At group time, hold up clothing items and ask the children who would wear it. Include baby clothes, sports uniforms and occupational clothing, ladies clothes, men's clothes, etc.

Group Time

Look Closely

While the children are sitting on the floor in a circle, call out the clothes items that one child is wearing. For example, say, "I see someone who is wearing a red shirt and pants." The children can look around the circle and say the name of the child who is wearing those items.

Cooking

1. Graham Crackers

Wear chef uniforms, and make your own graham crackers for snack.

1/2 cup margarine
2/3 cup brown sugar
1/2 cup water
2 3/4 cups graham flour
1/2 teaspoon salt
1/2 teaspoon baking powder
1/8 teaspoon cinnamon

Beat margarine and sugar till smooth and creamy. Add the remainder of the ingredients and mix well. Let the mixture sit for

30 to 45 minutes. Sprinkle flour on a board or tabletop. Roll out dough to 1/8 inch thick. Cut the dough into squares, logs, or whatever. Place on an oiled cookie sheet. Bake at 350 degrees for 20 minutes until lightly brown. This recipe should produce a sufficient quantity for eight children.

2. Irish Gingerbread

1 or 2 teaspoons butter
2 cups flour
1 1/2 teaspoon baking soda
1 teaspoon cinnamon
1 teaspoon ground ginger
3/4 teaspoon salt
1 egg
2 egg yolks
1 cup molasses
1/2 cup soft butter
1/2 cup sugar
1/2 cup quick-cooking oatmeal
1 cup hot water

Preheat the oven to 350 degrees. Grease the bottom of the baking pan with 1 or 2 teaspoons of butter. Measure the flour, baking soda, cinnamon, ginger, and salt; sift them together onto a piece of waxed paper. In a mixing bowl, combine the butter with the sugar by stirring them with the mixing spoon until they are blended. Add the egg and egg yolks. With the mixing spoon, beat the mixture until it is fluffy. Stir in the molasses.

Add the sifted dry ingedients, the oatmeal, and the hot water one fourth at a time to the egg and molasses mixture, stirring after each addition. Pour the mixture into the greased pan. Bake 50 to 55 minutes. Test with a toothpick. Make gingerbread people with cookie cutters. Decorate: make clothes for the gingerbread people using coconut, nuts, raisins, etc.

Source: Touff, Terry, & Ratner, Marilyn. (1974). *Many Hands Cooking*. New York: Thomas Y. Crowell Co.

3. Pita or Pocket Bread

1 package of yeast
1/4 cup of lukewarm water
3 cups of flour
    (white, whole wheat, or any combination)
2 teaspoons of salt

Dissolve the yeast in the water and add the flour and salt. Stir into a rough sticky ball. Knead on a floured board or table until smooth, adding more flour, if necessary. Divide the dough into 6 balls and knead each ball until smooth and round. Flatten each ball with a rolling pin until 1/4 inch thick and about 4 to 5 inches in diameter.

Cover the dough with a clean towel and let it rise for 45 minutes. Arrange the rounds upside down on baking sheets. Bake in a 500-degree oven for 10 to 15 minutes or until brown and puffed in the center. The breads will be hard when they are removed from the oven, but will soften and flatten as they cool. When cooled, split or cut the bread carefully and fill with any combination of sandwich filling.

Dramatic Play Clothes

The following list contains names of clothing articles to save for use in the dramatic play area:

aprons	leotards	shoes	shorts
boots	swimsuits	slippers	sweatsuits
pajamas	socks	robes	suspenders
shirts	purses	slacks	billfolds
dresses	jewelry	sweaters	ties
skirts	rings	coats	belts
hats	bracelets	earmuffs	
gloves/mittens	necklaces	raincoats	
scarves	clip-on earrings	snow pants	

Books

The following books can be used to complement this theme:

Burton, Marilee Robin. (1994). *My Best Shoes*. Illus. by James E. Ransome. New York: William Morrow.

Havill, Juanita. (1993). *Jamaica and Brianna*. Illus. by Anne Sibley O'Brien. Boston: Houghton Mifflin.

Hilton, Nette. (1991). *The Long Red Scarf*. Illus. by Margaret Power. Minneapolis: Carolrhoda Books.

Howard, Elizabeth Fitzgerald. (1991). *Aunt Flossie's Hats and Crab Cakes Later*. Illus. by James Ransome. New York: Clarion Books.

Hurwitz, Johanna. (1993). *New Shoes for Silvia*. Illus. by Jerry Pinkney. New York: William Morrow.

Keller, Holly. (1995). *Rosata*. New York: Greenwillow.

London, Jonathan. (1992). *Froggy Gets Dressed*. Illus. by Frank Remkiewicz. New York: Viking.

Mendel, Lydia J. (1993). *All Dressed Up and Nowhere to Go*. Illus. by Normand Chartier. Boston: Houghton Mifflin.

Miller, Margaret. (1988). *Whose Hat?* New York: William Morrow.

Morris, Ann. (1989). *Hats, Hats, Hats*. Photos by Ken Heyman. New York: Lothrop, Lee & Shepard.

Morris, Ann. (1995). *Shoes, Shoes, Shoes*. New York: Lothrop, Lee & Shepard.

Murphy, Stuart. (1996). *A Pair of Socks*. Illus. by Lois Ehlert. New York: HarperCollins.

Neitzel, Shirley. (1992). *The Dress I'll Wear to the Party*. Illus. by Nancy Winslow Parker. New York: Greenwillow.

Neitzel, Shirley. (1989). *The Jacket I Wear in the Snow*. Illus. by Nancy Winslow Parker. New York: Greenwillow.

O'Brien, Claire. (1997). *Sam's Sneaker Search*. Illus. by Charles Fuge. New York: Simon & Schuster.

Patrick, Denise Lewis. (1993). *Red Dancing Shoes*. Illus. by James Ransome. New York: William Morrow.

Pearson, Tracey Campbell. (1997). *The Purple Hat*. New York: Farrar, Straus & Giroux.

Serfozo, Mary. (1993). *Benjamin Bigfoot*. Illus. by Joseph A. Smith. New York: Margaret McElderry.

Small, David. (1996). *Fenwick's Suit*. New York: Farrar, Straus & Giroux.

Stoeke, Janet Morgan. (1994). *A Hat for Minerva Louise*. New York: Dutton.

Multimedia

The following multimedia products can be used to complement this theme:

Jenkins, Ella. "One Two Buckle My Shoe" on *Ella Jenkins Live at the Smithsonian* [video]. (1991). Washington, D.C.: Smithsonian/Folkways.

London, Jonathan. *Froggy Gets Dressed* [cassette and book]. (1997). New York: Penguin Books.

Parker, Dan. *Teach Me About Getting Dressed* [cassette and book]. (1988). Fallbrook, CA: Living Skills Music.

Scullard, Sue. *The Flyaway Pantaloons* [video]. (1992). Pine Plains, NY: Live Oak Media.

Recordings and Song Titles

The following recordings can be used to complement this theme:

Journey into Space—"My Space Suit"

Listen with Your Ears—"I Have Swimsuits"

Self Help Skills—"I Wear Clean Clothes"

More Songs About Me—"If You Have This On . . . Stand Up, Sit Down"

THEME 16

Alarm

flashing light,
car horn,
fire, sirens

Written

books, newspapers,
magazines, letters,
cards, words

Verbal

talking
singing
sounds
foreign accents
disabilities

Communication

Equipment

telephone,
television,
typewriter,
telegraph,
FAX, radio, records,
video recorder,
cassette player,
computer, email

Visual

letters
numbers
signs
pictures
art
artifacts

Nonverbal

listening
body movements
sign language
dancing
pantomime
drawings

Theme Goals

Through participating in the experiences provided by this theme, the children may learn:

1. Visual communication skills.
2. Nonverbal communication skills.
3. Verbal communication skills.
4. Communication equipment.

Concepts for the Children to Learn

1. Talking is a form of communication.
2. Listening is a way to communicate.
3. Our hands can communicate.
4. Our faces can communicate.
5. Sign language is a way of communication.
6. The telephone is a communication tool.
7. Letters and cards are a way of communicating.
8. Machines can transmit messages.
9. Typewriters, televisions, radios, and computers are equipment for communicating.
10. Signs are a way of communicating.
11. Books are a form of communication.

Vocabulary

1. **communication**—sharing information.
2. **typewriter**—a machine that prints letters.
3. **newspaper**—words printed on paper.
4. **sign language**—making symbols with our hands to communicate.
5. **Braille**—a system of printing for blind people.
6. **alphabet**—letter symbols that are used to write a language.
7. **signs**—symbols.
8. **card**—a piece of folded paper with a design. Cards are sent to people on special occasions: birthdays, holidays, celebrations, or when ill.
9. **letter**—paper with a written or typed message.

156

Bulletin Board

The purpose of this bulletin board is to assist older children in learning their home telephone number. Construct a telephone and receiver for each child. See the illustration. Affix each child's telephone number to the telephone. Laminate this card. For younger children, receivers can be attached to the telephones but left off the hook. The children can hang up their receiver when they arrive at school. Older children can match their receiver to their number and correct themselves by the color match. Later, white receivers for each child could be used to see if they know their telephone number. Telephones can be prepared for dialing by fastening the rotary dial with a brass fastener. Then the children can practice calling home by dialing their own number.

Parent Letter

Dear Parents,

We will begin talking about communication or how we share our ideas with others. Through this unit the children will become aware of the different ways we communicate: Through our voices, letters, using hand signals, and body language. They will also become familiar with machines that are used to communicate, such as the television, radio, computer, typewriter, and telephone.

AT SCHOOL

Some of the learning experiences planned for this unit include:

- a sign language demonstration.
- a phone booth in the dramatic play area.
- a typewriter and computer in the writing center.
- songs and books about communication.
- a wireless telephone on the science table.

AT HOME

It is important for children to learn their telephone number for safety purposes. Help your children learn your home telephone number. (This is also something we will be practicing at school.) To make practicing more fun, construct a toy telephone with your child. Two paper cups or empty tin cans and a long piece of rope, string, or yarn are needed to make a telephone. Thread the string through the two cups and tie knots on the ends. Have two people hold the cups and pull the string taut. Take turns talking and listening. The sound vibrations travel through the string—and you won't hear a busy signal!

Enjoy your children as you share concepts and experiences related to communication.

158

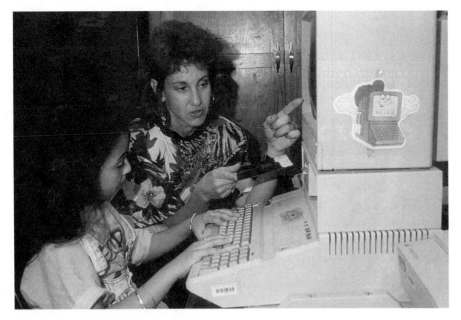

Computers are one way to communicate.

Music

1. **"Call a Friend"**
   (Sing to the tune of "Row, Row, Row Your Boat")

   Call, call, call a friend.
   Friend, I'm calling you.
   Hi, hello, how are you?
   Very good, thank you!

2. **"A Letter, A Letter"**
   (Sing to the tune of "A Tisket, A Tasket")

   A letter, a letter, I can make a letter.
   I take my arms and take my legs and I
     can make a _____.

   Encourage the children to make letters of
   the alphabet with their body parts.

   Source: Wirth, Stassevitch, Shotwell, and Stemmler. *Musical Games, Fingerplays and Rhythmic Activities for Early Childhood.*

3. **"Twinkle, Twinkle Traffic Light"**
   (Sing to the tune of "Twinkle, Twinkle Little Star")

   Twinkle, twinkle traffic light
   Standing on the corner bright.
   Green means go, we all know

   Yellow means wait, even if you're late.
   Red means STOP!
     (pause)
   Twinkle, twinkle traffic light
   Standing on the corner bright.

4. **"I'm a Little Mail Carrier"**
   (Sing to the tune of "I'm a Little Teapot")

   I'm a little mail carrier, short and stout.
   Here is my hat, and here is my pouch.
     (point to head, point to side)
   I walk around from house to house,
   Delivering mail from my pouch.
     (pretend to take things out of a bag)

Fingerplays

BODY TALK

   When I smile, I tell you I'm happy.
     (point at the corner of mouth)
   When I frown I tell you that I'm sad.
     (pull down corners of mouth)
   When I raise my shoulders and tilt my
     head I tell you "I don't know."
     (raise shoulders, tilt head, raise hands,
     shake head)

HELPFUL FRIENDS

Mail carriers carry a full pack
Of cards and letters on their backs.
   (hold both hands over one shoulder)
Step, step, step! Now ring, ring, ring!
   (step in place and pretend to ring bell)
What glad surprises do they bring?

MY HANDS

My hands can talk
In a special way.
These are some things
They help me to say:
"Hello"
   (wave)
"Come Here"
   (beckon toward self)
"It's A-OK"
   (form circle with thumb and pointer)
"Now Stop"
   (hand out, palm up)
"Look"
   (hands shading eyes)
"Listen"
   (cup hand behind ear)
Or "It's far, far away"
   (point out into the distance)
And "Glad to meet you, how are you
   today."
   (shake neighbor's hand)

Science

1. Telephones

Place telephones, real or toy, in the classroom to encourage the children to talk to each other. Also, make your own telephones by using two large empty orange juice concentrate cans. After washing the cans, connect with a long string. The children can pull the string taut. Then they can take turns talking and listening to each other.

2. Sound Shakers

Using identical small orange juice cans, pudding cups, or empty film containers, fill pairs of the containers with different objects. Included may be sand, coins, rocks, rice, salt, etc. Replace the lids. Make sure to secure the lids with glue or heavy tape to avoid spilling. To make the containers self-correcting, place numbers or like colors on the bottoms of the matching containers.

3. Feely Box

Prepare a feely box which includes such things as tape cassette, pen, pencil, block letters, an envelope, and anything else that is related to communication. The children can place their hand in the box and identify objects using their sense of touch.

4. Training Telephones

Contact your local telephone company to borrow training telephones. Place the telephone on the science table along with a chart listing the children's telephone numbers. The children can sort, match, and classify the wires.

5. Vibrations

Encourage the children to gently place their hand on the side of the piano, guitar, record player, radio, television, etc., in order to feel the vibrations. Then have the children feel their own throats vibrate as they speak. A tuning fork can also be a teaching aid when talking about vibrations.

6. Telephone Parts

Dismantle an old telephone and put it on the science table for the children to discover and explore the parts.

Dramatic Play

1. Post Office

In the dramatic play area place a mailbox, envelopes, old cards, paper, pens, old stampers, ink pads, hats, and mailbags. During self-selected or self-initiated play periods, the children can play post office.

2. **Telephone Booth**

Make a telephone booth from a large refrigerator-sized cardboard box. Inside, place a toy phone. Place in the dramatic play area.

3. **Television**

Obtain a discarded television console to use for puppetry or storytelling experiences. Remove the back and set, leaving just the wooden frame. If desired, make curtains.

4. **Radio Station**

Place an old microphone, or one made from a styrofoam ball and cardboard, with records in the dramatic play area.

5. **Puppet Show**

Place a puppet stand and a variety of puppets in the dramatic play area for the children to use during the self-selected or self-directed play period.

Arts and Crafts

1. **Record Player Art**

Place a piece of round paper or a paper plate with a hole punched in the center on a record player turntable. Turn the record player on. The children can use crayons or markers to draw softly on the paper while the record player is spinning.

2. **Easel Idea**

Cut easel paper in the shape of a book, record, radio, or other piece of communication equipment.

3. **Traffic Lights**

Provide red, yellow, and green circles, glue, and construction paper for the children to create a traffic light.

4. **Stationery**

Provide the children with various stencils or stamps to make their own stationery. It can be used for a gift for a parent or a special person. Children could then dictate a letter to a relative or friend.

Large Muscle

Charades

Invite children one at a time to come to the front of the group. Then whisper something in the child's ear, like "You're very happy." The child then uses his hands, face, feet, arms, etc., to communicate this feeling to the other children. The group of children then identifies the demonstrated feeling.

Field Trips/ Resource People

1. **Post Office**

Visit a local post office. Encourage the children to observe how the mail is sorted.

2. **Phone Company**

Visit a local phone company.

3. **Radio Station**

Visit a local disc jockey at the radio station.

4. **Television Station**

If available, visit a local television station. Observe the cameras, microphones, and other communication devices.

5. **Sign Language Demonstration**

Invite someone to demonstrate sign language.

Fingerpaint Recipes

Liquid Starch Method

liquid starch
   (put in squeeze bottles)
dry tempera paint in shakers

Put about 1 tablespoon of liquid starch on the surface to be painted. Let the child shake the paint onto the starch. Mix and blend the paint. Note: If this paint becomes too thick, simply sprinkle a few drops of water onto the painting.

Soap Flake Method

Mix in a small bowl:

soap flakes
a small amount of water

Beat until stiff with an egg-beater. Use white soap on dark paper, or add colored tempera paint to the soap and use it on light-colored paper. This gives a slight three-dimensional effect.

Wheat Flour Paste

3 parts water
1 part wheat paste flour
coloring

Stir flour into water. Add coloring. (Wallpaper paste can be bought at low cost in wallpaper stores or department stores.)

Uncooked Laundry Starch

A mixture of 1 cup laundry/liquid starch, 1 cup cold water, and

3 cups soap flakes will provide a quick finger-paint.

Flour and Salt I

1 cup flour
1 1/2 cups salt
3/4 cup water
coloring

Combine flour and salt. Add water. This has a grainy quality, unlike the other fingerpaints, providing a different sensory experience. Some children enjoy the different touch sensation when 1 1/2 cups salt are added to the other recipes.

Flour and Salt II

2 cups flour
2 teaspoons salt
3 cups cold water
2 cups hot water
coloring

Add salt to flour, then pour in cold water gradually and beat mixture with egg beater until it is smooth. Add hot water and boil until it becomes clear. Beat until smooth, then mix in coloring. Use 1/4 cup food coloring to 8 to 9 ounces of paint for strong colors.

Instantized Flour Uncooked Method

1 pint water (2 cups)
1 1/2 cups instantized flour
   (the kind used to thicken gravy)

Put the water in the bowl and stir the flour into the water. Add color. Regular flour may be lumpy.

Cooked Starch Method

1 cup laundry starch
   dissolved in a small
   amount of cold water
5 cups boiling water added
   slowly to dissolve starch
1 tablespoon glycerine
   (optional)

Cook the mixture until it is thick and glossy. Add 1 cup mild soap flakes. Add color in separate containers. Cool before using.

Cornstarch Method

Gradually add 2 quarts water to 1 cup cornstarch. Cook until clear and add 1/2 cup soap flakes (like Ivory Snow). A few drops of glycerine or oil of winter-green may be added.

Flour Method

Mix 1 cup flour and 1 cup cold water. Add 3 cups boiling water and bring all to a boil, stirring constantly. Add 1 tablespoon alum and coloring. Paintings from this recipe dry flat and do not need to be ironed.

Math

Phone Numbers

Make a list of the children's names and telephone numbers. Place the list by a toy, trainer, or unhooked telephone.

Social Studies

Thank You

Let the children dictate a group thank-you letter to one of your resource visitors or field trip representatives. Before mailing the letter, provide writing tools for children to sign their names.

Group Time
(games, language)

1. **Telephone**

   Play the game "telephone" by having the children sit in a circle. Begin by whispering a short phrase into a child's ear. That child whispers your message to the next child. Continue until the message gets to the last child. The last child repeats the message out loud. It is fun to see how much it has changed. (This game is most successful with older children.)

2. **What's Missing?**

   Place items that are related to communication on a tray. Include a stamp, a telephone, a record, a pocket radio, etc. The children can examine the objects for a few minutes. After this they should close their eyes while you remove an object. Then let the children look at the tray and identify which object is missing.

3. **Household Objects Sound Like . . .**

   Make a tape of different sounds around the house. Include a radio, television, alarm clock, telephone, vacuum cleaner, flushing toilet, door bells, egg timer, etc. Play the tape for the children, letting them identify the individual sounds.

Cooking

Edible Envelope

Spread peanut butter on a graham cracker. Add raisins to represent an address and a stamp.

Books

The following books can be used to complement this theme:

Aliki. (1993). *Communication*. New York: Greenwillow.

Aliki. (1996). *Hello! Good-Bye*. New York: Greenwillow.

Bornstein, Harry. (1992). *Nursery Rhymes from Mother Goose: Told in Signed English*. Washington, D.C.: Kendall Green Publications.

Brown, Marc Tolon. (1997). *Arthur's TV Trouble*. Boston: Little, Brown. (Pbk)

Brown, Ruth. (1991). *Alphabet Times Four: An International ABC*. New York: Dutton.

Buck, Nola. (1996). *Sid and Sam*. Illus. by G. Brian Karas. New York: HarperCollins.

Coffelt, Nancy. (1995). *The Dog Who Cried Woof*. Orlando: Harcourt Brace.

Gibbons, Gail. (1993). *Puff—Flash—Bang: A Book about Signals*. New York: William Morrow.

King, Mary Ellen. (1997). *A Good Day for Listening*. Morehouse Publishing.

Klove, Lars. (1996). *I See a Sign*. New York: Aladdin Paperbacks.

Leedy, Loreen. (1990). *The Furry News: How to Make a Newspaper*. New York: Holiday House.

Lester, Helen. (1995). *Listen, Buddy*. Illus. by Lynn Munsinger. Boston: Houghton Mifflin.

Nelson, Nigel. (1994). *Codes*. Illus. by Tony De Saulles. Cincinnati, OH: Thomson Learning.

Nelson, Nigel. (1994). *Writing and Numbers*. Illus. by Tony De Saulles. Cincinnati, OH: Thomson Learning.

Oxlade, Chris. (1997). *Electronic Communication*. Illus. by Colin Mier. New York: Franklin Watts.

Peterson, Jeanne Whitehouse. (1994). *My Mama Sings*. Illus. by Sandra Speidel. New York: HarperCollins.

Rankin, Laura. (1991). *The Handmade Alphabet*. New York: Dial Books.

Shapiro, Arnold. (1997). *Mice Squeak, We Speak*. Illus. by Tomie de Paola. New York: G. P. Putnam.

Showers, Paul. (1991). *Listening Walk*. Revised ed. New York: HarperCollins.

Weller, Janet. (1997). *The Written Word*. Illus. by Colin Mier. New York: Franklin Watts.

Wheeler, Cindy. (1998). *More Simple Signs*. New York: Viking.

Multimedia

The following multimedia products can be used to complement this theme:

Bailey's Book House [CD-ROM]. (1995). Redmond, WA: Edmark.

Be a Better Listener [video]. (1995). Pleasantville, NY: Sunburst Communications.

Exciting People, Places and Things [video]. (1989). Washington, D.C.: Gallaudet University Press.

Lonnquist, Ken and others. *Sign Songs: Fun Songs to Sign and Sing* [video]. (1994). Madison, WI: Aylmer Press.

Reader Rabbit's Ready for Letters [computer program]. (1994). Learning Company.

Tossing, Gaia. *Sing 'n Sign for Fun!* [compact disc]. (1995). Glenview, IL: Heartsong.

Recordings and Song Titles

The following recordings can be used to complement this theme:

Gaia—*Sign 'n Sing for Fun* (Sign Language)

Gaia—*Sign, Dance 'n Sing* (Sign Language)

Tony Chestnut (The Learning Station)— "Imagination, Communication"

THEME 17

Construction Tools

Safety

storage, use, care,
electrical,
sharpness,
child-proof

Types

electric
gas
left-hand
right-hand
large

Names

drill,
wrench,
screwdriver,
saw, hammer,
pliers, clamp,
level, wedge,
ruler, plane,
pencil, chalk,
scissors

Uses

clamp
drill holes
measure
cutting
pounding
building

Theme Goals

Through participating in the experiences provided by this theme, the children may learn:

1. Types of tools.
2. Names of common tools.
3. Functions of tools.
4. Tool safety.

Concepts for the Children to Learn

1. Tools can be electric or hand-powered.
2. Tools are helpful when building.
3. Pliers, tweezers, and clamps hold things.
4. Drills, nails, and screws make holes.
5. Planes, saws, and scissors cut materials.
6. Hammers and screwdrivers are used to put in and remove nails and screws.
7. Rulers are used for measuring.
8. To be safe, tools need to be handled with care.
9. Goggles should be worn to protect our eyes when using tools.
10. After use, tools need to be put away.

Vocabulary

1. **tool**—an object to help us.
2. **drill**—a tool that cuts holes.
3. **wrench**—a tool that holds things.
4. **screwdriver**—a tool that turns screws.
5. **saw**—a cutting tool with sharp edges.
6. **hammer**—a tool used to insert or remove objects such as nails.
7. **pliers**—a tool used for holding.
8. **clamp**—a tool used to join or hold things.
9. **ruler**—a measuring tool.
10. **wedge**—a tool used for splitting.
11. **plane**—a tool used for shaving wood.

Bulletin Board

The purpose of this bulletin board is to develop awareness of tool types, as well as to foster visual discrimination skills. A shadow tool match bulletin board can be constructed by drawing six or seven tool pieces on tagboard. See the illustration. These pieces can be colored and then cut out. Next, trace the tools on black construction paper to make shadows of each piece. These shadow pieces can be attached to the bulletin board. Magnet pieces can be applied to both the shadows and the colored tool pieces. Otherwise, a pushpin can be placed above the shadow and a hole can be punched in the colored tool piece. The children can match the colored tool piece to its corresponding-shaped shadow.

Parent Letter

Dear Parents,

Construction tools will be the focus of our next curriculum unit. This unit will help your child become more aware of many kinds of tools, their purposes, and tool safety. While exploring the classroom activities, the children will have opportunities to use many hand tools at the woodworking bench.

AT SCHOOL

Some of the activities the children will participate in include:

- painting with screwdrivers and wrenches.
- exploring wood shavings in the sensory table.
- setting up a mechanic's shop where the children can pretend to fix cars.
- a visit on Wednesday from Mr. Smith, a local shoe repairer. Mr. Smith will show us the tools and techniques he uses to repair shoes.

AT HOME

To develop language skills, recall with your child the tools you use in your home—from cooking and cleaning tools to gardening tools. Count the number of tools that are in each room of your house. Which room contains the most tools? This will promote the mathematical concepts of rational counting and vocabulary concepts of most and least.

Have fun with your child!

Construction tools help people build tall buildings.

Music

"This Is the Way"
(Sing to the tune of "Mulberry Bush")

This is the way we saw our wood,
  saw our wood, saw our wood.
This is the way we saw our wood,
  so early in the morning.

Other verses: pound our nails
          drill a hole
          use a screwdriver

Fingerplays

CARPENTER'S HAMMER

The carpenter's hammer goes rap, rap, tap
  (make hammer motion)
And his saw goes see, saw, see.
  (make saw motions)
He planes and measures and hammers and
  saws
  (act out each one)
While he builds a house for me.
  (draw house with index fingers)

JOHNNY'S HAMMER

Johnny works with one hammer, one
  hammer, one hammer.
Johnny works with one hammer, then he
  works with two.

Say the same words adding one hammer
each time. Children are to pretend to
hammer using various body parts.

Verse 1:   1 hand hitting leg.
Verse 2:   2 hands hitting legs.
Verse 3:   use motions for verses 1 and 2,
       plus tap one foot.
Verse 4:   verses 1, 2, and 3 plus tap other
       foot.
Verse 5:   verses 1 to 4, plus nod head. At
       the end of verse 5 say, "Then he
       goes to sleep," and place both
       hands by side of head.

You can also change the name used in the
fingerplay to include names of children in
your classroom.

169

THE COBBLER

Cobbler, cobbler, mend my shoe.
  (point to shoe)
Get it done by half past two.
  (hold up two fingers)
Half past two is much too late.
Get it done by half past eight.
  (hold up eight fingers)

Science

1. Exploring Levels

Place levels and wood scraps on a table for the children to explore while being closely supervised.

2. Hammers

Collect a variety of hammers, various-sized nails, and wood scraps or styrofoam. Allow the children to practice pounding using the different tools and materials.

3. The Wide World of Rulers

Set up a display with different types and sizes of rulers. Include the reel type. Paper and pencils can also be added to create interest.

Dramatic Play

1. The Carpenter

Place a carpentry box with scissors, rulers, and masking tape in the woodworking area. Also, provide large cardboard boxes and paint, if desired.

2. Shoemaker Store

Set up a shoemaker's store. Provide the children with shoes, toy hammers, smocks, cash registers, and play money. The children can act out mending, buying, and selling shoes.

Arts and Crafts

1. Rulers

Set rulers and paper on the table. The children can then experiment creating lines and geometric shapes.

2. Tool Print

Pour a small amount of thick, colored tempera paint in a flat pan. Also, provide the children with miniature tools such as wrenches, screwdrivers, and paper. The children then can place the tools in the paint pan, remove them, and print on paper.

Sensory

1. Scented Playdough

Prepare playdough and add a few drops of extract such as peppermint, anise, or almond. Also, collect a variety of scissors, and place in the art area with the playdough.

2. Wood Shavings

Place wood shavings in the sensory table along with scoops and pails.

Large Muscle

The Workbench

In the woodworking area place various tools, wood, and goggles for the children to use. It is very important to discuss the safety and limits used when at the workbench prior to this activity. An extra adult is helpful to supervise this area.

Field Trips/ Resource People

1. Shoe Repair Store

Visit a shoe repair store. Observe a shoe being repaired.

2. Woodworker

Invite a parent or other person into the classroom who enjoys woodworking as a hobby.

Math

1. Use of Rulers

Discuss how rulers are used. Provide children with rulers so that they may measure various objects in the classroom. Allow them to compare the lengths. Also, measure each child and construct a chart including each child's height.

2. Weighing Tools

Place scales and a variety of tools on the math table. Let the children explore weighing the tools.

Science Materials and Equipment

Teachers need to continuously provide science materials for the classroom. Materials that can be collected include:

acorns and other nuts	flowers	paper bags	scissors—assorted sizes
aluminum foil	gears	paper of various types	screen wire
ball bearings	insect nests	paper rolls and spools	sieves, sifters, and funnels
balloons	insects	plants	seeds
binoculars	jacks	plastic bags	spatulas
bird nests	kaleidoscope	plastic containers with lids—many sizes	sponges
bones	locks and keys		stones
bowls and cups	magnets of varying strengths, sizes		string
cocoon	magnifying glasses with good lenses	plastic tubing	styrofoam
corks		pots, pans, trays, muffin tins	tape
discorded clock	marbles		thermometers
dishpans	measuring cups and spoons	prisms	tongs and tweezers
drinking straws		pulleys	tools—hammer, pliers
drums	microscope	rocks	
egg cartons	milk cartons	rubber tubing	tuning forks
eggbeaters	mirrors—all sizes	ruler	waxed paper
eyedroppers and basters	moths	safety goggles— child size	weeds
fabric scraps	musical instruments	sandpaper	wheels
filter paper	newspapers	scales	wood and other building materials
flashlight	nails, screws, bolts		

Social Studies

1. Tool Safety

Discuss the safe use of tools. Allow the children to help decide what classroom rules are necessary for using tools. Make a chart containing these rules to display in the woodworking area.

2. Helper Chart

Design a helper chart for the children to assist with cleanup and care of the classroom tools. Each day select new children to assist, assuring that everyone gets a turn. To participate, the children can be responsible for cleaning the dirty tools and putting them away.

Group Time
(games, language)

1. Tool of the Day

Each day of this unit, introduce a "tool of the day." Explain how each tool is used and who uses it. If possible, leave the tool out for children to use on the woodworking bench.

2. Thank-You Letter

Using a pencil as a tool, let the children dictate a thank-you note to any resource person or field trip site coordinator who has contributed to the program.

Cooking

"Hands On" Cookies

3 cups brown sugar
3 cups margarine or butter
6 cups oatmeal
1 tablespoon baking soda
3 cups flour

Place all of the ingredients in a bowl. Let the children use clean child-size wooden hammers to mash and knead. Form into small balls and place on ungreased cookie sheet. Butter the bottom of a glass. Dip the bottom of the glass into a saucer with sugar. Use the glass to flatten the balls. Bake in an oven preheated to 350 degrees for 10 to 12 minutes. Makes 15 dozen.

Books

The following books can be used to complement this theme:

Barton, Byron. (1995). *Tools*. New York: HarperCollins. (Board book)

Brady, Peter. (1996). *Bulldozers*. Mankato, MN: Bridgestone Books.

Gibbons, Gail. (1990). *How a House Is Built*. New York: Holiday House.

Gibbons, Gail. (1982). *Tool Book*. New York: Holiday House.

Hoban, Tana. (1997). *Construction Zone*. New York: Greenwillow.

Klinting, Lars. (1996). *Bruno the Carpenter*. New York: Holt.

Miller, Margaret. (1990). *Who Uses This?* New York: Greenwillow.

Morris, Ann. (1992). *Tools*. Photos by Ken Heyman. New York: Lothrop, Lee & Shepard.

Neitzel, Shirley. (1997). *The House I'll Build for the Wren*. Illus. by Nancy Winslow Parker. New York: Greenwillow.

Radford, Derek. (1994). *Building Machines and What They Do*. Reprint edition. Cambridge, MA: Candlewick Press.

Robbins, Ken. (1993). *Power Machines*. New York: Holt.

Rockwell, Anne F. (1990). *Toolbox*. New York: Aladdin.

Wallace, John. (1997). *Building a House with Mr. Bumble*. Cambridge, MA: Candlewick Press.

Multimedia

The following multimedia products can be used to complement this theme:

Big Job [CD-ROM]. (1995). Bethesda, MD: Discovery Communications, Inc.

Let's Build a House [video]. (1996). San Diego, CA: Video Connections.

Macaulay, David. *The Way Things Work* [CD-ROM]. (1994). New York: Dorling Kindersley Multimedia.

There Goes a Bulldozer [video]. (1993). Van Nuys, CA: Live Action Video for Kids.

Recordings and Song Titles

The following recordings can be used to complement this theme:

People in Our Neighborhood—"The Community Helper Hop" (Construction workers)—builders, carpenters, bricklayers, plasterers, painters, plumbers, electricians

Cars, Trucks and Trains—"Cement Mixer," "Ding Dong Digger (The Power Shovel)"

THEME 18

Uses

packaging liquids/solids
carrying items

Containers

Types

boxes
jars
cans
bags
bottles
pockets
baskets

Materials

glass
aluminum
steel
cardboard
paper
plastic
fabric
wood

Theme Goals

Through participating in the experiences provided by this theme, the children may learn:

1. Types of containers.
2. Materials used to make containers.
3. Container uses.

Concepts for the Children to Learn

1. There are many kinds of containers.
2. Containers are used to hold something.
3. Containers can be made from many materials.
4. Boxes are usually made from cardboard.
5. Cans are made from aluminum or steel.
6. Jars are usually made from glass.
7. Bags can be paper, plastic, or fabric.
8. Bottles are made from glass or plastic.
9. Pockets are usually made from fabric.
10. Baskets can be made from wood or plastic.
11. Many items are sold in containers.

Vocabulary

1. container—a box, jar, can, etc. used to hold something.
2. pocket—a small bag sewed into clothing.
3. bottle—container for holding liquids that has a narrow neck that can be closed with a stopper.
4. bag—container made of paper, cloth, or plastic that can be closed at the top.

Bulletin Board

The purpose of this bulletin board is to promote the development of visual discrimination and memory skills. Create the containers by sketching them onto heavy tagboard. Use felt-tip markers to add color and/or details. Laminate and cut out the containers. Trace the cutout container pieces onto black construction paper. Cut out these pieces and attach to the bulletin board. A magnet strip should be attached to the containers and the shadow pieces. The children can match each container shape to its shadow on the bulletin board.

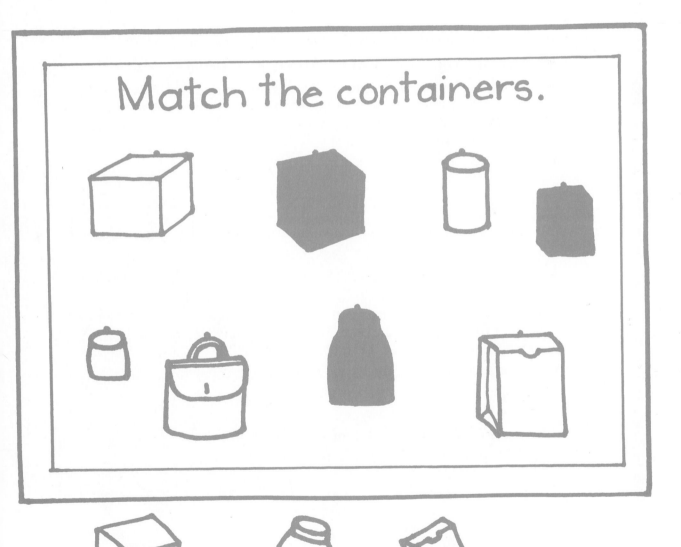

Parent Letter

Dear Parents,

Try to imagine a world without boxes, jars, bags, baskets, or pockets. It's hard to do! There are so many kinds of containers—we use them every day and probably never realize it. This week at school we will focus on the subject of containers. The children will learn about types of containers, typical materials used to make containers, and items that come in containers.

AT SCHOOL

As we learn about containers this week at school, the children will:

⊚ make prints with plastic berry baskets and paint in the art area.

⊚ work in our classroom grocery store set up in the dramatic play area. We could use your help. Please save and send empty, clean food containers to school. We will use the boxes, bottles, and jars as grocery items in the dramatic play area. Thank you.

⊚ sort various containers by type and materials.

AT HOME

You can help your child make discoveries about containers. A few things to try include:

⊚ look in your refrigerator or kitchen and find containers. How many are boxes, cans, bottles, etc.?

⊚ make a milk carton bird feeder. Cut a large rectangle in the side of a half-gallon milk carton. Fill the bottom of the carton with birdseed. Hang the bird feeder outside where it can be observed.

⊚ find some books at the library about containers. A few to look for:

The Paper Bag Princess by Robert Munsch

Katy-No-Pocket by Emmy Payne

Pocket for Corduroy by Don Freeman

Have a good week!

178

Music

1. **"I Have Something in My Pocket"**
   (traditional)

   I have something in my pocket that
      belongs across my face.
   I keep it very close at hand in a most con-
      venient place.
   I'm sure you couldn't guess it if you'd take
      a long, long while.
   So, I'll take it out and put it on,
   It's a great, big, happy smile.

2. **"Tony Has Three Pockets"**
   (Sing to the tune of "Mary Wore a Red Dress")

   Tony has three pockets,
   Three pockets, three pockets.
   Tony has three pockets,
   On his shirt today.

   Insert individual children's names and substitute articles of clothing that could have
   pockets, such as a dress, slacks, jacket, etc.

3. **"A Tisket, a Tasket"**
   (traditional)

   A tisket, a tasket, a green and yellow basket.
   I wrote a letter to my love
   And on the way I dropped it.
   I dropped it, I dropped it
   And on the way I dropped it.
   I wrote a letter to my love
   And on the way I dropped it.

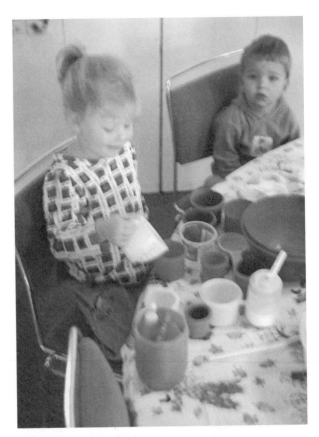

**Children develop hand-eye coordina-
tion skills by pouring liquids from
one container to another.**

Fingerplays

THERE WAS A LITTLE TURTLE
by Vachel Lindsay

   There was a little turtle,
      (make small circle with hands)
   He lived in a box.
      (make box with both hands)

   He swam in a puddle,
      (wiggle hands)
   He climbed on the rocks.
      (climb fingers of one hand up over
      the other)

   He snapped at a mosquito,
      (clap hands)
   He snapped at a flea,
      (repeat)
   He snapped at a minnow,
      (repeat)
   He snapped at me!
      (point to self)

   He caught the mosquito,
      (catching motion with hands and arms)
   He caught the flea,
      (repeat)
   He caught the minnow,
      (repeat)
   But he didn't catch me!
      (shake head from side to side)

179

Sensory

The following materials can be added to the sensory table:

- ◉ plastic bottles, funnels, and colored water.
- ◉ plastic jars, animals, and sand.
- ◉ berry baskets, plastic zoo animals, and grains.
- ◉ ziplock bags, scoops, and sand.

Math

1. Container Sort

Collect various containers and place in a laundry basket. Encourage children to find ways to sort the containers. Containers could be sorted by type, size, or construction material.

2. Pocket Count

During a group time, have the children individually stand up and take note of the pockets on his or her clothes. Assist in counting the number of pockets each child has. If appropriate, the information could be recorded and put on a graph to be displayed. Repeat the activity on a different day and compare the results.

3. How Many?

Place a number of small objects (such as paper clips, dice, marbles, buttons) in a clear plastic bag or a jar. Let children guess how many of the objects are in the bag. Count the objects together. Repeat with a different number of objects.

Large Muscle

Box Obstacle Course

Collect large cardboard boxes. Open the tops and bottoms and lay boxes on their sides to create tunnels. Place the boxes in a maze-type course and children can discover ways to complete the course. They could run, walk, crawl, or hop from beginning to end.

Science

1. Insect Keeper

Collect milk cartons or similar-sized cardboard boxes. For each insect keeper, cut a rectangle out of each side of a clean carton or box. Glue or tape the top closed. Decorate if desired. After an insect or two are found, put the insects, along with a twig and grass, in the carton. Quickly insert box in the leg portion of an old nylon stocking (or cover with netting) and use a twist tie or rubber band to fasten the top.

2. Rubber Band Guitar

Each child will need a small box or carton, such as an individual cereal box, check box, or half-pint milk carton. For each "guitar" cut a rectangle in one side of a box or carton. Decorate as desired. Wrap each container with four or five rubber bands. The children can pluck or strum the rubber bands to create sounds.

3. Wave Jar

Fill a jar half full with water. Add a few drops of food coloring, if desired. Pour mineral oil to fill the jar. Secure the lid tightly. Watch what happens as the jar is gently tilted back and forth. Individual wave jars can be made using baby food jars.

4. Sound Jars or Boxes

Collect 10 film canisters or 10 identical small boxes. Fill the containers, as pairs, with five different materials such as popcorn kernels, pennies, sand, nails, cotton balls, rubber bands, paper clips, etc. Secure caps or lids and place containers on a table. Encourage children to shake the containers to find the matching sound containers.

5. Musical Jars

Fill five or six identical-sized jars with varying amounts of water. Add drops of food coloring to water if desired. Encourage children to gently tap the sides of the jars with a metal spoon to create sounds. The jars will produce low to high sounds. Some children may be able to arrange the jars from lowest to highest sounds.

6. Fish in a Bottle

Save and clean a two-liter plastic soda bottle. Fill the bottle one-quarter full with water. Add a few drops of blue food coloring to the water and swirl to mix. Barely blow up some small balloons and tie ends closed. Use a permanent marker to draw eyes, gills, and mouths on balloons to make them look like fish. Push the balloons into the bottle and securely fasten the cap of the bottle. Hold the bottle on its side and it will look like fish in the water. Gently rock bottle back and forth to create waves.

Dramatic Play

Grocery Store

To create a grocery store in the dramatic play area, provide props such as a cash register, posters of various foods, smocks or shirts, paper and plastic grocery bags, and empty, clean food containers. A note can be sent home requesting help with this project. Set food containers on shelves or in baskets to resemble a grocery store.

Arts and Crafts

1. Basket Prints

Collect plastic berry baskets, construction paper, and paints. Pour paint(s) into shallow trays. Have the children dip the bottom of the plastic berry baskets in paint, then press them on construction paper.

2. Jar Prints

Save and clean baby food jars. Provide the jars, construction paper, and paint(s). Pour the paint(s) into individual trays, just covering the bottoms. Children can turn the jars over and dip the tops of the baby food jars in the paint, then press them on their paper to create prints.

3. Ziplock Bag Painting

Materials needed include tempera paints and small ziplock bags—one per child. Ask each child which two colors of paint he or she would like. Put a small amount of the two colors of paint into a ziplock bag. Carefully seal the bags. Apply cellophane or masking tape for added safety. The children can then squeeze their bags to mix the colors. The bag can be placed on a table and fingers can be used to fingerpaint without getting messy.

4. Colored Salt Jars

Create several colors of salt (or sand) by adding teaspoons of tempera paint powder to bowls of salt. Stir well. Collect baby food jars and lids. To create a colored salt jar, the children spoon colored salt into the jar, creating layers of beautiful colors. Fill jars to the top and secure lid tightly. If desired, squeeze glue around the jar rim before placing lid on.

Group Time
(games, language)

1. Mystery Box

Collect a box with a lid. Color or decorate as desired. Secretly place an object inside the box. At group time, begin by saying, "There is something in my box. What do you think it might be?" Give identifying clues until the children guess what the object is.

2. Cookie Jar

Have the children sit on the floor, with their legs crossed, in a circle formation. The children should repeat a rhythmic chant with the teacher while clapping their hands together and then clapping their hands on their thighs. The chant is as follows:

Someone took a cookie from the cookie jar.
Who took a cookie from the cookie jar?
Mara took a cookie from the cookie jar.
(Mara): Who me?
(All): Yes, you!
(Mara): Couldn't be!
(All): Then who?
(Mara, naming another child): —— took
    a cookie from the cookie jar.

Use each child's name.

3. Hiding Game

Collect three small boxes. Set out the boxes in a row and place a bean or button under one of the boxes. While the children watch, move the order of the cups several times. Ask the children to guess which cup the bean is under. The bean or button can be hid again and the game repeated.

Cooking

1. Container Cookies

1/2 cup butter or margarine
1/2 cup shortening
1 cup sugar
1 egg
2 tablespoons milk
1/2 teaspoon vanilla
2 1/4 cups flour
1/2 teaspoon baking soda
1/2 teaspoon salt

Filling choices:
pie filling—any flavor
jam or jelly
peanut butter
chopped nuts
chocolate chips
raisins
toasted coconut
sugar

Beat butter (or shortening) in a large mixing bowl with an electric mixer on medium speed, about 30 seconds. Add sugar and beat until fluffy. Add egg, milk, and vanilla. Beat well. In a medium mixing bowl, combine flour, baking soda, and salt. With electric mixer on low, gradually add the flour mixture to the butter mixture, beating well. Cover and chill dough in the freezer about 20 minutes or until firm to handle. Divide dough in half. Shape each half into a roll 3 inches thick and 3 inches long. Wrap in plastic wrap. Freeze at least 6 hours or up to 6 months.

When ready to bake the cookies, preheat oven to 375 degrees. Unwrap one roll of dough. Slice the roll crosswise to make 16 slices about 1/8-inch thick. Repeat with the other roll. Place half of the slices 2 inches apart on ungreased cookie sheets. In the center of the circles, place 2 teaspoons of desired filling(s). Top each with a plain slice of dough. Press a floured fork around the edges to seal well. Sprinkle with a little sugar.

Bake for 12 to 15 minutes or until edges are golden brown. Place cookies on rack to cool.

2. Butter in a Jar

Pour 1/3 cup of whipping cream in a clean small jar. Secure lid tightly. Allow children to take turns shaking the jar until a lump of butter forms. This will take several minutes. Pour off liquid, add a dash of salt, and stir. Spread butter on crackers to enjoy.

3. Pita Pocket Sandwiches

Use pita bread to create yummy pocket sandwiches. Cut rounds of pita bread in half, creating pocket-shaped pieces. Fill with favorite sandwich ingredients.

Try:

Sloppy Joe's
Peanut butter and jelly
Tuna salad
Ham and cheese

182

Books

The following books can be used to complement this theme:

Boivin, Kelly. (1991). *What's in a Box?* Illus. by Janice Skivington. Chicago: Children's Press.

Carter, David A. (1990). *More Bugs in Boxes Pop-Up Book: A Pop-Up Book about Color.* New York: Simon & Schuster.

King, Stephen Michael. (1996). *A Special Kind of Love.* New York: Scholastic.

Lillegard, Dee. (1992). *Sitting in My Box.* Illus. by Jon Agee. New York: Puffin. (Pbk)

Rau, Dana Meachen. (1997). *A Box Can Be Many Things.* Illus. by Paige Bellin-Frye. Chicago: Children's Press.

Stevenson, James. (1997). *The Mud Flat Mystery.* New York: Greenwillow.

Stock, Catherine. (1994). *Sophie's Bucket.* Orlando: Harcourt Brace. (Pbk)

Tibo, Gilles. (1995). *Simon and His Boxes.* Plattsburgh, NY: Tundra Books.

Westcott, Nadine. (1990). *There's a Hole in the Bucket.* New York: Harper & Row.

Multimedia

The following multimedia product can be used to complement this theme:

Carter, David A. *How Many Bugs in a Box?* [CD-ROM]. (1996). Simon & Schuster Interactive.

THEME 19

Creative Movement

Accessories
ballet shoes
tap shoes
costumes
makeup

Feelings
happy
sad
angry
surprised

Dancers
ballet
tap
jazz
social
folk
modern
street dancing
line dancing
hula

Body Movements
twist
slide
wave arms
yoga
alone
with partner
in group
shapes
sports
pantomime

Sound Sources
record player
tape recorder
compact disc player
drums
guitar
rhythm sticks
music
self

Theme Goals

Through participating in the experiences provided by this theme, the children may learn:

1. Creative movement accessories.
2. Creative movement sound sources.
3. Body movements used in creative movement.
4. Expression of feelings through creative movement.
5. Types of dancers.

Concepts for the Children to Learn

1. People can dance to music.
2. The record player, tape recorder, and compact disc player are all sound sources used for dance.
3. Dancing and moving can be done alone, with a partner, or in a group.
4. Our bodies can move in many different ways.
5. Ballet, tap, jazz, and social are some types of dances.
6. Happy, sad, angry, and surprised are feelings that can be expressed through dance.
7. Some dancers wear special costumes and makeup.
8. Ballet and tap dancers wear special shoes.
9. Our bodies can move to the sound of drums, guitars, and rhythm sticks.
10. We can twist, slide, and wave our arms during dance.

Vocabulary

1. **dance**—a pattern of body movements.
2. **movement**—change in body position.
3. **ballet**—movement that usually tells a story.
4. **music**—sounds made by instruments or voices.

Bulletin Board

The purpose of this bulletin board is to promote the development of one-to-one correspondence skills and to match a set to a written numeral. Construct tank tops, each of a different color, from a sheet of tagboard. See the illustration. Print a numeral that would be developmentally appropriate for the group of children on each tank top. Draw a corresponding number of black dots below each numeral. Construct a tutu ruffle from white tagboard for each top. Place colored dots on each ruffle. Trace ruffles onto black construction paper. Laminate all pieces. Staple tank tops and shadow ruffles to bulletin board. The children can match the ruffles with dots to the corresponding tank top, using holes in white ruffles and pushpins in shadow ruffles.

Parent Letter

Dear Parents,

Children love to dance, and they are constantly on the move. We will begin a curriculum unit on creative movement. Throughout the classroom activities the children will discover the different ways our bodies move, and also learn about various forms of dance. Some of the activities include:

- singing songs and moving to music.
- dancing in the dance studio that will be set up in the dramatic play area.
- watching other people move.
- participating in an aerobics class.

FIELD TRIP

On Thursday, at 2:30 p.m., we will be taking a bus to a dance studio. At the studio, we will observe dancers and learn a few steps from a dance instructor. To assist with the trip, we need several parents to accompany us. Please call the school if you are available.

AT HOME

As your child develops, you will observe increased control and interest in perfecting and improving motor skills. To foster the development of large muscle skills, balance, and body coordination, provide opportunities each day for vigorous play. Give suggestions, such as "How fast can you hop?" "How far can you hop on one foot?" etc. Also, ask your child to walk on a curved line, a straight line, or a balance beam.

Enjoy your child!

188

Fingerplays

The following circle games are from *Finger Frolics: Fingerplays for Young Children* by Cromwell, Hibner, and Faitel. (Partner Press: 1983).

HOP AND TWIRL

Make a circle and we'll go around.
First walk on tiptoe so we don't make a sound.
Tip, toe, around we go.
Then hop on our left foot, and then on our right.
Then hop together. What a funny sight!
Now stop hopping and twirl around
Now we're ready to settle down.

A CIRCLE

Around in a circle we will go.
Little tiny baby steps, make us go very slow.
And then we'll take some great giant steps,
As big as they can be.
Then in our circle we'll stand quietly.

STAND IN A CIRCLE

Stand in a circle and clap your hands.
Clap, clap, clap, clap.
Now put your hands over your head.
Slap, slap, slap, slap.
Now hands at your sides and turn around.
Then in our circle we'll all sit down.

ONE TO TEN CIRCLE

Let's make a circle and around we go,
Not too fast and not too slow.
One, two, three, four, five, six, seven, eight, nine, ten,
Let's face the other way and go around again.
One, two, three, four, five, six, seven, eight, nine, ten.

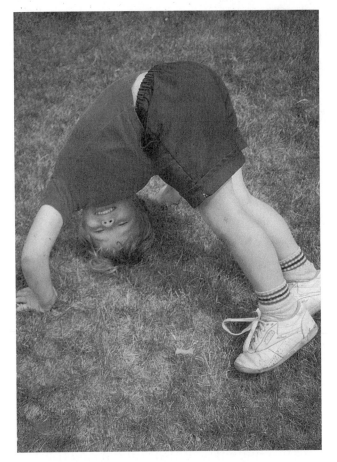

Exercise can be a form of creative movement.

PARTNER GAME

Pick a partner, take a hand.
Then in a circle partners stand.
Take two steps forward,
And two steps back.
Then bow to your partner
And clap, clap, clap.
Wrap your elbows
And around you go.
Not too fast and not too slow.
Change elbows.
Go around again.
Then stand in a circle
And count to ten.

Science

1. Magnet Dancers

On a piece of tagboard, draw pictures of three-inch dancers. Stickers or pictures from magazines can also be used. Cut the dancers out and attach paper clips to the back side. Use a small box and a magnet to make these dancers move. Hold the dancers up on one side of the box and move the dancer up by holding and moving a magnet on the other side of the box.

2. Kaleidoscopes

On the science table, put a number of kaleidoscopes. The tiny figures inside appear to be dancing.

3. Dancing Shoes

Place various types of dancing shoes at the science table. Let the children compare the shape, size, color, and texture of the shoes. The children may also enjoy trying the shoes on for size and dancing in them.

Dramatic Play

1. Dance Studio

Add to the dramatic play area tap shoes, tutus, ballet shoes, tights, and leotards. Provide a record player with records or tape player with tapes.

2. Fitness Gym

Add to the dramatic play area a small mat, head bands, wrist bands, sweat shirts, sweat pants, leotards, and music.

Arts and Crafts

1. Stencils

The teacher can construct stencils from tagboard. Shapes such as shoes, ballerinas, circles, etc., can be made and added to the art table for use during self-selected activity periods.

2. Musical Painting

Provide a tape recorder with headphones and a tape of children's music or classical music at the easel. The children can listen and move their brushes to the music if desired.

Large Muscle

1. Streamer/Music Activity

In the music area provide streamers. Play a variety of music, allowing the children, if desired, to move to the different rhythms.

2. Do As I Say

Provide the children verbal cues for moving. For example, say, "Move like you are sad," "Show me that you are tired," "You just received a special present," or "Show me how you feel."

3. Animal Movement

Ask a child to act out the way a certain animal moves. Examples include: frog, spider, caterpillar, butterfly, etc.

4. Balance

Add a balance beam or balance strip to the indoor or outdoor environment.

5. Roly-Poly

The children can stretch their bodies out on the floor. When touched by a teacher, the child rolls into a tight ball.

6. Dancing Cloud

Using an inflated white balloon or ball, let the children stand in a circle and bounce or hit it to each other.

7. Obstacle Course

Set up an obstacle course indoors or outdoors depending on the weather. Let the children move their bodies in many different ways. They can run or crawl through the course. Older children may enjoy hopping or skipping.

Field Trips/ Resource People

1. **Field Trips**
   - dance studio
   - health club
   - gymnasium

2. **Resource People**

   Invite the following people to class to talk with the children:
   - a dancer or dance instructor
   - gymnast
   - aerobics instructor

Math

1. **Matching Leotards to Hangers**

   Using plastic hangers, prepare a numeral on each of the hangers. Provide the children with a box of leotards. Have a printed numeral on each. Encourage the children to match the numbered leotard with the identically numbered hanger.

2. **Following Steps**

   Using tagboard, cut out some left feet and right feet. Write the numerals from one to ten on the feet and arrange them in numerical order. Place the footprints on the floor, securing them with masking tape. Encourage the children to begin the walk on the numeral one and continue in the correct sequence.

3. **Ballet Puzzle**

   Purchase a large poster of a ballet dancer. Laminate the poster or cover it with clear contact paper. Cut the poster into several

large shapes. Place the puzzle in the manipulative area. During self-selected play periods, the children can reconstruct the puzzle.

Social Studies

Social Dancing

Let each child choose a partner. Encourage the children to hold hands. Play music as a background, so the partners can move together.

Group Time (games, language)

1. **Balloon Bounce**

   Blow up balloons for the children to use at group time. Play music and have children bounce the balloons up in the air. Let the balloons float to the ground when the music ends. Supervision is required for this activity. Broken balloons should be immediately removed from the environment.

2. **Toy Movements**

   Form a circle and move like different toys. Try to include as many actual toys as you can, so that the children can observe each toy moving, and then can more easily pretend to be that toy.
   - jack-in-the-box
   - wind-up dolls
   - roll like a ball
   - skates

3. **Rag Doll**

   Repeat the following poem as the child creates a dance with a rag doll.

   If I were a rag doll
   And I belonged to you,
   Whenever I would try to dance,
   This is what I'd do.

Movement Activities

Listen to the Drum

Accessory: drum
fast
slow
heavy
soft
big
small

Choose a Partner

Make a big shape
go over
go under
go through
go around

To Become Aware of Time

Run very fast
Walk very slowly
Jump all over the floor quickly
Sit down on the floor slowly
Slowly grow up as tall as you can
Slowly curl up on the floor as small as possible

To Become Aware of Space

Lift your leg up in front of you
Lift it up backwards, sideways
Lift your leg and step forward, backwards, sideways, and around and around
Reach up to the ceiling
Stretch to touch the walls
Punch down to the floor

To Become Aware of Weight

To feel the difference between heavy and light, the child should experiment with his own body force.

Punch down to the floor hard
Lift your arms up slowly and gently
Stomp on the floor
Walk on tiptoe
Kick out one leg as hard as you can
Very smoothly and lightly slide one foot along the floor

Moving Shapes

1. Try to move about like something huge and heavy: elephant, tug boat, bulldozer.
2. Try to move like something small and heavy: a fat frog, a heavy top.
3. Try moving like something big and light: a beach ball, a parachute, a cloud.
4. Try moving like something small and light: a feather, a snowflake, a flea, a butterfly.

Put Yourself Inside Something

(bottle, box, barrel)
You're *outside* of something—now get into it
You're *inside* of something—now get out of it
You're *underneath* something
You're *on top of* something
You're *beside* or *next to* something
You're *surrounded* by it

Pantomime

1. You're going to get a present. What is the shape of the box? How big is the box? Feel it. Hold it. Unwrap it. Take it out. Put it back in.
2. Think about an occupation. How does the worker act?
3. Show me that it is cold, hot.
4. You are two years old (sixteen, eighty, etc.)
5. Show me: It's very early in the morning, late in the afternoon.
6. Show me: What is the weather like?
7. Pretend you are driving, typing, raking leaves.
8. Take a partner. Pretend you're playing ball.

Cooking

1. Orange Buttermilk Smoothie

1 quart buttermilk
3 cups orange juice
1/2 teaspoon cinnamon
1/4 cup honey

Blend in a blender until the mixture is smooth. Enjoy!

2. Indian Flat Bread

2 cups all-purpose flour
1/4 cup unflavored yogurt
1 egg, slightly beaten
1 1/2 teaspoons baking powder
1 teaspoon sugar
1/4 teaspoon salt
1/4 teaspoon baking soda
1/2 cup milk
vegetable oil
poppy seeds

Mix all ingredients except milk, vegetable oil, and poppy seeds. Stir in enough milk to make a soft dough. Turn dough onto lightly floured surface. Knead until smooth, about 5 minutes. Place in greased bowl; turn greased side up. Cover and let rest in warm place 3 hours.

Divide dough into 6 or 8 equal parts. Flatten each part on lightly floured surface, rolling it into a 6-inch x 4-inch leaf shape about 1/4 inch thick. Brush with vegetable oil; sprinkle with poppy seeds.

Place 2 cookie sheets in oven; heat oven to 450 degrees. Remove hot cookie sheets from oven; place breads on cookie sheets. Bake until firm, 6 to 8 minutes. Makes 6 to 8 breads.

Source: *Betty Crocker's International Cookbook*. (1980). New York: Random House.

Books

The following books can be used to complement this theme:

Auch, Mary Jane. (1995). *Hen Lake*. New York: Holiday House.

Duvall, Jill D. (1997). *Meet Rory Hohenstein, a Professional Dancer*. Photos by Lili S. Duvall. Chicago: Children's Press.

Esbensen, Barbara Juster. (1995). *Dance with Me*. Illus. by Megan Lloyd. New York: HarperCollins.

Gauch, Patricia Lee. (1992). *Bravo, Tanya*. Illus. by Satomi Ichikawa. New York: Philomel Books.

Gauch, Patricia Lee. (1994). *Tanya and Emily in a Dance for Two*. Illus. by Satomi Ichikawa. New York: Philomel Books.

Gray, Libba Moore. (1995). *My Mama Had a Dancing Heart*. Illus. by Raul Colon. New York: Orchard Books.

Grimm, Jakob. (1996). *The Twelve Dancing Princesses*. Retold by Jane Ray. New York: Dutton.

Isadora, Rachel. (1993). *Lili at Ballet*. New York: G. P. Putnam.

Isadora, Rachel. (1997). *Lili Backstage*. New York: G. P. Putnam.

King, Sandra. (1993). *Shannon: An Ojibway Dancer*. Minneapolis: Lerner Publications.

Kroll, Virginia L. (1996). *Can You Dance, Dalila?* Illus. by Nancy Carpenter. New York: Simon & Schuster.

Lee, Jeanne M. (1991). *Silent Lotus*. New York: Farrar, Straus & Giroux.

Loredo, Elizabeth. (1997). *Boogie Bones*. Illus. by Kevin Hawkes. New York: G. P. Putnam.

Lowery, Linda. (1995). *Twist with a Burger, Jitter with a Bug*. Boston: Houghton Mifflin.

O'Connor, Jane. (1993). *Nina, Nina Ballerina*. Illus. by DyAnne DiSalvo-Ryan. New York: Grosset & Dunlap.

Patrick, Denise Lewis. (1993). *Red Dancing Shoes*. Illus. by James E. Ransome. New York: Tambourine.

Schomp, Virginia. (1997). *If You Were a . . . Ballet Dancer*. Tarrytown, NY: Marshall Cavendish.

Thomassie, Tynia. (1996). *Mimi's Tutu*. Illus. by Jan Spivey Gilchrist. New York: Scholastic.

Walsh, Ellen Stoll. (1993). *Hop Jump*. New York: Harcourt Brace.

Waters, Kate. (1990). *Lion Dancer: Ernie Wan's Chinese New Year*. New York: Scholastic.

Wilder, Laura Ingalls. (1994). *Dance at Grandpa's: Adapted from the Little House Books*. New York: HarperCollins.

Multimedia

The following multimedia products can be used to complement this theme:

All-Time Favorite Dances [compact disc or cassette]. (1991). Longbranch, NJ: Kimbo Educational.

Dance With Us: A Creative Movement Video [video]. (1994). Pleasantville, NY: Sunburst.

Jack, David. *David Jack . . . Live!: Makin' Music, Makin' Friends* [video]. (1991). Leucadia, CA: Ta-Dum Productions.

Jack, David. *Gotta Hop* [cassette]. (1990). Leucadia, CA: Ta-Dum Productions.

Jenkins, Ella. *Growing Up With Ella Jenkins: Rhythms, Songs and Rhymes* [cassette]. (1990). Rockville, MD: Smithsonian Folkways.

Stewart, Georgiana Liccione. *Children of the World: Multi-Cultural Rhythmic Activities* [cassette]. (1991). Long Branch, NJ: Kimbo Educational.

Recordings and Song Titles

The following recordings can be used to complement this theme:

Everybody Dance

Gotta Dance

Motown Dances

A to Z, the Animals and Me

Children of the World

Where Is Thumbkin?

Preschool Action Time

Joining Hands in Other Lands

A World of Parachute Play

Yes, I Can Sing Songs with RONNO

People in Our Neighborhood

THEME 26

Sources

cows
goats
sheep
llamas

Forms

fresh
frozen
canned

Dairy Products

Storing

cartons
bottles
pails
bags
boxes

Places to Purchase

supermarkets
minimarts
cheese factories
restaurants

Types

butter
cream cheese
cottage cheese
cheddar cheese
mozzarella cheese
milk
ice cream
yogurt

Theme Goals

Through participating in the experiences provided by this theme, the children may learn:

1. Sources of dairy products.
2. Types of dairy products.
3. Forms of dairy products.
4. Places dairy products can be purchased.
5. Containers used to hold dairy products.

Concepts for the Children to Learn

1. Cows, goats, sheep, and llamas provide milk.
2. Milk can be used to make butter, cheese, ice cream, and yogurt.
3. There are many kinds of cheese such as cottage cheese, cream cheese, cheddar cheese, mozzarella, and colby.
4. Dairy products can be purchased fresh, frozen, canned, or processed.
5. We can buy dairy products at supermarkets, minimarts, cheese factories, and restaurants.
6. Cartons, bottles, pails, bags, and boxes are used to store dairy products.
7. Dairy products are good food choices.

Vocabulary

1. **dairy product**—a product made from milk.
2. **can**—to prepare food for future use.
3. **frozen**—food that is kept cold.
4. **cheese factory**—a place where cheese is made or sold.
5. **carton**—a box or container to hold food or other objects.
6. **cream**—the yellowish part of milk.
7. **yogurt**—a milk product that can be flavored with fruit.
8. **minimart**—a very small store.

Bulletin Board

The purpose of this bulletin board is to help children become aware of ice cream as a dairy product, as well as recognize the printed word. This is designed as a check-in or attendance bulletin board. Each child is provided a bulletin board piece with his name on it. When the children arrive each day at school, they should be encouraged to place their names on the bulletin board.

To create the bulletin board, cut an ice cream cone out of tagboard or construction paper for each child in the class. Color or decorate each cone as desired. Print the child's name on the ice cream cone. Laminate the pieces or cover with clear contact paper. Use pushpins or adhesive magnet pieces to attach the ice cream cones to the bulletin board.

Parent Letter

Dear Parents,

Did you know that the average person in the United States consumes about 550 pounds of dairy products each year? Dairy products provide us with one of our main sources of protein. We will be learning about dairy products in our classroom. The children will learn sources of dairy products, types of dairy products, forms of dairy products, places dairy products can be purchased, and containers used to hold dairy products.

AT SCHOOL

Some of the learning activities the children will participate in include:

- preparing milkshakes, homemade vanilla pudding, and strawberry yogurt in the cooking area.
- creating a dairy collage, yogurt print cups, and ice cream cone sponge paints in the art area.
- hearing stories related to the story theme.
- visiting the dairy department of a grocery store.
- looking at books featuring dairy products.
- identifying foods prepared with dairy products.

AT HOME

At home you can reinforce the dairy product concepts by:

- encouraging your child to prepare instant pudding with you for snack or a dessert.
- have your child identify the foods being served at mealtimes that are dairy products.
- browse through newspaper ads or magazines and have your child identify dairy products.
- take your child grocery shopping and have him/her show you where the dairy section of the store is located.

Enjoy your child!

198

Milk is a dairy product.

Music

1. **"The Farmer in the Dell"**

    The farmer in the dell,
    The farmer in the dell,
    Hi-ho, the dairy-o
    The farmer in the dell.

    Continue with additional verses:

    The farmer takes the wife/husband
    The wife/husband takes the nurse.
    The nurse takes the dog.
    The dog takes the cat.
    The cat takes the rat.
    The rat takes the cheese.

    The final verse:

    The cheese stands alone.
    The cheese stands alone.
    Hi-ho, the dairy-o,
    The cheese stands alone.

2. **"Old McDonald Had a Farm"**
    (traditional)

3. **"We Like Ice Cream"**
    (Sing to the tune of "Are You Sleeping?")

    We like ice cream, we like ice cream.
    Yes, we do! Yes, we do!
    Vanilla and strawberry,
    Chocolate and mint.
    Yum, yum, yum.
    Yum, yum, yum!

4. **"Drink Your Milk"**
    (Sing to the tune of "My Darling Clementine")

    Drink your milk.
    Drink your milk.
    Drink your milk every day.
    It is good for your teeth and bones.
    Drink your milk everyday.

5. **"Cows"**
    (Sing to the tune of "Mulberry Bush")

    This is the way we feed the cows,
    Feed the cows, feed the cows.
    This is the way we feed the cows,
    On the dairy farm each day.

    This is the way we milk the cows,
    Milk the cows, milk the cows.
    This is the way we milk the cows,
    On the dairy farm each day.

Fingerplays

ICE CREAM

I'm licking my ice cream.
I'm licking it fast.
It's dripping down my arm.
It's disappearing fast.

LITTLE MISS MUFFET

Little Miss Muffet
Sat on a tuffet
Eating her curds and whey.
Along came a spider
And sat down beside her
And frightened Miss Muffet away!

THIS LITTLE COW

This little cow eats grass.
   (hold up fingers of one hand, bend down
   one finger)
This little cow eats hay.
   (bend down another finger)
This little cow drinks water.
   (bend down another finger)
And this little cow does nothing.
   (bend down another finger)
But lie and sleep all day.

Science

1. Make Butter

Fill baby food jars half-full with whipping cream and replace lids. The children can take turns shaking the jars until the cream separates. (The mixture will first look like whipping cream, then like overwhipped cream, and finally it will be obvious that separation has occurred.) Pour off the remaining liquid. Rinse the butter in cold water several times and drain. Add salt to taste. Let the children spread the butter on crackers or bread.

2. Making Ice Cream

Collect the following ingredients:

1 cup milk
1/2 cup sugar
1/4 teaspoon salt
3 beaten egg yolks
1 tablespoon vanilla
2 cups whipping cream

In a saucepan, combine milk, sugar, salt, and egg yolks. Stir constantly over medium heat until bubbles appear around the edge of the pan. Cool mixture at room temperature. Stir in vanilla and whipping cream. Pour into an ice cream maker and follow the manufacturer's directions. (Recipe makes 1 quart of ice cream.)

3. Science Table Additions

Additions to the science table may include:

- pictures of dairy cows.
- books about milking cows and dairy animals.
- containers of grain, corn, and hay along with magnifying glasses.
- pictures of goats, sheep, and llamas.

Dramatic Play

1. Ice Cream Shop

Clothes and props for an ice cream shop can be placed in the dramatic play area. Include items such as empty, clean ice cream pails and cartons, ice cream scoops, plastic parfait glasses and bowls, plastic spoons, empty ice cream cone boxes, napkins, aprons, and a cash register with play money. Prepare and display posters in the area that portray various ice cream products and flavors.

2. Dairy Farm

Turn the dramatic play center into a dairy farm where the children can pretend to do chores. Display pictures of farms and cows and provide overalls, boots, hats, pails, hoses, and other appropriate props.

3. **Grocery Store—Dairy Department**

Set up the dramatic play area to resemble the dairy department of a grocery store. Include props such as milk cartons, cottage cheese containers, yogurt cups, sour cream containers, ice cream pails and cartons, butter boxes, cheese packages, and a cash register. Display pictures of dairy foods.

Arts and Crafts

1. **Buttermilk Chalk Pictures**

Dip colored chalk into a small container of buttermilk or brush construction paper with buttermilk. Use the chalk to create designs on construction paper.

2. **Dairy Product Paint Containers**

Use empty dairy product containers to hold paint for use at the art table or easel. Examples include milk cartons, yogurt cups, and cottage cheese containers.

3. **Whipped Soap Painting**

The following mixture can be made to represent ice cream or cottage cheese. Mix one cup of Ivory Snow flakes with 1/2 cup of warm water in a bowl. The children can beat the mixture with a hand eggbeater until it is fluffy. Add more water, if necessary. Apply mixture with paint brushes or fingers to construction paper. For a variation, food coloring can be added to the paint mixture.

4. **Ice Cream Cone Sponge Painting**

Cut sponges into shapes of ice cream cones and scoops of ice cream. Provide shallow trays of various colors of paints. Designs are created by dipping the sponge in the paint and then pressing it onto a piece of construction paper.

5. **Yogurt Cup Prints**

Collect empty yogurt cups of various shapes and sizes. Wash them thoroughly. Prepare shallow trays of paint. Create designs by inverting a yogurt cup, dipping it into the paint, and then applying it to construction paper. Repeat the process as desired.

6. **Dairy Collage**

Provide magazines that contain pictures of dairy products for the children to cut out. The pictures can be glued to a piece of construction paper, tagboard, or a paper plate for the children to create a collage.

Sensory

Add to the sensory table:

- sand, scoops, and empty milk cartons.
- water and empty, clean yogurt and cottage cheese containers.
- cotton balls, spoons, ice cream scoops, bowls, and empty, clean ice cream pails.

Field Trips

1. **The Grocery Store**

Visit a grocery store and locate the dairy section. Look at the types of dairy products available.

2. **Ice Cream Shop**

Take a trip to an ice cream shop. Count the flavors of ice cream available. Purchase a cone for each of the children.

3. **Dairy Farm**

Visit a dairy farm. Ask the farmer to show the housing, equipment, and food supplies needed to care for dairy cows.

Math

1. Dairy Sort

Collect different types of food-product containers, including dairy products. Place all of the containers in a basket. Encourage the children to sort out the containers representing dairy products from the other food-product containers.

2. Dairy Lids

Collect lids and caps from milk jugs. They can be recycled and used for game pieces, creating patterns, and counting activities.

3. Favorite Ice Cream Graph

The children can assist in making a graph of their favorite ice cream flavors. Begin by printing the caption, "Our Favorite Ice Cream Flavors," across the top of a piece of tagboard. Draw or paste pictures of different flavors of ice cream along the left-hand side of the tagboard. Each child's name or picture is placed next to the picture of his favorite ice cream flavor. The results of the graph should be shared with the children using math vocabulary words: most, more, fewer, least, etc. Display the graph for further reference.

Additional graphs could be made depicting the children's favorite flavors of yogurt, cheese, or milk.

Social Studies

1. Sharing a Treat

Prepare a dairy food with the children and share it with another class, senior citizens group, or other community group.

2. Role of the Dairy Farmer

Invite a dairy farmer to the classroom to discuss his occupation. The equipment and tools used to farm could also be shown and discussed.

Group Time
(games, language)

1. Dairy Charts

Print the caption, "Foods Made from Milk," across the top of a piece of tagboard. During group time, present the chart and record the children's responses. Display the chart and refer to it throughout the theme.

Additional language charts could be made about types of cheeses, ice cream, and yogurt.

2. Cheese Tasting Party

Cut various types of cheese into small slices or pieces. Place the cheese pieces on paper plates for the children to taste. Discuss types of cheeses, textures, flavors, and colors.

Cooking

1. Milk Shake

For each shake, combine 1/2 cup of vanilla ice cream and one cup of milk in a blender. If desired, flavor the shake with one of the following: 1/2 cup fresh berries, 1/2 banana, two tablespoons of peanut butter, or two tablespoons chocolate syrup.

2. Grilled Cheese Sandwich

Assist the children in making cheese sandwiches. Provide plastic knives for the children to spread soft butter or margarine on the outside of sandwiches. Turn over and place a cheese slice between the two pieces of bread.

Under adult supervision, place the sandwiches on a heated skillet or electric grill until golden brown, turning once.

3. Homemade Vanilla Pudding

1/8 teaspoon salt
2 cups milk
2 slightly beaten egg yolks
1 tablespoon softened butter or margarine
2 teaspoons vanilla

Combine cornstarch, sugar, and salt in a medium saucepan. Stir in the milk. Over medium heat, cook and stir constantly until the mixture thickens and comes to a boil. Stir and boil one minute. In a small bowl, blend half of the hot mixture into the egg yolks. Pour the egg mixture back into the saucepan and cook until the mixture boils, stirring constantly. Remove the pan from the heat and add the butter and vanilla. Allow the pudding to cool slightly and spoon into a serving bowl or individual dishes. Refrigerate. (This recipe makes four servings.)

4. Strawberry Yogurt Surprise

3-oz. package strawberry-flavored gelatin
1 cup boiling water
1/2 cup cold water
1 cup strawberry yogurt

Dissolve gelatin in the boiling water. Stir in cold water. Chill until thickened but not set. Beat gelatin and fold in yogurt. Pour into serving dish. Refrigerate until firm. (This recipe makes four servings.)

Books

The following books can be used to complement this theme:

Aliki. (1992). *Milk: From Cow to Carton.* Rev. ed. New York: HarperCollins.

Asch, Frank. (1992). *Milk and Cookies.* Milwaukee: Gareth Stevens.

Barton, Byron. (1995). *Wee Little Woman.* New York: HarperCollins.

Brady, Peter. (1996). *Cows.* Illus. by William Munoz. Bridgestone Books.

Ericsson, Jennifer A. (1993). *No Milk.* Illus. by Ora Eitan. New York: Tambourine Books.

Fowler, Allan. (1992). *Thanks to Cows.* Chicago: Children's Press.

Gibbons, Gail. (1985). *The Milk Makers.* New York: Simon & Schuster.

Godfrey, Neale S. (1995). *Here's the Scoop: Follow an Ice-Cream Cone Around the World.* Illus. by Randy Verougstraete. Morristown, NJ: Silver Burdett Press.

Grossman, Bill and Victoria Chess. (1991). *Tommy at the Grocery Store.* New York: HarperCollins. (Pbk)

Jackson, Ellen. (1995). *Brown Cow, Green Grass, Yellow Mellow Sun.* Illus. by Victoria Raymond. New York: Hyperion.

Keillor, Garrison. (1996). *The Old Man Who Loved Cheese.* Illus. by Anne Wilsdorf. Boston: Little, Brown.

Keller, Stella and John Holm. (1990). *Ice Cream.* Austin, TX: Raintree/Steck Vaughn.

Mazan, Barbara S. (1994). *Pass the Cheese Please.* Illus. by Paul Harvey. Newbridge. (Pbk)

Older, Jules. (1997). *Cow.* Illus. by Lyn Severance. Watertown, MA: Charlesbridge Publishers.

Peterson, Cris. (1994). *Extra Cheese, Please! Mozzarella's Journey from Cow to Pizza.* Illus. by Alvis Upitis. Honesdale, PA: Boyds Mills Press.

Reid, Mary Ebeltoft. (1997). *Let's Find Out About Ice Cream.* New York: Scholastic. (Pbk)

Schertle, Alice. (1994). *How Now Brown Cow?* Illus. by Amanda Schaffer. San Diego, CA: Browndeer Press.

Seymour, Tres. (1993). *Hunting the White Cow.* Illus. by Wendy Anderson Halperin. New York: Orchard Books.

Van Laan, Nancy. (1993). *Tiny Tiny Boy and the Big Big Cow: A Scottish Folk Tale.* Illus. by Marjorie Priceman. New York: Knopf.

Multimedia

The following multimedia products can be used to complement this theme:

From Moo to You [CD-ROM]. (1996). Westmont, IL: Dairy Council of Wisconsin.

Let's Go to the Ice Cream and Yogurt Factory [video]. (1996). Burlington, VT: Vermont Story Works.

Make Mine Milk [video]. Sky Dog Productions.

Milk Cow, Eat Cheese [video]. (1995). Gig Harbor, WA: Real World Video.

Paterson, Katherine. *Smallest Cow in the World* [cassette and book]. (1996). Harper Audio.

T H 21 E M E

Tools

dental floss
toothbrush
mirror
toothpaste
toothpick
fluoride rinse

Job

checks teeth
treats teeth
fills cavities
medical treatment
prevention training
braces

Dentist

Furnishings

chairs
desk
patient's chair
telephone
file cabinet

Equipment

lights
x-ray machine

Helpers

hygienist
receptionist

Theme Goals

Through participating in the experiences provided by this theme, the children may learn:

1. How the dentist helps us.
2. Dentist's tools.
3. The name of a dental assistant.
4. Proper tooth care.
5. Dental equipment.
6. Dental office furnishings.

Concepts for the Children to Learn

1. The dentist helps keep our teeth healthy.
2. Teeth are used to chew food.
3. Teeth should be brushed after each meal.
4. A hygienist helps the dentist.
5. A dentist removes decay from our teeth.
6. Pictures of our teeth are called X rays.
7. A toothbrush and paste are used to clean teeth.
8. Dental floss helps clean between teeth.
9. The dentist's office has special machines.

Vocabulary

1. **toothbrush**—a brush to clean teeth.
2. **toothpaste**—a paste to clean our teeth.
3. **dentist**—a person who helps to keep our teeth healthy.
4. **teeth**—used to chew food.
5. **hygienist**—the dentist's assistant.
6. **cavity**—tooth decay.
7. **toothpick**—a stick-like tool used for removing food parts between our teeth.
8. **dental floss**—a string used to clean between the teeth.

206

Bulletin Board

The purpose of this bulletin board is to promote the development of a positive self-concept and assist in developing name recognition skills. Prepare an attendance bulletin board by constructing a toothbrush out of tagboard for each student and teacher. See the illustration. Color the toothbrushes with colored felt-tip markers and print the children's names on them. Laminate. Punch holes in each toothbrush. Check who has brushed their teeth by observing the toothbrush hung on the bulletin board.

Parent Letter

Dear Parents,

We are continuing our study of community helpers with a unit on the dentist. The dentist is an important helper for us because our teeth are very important. Children are very aware of their teeth at this age. Many of the older five-year-olds will soon begin losing their baby teeth. Through the experiences provided in this curriculum unit, the children may learn that the dentist is a person who helps us keep our teeth healthy. They will also spend some time learning about the importance and techniques of proper tooth care.

AT SCHOOL

Some of the experiences planned for the unit include:

- making toothpaste.
- string painting with dental floss at the art table.
- painting with discarded toothbrushes at the easel.
- exploring tools that a dentist uses.

SPECIAL VISITOR

On Tuesday, January 13, we will meet Mrs. Jones, the dental hygienist at Dr. Milivitz's dental clinic. Mrs. Jones will discuss proper toothbrushing and will pass out toothbrush kits. You are invited to join our class at 10:00 a.m. for her visit.

AT HOME

Good habits start young! Dental cavities are one of the most prevalent diseases among children. It has been estimated that 98 percent of school-aged children have at least one cavity. You and your child can spend some time each day brushing your teeth together. Sometimes a child will more effectively brush if someone else is with him. It is important for children to realize that they are the primary caretakers of their teeth!

Have fun with your child!

208

Children usually enjoy brushing their teeth.

Music

1. **"Brushing Teeth"**
   (Sing to the tune of "Mulberry Bush")

   This is the way we brush our teeth,
      brush our teeth, brush our teeth.
   This is the way we brush our teeth,
      so early in the morning.

2. **"Clean Teeth"**
   (Sing to the tune of "Row, Row, Row Your Boat")

   Brush, brush, brush your teeth
   Brush them every day.
   We put some toothpaste on our brush
   To help stop tooth decay.

Fingerplays

MY TOOTHBRUSH

  I have a little toothbrush.
    (use pointer finger)
  I hold it very tight.
    (make hand into fist)
  I brush my teeth each morning,
    and then again at night.
    (use pointer finger and pretend to brush)

MY FRIEND THE TOOTHBRUSH

  My toothbrush is a tool.
  I use it every day.
  I brush and brush and brush and brush
    to keep the cavities away.
    (pretend to brush teeth)

Science

1. **Tools**

   Place some safe dental products on the sensory table. Include a mirror, dental floss, toothbrush, toothpaste, etc. A dentist may even lend you a model of a set of teeth.

2. **Acid on Our Teeth**

   Show the children how acid weakens the enamel of your teeth. Place a hard-boiled egg into a bowl of vinegar for 24 hours. Observe how the egg shell becomes soft as it decalcifies. The same principle applies to our teeth if the acid is not removed by brushing. (This activity is only appropriate with older children.)

3. Making Toothpaste

In individual plastic bags, place 4 teaspoons of baking soda, 1 teaspoon salt, and 1 teaspoon water. Add a drop of food flavoring extract such as peppermint, mint, or orange. The children can mix their own toothpaste.

4. Sugar on Our Teeth

Sugar found in sweet food can cause cavities on tooth enamel if it is not removed by rinsing or brushing. To demonstrate the effect of brushing, submerge white eggshells into a clear glass of cola for 24 hours. Observe the discoloration of the eggshell. Apply toothpaste to toothbrush. Brush the eggshell, removing the stain. Ask the children, "What caused the stain?"

Arts and Crafts

1. Easel Ideas
- paint with discarded toothbrushes
- paint on tooth-shaped easel paper

2. Toothbrushes and Splatter Screen

Provide construction paper, splatter screens, and discarded toothbrushes. The children can splatter paint onto the paper using the toothbrush as a painting tool.

3. Dental Floss Painting

Provide thin tempera paint, paper, and dental floss. The child can spoon a small amount of paint onto their paper and can hold on to one end of the dental floss while moving the free end through the paint to make a design.

Sensory

Additions to the Sensory Table
- toothbrushes and water
- peppermint extract added to water

Large Muscle

1. Drop the Toothbrush

Set a large, plastic open-mouth bottle on the floor. Encourage the children to try to drop the toothbrushes into the mouth of the bottle.

2. Sugar, Sugar, Toothbrush

Play like "Duck, Duck, Goose." The toothbrush tries to catch the "sugar" before it gets around the circle to where the "toothbrush" was sitting. Game can continue until interest diminishes.

Field Trips/ Resource People

1. The Dentist

Visit the dentist's office. Observe the furnishings and equipment.

2. The Hygienist

Invite a dental hygienist to visit the classroom. Ask the hygienist to discuss tooth care and demonstrate proper brushing techniques. After the discussion, provide each child with a disclosing tablet to check their brushing habits.

Group Time
(games, language)

Pass the Toothpaste

Play music and pass a tube of toothpaste around the circle. When the music stops, the person who is holding the toothpaste stands up and claps his hands three times (or some similar action). Repeat the game.

Cooking

1. **Happy Teeth Snacks**
   - apple wedges
   - orange slices
   - asparagus
   - cheese chunks
   - milk
   - cucumber slices
   - cauliflower pieces

2. **Smiling Apples**

   apples, cored and sliced
   peanut butter
   mini-marshmallows, raisins, or peanuts

   Spread peanut butter on one side of each apple slice. Place three to four mini-marshmallows, raisins, or peanuts on the peanut butter of one apple slice. Top with another apple slice, peanut butter side down.

Books

The following books can be used to complement this theme:

Adler, David A. (1997). *A Young Cam Jansen and the Lost Tooth.* Illus. by Susanna Natti. New York: Viking.

Falwell, Cathryn. (1996). *Dragon Tooth.* New York: Clarion Books.

Finnegan, Evelyn M. (1995). *My Little Friend Goes to the Dentist.* Illus. by Diane R. Houghton. Scituate, MA: Little Friend Press.

Gomi, Taro. (1994). *The Crocodile and the Dentist.* Brookfield, CT: Millbrook Press.

Hall, Kirsten. (1994). *The Tooth Fairy.* Illus. by Nan Brooks. Chicago: Children's Press.

Hoban, Lillian. (1987). *Arthur's Loose Tooth: Story and Pictures.* New York: HarperCollins.

Luttrell, Ida. (1997). *Milo's Toothache.* Illus. by Enzo Giannini. New York: Puffin. (Pbk)

MacDonald, Amy. (1996). *Cousin Ruth's Tooth.* Illus. by Marjorie Priceman. Boston: Houghton Mifflin.

Paxton, Tom. (1996). *The Story of the Tooth Fairy.* Illus. by Rob Sauber. New York: William Morrow.

Ready, Dee. (1997). *Dentists.* Chicago: Children's Press.

Rockwell, Harlow. (1987). *My Dentist.* New York: William Morrow.

Showers, Paul. (1991). *How Many Teeth?* New York: HarperCollins. (Pbk)

Multimedia

The following multimedia products can be used to complement this theme:

Goofy Over Dental Health [video]. (1991). Newton, PA: Disney Educational Productions.

McPhail, David M. *The Bear's Toothache* [book and cassette]. (1986). Pine Plains, NY: Live Oak Media.

Parker, Dan. *Teach Me About the Dentist* [cassette and book]. (1988). Fallbrook, CA: Living Skills Music.

Recording and Song Title

The following recording can be used to complement this theme:

People in Our Neighborhood—"Doctor, Doctor"

T H 22 E M E

Tools
rubber hammer,
stethoscope,
thermometer,
scale, medicine

Kinds
eye, ear,
feet, teeth,
community helpers,
animal, baby

Doctors
and Nurses

Clothing
white lab coat
gloves
masks

Places of
Work
hospitals
clinics
home care
schools

Purposes
help people
help animals
well care

Theme Goals

Through participating in the experiences provided by this theme, the children may learn:

1. Kinds of doctors and nurses.
2. Places doctors and nurses work.
3. Tools used by doctors and nurses.
4. Clothing worn by doctors and nurses.
5. How doctors and nurses help people and animals.

Concepts for the Children to Learn

1. A man or woman can be a doctor or nurse.
2. Doctors and nurses are community helpers.
3. Doctors and nurses help to keep people and animals healthy.
4. Doctors and nurses work in hospitals and clinics.
5. Lab coats, gloves, and masks are clothing doctors and nurses may wear.
6. Special doctors and nurses care for our eyes, ears, feet, and teeth.
7. A stethoscope is a tool used to check heartbeats and breathing.
8. Thermometers are used to check body temperature.

Vocabulary

1. **doctor**—a man or woman who helps keep our bodies healthy.
2. **nurse**—a man or woman who usually assists the doctor.
3. **stethoscope**—a tool used for checking heartbeat and breathing.
4. **thermometer**—tool for checking body temperature.
5. **patient**—a person who goes to see a doctor.
6. **pediatrician**—a children's doctor.
7. **veterinarian**—an animal doctor.
8. **ophthalmologist**—an eye doctor.

214

Bulletin Board

The purpose of this bulletin board is to develop skills in identifying written numerals and matching sets to numerals. Construct bandages out of manilla tagboard as illustrated or use purchased adhesive bandages. Laminate. Collect small boxes and cover with white paper if necessary. The number of boxes will be dependent upon the developmental age of children. Plastic bandage boxes or 16-count crayon boxes may be used. On each box place a numeral. Affix the box to a bulletin board by stapling. The children can place the proper number of bandages in each box.

Parent Letter

Dear Parents,

I hope everyone in your family is happy and healthy! Speaking of healthy, we are starting a unit on doctors and nurses. The children will be learning about the different types of doctors and nurses and how they help people. They also will be introduced to some of the tools used by doctors and nurses.

AT SCHOOL

A few of the learning experiences planned include:

- listening to the story, *Tommy Goes to the Doctor*.
- taking our temperatures with forehead strips and recording them on a chart in the science area.
- dressing up as doctors and nurses in the dramatic play area.
- experimenting with syringes (no needles!) and water at the sensory table.
- listening to and looking at books related to doctors and nurses.
- viewing the video titled *Hospital*.

AT HOME

There are many ways to integrate this curriculum unit into your home. To begin, discuss the role of your family doctor. Talk about your child's visit to a physician. This will help to alleviate anxiety and fears your child may have about the procedures and setting.

Let your child help you prepare this nutritious snack at home. We will be making it for Wednesday's snack as well.

Peanut Butter Balls

1/2 cup peanut butter
1/2 cup honey
3/4 to 1 cup powdered milk

Combine all of the ingredients in a bowl. Shape the mixture into small balls and roll in chopped nuts, coconut, or graham cracker crumbs, if desired.

Model positive attitudes toward health for your child.

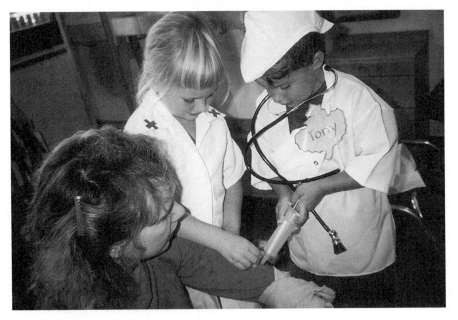

Girls and boys can be doctors or nurses.

Music

1. **"The Doctor in the Clinic"**
   (Sing to the tune of "Farmer in the Dell")

   The doctor in the clinic.
   The doctor in the clinic.
   Hi-ho the derry-o,
   The doctor in the clinic.

   The doctor takes a nurse . . .
   The nurse takes a patient . . .
   The patient gets help . . .
   The patient gets better . . .

2. **"To the Hospital"**
   (Sing to the tune of "Frere Jacques")

   To the hospital, to the hospital,
   We will go, we will go.
   We will see the doctors,
   And we'll see the nurses,
   Dressed in white, dressed in white.

Fingerplays

MISS POLLY'S DOLLY

Miss Polly had a dolly that was sick, sick, sick.
   (cradle arms and look sad)
She called for the doctor to come quick, quick, quick.
   (clap hands three times)
The doctor came with his coat and his hat.
   (point to your shirt and head)
And rapped on the door with a rap, rap, rap.
   (pretend to knock three times)
He looked at the dolly and he shook his head
   (shake head)
And he said, "Miss Polly, put her straight to bed."
   (shake finger)
Then he wrote on a paper for some pills, pills, pills.
   (hold left hand out flat, pretend to write with right hand)
I'll be back in the morning with my bill, bill, bill.
   (hold left hand out flat, wave it up and down as if waiting to be handed cash)

Note: The doctor may be male or female. Substitute pronouns.

DOCTOR DAY

My father said,
"It's doctor day,"
Then he and I
We're on our way
To see our friend
The doctor who
Would check me out
As doctors do.
She had more things
Than I can tell
To help her keep
The people well.
She checked me up
And all the while
She wore a big
And friendly smile.
So now I hope
That someday you
May go to see
The doctor too!

Source: Wilmes, Liz & Dick. (1983). *Everyday Circle Times*.
Illinois: Building Blocks Publishing.

Science

1. **Thermometer**

   Place a variety of unbreakable thermometers on the science table. Include a candy,
   meat, and an outdoor thermometer. Also
   include a strip thermometer that can be
   safely used on children's foreheads.

2. **Casts**

   Ask personnel at a local hospital to save
   clean, discarded casts. Place the casts on
   the science table, allowing the children to
   observe the materials, try them on for size,
   as well as feel their weight. The children
   may also enjoy decorating the casts.

3. **Stethoscope**

   Place a stethoscope on the science table for
   the children to experiment with. After each
   child uses it, wipe the ear plugs with alco-
   hol to prevent the transmission of disease.

4. **Doctors' Tools**

   In a feely box place several tools that a doctor uses. Include a thermometer, gauze,
   stethoscope, rubber hammer, and a tongue
   depressor.

5. **Making Toothpaste**

   Mix four teaspoons baking soda, one teaspoon salt, and one teaspoon peppermint
   flavoring. Then add just enough water to
   form a thick paste.

Dramatic Play

1. **Doctors and Nurses**

   Make a prop box for a doctor and nurse.
   Include a white coat, rubber gloves, a thermometer, gauze, tape, masks, eye droppers,
   tongue depressors, eye chart, cots, blankets,
   pencil and paper, empty and washed medicine bottles, a stethoscope, a scale, and
   syringes without needles. A first-aid kit
   including gauze and tape, bandages, butterflies, a sling, and ace bandages can be
   placed in this box. Place the prop boxes in
   the dramatic play area.

2. **Animal Clinic**

   Place stuffed animals with the doctor tools
   in the dramatic play area.

3. **Eye Doctor Clinic**

   Ask a local eye doctor for discontinued eye
   glass frames. Place the frames with a wall
   chart in the dramatic play area.

Arts and Crafts

1. **Cotton Swab Painting**

   Place cotton swabs, cottonballs, and tempera paint on a table in the art area. The
   cotton swabs and balls can be used as
   painting tools.

218

2. Body Tracing

Trace the children's bodies by having them lie down on a large piece of paper. The body shape can be decorated at school by the child with crayons and felt-tip markers. The shapes could also be taken home and decorated with parental assistance.

3. Eye Dropper Painting

Provide eye droppers, thin tempera paint, and absorbent paper. Designs can be made by using the eye dropper as a painting tool. Another method is to prepare water colored with food coloring in muffin tins. Using heavy paper towels with construction paper underneath for protection, the children will enjoy creating designs with the colored water.

Field Trips/ Resource People

1. Doctor's Office

Visit a doctor's office.

2. Resource Person

Invite a nurse or doctor to visit the classroom. Encourage them to talk briefly about their jobs. They can also share some of their tools with the children.

3. The Hospital

Visit a local hospital.

Math

1. Weight and Height Chart

Prepare a height and weight chart out of tagboard. Record each child's height and weight on this chart. Repeat periodically throughout the year to note physical changes.

2. Tongue Depressor Dominoes

Make a set of dominoes by writing on tongue depressors. Divide each tongue depressor in half with a felt-tip marker. On each half place a different number of dots. Consider the children's developmental level in determining the number of dots to be included. Demonstrate to interested children how to play dominoes.

3. Bandage Lotto

Construct a bandage lotto game using various sizes and shapes of bandages. Place it on a table for use during self-selected activity time.

Social Studies

Pictures

Display various health-related pictures in the room at the children's eye level, including doctors and nurses. Pictures should depict males and females in these health-related fields.

Group Time
(games, language)

1. Doctor, Doctor, Nurse

Play "Duck, Duck, Goose" inserting the words, "Doctor, Doctor, Nurse."

2. What's Missing?

Place a variety of doctors' and nurses' tools on a large tray. Tell the children to close their eyes. Remove one item from the tray. Then have the children open their eyes and guess which item has been removed. Continue playing the game using all of the items as well as providing an opportunity for each child.

Cooking

1. **Mighty Mixture**

   Mix any of the following:

   A variety of dried fruit (apples, apricots, pineapple, raisins)

   A variety of seeds (pumpkin, sunflower)

   A variety of nuts (almond, walnuts, pecans)

2. **Vegetable Juice**

   Prepare individual servings of vegetable juice in a blender by adding 1/2 cup of cut-up vegetables and 1/4 cup water. Salt to taste. Vegetables that can be used include: celery, carrots, beets, tomatoes, cucumbers, and zucchini.

Books

The following books can be used to complement this theme:

Brazelton, T. Berry. (1996). *Going to the Doctor.* Photos by Alfred Womack. Reading, MA: Addison Wesley.

Dooley, Virginia. (1996). *Tubes in My Ears: My Trip to the Hospital.* Illus. by Miriam Katin. Greenvale, NY: Mondo Publications. (Pbk)

Fine, Anne. (1992). *Poor Monty.* Illus. by Clara Vulliamy. New York: Clarion Books.

Flanagan, Alice K. (1997). *Ask Nurse Pfaff, She'll Help You.* Photos by Christine Osinski. Chicago: Children's Press.

Howe, James. (1994). *The Hospital Book.* Photos by Mal Warshaw. New York: William Morrow.

Kuklin, Susan. (1988). *Taking My Cat to the Vet.* Minneapolis: Bradbury Press.

Miller, Marilyn. (1996). *Behind the Scenes at the Hospital.* Illus. by Ingo Fast. Austin, TX: Raintree/Steck Vaughn.

Moses, Amy. (1997). *Doctors Help People.* Mankato, MN: Child's World.

Ready, Dee. (1997). *Doctors.* Chicago: Children's Press.

Ready, Dee. (1997). *Nurses.* Chicago: Children's Press.

Redberg, Rita F. et al. (1996). *You Can Be a Woman Cardiologist.* Culver City, CA: Cascade Pass. (Pbk)

Rogers, Fred. (1997). *Going to the Hospital.* Illus. by Jim Judkis. New York: G. P. Putnam.

Rosenberg, Maxine B. (1997). *Mommy's in the Hospital Having a Baby.* Photos by Robert Maass. New York: Clarion Books.

Schomp, Virginia. *If You Were a Veterinarian.* (1998). Tarrytown, NY: Marshall Cavendish.

Multimedia

The following multimedia products can be used to complement this theme:

Come See What the Doctor Sees [video]. (1994). Half Moon Bay, CA: Visual Mentor.

Emergency 911 [video]. (1994). Washington, D.C.: National Geographic.

Hospital [video]. (1990). Washington, D.C.: National Geographic.

Rogers, Fred. *Mister Rogers' Neighborhood: Doctor* [video]. (1996). CBS/Fox Home Video.

Ronno. "Doctor Doctor" on *People in Our Neighborhood* [cassette]. (1996). Long Branch, NJ: Kimbo Educational.

When I Grow Up I Wanta Be [video]. (1994). Birmingham, AL: Five Points South.

Recording and Song Title

The following recordings can be used to complement this theme:

People in Our Neighborhood—"Doctor, Doctor"

THEME 23

Dogs

Sizes
large
medium
small

Body Parts
fur, four legs,
paws, tail,
ears, eyes,
nose, mouth

Food
water
dog food
scraps

Safety
diseases
rabies
wild dogs
strange dogs

Supplies
collars
bones
leashes
brushes

Colors
yellow, brown,
black, white,
mixed

Care
exercise,
food, water,
sleep,
grooming,
medical, fleas

Occupational Uses
police/security dog,
seeing eye dog,
hunting, farming

Homes
dog houses
kennels
house

Theme Goals

Through participating in the experiences provided by this theme, the children may learn:

1. Dog's body parts.
2. Types of dogs.
3. Dogs need special care.
4. Dogs can be trained to do special tasks and tricks.

Concepts for the Children to Learn

1. There are many different sizes of dogs.
2. Dogs have a keen sense of smell and hearing.
3. Dogs growl and bark to communicate.
4. Dogs may bark at strangers to protect their owners and their space.
5. Dogs have legs, eyes, ears, a mouth, nose, and tail.
6. Dogs have fur on their skin.
7. Dogs enjoy being handled carefully and gently.
8. Some dogs help people.
9. There are many different colors, sizes, and kinds of dogs.
10. Dogs need food, water, and exercise every day.
11. Dogs can be taught to do tricks.

Vocabulary

1. **puppy**—a baby dog.
2. **pet**—an animal kept for pleasure.
3. **paw**—the dog's foot.
4. **veterinarian**—an animal doctor.
5. **guide dog**—a dog trained to help blind people.
6. **leash**—a rope, chain, or cord that attaches to a collar.
7. **collar**—a band worn around the dog's neck.
8. **obedience school**—a school where dogs are taught to obey.
9. **whiskers**—stiff hair growing around the dog's nose, mouth, and eyes.
10. **bone**—an object a dog uses to chew on.
11. **coat**—hair or fur covering the skin.
12. **doghouse**—a place for dogs to sleep and keep warm.

Bulletin Board

The purpose of this bulletin board is to develop color recognition and matching skills. Prepare the bulletin board by cutting dog shapes out of tagboard or construction paper. Add details using felt-tip markers. Use rubber cement to attach a different colored paper collar to each dog's neck. Also, cut out dog dishes from colored construction paper. Attach the pieces to the bulletin board as illustrated. Attach lengths of yarn or string for children to match the color of each dog's collar to the corresponding dog dish.

Parent Letter

Dear Parents,

We will begin a curriculum unit on a favorite subject of children of all ages—dogs! Through the classroom activities, we will be learning about a dog's basic physical features such as coat and body parts. We will also learn about caring for a dog, the roles of dogs in people's lives, dog training, as well as factors families need to consider when choosing a dog. This curriculum unit is designed to encourage the children to develop an awareness of and respect for dogs as pets.

AT SCHOOL

Some of the learning experiences planned include:

- creating paw prints at the art table (dipping paw-shaped sponges into paint and applying them to paper).
- sorting various-sized dog biscuits.
- listening to the children's stories about their own dogs.
- setting up a "pet store" in the dramatic play area, complete with stuffed animals and many dog accessories.
- baking dog biscuits!

AT HOME

To foster parent-child interaction and reinforce some of the concepts we are working on at school, try some of the following ideas:

- Look through magazines to find pictures of dogs and puppies. Help your child tear out pictures of dogs and puppies. This activity is good for the development of fine motor and visual discrimination skills. An interesting collage can be made by gluing these pictures onto a piece of paper.
- If you don't have access to a dog, visit a pet shop to observe the puppies. At the same time note all of the dog supplies available.

Enjoy your child!

Music

1. **"Bingo"**

   There was a farmer who had a dog
   And Bingo was his name-o.
   B-I-N-G-O
   B-I-N-G-O
   B-I-N-G-O
   And Bingo was his name-o.

2. **"Six Little Dogs"**
   (Sing to the tune of "Six Little Ducks")

   Six little dogs that I once knew,
   fat ones, skinny ones, fair ones too.
   But the one little dog with the brown
      curly fur,
   He led the others with a grr, grr, grr.
   Grr, grr, grr
   Grr, grr, grr
   He led the others with a grr, grr, GRR!

What is your favorite breed of dog?

Fingerplays

FRISKY'S DOGHOUSE

   This is Frisky's doghouse;
      (pointer fingers touch to make a roof)
   This is Frisky's bed;
      (motion of smoothing)
   Here is Frisky's pan of milk;
      (cup hands)
   So that he can be fed.

   Frisky has a collar
      (point to neck with fingers)
   With his name upon it, too;
   Take a stick and throw it,
      (motion of throwing)
   He'll bring it back to you.
      (clap once)

FIVE LITTLE PUPPIES

   Five little puppies were playing in the sun.
      (hold up hands, fingers extended)
   This one saw a rabbit, and he began to run.
      (bend down first finger)
   This one saw a butterfly, and he began to
      race.
      (bend down second finger)
   This one saw a cat, and he began to chase.
      (bend down third finger)
   This one tried to catch his tail, and he went
      round and round.
      (bend down fourth finger)
   This one was so quiet, he never made a
      sound.
      (bend down thumb)

FIVE LITTLE PUPPIES

   Five little puppies jumping on the bed,
      (hold up five fingers)
   One fell off and bumped his head,
      (hold up one finger—tap head)
   Mama called the doctor and the doctor
      said,
   "No more puppies jumping on the bed."
      (shake index finger)

Science

1. Additions to the science table or area may include:
   - a magnifying glass with bones, dog hair, and dog food.
   - dog tags of different sizes, including some with squeakers.
   - a balance scale and dry dog food.
2. During a cooking activity, prepare dog biscuits. The recipe is listed under cooking.

Dramatic Play

1. **Pet Store**

   Simulate a pet store using stuffed animals. Include a counter complete with cash register and money. Post a large sign that says, "Pet Store." Set out many stuffed dogs with collars and leashes. Children will enjoy pretending they have a new pet.

2. **Veterinarian's Office**

   Use some medical equipment and stuffed dogs to create a veterinarian's office.

3. **Pet Show**

   Encourage the children to bring a stuffed animal to school. Children can pretend that their stuffed animals can do tricks. Have ribbons available for them to look at and award to each other.

4. **Dog House**

   Construct a dog house from a large cardboard box. Provide dog ears and tails for the children to wear as they imitate the pet.

Arts and Crafts

1. **Paw Prints**

   Make stamps out of erasers, sponges, or with the child's fist.

2. **Dog Puppets**

   Provide socks, paper bags, and/or paper plates to make dog puppets.

3. **Dog Masks**

   Use fake fur ears and pipe cleaners for whiskers.

4. **Bone Printing**

   Provide different meat bones, a tray of tempera paint, and paper to make prints.

5. **Bone Painting**

   Cut easel paper in bone shapes.

6. **Dog Collages**

   Provide dog pictures cut out of magazines to make a collage.

Large Muscle

1. Encourage the children to dramatize the following movements:
   - a big dog
   - a tiny dog
   - a dog with heavy steps
   - a dog with light steps
   - a happy dog
   - a sad dog
   - a mad dog
   - a loud dog
   - a quiet dog
   - a hungry dog
   - a tired dog
   - a curious dog
   - a sick dog

2. **Dog Hoops**

   Provide hoops for the children to jump through as they imitate dogs.

3. **Scent Walk**

   Place prints of dog paws on the play yard leading to different activities. Encourage the child to crawl to each activity.

4. Tracks

If snow is available, make tracks with boots that have different treads. Encourage children to follow one track.

5. Bean Bag Bones

Provide round bean bags or make special bone-shaped bean bags. Encourage the children to throw them into a large dog food bowl.

Field Trips/ Resource People

1. Pet Store

Take a field trip to a pet store. While there ask the manager how to care for dogs. Observe the different types of cages, collars, leashes, food, and toys.

2. Veterinarian Office

Take a field trip to a veterinarian's office or animal hospital. Compare its similarities and differences to a doctor's office.

3. Kennel

Visit a kennel and observe the different sizes of cages and dogs.

4. Variety Store

Visit a variety store and observe pet accessories.

5. Grocery Store

Take a field trip to the grocery store and purchase the ingredients needed to make dog biscuits.

6. Dog Trainer

Invite an obedience trainer to talk about teaching dogs.

7. Additional Resource People

- veterinarian
- pet store owner
- parents (bring in family dogs)
- humane society representative
- representative from a kennel
- dog groomer
- person with a seeing eye dog (guide dog)

Math

1. Dog Bones

Cut dog bone shapes of four different sizes from tagboard. Encourage the children to sequence them.

2. Classifying Dog Biscuits

Purchase three sizes of dog biscuits. Using dog dishes, have the children sort them according to size and type.

3. Weighing Biscuits

Using the scale, encourage the children to weigh different sizes and amounts of dog biscuits.

Social Studies

1. Share Your Dog

Individually invite the parents to bring their child's pet to school.

2. Pictures of Dogs

Display pictures of different types of dogs.

3. Bulletin Board

Prepare a bulletin board with pictures of the children's dogs.

4. Slides

Take slides of field trips and of resource people. Share them at group time. (This slide series may be shared with parents at meetings or coffees.)

5. **Dog Biscuits**

   Prepare dog biscuits and donate to the local animal shelter. (See Cooking.)

6. **Chart**

   Make a chart including the children's name, type of pet, size of pet, and the name of the pet. Count the number of dogs, cats, birds, etc. Discuss the most popular names.

7. **Dogs**

   Using pictures or a real dog, talk about a dog's body. Some dogs have long noses so they can smell things very well; others have short hair to live in hot climates. Discuss why some dogs are good guard dogs. Discuss how dogs' tongues help them to cool off on hot days. Also talk about what else a dog's rough tongue is used for.

Group Time
(games, language)

1. **The Dog Catcher**

   Hide stuffed dogs or those cut from construction paper around the classroom and have children find them.

2. **Child-created Stories**

   Bring in a picture of a dog or stuffed dog. Encourage the children to tell you a story about the picture or the stuffed dog. While the child speaks, record the words. Place the story in the book corner.

3. **Dog Chart**

   Make a chart listing the color of each child's dog. A variation would be to have the children state their favorite color of dog. This activity can be repeated using size.

4. **Doggie, Doggie, Where's Your Bone?**

   Bring in a clean bone or a bone cut from construction paper. Sit the children in a circle. Choose one child to be the dog.

Have the child pretending to be the dog sit in the middle. The doggie closes his eyes. A child from the circle sneaks up and takes the bone. Children call, "Doggie, doggie, where's your bone? Someone stole it from your home!" The "dog" gets three guesses to find out who has the bone.

5. **The Lost Dog**

   (This is a variation of the "Dog Catcher" game.) Using the children's stuffed animals from home, have the children trade dogs so that each is holding another's pet. One child begins by hiding the dog he is holding while the other children cover their eyes. He tells the owner, "Your dog is lost, but we can help you find it." As the dog owner looks, he can put the pet he is holding on his carpet square to free both hands. The group gives "hot" and "cold" clues to indicate whether the child is close to or far away from the pet. When the child finds his pet, he is the next one to hide a pet.

Cooking

1. **Hot "Dog" Kebabs on a Stick**

   paper plates and napkins
   skewers
   1 package hot dogs
   2 green peppers, cut up
   cherry tomatoes

   Place 2 pieces of green pepper, 2 cherry tomatoes, and 2 hot dog pieces on each child's plate. Show the children how to thread the ingredients on skewers. Bake the kabobs in a preheated oven for 15 minutes at 350 degrees.

2. **Dog Biscuits**

   2 1/2 cups whole wheat flour
   1/2 cup powdered dry milk
   1/2 teaspoon salt
   1/2 teaspoon garlic powder
   6 tablespoons margarine, shortening, or
      meat drippings
   1 egg
   1 teaspoon brown sugar
   1/2 cup ice water

Combine flour, milk, salt, and flour. Cut in the shortening. Mix in egg. Add enough water until mixture forms a ball. Pat the dough to a half-inch thickness on a lightly oiled cookie sheet. Cut with cutters and remove scraps. Bake 25 to 30 minutes at 350 degrees. This recipe may be varied by adding pureed soup greens, protein powder, etc.

3. Dogs-in-a-Blanket

cheese crust
    1/2 teaspoon salt
    pinch baking powder
    1 cup white flour
    1/4 cup shortening
    1/4 cup water
    1/4 cup finely shredded cheddar cheese

hot dogs

Stir the dry ingredients in a large bowl. Cut in shortening and then add 1/4 cup water. Stir with a fork and add more water only if necessary to work in flour. Add cheese and knead together. Cut the cheese pie crust in strips and wrap each around a whole or half of a hot dog. Bake at 350 degrees until crust is light brown.

Source: Warren, Jean. (1982). *Super Snacks*. Alderwood Manor, WA: Warren Publishing House.

4. Hush Puppies

vegetable oil
2 1/4 cups yellow cornmeal
1 teaspoon salt
2 tablespoons finely chopped onion
3/4 teaspoon baking soda
1 1/2 cups buttermilk

Heat oil (about 1 inch deep) to 375 degrees. Mix cornmeal, salt, onion, and baking soda in a bowl. Add buttermilk. Drop by spoonfuls into hot oil. Fry until brown about 2 minutes.

Books

The following books can be used to complement this theme:

Boland, Janice D. (1996). *A Dog Named Sam.* Illus. by G. Brian Karas. New York: Dial Books.

Coffelt, Nancy. (1995). *Dog Who Cried Woof.* New York: Harcourt Brace.

Cole, Joanna. (1991). *My Puppy Is Born.* Revised and newly illustrated. Photos by Margaret Miller. New York: William Morrow.

Copeland, Eric. (1994). *Milton, My Father's Dog.* Plattsburgh, NY: Tundra.

Ernst, Lisa Campbell. (1992). *Walter's Tail.* New York: Simon & Schuster.

Gibbons, Gail. (1996). *Dogs.* New York: Holiday House.

Gliori, Debi. (1996). *The Snow Lambs.* New York: Scholastic.

Gregory, Nan. (1995). *How Smudge Came.* Illus. by Ron Lightburn. New York: Red Deer College Press.

Hall, Donald. (1994). *I Am the Dog, I Am the Cat.* Illus. by Barry Moser. New York: Dial Books.

Harper, Isabelle. (1994). *My Dog Rosie.* Illus. by Barry Moser. New York: Scholastic.

Harper, Isabelle. (1996). *Our New Puppy.* Illus. by Barry Moser. New York: Scholastic.

Hesse, Karen. (1993). *Lester's Dog.* Illus. by Nancy Carpenter. New York: Crown Publishers.

Masurel, Claire. (1997). *No, No, Titus!* Illus. by Shari Halpern. New York: North South Books.

McGeorge, Constance W. (1994). *Boomer's Big Day.* Illus. by Mary Whyte. San Francisco: Chronicle.

Moore, Eva. (1996). Buddy: *The First Seeing Eye Dog.* Illus. by Don Bolognese. New York: Scholastic.

Osofsky, Audrey. (1992). *My Buddy.* Illus. by Ted Rand. New York: Holt.

Robertus, Polly M. (1991). *The Dog Who Had Kittens*. Illus. by Janet Stevens. New York: Holiday House.

Rylant, Cynthia. (1991). *Bookshop Dog.* New York: Scholastic.

Rylant, Cynthia. (1994). *Mr. Putter and Tabby Walk the Dog.* Illus. by Arthur Howard. Orlando: Harcourt Brace.

Siracusa, Catherine. (1991). *Bingo, the Best Dog in the World.* Illus. by Sidney Levitt. New York: HarperCollins.

Wells, Rosemary. (1997). *McDuff Moves In.* Illus. by Susan Jeffers. New York: Hyperion.

Wild, Margaret. (1994). *Toby.* Illus. by Noela Young. New York: Ticknor & Fields.

Zolotow, Charlotte. (1995). *Old Dog.* Revised and newly illustrated. Illus. by James Ransome. New York: HarperCollins.

Multimedia

The following multimedia products can be used to complement this theme:

"Bingo" on *Six Little Ducks: Classic Children's Songs* [cassette or CD]. (1997). Kimbo Educational.

Dog [video]. Eyewitness Videos. Available from Kimbo Educational.

World of Pets: Dogs [video]. (1985). National Geographic Society.

Pets: See How They Grow [video]. Sony. Available from Kimbo Educational.

"Puppy Dog" on *Walk Like the Animals* by Georgiana Liccione Stewart [cassette]. Kimbo Educational.

Robertus, Polly M. *Dog Who Had Kittens* [video]. (1992). Live Oak Media.

Wagging Tails: The Dog and Puppy Music Video [video]. (1994). Forney Miller Film & Video; distributed by New Market Sales.

Recordings and Song Titles

The following recordings can be used to complement this theme:

Six Little Ducks—"B-I-N-G-O"

Tony Chestnut (The Learning Station)— "How Much Is That Doggie?"

THEME 24

Easter

Special Foods
colored eggs
hot cross buns
candies

Symbols
baskets
rabbits
eggs
chicks/ducks
bonnets

Spring Holiday
new life,
religious for
some people*

Celebrations
egg hunts
parades

* Some center personnel may elect to include an Easter theme with an emphasis on the spring holiday as opposed to the traditional religious emphasis.

Theme Goals

Through participating in the experiences provided by this theme, the children may learn:

1. Easter traditions.
2. Easter symbols.
3. Boiled eggs can be dyed and decorated for Easter.
4. Care of rabbits.

Concepts for the Children to Learn

1. Easter is a holiday.
2. Many families celebrate Easter.
3. At Eastertime eggs are decorated.
4. There are many symbols of Easter, including baby animals, baskets, rabbits, and eggs.
5. Baskets filled with eggs and candy may be hidden.
6. Baby animals born in the Spring are a sign of new life.
7. Bonnets (hats) may be worn at Easter time.

Vocabulary

1. **Easter**—a holiday in Spring.
2. **basket**—a woven container.
3. **hatch**—to break out of a shell.
4. **dye**—to change the color.
5. **duckling**—a baby duck.
6. **chick**—a baby chicken.
7. **lamb**—a baby sheep.
8. **bunny**—a baby rabbit.
9. **holiday**—a day of celebration.
10. **Spring**—the season of the year when plants begin to grow.
11. **bonnet**—a kind of hat.

Bulletin Board

The purpose of this bulletin board is to promote correspondence of sets to the written numeral. Construct baskets out of stiff tagboard. Write a numeral beginning with the number one on each basket as illustrated. Carefully attach these to the bulletin board by stapling all the way around the round bottom of the baskets. Construct many small Easter eggs. Encourage the children to deposit the corresponding number of Easter eggs in the numbered baskets. Care needs to be taken when removing the eggs. The number of baskets provided should reflect the developmental level of the children. If available, you might want to try using lightweight Easter baskets. They are harder to hang up, but may prove to be more sturdy.

Parent Letter

Dear Parents,

"Here comes Peter Cottontail, hopping down the bunny trail. . . ." Easter is on its way, and is the curriculum theme we will explore. This is an exciting holiday for children. Through the planned learning experiences, the children will learn ways that families celebrate Easter and the symbols representing Easter. Included will be customs such as the Easter bunny, Easter baskets, and foods that are usually associated with Easter.

AT SCHOOL

Learning experiences planned to reinforce concepts of Easter include:

- a special visitor for the week—a rabbit! The children will assist in taking care of the rabbit.
- a hat shop in the dramatic play area with materials to create Easter bonnets.
- Easter grass and plastic eggs in the sensory table.
- an egg hunt! On Friday, we will search our play yard for hidden eggs and place them in our baskets.
- listening to Easter stories.

AT HOME

To establish a sense of family history, recall family Easter celebrations that you have had in the past with your child. What special things does your family do together on this holiday? And, of course, dye some Easter eggs!

Be adventurous and try some dyes from natural materials. Natural dying is not new; natural dyes were the original Easter egg colors the world over. To make purple eggs purchase a box of frozen blackberries. Thaw and place in a saucepan. Add eggs and cover with water plus 1 tablespoon of vinegar. Bring the water to a boil and simmer for 20 minutes. Afterward, take the pan off the heat source and let stand for approximately 20 minutes.

To make gold eggs use powdered tumeric. Place eggs in a saucepan and add enough water to cover. Then, add 3 tablespoons of tumeric and bring to a boil. Simmer for 20 minutes. Remove from heat source and cool.

To create pale green eggs, cut spinach and place in the bottom of a pan. Add enough water to cover and add eggs. Bring to a boil and simmer for 20 minutes. Remove from heat and allow to set for more intense color.

From all of us,

234

Children enjoy being read Easter stories.

Music

1. "Did You Ever See a Rabbit?"
(Sing to the tune of "Did You Ever See a Lassie?")

Did you ever see a rabbit, a rabbit, a rabbit?
Did you ever see a rabbit, a rabbit on Easter morn?
He hops around so quietly
And hides all the eggs.
Did you ever see a rabbit, on Easter morn?

2. "Easter Bunny"
(Sing to the tune of "Ten Little Indians")

Where, oh, where is the Easter Bunny,
Where, oh, where is the Easter Bunny,
Where, oh, where is the Easter Bunny,
Early Easter morning?

Find all the eggs and put them in a basket,
Find all the eggs and put them in a basket,
Find all the eggs and put them in a basket,
Early Easter morning.

3. "Easter Eggs"
(Sing to the chorus of "Jingle Bells")

Easter eggs, Easter eggs,
Hidden all around.
Come my children look about
And see where they are found.

Easter eggs, Easter eggs,
They're a sight to see.
One for Tom and one for Ann
And a special one for me!

Insert names of children in your classroom.

4. "Easter Eggs"
(Sing to the tune of "Mama's Little Baby Loves Shortnin'")

Easter eggs here and there,
Easter eggs everywhere.
What's the color of the
Easter egg here?

Fingerplays

FIVE LITTLE EASTER EGGS

Five little Easter eggs lovely colors wore;
Mother ate the blue one and then there were four.
Four little Easter eggs, two and two, you see;
Daddy ate the red one, and then there were three.
Three little Easter eggs; before I knew
Sister ate the yellow one, then there were two.
Two little Easter eggs; oh what fun.

Brother ate the purple one, then there was
one.
One little Easter egg; see me run!
I ate the very last one, and then there were
none!

This could be a fingerplay or could be done
with colored finger puppet eggs with the
children holding a particular color coming
forward when that color is named.

Source: Peck, Don. (1975). *Fingerplays that Motivate*. Minneapolis: T. S. Denison and Company.

KITTY AND BUNNY

Here is a kitty.
(make a fist with one hand)
Here is a bunny.
(hold up other hand with pointer and
middle fingers up straight)
See his tall ears so pink and funny?
(wiggle the two extended fingers)
Kitty comes by and licks his face;
(extend thumb and wiggle near the
bunny)
And around and around the garden they
race.
(make circular motions with hands)
And then without a single peep,
They both lie down and go to sleep.
(fold hands)

Source: Peck, Don. (1975). *Fingerplays that Motivate*. Minneapolis: T. S. Denison and Company.

EASTER BUNNY

Easter Bunny, Easter Bunny
(make "ears" at head with arms outstretched)
Pink and white
Come fill my basket
(make filling motion)
Overnight
(pretend to sleep, lay head on hands)

Source: Overholser, Kathy. (1979). *Let Your Fingers Do the
Talking*. Minneapolis: T. S. Denison and Company.

THE DUCK

I waddle when I walk.
(hold arms elbow high and twist trunk
side to side, or squat down)
I quack when I talk.
(place palms together and open and
close)
And I have webbed toes on my feet.
(spread fingers wide)
Rain coming down
Makes me smile, not frown
(smile)
And I dive for something to eat.
(put hands together and make diving
motion)

MY RABBIT

My rabbit has two big ears
(hold up index and middle fingers for
ears)
And a funny little nose.
(join other three fingers for nose)
He likes to nibble carrots
(move thumb away from other two
fingers)
And he hops wherever he goes.
(move whole hand jerkily)

Science

1. **Incubate and Hatch Eggs**

Check the yellow pages of your telephone
book to see if any hatcheries are located in
your area.

2. **Dyeing Eggs**

Use natural products to make egg dye.
Beets—deep red; onions—yellow (add soda
to make bright yellow); cranberries—light
red; spinach leaves—green; and blackberries—blue. To make dyed eggs pick two or
three colors from the list. Make the dye by
boiling the fruit or vegetable in small
amounts of water. Let the children put a
cool hard-boiled egg in a nylon stocking
and dip it into the dye. Keep the egg in the
dye for several minutes. Pull out the nylon

and check the color. If it is dark enough, place the egg on a paper towel to dry. If children want to color the eggs with crayons before dying, you can show how the wax keeps liquid from getting on the egg.

3. **Science Table Additions**
   - ◉ bird nests
   - ◉ empty bird eggs
   - ◉ different kinds of baskets
   - ◉ an incubator
   - ◉ newly planted seeds
   - ◉ flowers still in bud (children can watch them open)
   - ◉ pussy willows

4. **Basket Guessing**

   Do reach-and-feel using a covered basket. Place an egg, a chick, a rabbit, a doll's hat, some Easter grass, etc., in a large Easter basket. Let the children place their hands into the basket individually and describe the objects they are feeling.

Dramatic Play

1. **Flower Shop**

   Plan a flower shop for the dramatic play area. Include spring plants, baskets, and Easter lilies.

2. **Egg Center**

   Create a colored egg center to be used during self-directed play. Some children put stickers on plastic eggs, some sell the eggs, and others buy them.

3. **Costume Shop**

   Place costumes for bunny use, Easter baskets, and Easter eggs in the dramatic play area. The children can take turns hiding the eggs and going on hunts.

4. **A Bird Nest**

   Place a nest with eggs in the dramatic play area. Also provide bird masks, a perch, and other bird items in the area for use during self-initiated play.

5. **Easter Clothes**

   Bring in Easter clothes for the children to dress up in. Suits, dresses, hats, purses, gloves, and dress-up shoes should be included.

6. **Hat Shop**

   Make a hat shop. Place hats with ribbons, flowers, netting, and other decorations in the dramatic play area. The children can decorate the hats. If the children are interested, plan an Easter Parade.

Arts and Crafts

1. **Easter Collages**

   Collect eggshells, straw, Easter grass, or plant seeds for making collages. Place on art table with sheets of paper and glue.

2. **Colorful Collages**

   Use pastel-colored sand and glue to make collages.

3. **Wet Chalk Eggs**

   Use wet chalk to decorate paper cut in the shape of eggs in pastel colors. Show the children the difference between wetting the chalk in vinegar and water. The vinegar color will be brighter.

4. **Easel Ideas**

   Cut egg-shaped easel paper or basket-shaped paper. Clip to the easel. Provide pastel paints at the easel. To make the paint more interesting add glitter.

5. **Milk Carton Easter Baskets**

   Cut off the bottom four inches of milk cartons. Provide precut construction or wallpaper to cover the baskets, and yarn. Include small bits of paper or bright cloth to glue on. Make a handle using a thin strip of paper that is stapled to the carton. Use the baskets for the children's snack.

6. Plastic Easter Baskets

Easter baskets can be made by using the green plastic baskets that strawberries and blueberries come in from the grocery store. Cut thin strips of paper that children can practice weaving through the holes. This activity is most successful with older children.

7. Color Mixing

Provide red, yellow, and blue dyed water in shallow pans. Provide the children with medicine droppers and absorbent paper cut in the shape of eggs. Also, the children can use medicine droppers to apply color to the paper. Observe what happens when the colors blend together.

8. Rabbit Ears

Construct rabbit ears out of heavy paper. Attach them to a band that can be worn around the head, fitting it for size. These ears may stimulate creative movement as well as dramatic play.

9. Shape Rabbit

Provide a large, a medium, and four small circles cut from white paper, as well as two tall thin triangles. Show the children how to put these shapes together to make a rabbit.

Sensory

1. Sensory Table Activities

Add to the sensory table:

- cotton balls with scoops and measuring cups
- birdseed or beans
- straw or hay and plastic eggs
- plastic chicks and ducks with water
- Easter grass, eggs, small straw mats
- dirt with plastic flowers and/or leaves
- dyed, scented water and water toys
- sand, shovels, and scoops

2. Clay Cutters

Make scented clay. Place on the art table with rabbit, duck, egg, and flower cookie cutters for the children to use during self-directed or self-initiated play.

Large Muscle

1. Bunny Trail

Set up a bunny trail in the classroom. Place tape on the floor and have children hop over the trail. To make it more challenging, add a balance beam to resemble a bridge.

2. Eggs in the Basket

The children can practice throwing egg-shaped or regular bean bags into a large basket or bucket.

3. Rabbit Tag

Make the egg-shaped bean bags to play rabbit tag. To play the game, the children stand in a circle, with one child being the rabbit. The rabbit walks around the circle with a bean bag balanced on his head, and drops a second bean bag behind the back of another child. The second child must put the bean bag on his head and follow the rabbit around the circle once. Each child must keep the bean bag balanced—if it drops, it must be picked up and replaced on the head. If the rabbit is tagged, he chooses the next rabbit. If the rabbit returns to the empty spot in the circle, the second child becomes the rabbit. This is an unusual game in that the action is fairly slow, but it's still very exciting.

4. Egg Rolling

Place mats on the floor and have children roll across with their arms at their sides. For older children, you can place the mat on a slightly inclined plane and have children roll down, then try to have them roll back up, which is more challenging.

Field Trips

1. The Farm

Take a trip to a farm to see the new baby animals.

2. The Hatchery

Visit a hatchery on a day that they are selling baby chicks.

3. Neighborhood Walk

Take a walk around the neighborhood and look for signs of new life.

4. Rabbit Visit

Bring some rabbits to school for the children to observe.

Math

1. Egg Numerals

Collect five large plastic eggs, such as the kind that nylon stockings can be purchased in. Put numerals from one to five (or ten, for older children) on the eggs. Let the children place the correct number of cotton balls or markers into each egg.

2. Easter Seriation

Cut different-sized tagboard eggs, chicks, ducks, and rabbits. The children can place the items in a row from the smallest to the largest.

Social Studies

1. Family Easter Traditions

During large group, ask the children what special activities their families do to celebrate Easter. Their families may go to church, eat together, have egg hunts, or do other things that are special on this day.

2. Sharing Baskets

Decorate eggs or baskets to give to a home for the elderly. If possible, take a walk and let the children deliver them.

Group Time
(games, language)

1. The Last Bunny

This is a game for ten or more players. It is more fun with a large number. An Easter rabbit is chosen by counting out or drawing straws. All the other players stand in a circle. The Easter rabbit walks around the circle and taps one player on the back saying, "Have you seen my bunny helper?" "What does it look like?" asks the player and the Easter rabbit describes the bunny helper. He may say, "She is wearing a watch and blue shoes." The player tries to guess who it is. When he names the right person, the Easter rabbit says, "That's my helper!" and the other player chases the bunny helper outside and around the circle. If the chaser catches the bunny helper before he can return to his place the chaser becomes the Easter rabbit. If the bunny helper gets there first then the first Easter rabbit must try again. The Easter rabbit takes the place in the circle of whoever is the new Easter rabbit.

Source: Rockwell, Anne. (1973). *Games and How to Play Them*. New York: Thomas Y. Crowell Co.

2. Outdoor Egg Hunt

Plan an egg hunt outdoors, if possible. Hide the boiled eggs that the children have decorated, candy eggs in wrappers, or small Easter candies in clear plastic bags. The children can use the baskets they have made to collect their eggs, then, weather permitting, eat the boiled eggs for a snack outdoors.

Easter Eggs

Where did the custom of coloring Easter eggs come from? No one knows for sure. In any case, the Easter holiday centers around eggs for young children. Here are some projects you might like to try.

- To hard-cook eggs: Place eggs in a saucepan and add enough cold water to cover at least 1 inch above the eggs. Heat rapidly to boiling and remove from heat. Cover the pan and allow to stand for 22 to 24 minutes. Immediately cool the eggs in cold water.

- Make a vegetable dye solution by adding a teaspoon of vinegar to 1/2 cup of boiling water. Drop in food coloring and stir. The longer the egg is kept in the dye, the deeper the color will be.

- Add a teaspoonful of salad oil to a dye mixture and mix in the oil well. This results in a dye that produces swirls of color. Immerse the egg in the dye for a few minutes.

- Draw a design on an egg with a crayon before dying it. The dye will not take to the areas with the crayon marks and the design will show through.

- Wrap rubber bands, string, yarn, or narrow strips of masking tape around an egg to create stripes and other designs. Dip the egg in a dye and allow to dry before removing the wrapping.

- Drip the wax of a lighted birthday candle over an egg or draw a design on the egg using a piece of wax. Place the egg in dye. Repeat process again, if desired, dipping the egg in another color of dye. (Note: The lighted candle is to be used by an adult only.)

- Felt-tip markers can be used to decorate dyed or undyed eggs.

- Small stickers can be used on eggs.

- Craft items such as sequins, glitter, and ribbons and small pom-poms can be used with glue to decorate eggs.

- Apply lengths of yarns, string, or thread to the eggs with glue, creating designs, and allow to dry.

- Egg creatures can be created by using markers, construction paper, feathers, ribbon, lace, cotton balls, fabric, and buttons. To make an egg holder, make small cardboard or construction paper cylinders. A toilet paper or paper towel tube can be cut to make stands as well.

- Save the shells from the eggs to use for eggshell collages. Crumble the shells and sprinkle over a glue design that has been made on paper or cardboard.

Cooking

1. **Decorating Cupcakes**

   Let the children use green frosting, dyed coconut shreds, and jelly beans to decorate cupcakes and put them into an Easter basket. As a last touch, add a pipe cleaner handle. Cake mixes can be used to make the cupcakes. Follow the directions on the box. Place paper liners in a muffin pan to ensure easy removability.

2. **Bunny Food**

   Carrot sticks, celery, and lettuce can be available for snack.

3. **Egg Sandwiches**

   Use the boiled eggs the children have decorated to make egg salad or deviled eggs for snack time.

4. **Carrot and Raisin Salad**

   4 cups grated carrots
   1 cup raisins
   1/2 cup mayonnaise or whipped salad dressing

   Place ingredients in a bowl and mix thoroughly.

5. **Bunny Salad**

   For each serving place one lettuce leaf on a plate. Put one canned pear half with the cut side down on top of the lettuce leaf. Add sections of an orange to represent the ears. Decorate the bunny face by adding grated carrots, raisins, nuts, or maraschino cherries to make eyes, a nose, and a mouth.

Books

The following books can be used to complement this theme:

Adams, Adrienne. (1991). *Easter Egg Artists.* Madison, WI: Demco Media.

Auch, Mary Jane. (1992). *The Easter Egg Farm.* New York: Holiday House.

Auch, Mary Jane. (1996). *Eggs Mark the Spot.* New York: Holiday House.

Barth, Edna. (1981). *Lilies, Rabbits, and Painted Eggs: The Story of the Easter Symbols.* Boston: Houghton Mifflin. (Pbk)

Fisher, Aileen Lucia. (1997). *The Story of Easter.* Illus. by Stefano Vitale. New York: HarperCollins.

Gibbons, Gail. (1989). *Easter.* New York: Holiday House.

Hallinan, P. K. (1993). *Today Is Easter!* Nashville, TN: Ideals Childrens Books. (Pbk)

Hopkins, Lee Bennett. (1993). *Easter Buds Are Springing: Poems for Easter.* Illus. by Tomie De Paola. Honesdale, PA: Boyds Mills Press.

Kennedy, Pamela. (1991). *An Easter Celebration: Traditions and Customs from Around the World.* Nashville, TN: Ideals Childrens Books.

McDonnell, Janet. (1993). *The Easter Surprise.* Illus. by Linda Hohag. Chicago: Children's Press.

Milich, Melissa. (1997). *Miz Fannie Mae's Fine New Easter Hat.* Illus. by Yong Chen. Boston: Little, Brown.

Nielsen, Shelly. (1992). *Celebrating Easter.* Minneapolis: Abdo & Daughters.

Polacco, Patricia. (1992). *Chicken Sunday.* New York: Philomel Books.

Polacco, Patricia. (1988). *Rechenka's Eggs.* New York: G. P. Putnam.

Zolotow, Charlotte. (1998). *The Bunny Who Found Easter.* Boston: Houghton Mifflin.

Multimedia

The following multimedia products can be used to complement this theme:

Auch, Mary Jane. *Easter Egg Farm* [book and cassette]. (1995). Pine Plains, NY: Live Oaks Media.

"Easter Egg Hunt" on *Holiday Songs for All Occasions* [cassette]. Kimbo Educational.

"Easter Time Is Here Again" on *Holiday Songs and Rhythms* [compact disc]. (1997). Freeport, NY: Activity Records, Inc.; Educational Activities, Inc.

Max's Chocolate Chicken and Other Stories for Young Children [video]. (© 1993). Weston, CT: Children's Circle Home Video; Los Angeles, distributed by Wood Knapp Video.

"Peter Cottontail" on *Holidays and Special Times* [cassette] (1989). Sung by Greg Scelsa and Steve Millang. Los Angeles, CA: Youngheart Records.

Recordings and Song Titles

The following recordings can be used to complement this theme:

Holiday Piggyback Songs—"So Early Easter Morning," "Bunny-Pokey," "Like a Bunny Would"

Holiday Songs for All Occasions—"Easter Egg Hunt"

Holiday Action Songs—"The Black Top Hat & the Easter Bonnett," "The Lonely Ducks," "The Easter Basket," "Rolling Down the Hill," "The Wandering Goose," "The Easter Bunny"

Singing Calendar—"April"

THEME 25

Eggs

Shapes
round (toad, frog)
oval (bird)
spherical (tortoise)

Sizes
small (insect)
large (ostrich)

Colors
clear, white,
tan, black,
blue, speckled

Kinds
bird; insect;
spider; toad;
frog; fish;
reptile: snake,
lizard, turtle,
alligator, crocodile

Locations
nests, trees, grass,
rock ledges,
sand, lakes, ponds,
oceans,
grocery stores

Uses
food for humans
(bird eggs),
food for animals,
preparation of
vaccines (bird eggs),
cosmetics (bird eggs)

Theme Goals

Through participating in the experiences provided by this theme, the children may learn:

1. Animals that produce eggs.
2. Colors of eggs.
3. Sizes of eggs.
4. Shapes of eggs.
5. Places to find eggs.
6. Uses of eggs.

Concepts for the Children to Learn

1. An egg is the first stage in the development of an animal.
2. Eggs are made by the female.
3. Many kinds of animals lay eggs (birds, fish, turtles, insects, spiders, snakes).
4. Birds are the only animals that sit on their eggs to keep them warm.
5. Eggs can be different colors.
6. Eggs range in size from tiny eggs, such as insects' eggs, to very large eggs, like that of an ostrich.
7. Birds lay only a few eggs at a time. Other animals may lay thousands of small eggs.
8. Bird eggs are generally oval in shape. Other animals have eggs that are different shapes.
9. Eggs can be found in a variety of places.
10. Some people eat chicken eggs.
11. Chicken eggs can be prepared to be eaten in many ways (boiled, scrambled, fried, poached).
12. Chicken eggs are sold in grocery stores by the dozen.
13. Chicken eggs are also used to prepare vaccines, animal feeds, fertilizers, and some cosmetics.

Vocabulary

1. **egg**—a roundish object covered with a shell or membrane that is laid by the female of birds, reptiles, fish, and amphibians.
2. **shell**—the outer covering of most eggs.
3. **incubate**—to sit on eggs in order to hatch them.
4. **incubator**—a machine-type box for keeping bird eggs at a certain temperature so that they will hatch.
5. **hatch**—to come out of an egg.

244

Bulletin Board

The purpose of this bulletin board is to promote correspondence skills. To prepare the bulletin board pieces, trace and cut the nests from yellow tagboard. Then trace and cut the eggs from white tagboard. Attach dots and print numerals on each nest as illustrated. The number of nests prepared and numerals utilized should be developmentally approximate for the group of children.

Parent Letter

Dear Parents,

We will be having an "egg-stra" special week as we make discoveries about eggs. We usually think of chicken eggs when we hear the word "egg"—but there are so many animals that lay different kinds of eggs. Your child will learn about many animals that lay eggs, places eggs can be found, and uses of eggs during our week focusing on the theme of eggs.

AT SCHOOL

A few of the week's highlights include:

- Going on an egg walk! Weather permitting, we plan on walking through the park to look for various types of eggs, looking underneath logs and leaves. Care to join us?
- Creating mosaic designs with eggshells. You can help us by saving and cleaning eggshells. Please bring them to school by Friday morning.
- Observing chicken eggs in an incubator. Mr. Johnson (Matt's Dad) will be bringing an incubator and five fertilized eggs for us to watch. Chicken eggs hatch in about 21 days. We'll keep you posted!

AT HOME

There are many ways to bring our egg unit into your home. Some ideas to try include:

- preparing a meal or snack with your child that uses eggs as an ingredient.
- comparing the sizes of small, medium, large, and extra large eggs while at a grocery store with your child.
- going to the library and checking out children's books about eggs. Some titles to look for:

    Hatch, Egg, Hatch! by Shen Roddie

    Chickens Aren't the Only Ones by Ruth Heller

    Egg: A Photographic Story of Hatching by Robert Burton

Have an "egg-cellent" week!

246

Music

1. "Here's a Little Birdie"
(Sing to the tune of "I Know a Little Pussy")

Here's a little birdie
Hatching from its shell.
First comes its beak,
Then comes its head.
He's working very, very hard,
His wings he gives a flap.
Then he lays down to rest and dry off,
Now what do you think of that?!
Peck, peck, peck, peck, peck, peck,
    peck, peck,
Peep!

2. "Egg Choices"
(Sing to the tune of "If You're Happy and You Know It")

If you like your eggs scrambled,
Clap your hands. (clap, clap)
If you like your eggs scrambled,
Clap your hands. (clap, clap)
If you like your eggs scrambled,
And it's your favorite way to make 'em,
If you like your eggs scrambled,
Clap your hands. (clap, clap)

Additional verses:

If you like your eggs fried,
Touch your toes . . .

If you like your eggs hard boiled,
Snap your fingers . . .

3. "Red Hen, Red Hen"
(Sing to the tune of "Baa, Baa, Black Sheep")

Red hen, red hen, have you eggs for me?
Yes, sir. Yes, sir. A lot as you can see.
One to hard boil.
Another one to fry.
One to scramble.
And Easter eggs to dye.
Red hen, red hen, have you eggs for me?
Yes, sir. Yes, sir. A lot as you can see.

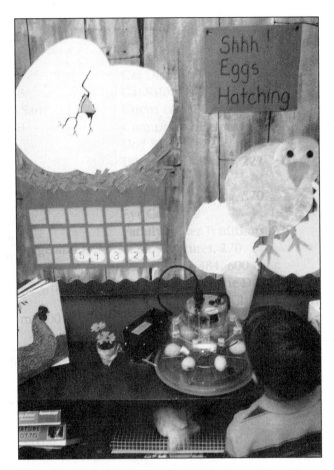

Observing eggs hatching is a science experience.

Fingerplays

EGGS IN A NEST

Here's an egg in a nest up in a tree.
    (make fist with right hand and place in
    palm of cupped left hand)
What's inside? What can it be?
    (shrug shoulders)
Peck, peck, peck,
Peep, peep, peep.
Out hatches a little bird,
    (wiggle fingers or fisted hand)
Cute as can be!

MY TURTLE

This is my turtle,
  (make fist and extend thumb)
He lives in a shell.
  (hide thumb in fist)
He likes his home very well.
He pokes his head out when he wants to
  eat
  (extend thumb)
And pulls it back in when he wants to
  sleep.
  (hide thumb in fist)

HATCHING CHICKENS

Five eggs and five eggs
  (hold up one hand and then the other)
Are underneath a hen.
Five eggs and five eggs
  (hold up all fingers)
And that makes ten.
The hen keeps the eggs warm for three long
  weeks
  (hold up three fingers)
Snap go the shells with tiny little beaks.
  (snap fingers)
Crack, crack, the shells go.
  (clap four times)
The chickens, every one,
Fluff out their feathers
In the warm spring sun.
  (make circle of arms)

Sensory

Add to the sensory table:

- grains, egg cartons, and plastic eggs.
- water, plastic fish, and strainers.
- water, plastic frogs/toads, and berry baskets.
- sand and plastic reptile and amphibian toys.

Math

1. **Balancing Eggs**

   Provide a balance scale and a hard-boiled egg. If appropriate, children can estimate how many of a specific object (crayons, cubes, blocks) they think will balance the egg. Then the children can count (and possibly record) the actual number it takes to balance the egg. The activity can be repeated with various objects. Results can be compared.

2. **Egg Sort**

   Create and cut various egg shapes out of construction paper or tagboard. Decorate pieces as desired. Laminate pieces for durability. Encourage children to sort the eggs by various attributes such as size, color, and patterns.

3. **Egg Carton Math**

   Using a permanent marker, randomly number the egg cups in an egg carton from 1 to 12 (or use fewer numerals or sets of dots, if appropriate). Put a button or bread tag in the carton and close the lid. Children shake the carton, open the lid, and identify the number the piece landed on.

Social Studies

Ukrainian Eggs

Ukrainian Easter eggs, known as pysanky, feature colorful, intricate designs. Some people are skilled in this Ukrainian art. If possible, a collection of Ukrainian eggs could be shown to the children. Ideally, the art could be demonstrated to the children. Contact your high school art department, library, or university for names of individuals who could share this art with the children.

Large Muscle

1. Egg Maze

Create a maze on the floor using classroom blocks. Older children may be able to help! Then, encourage children to roll and push a hard-boiled or plastic egg through the maze as quickly as possible. Tools such as brushes, small brooms, or spoons could be used to roll the egg.

2. Egg Relay

In this activity, a spoon is used to transport a hard-boiled egg from one location to another. The game can be played individually or children can be in teams, if appropriate.

Science

1. Eggshell Garden

Save and clean eggshell halves. Provide potting soil and seeds (such as radish, marigold). Have children fill each shell with soil and a few seeds. Add a spoonful of water to each shell. Place eggshell halves in the cups of an empty egg carton. Once the plants have grown, they can be transplanted into the ground or a larger container, after crushing the eggshells.

2. Will an Egg Float?

All fresh, raw chicken eggs sink in water. However, salt mixed or dissolved in water can make an egg float. Place a raw egg in a clear glass filled with water. If appropriate, older students can count and record how many individual teaspoons of salt are mixed in the water to make the egg float.

3. Vinegar and Eggs

Gently place a raw egg in a clear glass or jar filled with vinegar. Observe what happens to the egg over a period of three to four days. (After two days, the shell will soften and begin to disappear. After three days, most of the calcium will have dissolved, leaving only a bladder.)

4. Egg to Frog (or Toad)

Hatching frog or toad eggs is a great way to observe eggs. In the spring, search local ponds for jelly-like masses of eggs. They are usually found underwater among weeds or grasses near shore. Prepare a tank or glass jar for the eggs/tadpoles. Changes occur fast and children will be able to observe them. (If ponds are not locally accessible, check a biological supply house or with a high-school biology teacher.)

5. Hatching Chicken Eggs

Contact a chicken farmer or your high-school biology department to find out about borrowing an incubator and obtaining fertilized eggs. Follow the directions closely for setting up the incubator and maintaining its temperature and humidity. Stress to the children the importance of not disturbing the incubator. Keep a camera handy to record the hatching process.

Dramatic Play

1. Grocery Store

Ask parents to save empty, clean food containers (boxes, jars, plastic bottles, etc.) to be used as props and supplies for a grocery store. Include empty, clean egg cartons of various-sized eggs.

2. House

Provide empty, clean egg cartons, egg beaters, wire whips, bowls, small frying pans and turners as additional props to the housekeeping area.

3. Bird Store

Create a bird store in the dramatic play area. Display posters and pictures of birds. Provide clean bird cages, stuffed toy and craft birds, and plastic bird eggs. Check out bird books from the library and include in the area.

Arts and Crafts

1. Eggshell Mosaic

Save and clean eggshells. Children can color eggshells with markers or paint. Then, have children spread glue on a piece of cardboard, tagboard, or construction paper. Eggshells can be broken into smaller pieces and placed in the glue to create a design.

2. Egg Carton Caterpillar

Collect cardboard egg cartons, pipe cleaners, crayons, markers, and paint. Cut egg cartons in half lengthwise. Help children fold a pipe cleaner in half and poke it into the top of the first section of the egg carton to represent the antennas. Children can then use the other materials as desired to decorate their caterpillar.

3. Painting with Feathers

Provide construction paper, feathers (available at craft stores), and paint. Children can use the feathers to apply the paint to the paper.

4. Clay Eggs

Children can use clay or playdough to create various sizes and colors of eggs. Allow to dry if desired.

Field Trips/ Resource People

1. Farm

Plan a field trip to a farm where children can observe young chickens, turkeys, or ducks.

2. Zoo

Eggs of many reptiles, amphibians, and birds may be observed at some zoos.

3. 4-H Agent

Contact your local 4-H agent for information regarding area people involved in hatcheries. Invite one to talk to the children about eggs and incubators.

4. Grocery Store

While at the grocery store, observe the egg section.

Group Time (games, language)

1. Egg Habitats

Ask the children, "If you could go looking for an egg right now, where would you look?" Have children name places eggs can be found—nests, grass, water, sand, ponds, sea, trees. Record the children's responses on a large sheet of paper or tagboard. Display the sheet in the classroom.

2. Game: "Egg, egg, who's got the egg?"

For this game, a plastic, paper, or hard-boiled egg can be used. The children sit in a circle formation. One child is chosen to be the chicken or bird and sits in the center of the circle with the egg in front of him or her. The "chicken" closes his eyes. A child from the circle is silently chosen to sneak up and take the egg. All children then put their hands behind their backs and call, "Egg, egg, who's got the egg?" The "chicken" then has three chances to guess who is holding the egg.

Cooking

1. Noodle Nests

12 ounces butterscotch chips
3 cups chow-mein noodles
1 1/4 cup roasted peanuts
optional: jelly beans

Melt butterscotch chips in microwave or saucepan over low heat. Stir in noodles and

250

peanuts. Drop by teaspoonfuls onto waxed paper. Immediately top with jelly beans if desired. Let stand until firm. Makes about 36 pieces.

2. Egg Foo Young

6 eggs
1/4 cup instant minced onion
2 tablespoons chopped green pepper
1/2 teaspoon salt
dash of pepper
16-ounce can bean sprouts, drained

Sauce:
1 tablespoon cornstarch
2 teaspoons sugar
1 cube chicken bouillon
dash of ginger
1 cup water
2 tablespoons soy sauce

Heat oven to 300 degrees. In large bowl, beat eggs well. Add remaining ingredients, except sauce ingredients. Mix well. Heat 2 tablespoons oil in large skillet. Drop egg mixture by tablespoonfuls into skillet. Fry until golden. Turn and brown other side. Drain on paper towel. If necessary, add additional oil to skillet and cook remaining egg mixture. Keep warm in 300-degree oven while preparing sauce. Combine first 4 ingredients in small saucepan. Add water and soy sauce. Cook until mixture boils and thickens, stirring constantly.

3. Southwestern Eggs

1 pound bulk chorizo or pork sausage
1/2 cup chopped onion
1 1/4 cups salsa
4 eggs
3/4 cup shredded mozzarella cheese

Cook sausage and onion in 10-inch skillet until sausage is brown; drain. Stir in salsa and heat. Spread mixture evenly in skillet. Make 4 indentations in mixture with back of spoon. Break 1 egg into each indentation. Cover and cook over low heat about 12 minutes or until whites are set and yolks have thickened. Sprinkle with cheese. Serve with sour cream if desired.

4. Painted Egg Cookies

1/3 cup butter or margarine
1/4 cup sugar
1 egg
2/3 cup honey
3/4 teaspoon vanilla
2 3/4 cups flour
1 teaspoon baking soda
1/2 teaspoon salt

"Paint":
1 egg yolk
1/4 teaspoon water
food coloring

In a large mixing bowl, beat butter and sugar until fluffy. Add egg, honey, and vanilla. Beat well. Combine flour, baking soda, and salt. Gradually add flour mixture to butter mixture. Beat well. Cover and chill 1 hour.

Set oven to 350 degrees. Grease cookie sheets if necessary. Divide dough in half, keeping one half chilled. Roll dough on a lightly floured surface to a 1/4-inch thickness. Cut with egg-shaped (oval) cookie cutter. Place 1 inch apart on cookie sheets. Repeat with remaining dough.

Beat egg yolk and water in a small mixing bowl. Divide yolk mixture between 3 or 4 small bowls. Add 2 to 3 drops of different food colors to each bowl and mix well. With a clean small paint brush or cotton swab, paint cookies as desired. Bake 6 to 8 minutes or until golden.

Books

The following books can be used to complement this theme:

Burton, Robert. (1994). *Egg: A Photographic Story of Hatching*. Photos by Kim Taylor. New York: Dorling Kindersley.

Butrum, Ray. (1998). *I'm Sorry You Can't Hatch an Egg*. Sisters, OR: Multnomah Press.

De Bourgoing, Pascale. (1992). *The Egg*. Illus. by RenGe Mettle. New York: Scholastic.

Ernst, Lisa Campbell. (1992). *Zinnia and Dot*. New York: Viking.

Fowler, Allan. (1993). *The Chicken or the Egg!* Chicago: Children's Press.

Heller, Ruth. (1981). *Chickens Aren't the Only Ones*. New York: G. P. Putnam.

Humphrey, Paul. (1996). *Frog's Eggs*. Austin, TX: Raintree/Steck Vaughn. (Pbk)

Jenkins, Priscilla Belz. (1995). *A Nest Full of Eggs*. Illus. by Lizzy Rockwell. New York: HarperCollins.

Johnson, Sylvia A. (1992). *Inside an Egg*. Photos by Kiyoshi Shimizu. Minneapolis: Lerner Publishing. (Pbk)

Joyce, William. (1992). *Bently and Egg*. New York: HarperCollins.

Lionni, Leo. (1994). *An Extraordinary Egg*. New York: Knopf.

Polacco, Patricia. (1988). *Rechenka's Eggs*. New York: G. P. Putnam.

Reasoner, Charles. (1994). *Who's Hatching?* (A Sliding Surprise Book) New York: Price Stern Sloan.

Ruurs, Margriet. (1997). *Emma's Eggs*. Illus. by Barbara Spurll. New York: Stoddart Kids.

Seuss, Dr. (1992). *Scrambled Eggs Super!* New York: Random House.

Multimedia

The following multimedia products can be used to complement this theme:

Kids Get Cooking: The Egg [video]. (1987). Newton, MA: Kidviz.

Palmer, Hap. "Humpty Dumpty" on *Hap Palmer Sings Classic Nursery Rhymes* [cassette]. (1991). Freeport, NY: Educational Activities.

Polacco, Patricia. *Rechenka's Eggs* [video]. (1992). Lincoln, NE: GNP.

Recording and Song Title

The following recording can be used to complement this theme:

Rock 'n' Roll Songs That Teach (The Learning Station)—"Green Eggs and Ham"

THEME 2d

Fall

Changes
leaves turn color
temperature cooler
darker earlier

Clothing
sweaters
scarves
long-sleeved shirts
long pants
blankets

Holidays
Labor Day
Halloween
Thanksgiving

Activities
football
raking leaves
walks
bike rides
harvesting foods
camping
soccer

Theme Goals

Through participating in the experiences provided by this theme, the children may learn:

1. Characteristics of fall weather.
2. Fall holidays.
3. Fall clothing.
4. Fall activities.

Concepts for the Children to Learn

1. Fall is one of the four seasons.
2. Fall is the season between summer and winter.
3. Some trees change color in the fall.
4. In some places the weather becomes cooler in the fall.
5. The day becomes shorter in the fall.
6. Leaves fall from some trees in the fall.
7. Labor Day, Halloween, and Thanksgiving are some fall holidays.
8. Scarfs and sweaters may need to be worn in the fall in some areas.
9. Pumpkins and apples can be harvested in the fall.
10. Football is a fall sport.
11. Blankets are usually needed on our beds in the fall in some places.

Vocabulary

1. **fall**—the season between summer and winter.
2. **Halloween**—the holiday when people wear costumes and go trick or treating.
3. **Thanksgiving**—a holiday to express thanks.
4. **Labor Day**—a holiday to honor working people.
5. **season**—a time of the year.

Bulletin Board

The purpose of this bulletin board is to foster a positive self-concept as well as develop skills of name recognition. Construct an acorn for each child. Print the children's names on the acorns. See illustration. Laminate and punch holes in the acorns. Children can hang their acorns on a pushpin on the bulletin board when they arrive.

Parent Letter

Dear Parents,

Where we live, the days are getting shorter, the temperature is getting colder, and the leaves are changing color. It's the perfect time to introduce our next unit—fall. By participating in the experiences provided throughout this unit, children will become more aware of changes that take place in the fall and common fall activities.

AT SCHOOL

A few of this week's learning experiences include:

- recording the temperature and the changing colors of the leaves.
- making leaf rubbings in the art area.
- raking leaves on our playground during outdoor time.

We will also be taking a fall walk around the neighborhood to observe the trees in their peak changes. We will be leaving Thursday at 10:00 a.m. Please feel free to join us. It will be a scenic tour.

AT HOME

To develop classification skills help your child sort leaves by their color, type, or size.

Fingerplays promote language and vocabulary skills. This fingerplay is one we will be learning this week. Enjoy it with your child at home!

Autumn

Autumn winds begin to blow.
  (blow)
Colored leaves fall fast and slow.
  (make fast and slow motions with hands)
Twirling, whirling all around,
  (turn around)
'Til at last, they touch the ground.
  (fall to the ground)

Enjoy your child as you explore experiences related to the unit on fall.

256

Leaves turn different colors during the fall.

Music

1. **"Little Leaves"**
   (Sing to the tune of "Ten Little Indians")

   One little, two little, three little leaves.
   Four little, five little, six little leaves.
   Seven little, eight little, nine little leaves.
   Ten little leaves fall down.

2. **"Happy Children Tune"**
   (Sing to the tune of "Did You Ever See a Lassie?")

   Happy children in the autumn,
   In the autumn, in the autumn.
   Happy children in the autumn
   Do this way and that.

   While singing the song, children can keep time by pretending to rake leaves, jump in the leaves, etc.

3. **"Pretty Leaves Are Falling Down"**
   (Sing to the tune of "London Bridges")

   Pretty leaves are falling down, falling down, falling down.
   Pretty leaves are falling down, all around the town.
      (wiggle fingers)

Let's rake them up in a pile, in a pile, in a pile.
Let's rake them up in a pile, all around the town.
   (make raking motions)

Let's all jump in and have some fun, have some fun, have some fun.
Let's all jump in and have some fun, all around the town.
   (jump into circle)

Fingerplays

AUTUMN

Autumn winds begin to blow.
   (blow)
Colored leaves fall fast and slow.
   (make fast and slow falling motions with hands)
Twirling, whirling all around
   (turn around)
'Til at last, they touch the ground.
   (fall to the ground)

LEAVES

Little leaves fall gently down
Red and yellow, orange and brown.
  (flutter hands as leaves falling)
Whirling, whirling around and around.
  (turn around)
Quietly without a sound.
  (put finger to lips)
Falling softly to the ground
  (begin to fall slowly)
Down and down and down and down.
  (lie on floor)

LITTLE LEAVES

The little leaves are falling down
  (use hands to make falling motion)
Round and round, round and round.
  (turn around)
The little leaves are falling down,
  (use hands to make falling motion)
Falling to the ground.
  (fall to ground)

TWIRLING LEAVES

The autumn wind blows—Oooo Oooo
  Oooo.
  (make wind sounds)
The leaves shake and shake then fly into
  the sky so blue.
  (children shake)
They whirl and whirl around them, twirl
  and twirl around.
  (turn around in circles)
But when the wind stops, the leaves sink
  slowly to the ground.
Lower, lower, lower, and land quietly without a sound.
  (sink very slowly and very quietly)

Science

1. Leaf Observation

Collect leaves from a variety of trees. Place them and a magnifying glass on the science table for the children to explore.

2. Temperature Watch

Place a thermometer outside. A large cardboard thermometer can also be constructed out of tagboard with movable elastic or ribbon for the mercury. The children can match the temperature on the cardboard thermometer with the outdoor one.

3. Weather Calendar

Construct a calendar for the month. Record the changes of weather each day by attaching a symbol to the calendar. Symbols should include clouds, sun, snow, rain, etc.

4. Color Change Sequence

Laminate or cover with contact paper, several leaves of different colors. The children can sort, count, and classify the leaves.

Dramatic Play

1. Fall Wear

Set out warm clothes such as sweaters, coats, hats, and blankets to indicate cold weather coming on. The children can use the clothes for dressing up.

2. Football

Collect football gear including balls, helmets, and jerseys and play on the outdoor playground.

Arts and Crafts

1. Fall Collage

After taking a walk to collect objects such as grass, twigs, leaves, nuts, and weeds, collages can be made in the art area.

2. Leaf Rubbings

Collect leaves, paper, and crayons and show the children how to place several leaves under a sheet of paper. Using the flat edge of crayon color rub over paper. The image of the leaves will appear.

Nature Recipes

Cattails

Use them in their natural color or tint by shaking metallic powder over them. Handle carefully. The cattail is dry and feels crumbly. It will fall apart easily.

Crystal Garden*

Place broken pieces of brick or terra cotta clay in a glass bowl or jar. Pour the following solution over this:

4 teaspoons water
1 teaspoon ammonia
4 teaspoons bluing
1 teaspoon Mercurochrome
4 teaspoons salt

Add more of this solution each day until the crystal garden has grown to the desired size. (Adult supervision required.)

* This activity should be carefully observed if in a classroom with preschool children.

Drying Plants for Winter Bouquets

Strip the leaves from the flowers immediately. Tie the flowers by their stems with string and hang them with the heads down in a cool dry place away from the light. Darkness is essential for preserving their color. Thorough drying takes about 2 weeks.

Preserving Fall Leaves

Place alternate layers of powdered borax and leaves in a box. The leaves must be completely covered. Allow them to stand for four days. Shake off the borax and wipe each with liquid floor wax. Rub a warm iron over a cake of paraffin, then press the iron over front and back of leaves.

Preserving Magnolia Leaves

Mix two parts of water with one part of glycerine. Place stems of the magnolia leaves in the mixture and let them stand for several days. The leaves will turn brown and last several years. Their surface may be painted or sprayed with silver or gold paint.

Pressing Wild Flowers

When gathering specimens, include the roots, leaves, flowers and seed pods. Place between newspapers, laying two layers of blotters underneath the newspaper and two on top to absorb the moisture. Change the newspapers three times during the week. Place between two sheets of corrugated cardboard and press. It usually takes seven to ten days to press specimens. Cardboard covered with cotton batting is the mounting base. Lay the flower on the cotton and cover with cellophane or plastic wrap to preserve the color.

Treating Gourds

Soak gourds for two hours in water. Scrape them clean with a knife. Rub with fine sandpaper. While still damp cut an opening to remove seeds.

---

3. **Pumpkin Seed Collage**

Wash and dry pumpkin seeds and place them in the art area with glue and paper. The children can make pumpkin seed collages.

4. **Leaf Spatter Painting**

Use a lid from a box that is approximately 9 inches × 12 inches × 12 inches. Cut a rectangle from top of lid leaving a 1 1/2-inch border. Invert the lid and place a wire screen over the opening. Tape the screen to the border. Arrange the leaves on a sheet of paper. Place the lid over the arrangement. Dip a toothbrush into thin tempera paint and brush across screen. When the tempera paint dries, remove the leaves.

Sensory

Leaves

Place a variety of leaves in the sensory table. Try to include moist and dry examples for the children to compare.

Large Muscle

Raking Leaves

Child-sized rakes can be provided. The children can be encouraged to rake leaves into piles.

Field Trips

1. **Neighborhood Walk**

   Take a walk around the neighborhood when the leaves are at their peak of changing colors. Discuss differences in color and size.

2. **Apple Orchard**

   Visit an apple orchard. Observe the apples being picked and processed. If possible let children pick their own apples from a tree.

3. **Pumpkin Patch**

   Visit a pumpkin patch. Discuss and observe how pumpkins grow, their size, shape, and color. Let the children pick a pumpkin to bring back to the classroom.

Math

1. **Weighing Acorns and Pine Cones**

   A scale, acorns, and pine cones for the children to weigh can be added to the science table.

2. **Leaf Math**

   Out of construction paper or tagboard, prepare pairs of various-shaped leaves. The children can match the identical leaves.

Social Studies

Bulletin Board

Construct a bulletin board using bare branches to represent a tree. Cut out leaves from colored construction paper and print one child's name on each. At the beginning of the day, children can hang their name on the tree when they arrive.

Cooking

1. **Apple Banana Frosty**

   1 golden delicious apple, diced
   1 peeled sliced banana
   1/4 cup milk
   3 ice cubes

   Blend all the ingredients in a blender. Serves 4 children.

2. **Apple Salad**

   6 medium apples
   1/2 cup raisins
   1/2 teaspoon cinnamon
   1/2 cup chopped nuts
   1/4 cup white grape juice

   Peel and chop the apples. Mix well and add the remaining ingredients. Serves 10 children.

Books

The following books can be used to complement this theme:

Arnosky, Jim. (1993). *Every Autumn Comes the Bear.* New York: G. P. Putnam.

Bunting, Eve. (1997). *The Pumpkin Fair.* Illus. by Eileen Christelow. New York: Clarion Books.

Ehlert, Lois. (1991). *Red Leaf, Yellow Leaf.* Orlando: Harcourt Brace.

Fowler, Allan. (1992). *How Do You Know It's Fall?* Chicago: Children's Press.

Fowler, Allan. (1993). *It Could Still Be a Leaf.* Chicago: Children's Press.

George, Lindsay Barrett. (1995). *In the Woods: Who's Been Here?* New York: Greenwillow.

Hall, Zoe. (1994). *It's Pumpkin Time!* Illus. by Shari Halpern. New York: Scholastic.

Hoban, Lillian. (1996). *Arthur's Back to School Day.* New York: HarperCollins.

Hunter, Anne. (1996). *Possum's Harvest Moon.* Boston: Houghton Mifflin.

Hutchings, Amy. (1994). *Picking Apples and Pumpkins.* Illus. by Richard Hutchings. St. Paul, MN: Cartwheel Books. (Pbk)

Lotz, Karen E. (1993). *Snowsong Whistling.* Illus. by Elisa Kleven. New York: Dutton.

Maass, Robert. (1992). *When Autumn Comes.* Owlet. (Pbk)

Maestro, Betsy C. (1994). *Why Do Leaves Change Color?* Illus. by Loretta Krupinski. New York: HarperCollins.

Moore, Elaine. (1995). *Grandma's Smile.* Illus. by Dan Andreasen. New York: Lothrop, Lee & Shepard.

Robbins, Ken. (1998). *Fall Leaves.* New York: Scholastic.

Rockwell, Anne F. (1989). *Apples and Pumpkins.* Illus. by Lizzy Rockwell. New York: Simon & Schuster.

Russo, Marisabina. (1994). *I Don't Want to Go Back to School.* New York: Greenwillow.

Saunders-Smith, Gail. (1997). *Autumn Leaves.* Mankato, MN: Pebble Books.

Schweninger, Ann (1993). *Autumn Days.* New York: Puffin. (Pbk)

Simon, Seymour. (1993). *Autumn Across America.* New York: Hyperion.

White, Linda. (1996). *Too Many Pumpkins.* Illus. by Megan Lloyd. New York: Holiday House.

Zagwyn, Deborah Turney. (1997). *The Pumpkin Blanket.* Berkeley, CA: Tricycle Press.

Multimedia

The following multimedia products can be used to complement this theme:

Bingham, Bing. "The First Day of School" on *A Rainbow of Songs* [cassette]. Available from Kimbo Educational.

James, Dixie and Linda Becht. *The Singing Calendar* [cassette]. Kimbo Educational.

Maestro, Betsy C. *Why Do Leaves Change Color?* Illus. by Loretta Krupinski. [Book and cassette]. (1996). Harper Audio.

What Is a Leaf? [video]. (1991). Washington, D.C.: National Geographic.

White, Linda. *Too Many Pumpkins* [video]. (1997). Live Oak Productions.

Recording and Song Title

The following recording can be used to complement this theme:

Piggyback Songs—"Autumn," "Season Song," "Leaves"

T H E M E 27

Activities

celebrations
eating
reading
playing
working
reunions
vacationing

Types

single parents
two parents
blended
extended

Families

Members

stepparents,
mothers, fathers,
sisters, brothers,
grandmothers,
grandfathers,
aunts, uncles,
nephews, nieces,
cousins,
adopted members,
deceased members

Theme Goals

Through participating in the experiences provided by this theme, the children may learn:

1. The members in a family.

2. Roles of family members.

3. Family activities.

Concepts for the Children to Learn

1. A family is a group of people who live together.

2. Mothers, fathers, sisters, and brothers are family members.

3. Grandmothers, grandfathers, aunts, uncles, cousins, nephews, and nieces are family members.

4. Camping, eating, working, reading, and watching television are all family activities.

5. Each family is a special group of people.

6. Families teach us about our world.

7. Family members care for us.

8. There are many types of families: one-parent, two-parent, blended, and extended.

Vocabulary

1. **mother**—female parent.

2. **father**—male parent.

3. **children**—young people.

4. **sister**—a girl having the same parents as another person.

5. **brother**—a boy having the same parents as another person.

6. **grandmother**—mother of a parent.

7. **grandfather**—father of a parent.

8. **cousin**—son or daughter of an uncle or aunt.

9. **aunt**—sister of a parent.

10. **uncle**—brother of a parent.

11. **nephew**—son of a brother or sister.

12. **niece**—daughter of a brother or sister.

13. **love**—feeling of warmth toward another.

14. **family**—people living together.

15. **one-parent family**—a child or children who lives with only one parent, a father or mother.

16. **blended**—people from two or more families living together.

17. **extended**—includes aunts, uncles, grandparents, and cousins.

Bulletin Board

The purpose of this bulletin board is to foster an awareness of various family sizes, as well as to identify family members. Construct a name card for each child from tagboard. Print each child's name on one of the tagboard pieces. Then cut people figures as illustrated. Laminate the name cards and people. Staple the name cards to a bulletin board as illustrated. Individually, the children can affix the people in their family after their name using tape, sticky putty, or a stapler.

Parent Letter

Dear Parents,

Our next unit will focus on families. Through this unit, the children will develop an understanding of various family patterns. They will also discover what family members do for each other, as well as activities that families can participate in together.

AT SCHOOL

A few of this unit's highlights include:

- creating pictures of our families on a bulletin board.
- looking at photographs of classmates' families. To assist us with this unit, please send a picture of your family to school with your child. We will place the photograph in a special photo album to look at in the reading area.

AT HOME

There are several activities you can do at home to foster the concepts of this unit. Begin by looking through family photographs with your child. While doing this discuss family traditions or customs. You can also encourage your child to dictate a letter to you to write to a grandparent or other relative. Plan and participate in a family activity. This could be as simple as taking a walk together or going on a picnic.

We invite you and your family to visit us. This includes moms, dads, brothers, sisters, grandparents, and other relatives! If you are interested in coming, please let me know!

From all of us,

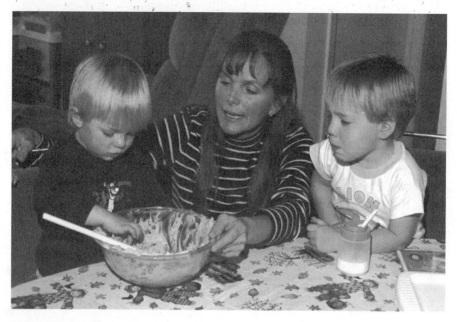

Families are an important part of life.

Music

"Family Helper"
(Sing to the tune of "Here We Are Together")

It's fun to be a helper, a helper, a helper.
It's fun to be a helper, just any time.
Oh, I can set the table, the table, the table.
Oh, I can set the table at dinner time.
Oh, I can dry the dishes, the dishes, the dishes.
Oh, I can dry the dishes, and make them shine.

Fingerplays

MY FAMILY

If you peek in my room at night,
 (stand on toes as if peeking)
My family you will see,
 (nod head)
They kiss my face and tuck me in tight,
 (kiss into the air)
Why? Because they love me!
 (hug yourself)

SEE MY FAMILY

See my family? See them all?
 (hold up all five fingers)
Some are short
 (hold up thumb)
Some are tall
 (hold up middle finger)

Let's shake hands. "How do you do?"
 (grasp hands and shake)
See them bow? "How are you?"
 (bend fingers)

Father,
 (hold up middle finger)
Mother,
 (hold up pointer finger)
Sister,
 (hold up ring finger)
Brother,
 (hold up thumb)
And me.
 (hold up pinky finger)

THIS IS THE MOTHER

This is the mother, kind and dear.
  (make a fist, then point to the thumb)
This is the father sitting near.
  (show each finger in turn)
This is the brother, strong and tall.
This is the sister, who plays with her ball.
This is the baby, the littlest of all.
See my whole family large and small?
  (wiggle all fingers)

I LOVE MY FAMILY

Some families are large.
  (spread arms out wide)
Some families are small.
  (bring arms close together)
But I love my family
  (cross arms over chest)
Best of all!

A GOOD HOUSE

This is the roof of the house so good.
  (make roof with hands)
These are the walls that are made of wood.
  (hands straight, palms parallel)
These are the windows that let in the light.
  (thumbs and forefingers form window)
This is the door that shuts so tight.
  (hands straight by side)
This is the chimney so straight and tall.
  (arms up straight)
Oh! What a good house for one and all!

All fingerplays taken from Cromwell, Faitel & Hibner. (1983). *Finger Frolics: Fingerplays for Young Children*. Michigan: Partner Press.

Science

1. Sounds

Tape different sounds from around the house that families hear daily, such as a crying baby, brushing teeth, telephone ringing, toilet flushing, doorbell ringing, water running, electric shaver, alarm clock, etc. Play the tape for the children to identify the correct sound.

2. Feely Box

Place objects pertaining to a family into a box. Include items such as a baby rattle, a toothbrush, a comb, baby bottle, etc. The children feel the objects and try to identify them.

3. Animal Families

Gerbils or hamsters with young babies in a cage can be placed on the science table. Observe daily to see how they raise their babies. Compare the animal behavior to the children's own families.

Dramatic Play

1. Baby Clothing

Arrange the dramatic play area for washing baby dolls. Include a tub with soapy water, washcloths, drying towels, play clothes, brush, and comb.

2. Family Picnic

Collect items to make a picnic basket. Include paper napkins, cups, plates, plastic eating utensils, etc.

3. Dollhouse

Set up a large dollhouse for children to play with. These can be constructed from cardboard. Include dolls to represent several members of a family.

Arts and Crafts

1. Family Collage

The children can cut out pictures of people from magazines. The pictures can be pasted on a sheet of paper to make a collage.

2. My Body

Trace each child's body on a large piece of paper. The children can use crayons and felt-tip markers to color their own body picture. When finished, display the pictures around the room or in the center's entrance.

Sensory

1. Washing baby dolls in lukewarm, soapy water
2. Washing dishes in warm water
3. Washing doll clothes and hanging them up to dry
4. Cars and houses placed on top of several inches of sand

Large Muscle

Neighborhood Walk

Take a walk through a neighborhood and have children identify different homes. Observe the colors and sizes of the homes.

Resource People

Family Day

Invite moms, dads, sisters, brothers, grandfathers, grandmothers, and other family members to a tea at your center.

Math

1. **Families—Biggest to Smallest**

   Cut out from magazines several members of a family. The children can place the members from largest to smallest, and then smallest to largest. They can also identify each family member as the biggest and the smallest.

2. **Family Member Chart**

   Graph the number of family members for each child's family in the classroom.

Social Studies

Family Pictures

1. Display posters of all types of families. Discuss at group time ways that families help and care for each other.
2. Ask each child to bring in a family picture. Label each child's picture and place on a special bulletin board with the caption, "Our Families."
3. Discuss the Muslim celebration of Ramadan. Each year Muslims around the world observe the religious period of Ramadan by refraining from food, water, television, and other activities from sunrise to sunset. The fasting lasts for 28 days. Fasting teaches patience, discipline, and humility. Families and friends gather before sunrise (*Suhour*) and after sunset for meals. When it is time to break the fast (*Iftar*), the first thing one should eat is dates. Children learn that the Prophet Mohammed broke his fast on dates. Families then mostly have soup, because it is easy on the stomach and also helps rehydrate the thirsty.

Group Time
(games, language)

A Hundred Ways to Get There

During outdoor or group play, form a large circle. Begin the game by choosing a child to cross the circle by skipping, hopping, jumping, crawling, running, etc. Once the circle has been crossed the child takes the place of another person who then goes across the circle in another manner. Each child can try to think of something new.

Cooking

1. **Peanut Butter and Jelly**

   Cut whole wheat bread into house shapes for snack one day. Put peanut butter, raisins, and jelly on the table with knives. Let children choose their own topping.

2. Gingerbread Families

Use the following recipe to create gingerbread families.

1 1/2 cups whole wheat pastry flour
1 teaspoon baking soda
1/2 teaspoon salt
1/2 teaspoon ginger
1 teaspoon cinnamon
1/4 cup oil
1/4 cup maple syrup
1/4 cup honey
1 large egg

Preheat oven to 350 degrees. Measure all of the dry ingredients into a bowl and mix well. Measure all wet ingredients into a second bowl and mix well. Add the two mixtures together. Pour the combined mixture into an 8-inch square pan and bake for 30 to 35 minutes. When cool, roll the gingerbread dough into thin slices and provide cookie cutters for children to cut their family. Decorate the figures with raisins, peanut butter, wheat germ, etc. Enjoy for snack time.

3. Raisin Bran Muffins

4 cups raisin bran cereal
2 1/2 cups all-purpose flour
1 cup sugar
1/2 cup chopped walnuts
2 1/2 teaspoons baking soda
1 teaspoon salt
2 eggs, beaten
2 cups buttermilk
1/2 cup cooking oil

Stir the cereal, flour, sugar, nuts, baking soda, and salt together in a large mixing bowl. In a separate bowl beat the eggs, buttermilk, and oil together. Add this mixture to the dry ingredients and stir until moistened. The batter will be thick. Spoon the batter into greased or lined muffin cups, filling 3/4 full. Bake in a 375-degree oven for 20 to 25 minutes and remove from pans.

4. Kabbat Hamudth

(Meatball soup served during Ramadan, a Muslim celebration)

For the meatballs:

1 pound choice ground beef
14-oz. box cream of rice
1/2 teaspoon salt

Combine ingredients and mix well. Add a little water if necessary. Puree in small batches. Divide mixture into 30 balls. Cover and chill.

For the stuffing:

1 medium onion, chopped
1/2 pound choice ground beef
1 cup drained chickpeas, cut in half
1/4 cup chopped fresh parsley
1 scant teaspoon ground allspice

Brown onions and beef in a 10-inch skillet. Drain fat and add remaining stuffing ingredients. Set aside.

To form meatballs flatten each ball with your fingertips. Place 2–3 teaspoons of the stuffing in the center and reform beef into a ball around the stuffing. Cover and chill.

For the soup:

2–3 medium onions, quartered
1 pound turnips, chopped
2 tablespoons olive oil
16 cups beef broth
1 pound Swiss chard, coarsely chopped
1 cup drained canned chickpeas
1 teaspoon ground allspice (optional)
Salt and pepper to taste
3–4 tablespoons finely chopped fresh mint
    leaves or 2 teaspoons dried
1/2 cup lemon juice

Sauté onions and turnips in olive oil until onions are translucent. Bring broth to boil, lower heat, add onions, turnips, Swiss chard, and chickpeas. Season with allspice, salt, and pepper. Simmer until turnips are soft. Add mint and lemon juice. About 20 minutes before serving add meatballs.

Serve in bowls with 2–3 meatballs per serving. Caution must be taken regarding the temperature of the soup.

Snack Ideas

MILK

1. Dips (yogurt, cottage cheese, cream cheese)
2. Cheese (balls, wedges, cut-outs, squares, faces, etc.)
3. Yogurt and fruit
4. Milk punches made with fruits and juices
5. Conventional cocoa
6. Cottage cheese (add pineapple, peaches, etc.)
7. Cheese fondues (pre-heated, no open flames in classroom)
8. Shakes (mix fruit and milk in a blender)

MEAT

1. Meat strips, chunks, cubes (beef, pork, chicken, turkey, ham, fish)
2. Meatballs, small kabobs
3. Meat roll-ups (cheese spread, mashed potatoes, spinach, lettuce leaves, or tortillas)
4. Meat salads (tuna, other fish, chicken, turkey, etc.) as spreads for crackers, stuffing for celery, rolled in spinach or lettuce
5. Sardines
6. Stuffing for potatoes, tomatoes, squash

EGGS

1. Hard boiled
2. Deviled (use different flavors)
3. Egg salad spread
4. Eggs any style that can be managed
5. Egg as a part of other recipes
6. Eggnog

FRUITS

1. Use standard fruits, but be adventurous: pomegranates, cranberries, pears, peaches, apricots, plums, berries, pineapples, melons, grapes, grapefruit, tangerines
2. Kabobs and salads
3. Juices and juice blends
4. In muffins, yogurt, milk beverages
5. Fruit "sandwiches"
6. Stuffed dates, prunes, etc.
7. Dried fruits (raisins, currants, prunes, apples, peaches, apricots, dates, figs)

VEGETABLES

1. Variety—sweet and white potatoes, cherry tomatoes, broccoli, cauliflower, radishes, peppers, mushrooms, zucchini, all squashes, rutabaga, avocados, eggplant, okra, pea pods, turnips, pumpkin, sprouts, spinach
2. Almost any vegetable can be served raw with or without dip
3. Salads, kabobs, cutouts
4. Juices and juice blends
5. Soup in a cup (hot or cold)
6. Stuffed—celery, cucumbers, zucchini, spinach, lettuce, cabbage, squash, potatoes, tomatoes
7. Vegetable spreads
8. Sandwiches

DRIED PEAS AND BEANS

1. Peanuts, kidney beans, garbanzos, limas, lentils, yellow and green peas, pintos, black beans
2. Beans and peas mashed as dips or spreads
3. Bean, pea, or lentil soup in a cup
4. Roasted soybean-peanut mix
5. Three-bean salad

PASTAS

1. Different shapes and thicknesses
2. Pasta with butter and poppy seeds
3. Cold pasta salad
4. Lasagne noodles (cut for small sandwiches)
5. Chow mein noodles (wheat or rice)

BREADS

1. Use a variety of grains—whole wheat, cracked wheat, rye, cornmeal, oatmeal, bran, grits, etc.
2. Use a variety of breads—tortillas, pocket breads, crepes, pancakes, muffins, biscuits, bagels, popovers, English muffins
3. Toast—plain, buttered, with spreads, cinnamon
4. Homemade yeast and quick breads

5. Fill and roll up crepes, pancakes
6. Waffle sandwiches

CEREALS, GRAINS, SEEDS

1. Granola
2. Slices of rice loaf or rice cakes
3. Dry cereal mixes (not pre-sweetened)
4. Seed mixes (pumpkin, sunflower, sesame, poppy, caraway, etc.)
5. Roasted wheat berries, wheat germ, bran as roll-ins, toppings, or as finger mix
6. Popcorn with toppings of grated cheese, flavored butters, mixed nuts
7. Stir into muffins or use as a topping

Books

The following books can be used to complement this theme:

Buckley, Helen E. (1994). *Grandfather and I*. Illus. by Jan Ormerod. New York: Lothrop, Lee & Shepard.

Buckley, Helen E. (1994). *Grandmother and I*. Illus. by Jan Ormerod. New York: Lothrop, Lee & Shepard.

De Paola, Tomie. (1996). *The Baby Sister*. New York: G. P. Putnam.

Flournoy, Valerie. (1995). *Tanya's Reunion*. Illus. by Jerry Pinkney. New York: Dial Books.

Hausherr, Rosemarie. (1997). *Celebrating Families*. New York: Scholastic.

Johnson, Angela. (1991). *One of Three*. Illus. by David Soman. New York: Orchard Books.

Johnson, Angela. (1990). *When I Am Old with You*. Illus. by David Soman. New York: Orchard Books.

Jones, Rebecca C. (1995). *Great Aunt Martha*. Illus. by Shelley Jackson. New York: Dutton.

Knight, Margy Burns. (1994). *Welcoming Babies*. Illus. by Anne Sibley O'Brien. Gardner, ME: Tilbury House.

Kroll, Virginia L. (1994). *Beginnings: How Families Came to Be*. Illus. by Stacey Schuett. Niles, IL: Albert Whitman & Co.

Kuklin, Susan. (1992). *How My Family Lives in America*. Minneapolis: Bradbury Press.

Lakin, Patricia. (1994). *Dad and Me in the Morning*. Illus. by Robert G. Steele. Niles, IL: Albert Whitman & Co.

Leedy, Loreen. (1995). *Who's Who in My Family*. New York: Holiday House.

Maynard, Christopher. (1997). *Why Are All Families Different? Questions Children Ask About Families*. New York: Dorling Kindersley.

Morris, Ann. (1995). *The Daddy Book*. Photos by Ken Heyman. Parsippany, NJ: Silver Press.

Morris, Ann. (1995). *The Mommy Book*. Photos by Ken Heyman. Parsippany, NJ: Silver Press.

Pellegrini, Nina. (1991). *Families Are Different*. New York: Holiday House.

Rosenberg, Maxine B. (1991). *Brothers and Sisters*. Photos by George Ancona. New York: Clarion Books.

Rotner, Shelley and Sheila M. Kelly. (1997). *Lots of Dads*. New York: Dial Books.

Rotner, Shelley and Sheila M. Kelly. (1996). *Lots of Moms*. New York: Dial Books.

Russo, Marisabina. (1998). *When Mama Gets Home*. New York: Greenwillow.

Schindel, John. (1995). *Dear Daddy*. Illus. by Dorothy Dononue. Niles, IL: Albert Whitman & Co.

Schwartz, Amy. (1994). *A Teeny Tiny Baby.* New York: Orchard Books.

Stevenson, Harvey. (1994). *Grandpa's House.* New York: Hyperion.

Vigna, Judith. (1997). *I Live with Daddy.* Niles, IL: Albert Whitman & Co.

Wild, Margaret. (1994). *Our Granny.* Illus. by Julie Vivas. New York: Ticknor & Fields.

Williams, Vera B. (1990). *More More More Said the Baby.* New York: Greenwillow.

Zamorano, Ana. (1997). *Let's Eat!* Illus. by Julie Vivas. New York: Scholastic.

Byars, Betsy. *My Brother Ant* [cassette and book]. (1998). Prince Frederick, MD: Recorded Books.

Daddy Doesn't Live with Us [video]. (1994). Sunburst.

My Family, Your Family [video]. (1994). Sunburst.

New Baby in My House [video]. (1993). Children's Television Workshop/ distributed by Sony Wonder.

We're a Family [video]. (1992). Sunburst.

Multimedia

The following multimedia products can be used to complement this theme:

A Kid's Guide to Families [video]. Available from Kimbo Educational.

Recording and Song Title

The following recording can be used to complement this theme:

Songs for You and Me—"A Family Song"

274

THEME 28

Shelters

tanks
farm
barns
stables
sheds

Kinds

horses
cows
chickens
pigs
goats
sheep
fish

Farm Animals

Sounds

Uses

transportation
milk
food

Care

food
corn
hay
oats
silage
water
shelter

Theme Goals

Through participating in the experiences provided by this theme, the children may learn:

1. Names of farm animals.
2. Uses for farm animals.
3. Farm animal shelters.
4. Food for farm animals.
5. Sounds of farm animals.

Concepts for the Children to Learn

1. A farm animal lives on a farm.
2. Barns, stables, and sheds are homes for farm animals.
3. Horses are farm animals that can be used for transportation.
4. Cows, chickens, pigs, sheep, and goats are farm animals.
5. Some cows and goats give milk.
6. Farm animals eat corn, hay, oats, and silage.
7. A farmer cares for farm animals.
8. We can recognize some farm animals by their sounds.
9. Some farm animals supply us with food such as milk, meat, and eggs.

Vocabulary

1. **herd**—a group of animals.
2. **stable**—building for horses and cattle.
3. **farmer**—person who cares for farm animals.
4. **barn**—building to house animals and store grain.

Bulletin Board

The purpose of this bulletin board is to foster visual, perceptual, and numeral recognition skills. Out of tagboard, construct red barns as illustrated. The number of barns constructed will depend upon the maturity of your group of children. Place a numeral on each red barn. Construct the same number of black barns by tracing around the red barns onto black construction paper. After cutting out, place small white circles (dots from paper punch) onto the black barns. Laminate all barns. Staple black barns to the board. Punch a hole in each red barn window. During self-selected activity periods the children can hang red barns on pushpins of corresponding black barns.

Parent Letter

Dear Parents,

Farm animals will be the focus of our next curriculum unit. The children will be learning the many different ways that farm animals help us. They will also become aware of the difference between pets and farm animals. The children will also discover that farm animals need homes and food.

AT SCHOOL

Some of the learning activities scheduled for this week include:

- making a barn out of a large cardboard box for the dramatic play area.
- tasting different kinds of eggs, milk, and cheese for breakfast one day.
- at the science table, observing and comparing the many grains and seeds farm animals eat.
- dressing up like farmers and farm animals.
- making buttermilk chalk pictures.
- listening to stories about farm animals.
- reciting fingerplays representing farm animals.

AT HOME

There are many ways you can integrate this unit into your family life. To stimulate imagination and movement skills ask your child to imitate different farm animals by walking and making that animal's noise. Also, your child will be learning this rhyme at school. You can also recite it at home to foster language skills.

If I Were a Horse

If I were a horse, I'd gallop all around.
  (slap thighs and gallop in a circle)
I'd shake my head and say "Neigh, neigh."
  (shake head)
I'd prance and gallop all over town.

Enjoy your child as you explore experiences related to farm animals.

Seesaws can be pretend horses.

Music

1. **"Old MacDonald Had a Farm"**
   (traditional)

2. **"The Animals on the Farm"**
   (Sing to the tune of "The Wheels on the Bus")

   The cows on the farm go moo, moo, moo.
   Moo, moo, moo, moo, moo, moo.
   The cows on the farm go moo, moo, moo
       all day long.

   The horses on the farm go neigh, neigh,
       neigh.
   Neigh, neigh, neigh, neigh, neigh, neigh.
   The horses on the farm go neigh, neigh,
       neigh all day long.

   (pigs—oink)
   (sheep—baa)
   (chicken—cluck)
   (turkeys—gobble)

3. **"The Farmer in the Dell"**
   (traditional)

   The farmer in the dell,
   The farmer in the dell,
   Hi-ho the dairy-o
   The farmer in the dell.

   The farmer takes a wife/husband.
   The farmer takes a wife/husband.
   Hi-ho the dairy-o
   The farmer in the dell.

   (The other verses are:)
   The wife/husband takes the child
   The child takes the nurse
   The nurse takes the dog
   The dog takes the cat
   The cat takes the rat
   The rat takes the cheese.

   (The final verse:)
   The cheese stands alone.
   The cheese stands alone.
   Hi-ho the dairy-o
   The cheese stands alone.

Fingerplays

THIS LITTLE COW

This little cow eats grass.
  (hold up one hand, fingers erect, bend
  down one finger)
This little cow eats hay.
  (bend down another finger)
This little cow drinks water.
  (bend down another finger)
And this little cow does nothing.
  (bend down another finger)
But lie and sleep all day.

IF I WERE A HORSE

If I were a horse, I'd gallop all around.
  (slap thighs and gallop in a circle)
I'd shake my head and say "Neigh, neigh."
  (shake head)
I'd prance and gallop all over town.

THIS LITTLE PIG

This little pig went to market.
  (point to one finger at a time)
This little pig stayed home.
This little pig had roast beef.
This little pig had none.
This little pig cried, "Wee, wee, wee"
And ran all the way home.

EIGHT BABY PIGS

Two mother pigs lived in a pen.
  (thumbs)
Each had four babies and that made ten.
  (fingers of both hands)
These four babies were black and white.
  (fingers of one hand)
These four babies were black as night.
  (fingers of other hand)
All eight babies loved to play
  (wiggle fingers)
And they rolled in the mud all day!
  (roll hands)

THE FARM

The cows on the farm go, "Moo-oo,
  moo-oo";
The rooster cries, "Cock-a-doodle-doo";
The big brown horse goes, "Neigh, neigh";
The little lamb says, "Baa," when he wants
  to play.
The little chick goes, "Peep, peep, peep";
The cat says, "Meow," when it's not asleep;
The pig says, "Oink," when it wants to eat.
And we all say, "Hello," when our friends
  we meet.

Source of fingerplays: Cromwell, Hibner & Faitel. (1983).
Finger Frolics: Fingerplays for Young Children. Michigan:
Partner Press.

Science

1. **Sheep Wool**

   Place various types of wool on a table for
   the children to observe. Included may be
   wool clippings, lanolin, dyed yarn, yarn
   spun into thread, wool cloth, wool articles
   such as mittens and socks.

2. **Feathers**

   Examine various types of feathers. Use a
   magnifying glass. Discuss their purposes
   such as keeping animals warm and helping
   ducks to float on water. Add the feathers to
   the water table to see if they float. Discuss
   why they float.

3. **Tasting Dairy Products**

   Plan a milk-tasting party. To do this, taste
   and compare the following types of milk
   products: cow milk, goat milk, cream,
   skimmed milk, whole milk, cottage cheese,
   sour cream, butter, margarine, and buttermilk.

4. **Eggs**

   Taste different kinds of eggs. Let children
   choose from scrambled, poached, deviled,
   hard-boiled, and fried. This could also be
   integrated as part of the breakfast menu.

5. Cheese Types

Observe, taste, and compare different kinds of cheese. Examples include swiss, cheddar, colby, cottage cheese, and cheese curds.

6. Egg Hatching

If possible, contact a hatchery to borrow an incubator. Watch the eggs hatch in the classroom.

7. Feels from the Farm

Construct a feely box containing farm items. Examples may include an ear of corn, hay, sheep wool, a turkey feather, hard-boiled egg, etc.

Dramatic Play

1. Farmer

Clothes and props for a farmer can be placed in the dramatic play area. Include items such as hats, scarves, overalls, boots, etc.

2. Saddle

A horse saddle can be placed on a bench in the classroom. The children can take turns sitting on it, pretending they are riding a horse.

3. Barn

A barn and plastic animals can be added to the classroom. The children can use blocks as accessories to make pens, cages, etc.

4. Veterinarian

Collect materials to make a veterinarian prop box. Stuffed animals can be used as patients.

Arts and Crafts

1. Yarn Collage

Provide the children with several types and lengths of yarn. Include clipped yarn, yarn fluffs, frayed yarn in several different colors, along with paper.

2. Texture Collage

On the art table provide several colors, shapes, and types of fabric for creating a texture collage during the self-selected activity period for the children.

3. Grain and Seed Collage

Corn, wheat, hay, oats, barley, and grains that farm animals eat can be placed on the art table. Paper and glue or paste should also be provided.

4. Buttermilk Chalk Picture

Brush a piece of cardboard with 2 to 3 tablespoons of buttermilk or dip chalk in buttermilk. Create designs using colored chalk as a tool.

5. Farm Animal Mobiles

Cut pictures of farm animals from magazines and hang them from hangers or branches.

6. Eggshell Collages

Collect eggshells and crush into pieces. Place the eggshells in the art area for the children to glue on paper. Let dry. If desired, the shells can be painted. If preparation time is available, eggshells can be dyed with food coloring by teacher prior to the activity.

7. Sponge Prints

Cut farm animal shapes out of sponges. If a pattern is needed, cut out of a coloring book. Once cut, the sponge forms can be dipped into a pan of thick tempera paint and used as a tool to apply a design.

Sensory

Add to the Sensory Table

- Different types of grain, such as oats, wheat, barley, and corn, and measuring devices
- Wool and feathers
- Sand and plastic farm animals
- Provide materials to make a barnyard. Include soil, hay, farm animals, barns, farm equipment toys, etc.

Large Muscle

1. **Trikes**

   During outdoor play, encourage children to use trikes and wagons for hauling.

2. **Barn**

   Construct a large barn out of a large cardboard box. Let all the children help paint it outdoors. When dry, the children can play in it.

Field Trips/ Resource People

1. **Farmer**

   Invite a farmer to talk to the children. If possible, have him bring a smaller farm animal for the children to touch and observe.

2. **The Farm**

   Visit a farm. Observe the animals and machinery.

3. **Milk Station**

   Visit a milk station if there is one in your area.

4. **Grocery Store**

   Visit the dairy section of a grocery store. Look for dairy products.

Math

1. **Puzzles**

   Laminate several pictures of farm animals; coloring books are a good source. Cut the pictures into puzzles for the children.

2. **Grouping and Sorting**

   Collect plastic farm animals. Place in a basket and let the children sort them according to size, color, where they live, how they move, etc.

Social Studies

Farm Animal of the Day

Throughout the week let children take care of and watch baby farm animals. Suggestions include a piglet, chicks, small ducks, rabbit, or lamb.

Group Time
(games, language)

1. **"Duck, Duck, Goose"**

   Sit the children in a circle. Then choose one child to be "it." This child goes around the circle and touches each of the other children on the shoulder and says "Duck, Duck, Goose." The child who is tapped as "goose" gets up and chases the other child around the circle. The first child who returns back to the empty spot sits down and the other child proceeds with the game of tapping children on the shoulder until someone else is tapped as the goose.

2. **Thank You**

   Write a thank-you note as a follow-up activity after a field trip or a visit from a resource person.

Miscellaneous

Transition

During transition time encourage the children to imitate different farm animals. They may gallop like a horse, hop like a bunny, waddle like a duck, move like a snake, etc.

Cooking

1. Make Butter

Fill baby food jars half-full with whipping cream. Allow the children to take turns shaking the jars until the cream separates. First it will appear like whipping cream, then like overwhipped cream, and finally an obvious separation will occur. Then pour off liquid and taste. Wash the butter in cold water in a bowl several times. Drain off milky liquid each time. Taste and then wash again until nearly clear. Work the butter in the water with a wooden spoon as you wash. Add salt to taste. Let the children spread the butter on crackers or bread.

2. Make Cottage Cheese

Heat one quart of milk until lukewarm. Dissolve one rennet tablet in a small amount of the milk. Stir the rennet mixture into remaining milk. Let the mixture stand in a warm place until set. Drain the mixture through a strainer lined with cheesecloth. Bring the corners of the cloth together and squeeze or drain the mixture. Rinse the mixture with cold water and drain again. Add a small amount of butter and salt.

3. Purple Cow Drink Mix

1/2 gallon milk
1/2 gallon grape juice
6 ice cubes
blender

Mix the ingredients in a blender for one minute. Drink. Enjoy! This recipe will serve approximately 20 children.

4. Animal Crackers

Serve animal crackers and peanut butter for snack.

5. Hungry Cheese Spread

1 8-ounce goat cheese or 8-ounce soft cream cheese
1/4 cup soft butter
1 teaspoon salt
1 tablespoon paprika
1 teaspoon dry mustard
1 1/2 tablespoons caraway seeds

Blend the cheese and butter in the mixing bowl. Add the remaining ingredients. Mix them well. Put the blended cheese into a small serving bowl. Chill in the refrigerator for at least 30 minutes before serving.

Source: Cooper, Terry Touff, & Ratner, Marilyn. (1974). *Many Hands Cooking*. New York: Thomas Y. Crowell Company.

6. Corn Bread

2 cups cornmeal
1 teaspoon salt
1/2 teaspoon baking soda
1 1/2 teaspoons baking powder
1 tablespoon sugar
2 eggs
1 1/2 cups buttermilk
1/4 cup cooking oil

Heat oven to 400 degrees. Sift cornmeal, salt, soda, baking powder, and sugar into a bowl. Stir in unbeaten eggs, buttermilk, and cooking oil until all ingredients are mixed. Pour the batter into a greased 9-inch × 9-inch pan or cob-formed pans. Bake for 30 minutes until lightly browned.

Books

The following books can be used to complement this theme:

Aliki. *Milk from Cow to Carton.* (1992). Revised ed. New York: HarperCollins.

Brown, Craig. (1994). *In the Spring.* New York: Greenwillow.

Edwards, Pamela Duncan. (1998). *The Grumpy Morning.* Illus. by Loretta Krupinski. New York: Hyperion.

Ehrlich, Amy. (1993). *Parents in the Pigpen, Pigs in the Tub.* Illus. by Steven Kellogg. New York: Dial Books.

Fleming, Denise. (1994). *Barnyard Banter.* New York: Holt.

Fowler, Allan. (1992). *Thanks to Cows.* San Francisco: Children's Book Press.

Gibbons, Gail. (1998). *Farming.* New York: Holiday House.

Gray, Libba Moore. (1997). *Is There Room on the Feather Bed?* Illus. by Nadine Bernard Westcott. New York: Orchard Books.

Hutchins, Pat. (1994). *Little Pink Pig.* New York: Greenwillow.

Jackson, Ellen. (1995). *Brown Cow, Green Grass, Yellow Mellow Sun.* Illus. by Victoria Raymond. New York: Hyperion.

Lesser, Carolyn. (1995). *What a Wonderful Day to Be a Cow.* Illus. by Melissa Bay Mathis. New York: Knopf.

MacLachlan, Patricia. (1994). *All the Places to Love.* Illus. by Mike Wimmer. New York: HarperCollins.

Masurel, Claire. (1997). *No, No, Titus!* Illus. by Shari Halpern. New York: North South Books.

McDonnell, Flora. (1994). *I Love Animals.* Cambridge, MA: Candlewick Press.

Older, Jules. (1997). *Cow.* Illus. by Lyn Severance. Watertown, MA: Charlesbridge Publishers.

Plourde, Lynn. (1997). *Pigs in the Mud in the Middle of the Road.* Illus. by John Schoenherr. New York: Scholastic.

Sykes, Julie. (1996). *This and That.* Illus. by Tanya Linch. New York: Farrar, Straus & Giroux.

Tafuri, Nancy. (1994). *This Is the Farmer.* New York: Greenwillow.

Tresselt, Alvin. (1991). *Wake Up, Farm.* Newly illus. by Carolyn Ewing. New York: Lothrop, Lee & Shepard.

Waddell, Martin. (1992). *Farmer Duck.* Illus. by Helen Oxenbury. Cambridge, MA: Candlewick Press.

Wormell, Christopher. (1995). *A Number of Animals.* Mankato, MN: Creative Editions.

Ziefert, Harriet. (1996). *Who Said Moo?* Illus. by Simms Taback. New York: HarperCollins.

Multimedia

The following multimedia products can be used to complement this theme:

Cows [video]. (1995). Churchill Media.

Let's Go to the Farm [video]. (1994). With Mac Parker. Burlington, VT: Vermont Story Works.

Rosenthal, Phil. "Little White Duck" on *Animal Songs* [sound disc]. (1996). Guilford, CT: American Melody.

See How They Grow: Farm Animals [video]. (1993). New York: Sony Music Entertainment.

We're Goin' to the Farm [video]. (1994). Minneapolis: Shortstuff Entertainment.

Recordings and Song Titles

The following recordings can be used to complement this theme:

"Farmer in the Dell"—*Singing Games for Little People, Preschool Aerobic Fun, Diaper Gym*

Preschool Action Time—"Farmer's Friends"

Singable Nursery Rhymes—"This Little Piggy," "Mary Had a Little Lamb," "Baa, Baa Black Sheep"

Nursery Rhymes for Little People—"Baa, Baa Black Sheep," "Mary Had a Little Lamb"

Six Little Ducks—"Old MacDonald Had a Farm," "Six Little Ducks," "Little White Duck," "B-I-N-G-O"

A to Z, the Animals and Me—"Neat Nanny Goat," "Piggly, Wiggly, Pizza Pig," "Skiing Sheep"

Lullaby Time for Little People—"All the Pretty Horses"

Musical Playtime Fun—"Animal Parade"

It's Fun to Clap—"Here Comes the Cow," "Hop Like a Bunny"

Where Is Thumbkin?—"Five Fat Turkeys Are We"

Holiday Action Songs—"Strutting Turkey," "Wandering Goose"

T H E M E 29

Causes

people
situations
sickness

Verbal

yelling
crying
talking
singing
laughing

Feelings

Types

happy
sad
lonely
tired
surprised
angry
excited
friendly
afraid
hungry
loving
depressed

Nonverbal

frowning
jumping
hitting
petting
hugging
kissing

Theme Goals

Through participating in the experiences provided by this theme, the children may learn:

1. Types of feelings.
2. Verbal expressions of feelings.
3. Nonverbal expressions of feelings.
4. Causes for our feelings.

Concepts for the Children to Learn

1. Everyone has feelings.
2. Feelings show how we feel.
3. Feelings change.
4. Happy, sad, excited, and surprised are types of feelings.
5. Happy people usually smile.
6. Sad people sometimes cry.

Vocabulary

1. **feelings**—expressed emotions.
2. **happy**—a feeling of being glad.
3. **smile**—a facial expression of pleasure or happiness.
4. **surprise**—a feeling from something unexpected.
5. **sad**—the feeling of being hurt or unhappy.
6. **afraid**—the feeling of being unsure of or frightened about something.

Bulletin Board

The purpose of this bulletin board is to help the children become aware of feelings, as well as recognize their printed names. Prepare individual name cards for each child. Then prepare different expressive faces such as happy, sad, and angry. Staple faces to top of bulletin board. See the illustration for an example. If available, magnetic strips may be added to the bulletin board under faces and pieces affixed to name cards, or pushpins may be placed on the board and holes punched in name cards. The children may place their names under the face they decide they feel when arriving at school. Later, during large group time, the board can be reviewed to see if any of the children's feelings have changed.

Parent Letter

Dear Parents,

Emotions and feelings will be the focus of our next curriculum unit. Throughout each day, the children experience many feelings, ranging from happiness to sadness. The purpose of this unit is to have the children develop an understanding of feelings. Feelings are something we all share, and feelings are acceptable. We will also be exploring ways of expressing different feelings.

AT SCHOOL

Some of the learning experiences planned for this unit include:

- listening and discussing the book *Alexander and the Terrible, Horrible, No Good, Very Bad Day* by Judith Viorst.
- singing songs about our feelings.
- drawing and painting to various types of music.
- expressing feelings through music.

OUR SPECIAL VISITOR

"Clancy the Clown" will be visiting the children on Thursday at 3:00 p.m. The children are all looking forward to this special visitor. You are encouraged to join us and share their excitement.

AT HOME

To help your child identify situations that elicit feelings, have your child cut or tear pictures from discarded magazines that depict events or situations that make your child feel happy or sad. These pictures can then be glued or pasted on paper to create a feelings collage.

Talking with your child about your feelings will encourage parent-child communication. Tell your child what things make you feel various ways. Then ask your child to share some feelings.

Make your child happy today!

Music

1. **"Feelings"**
   (Sing to the tune of "Twinkle, Twinkle Little Star")

   I have feelings.
   You do, too.
   Let's all sing about a few.

   I am happy.
      (smile)
   I am sad.
      (frown)
   I get scared.
      (wrap arms around self)
   I get mad.
      (make a fist and shake it)

   I am proud of being me.
      (hands on hips)
   That's a feeling too, you see.
   I have feelings.
      (point to self)
   You do, too.
      (point to someone else)
   We just sang about a few.

2. **"If You're Happy and You Know It"**
   (traditional)

   If you're happy and you know it
   Clap your hands.
      (clap twice)
   If you're happy and you know it
   Clap your hands.
      (clap twice)
   If you're happy and you know it
   Then your face will surely show it.
   If you're happy and you know it
   Clap your hands.
      (clap twice)

   For additional verses, change the emotions and actions.

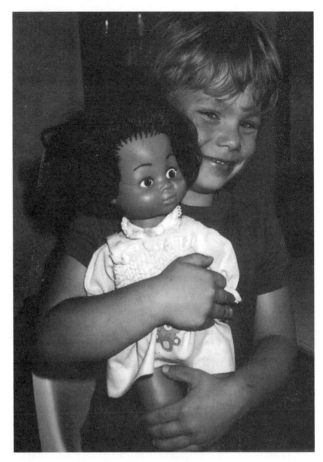

How do you feel today?

Fingerplays

FEELINGS

Smile when you're happy.
Cry when you are sad.
Giggle if it's funny.
Get angry if you're mad.

Source: Wilems, Dick. *Everyday Circle Times.*

I LOOKED INSIDE MY LOOKING GLASS

I looked inside my looking glass
To see what I could see.
It looks like I'm happy today,
Because that smiling face is me.

STAND UP TALL

Stand up tall
Hands in the air.
Now sit down
In your chair.
Clap your hands
And make a frown.
Smile and smile.
Hop like a clown.

Science

1. Sound Tape

Tape various noises that express emotions; suggestions include sounds such as laughter, cheering, growling, shrieking, crying, etc. Play these sounds for the children letting them identify the emotion. They may also want to act out the emotion.

2. Communication without Words

Hang a large screen or sheet with a bright light behind it. The children can go behind the screen and act out various emotions. Other children guess how they are feeling.

3. How Does It Feel?

Add various pieces of textured materials to the science table. Include materials such as soft fur, sandpaper, rocks, and cotton. Encourage the children to touch each object and explain how it feels.

Dramatic Play

1. Flower Shop

Plastic flowers, vases, and wrapping paper can be placed in the dramatic play area. Make a sign that says "Flower Shop." The children may want to arrange, sell, deliver, and receive flowers.

2. Post Office

Collect discarded greeting cards and envelopes. The children can stamp and deliver the cards to one another.

3. Puppet Center

A puppet center can be added to the dramatic play area. Include a variety of puppets and a stage.

Arts and Crafts

1. Drawing to Music

Play various types of music including jazz, classical, and rock and let the children draw during the self-selected activity period. Different tunes and melodies might make us feel a certain way.

2. Playdough

Using playdough is a wonderful way to vent feelings. Prepare several types and let the children feel the different textures. Color each type a different color. Add a scent to one and to another add a textured material such as sawdust, rice, or sand. A list of playdoughs can be found later in this theme.

3. Footprints

Mix tempera paint. Pour the paint into a shallow jelly roll pan approximately 1/4 inch deep. The children can dip their feet into the pan. After this, they can step directly onto paper. Using their feet as an application tool, footsteps can be made. This activity actually could be used to create a mural to hang in the hall or lobby.

Sensory

Texture Feelings

Various textures can create feelings. Let the children express their feelings by adding the following to the sensory table:

- cotton
- water (warm or with ice)
- black water

292

- blue water
- sand
- pebbles
- dirt with scoops
- plastic worms with water

Large Muscle

1. **Mirrors**

   The children should sit as pairs facing each other. Select one child to make a "feeling face" at the partner. Let the other child guess what feeling it is. A variation of this activity would be to have partners face each other. When one child smiles, the partner is to imitate his feelings.

2. **Simon Says**

   Play "Simon Says" using emotions:
   "Simon Says walk in a circle feeling
     happy . . ."
   "Simon Says walk in a circle feeling
     sad . . ."

Resource People

1. **A Clown**

   Invite a clown to the classroom. You may ask the clown to dress and apply makeup for the children. After the clown leaves provide makeup for the children.

2. **Musician**

   Invite a musician to play a variety of music for the children to express feelings.

3. **Florist**

   Invite a florist to visit your classroom and show how flowers are arranged. Talk about why people send flowers. If convenient, the children could visit the florist, touring the greenhouses.

Math

Face Match

Collect two small shoe boxes. On one shoe box draw a happy face. On the other box, draw a sad face. Cut faces of people from magazines. The children can sort the pictures accordingly.

Social Studies

Pictures

Share pictures of individuals engaged in different occupations such as doctors, firefighters, beauticians, florists, nurses, bakers, etc. Discuss how these individuals help us and how they make us feel.

Group Time
(games, language)

Happy Feeling

Discuss happiness. Ask each child one thing that makes him happy. Record each answer on a "Happiness Chart." Post the chart for the parents to observe as they pick up their children.

Cooking

1. **Happy Rolls**

   1 package of fast-rising dry yeast
   1 cup warm water
   1/3 cup sugar
   1/3 cup cooking oil
   3 cups flour
   a dash of salt

   Measure the warm water and pour it into a bowl. Sprinkle the yeast on top of the water. Let the yeast settle into the water.

Mix all of the ingredients in a large bowl. Place the dough on a floured board to knead it. Demonstrate how to knead, letting each of the children take turns kneading the bread. This is a wonderful activity to work through emotions. After kneading it for about 10 minutes, put the ball of dough into a greased bowl. If kneaded sufficiently, the top of the dough should have blisters on it. Cover the bowl and put in the sun or near heat. Let it rise for about an hour or until doubled. Take the dough out of the bowl. Punch it down, knead for several more minutes and then divide the dough into 12 to 15 pieces. Roll each piece of dough into a ball. Place each ball on a greased cookie sheet. Let the dough rise again until doubled. Bake at 450 degrees for 10 to 12 minutes. A happy face can be drawn on the roll with frosting.

2. **Berry "Happy" Shake—Finland**

10 fresh strawberries or 6 tablespoons
   sliced strawberries in syrup, thawed
2 cups cold milk
1 1/2 tablespoons sugar or honey

Wash the strawberries (if fresh) and cut out the stems. Cut the strawberries into small pieces. (If you are using frozen strawberries, drain the syrup into a small bowl or cup and save it.) Pour the milk into the mixing bowl. Add the strawberries. If you are using fresh strawberries, add the sugar or honey. If you are using frozen strawberries, add 3 tablespoons of the strawberry syrup instead of sugar. Beat with the egg beater for 1 minute. Pour the drink into glasses.

Source: Touff, Terry, & Ratner, Marilyn. (1974). *Many Hands Cooking*. New York: Thomas Y. Crowell Company.

3. **Danish Smile Berry Pudding**

1 10-ounce package frozen raspberries,
   thawed
1 10-ounce package frozen strawberries,
   thawed
1/4 cup cornstarch
2 tablespoons sugar
1/2 cup cold water
1 tablespoon lemon juice
slivered almonds

Puree berries in blender or press through sieve. Mix cornstarch and sugar in 1 1/2-quart saucepan. Gradually stir in water; add puree. Heat to boiling, stirring constantly. Boil and stir 1 minute. Remove from heat. Stir in lemon juice. Pour into dessert dishes or serving bowl. Cover and refrigerate at least 2 hours. Sprinkle with almonds; serve with half-and-half if desired. Makes 6 servings.

Source: *Betty Crocker's International Cookbook*. (1980). New York: Random House.

Recipes for Doughs and Clays

Clay Dough

3 cups flour
3 cups salt
3 tablespoons alum

Combine ingredients and slowly add water, a little at a time. Mix well with spoon. As mixture thickens, continue mixing with your hands until it has the feel of clay. If it feels too dry, add more water. If it is too sticky, add equal parts of flour and salt.

Playdough

2 cups flour
1 cup salt
1 cup hot water
2 tablespoons cooking oil
4 teaspoons cream of tartar
food coloring

Mix well. Knead until smooth. This dough may be kept in a plastic bag or covered container and used again. If it gets sticky, more flour may be added.

Favorite Playdough

Combine and boil until dissolved:

2 cups water
1/2 cup salt
food coloring or tempera paint

Mix in while very hot:

2 tablespoons cooking oil
2 tablespoons alum
2 cups flour

Knead (approximately 5 minutes) until smooth.

Store in covered airtight containers.

Oatmeal Dough

2 cups oatmeal
1 cup flour
1/2 cup water

Combine ingredients. Knead well. This dough has a very different texture, is easily manipulated, and looks different. Finished projects can be painted when dry.

Baker's Clay #1

1 cup cornstarch
2 cups baking soda
1 1/2 cups cold water

Combine ingredients. Stir until smooth. Cook over medium heat, stirring constantly until mixture reaches the consistency of slightly dry mashed potatoes.
Turn out onto plate or bowl, covering with damp cloth. When cool enough to handle, knead thoroughly until smooth and pliable on cornstarch-covered surface.
Store in tightly closed plastic bag or covered container.

Baker's Clay #2

4 cups flour
1 1/2 cups water
1 cup salt

Combine ingredients. Mix well. Knead 5 to 10 minutes. Roll out to 1/4-inch thickness. Cut with decorative cookie cutters or with a knife. Make a hole at the top.
Bake at 250 degrees for 2 hours or until hard. When cool, paint with tempera paint and spray with clear varnish or paint with acrylic paint.

Cloud Dough

3 cups flour
1 cup oil
scent (oil of peppermint, wintergreen, lemon, etc.)
food coloring

Combine ingredients. Add water until easily manipulated (about 1/2 cup).

Sawdust Dough

2 cups sawdust
3 cups flour
1 cup salt

Combine ingredients. Add water as needed. This dough becomes very hard and is not easily broken. It is good to use for making objects and figures that one desires to keep.

Salt Dough

4 cups salt
1 cup cornstarch

Combine with sufficient water to form a paste. Cook over medium heat, stirring constantly.

(continued)

Recipes for Doughs and Clays
(continued)

Peanut Butter Playdough

2 1/2 cups peanut butter
2 tablespoons honey
2 cups powdered milk

Mix well with very clean hands. Keep adding powdered milk until the dough feels soft, not sticky. This is a dough that can be eaten.

Variations:
1. Cocoa or carob powder can be added for chocolate flavor.
2. Raisins, miniature marshmallows, or chopped peanuts may be added or used to decorate finished shapes.

Each child can be given dough to manipulate and then eat.

Cooked Clay Dough

1 cup flour
1/2 cup cornstarch
4 cups water
1 cup salt
3 or 4 pounds flour
food coloring if desired

Stir slowly and be patient with this recipe. Blend the flour and cornstarch with cold water. Add salt to the water and boil. Pour the boiling salt and water solution into the flour and cornstarch paste and cook over hot water until clear. Add the flour and coloring to the cooked solution and knead. After the clay has

been in use, if too moist, add flour; if dry, add water. Keep in covered container. Wrap dough with damp cloth or towel. This dough has a very nice texture and is very popular with all age groups. May be kept 2 or 3 weeks.

Playdough

5 cups flour
2 cups salt
4 tablespoons cooking oil
add water to right consistency

Powdered tempera may be added in with flour, or food coloring may be added to finished dough. This dough may be kept in plastic bag or covered container for approximately 2 to 4 weeks. It is better used as playdough rather than leaving objects to harden.

Used Coffee Grounds

2 cups used coffee grounds
1/2 cup salt
1 1/2 cups oatmeal

Combine ingredients and add enough water to moisten. Children like to roll, pack, and pat this mixture. It has a very different feel and look, but it's not good for finished products. It has a very nice texture.

Mud Dough

2 cups mud
2 cups sand
1/2 cup salt

Combine ingredients and add enough water to make pliable. Children like to work with this mixture. It has a nice texture and is easy to use. This cannot be picked up to save for finished products easily. It can be used for rolling and cutouts.

Soap Modeling

2 cups soap flakes

Add enough water to moisten and whip until consistency is right for molding. Use soap such as Ivory Snow, Dreft, Lux, etc. Mixture will have very slight flaky appearance when it can be molded. It is very enjoyable for all age groups and is easy to work. Also, the texture is very different from other materials ordinarily used for molding. It may be put up to dry, but articles are very slow to dry.

Soap and Sawdust

1 cup whipped soap
1 cup sawdust

Mix well together. This gives a very different feel and appearance. It is quite easily molded into different shapes by all age groups. May be used for 2 to 3 days if stored in tight plastic bag.

Books

The following books can be used to complement this theme:

Berry, Joy. (1996). *Let's Talk About* series. Illus. by Maggie Smith. New York: Scholastic. *Feeling Afraid; Feeling Angry; Feeling Sad.* (Pbk).

Brown, Laurie Krasny. (1996). *When Dinosaurs Die: A Guide to Understanding Death.* Illus. by Marc Tolon Brown. Boston: Little, Brown.

Carle, Eric. (1995). *The Very Lonely Firefly.* New York: Philomel Books.

Carlson, Nancy L. (1997). *ABC I Like Me.* New York: Viking.

Conlin, Susan et al. (1991). *All My Feelings at Preschool: Nathan's Day.* Seattle, WA: Parenting Press.

Crary, Elizabeth. *Dealing with Feelings* series. Illus. by Jean Whitney. Seattle, WA: Parenting Press. *I'm Excited.* (1996); *I'm Frustrated.* (1992); *I'm Furious.* (1996); *I'm Mad.* (1992); *I'm Proud.* (1992); *I'm Scared.* (1996).

Curtis, Munzee. (1997). *When the Big Dog Barks.* Illus. by Susan Ayishai. New York: Greenwillow.

Egan, Tim. (1996). *Metropolitan Cow.* Boston: Houghton Mifflin.

Emberley, Ed. (1997). *Glad Monster, Sad Monster: A Book About Feelings.* Illus. by Anne Miranda. Boston: Little, Brown.

Emberley, Ed. (1993). *Go Away, Big Green Monster!* Boston: Little, Brown.

Hamilton, Dewitt. (1995). *Sad Days, Glad Days: A Story About Depression.* Illus. by Gail Owens. Morton Grove, IL: Albert Whitman and Co.

Krueger, David. (1996). *What Is a Feeling?* Seattle, WA: Parenting Press.

Lachner, Dorothea. (1995). *Andrew's Angry Words.* Illus. by Tjong-Khing The. New York: North South Books.

Havill, Juanita. (1993). *Jamaica and Brianna.* Illus. by Anne Sibley O'Brien. Boston: Houghton Mifflin.

Joosse, Barbara M. (1991). *Mama, Do You Love Me?* Illus. by Barbara Lavalle. San Francisco: Chronicle Books.

Roth, Susan L. (1997). *My Love for You.* New York: Dial Books.

Seuss, Dr. (1996). *My Many Colored Days.* Edited by Lou Fancher; illus. by Steve Johnson. New York: Knopf.

Waddell, Martin. (1993). *Let's Go Home, Little Bear.* Illus. by Barbara Firth. Cambridge, MA: Candlewick Press.

Ward, Heather P. (1994). *I Promise I'll Find You.* Illus. by Sheila McGraw. Buffalo, NY: Firefly Books.

Multimedia

The following multimedia products can be used to complement this theme:

Berenstain Bears in the Dark [CD-ROM]. (1996). New York: Random House/Broderbund.

Groark Learns About Prejudice [video]. (1996). Featuring Randel McGee. Elkind & Sweet Communications/distributed by Live Wire Media.

I Get So Mad! [video]. (1993). Sunburst Communications.

Murphy, Jane. *Songs for You and Me: Kids Learn About Feelings and Emotions* [cassette]. Kimbo Educational.

Recordings and Song Titles

The following recordings can be used to complement this theme:

Get Up and Grow—"A Friend in Need," "It's a Great Day," "It's All Right," "Squabbles Hugs"

Nelson Gill / *Friends*—"Friends"

Gaia—*Sing 'n Sign for Fun,* "I Sign Like This," "Feeling Signs"

Songs for You and Me—"The Angry Song"

Singing, Moving and Fun—"Angry," "Sad," "Scared"

Piggyback Songs—"How Are You Today—Please?"

Where Is Thumbkin?—"If You're Happy and You Know It"

Toddlers on Parade—"Moods"

Yes, I Can Songs (with RONNO)—"Happy Rappy"

THEME

Job

fight fires
inspect buildings
teach fire safety
provide medical
treatment

Clothing

hats, coats,
masks, boots,
gloves, uniforms

Vehicles

fire trucks
water trucks
fire chief car
ambulance
police car

Firefighters

Safety

when to use
house
person
how to get them
false alarms
matches
cooking
smoking

Equipment

fire hydrant,
fire extinguisher,
hose, nozzles, ax,
ladders, telephone,
communication radios,
water

Fire Station

garage
workroom
kitchen
bedroom
dalmatians

Theme Goals

Through participating in the experiences provided by this theme, the children may learn:

1. The firefighter's job.
2. Firefighter's clothing.
3. Vehicles used by firefighters.
4. Firefighting equipment.
5. Areas inside a fire station.

Concepts for the Children to Learn

1. Men and women who fight fires are called firefighters.
2. Firefighters help keep our community safe.
3. Firefighters wear special hats and clothing.
4. The fire station has a garage, kitchen, workroom, and sleeping rooms.
5. The fire station has a special telephone number.
6. Ladders and water hoses are needed to fight fires.
7. Fire and water trucks are driven to fires.
8. Firefighters check buildings to make sure they are safe.
9. Firefighters teach us fire safety.
10. Fire extinguishers can be used to put out small fires.
11. Fire drills teach us what to do in case of a fire.

Vocabulary

1. **fire alarm**—a sound that warns people about fire.
2. **fire drill**—practice for teaching people what to do in case of a fire.
3. **fire extinguisher**—equipment that puts out fires.
4. **hose**—a tube that water flows through.
5. **helmet**—a protective hat.
6. **fire engine**—trucks carrying tools and equipment needed to fight fires.
7. **fire station**—a building that provides housing for firefighters and fire trucks.

Bulletin Board

The purpose of this bulletin board is to develop an awareness of clothing worn by firefighters and to reinforce color matching skills. From tagboard construct five firefighter hats. Color each hat a different color. Then construct five firefighter boots from tagboard. Color coordinate boots to match the hats. Laminate all of the pieces. Staple hats in two rows across the top of the bulletin board as illustrated. Staple boots in a row across the bottom of the bulletin board. Affix matching yarn to each hat. Children can match each hat to its corresponding colored boot by winding the string around a push-pin in the top of the boot.

Parent Letter

Dear Parents,

Because next week is Fire Prevention Week, we have decided that it would be fun and educational to focus on some very important community helpers—firefighters. The children will become more aware of the role of the firefighter, clothing worn by firefighters, and the fire station. We will also be learning how to use the telephone to call the emergency fire number.

AT SCHOOL

We have many activities planned for this unit! On Monday, we will paint a large box to create our own fire engine to use during the week in the dramatic play area. On Tuesday, a real fire engine will visit the parking lot, so the children can see how many tools firefighters need to take along on the job. We'll also be making fire helmets, and practicing our fire drill procedures.

AT HOME

To ensure your family's safety, talk with your child about what would happen in the event of a fire in your house. You can do this calmly, without frightening your child. Practice taking a fire escape route from the child's bedroom, the playroom, kitchen, and other rooms of your house. Establish a meeting place so that family members can go to the same location in the event of a fire.

Enjoy your child as you share the importance of safety in the event of a fire.

A unit on firefighters provides an opportunity to practice fire drills.

Music

"Down by the Station"

Down by the station early in the morning
See the great big fire trucks all in a row.
Hear the jangly fire bell sound a loud alarm
now—
Chug chug, clang clang, off we go!

Fingerplay

TEN BRAVE FIREFIGHTERS

Ten brave firefighters sleeping in a row.
   (fingers curled to make sleeping men)
Ding, dong, goes the bell
   (pull down on the bell cord)
And down the pole they go.
   (with fists together make hands slide
   down the pole)
Off on the engine, oh, oh, oh!
   (pretend you are steering the fire engine
   very fast)
Using the big hose, so, so, so.
   (make a nozzle with fist to use hose)

When all the fire's out, home so slow.
Back to bed, all in a row.
   (curl all fingers again for sleeping firefighters)

Source: Adapted from Cromwell, Liz, & Hibner, Dixie. (1976). *Finger Frolics*. Mt. Ranier, MD: Gryphon House.

Dramatic Play

1. **Firefighters**

   Place firefighting clothes such as hats, boots, and coats for children to wear. Sometimes fire station personnel will allow schools to borrow some of their clothing and equipment. Also, provide a bell to use as an alarm. A vacuum cleaner hose or a length of garden hose can be included to represent a water hose to extend play.

2. **Fire Truck**

   A fire truck can be cut from a cardboard refrigerator box. The children may want to paint the box yellow or red. A steering wheel and chairs may be added.

Arts and Crafts

1. Firefighters' Hats

Provide materials for the children to make fire hats. The hats can be decorated with foil, crayons, or paint. The emergency number 911 may be printed on the crown.

2. Charcoal Drawings

Provide real charcoal at the easels to be used as an application tool.

3. Crayon Melting

Place waxed crayons and paper on the art table for the children to create a design during self-initiated or self-directed play. Place a clean sheet of paper over the picture. Apply a warm iron. Show the children the effect of heat. This activity needs to be carefully supervised. The caption "crayon melting" may be printed on a bulletin board. On the board place the children's pictures, identifying each by name in the upper left-hand corner.

Sensory

1. Fill the sensory table with water. Provide cups and rubber tubing to resemble hoses and funnels.
2. Place sand in the sensory table. Add fire engines, firefighter dolls, popsicle sticks to make fences, and blocks to make buildings or houses.

Large Muscle

1. Firefighter's Workout

Lead children in a firefighter's workout. Do exercises like jumping jacks, knee bends, leg lifts, and running in place. Ask children why they think firefighters need to be in good physical condition for their jobs.

2. Obstacle Course

Make an obstacle course. Let children follow a string or piece of tape under chairs or tables, over steps, and across ladders. This activity can be planned for indoors or outdoors.

Field Trips/ Resource People

1. Fire Station

Take a trip to a fire station. Observe the clothing worn by firefighters, the building, the vehicles, and the tools.

2. Firefighter

Invite a firefighter to bring a fire truck to your school. Ask the firefighter to point out the special features such as the hose, siren, ladders, light, and special clothing kept on the truck. If permissable and safe, let the children climb onto the truck.

Math

1. Sequencing

Cut a piece of rubber tubing into various lengths. The children can sequence the pieces from shortest to longest.

2. Emergency Number

Contact your local telephone company for trainer telephones to use. If developmentally appropriate, teach the children how to dial a local emergency number.

Social Studies

1. Safety Rules

Discuss safety rules dealing with fire. Let children generate ideas about safety. Write their ideas on chart paper and display. Discuss why fire drills are a good idea.

2. **Fire Inspection Tour**

   Tour the classroom or building looking for fire extinguishers, emergency fire alarm boxes, and exits.

3. **Fire Drill**

   Schedule a fire drill. Prior to the drill talk to the children about fire drill procedures.

Group Time
(games, language)

Language Experience

Review safety rules. Write the rules on a large piece of paper. These rules can also be included in a parent letter as well as posted in the classroom.

Cooking

Firehouse Baked Beans

Purchase canned baked beans. To the beans, add cut-up hot dogs and extra catsup. Heat and serve for snack.

Books

The following books can be used to complement this theme:

Flanagan, Alice K. (1997). *Ms. Murphy Fights Fires*. Photos by Christine Osinski. Chicago: Children's Press.

Hines, Gary. (1993). *Flying Firefighters*. Illus. by Anna Grossnickle Hines. New York: Clarion Books.

Kallen, Stuart A. (1997). *The Fire Station*. Minneapolis: Abdo & Daughters.

Kuklin, Susan. (1993). *Fighting Fires*. New York: Simon & Schuster.

Kunhardt, Edith. (1995). *I'm Going to Be a Fire Fighter*. St. Paul, MN: Cartwheel Books. (Pbk)

Lakin, Pat. (1995). *The Fire Fighter: Where There's Smoke*. Austin, TX: Raintree/ Steck Vaughn.

Packard, Mary. (1995). *I'm a Fire Fighter*. Illus. by Julie Durrell. Madison, WI: Demco Media.

Ready, Dee. (1997). *Fire Fighters*. Danbury, CT: Grolier Pub.

Simon, Norma. (1995). *Fire Fighters*. Illus. by Pam Paparone. New York: Simon & Schuster.

Winkleman, Katherine. (1994). *Firehouse*. Illus. by John S. Winkleman. New York: Walker & Co.

Multimedia

The following multimedia products can be used to complement this theme:

Big Job [CD-ROM]. (1995). Bethesda, MD: Discovery Communications, Inc.

BigRed [video]. (1993). Mill Valley, CA: Fire Dog Pictures.

Fire and Rescue [video]. (1993). Montpelier, VT: Focus Video Productions.

Fire Safety for Kids [video]. (1995). South Burlington, VT: Children's Video Development.

Fire Station [video]. (1990). Washington, D.C.: National Geographic.

Firefighter [CD-ROM]. (1994). New York: Simon & Schuster Interactive.

Sound the Alarm: Firefighters at Work [video]. (1994). Bohemia, NY: Rainbow Educational Media.

Recording and Song Title

The following recording can be used to complement this theme:

People in Our Neighborhood—"Safety Pros Know" (firefighter, fire chief, fire inspector, police)

T H 31 E M E

Size

small
medium
large
very large

Habitat

lakes
oceans
ponds
rivers
fish farms
aquariums

Foods

insects
snails
worms
other fish
fish food
cornmeal

Fish

Colors

blue
brown
grey
black
orange
white

Kinds

Northern pike
seahorse
guppies
catfish
shark
eel

Parts

eyes
fins
gills
scales
mouth
tail

Importance

food
entertainment
sports
pets

Theme Goals

Through participating in the experiences provided by this theme, the children may learn:

1. Homes for fish.
2. The importance of fish.
3. Colors of fish.
4. Care of fish.
5. Kinds of fish.
6. Sizes of fish.
7. Parts of fish.

Concepts for the Children to Learn

1. Most fish have eyes, fins, gills, scales, a mouth, and tail.
2. Fish vary in size. They may be small, medium, large, or very large.
3. Blue, brown, grey, white, black, and orange are colors of fish.
4. Fish may live in lakes, oceans, ponds, rivers, fish farms, and aquariums.
5. Fish need food and water to live.
6. Insects, snails, other fish, plants, worms, fish food, and cornmeal are foods fish eat.
7. There are many kinds of fish. Some kinds include Northern pike, seahorse, guppies, catfish, shark, and eel.
8. Fish are important to people. (They provide food, entertainment, pets, and sport.)

Vocabulary

1. **scales**—skin covering of fish and other reptiles.
2. **gills**—the part of the fish body that helps it get air.
3. **fin**—the part that moves to help fish swim.
4. **tail**—the end body part that helps fish move.
5. **fish farm**—a place to raise fish for food.
6. **school**—a group of fish.

Bulletin Board

The purpose of this bulletin board is to promote identification of written numerals, as well as matching a set to a written numeral. To prepare the bulletin board begin by drawing and cutting fish shapes from construction paper. Decorate the fish as desired and print a numeral on each fish. Make another set of identical fish shapes from black construction paper to create fish "shadows." Cut small circles out of white construction paper to represent the fish air bubbles. Staple the fish shadows to the bulletin board. Above each fish shadow, staple a set of air bubbles. Children can then match the numerals on the fish to the corresponding set of air bubbles. The fish can be attached to the bulletin board with pushpins or small adhesive magnet pieces.

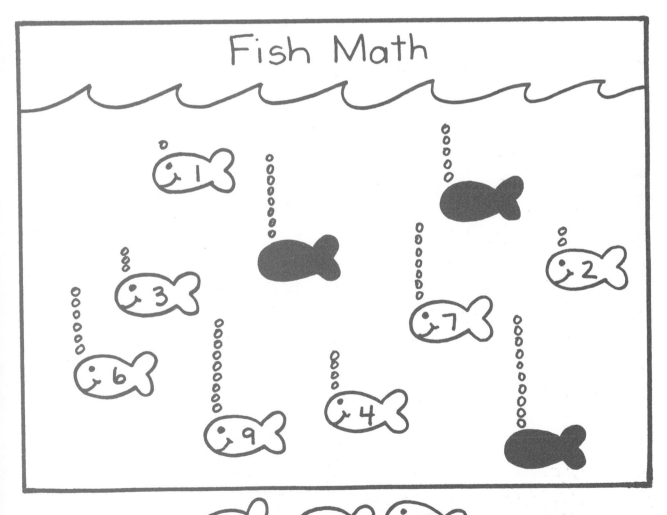

Parent Letter

Dear Parents,

Our next theme will focus on fish. Through participating in the experiences provided by this theme, the children will learn the color, size, kinds, and parts of a fish. They will also learn where fish live and the role fish play in our lives.

AT SCHOOL

Learning experiences that have been planned to complement this theme include:

- visiting a pet store to observe different types and colors of fish. We will also purchase fish to bring back to our classroom.
- listening to the story *Fish Eyes* by Lois Ehlert.
- sorting, counting, and eating various fish-shaped crackers.
- fishing in the dramatic play area.
- observing minnows in the sensory table.

AT HOME

- prepare a tuna salad using a favorite recipe with your child.
- point out fishing gear in the sports section of a department store or in a catalog.
- check out children's books about fish from the library. Look for:
  Fishes by Brian Wildsmith.
  Fish Is Fish and *Swimmy* by Leo Lionni.
  Gone Fishing by Earlene R. Long.
  A Million Fish . . . More or Less by Patricia C. McKissack.

How many fish can you catch?

Music

1. **"I'm a Little Fish"**
   (Sing to the tune of "I'm a Little Teapot")

   I'm a little fish in the lake so blue,
   There are so many things that I can do.
   I can swim around with my tail and fin.
   The water's fine—just jump right in.

2. **"Goldfish"**
   (Sing to the tune of "Have You Ever Seen a Lassie?")

   Have you ever seen a goldfish, a goldfish,
   a goldfish?
   Have you ever seen a goldfish, just swim-
   ming all around?
   He swims this way and that way,
   And this way and that way.
   Have you ever seen a goldfish, just swim-
   ming all around?

3. **"Six Little Fish"**
   (Sing to the tune of "Six Little Ducks")

   Six little fish that I once knew,
   Fat ones, skinny ones, fair ones, too.
   But the one little fish who was the leader of
   the crowd.
   He led the other fish around and around.

Fingerplays

FISH STORY

One, two, three, four, five
   (hold up fingers while counting)
Once I caught a fish alive.
Six, seven, eight, nine, ten
   (hold up additional fingers)
Then I let it go again.
Why did I let it go?
Because it bit my finger so.
Which finger did it bite?
The little finger on the right.
   (hold up pinky on the right hand)

DIVE LITTLE GOLDFISH

Dive, little goldfish one.
   (hold up one finger)
Dive, little goldfish two.
   (hold up two fingers)
Dive, little goldfish three
   (hold up three fingers)
Here is food, you see!
   (sprinkling motion with fingers)
Dive, little goldfish four.
   (hold up four fingers)

Dive, little goldfish five.
(hold up five fingers)
Dive, little goldfish six.
(hold up six fingers)
I like your funny tricks.

Source: Scott, Louise Binder. *Rhymes for Learning Times.*

GOLDFISH PETS

One little goldfish lives in a bowl.
(hold up one finger)
Two little goldfish eat their food whole.
(hold up two fingers)
Three little goldfish swim all around.
(hold up three fingers)
Although they move, they don't make a
sound.
Four little goldfish have swishy tails.
(hold up four fingers)
Five little goldfish have pretty scales.
(hold up five fingers)

Source: Scott, Louise Binder. *Rhymes for Learning Times.*

Science

1. Aquarium

Set up an aquarium to place on the science
table. Let the children take turns feeding
the fish. Provide pictures and books about
fish.

2. Balance Scale

Place on the science table a balance scale
and clean aquarium rocks. The children
can use spoons and measuring cups to
transfer the rocks into the scale containers.
After this, they can experiment with the
balance.

3. Fish Tasting Party

Plan a tasting party. Prepare fish using different methods such as baked, broiled,
fried, and prepared in a casserole. The
results of the children's favorite fish preparation can be discussed and charted.

Dramatic Play

1. Gone Fishing

Set up a fishing area in the dramatic play
center. Provide props such as a wooden
rocking boat, small wading pool, life vests,
hats, tackle boxes, nets, and fishing poles.
Fishing poles can be made by attaching
string to a short dowel or paper towel tube.
Tie a small magnet to the end of the string.
Attach paper clips to the construction
paper fish. Then, go fishing!

2. Bait and Tackle Shop

Provide props to simulate a bait and tackle
shop in the dramatic play area. Items can
include a cash register, play money, plastic
or paper fish of varying sizes, nets, fishing
lures (remove hooks), tackle boxes, coolers,
fishing poles, and life vests. Display pictures of fish and people fishing.

Arts and Crafts

1. Aquarium Crayon Resist

After observing fish or listening to stories
about fish, encourage the children to use
crayons to draw fish on a piece of white
construction paper. Then, the children can
paint over their crayon drawing with a thin
wash of blue tempera or water color. The
wax will repel the water paints leaving an
interesting effect.

2. Fish Sponge Painting

Cut sponges into fish shapes. Place the
sponges on the art table with paper and
several shallow trays of paint. Use thick
tempera paint the color of fish. Also provide paper. The children can make prints
by dipping the sponges into the paint and
then pressing them onto paper.

3. Fish Rubbings

Cut fish shapes out of tagboard, adding
details as desired. Place the fish shapes on
the art table along with paper and crayons.
The children can create designs by placing

312

a tagboard fish beneath a piece of paper and rubbing over the top of the paper with a crayon. Repeat as discussed.

4. **Tackle Box Paint Container**

Use a discarded, clean tackle box as a container to hold paints at the art table. Paints can be placed in individual compartments, providing several choices for the children.

Sensory

1. **Aquarium Rocks**

Place a bag of clean aquarium rocks in the sensory table. Provide cups, bowls, and pails for the children's use. Add water, if desired.

2. **Plastic Fish**

Purchase small plastic fish and place in the sensory table with water, strainers, and pails.

3. **Minnows**

Purchase minnows from a bait store. Place the minnows in a sensory table filled with cold water. Stress the importance of being gentle with the fish and follow through with limits set for the activity. After participating in this activity, the children need to wash their hands.

4. **Plastic Boats**

Place small plastic boats in a sensory table filled with water. Also provide small plastic people to ride and fish in the boats.

Field Trips/ Resource People

1. **Lake, Pond, or Stream**

If possible, visit a small body of water to observe fish habitat. Watch for people fishing. (For safety purposes, the body of water will have to be carefully chosen. Likewise, additional supervision may be required.)

2. **Pet Store**

Visit a pet store to see many types of fish, as well as aquariums and fish supplies. Purchase one or more goldfish to take back to your classroom.

3. **Bait and Tackle Shop**

Make arrangements to visit a bait and tackle shop. Observe the many types of fishing poles and lures, as well as boat safety items.

4. **State or National Fish Hatchery**

These make a wonderful field trip. They also have coloring books, etc., for the children.

5. **Fish Sportsman or Sportswoman**

Invite a parent or another person who enjoys fishing to come talk with the children. Ask the person to bring fishing gear and pictures of fishing trips as well as fish caught.

Math

1. **Sort the Fish**

Purchase a variety of small plastic fish or construct some out of tagboard. Put them in a large pail. The children can sort the fish by size, color, and type.

2. **Fish Seriation/Measurement**

Trace and cut shapes out of construction paper. Encourage the children to place them in order from smallest to largest. If developmentally appropriate, provide rulers and yardsticks for the children to measure the fish.

3. **Fishbowl Math**

Print numerals or sets of dots on small plastic fish. Place the fish in a clean bowl or container. The children can use small nets to take turns scooping out a fish and stating the numeral or counting the dots.

4. Fish Cracker Sort

Purchase a variety of flavors of small fish-shaped crackers. For each child, place a few of each kind of cracker in a paper cup. Before eating the crackers, encourage the children to sort the crackers. If appropriate, the children can count the number of each cracker flavor.

Group Time
(games, language)

1. Fish Memory Game

Collect items associated with fish and place on a tray. At group time, show the tray containing the items and name them. To play the game, cover the tray with a towel. Then ask the children to recall the names of items on the tray. To vary the game, play again, this time removing an item from the tray while covered. The children then try to name the item missing from the tray. To ensure success, begin the activity with few objects. Additional objects can be added depending upon the developmental maturity of the children.

2. Go Fish!

Cut fish shapes out of various colors of construction paper. Attach a paper clip to each fish. Make a fishing pole by tying a string to a short dowel. Attach a small magnet to the end of the string. At group time, present the fishing pole and fish. Place the fish on the floor and allow the children to take turns fishing. As a fish is caught, the child removes it from the magnet and names the color. Repeat until all of the children have had a turn. The game can be varied by drawing a basic shape and printing a numeral or a letter on each fish for the children to identify.

Cooking

1. Swimming Fish Snack

8 ounces soft cream cheese
blue food coloring
1 box rectangular-shaped crackers
2 cups small fish-shaped crackers
   (any flavor)

Add a few drops of blue food coloring to the cream cheese and stir. For each serving, spread cream cheese on a large, rectangular cracker. Place a few fish-shaped crackers on top of the cream cheese.

2. Fish Mix Snack

2 cups toasted oat cereal
2 cups pretzel sticks
2 cups small fish-shaped crackers
   (any flavor)
1/4 cup melted margarine
2 teaspoons Worcestershire sauce

Combine oat cereal, pretzels, and fish-shaped crackers in a bowl. In a small bowl, stir together melted margarine and Worcestershire sauce. Drizzle over cereal mixture and toss to coat evenly. Transfer into 13×9 baking pan and bake in a 300-degree oven for 30 minutes, stirring occasionally. Remove from oven and cool. Makes approximately 6 cups.

3. Tuna Salad

1 can of tuna (3 1/4-ounce), drained
1/4 cup mayonnaise, salad dressing, or
   plain yogurt
1/4 cup finely chopped apple
3 tablespoons sunflower seeds
4 slices of bread or 2 English muffins

Combine the tuna, mayonnaise, apple, and sunflower seeds in a bowl. Chill if desired. Toast the bread or English muffins. Spread tuna mixture on toasted muffins. (Makes four servings.)

4. Tartar Sauce for Fish Sticks

1/2 cup mayonnaise or salad dressing
1 tablespoon finely chopped pickle or
    pickle relish
1 teaspoon dried parsley
1/2 teaspoon grated onion or onion flakes

Combine all ingredients and chill. Bake
frozen fish sticks as directed on the package
and serve with tartar sauce.

Books

The following books can be used to
complement this theme:

Adams, Georgie. (1993). *Fish, Fish, Fish.*
    New York: Dial Books.

Aliki. (1993). *My Visit to the Aquarium.*
    New York: HarperCollins.

Arnosky, Jim. (1993). *Crinkleroot's 25 Fish
    Every Child Should Know.* New York:
    Simon & Schuster.

Bailey, Donna. (1990). *Fishing.* Austin, TX:
    Raintree/Steck Vaughn.

Boyle, Doe. (1997). *Coral Reef Hideaway:
    The Story of a Clown Anemonefish.*
    Illus. by Steven James Petruccio.
    Norwalk, CT: Soundprints Corp.

Clark, Elizaabeth. (1990). *Fish.* Illus. by
    John Yates. Minneapolis: Carolrhoda
    Books.

Cole, Joanna. (1997). *Magic School Bus
    Goes Upstream: A Book About Salmon
    on Migration.* Illus. by Bruce Degen.
    New York: Scholastic. (Pbk)

Dunphy, Madeleine. (1998). *Here Is the
    Coral Reef.* Illus. by Tom Leonard.
    New York: Hyperion.

Ehlert, Lois. (1990). *Fish Eyes: A Book You
    Can Count On.* New York: Harcourt
    Brace.

Evans, Mark. (1993). *Fish: Practical Guide
    to Caring for Your Fish.* New York:
    Dorling Kindersley.

Fowler, Allan. (1995). *The Best Way to See a
    Shark.* Chicago: Children's Press.

Gibbons, Gail. (1992). *Sharks.* New York:
    Holiday House.

Holmes, Kevin J. (1998). *Sharks.* Chicago:
    Children's Press.

Johnston, Tony. (1996). *Fishing Sunday.*
    Illus. by Barry Root. New York:
    William Morrow.

Jonas, Anne. (1995). *Splash!* New York:
    Greenwillow.

Ling, Mary. (1991). *Amazing Fish.* Photos
    by Jerry Young. New York: Knopf.

McKissack, Patricia. (1992). *A Million
    Fish—More or Less.* Illus. by Dena
    Schutzer. New York: Knopf.

Morley, Christine et al. (1997). *Me and My
    Pet Fish.* Chicago: World Book.

Pfeffer, Wendy. (1996). *What's It Like to Be
    a Fish?* Illus. by Holly Keller. New
    York: HarperCollins.

Pfister, Marcus. (1992). *The Rainbow Fish.*
    Translated by J. Alison James. New
    York: North South Books.

Pfister, Marcus. (1995). *Rainbow Fish to the
    Rescue.* Illus. by J. Alison James. New
    York: North South Books.

Ryder, Joanne. (1997). *Shark in the Sea.*
    Illus. by Michael Rothman. New
    York: William Morrow.

Samson, Suzanne. (1995). *Sea Dragons and
    Rainbow Runners: Exploring Fish with
    Children.* (1995). Illus. by Preston Neel.
    Niwot, CO: Roberts Rinehart Pub.

Sharp, N. L. (1993). *Today I'm Going
    Fishing with My Dad.* Illus. by Chris L.
    Demarest. Honesdale, PA: Boyds Mills
    Press.

Van Laan, Nancy. (1998). *Little Fish, Lost.*
    Illus. by Jane Conteh-Morgan. New
    York: Simon & Schuster.

Wallace, Karen. (1993). *Think of an Eel.*
    Illus. by Mike Bostock. Cambridge,
    MA: Candlewick Press.

Wood, Jakki. (1998). *Across the Big Blue
    Sea: An Ocean Wildlife Book.*
    Washington, D.C.: National
    Geographic.

Multimedia

The following multimedia products can be used to complement this theme:

Eastman, David. *What Is a Fish?* [video]. (1993). Northbrook, IL: Film Ideas.

Exploring the World of Fish [video]. (1992). Troy, MI: Anchor Bay Entertainment.

Fish [video]. Eyewitness Videos. Available from Kimbo Educational.

Tell Me Why: Fish, Shellfish, Underwater Life. [video]. (1987). Marina del Rey, CA: Tell Me Why.

Wet & Wild: Under the Sea with OWL/TV [video]. (1994). Toronto, ON: Children's Group Inc.

World of Pets: Fish [video]. (1985). Washington, D.C.: National Geographic.

Recordings and Song Titles

The following recordings can be used to complement this theme:

What's in the Sea?

Piggyback Songs—"I'm a Fish"

Science in a Nutshell—"Down, Down Below"

Musical Playtime Fun—"Five Gray Sharks"

THEME 32

Containers
vases
pots
window boxes
planters

Parts
petals
stem
leaves
roots
buds
seeds

Flowers

Uses
beauty
decoration
perfume
dye for clothing
gifts
ceremonial
food

Care
water
soil
sunshine
air
pollination (bees)

Names
violet
tulip
carnation
rose
lilac
lily
sunflower
orchid
magnolia
petunia
marigold
pansy

Location
wild
soil
water
greenhouses
gardens
homes

Theme Goals

Through participating in the experiences provided by this theme, the children may learn:

1. Parts of the flower.
2. Flowers have names.
3. Places flowers grow.
4. Uses of flowers.
5. Containers that hold flowers.
6. Care of flowers.

Concepts for the Children to Learn

1. A flower is a plant.
2. Flowers add beauty to our world.
3. Flowers can be used for decoration.
4. Most flowers have a smell.
5. Vases, pots, window boxes, and planters are all flower containers.
6. Flowers need soil, water, sunshine, and air to grow.
7. Sometimes flowers are given to people for special reasons, such as holidays, birthdays, or if someone goes to the hospital.

Vocabulary

1. **flower**—part of a plant that blossoms.
2. **petal**—colored part of a flower.
3. **seed**—produces a new plant.
4. **stem**—the trunk of the plant.
5. **leaves**—growth from the stem.
6. **greenhouse**—a glass house for growing plants.
7. **root**—the part of the plant that usually grows down into the soil.

Bulletin Board

The purpose of this bulletin board is to develop color matching skills, as well as to foster the correspondence of sets to written numerals. Cut large numerals out of tagboard. Color each number a different color. Next, create tulips out of tagboard. The number will depend upon the maturity of the children. Color each tulip the same color as its corresponding numeral: for example, three blue tulips for a blue numeral 3. The children can hang the appropriate number of tulips on the bulletin board next to each numeral. Moreover, the children can match the colored tulips to the corresponding colored numeral to make this activity self-correcting.

Parent Letter

Dear Parents,

Hello! As spring arrives and all the flowers begin to bloom, we will begin a unit on flowers. Through this unit the children will learn about the care, uses, and parts of a flowering plant.

AT SCHOOL

Some of the learning experiences planned to help the children make discoveries about flowers include:

- listening to the story, *Dandelion* by Ladislav Svatos.
- observing and measuring the growth of various flowers.
- visiting a floral shop.
- playing a flower beanbag toss game.
- reciting fingerplays.
- planting seeds.

AT HOME

You can integrate the concepts included in this unit into your home in many ways. If you are planning to plant a garden in your yard this spring, let your child help you. It might even be fun to section off a small part of your garden for your child to grow flowers and care for them. Another activity would be to examine the plants and flowers you have growing in your house. Also, let your child send flowers to someone special.

To develop language skills, we will be learning this fingerplay in school. Let your child teach it to you.

Daisies

One, two, three, four, five
  (pop up fingers, one at a time)
Yellow daisies all alive.
Here they are all in a row.
  (point to fingers standing)
The sun and the rain will help them grow.
  (make a circle with fingers,
  flutter fingers for rain)

Enjoy your child!

Music

"Flowers"
(Sing to the tune of "Pop! Goes the Weasel")

All around the forest ground
There's flowers everywhere.
There's pink, yellow, and purple, too.
Here's one for you.

Fingerplays

MY GARDEN

This is my garden
  (extend one hand forward, palm up)
I'll rake it with care
  (raking motion with fingers)
And then some flower seeds
  (planting motion)
I'll plant in right there.
The sun will shine
  (make circle with hands)
And the rain will fall
  (let fingers flutter down to lap)
And my garden will blossom
  (cup hands together, extend upward
  slowly)
And grow straight and tall.

DAISIES

One, two, three, four, five
  (pop up fingers, one at a time)
Yellow daisies all alive.
Here they are all in a row.
  (point to fingers standing)
The sun and the rain will help them grow.
  (make a circle with fingers, flutter fingers
  for rain)

FLOWER PLAY

If I were a little flower
Sleeping underneath the ground,
  (curl up)
I'd raise my head and grow and grow
  (raise head and begin to grow)
And stretch my arms and grow and grow
  (stretch arms)
And nod my head and say,
  (nod head)
"I'm glad to see you all today."

Children learn science concepts by growing flowers.

Science

1. **Flowers**

   Place a variety of flowers on the science table. Encourage the children to compare the color, shape, size, and smell of each flower.

2. **Planting Seeds**

   Plant flower seeds in a styrofoam cup. Save the seed packages and mount on a piece of tagboard. Place this directly behind the containers on the science table. Encourage the children to compare their plants. When the plant starts growing, compare the seed packages to the plant growth.

3. **Carnation**

Place a white carnation in a vase containing water with red food coloring added. Watch the tips of the carnation petals gradually change colors. Repeat the activity using other flowers and colors of water.

4. **Observing and Weighing Bulbs**

Collect flower bulbs and place in the science table. Encourage the children to observe the similarities and differences. A balance scale can also be added.

5. **Microscopes**

Place petals from a flower under a microscope for the children to observe.

Dramatic Play

1. **Garden**

Aprons, small garden tools, a tin of soil, seeds, watering cans, pots, and vases can all be provided. Pictures of flowers with names on them can be hung in the classroom.

2. **Gardener**

Gather materials for a gardener prop box. Include gloves, seed packets, sun hat, hoe, stakes for marking, watering cans, etc.

3. **Flower Shop**

In the dramatic play area, set up a flower shop complete with plastic flowers, boxes, containers, watering cans, misting bottle, and cash register. Artificial corsages would also be a fun addition.

4. **Flower Arranging**

Artificial flowers and containers can be placed in the dramatic play area. The children can make centerpieces for the lunch table. Also, a centerpiece can be made for the science table, the lobby, and the secretary, director, or principal.

Arts and Crafts

1. **Muffin Cup Flowers**

For younger children, prepare shapes of flowers and leaves. The older children may be able to do this themselves. Attach the stems and leaves to muffin tin liners. Add a small amount of perfume to the flower for interest.

2. **Collage**

Cut pictures of flowers from seed catalogs. With these flowers, create a collage.

3. **Easel**

Cut easel paper into flower shapes.

4. **Seed Collages**

Place a pan containing a variety of seeds in the middle of the art table. In addition, supply glue and paper for the children to form a collage.

5. **Egg Carton Flowers**

Cut the sections of an egg container apart. Attach pipe cleaners for stems and decorate with watercolor markers.

6. **Flower Mobile**

Bring in a tree branch and hang from the classroom ceiling. Let the children make flowers and hang them on the branch for decoration.

7. **Paper Plate Flowers**

Provide snack-sized paper plates, markers, crayons, and colored construction paper. The children may use these materials to create a flower.

Sensory

Add to the sensory table:

⑤ soil and plastic flowers

⑤ water and watering cans

Field Trips/ Resource People

1. Florist

Arrange to visit a local floral shop. Observe the different kinds of flowers. Then watch the florist design a bouquet or corsage.

2. Walk

Walk around the neighborhood observing different types and colors of flowers.

Math

1. Flower Growth

Prepare sequence cards representing flowers at various stages of growth. Encourage the children to sequence them.

2. Flower Match

Cut pictures of flowers from magazines or seed catalogs. If desired, mount the pictures. The children can match them by kind, size, color, and shape.

3. Measuring Seed Growth

Plant several types of seeds. At determined intervals, measure the growth of various plants and flowers. Maintain a chart comparing the growth.

Group Time
(games, language)

Hide the Flower

Choose one child to look for the flower. Ask him to cover his eyes. Ask another child to hide a flower. After the flower is hidden and the child returns to the group, instruct the first child to uncover his eyes and find the flower. Clues can be provided. For example, if the child aproaches the area where the flower is hidden, the remainder of the children can clap their hands.

Cooking

1. Fruit Candy

Fruit grows on trees and plants. A flower blossom grows on the trees or plants. The flowers produce fruit.

1 pound dried figs
1 pound dried apricots
1/2 pound dates
2 cups walnuts
1/2 cup raisins
1/2 cup coarsely chopped walnuts

Put fruit and 2 cups of walnuts through a food grinder. Mix in the 1/2 cup of chopped walnuts and press into a buttered 9-inch × 13-inch pan. Chill and enjoy!

2. China—Egg Flower Soup

Watch an egg turn into a flower. Chinese cooks say that the cooked shreds of egg afloat in this soup look like flower petals.

1 tablespoon cornstarch
2 tablespoons cold water
1 egg
3 cups clear canned chicken broth
1 teaspoon salt
1 teaspoon chopped scallion or parsley (optional)

Put the cornstarch into a small bowl and gradually add water, stirring it with a fork until you no longer see any lumps. Break the egg into another small bowl and beat it with the fork. Pour the broth into the saucepan. Bring it to a boil over high heat. Add the salt. Give the cornstarch and water mixture a quick stir with the fork. Add it to the soup. Stir the soup with a spoon until it thickens and becomes clear (about one minute). Slowly pour the beaten egg into the soup. The egg will cook in the hot soup and form shreds. When all the egg has been added, stir once. Turn off the heat. Pour the soup into 4 soup bowls. Top if desired with chopped scallion or parsley for decorations.

Source: Touff, Terry, & Ratner, Marilyn. (1974). *Many Hands Cooking*. New York: Thomas Y. Crowell Company.

3. Dandelion Salad

6 cups young dandelion leaves, picked before flower blossoms
croutons, hard-boiled eggs, vegetables (optional)
dressing

Thoroughly wash the dandelion greens, removing stems and roots. Tear the leaves into small pieces and place in bowls. Add optional ingredients. Toss with salad dressing.

Books

The following books can be used to complement this theme:

Barker, Cicely Mary. (1998). *Flower Fairies of the Spring: A Celebration.* New York: Frederick Warne.

Barker, Cicely Mary. (1996). *Flower Fairies: The Meaning of Flowers.* New York: Frederick Warne.

Bryant-Mole, Karen. (1996). *Flowers.* Austin, TX: Raintree/Steck Vaughn.

Bunting, Eve. (1994). *Flower Garden.* Illus. by Kathryn Hewitt. Orlando: Harcourt Brace.

Burnie, David. (1992). *Flowers.* New York: Dorling Kindersley.

Cole, Henry. (1995). *Jack's Garden.* New York: Greenwillow.

Cole, Joanna. (1995). *The Magic School Bus Plants Seeds: A Book About How Living Things Grow.* Illus. by Bruce Degen. New York: Scholastic. (Pbk)

De Paola, Tomie. (1994). *The Legend of the Poinsettia.* New York: G. P. Putnam.

Ford, Miela. (1995). *Sunflower.* Illus. by Sally Noll. New York: Greenwillow.

King, Elizabeth. (1993). *Backyard Sunflower.* New York: Dutton.

Lobel, Anita. (1990). *Alison's Zinnia.* New York: Greenwillow.

Lucht, Irmgard. (1995). *The Red Poppy.* Illus. by Frank Jacoby-Nelson. New York: Hyperion.

Marzollo, Jean. (1996). *I'm a Seed.* Madison, WI: Demco Media.

Pallotta, Jerry. (1990). *Flower Alphabet Book.* Illus. by Leslie Evans. Watertown, MA: Charlesbridge Publishers.

Pomeroy, Diana. (1997). *Wildflower ABC: An Alphabet of Potato Prints.* Orlando: Harcourt Brace.

Robbins, Ken. (1990). *A Flower Grows.* New York: Dial Books.

Samson, Suzanne. (1994). *Fairy Dusters and Blazing Stars: Exploring Wildflowers With Children.* Illus. by Neel Preston. Niwot, CO: Roberts Rinehart Publishers.

Sun, Chyng-Feng. (1996). *Cat and Cat-Face.* Illus. by Lesley Liu. Boston: Houghton Mifflin.

Multimedia

The following multimedia products can be used to complement this theme:

Flowers & Seeds [video]. (1994). Princeton, NJ: Films for the Humanities.

Flowers, Plants and Trees [video]. (1987). *Tell Me Why* series. Marina Del Rey, CA: Penguin Productions.

Raffi. *"Spring Flowers"* on Bananaphone [compact disc]. (1994). Cambridge, MA: Shoreline. Available from Kimbo Educational.

Recordings and Song Titles

The following recordings can be used to complement this theme:

Piggyback Songs—"Flower Garden"

Science in a Nutshell—"Dandelion Seed," "I'm Going to Plant a Garden"

Rainbow of Songs—"In Grandma's Garden"

Singable Nursery Rhymes—"Mary, Mary, Quite Contrary"

T H E M E 33

Friends

Activities
play
share
learn
talk
listen
work

Who
self
mothers
fathers
brothers
sisters
cousins
relatives
boys
girls
neighbors
pets

Places
school
neighborhood
home
park

Why
to help
to enjoy

Theme Goals

Through participating in the experiences provided by this theme, the children may learn:

1. Who friends are.
2. Why we have friends.
3. Activities we can do with our friends.
4. Places we can make friends.

Concepts for the Children to Learn

1. A friend is someone who I like and who likes me.
2. My friends are special to me.
3. We have friends at school.
4. Our brothers and sisters can be our friends.
5. Friends can help us with our work.
6. We play with our friends.
7. We share and learn with friends.
8. Friends talk and listen to us.
9. A pet can be a friend.
10. Friends can be boys or girls.

Vocabulary

1. **friend**—a person we enjoy.
2. **sharing**—giving and taking turns.
3. **like**—feeling good about someone or something.
4. **giving**—sharing something of your own with others.
5. **cooperating**—working together to help someone.
6. **togetherness**—being with one another and sharing a good feeling.
7. **pal or buddy**—another word for friend.

Bulletin Board

The purpose of this bulletin board is to help the children recognize their own and their friends' names. The bulletin board can also be used by the teacher as an attendance check. Prepare the board by constructing name cards for each child as illustrated. Then laminate and punch holes in each card. When the children arrive at school, they can attach their name card to the bulletin board with a pushpin.

Parent Letter

Dear Parents,

We will be starting a curriculum unit on friends, which will include discovering people of all ages and even animal friends. The children have made many new friends at school with whom they are learning to take turns, cooperate, work, and play. Through this unit, the children will become more aware of what a friend is and activities friends can do together. Moreover, they will learn the importance of prosocial behavior.

AT SCHOOL

Highlights of the learning experiences in this unit include:

⑤ making friendship fortune cookies.

⑤ sending notes to pen pals.

⑤ creating a friendship chain with strips of paper.

⑤ looking at pictures of our friends at school in our classroom photo album.

⑤ reciting fingerplays related to friendships.

⑤ singing songs related to friends.

AT HOME

Your child may enjoy looking at photo albums of family and friends. Perhaps a friend could be invited to come and play with your child. We will be learning a poem about friends to promote an enjoyment of language and poetry.

Friends

I like my friends,
So when we are at play,
I try to be very kind,
and nice in every way.

Be your child's best friend!

328

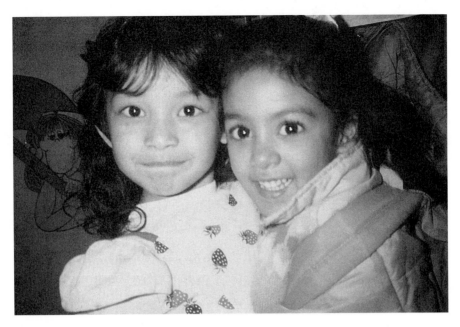

Tina is my best friend!

Music

1. **"Do You Know This Friend of Mine?"**
(Sing to the tune of "The Muffin Man")

Do you know this friend of mine,
This friend of mine,
This friend of mine?
Do you know this friend of mine?
His name is _____.

Yes, we know this friend of yours,
This friend of yours,
This friend of yours.
Yes, we know this friend of yours.
His name is _____.

2. **"The More We Are Together"**
(Sing to the tune of "Have You Ever Seen a Lassie?")

The more we are together, together,
together,
The more we are together, the happier we'll
be.
For your friends are my friends, and my
friends are your friends.
The more we are together the happier we'll
be.

We're all in school together, together,
together,
We're all in school together, and happy
we'll be.
There's Ali and Keisha and Jenny and Ben,
There's _____ and _____ and _____ and
_____.
We're all in school together and happy
we'll be.

Insert names of children in your classroom.

3. **"Beth Met a Friend"**
(Sing to the tune of "The Farmer in the Dell")

Beth met a friend,
Beth met a friend,
When she came to school today,
Beth met a friend.

Insert names of children in your classroom
for each verse.

Fingerplays

FRIENDS

I like my friends.
So when we are at play,
I try to be very kind
and nice in every way.

FIVE LITTLE FRIENDS

(hold up five fingers; subtract one with
each action)

Five little friends playing on the floor,
One got tired and then there were four.
Four little friends climbing in a tree,
One jumped down and then there were
   three.
Three little friends skipping to the zoo,
One went for lunch and then there were
   two.
Two little friends swimming in the sun,
One went home and then there was one.
One little friend going for a run,
Decided to take a nap and then there were
   none.

Science

1. **Comparing Heartbeats**

   Provide stethoscopes for the children to listen to their friends' heartbeats.

2. **Fingerprints**

   Ink pads and white paper can be provided
   for the children to make fingerprints. Also,
   a microscope can be provided to encourage
   the children to compare their fingerprints.

3. **Friends' Voices**

   Tape the children's voices throughout the
   course of the day. The following day, leave
   the tape recorder at the science table. The
   children can listen to the tape and try to
   guess which classmate is talking.

4. **Animal Friends**

   Prepare signs for the animal cages listing
   the animal's daily food intake and care.

Dramatic Play

1. **Puppet Show**

   Set up a puppet stage with various types of
   puppets. The children can share puppets
   and act out friendships using the puppets
   in various situations.

2. **A Tea Party**

   Provide dress-up clothes, play dishes, and
   water in the dramatic play area.

Arts and Crafts

1. **Friendship Chain**

   Provide strips of paper for the older children to print their names on. For those
   children who are not interested or unable,
   print their names for them. When all the
   names are on the strips of paper, the children can connect them to make a chain.
   The chain should symbolize that everyone
   in the class is a friend.

2. **Friendship Collage**

   Encourage the children to find magazine
   pictures of friends. These pictures can be
   pasted on a large sheet of paper for a collage. Later the paper can be used for decoration and discussion in the lobby or
   hallway.

3. **Friendship Exchange Art**

   Provide each child with a piece of construction paper with "To: _____" printed in
   the upper left corner and "From: _____"
   printed on the bottom. The teacher assists
   the children in printing their names on the
   bottom and the name of the person to
   their right on the top of the paper. Using

paper scraps, tissue paper squares, fabric scraps, and glue, each child will construct a picture for a friend. When finished, have each child pass the paper to the friend it was made for.

Sensory

The sensory table is an area where two to four children can make new friends and share. Materials that can be added to the sensory table include:

- shaving cream
- playdough
- sand with toys
- water with boats
- wood shavings
- Silly Putty

Mix equal parts of white glue and liquid starch. Food coloring can be added for color. Store in an airtight container.

- dry pasta with scoops and a balance scale
- goop

Mix water and cornstarch. Add cornstarch to the water until you get the consistency that you want.

Large Muscle

1. **Double Balance Beam**

   Place two balance beams side by side and encourage two children to hold hands and cross together.

2. **Bowling Game**

   Set up pins or plastic bottles. With a ball, have the children take turns knocking down the pins.

3. **Outdoor Obstacle Course**

   Design an obstacle course outdoors that is specifically designed for two children to go

through at one time. Use balance beams, climbers, slides, etc. Short and simple obstacle courses seem to work the best.

Field Trips/ Resource People

1. **The Zoo**

   Take a trip to the zoo to observe animals.

2. **The Nursing Home**

   Visit a nursing home allowing the children to interact with elderly friends.

3. **Resource People**

   Invite the following community helpers into the classroom:

   - police officer
   - trash collector
   - janitor/custodian
   - firefighter
   - doctor, nurse, dentist
   - principal or director

Math

1. **Group Pictures**

   Take pictures of the children in groups of 2, 3, 4, etc. Make separate corresponding number cards. The children then can match the correct numeral to the picture card.

2. **Friend Charts**

   Take individual pictures of the children and chart them according to hair color, eye color, etc. Encourage the children to compare their looks to the characteristics of their friends.

Transition Activities

CLEAN UP

"Do You Know What Time It Is?"
(Sing to the tune of "The Muffin Man")

Oh, do you know what time it is,
What time it is, what time it is?
Oh, do you know what time it is?
It's almost clean-up time.
  (Or, it's time to clean up.)

"Clean-up Time"
(Sing to the tune of "London Bridge")

Clean-up time is already here,
Already here, already here.
Clean-up time is already here,
Already here.

"This Is the Way"
(Sing to the tune of "Mulberry Bush")

This is the way we pick up our toys,
Pick up our toys, pick up our toys.
This is the way we pick up our toys,
At clean-up time each day.

"Oh, It's Clean-up Time"
(Sing to the tune of "Oh, My Darling Clementine")

Oh, its clean-up time,
Oh, it's clean-up time,
Oh, it's clean-up time right now.
It's time to put the toys away,
It is clean-up time right now.

"A Helper I Will Be"
(Sing to the tune of "The Farmer in the Dell")

A helper I will be.
A helper I will be.
I'll pick up the toys and put them away.
A helper I will be.

"We're Cleaning Up Our Room"
(Sing to the tune of "The Farmer in the Dell")

We're cleaning up our room.
We're cleaning up our room.
We're putting all the toys away.
We're cleaning up our room.

"It's Clean-up Time"
(Sing to the chorus of "Looby Loo")

It's clean-up time at school.
It's time for boys and girls
To stop what they are doing
And put away their toys.

"Time to Clean Up"
(Sing to the tune of "Are You Sleeping?")

Time to clean up.
Time to clean up.
Everybody help.
Everybody help.
Put the toys away, put the toys away.
Then sit down. (Or, then come here.)

Specific toys can be mentioned in place of "toys."

"Clean-up Time"
(Sing to the tune of "Hot Cross Buns")

Clean-up time.
Clean-up time.
Put all of the toys away.
It's clean-up time.

ROUTINES

"Passing Around"
(Sing to the tune of "Skip to My Loo")

Brad, take a napkin and pass them to Sara.
Sara, take a napkin and pass them to Tina.
Tina, take a napkin and pass them to Eric,
Passing around the napkins.

Fill in appropriate child's name and substitute napkin for any object that needs to be passed at meal time.

"Put Your Coat On"
(Sing to the tune of "Oh, My Darling Clementine")

Put your coat on.
Put your coat on.
Put your winter coat on now.
We are going to play outside.
Put your coat on right now.

Change coat to any article of clothing.

"Time to Go Outside"
(Sing to the tune of "When Johnny Comes Marching Home")

When it's time for us to go outside
To play, to play,

We find a place to put our toys
Away, away.
We'll march so quietly to the door.
We know exactly what's in store
When we go outside to play for a little while.

"We're Going on a Walk"
(Sing to the tune of "The Farmer in the Dell")

We're going for a walk.
We're going for a walk.
Hi-ho, the dairy-o,
We're going for a walk.

Additional verses:
What will we wear?
What will we see?
How will we go?
Who knows the way?

"Find a Partner"
(Sing to the tune of "Oh, My Darling Clementine")

Find a partner, find a partner,
Find a partner right now.
We are going for a walk.
Find a partner right now.

"Walk Along"
(Sing to the tune of "Clap Your Hands")

Walk, walk, walk along,
Walk along to the bathroom.
____ and ____ walk along,
Walk along to the bathroom.

Change walk to any other types of movement— jump, hop, skip, crawl.

"We're Going . . ."
(Sing to the tune of "Go in and out the Window")

We're going to the bathroom,
We're going to the bathroom,
We're going to the bathroom,
And then we'll wash our hands.

"It's Time to Change"
(Sing to the tune of "Hello, Everybody")

It's time to change, yes indeed,
Yes indeed, yes indeed.
It's time to change, yes indeed
Time to change groups.
  (Or, Time to go outside.)

Social Studies

Friends Bulletin Board

Ask the children to bring pictures of their friends into the classroom. Set up a bulletin board in the classroom where these pictures can be hung for all to see. Remind the children that friends can be family members and animals too.

Cooking

1. **Pound Cake Brownies**

   3/4 cup butter or margarine, softened
   1 cup sugar
   3 eggs
   2 1-ounce squares unsweetened chocolate, melted and cooled
   1 teaspoon vanilla
   1 1/4 cups all-purpose flour
   1/2 teaspoon baking powder
   1/4 teaspoon salt
   1/2 cup chopped nuts

   Cream butter and sugar; beat in eggs. Blend in chocolate and vanilla. Stir flour with baking powder and salt. Add to creamed mixture. Mix well. Stir in nuts. Spread in a greased 9- × 9- × 2-inch baking pan. Bake at 350 degrees for 25 to 30 minutes. Cool. If desired, sift powdered sugar over the top. Cut into bars. Yields 24 bars.

Books

The following books can be used to complement this theme:

Aliki. (1995). *Best Friends Together Again.* New York: Greenwillow.

Carlson, Nancy L. (1994). *How to Lose All Your Friends.* New York: Viking.

Caseley, Judith. (1991). *Harry and Willy and Carrothead.* New York: Greenwillow.

Champion, Joyce. (1993). *Emily and Alice.* Illus. by Sucie Stevenson. Orlando: Harcourt Brace.

Cote, Nancy. (1993). *Palm Trees.* New York: Four Winds.

Dugan, Barbara. (1992). *Loop the Loop.* Illus. by James Stevenson. New York: Greenwillow.

Egan, Tim. (1996). *Metropolitan Cow.* Boston: Houghton Mifflin.

Fuchs, Diane Marcial. (1995). *A Bear for All Seasons.* Illus. by Kathryn Brown. New York: Holt.

Haville, Juanita. (1993). *Jamaica and Brianna.* Illus. by Anne Sibley O'Brien. Boston: Houghton Mifflin.

Hoban, Russell. (1994). *Best Friends for Frances.* Illus. by Lillian Hoban. New York: HarperCollins.

Hutchins, Pat. (1993). *My Best Friend.* New York: Greenwillow.

Hutchins, Pat. (1996). *Titch and Daisy.* New York: Greenwillow.

Leedy, Loreen. (1996). *How Humans Make Friends.* New York: Holiday House.

Mavor, Salley. (1997). *You and Me: Poems of Friendship.* New York: Orchard Books.

Monson, A. M. (1997). *Wanted: Best Friend.* Illus. by Lynn Munsinger. New York: Dial Books.

Morris, Ann. (1990). *Loving.* Photos by Ken Heyman. New York: Lothrop, Lee & Shepard.

Naylor, Phyllis Reynolds. (1991). *King of the Playground.* Illus. by Nola Langner Malone. Colchester, CT: Atheneum.

Polacco, Patricia. (1992). *Chicken Sunday.* New York: Philomel Books.

Polacco, Patricia. (1992). *Mrs. Katz and Tush.* New York: Bantam.

Raschka, Chris. (1993). *Yo! Yes?* New York: Orchard Books.

Reiser, Lynn. (1997). *Best Friends Think Alike.* New York: Greenwillow.

Reiser, Lynn. (1993). *Margaret and Margarita/Margarita y Margaret.* New York: Greenwillow.

Spohn, Kate. (1996). *Dog and Cat Shake a Leg.* New York: Viking.

Waber, Bernard. (1995). *Gina.* Boston: Houghton Mifflin.

Multimedia

The following multimedia products can be used to complement this theme:

Berenstain Bears Get in a Fight [CD-ROM]. (1995). Random House/Broderbund.

Brown, Marc. *Arthur's Birthday* [CD-ROM]. (1994). Random House/Broderbund.

Hartmann, Jack. *Make a Friend, Be a Friend: Songs for Growing Up and Growing Together with Friends* [sound cassette]. (1990). Educational Activities.

Recordings and Song Titles

The following recordings can be used to complement this theme:

Get Up and Grow—"A Friend in Need"

Nelson Gill / *Friends*—"Friends"

Tony Chestnut (The Learning Station)— "I Like Friends"

THEME 34

Characteristics

seeds, fruits, vegetables,
shapes, sizes, colors

Growth

sunlight
water

Fruits
and
Vegetables

Forms

fresh
frozen
canned

Kinds

kiwi, bananas,
corn, beans,
squash, mangoes,
apricots, cherries,
green beans

Preparation

peel, raw,
cook, frozen,
canned, dried

Places
Grown

yard
garden
trees
vines
underground

Theme Goals

Through participating in the experiences provided by this theme, the children may learn:

1. Names of common fruits and vegetables.
2. Purposes of fruits and vegetables.
3. Places fruits and vegetables are grown.
4. Preparation of fruits and vegetables.
5. Tastes of fruits and vegetables.
6. Fruit or vegetable seeds.

Concepts for the Children to Learn

1. There are many kinds of fruits and vegetables.
2. Fruits and vegetables come in many shapes, sizes, and colors.
3. Fruits and vegetables need sunlight and water to grow.
4. Fruits and vegetables can be bought fresh, frozen, or canned.
5. Some people grow fruits and vegetables in gardens.
6. Fruits and vegetables have different names.
7. Most fruits and vegetables can be eaten raw or cooked.
8. Some fruits and vegetables we eat with skin; some we need to peel first.
9. Some fruits have seeds.

Vocabulary

1. **fruit**—usually a sweet-tasting part of a plant.
2. **vegetable**—part of a plant that can be eaten.
3. **garden**—ground used to grow plants.
4. **produce**—agriculture products such as fruits and vegetables.
5. **vine**—plant with long, slender stem.

6. **cook**—prepare food by heating.

7. **frozen**—chilled or refrigerated to make solid.

8. **seeds**—part of a plant used for growing a new crop and edible in some plants (sunflower, pumpkin).

9. **roots**—parts of a plant that grow downward into the soil and are edible in some plants (potatoes, turnips, radishes, onions, and carrots).

10. **soil**—portion of earth; dirt used for growing.

11. **sprout**—to begin to grow.

12. **stems**—part of a plant used for transporting food and water and edible in some plants (celery).

13. **ripe**—ready to be picked and eaten.

Bulletin Board

The purpose of this bulletin board is to observe the growth of a lima bean seed. Prepare by placing a moist paper towel in a small plastic bag, along with a lima bean seed. Sprouting will occur faster if the seeds have been pre-soaked overnight. Staple each bag to the bulletin board as illustrated and place a child's name beside each one. Additional watering may be needed throughout this unit.

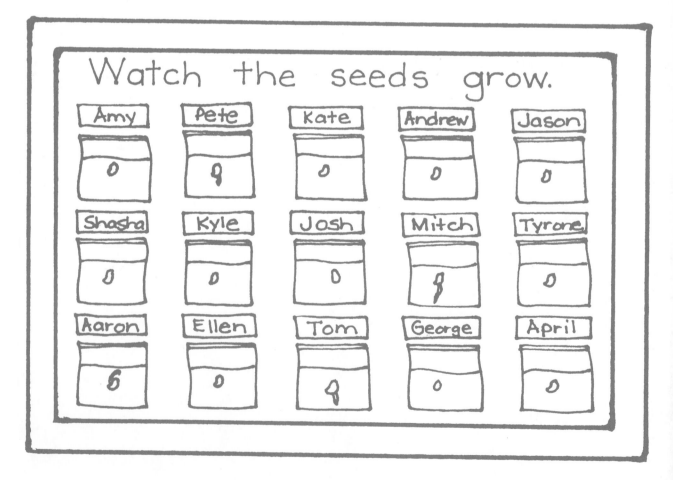

Parent Letter

Dear Parents,

Hello again! We hope that everyone in your family is healthy and happy. Speaking of health, we are starting a new curriculum unit on fruits and vegetables. Through the experiences planned for this unit, the children will become aware of many fruits and vegetables and how they are grown. Also, they will discover how many different fruits and vegetables taste.

AT SCHOOL

Some of the many fun-filled learning activities scheduled for this unit are:

- planting lima bean seeds to sprout. Take a look at our bulletin board this week.
- playing the role of a gardener/farmer in the dramatic play area.
- matching pictures of vegetables to where they are grown (trees, vines, underground, etc.).
- having a fruit and vegetable tasting party during snack.
- visiting a produce section at the grocery store.
- listening to a story called *What Was It Before It Was Orange Juice?* by Jane Belk Moncure.

AT HOME

There are many ways you can integrate the concepts included in this unit into your family life. To help develop memory and language skills, ask your child which vegetables or fruits he tried during the week. Then let your child help you prepare them at home. Cooking often tempts a child to try new foods. Also, here is a great dip recipe we will be making for snack on Tuesday that you may want to make at home also.

Vegetable Dip

1 cup yogurt	1 tablespoon dill weed
1 cup mayonnaise	1 teaspoon seasoned salt

Mix all ingredients and chill. Serve with fresh raw vegetables.

We still need two more helpers to assist us with our field trip on Thursday to the grocery store. Let me know if you are available. The children enjoy having parents join in our activities.

Enjoy your child!

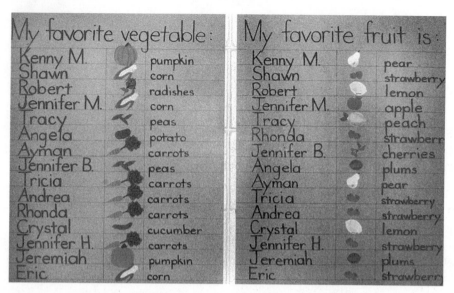

My favorite vegetable:			My favorite fruit is:		
Kenny M.		pumpkin	Kenny M.		pear
Shawn		corn	Shawn		strawberry
Robert		radishes	Robert		lemon
Jennifer M.		corn	Jennifer M.		apple
Tracy		peas	Tracy		peach
Angela		potato	Rhonda		strawberr
Ayman		carrots	Jennifer B.		cherries
Jennifer B.		peas	Angela		plums
Tricia		carrots	Ayman		pear
Andrea		carrots	Tricia		strawberry
Rhonda		carrots	Andrea		strawberry
Crystal		cucumber	Crystal		lemon
Jennifer H.		carrots	Jennifer H.		strawberry
Jeremiah		pumpkin	Jeremiah		plums
Eric		corn	Eric		strawberr

Trying different fruits and vegetables and listing favorites is a good activity.

Music

1. "The Vegetable Garden"
(Sing to the tune of "Mulberry Bush")

Here we go 'round the vegetable garden,
The vegetable garden, the vegetable
   garden,
Here we go 'round the vegetable garden,
So early in the morning.

Other verses:
This is the way we pull the weeds . . .
This is the way we water the plants . . .
This is the way we eat the vegetables . . .

2. "Vegetables"
(Sing to the tune of "Mary Had a Little Lamb")

I'm a tomato, red and round,
Red and round, red and round.
I'm a tomato, red and round,
Seated on the ground.

I'm a corn stalk, tall and straight,
Tall and straight, tall and straight.
I'm a corn stalk, tall and straight
And I taste just great.

Fingerplays

MY GARDEN

This is my garden
   (extend one hand forward, palm up)
I'll rake it with care
   (make raking motion on palm with three
   fingers of other hand)
And then some seeds
   (planting motion)
I'll plant in there.
The sun will shine
   (make circle with arms)
And the rain will fall
   (let fingers flutter down to lap)
And my garden will blossom
   (cup hand together, extend upward
   slowly)
And grow straight and tall.

DIG A LITTLE HOLE

Dig a little hole.
   (dig)
Plant a little seed.
   (drop seed)
Pour a little water.
   (pour)
Pull a little weed.
   (pull and throw)

Chase a little bug.
    (chasing motion with hands)
Heigh-ho, there he goes.
    (shade eyes)
Give a little sunshine
    (circle arms over head)
Grow a little bean!
    (hands grow upward)

APPLE TREE

Way up high in the apple tree
    (hold arms up high)
Two little apples smiled at me.
    (look at two hands up high)
I shook that tree as hard as I could.
    (shake arms)
Down came the apples,
    (arms fall)
Mmm, were they good!
    (rub tummy)

BANANAS

Bananas are my favorite fruit.
    (make fists as if holding banana)
I eat one every day.
    (hold up one finger)
I always take one with me
    (act as if putting one in pocket)
When I go out to play.
    (wave good-bye)
It gives me lots of energy
    (make a muscle)
To jump around and run.
    (move arms as if running)
Bananas are my favorite fruit.
    (rub tummy)
To me they're so much fun!
    (point to self and smile)

VEGETABLES AND FRUITS

The food we like to eat that grows
On vines and bushes and trees
Are vegetables and fruits, my friends,
Like cherries, grapes, and peas.
Apples and oranges and peaches are fruits
And so are tangerines,
Lettuce and carrots are vegetables,
Like squash and beans.

Science

1. **Cut and Draw**

    Cut out or draw many different fruits and vegetables from tagboard or construction paper scraps. Also make a tree, a vine, and some soil. Have children classify the fruit by where it's grown—on a tree, on a vine, or underground.

2. **Tasting Center**

    Cut small pieces of various fruits and set up a tasting center. Encourage the children to taste and compare different fruits and vegetables.

3. **Tasting Party**

    Plan a vegetable tasting party. Cut small pieces of vegetables. Also, have children taste raw vegetables and compare them to the same vegetable cooked.

4. **Identify by Smelling**

    Place one each of several fruits and vegetables in small cups and cover with aluminum foil. Punch a small hole in the top of the aluminum foil. Then have the children smell the cups and try to identify each fruit or vegetable.

5. **Carrot Tops in Water**

    Cut off the top of a carrot and place it in a shallow dish of water. Observe what happens day to day. Given time, the top of the carrot should sprout.

6. **Colored Celery Stalks**

    Place celery stalks into water colored with food coloring. Observe what happens to the leaves of celery.

Dramatic Play

Grocery Store

Plan a grocery store containing many plastic fruits and vegetables, a cash register, grocery bags, and play money if available. The children can take turns being a produce clerk, cashier, and price tagger.

Arts and Crafts

1. **Fruit and Vegetable Collage**

   Make a fruit and vegetable collage. Have children draw or cut their favorite fruits and vegetables from magazines and paste on paper.

2. **Seeds**

   Save several seeds from fruits and vegetables for the children to make a seed collage. When seeds are securely glued, children can also paint them if desired. The collage can be secured to a bulletin board.

3. **Cutting Vegetable and Fruit Shapes**

   Cut easel paper into a different shape of fruit or vegetable every day.

4. **Mold with Playdough**

   The children can mold and create fruits and vegetables out of clay and playdough. Another option would be to color and scent the playdough. Examples might include orange-smelling orange, lemon-smelling yellow, banana-smelling yellow.

5. **Potato Prints**

   Cut potatoes in half. The children can dip them in paints and stamp the potatoes on a large sheet of paper.

6. **Paint with Celery Leaves**

   Mix some thin tempera paint. Use celery leaves as a painting tool.

Sensory

Preparing Fruits and Vegetables

Wash vegetables and fruits to prepare for eating at snack time.

Large Muscle

Place hoes, shovels, rakes, and watering cans around the outdoor sand area.

Field Trips

1. **Grocery Store**

   Take a trip to the grocery store to visit the produce department. Ask the clerk to show the children how the food is delivered.

2. **Visiting a Farm**

   Visit a farm. Ask the farmer to show the children the fruits and vegetables grown on the farm.

3. **Visit a Farmers' Market**

   Visit a farmers' market. Purchase fruits and vegetables that can be used for snacks.

4. **Visit an Orchard**

   Visit an apple or fruit orchard. Observe how the fruit is grown. If possible, pick some fruit to bring back to the classroom.

Math

1. **Fruit and Vegetable Match**

   Cut out various fruits and vegetables from a magazine. Trace their shapes onto tagboard. Have children match the fruit or vegetable to the correct shape on the tagboard.

2. Seriation

Make five sizes of each vegetable or fruit you want to use. Have children place in order from smallest to largest, or largest to smallest.

3. Measuring

The children can measure their bean sprouts. Maintain a small chart of their measurements.

4. Parts and Wholes

Cut apples in half at snack time to introduce the concepts of parts and whole.

5. Grouping Pictures

Cut pictures of fruits and vegetables for the children to sort according to color, size, and shape.

Social Studies

1. Field Trip to a Garden

Plan a field trip to a large garden. Point out different fruits and vegetables. If possible, have the children pull radishes and carrots.

2. Hang Pictures

On a bulletin board in the classroom hang pictures of fruits and vegetables.

3. Fruit and Vegetable Book

The children can make a fruit and vegetable book. Possible titles include "My favorite fruit is," "My favorite vegetable is," "I would like to grow," and "I would most like to cook." The children can paste pictures or adhere stickers to the individual pages.

Group Time
(games, language)

1. Carrot, Carrot, Corn

Play "Duck, Duck, Goose," but substitute "Carrot, Carrot, Corn."

2. Hot Potato

The children sit in a circle and the teacher gives one child a potato. Teacher then plays lively music and the children pass potato around the circle. When the music suddenly stops, the child with the potato must stand up and say the name of a fruit or vegetable. Encourage children to think of a fruit or vegetable that hasn't been named yet.

Cooking

1. Vegetable Dip

1 cup plain yogurt
1 cup mayonnaise
1 tablespoon dill weed
1 teaspoon seasoned salt

Mix all the ingredients together and chill. Serve with fresh raw vegetables.

2. Ants on a Log

Cut celery into pieces and spread with peanut butter. Top with raisins, coconut, or grated carrots. (Celery is difficult for younger children to chew.)

3. Applesauce

4 apples
1 tablespoon water
2 tablespoons brown sugar or honey

Wash the apples and cut into small pieces. Dip the pieces into water and roll in brown sugar or honey. Serves 8.

4. Banana Rounds

4 medium bananas
1/2 cup yogurt
3 tablespoons honey
1/8 teaspoon nutmeg
1/8 teaspoon cinnamon
1/4 cup wheat germ

The children can participate by peeling the bananas and slicing into "rounds." Measure the spices, wheat germ, and honey. Blend this mixture with yogurt and bananas. Chill prior to serving. Serves 8.

5. Middle East Date and Banana Dessert

4 ounces (1 cup) pitted dates, cut up
2 bananas, thinly sliced
2 to 3 teaspoons finely shredded lemon
   peel
1/2 cup half and half
sliced almonds (optional)

Alternate layers of dates and bananas in serving dish or dessert dishes. Sprinkle with lemon peel. Pour half and half over top. Cover and refrigerate at least 4 hours. Just before serving sprinkle with almonds. Makes 3 to 4 servings.

Source: *Betty Crocker's International Cookbook.* (1980). New York: Random House.

6. Finnish Strawberry Shake

20 fresh strawberries
4 cups milk
3 tablespoons sugar

Wash strawberries and remove stems. Cut strawberries into small pieces. Combine milk, sugar, and strawberries in a large mixing bowl or blender. Beat with an eggbeater or blend for 2 minutes. Pour strawberry shakes into individual glasses. Makes 4 to 8 servings.

Variation: Raspberries or other sweet fruit may be used instead.

7. Banana Sandwiches

1/2 or 1 banana per child
peanut butter

Peel the bananas and slice them in half lengthwise. Spread peanut butter on one half of the banana and top with the other half.

Cooking Vocabulary

The following vocabulary words can be introduced through cooking experiences:

bake	cut	grill	pit	spread
beat	dice	grind	pour	sprinkle
boil	dip	heat	roast	squeeze
broil	drain	knead	roll	stir
brown	freeze	marinate	scrape	strain
chop	frost	measure	scrub	stuff
cool	fry	mince	shake	tear
core	garnish	mix	shread	toast
cream	grate	pare	sift	whip
cube	grease	peel	simmer	

Books

The following books can be used to complement this theme:

Brown, Laurene Krasny. (1995). *The Vegetable Show*. Boston: Little, Brown.

Caseley, Judith. (1990). *Grandpa's Garden Lunch*. New York: Greenwillow.

Charles, N. N. (1994). *What Am I?: Looking Through Shapes at Apples and Grapes*. Illus. by Leo and Diane Dillon. New York: Scholastic.

Ehlert, Lois. (1994). *Eating the Alphabet: Fruits & Vegetables from A to Z*. Orlando: Harcourt Brace.

Fowler, Allan. (1995). *Corn—On and Off the Cob*. Chicago: Children's Press. (Pbk)

Fowler, Allan. (1996). *It's a Fruit, It's a Vegetable, It's a Pumpkin*. Illus. by Robert L. Hillerich. Chicago: Children's Press.

French, Vivian. (1995). *Oliver's Vegetables*. Illus. by Alison Bartlett. New York: Orchard Books.

Gershator, Phillis. (1996). *Sweet, Sweet Fig Banana*. Illus. by Fritz Millvoix. Niles, IL: Albert Whitman & Co.

Greenstein, Elaine. (1996). *Mrs. Rose's Garden*. New York: Simon & Schuster.

Hall, Zoe. (1996). *The Apple Pie Tree*. Illus. by Shari Halpern. New York: Scholastic.

Hoban, Tana. (1995). *Animal, Vegetable, or Mineral?* New York: Greenwillow.

Maestro, Betsy C. (1992). *How Do Apples Grow?* Illus. by Giulio Maestro. New York: HarperCollins.

Patent, Dorothy Hinshaw. (1991). *Where Food Comes From*. Illus. by William Munoz. New York: Holiday House.

Powell, Jillian. *Fruit*. Austin, TX: Raintree/Steck Vaughn, 1997.

Robinson, Fay. (1994). *Vegetables, Vegetables*. Chicago: Children's Press.

Robson, Pam. (1998). *Banana*. Chicago: Children's Press.

Robson, Pam. (1998). *Corn*. Chicago: Children's Press.

Rylant, Cynthia. (1995). *Mr. Putter and Tabby Pick the Pears*. Orlando: Harcourt Brace.

Seabrook, Elizabeth. (1997). *Cabbages and Kings*. Illus. by Jamie Wyeth. New York: Viking.

Sekido, Isamu. (1993). *Fruits, Roots, and Fungi: Plants We Eat*. Minneapolis: Lerner Publications.

Wiesner, David. (1992). *June 29, 1999*. New York: Clarion Books.

Multimedia

The following multimedia products can be used to complement this theme:

5-a-Day Adventures [CD-ROM]. (1994). San Mateo, CA.: Dole Food Company.

Bingham, Bing. "Goober Peas" on *A Rainbow of Songs* [cassette]. Available from Kimbo Educational.

Cranberry Bounce [video]. (1991). DeBeck Educational Video.

Fruit: Close Up and Very Personal [video]. (1995). Geneva, IL: Stage Fright Productions.

Scelsa, Greg and Steve Millang. "I Like Potatoes" on *We All Live Together—Volume 5* [cassette or CD]. Available from Kimbo Educational.

Recordings and Song Titles

The following recordings can be used to complement this theme:

Piggyback Songs—"Vegetable Soup Song," "Vegetables"

Songs about Me—"Do You Like Fruit?," "Do You Like Meat?"

More Songs about Me—"Do You Like Vegetables?," "Do You Like Dessert?"

Songs about Native Americans—"Food for My Family"

Joining Hands in Other Lands—"The Food Song," "Caribbean Mango Song"

A to Z, the Animals and Me—"Vixen Who Makes Vegetable Soup"

Where Is Thumbkin?—"Apples and Bananas," "Peanut Butter Song"

Get Up and Grow—"Let's Sing about Food"

Fun 'n' Friendly (RONNO)—"Veggie Power"

Musical Playtime Fun—"Snack Time"

Self Help Skills—"I Always Eat What's on My Plate," "I Eat with My Mouth Closed"

T H E M E 35

Types

rock
flower
vegetable
terrarium
window box
indoor
community
rooftop

Purpose

food
beauty
hobby

Gardens

Tools

hoe
rake
spade
hose
watering can

Needs

sunshine
water
fertilizer
warmth
soil

Plants

bulbs
seeds
plants
roots

Theme Goals

Through participating in the experiences provided by this theme, the children may learn:

1. Purposes of gardens.
2. Types of gardens.
3. Tools used for gardening.
4. Care of gardens.
5. Types of plants grown in a garden.

Concepts for the Children to Learn

1. Plants are living things.
2. Plants need sunshine, water, soil, fertilizer, and warmth to grow.
3. Gardens produce food and beautiful flowers.
4. We plant gardens by placing bulbs, seeds, plants, or roots in the ground.
5. Weeds are plants that do not bear fruit. They take water and food from our garden plants.
6. Fruits, vegetables, and flowers can be planted in our gardens.

Vocabulary

1. **bulb**—a type of seed.
2. **flower**—part of the plant that has colored petals.
3. **garden**—a place to grow plants.
4. **greenhouse**—building for growing plants and flowers.
5. **leaf**—flat green part of a plant.
6. **rake**—a tool with teeth or prongs.
7. **soil**—top of the ground.
8. **root**—part of the plant that grows into the ground.
9. **seed**—part of the plant from which a new plant will grow.
10. **stem**—part of the plant that holds the leaves and flowers.
11. **vegetable**—a plant that can be eaten.
12. **weed**—plant that is not needed.

Bulletin Board

The purpose of this bulletin board is to foster visual discrimination skills. To prepare the bulletin board, construct five or six watering cans out of tagboard. Color each one a different color with felt-tip markers and hang on the bulletin board. Attach a string to each watering can. Next, construct the same number of small rakes out of tagboard. Color each one using the same colors you used for the watering cans. Attach a pushpin to the top of each rake. The children can match each watering can to the corresponding colored rake by winding the string around the correct pushpin.

Parent Letter

Dear Parents,

"Mary, Mary, quite contrary, how does your garden grow?" That familiar nursery rhyme sums up our next curriculum unit—gardens! We will be exploring flower and vegetable gardens, as well as finding out about the work involved in planning and maintaining gardens and garden tools.

AT SCHOOL

Some of the learning experiences planned to foster concepts related to gardens include:

- enjoying a flower shop set up in the dramatic play area.
- dramatizing the story of *The Big Turnip*.
- preparing a section of our play yard for a garden. The children will help decide which seeds to plant.
- playing with mud in the sensory table.

AT HOME

If you have a garden, ask your child to help you water, weed, and care for it. If you don't have a garden, take a walk and observe how many plants you can find that are cared for by people. What are the plants? What colors are they? How are they cared for?

Cut the tops of carrots off 1/4 inch from the stem to make a carrot-top garden. Place carrot tops in a shallow pie tin and pour 1/4 inch of water in the tin. Soon roots will appear, the greens will grow, and your child will be able to observe the growth.

Enjoy your child!

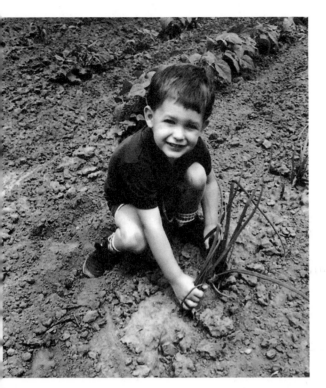

Watching a garden grow is a long-term science experience.

Music

"A Little Seed"
(Sing to the tune of "I'm a Little Teapot")

Here's a little seed in the dark, dark ground.
Out comes the warm sun, yellow and
  round.
Down comes the rain, wet and slow.
Up comes the little seed, grow, grow, grow!

Fingerplays

SEEDS

Some little seeds have parachutes
To carry them around
  (cup hand downward)
The wind blows them swish, swish, swish.
  (flip fingers outward from parachute)
Then gently lays them on the ground.
  (let hand gently float down and rest
  on lap)

RELAXING FLOWERS

Five little flowers standing in the sun
  (hold up five fingers)
See their heads nodding, bowing one by
  one?
  (bend fingers several times)
Down, down, down comes the gentle rain
  (raise hands, wiggle fingers, and lower
  arms to simulate falling rain)
And the five little flowers lift their heads up
  again!
  (hold up five fingers)

HOW IT HAPPENS

A muddy hump,
  (make a fist using both hands)
A small green lump,
  (poke up thumbs together as one)
Two leaves and then
Two leaves again
  (raise forefinger of each hand from fist,
  then middle fingers)
And shooting up, a stem and cup.
  (put elbows, forearms, and hands
  together, fingers slightly curved)
One last shower,
  (rain movements with spread arms and
  fingers)
Then a flower.
  (elbows, forearms together with hands
  wide apart, palms up)

LITTLE FLOWERS

The sun comes out and shines so bright
  (join hands over head in circle)
Then we have a shower.
  (wiggle fingers coming down)
The little bud pushes with all its might
  (one hand in fist; other hand clasped
  over, move hands up slowly)
And soon we have a flower.
  (join thumbs and spread fingers for
  flower)

MR. CARROT

Nice Mr. Carrot
Makes curly hair.
   (hand on head)
His head grows underneath the ground,
   (bob head)
His feet up in the air.
   (raise feet)
And early in the morning
I find him in his bed
   (close eyes, lay head on hands)
And give his feet a great big pull
   (stretch legs out)
And out comes his head.

Science

1. Growing Grass

Germinate grass seeds by placing a damp sponge in a pie tin of water and sprinkling seeds on the sponge. The children will notice tiny sprouts after a few days. Experiment by putting one sponge in the freezer, one near a heat source, and one in a dark closet. Discuss what happens to each group of seeds.

2. Plants Contain Water

Cut off 1/4 inch from the bottom of a celery stalk. Fill a clear vase with water containing food coloring. Place the celery stalk in the vase. Encourage the children to observe color changes in the celery stalk. This activity can be repeated using a white carnation.

3. Planting Seeds

Purchase bean and radish seeds. If space permits, plant outdoors. Otherwise, place soil in planters indoors. Plant the seeds with the children. Identify the plants by pasting the seed packages on the planters. This will help the children to recognize the plants as they emerge from the soil.

4. The Science Table

Place a magnifying glass with different types of seeds and bulbs on the science table. During the week add fresh flowers, plant leaves, and dried plants.

5. Rooting a Sweet Potato

To root a sweet potato in water, push toothpicks halfway into the potato. Then place the potato in a glass of water with the toothpicks resting on the top rim. Make sure the end of the potato is immersed in water. Place the glass where it will receive adequate light. Maintain the water level so that the bottom of the potato is always immersed. Note that in a few weeks roots will grow out of the sides and bottom of the potato, and leaves will grow out of the top. The plant can be left in the water or replanted in soil. This activity provides the children an opportunity to observe root growth.

6. Worm Farm

Collect the following materials: large clear jar with a wide mouth, soil, earthworms, gravel, food for worms (lettuce, cornmeal, cereals). Place gravel and soil in the jar. Add the worms. Add food on the top of the dirt and keep the soil moist, but not wet. Tape black construction paper around outside of jar. The paper can be temporarily removed to observe the worms and see their tunnels.

Dramatic Play

1. Flower Shop

Create a flower shop by gathering plastic flowers and plants. If desired, flowers can be made from tissue paper and pipe cleaners. Collect different kinds of vases and also styrofoam or sponge blocks so the children can make flower arrangements. A cash register, aprons, money, and sacks can also be provided to encourage play.

2. Gardening Center

Gather tools, gloves, hats, seeds, and plastic flowers or plants. The children can pretend to plant and grow seeds. Provide seed catalogs and order blanks for children to choose seeds to order.

3. Fruit Stand

Set up a fruit stand by using plastic fruits and vegetables. Aprons, a cash register, market baskets or bags, and play money can also be used to encourage play. The children can take turns being the owner and the shopper.

4. Sandbox

The children can experiment with gardening tools in the sandbox.

Arts and Crafts

1. Collage

Make collages using all types of seeds and beans. This activity can also include cutting pictures from seed catalogs.

2. Leaf Rubbings

Take the children on a leaf walk. The children choose a couple of large leaves to bring back to school. Place the leaves between two sheets of paper and rub with flat, large crayons across the top sheet of paper.

3. Stencils

Cut stencils out of tagboard of various-shaped leaves or vegetables (see patterns). Laminate the stencils. The children can use crayons, pencils, or marking pens to make the leaf or vegetable outlines. These stencils can be used as the front of the "soup and salad" party invitations listed under social studies activities.

4. Decorating Vases

Collect tin cans or milk cartons for the children to use as vases. If cans are used, file the sharp edges or cover them with masking tape. The children can decorate the containers with colored paper, gift wrapping paper, or wallpaper. Greeting cards may also be useful for this activity.

Sensory

1. Sensory Activities

In the sensory table place:

- soil
- seeds
- plastic plants
- beans
- measuring cups
- balance scales
- worms
- miniature garden tools
- cut grass or hay

2. Fill and Guess

After showing and discussing several kinds of fruits or vegetables with children, place the fruits or vegetables in a bag. Individually let children reach in and touch one item. See if they can guess what it is before pulling it out of the bag. Older children may also be able to describe the item.

Large Muscle

Leaf Jumping

This is an active skill game that can be played indoors or outdoors. Cut out large cardboard leaves and arrange them in an irregular line, as they might appear on a stem. The closer they are together, the harder the game will be. Beginning at one end, each player tries to jump over the leaves without touching them. Older children may try to skip or hop over the leaves.

Field Trips/ Resource People

1. Field Trips

Take a field trip to:

- a flower garden
- a vegetable garden
- a flower shop
- a farmers' market
- a greenhouse
- a conservatory
- a park
- the produce section of a grocery store
- a natural food store

2. Resource People

- gardeners
- florist to demonstrate flower arranging

Math

1. Sorting Beans

Mix together several shapes and colors of large, dried beans. The children can sort the beans by size and color.

2. Inchworm Measuring

A good introduction for this activity is the story *Inch by Inch* by Leo Lionni. Cut 2 or 3 dozen inchworms out of felt. Then cut out flowers of various heights—with long or short stems. Encourage the children to place worms along stem from bottom to top of flower. How many inchworms tall is each flower? After this, have the children count the inchworms.

Social Studies

1. Salad and Soup Party

The children can plan and participate in a salad and soup party for their parents. The groceries will need to be purchased, cleaned, and prepared.

2. Plant Hunt

Go on a hunt to discover how many non-flowering plants such as algae, fungi, lichens, mosses, and ferns are found in the school yard. Make a display. How are these plants different from garden plants?

Group Time (games, language)

1. Huckle Buckle Bean Stalk

A small object such as a plastic flower or acorn may be used for hiding. All the players cover their eyes, except the one who hides the object. After it is hidden, the players stand up and begin to look for it. When one locates it, he doesn't let others know the placement. Instead he quietly takes a seat, saying "Huckle Buckle Bean Stalk." The game continues until all players have located the object. The first child to find the object usually hides it the next time. This game is appropriate for older children.

Cooking

1. Vegetable Soup

Begin with consommé or soup base. Add whatever vegetables, beans, etc., children want to add and can help to prepare. Make soup a day ahead so that all of the vegetables will be cooked thoroughly.

2. Indian—Cucumbers and Tomatoes with Yogurt

2 medium cucumbers
2 green onions with tops, chopped
1 teaspoon salt
2 tomatoes chopped
1/2 clove garlic, finely chopped
2 tablespoons snipped parsley
1/2 teaspoon ground cumin
1/8 teaspoon pepper
1 cup unflavored yogurt

354

Cut cucumbers lengthwise into halves. Scoop out seeds. Chop cucumbers. Mix cucumbers, green onions, and salt. Let stand 10 minutes. Add tomatoes. Mix remaining ingredients except yogurt. Toss with cucumber mixture. Cover and refrigerate at least 1 hour. Drain thoroughly. Just before serving, fold in yogurt. Makes 6 servings.

Source: *Betty Crocker's International Cookbook.* (1980). New York: Random House.

3. Lettuce or Spinach Roll-ups

On clean lettuce or spinach leaves, spread softened cream cheese or cottage cheese. If desired, sprinkle with grated carrots or chopped nuts. Roll them up. Chill and serve.

4. Carrot Cookies

1/2 cup honey
1 egg
1/2 cup margarine
1 cup whole wheat flour
1 1/4 teaspoons baking powder
1/4 teaspoon salt
1/2 cup rolled oats
1/2 cup wheat germ
1/2 cup grated raw carrots
1/2 cup raisins
1/2 cup nuts (optional)
1 teaspoon vanilla

Mix all ingredients in a bowl. Drop mixture by spoonfuls onto a lightly greased cookie sheet. Flatten each ball slightly. Bake in a 350-degree oven for approximately 12 minutes.

Books

The following books can be used to complement this theme:

Bunting, Eve. (1994). *Flower Garden*. Illus. by Kathryn Hewitt. Orlando: Harcourt Brace.

Cole, Henry. (1995). *Jack's Garden*. New York: Greenwillow.

Cutler, Jane. (1996). *Mr. Carey's Garden*. Illus. by G. Brian Karas. Boston: Houghton Mifflin.

Delaney, A. (1997). *Pearl's First Prize Plant*. New York: HarperCollins.

Dyjak, Elisabeth. (1995). *Bertha's Garden*. Illus. by Janet Wilkins. Boston: Houghton Mifflin.

Florian, Douglas. (1991). *Vegetable Garden*. New York: Harcourt Brace.

Glaser, Linda. (1996). *Compost!: Growing Gardens from Your Garbage*. Illus. by Anca Hariton. Brookfield, CT: Millbrook Press.

Godkin, Celia. (1998). *What About Lady-bugs?* Boston: Little, Brown. (Pbk)

Greenstein, Elaine. (1996). *Mrs. Rose's Garden*. New York: Simon & Schuster.

Hall, Zoe. (1994). *It's Pumpkin Time!* Illus. by Shari Halpern. New York: Scholastic.

Hines, Anna Grossnickle. (1997). *Miss Emma's Wild Garden*. New York: Greenwillow.

Joyce, William. (1996). *The Leaf Men: And the Brave Good Bugs*. New York: HarperCollins.

Llewellyn, Claire. (1991). *First Look at Growing Food*. Milwaukee: Gareth Stevens.

Moore, Elaine. (1994). *Grandma's Garden*. Illus. by Dan Andreasen. New York: Lothrop, Lee & Shepard.

Perkins, Lynne Rae. (1995). *Home Lovely*. New York: Greenwillow.

Ryder, Joanne. (1994). *My Father's Hands*. New York: William Morrow.

Rylant, Cynthia. (1993). *Everyday Garden*. New York: Simon & Schuster. (Board book)

Seabrook, Elizabeth. (1997). *Cabbages and Kings*. Illus. by Jamie Wyeth. New York: Viking.

Shannon, George. (1994). *Seeds*. Illus. by Steve Bjorkman. Boston: Houghton Mifflin.

Shories, Pat. (1996). *Over Under in the Garden: An Alphabet Book*. New York: Farrar, Straus & Giroux.

Stewart, Sarah. (1997). *The Gardener*. Illus. by David Small. New York: Farrar, Straus & Giroux.

Tamar, Erika. (1996). *The Garden of Happiness*. Illus. by Barbara Lambase. Orlando: Harcourt Brace.

Multimedia

The following multimedia products can be used to complement this theme:

"I'm Going to Plant a Garden" on *Science in a Nutshell* [cassette]. Available from Kimbo Educational.

Palmer, Hap. *Walter the Waltzing Worm* [cassette or CD]. Available from Kimbo Educational.

T H E M E 36

Symbols

jack-o'-lantern
(pumpkin),
witch, ghosts,
skeleton,
black cats

Colors

orange
black

Halloween

Activities

trick-or-treating
bobbing for apples
parties
costume parades
making costumes
wearing makeup
safety

Costumes and Masks

goblin
witch
ghost
television characters
clowns
animals
gypsy
cartoon characters
funny people

Theme Goals

Through participating in the experiences provided by this theme, the children may learn:

1. Halloween colors.
2. Halloween costumes and masks.
3. Halloween activities.
4. Halloween symbols.

Concepts for the Children to Learn

1. Orange and black are Halloween colors.
2. Costumes and masks are worn on Halloween.
3. Some children make their costumes and wear makeup.
4. A costume is clothing put on for pretending.
5. A mask is a covering we put over our face.
6. A pumpkin can be cut to look like a face.
7. Ghosts, black cats, and witches are symbols of Halloween.
8. People go trick-or-treating on Halloween.
9. A costume parade is a march with many children who are dressed in costumes.
10. Bobbing for apples is an activity at Halloween parties.

Vocabulary

1. **Halloween**—a day when children dress in costumes and go trick-or-treating.
2. **jack-o'-lantern**—a pumpkin cut to look like a face.
3. **trick-or-treat**—walking from house to house to ask for candy or treats.
4. **witch**—a make-believe person who wears black.
5. **ghost**—a make-believe person who wears all white.
6. **goblin**—a Halloween character.
7. **costume**—clothing worn to pretend.
8. **mask**—face covering worn when pretending.
9. **pretending**—acting like someone else.

Bulletin Board

The purpose of this bulletin board is to have the children practice visual discrimination skills. To prepare the bulletin board, construct pumpkins out of orange-colored tagboard. The number prepared will be dependent upon the developmental appropriateness for the group of children. An alternative would be to use white tagboard colored orange with paint or markers. Divide the pumpkins into pairs. Draw a different kind of face for each pair of pumpkins. Hang one pumpkin from each pair on the left side of the bulletin board as illustrated. Attach an orange string to each pumpkin. On the right side of the bulletin board, hang the matching pumpkins. See illustration. Attach a pushpin to each of these pumpkins. The child can match the faces on the pumpkins by winding the correct string around the correct pushpin.

Parent Letter

Dear Parents,

The month of October has a special holiday for children—Halloween! Consequently, our next theme will center on Halloween. Many learning experiences have been planned to promote an awareness of colors that are associated with Halloween, as well as symbols that represent Halloween such as pumpkins, black cats, bats, and witches.

AT SCHOOL

Some of the Halloween activities planned include:
- discussing Halloween safety procedures, especially while trick-or-treating.
- carving a jack-o'-lantern for the classroom.
- roasting pumpkin seeds and baking a pumpkin pie.
- trying on a variety of costumes in the dramatic play area.
- creating designs with pumpkin seeds and glue on paper.

HALLOWEEN PARTY!

We will be having a Halloween party on Friday. You are welcome to send a costume to school with your child that day. The costume can be simple. A funny hat, a pair of silly glasses, a wig, or a little makeup would be fine Halloween attire. We would appreciate it if you could send the costume and accessories in a bag that is labeled with your child's name. This will prevent a mix-up of belongings. We will dress in our costumes about 2:00 p.m. Then we will have a small party and parade around in our costumes. It should be a fun day. Join us!

AT HOME

To get into the spirit of Halloween and to help your child develop language skills, practice the following Halloween rhyme:

"Five Little Pumpkins"

Five little pumpkins sitting on a gate.
The first one said, "Oh my, it's getting late."
The second one said, "There are witches in the air."
The third one said, "But we don't care."
The fourth one said, "Let's run. Let's run."
The fifth one said, "It's Halloween fun!"
"Woooooooooo," went the wind,
And out went the lights.
And the five little pumpkins rolled out of sight.

To ensure a safe Halloween:
- Check to see if your child's costume is flame resistant or at least flame retardant.
- Children can easily trip in long garments. Be sure the hemline is several inches off the ground.
- Masks and hoods can slip and make it difficult for your child to see. If a mask is worn, be sure it is secure and that the holes for the eyes are properly positioned. An alternative to wearing a mask is to use makeup.
- Finally, check the batteries in the flashlight!

Have a safe and happy Halloween.

360

Music

1. **"Flying Witches"**
   (Sing to the tune of "When the Saints Come Marching In")

   Oh, when the witches
   Come flying by.
   Oh, when the witches come flying by,
   It will be Halloween night,
   When the witches come flying by.

2. **"One Little, Two Little, Three Little Pumpkins"**
   (Sing to the tune of "One Little, Two Little, Three Little Indians")

   One little, two little, three little pumpkins,
   Four little, five little, six little pumpkins,
   Seven little, eight little, nine little
       pumpkins,
   Ready for Halloween night!

3. **"Have You Made a Jack-O'-Lantern?"**
   (Sing to the tune of "Muffin Man")

   Have you made a jack-o'-lantern,
   A jack-o'-lantern, a jack-o'-lantern?
   Have you made a jack-o'-lantern
   For Halloween night?

Masks and pumpkins are symbols of Halloween.

Fingerplays

JACK-O'-LANTERN

   I am a pumpkin, big and round.
       (show size with arms)
   Once upon a time, I grew on the ground.
       (point to ground)
   Now I have a mouth, two eyes, and a nose.
       (point to each)
   What are they for, do you suppose?
       (point to forehead and "think")
   Why—I'll be a jack-o'-lantern on
       Halloween night.

FIVE LITTLE WITCHES

   Five little witches standing by the door.
       (hold up five fingers)
   One flew out and then there were four.
       (flying motion with hand)
   Four little witches standing by a tree.
       (four fingers)
   One went to pick a pumpkin and then
       there were three.
       (picking motion, then three fingers)
   Three little witches stirring their brew.
       (stir)
   One fell in and then there were two.
       (two fingers)
   Two little witches went for a run.
       (run with fingers)
   One got lost and then there was one.
       (one finger)

One little witch, yes, only one.
  (one finger)
She cast a spell and now there are none.
  (make motions as if to cast spell and
  then put hands in lap)

HALLOWEEN FUN

Goblins and witches in high pointed hats,
  (hands above head to form hat)
Riding on broomsticks and chasing black cats.
  (ride broomstick)
Children in costumes might well give a
  fright.
  (look frightened)
Get things in order for Halloween night.
We like our treats
  (nod head)
And we'll play no mean pranks.
  (shake head)
We'll do you no harm and we'll only say,
  "Thanks!"

THE JACK-O'-LANTERN

Three little pumpkins growing on a vine.
  (three fingers)
Sitting in the sunlight, looking just fine.
  (arms up like sun)
Along came a ghost who picked just one
  (one finger)
To take on home for some Halloween fun.
  (smile)
He gave him two eyes to see where he goes.
  (paint two eyes)
He gave him a mouth and a big handsome
  nose.
  (point to mouth and nose)
Then he put a candle in.
  (pretend to put in candle)
Now see how he glows.
  (wiggle fingers from center of body out
  until arms are extended)

I'VE A JACK-O'-LANTERN

I've a jack-o'-lantern
  (make a ball with open fist, thumb at top)
With a great big grin.
  (grin)
I've got a jack-o'-lantern
With a candle in.
  (insert other index finger up through
  bottom of first)

HALLOWEEN WITCHES

One little, two little, three little witches,
  (hold up one hand, nod fingers at each
  count)
Fly over the haystacks
  (fly hand in up-and-down motion)
Fly over ditches
Slide down moonbeams without any
  hitches
  (glide hand downward)
Heigh-ho! Halloween's here!

THE FRIENDLY GHOST

I'm a friendly ghost—almost!
  (point to self)
And I chase you, too!
  (point to child)
I'll just cover me with a sheet
  (pretend to cover self ending with hands
  covering face)
And then call "scat" to you.
  (uncover face quickly and call out "scat")

WITCHES' CAT

I am the witches' cat.
  (make a fist with two fingers extended
  for cat)
Meoow. Meoow.
  (stroke fist with other hand)
My fur is black as darkest night.
My eyes are glaring green and bright.
  (circle eyes with thumb and forefingers)
I am the witches' cat.
  (make a fist again with two fingers
  extended and stroke fist with other
  hand)

MY PUMPKIN

See my pumpkin round and fat.
  (make circle with hands, fingers spread
  wide, touching)
See my pumpkin yellow.
  (make a smaller circle)
Watch him grin on Halloween.
  (point to mouth, which is grinning
  wide)
He is a very funny fellow.

362

Science

1. Carve Pumpkins

Purchase several pumpkins. Carve them and save the seeds for roasting. An alternative activity would be to use a black felt-tip marker to draw facial features on the pumpkin. Pumpkins can also have added accessories. For example, a large carrot can be used for a nose, parsley for hair, cut green peppers for ears, radishes for eyes, and a small green onion can be placed in a cut mouth for teeth.

2. Roasting Pumpkin Seeds

Wash and dry pumpkin seeds. Then spread the seeds out on a cookie sheet to dry. Bake the seeds in a preheated oven at 350 degrees until brown. Salt, cool, and eat at snack time.

3. Plant Pumpkin Seeds

Purchase a packet of pumpkin seeds. Plant the pumpkin seeds in small paper cups. Set the paper cups with the pumpkin seeds in a sunny place. Water as needed. Observe daily to see if there is growth.

Dramatic Play

Costumes

Add Halloween costumes to the dramatic play area. (Some teachers purchase these at thrift stores or sales. From year to year they are stored in a Halloween prop box.)

Arts and Crafts

1. Spooky Easel

Provide orange and black paint at the paint easels.

2. Pumpkin Seed Pictures

Dye pumpkin seeds many colors. Place the seeds with paste and paper on a table in the art area. The children then can create their own pictures.

3. Crayon Wash

On the art table, place paper, light-colored crayons, tempera paint, and brushes. The children can draw on paper with light-colored crayons. After this, they can paint over the entire picture.

4. Masks

Yarn, paper plates, felt-tip markers, and any other accessories needed to make masks interesting can be placed on a table in the art area. If desired, yarn can be used as hair on the mask.

Sensory

1. Measuring Seeds

Pumpkin seeds and measuring cups can be added to the sensory table. The children will enjoy feeling and pouring seeds.

2. Goop

Add dry cornstarch to the sensory table. Slowly add enough water to make it a "goopy" consistency. If desired, add coloring to make it black or orange.

Large Muscle

Ghost, Ghost, Witch

This game is played like "Duck, Duck, Goose." Form a circle and kneel. Choose one child to be "it" and to walk around the outside of the circle chanting, "Ghost, ghost, ghost." When the child taps another child and says "witch," the tapped child chases the initiator around the circle, attempting to tag "it." If the child who is "it" returns to the empty child's spot before being tagged, he can sit in the circle. If not, the child continues walking around the circle, repeating the same procedure.

Field Trips/ Resource People

1. Pumpkin Patch

Visit a pumpkin patch. During the tour point out various-sized pumpkins. Discuss how the pumpkins grow, as well as their shapes, sizes, etc.

2. Halloween Safety

A police officer can be invited to talk with the children about Halloween safety.

Math

1. Counting Pumpkin Seeds

Cut circles from construction paper. The number needed will depend upon the developmental level of the children. Write a numeral on each paper circle and place each into a pie tin. The children may count enough pumpkin seeds into each tin to match the numeral on the circle.

2. Weighing Pumpkin Seeds

In the math area, place a scale and pumpkin seeds. The children may elect to experiment by balancing the scale with the pumpkin seeds.

Group Time (games, language)

1. Thank-you Note

Write a thank-you note to any resource person. Encourage all of the children to participate by sharing what they liked or saw.

2. Costume Parade

On Halloween day, the children can dress up in costumes and march around the room and throughout the school to music. If available, a walk to a local nursing home may be enjoyed by the children as well as the elderly.

Decorating a Pumpkin

While carving or decorating a pumpkin with the children you can discuss:

- the physical properties of pumpkins— color, texture, size, shape (both outside and inside).
- food category to which pumpkins belong.
- what other forms pumpkins can be made into after the shell is scooped out.
- where pumpkins grow (plant some of the seeds).
- what size and shape to make the features of the pumpkin, including eyes, nose, mouth, and what kind of expression to make.

Accessories:

1 bunch parsley (hair)
1 carrot (nose)
2 string beans (eyebrows)
2 radishes (eyes)
1 green pepper (ears)
1 stalk celery (teeth)
1 large pumpkin (head)

Prepare the pumpkin in the usual manner; that is, cut off the cap and scoop out the seeds inside. Save the seeds for roasting. If desired, individual vegetable pieces may be attached by carving or inserting toothpicks.

Cooking

1. Pumpkin Pie

1 unbaked pie shell
2 cups (16–17 ounces) pumpkin
1 can sweetened condensed milk
1 egg
1/2 teaspoon salt
2 teaspoons pumpkin pie spice

Blend all of the ingredients in a large mixing bowl. Pour the mixture into the pie shell. Bake the pie in an oven preheated to 375 degrees for 50 to 55 minutes or until a sharp knife blade inserted near center of pie is clean when removed. Cool and refrigerate the pie for 1 hour before serving. Top with whipped cream if desired.

2. Pumpkin Patch Muffins

3 cups flour
1 cup sugar
4 teaspoons baking powder
1 teaspoon salt
1 teaspoon pumpkin pie spice
1 cup milk
1 cup canned pumpkin
1/2 cup (1 stick) butter or margarine, melted
2 eggs, beaten

Sift the flour, sugar, baking powder, salt, and pumpkin pie spice into a large mixing bowl. Add the milk, pumpkin, melted butter, and eggs. Mix with a wooden spoon just until flour is moist. (Batter will be lumpy.) Place paper liners in the muffin tins and fill 2/3 full with batter. Bake in a preheated 400-degree oven 20 minutes or until muffins are golden. Cool in muffin tins 10 minutes on a wire rack. Remove muffins from muffin tins and finish cooling on wire racks. Pile into serving baskets and serve warm for snack.

3. Witches' Brew

5 cups cranberry juice, unsweetened
5 cups apple cider, unsweetened
1 or 2 cinnamon sticks
1/4 teaspoon ground nutmeg

Place ingredients in a large saucepan. Cover, heat, and simmer for 10 minutes. Serve warm.

4. Roasted Pumpkin Seeds

Soak pumpkin seeds for 24 hours in salt-water (1/4 cup salt to 1 cup water). Spread on cloth-covered cookie sheet and roast at 100 degrees for 2 hours. Turn oven off and leave seeds overnight.

5. Non-bake Pumpkin Pie

1 can prepared pumpkin pie
1 package vanilla instant pudding
1 cup milk

Mix and pour into baked pie shell or graham cracker pie shell.

Books

The following books can be used to complement this theme:

Andrews, Sylvia. (1995). *Rattlebone Rock.* Illus. by Jennifer Plecas. New York: HarperCollins.

Carlstrom, Nancy White. (1995). *Who Said Boo?: Halloween Poems for the Very Young.* Illus. by R. W. Alley. New York: Simon & Schuster.

Caseley, Judith. (1996). *Witch Mama.* New York: Greenwillow.

Dillon, Jana. (1992). *Jeb Scarecrow's Pumpkin Patch.* Boston: Houghton Mifflin.

Enderle, Judith Ross. (1992). *Six Creepy Sheep.* Illus. by John O'Brien. Honesdale, PA: Boyds Mills Press.

Hall, Zoe. (1994). *It's Pumpkin Time!* Illus. by Shari Halpern. New York: Scholastic.

Heinz, Brian J. (1996). *The Monsters' Test.* Illus. by Sal Murdocca. Brookfield, CT: Millbrook Press.

Johnston, Tony. (1990). *The Soup Bone.* Illus. by Margot Tomes. Orlando: Harcourt Brace.

Johnston, Tony. (1995). *Very Scary*. Illus. by Douglas Florian. Orlando: Harcourt Brace.

Lachner, Dorothea. (1997). *Meredith: The Witch Who Wasn't*. Illus. by Christa Unzner. New York: North South Books.

Levine, Abby. (1997). *This Is the Pumpkin*. Niles, IL: Albert Whitman & Co.

Martin, Bill. (1993). *Old Devil Wind*. Illus. by Barry Root. Orlando: Harcourt Brace.

Meddaugh, Susan. (1994). *Witches Supermarket*. Madison, WI: Demco Media.

Nikola-Lisa, W. (1997). *Shake Dem Halloween Bones*. Boston: Houghton Mifflin.

Pilkey, Dav. (1995). *Hallo-Wiener*. New York: Scholastic.

Roberts, Bethany. (1995). *Halloween Mice!* Illus. by Doug Cushman. New York: Clarion Books.

Shaw, Nancy. (1997). *Sheep Trick or Treat*. Boston: Houghton Mifflin.

Sierra, Judy. (1995). *The House That Drac Built*. Illus. by Will Hillenbrand. Orlando: Harcourt Brace.

Silverman, Erica. (1992). *Big Pumpkin*. Illus. by S. D. Schindler. New York: Macmillan.

Stock, Catherine. (1990). *Halloween Monster*. New York: Simon & Schuster.

Stutson, Caroline. (1993). *By the Light of the Halloween Moon*. Illus. by Kevin Hawkes. New York: Lothrop, Lee & Shepard.

Van Rynbach, Iris. (1995). *Five Little Pumpkins*. Honesdale, PA: Boyds Mills Press.

Wolff, Ferida. (1994). *On Halloween Night*. Illus. by Dolores Avendano. New York: Tambourine Books.

Multimedia

The following multimedia products can be used to complement this theme:

Gold, Andrew. *Andrew Gold's Halloween Howls* [compact disc]. (1996). Redway, CA: Music for Little People.

Halloween [video]. (1993). Niles, IL: United Learning.

Holidays for Children: Halloween [video]. Schlessinger Media.

Lavender, Cheryl. *Moans, Groans and Skeleton Bones* [compact disc]. (1993). Milwaukee, WI: Hal Leonard.

Palmer, Hap. "Have a Good Halloween Night" on *Holiday Songs and Rhythms* [compact disc]. (1997). Freeport, NY: Educational Activities.

Skiera-Zucek, Lois. *Halloween Fun* [cassette]. (1989). Long Branch, NJ: Kimbo Educational.

Recordings and Song Titles

The following recordings can be used to complement this theme:

Halloween Fun

Holiday Piggyback Songs—"Halloween Song," "Halloween Is Here," "Pumpkin Song"

Toddlers on Parade—"Ten Little Goblins"

Preschool Action Time—"Ten Little Pumpkins"

Holiday Action Songs—"Dress Up on Halloween," "The Round Fat Pumpkin," "The Merry Brownies," "The Funny Little Owl," "The Black Pussy Cats," "Jack-O'-Lantern"

T H E M E 37

Foods

latkes
honey-spice cookies
ka'achei sumsum
matzo

Symbols

menorah
Star of David
dreidel
synagogue/temple

Hanukkah
(Chanukah)

Celebration

lighting the menorah
gift giving
family togetherness

Theme Goals

Through participating in the experiences provided by this theme, the children may learn:

1. The story of Hanukkah.
2. Symbols of Hanukkah.
3. Hanukkah celebrations.

Concepts for the Children to Learn

1. Hanukkah is a Jewish holiday.
2. Hanukkah is a time for giving and sharing with others.
3. The menorah and the dreidel are symbols of Hanukkah.
4. Hanukkah is celebrated for eight days.
5. Some foods eaten during Hanukkah include latkes, honey-spice cookies, ka'achei sumsum, and matzo.

Vocabulary

1. **latkes**—potato pancakes eaten during Hanukkah.
2. **dreidel**—four-sided toy that spins like a top.
3. **Star of David**—a six-pointed star that is a Jewish symbol.
4. **menorah**—eight-branched candlestick. The middle or ninth candle is taller than the other eight and is called the shammash.
5. **Hanukkah**—eight-day Jewish festival of lights. A celebration of the Jewish people's fight long ago to keep the right to practice their religion. One candle is lighted on the menorah each day.

Bulletin Board

The purpose of this bulletin board is to develop an awareness of the passage of time as well as the math concept of sets. This bulletin board starts out with the base of the menorah. Each day of Hanukkah the children work together to construct a candle and a flame to add to the menorah. Candles and flames are most interesting when made using a wide variety of mediums: sequins, feathers, cut construction paper, yarn, etc.

Parent Letter

Dear Parents,

For the next eight days, we will be celebrating Hanukkah. Hanukkah commemorates the victory of the Jews over the Syrians. Hanukkah, also known as the Festival of Lights, is celebrated for eight days in either November or December. In 175 B.C. a Syrian King, Antiochus, ordered the Jewish Temple defiled. After the Syrians desecrated the Temple, Judah Maccabee formed a small but powerful army to defend the Jews. The Maccabees rebuilt the Temple and the legend states that when it was time to light the Temple lamp for rededication, there was only enough sacred oil to burn for one day. Miraculously, it burned for eight days!

Hanukkah is celebrated by the lighting of a special candelabra called a menorah. On the menorah there is one holder for each of the eight nights and one for the shammash. Shammash means helper in Hebrew; this is the candle that is used to light the others. The candles are lit beginning on the right side and moving to the left.

Each night, after the lighting of the menorah, the children are given small gifts. Traditionally this gift was "gelt": money to be used while playing the dreidel game.

Unlike most Jewish holidays, work and schooling continues during the eight-day celebration.

AT SCHOOL

Some of the learning experiences the children will participate in include:

- playing a game with a dreidel, which is similar to a toy top.
- preparing latkes (potato pancakes) for snack.
- creating wax-resist drawings at the art table.

Happy Hanukkah!

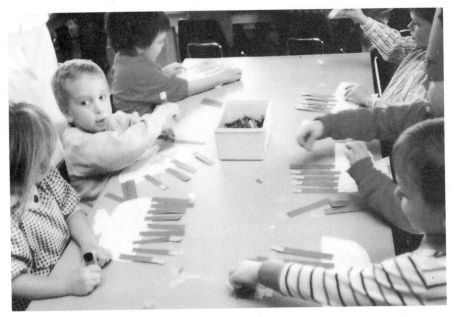

Learning about Hanukkah and other religious holidays is an important social studies activity.

Music

"Menorah Candles"
(Sing to the tune of "Twinkle, Twinkle, Little Star")

Twinkle, twinkle candles in the night,
Standing on the menorah bright,
Burning slow we all know,
Burning bright to give us light.
Twinkle, twinkle candles in the night,
Standing on the menorah bright.

Fingerplays

THE MENORAH CANDLE

I'm a menorah candle
  (stand, point at self)
Growing shorter you can see
  (bend down slowly)
Melting all my wax
  (go down more)
Until there's nothing left to see.
  (sit down)

HANUKKAH LIGHTS

One light, two lights, three lights, and four
  (hold up four fingers, one at a time)
Five lights, six lights, and three more,
  (hold up five fingers on other hand)
Twinkle, twinkle nine pretty lights,
  (move fingers)
In a golden menorah bright!
  (make cup with palm of hand)

MY DREIDEL

I have a little dreidel.
  (cup hands to form a square)
I made it out of clay.
  (move fingers in a molding motion)
And when it's dry and ready
  (flatten hands as if to hold in hand—
  palm up, pinkies together)
Then with it I will play.
  (pretend to spin dreidel on the floor)

Science

1. Potato Sprouts

Provide each child with a clear plastic cup. Fill the plastic cup half-full with water. Place a potato part way in the water supported by toothpicks to keep it from dropping into the jar. Put the end with tubers into the water. The other end should stick out of the water. Refill with fresh water as it evaporates and watch the roots begin to grow and leaves start to sprout.

2. Candle Snuffer

Demonstrate how a candle snuffer is used to put out a flame. (Check licensing regulations prior to the activity.)

3. Light

Light a candle. Discuss other sources of light. (Examples: sun, lamp, flashlight, traffic lights, etc.)

4. Sunlight Power

Fill two glasses half-full of warm water. Stir some flour into one glass. In the other, dissolve a little yeast in the water, then add flour. Now set them both in a warm place for an hour and watch the results.

Dramatic Play

1. Family Celebration

Collect materials for a special family meal. These may include dresses, hats, coats, plates, cups, plastic food, napkins, etc. The children can have a holiday meal.

2. Gift Wrapping Center

Collect various-sized boxes, wrapping paper, tape, and ribbon. The children can wrap presents for Hanukkah.

Sensory

Sand Temples

Fill the sensory table with sand and moisten until the sand begins to adhere. The children may pack sand into cans to mold into desired shapes and build sand temples from the molded forms.

Arts and Crafts

1. Star of David

Provide the children with triangles cut from blue construction paper. Demonstrate to the children how to invert one triangle over the other to form a star. The stars may be glued to construction paper.

2. Potato Art

Slice potatoes in half. The children may dip the potato halves in shallow pans containing various colors of tempera paint and then create designs on construction paper.

3. Hanukkah Handprints

Provide the children with construction paper, brushes, and tempera paint in shallow pans. Paint each of the children's hands with a brush that has been dipped in tempera paint. The children then may place their hands on the construction paper, creating handprints.

4. Dreidel Top

Collect and wash out 1/2-pint milk containers. Tape the top down so that the carton forms a square. Provide construction paper squares for the children to paste to the sides of the milk carton. The children may decorate with crayons or felt-tip markers. Upon completion, punch an unsharpened pencil through the milk container so that the children may spin it like a top.

5. **Star of David Mobile**

Provide each child with two drinking straws. Demonstrate to the children how to bend the straws so that they make triangles. Glue the straw triangles together, inverting one over the other to make a six-pointed star. Tie string to the star and hang from a window or ceiling. This activity is appropriate for 6-, 7-, and 8-year-olds.

Resource People

Invite a rabbi or parent of the Jewish faith to come and talk about Hanukkah and how it is celebrated.

Large Muscle

1. **Dreidel Dance**

The children can dance the dreidel dance by standing in a circle and spinning as they sing this song to the tune of "Row, Row, Row Your Boat."

Dreidel, dreidel, dreidel,
A-spinning I will go.
Speed it up and slow it down,
And on the ground I'll go!

2. **Frying Donuts—Dramatic Play**

Children can act out frying donuts as they sing this song to the tune of "I Have a Little Turtle."

I have a little donut,
It is so nice and light,
And when it's all done cooking,
I'm going to take a bite!

Frying donuts usually pop up and out of the frying oil when they are finished cooking. The children can act out these motions. The oil used in frying the donuts is significant in the Hanukkah celebration. It signifies the oil burned in the Temple lamp.

Math

1. **Sort the Stars**

Provide children with various-colored stars. The children can match the colors. A variation would be to have stars of various sizes. The children could sequence the stars from largest to smallest.

2. **Hanukkah Puzzles**

Mount pictures of a menorah and the Star of David on tagboard. Cut into pieces. Laminate. The number of pieces will depend upon the children's developmental age.

3. **Candle Holder and Candle Match**

Have a variety of candle holders set out with candles. The children will have to match the candles to the correct-sized candle holder.

Group Time
(games, language)

1. **Hot Potato**

Ask the children to sit in a circle. Provide one child with a real potato, a plastic potato, or a potato constructed from tagboard. Play music. As the music is playing, the children pass the potato around the circle until the music stops. The one holding the potato is out of the circle. The game continues until one child is left or the children no longer wish to play.

2. Dreidel Game

Each player starts with 10 to 15 pennies, nuts, or raisins. Each player places an object in the center of the circle. The dreidel is spun by one of the players, while the following verse is chanted:

I have a little dreidel.
I made it out of clay.
And when it's dry and ready.
Then with it I will play.

Whether the spinning player wins or loses depends on which side of the dreidel lands upward when it falls. The following may be used as a guide:

Nun (N) means nothing: player receives nothing from the pot.
Gimmel (G) means all: player receives everything from the pot.
Hay (H) means half: player takes 1/2 of the pot.
Shin (S) means put in: player adds two objects to the pot.

When one player has won all of the objects, the game is completed.

3. Gelt Hunt

Make a silver coin by cutting out a 4-inch round piece of cardboard and covering it with aluminum foil. Hide the coin (gelt) in the classroom and play a hide-and-seek game. For younger children hide the gelt in an obvious place.

(Gelt is the Yiddish word for money. Traditionally, small amounts of gelt are given to children each night of Hanukkah.)

Social Studies

1. Menorah

Glue eight wooden or styrofoam spools of equal size to a piece of wood, leaving a space in the middle. Glue a larger spool in the middle, thus having four smaller spools on each side. Spray with gold or silver paint. The menorah can be lit during the eight days of Hanukkah during group time. Explain the meaning of the menorah to the group as well.

2. Hanukkah Celebration

Display pictures at the child's eye level of the Hanukkah celebration. Examples would include such pictures as lighting the menorah, a family meal, etc.

3. Human Menorah

The children can make a human menorah by positioning themselves to resemble a menorah. A menorah is a lamp with nine flames that is used to celebrate Hanukkah. Two children can lie head-to-toe on the floor to form the base. Have nine children stand behind the base to form the candles. The tallest child can stand in the middle and be the shammash. The shammash is the center candle that lights the other candles. The children can make pretend flames out of construction paper for the candles to hold as if they were lit.

Cooking

1. Latkes

6 medium-sized potatoes washed, pared, and grated
1 egg
3 tablespoons flour
1/2 teaspoon baking powder

In a large bowl, mix the egg and the grated potatoes. Add the flour and baking powder. Drop by spoonfuls into hot cooking oil in a frying pan. Brown on both sides. Drain on paper towel. Latkes may be served with a spoonful of applesauce or sour cream.

2. Hanukkah Honey and Spice Cookies

1/2 cup (1 stick) margarine, softened
1/2 cup firmly packed dark brown sugar
1/2 cup honey
1 egg
2 1/2 cups unsifted flour
2 teaspoons ground ginger

374

1 teaspoon baking soda
1 teaspoon ground cinnamon
1 teaspoon ground nutmeg
1/2 teaspoon salt
1/4 teaspoon ground cloves

In a large mixing bowl cream margarine and sugar. Beat in honey and egg until well combined. In a small bowl combine flour, ginger, baking soda, cinnamon, nutmeg, salt, and cloves. Add to honey mixture. Beat on low speed until well blended. Cover dough and chill at least 1 hour or up to 3 days. Heat oven to 350 degrees. Grease cookie sheets. Set aside. Working quickly with 1/4 of the dough at a time, roll out on floured surface to 1/4-inch thickness. Cut into desired shapes, including a dreidel, menorah, or star. Using a spatula, place cookies on prepared cookie sheets 1 inch apart. Reroll scraps. Bake for 7 minutes. Transfer to wire racks to cool. Makes about 4 dozen cookies.

3. Ka'achei Sumsum—Bagel Cookies

4 cups of flour
1 cup margarine
1 teaspoon salt
3 tablespoons cake-form yeast
1 egg
1 cup lukewarm water
1/4 teaspoon sugar

Place yeast and sugar in a bowl. Pour over lukewarm water. Put in a warm place for 10 minutes or until yeast rises. Prepare a dough from the flour, margarine, salt, and dissolved yeast mixture. Cover dough with a towel, put in a warm place for 2 hours. When dough rises, take small pieces and roll into strips about 4 inches long. Join the ends to form a bagel. Brush each one with beaten egg and place on a greased baking sheet. Bake in a 350-degree oven for 20 to 30 minutes.

Source: Nahoum, Aldo (Ed.). (1970). *The Art of Israeli Cooking*. New York: Holt, Rinehart and Winston.

4. K'naidlach Soup

3 eggs
3 1/2 cups matzo meal
1/2 chicken bouillon cube
1 teaspoon celery leaves, chopped
nutmeg
juice of 1/2 lemon
salt
pepper

Beat eggs well. Add bouillon cube, salt, pepper, and a pinch of nutmeg. Add lemon juice and celery leaves. Continue to beat. Slowly add matzo meal, using a wooden spoon to stir. When matzo meal thickens, knead by hand. After matzo meal has been thoroughly kneaded, form small balls (1 inch). Arrange in a deep dish and leave in refrigerator for at least 3 hours. Prepare a clear chicken soup and when it reaches boiling, drop in matzo balls. Let cook for 10 to 12 minutes. Serve 3 to 4 balls per bowl of soup. Add lemon juice to taste.

Source: Nahoum, Aldo (Ed.). (1970). *The Art of Israeli Cooking*. New York: Holt, Rinehart and Winston.

Books

The following books can be used to complement this theme:

Adler, David A. (1997). *Chanukah in Chelm.* Illus. by Kevin O'Malley. New York: Lothrop, Lee & Shepard.

Adler, David A. (1995). *One Yellow Daffodil: A Hanukkah Story.* Illus. by Lloyd Bloom. San Diego, CA: Gulliver Books.

Conway, Diana Cohen. (1994). *Northern Lights: A Hanukkah Story.* Rockville, MD: Kar-Ben Copies.

Jaffe, Nina. (1992). *In the Month of Kislev: A Story for Hanukkah.* Illus. by Louise August. New York: Viking.

Kimmel, Eric A. (1996). *The Magic Dreidels: A Hanukkah Story.* Illus. by Katya Krenina. New York: Holiday House.

Kuskin, Karla. (1995). *A Great Miracle Happened There: A Chanukah Story.* Madison, WI: Demco Media.

Oberman, Sheldon. (1997). *By the Hanukkah Light.* Illus. by Neil Waldman. Honesdale, PA: Boyds Mills Press.

Penn, Malka. (1994). *The Miracle of the Potato Latkes: A Hanukkah Story.* Illus. by Giora Carmi. New York: Holiday House.

Polacco, Patricia. (1996). *Trees of the Dancing Goats.* New York: Simon & Schuster.

Rosen, Michael J. (1992). *Elijah's Angel: A Story for Chanukah and Christmas.* Illus. by Aminah B. L. Robinson. Orlando: Harcourt Brace.

Schnur, Steven. (1995). *The Tie Man's Miracle: A Chanukah Story.* Illus. by Stephen Johnson. New York: William Morrow.

Schotter, Roni. (1993). *Hanukkah!* Illus. by Marylin Hafner. Madison, WI: Demco Media.

Wax, Wendy, ed. (1993). *Hanukkah, Oh Hanukkah!: A Treasury of Stories, Songs, and Games to Share.* Illus. by John Speirs. New York: Bantam Doubleday.

Multimedia

The following multimedia products can be used to complement this theme:

Chanukah at Home [cassette]. (1988). Cambridge, MA: Rounder Records.

Holidays for Children: Hanukkah/Passover [video]. Schlessinger Media.

Lewis, Shari. *Lamb Chop's Special Chanukah!* [video]. (1995). Cypress, CA: Youngheart Music.

Palmer, Hap. "Hanukkah" on *Holiday Songs and Rhythms* [compact disc]. (1997). Baldwin, NY: Educational Activities.

Rosenthal, Margie. *Just in Time for Chanukah!* [compact disc]. (1987). Portland, OR: Sheera Recordings.

Recordings and Song Titles

The following recordings can be used to complement this theme:

Holiday Piggyback Songs—"Hanukkah, Hanukkah," "Hanukkah Menorah," "Dreidel Song," "The Latkes Are Frying in the Pan"

Children of the World—"The Dreidel Song"

Holiday Songs for all Occasions—"Hanukkah: Festival of Lights"

THEME 38

Materials

felt, plastic,
canvas, wool,
fur, yarn,
leather

Parts

crown
brim

Sizes

small
medium
large

Hats

Uses

ceremonial
occupational
protection
communication
decoration
religious
fraternal

Types

baseball
top hat
hard hat
bonnet
stocking cap
ski hat
cowboy hat
sombrero
helmet
hood
derby
graduation
birthday
yarmulka
headdresses
veils
turbans

Colors

red
blue
yellow
green
white
brown
purple
black

Theme Goals

Through participating in the experiences provided by this theme, the children may learn:

1. Types of hats.
2. Uses for hats.
3. Materials used to make hats.
4. Parts of a hat.
5. Colors and sizes of hats.

Concepts for the Children to Learn

1. Hats are worn on our heads.
2. Some hats keep us warm.
3. Felt, plastic, cloth, and yarn are all materials used to make hats.
4. Hats come in different sizes.
5. Hats come in different colors.
6. Some hats have special names.
7. Some hats can keep us cool.
8. Hats can be worn for fun.
9. Some people wear hats when they are working.
10. Most hats have a crown and a brim.

Vocabulary

1. **hat**—a covering for the head.
2. **crown**—top part of the hat.
3. **brim**—the part of a hat that surrounds the crown.

Bulletin Board

The purpose of this bulletin board is to have the children match the colored pieces to their corresponding shadow, thereby promoting the development of visual discrimination skills. To construct the bulletin board, draw different types of hats on white tagboard. Color the hats with watercolor markers and cut out. Trace the cut-out hats onto black construction paper to create shadows. Then cut the shadows out and attach to the bulletin board. A magnet piece or a pushpin can be fastened to the shadow. A magnet piece or a hole can be applied to the colored hats.

Parent Letter

Dear Parents,

Hats will be the focus of our next curriculum. Through this unit the children will become familiar with occupations and sports for which hats are worn, materials used to make hats, and purposes of hats such as for protection, decoration, and identification.

AT SCHOOL

Some of the learning activities planned include:

- playing in the Hat Store located in the dramatic play area.
- making paper plate hats at the art table.
- listening to and dramatizing the story *Caps for Sale*, by Esphyr Slobodkina.

SPECIAL REQUEST!

On Friday we will have a Hat Day. The children will show and wear hats that they have brought from home. If your child wishes to share a special hat, please label it and send it to school with your child in a paper bag. This will help us to keep track of which hat belongs to each child. Thank you for your help.

AT HOME

Ask your child to help you search the closets of your home for hats. To develop classification skills, discuss the colors and types of hats with your child. Are there more seasonal hats or sports hats? What are the hats made from? Why were those materials used?

Hats off to a fun unit!

Music

"My Hat"
(traditional song)

My hat it has three corners.
   (point to head, hold up three fingers)
Three corners has my hat.
   (hold up three fingers, point to head)
And had it not three corners
   (hold up three fingers)
It wouldn't be my hat.
   (shake head, point to head)

Variation: Make three-cornered paper hats to wear while acting out this song.

Science

What's It Made Of?

Hats representing a variety of styles and materials can be placed on the science table. Magnifying glasses can also be provided to allow the children to explore. They can look at, feel, and try on the hats.

- Before letting the children try on the hats, make sure the children do not have head lice.

Dramatic Play

1. **Sports Hats**

   Provide football helmets and jerseys, baseball hats, batters' helmets, and uniforms. Encourage the children to pretend they are football and baseball players.

2. **Construction Site**

   Provide the children with toy tools, blocks, and construction hard hats.

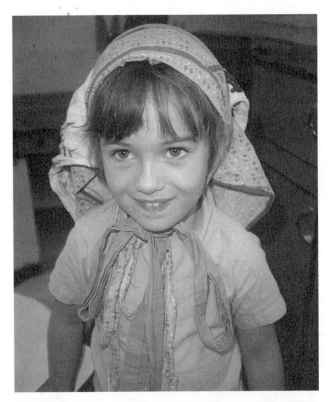

Hats serve many different functions and represent many different areas of the world.

3. **Hat Store**

   Firefighter hats, bonnets, top hats, hard hats, bridesmaids' hats, baby hats, etc., can all be made available in the hat store. Encourage the children to buy and sell hats using a cash register and play money.

Arts and Crafts

1. **Easel Ideas**
   - top hat–shaped paper
   - baseball cap–shaped paper
   - football helmet–shaped paper
   - graduation cap–shaped paper

2. **Paper Plate Hats**

Decorate paper plates with many different kinds of scraps, glitter, construction paper, and crepe paper. Punch a hole, using a paper punch, on each side of the hat. Attach strings so that the hat can be tied on and fastened under the chin.

Large Muscle

Hat Bean Bag Toss

Lay several large hats on the floor. Encourage the children to stand about two feet from the hats and try to throw the beanbags into the hats.

Field Trips

1. **Hat Store**

Visit a hat store or hat department of a store. Examine the different kinds, sizes, and colors of hats.

2. **Sports Store**

Visit a sporting goods store. Locate the hat section. Observe the types of hats used for different sports.

Math

1. **Hat Match**

Construct pairs of hat puzzles out of tagboard. On each pair, draw a different pattern. Encourage the children to mix the hats up and sort them by design.

2. **Hat Seriation**

Collect a variety of hats. The children can arrange them from smallest to largest and largest to smallest. Also, they can classify the hats by colors and uses.

Social Studies

Many of these activities lend themselves to group time situations.

1. **"Weather" or Not to Wear a Hat**

Discuss the different kinds of hats that are worn in cold weather. Ask questions such as, "What parts of our body does a hat keep warm?" "What kinds of hats do we wear when it is warm outside?" "How does a hat help to keep us cool?"

2. **Sports Hats**

Make an arrangement of different sports hats. Place a mirror close by. The children can try on the hats.

3. **Community Helpers**

Many people in our community wear hats as part of their uniform. Collect several of these hats, such as firefighter, police officer, mail carrier, baker, etc., and place in a bag for a small group activity. Identify one child at a time to pull a hat out of the bag. Once the hat is removed, the children can identify the worker. Older children may be able to describe the activities of the identified worker.

Group Time
(games, language)

1. **"My Favorite Hat Day"**

Encourage the children to share their favorite hats with the class on a specific day. Talk about each hat and ask where it was bought or found. Colors, sizes, and shapes can also be discussed.

2. **Dramatization**

Read the story, *Caps for Sale*. After the children are familiar with the storyline, they may enjoy acting out the story.

Cooking

The children may enjoy wearing baker's hats for the cooking experiences! Ask a bakery or fast-food restaurant to donate several for classroom use.

1. Cheese Crunchies

1/2 cup butter or margarine
1 cup all-purpose flour
1 cup shredded cheddar cheese
pinch of salt
1 cup rice cereal bits

Cut the butter into 6 or 8 slices and mix together with the flour, cheese, and salt. Use fingers or fork to mix. Knead in the cereal bits; then roll the dough into small balls or snakes. Press them down flat and place onto an ungreased cookie sheet. Bake at 325 degrees for approximately 10 minutes. Cool and serve for snack.

2. Hamantaschen from Israel

Children in Israel eat hamantaschen on the holiday of Purim. A hamantaschen is a pastry that represents the hat worn by the evil Haman, who plotted against the ancient Jews. Today, Israeli children dress in costumes, parade in the streets, and have parties on Purim.

7 tablespoons butter or margarine
1/3 cup sugar
2 eggs
2 1/2 cups flour
1/4 cup orange juice
1 teaspoon lemon juice
1 jar prune or plum jam

Cream the butter or margarine and sugar together in a large mixing bowl. Separate the eggs. Discard the whites. Add the yolk to the mixture and stir. Add the flour and juices to the mixture and mix to form dough. On a floured board, roll the dough to about 1/8-inch thickness. Use a cookie cutter to cut into 4-inch circles. Spoon a tablespoon of jam into the center of each circle and fold up 3 edges to create a triangle shape. Leave a small opening at the center. (Other fillings, such as poppy seeds or apricot jam, can be used.) Place the shaped dough on a cookie sheet and bake for 20 minutes in a 350-degree preheated oven. Serve for snack.

Hats

A variety of hats can be collected for use in the dramatic play area. Some examples are:

firefighter	party (birthday)	hard hats	bicycle helmet
police officer	nurse's cap	ski caps	pillbox
visor	railroad engineer	berets	sports:
sunbonnets	motorcycle helmet	top hat	football
sombrero	cloche	cowboy	baseball
straw hats	chef	stocking cap	
mantilla	sailor	mail carrier	

Books

The following books can be used to complement this theme:

Bancroft, Catherine. (1993). *Felix's Hat*. Illus. by Hannah Coale Gruenberg. New York: Simon & Schuster.

Brett, Jan. (1997). *The Hat*. New York: G. P. Putnam.

Carlson, Laurie. (1998). *Boss of the Plains: The Hat That Won the West*. Illus. by Holly Meade. New York: Dorling Kindersley.

Gardella, Tricia. (1997). *Casey's New Hat*. Illus. by Margot Apple. Boston: Houghton Mifflin.

Geringer, Laura. (1987). *A Three Hat Day*. Illus. by Arnold Lobel. New York: HarperCollins.

Hanel, Wolfram. (1995). *The Extraordinary Adventures of an Ordinary Hat*. Illus. by Christa Unzner-Fischer. New York: North South Books. (Pbk)

Howard, Elizabeth Fitzgerald. (1991). *Aunt Flossie's Hats (and Crab Cakes Later)*. Illus. by James Ransome. New York: Clarion Books.

Kalman, Bobbie. (1998). *Bandanas, Chaps, and Ten-Gallon Hats*. New York: Crabtree Publishing.

Keller, Holly. (1995). *Rosata*. New York: Greenwillow.

Malka, Lucy. (1995). *Fun with Hats*. Illus. by Melinda Levine. Greenvale, NY: Mondo Pub. (Pbk)

Milich, Melissa. (1997). *Miz Fannie Mae's Fine New Easter Hat*. Illus. by Yong Chen. Boston: Little, Brown.

Miller, Margaret. (1988). *Whose Hat?* New York: William Morrow.

Morris, Ann. (1989). *Hats, Hats, Hats*. Photos by Ken Heyman. New York: Lothrop, Lee & Shepard.

Oborne, Martine. (1997). *Juice the Pig*. Illus. by Axel Scheffler. New York: Holt.

Pearson, Tracey Campbell. (1997). *The Purple Hat*. New York: Farrar, Straus & Giroux.

Pratt, Pierre. (1992). *Follow That Hat!* Willowdale, ON: Annick Press.

Reed, Lynn Rowe. (1995). *Pedro, His Perro, and the Alphabet Sombrero*. New York: Hyperion.

Slobodkina, Esphyr. (1947). *Caps for Sale*. New York: W. R. Scott.

Smath, Jerry. (1995). *A Hat So Simple*. Mahwah, NJ: Troll. (Pbk)

Stoeke, Janet Morgan. (1994). *A Hat for Minerva Louise*. New York: Dutton.

THEME 39

Clothes

types

Exercise

running
aerobics
walking
bicycling

Tools

hairbrushes
toothbrushes
shampoo
soap
toothpaste

Health

Foods

fruits
vegetables
meats
dairy products
beans
legumes
breads
cereal
rice patties

People

doctors
dentists

Personal Habits

taking baths
brushing teeth
washing hair
taking naps
night sleep

Importance of

having a healthy body
having a rested body

Theme Goals

Through participating in the experiences provided by this theme, the children may learn:

1. Importance of good health.
2. Healthy foods.
3. Exercise clothes.
4. Tools used for health needs.
5. Exercises for health.
6. Health habits.
7. Health occupations.

Concepts for the Children to Learn

1. We need to take good care of our bodies.
2. Vitamins, shampoo, soap, and toothpaste are health aids.
3. Doctors and dentists provide health checkups.
4. Running, aerobics, and walking are all forms of exercise.
5. Fruits, vegetables, dairy products, beans, legumes, meat, breads, and cereals keep our bodies healthy.
6. Our bodies need rest.
7. Different types of clothing are worn during exercise.
8. Brushing teeth, washing hair, and bathing are ways to keep our bodies clean.
9. Hairbrushes and toothbrushes are health tools.

Vocabulary

1. **exercise**—moving body parts.
2. **health**—feeling good.
3. **nutrition**—eating foods that are good for our body.
4. **cleanliness**—keeping our body parts free from dirt.
5. **diet**—the food we eat.
6. **checkup**—a visit to a doctor to make sure you are healthy.

Bulletin Board

The purpose of this bulletin board is to have the children match the health aids to their corresponding shadow. Construct the health aid pieces from white tagboard. Include a toothbrush, toothpaste, comb, brush, and soap. Color the objects with colored felt-tip markers and laminate. Trace each of the health aids onto black construction paper to construct shadows as illustrated. Staple the shadow aids on the bulletin board either by affixing magnets or using pushpins. Then punch a hole in each of the health aid pieces, allowing the children to hang them on the appropriate shadow.

Parent Letter

Dear Parents,

We will be starting a unit on health. This unit will include many aspects of health. We will be discussing foods that are good for us, important personal habits, and exercise. Through this unit the children will develop an awareness of how important it is to keep their bodies healthy.

AT SCHOOL

Some of the learning experiences planned for the week include:

- tracing our bodies at the art center.
- visiting Dr. Thomas, the dentist, at her office.
- having a visit by an aerobics instructor.
- creating healthy snacks.
- weighing and measuring ourselves.

FIELD TRIP

Arrangements have been made to visit Dr. Thomas's office on Thursday of this week. Dr. Thomas will give us a tour of the dental clinic and show us various pieces of dental equipment. We will walk to her office, leaving school at 10:00 a.m., and return just in time for lunch. Please have your child at school by 10:00 a.m. if he wishes to participate. Parents, please feel free to join us.

JUST A REMINDER

If your child's toothbrush at school is missing, please send another one. We teach the importance of dental hygiene by brushing our teeth after all meals and snacks at school.

AT HOME

Cotton swabs may be used instead of brushes for painting. They may also be used to dot paper with different colors. Painting is a valuable sensory experience for a child. It provides an opportunity to experiment with color.

Teach your child healthy habits today!

Music

1. **"Brush Your Teeth"**
   by Raffi.

2. **"My Body"**
   (Sing to the tune of "Where Is Thumbkin?")

   This is my body.
   This is my body.
   It's the only one I've got.
   It's the only one I've got.
   I'm going to take good care of it.
   I'm going to take good care of it.
   Yes I am. Yes I am.

Fingerplay

BRUSHING TEETH

I jiggle the toothbrush again and again.
   (pretend to brush teeth)
I scrub all my teeth for awhile.
I swish the water to rinse them and then
   (puff out cheeks to swish)
I look at myself and I smile.
   (smile at one another)

Science

Soap Pieces

Add different kinds of soaps and a magnifying glass to the science area. Talk about what each one is used for.

Dramatic Play

1. **Health Club**

   Mats, fake weights (made from large tinker toys), headbands, and music to represent a health club can be placed in the dramatic play area.

Clean hands can prevent the spread of germs.

2. **Doctor's Office (Hospital)**

   White clothing, stethoscopes, strip thermometers, magazines, bandages, cots, sheets, and plastic syringes without needles can be placed in the dramatic play area to represent a hospital.

3. **Restaurant**

   Tables, tablecloths, menus, and tablets for taking orders can be placed in the dramatic play area. Paste pictures of food on the menus. A sign for the area could be "Eating for Health."

Arts and Crafts

1. Paper Plate Meals

Magazines for the children to cut food pictures from the five food groups should be provided. The pictures can be pasted on a paper plate to represent a balanced meal. Plates from microwave dinners, if thoroughly cleaned, work well, too.

2. Body Tracing

Instruct each child to lie on a large piece of paper. Trace the child's body and let him take the tracing home and decorate it with his parents. After this, it can be returned to school for display. This activity should help the children become aware of individual uniqueness and fosters parent-child interaction.

Sensory

Add shampoo or dish detergent to the sensory table.

Large Muscle

1. Weight Awareness

The object of this activity is to become aware of weight and to feel the difference between heavy and light. To do this, the child should experiment with body force. Exercise in the following ways: lift arms slowly and gently, stomp on the floor, walk on tiptoes, kick out one leg as hard as possible, very smoothly and lightly slide one foot along the floor. Music can be added to imitate aerobics.

2. Mini-Olympics

Set up various areas for jumping jacks, jogging, relays, and a "beanbag launch." For the "launch" put a beanbag on the top edge of a child's foot and launch it by kicking. Observe the distance each beanbag goes.

Field Trips/ Resource People

1. Take a field trip to:
- hospital
- health care facility
- doctor's office
- dentist's office
- beauty shop
- health club
- drugstore

2. Invite the following resource people to visit the classroom:
- doctor
- nurse
- dentist
- dietician
- aerobics instructor
- beautician

Math

1. Food Group Sorting

Create a food group display. To do this, encourage the children to bring empty food containers. The food containers can be sorted into food groups. This could be a small group activity or a choice during the self-selected play period.

2. Height and Weight Chart

Weigh and measure each of the children at various times throughout the year. Record the data on a chart. This chart can be posted in the classroom.

390

Group Time
(games, language)

Tasting Party

Prepare for a tasting party. Collect a wide variety of foods. For example, the children could experiment with bananas by dipping them in wheat germ, peanut butter, honey, raisins, etc. To extend this activity, charts can be prepared listing the children's favorite foods.

Cooking

Fruit Tree Salad

On a plate, place a lettuce leaf. On the lettuce, place a pineapple slice. Peel and slice a banana horizontally into 2-inch pieces, and place them on the pineapple. Drain 1 small can of fruit cocktail. Spoon the fruit over the bananas.

Books

The following books can be used to complement this theme:

Aliki. (1992). *I'm Growing.* New York: HarperCollins.

Barner, Bob. (1996). *Dem Bones.* New York: Chronicle Books.

Berger, Melvin. (1995). *Germs Make Me Sick.* Rev. ed. Illus. by Marylin Hafner. New York: HarperCollins.

Brown, Laurene Krasny and Marc Tolon Brown. (1990). *Dinosaurs Alive and Well! A Guide to Good Health.* Boston: Little, Brown.

Caffey, Donna. (1998). *Yikes—Lice!* Illus. by Patrick Girouard. Niles, IL: Albert Whitman.

Dooley, Virginia. (1996). *Tubes in My Ears: My Trip to the Hospital.* Illus. by Miriam Katin. Greenvale, NY: Mondo Pub.

Gosselin, Kim. (1998). *Taking Diabetes to School.* 2nd ed. Illus. by Moss Freedman. Manchester, MO: JayJo Books.

Janovitz, Marilyn. (1994). *Is It Time?* New York: North South Books.

Leedy, Loreen. (1994). *The Edible Pyramid: Good Eating Every Day.* New York: Holiday House.

London, Jonathan. (1992). *The Lion Who Had Asthma.* Illus. by Nadine B. Westcott. Beaver Dam, WI: Concept Books.

Newcome, Zita. (1997). *Toddlerobics.* New York: Candlewick Press.

Powell, Jillian. (1997). *Health Matters* series. Austin, TX: Raintree/Steck Vaughn. *Exercise and Your Health; Food and Your Health; Hygiene and Your Health.*

Rockwell, Harlow. (1987). *My Dentist.* New York: William Morrow.

Rockwell, Harlow. (1992). *My Doctor.* New York: Macmillan.

Showers, Paul. (1991). *How Many Teeth?* Newly illus. by True Kelley. New York: HarperCollins.

Showers, Paul. (1997). *Sleep Is for Everyone.* Illus. by Wendy Watson. New York: HarperCollins.

Teague, Mark. (1994). *Pigsty.* New York: Scholastic.

Thompson, Carol. (1997). *Piggy Washes Up.* New York: Candlewick Press.

Van Cleave, Janice. (1998). *Janice Van Cleave's Play and Find Out About the Human Body.* New York: Wiley.

Multimedia

The following multimedia products can be used to complement this theme:

Raffi. "Bathtime" on *Raffi in Concert with the Rise and Shine Band* [video]. (1988). Hollywood, CA: Troubadour Records.

Chef Combo's Fantastic Adventures in Tasting and Nutrition [kit]. (1996). Rosemont, IL: National Dairy Council.

Come See What the Doctor Sees [video]. (1994). Half Moon Bay, CA: Visual Mentor.

Goofy Over Dental Health [video]. (1991). Disney Educational Productions.

K-6 Classroom Gallery [CD-ROM]. (1997). Lancaster, PA: Classroom Connect.

Preschool Power! Jacket Flips and Other Tips [video]. (1991). Concept Associates.

Rock 'n' Roll Fitness Fun [compact disc or cassette]. (1989). Kimbo Educational.

Stewart, Georgiana. *Good Morning Exercises for Kids* [cassette]. (1987). Kimbo Educational.

Recordings and Song Titles

The following recordings can be used to complement this theme:

Get Up and Grow—"Brush Your Teeth," "I'm in the Tub," "Let's Sing about Food"

Piggyback Songs—"Good Grooming"

Positively Singable Songs—"Sticky, Sticky"

Make the Right Choice—"Say No to Drugs," "Please Don't Smoke"

Science in a Nutshell—"Hygiene," "Respiration"

People in Our Neighborhood—"Doctor, Doctor"—(RONNO)

Listen with Your Ears—"I Like to Wash" (Special Needs)

THEME 46

Homes

Materials
adobe
brick
straw
stone
wood
cement

Workers
carpenters
architects
painters
plumbers
electricians
masons
cabinet makers

Kinds
shelters/halfway houses
apartments
houseboats
trailers
houses
condominiums
duplexes
cabins
tents
huts
townhouses
solar

Rooms
living room
kitchen
bathroom
bedroom
den
dining room
closet
family room
office/study

Parts
roof
garage
basement
toilets
stairs
ceiling
floors
walls
doors
windows
cupboards
sinks
bathtubs

Theme Goals

Through participating in the experiences provided by this theme, the children may learn about:

1. Home builders.
2. Parts of a home.
3. Rooms in a home.
4. Kinds of homes.
5. Building materials.

Concepts for the Children to Learn

1. A home is a place to live.
2. Apartments, condominiums, trailers, and houses are all kinds of homes.
3. Most homes have a kitchen, bedroom, bathroom, and living room.
4. Homes can be built from brick, stone, wood, or cement.
5. The ceiling, floor, roof, and windows are parts of a home.
6. Construction workers build houses.
7. Homes come in many sizes.
8. Homes can be decorated many ways.

Vocabulary

1. **apartment**—a building including many homes.
2. **duplex**—a house divided into two separate homes.
3. **house**—a place to live.
4. **construction worker**—a person who builds.
5. **kitchen**—a room for cooking.
6. **bedroom**—a room for sleeping.
7. **architect**—a person who designs homes.

Bulletin Board

The purpose of this bulletin board is to promote the development of classification skills. Begin by drawing an unfurnished model of a home on a large sheet of tagboard as illustrated. Include the basic rooms such as kitchen, bedroom, and living room. Draw and cut furnishings to add to the home. Laminate home and furnishings. The children can place the furnishings in the proper room by using "fun tack" or magnetic strips on the furnishings.

Parent Letter

Dear Parents,

Homes will be the focus of our next curricular theme. Since everyone's home is unique we will be discussing how homes differ. We will also be discussing activities we do in our homes and the rooms in our homes.

AT SCHOOL

Some of our activities will include:

- constructing homes out of cardboard boxes and paper in the art area.
- acting out the story of *The Three Little Pigs* in the dramatic play area.
- building at the workbench.

A special activity will include making placemats, but we need your help. For our placemats we will need a few pictures of your family, home, or both. These will be glued to construction paper and laminated during our project. They will not be returned in their original form. Thank you!

This week we will also be taking a neighborhood tour to observe the various types of homes in the area. We will be taking our walk at 10:00 a.m. on Thursday. Please feel free to join us!

AT HOME

To develop observation skills, take your child on a walk around your neighborhood to look at the houses in your area. Talk about the different colors and sizes of dwellings.

Enjoy the time you spend with your child!

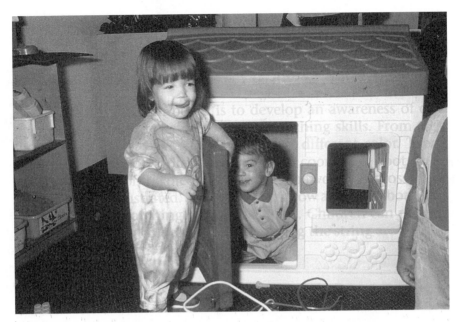

Playing house is an activity that builds interpersonal skills.

Music

"This Is the Way We Build Our House"
(Sing to the tune of "Here We Go 'Round the Mulberry Bush")

This is the way we build our house,
Build our house, build our house.
This is the way we build our house,
So early in the morning.

Other suggestions:
This is the way we paint the house.
This is the way we wash the car.
This is the way we rake the leaves.

Fingerplays

MY HOUSE

I'm going to build a little house
   (fingers make roof)
With windows big and bright
   (stand with arms in air)
Drifting out of sight.
In winter when the snowflakes fall
   (hands flutter down)

Or when I hear a storm
   (hand cupped to ear)
I'll go sit in my little house
   (sit down)
Where I'll be snug and warm.
   (cross arms over chest)

WHERE SHOULD I LIVE?

Where should I live?
In a castle with towers and a moat?
   (make a point with arms over head)
Or on a river in a houseboat?
   (make wavelike motions)
A winter igloo made of ice may be just the thing
   (pretend to pack snow)
But what would happen when it turned to spring?
   (pretend to think)
I like tall apartments and houses made of stone,
   (stretch up tall)
But I'd also like to live in a blue mobile home.
   (shorten up)
A cave or cabin in the woods would give me lots of space
   (stretch out wide)
But I guess my home is the best place!
   (point to self)

KNOCKING

Look at _____ knocking on our door.
(knock)
Look at _____ knocking on our door.
(knock)
Come on in out of the cold
(shiver)
Into our nice, warm home.
(rub hands together to be warm)

MY CHORES

In my home, I wash the dishes
(pretend to wash)
Vacuum the floor
(push vacuum)
And dust the furniture.
(dust)
Outside my home, I rake the leaves
(rake)
Plant the flowers
(plant)
And play hard all day.
(wipe sweat from forehead)
When the day is over
I eat my supper,
(eat)
Read a story
(read)
And go to sleep.
(put head on hands)

Science

Building Materials

Building materials and magnifying glasses should be placed in the science area. The children may observe and examine materials. Included may be wood, brick, canvas, tar paper, shingles, etc.

Dramatic Play

1. Tent Living

A small tent can be set up indoors or outdoors depending upon weather and space. Accessories such as sleeping bags, flashlights, rope, cooking utensils, and backpacks should also be provided if available.

2. Cardboard Houses

Collect large cardboard boxes. Place outdoors or in an open classroom area. The children may build their own homes. If desired, tempera paint can be used for painting the homes. Wallpaper may also be provided.

3. Cleaning House

Housecleaning tools such as a vacuum cleaner, dusting cloth, sponges, mops, and brooms can be placed in the dramatic play area. During the self-selected play periods the children may choose to participate in cleaning.

Arts and Crafts

1. Shape Homes

An assortment of construction paper shapes such as squares, triangles, rectangles, and circles should be placed on a table in the art area. Glue and large pieces of paper should also be provided.

2. Tile Painting

Ask building companies to donate cracked, chipped, or discontinued tiles. The children can paint tiles.

3. Homes I Like

The children can cut pictures of homes, rooms, appliances, and furniture from magazines. They can glue these pieces on large construction paper pieces. The construction paper can be stapled. A cover can also be added and labeled "Things in My Home."

4. Household Tracings

Several household items such as a spatula, wooden spoon, pizza cutter, or cookie cutter can be placed on the art table. Also include paper, scissors, and crayons. These items can be traced. Some of the older children may color and cut their tracings.

398

Sensory

1. Identifying Sounds

Record several sounds found in the home such as a vacuum cleaner, television, water running, and a toilet flushing. Encourage children to name sounds. For older children, this could also be played as a lotto game. Make cards containing pictures of sounds and vary pictures from card to card. When a sound is heard, cover the corresponding picture with a chip.

2. Sand Castles

Add wet sand to the sensory table. Provide forms to create buildings, homes, etc.
Caution: Examples may include empty cans, milk cartons, plastic containers, etc.

Large Muscle

Pounding Nails

Collect building materials such as soft pine scraps and styrofoam for the workbench.
Caution: Adult supervision is always required with this activity.

Field Trips/ Resource People

1. Neighborhood Walk

Walk around the neighborhood. Observe the construction workers' actions and tools.

2. Construction Site

If available visit a local construction site. Discuss the role of the construction worker.

3. Resource People

The following resource people could be invited to the classroom:

- builder
- painter
- architect
- electrician
- plumber

Math

My House

Construct a "My House" book for each child. On the pages write things like

My house has _____ steps.
My house is the color _____.
My house has _____ windows.
There are _____ doors in my house.
My house has _____ keyholes.

Other ideas could include the number of beds, people, pets, etc. Send this home with the child to complete with parents.

Social Studies

Room Match

Collect several boxes. On one box print "kitchen"; on another print "bathroom"; on another print "living room"; and on another print "bedroom." Then cut objects related to each of these rooms from catalogs. The children may sort objects by placing them in the appropriate boxes. For example, dishes, silverware, and a coffee pot would be placed in the box labeled kitchen.

Group Time
(games, language)

Construct a "My home is special because . . ." chart. Encourage the children to name a special thing about their homes. Display the chart at the children's eye level in the classroom for the week.

Cooking

Individual Pizza

English muffins   pizza sauce
grated mozzarella cheese

Spread a tablespoon of sauce on each muffin half. Sprinkle the top with grated cheese. Bake in a preheated oven at 375 degrees until cheese melts.

Books

The following books can be used to complement this theme:

Ackerman, Karen. (1992). *I Know a Place.* Illus. by Deborah Kogan Ray. Boston: Houghton Mifflin.

Ackerman, Karen. (1995). *The Sleeping Porch.* Illus. by Elizabeth Sayles. New York: William Morrow.

Arnold, Ted. (1987). *No Jumping on the Bed.* New York: Dutton.

Ballard, Robin. (1994). *Good-Bye House.* New York: Greenwillow.

Brown, Richard Eric. (1988). *100 Words About My House.* Orlando: Harcourt Brace.

Bunting, Eve. (1991). *Fly Away Home.* Illus. by Ronald Himler. New York: Clarion Books.

Delafosse, Claude, ed. (1998). *Houses.* New York: Scholastic.

Dorros, Arthur. (1992). *This Is My House.* New York: Scholastic.

Gibbons, Gail. (1990). *How a House Is Built.* New York: Holiday House.

Hill, Elizabeth Starr. (1991). *Evan's Corner.* Revised and newly illus. by D. Brodie. New York: Viking.

Hoberman, Mary Ann. (1978). *A House Is a House for Me.* Illus. by Betty Fraser. New York: Viking.

Kalman, Bobbie. (1994). *Homes Around the World.* New York: Crabtree Publishing.

Kuklin, Susan. (1992). *How My Family Lives in America.* Minneapolis: Bradbury Press.

McDonald, Megan. (1996). *My House Has Stars.* Illus. by Peter Catalanotto. New York: Orchard Books.

McGovern, Ann. (1997). *The Lady in the Box.* Illus. by Marni Backer. New York: Turtle Books.

Morris, Ann. (1992). *Houses and Homes.* Photos by Ken Heyman. New York: Lothrop, Lee & Shepard.

Rosen, Michael, ed. (1992). *Home.* New York: HarperCollins.

Rosen, Michael. (1996). *This Is Our House.* Illus. by Bob Graham. Cambridge, MA: Candlewick Press.

Rounds, Glen. (1996). *Sod Houses on the Great Plains.* New York: Holiday House.

Rylant, Cynthia. (1993). *Everyday House.* New York: Simon & Schuster. (Board book)

Saul, Carol P. (1995). *Someplace Else.* Illus. by Barry Root. New York: Simon & Schuster.

Shelby, Anne. (1996). *The Someday House.* Illus. by Rosanne Litzinger. New York: Orchard Books.

Williams, John. (1997). *Houses and Homes.* Austin, TX: Raintree/Steck Vaughn.

Multimedia

The following multimedia products can be used to complement this theme:

Community Construction Kit [CD-ROM]. (1998). Watertown, MA: Tom Snyder Productions.

Dig Hole, Build House [video]. (1994). Gig Harbor, WA: Real World Video.

Gryphon Bricks [CD-ROM]. (1996). San Diego, CA: Gryphon Software Corp.

Let's Build a House [video]. (1996). San Diego, CA: Video Connections.

A Silly, Noisy House [CD-ROM]. (1991). Santa Monica, CA: Voyager Company.

Insects and Spiders

Insects

TYPES
ants
beetles
bees
butterflies
moths
grasshoppers
crickets
mosquitoes
flies

BODY PARTS
6 legs
3 parts
feelers
wings

Movement

hop
crawl
fly
swim

Uses

pest control
pollination
food

Homes

hives (bees),
hills (ants),
webs (spiders),
water, grass,
ground, trees,
plants

Sounds

chirp
creak
buzz

Spiders

TYPES
daddy longlegs
tarantula
garden-variety

BODY PARTS
8 legs
2 parts

Theme Goals

Through participating in the experiences provided by this theme, the children may learn:

1. Ways to identify different insects and spiders.
2. Ways insects help us.
3. Ways spiders help us.
4. Places where spiders and insects live.
5. Ways that spiders and insects move from place to place.

Concepts for the Children to Learn

1. There are many kinds of insects.
2. Insects are different in many ways: size, shape, color, eyes, mouths, and number of wings.
3. Insects have six legs (three pairs) and, if winged, four wings.
4. Spiders have eight legs (four pairs) and no wings.
5. Insects and spiders come from eggs.
6. Insects can help us by making honey and pollinating fruits and flowers.
7. Spiders can help us by eating insect pests.
8. Most spiders spin a web.
9. Some insects fly, others walk.
10. Spiders spin a web to catch insects to eat.

Vocabulary

1. **insect**—small animal with three pairs of jointed legs.
2. **spider**—small animal with four pairs of legs.
3. **caterpillar**—the wormlike larva of a butterfly or moth.
4. **pollinate**—the way insects help flowers to grow.
5. **spiderling**—a baby spider.
6. **antennae**—feelers on an insect that stick out from the head.
7. **pupa**—intermediate stage of an insect; chrysalis.
8. **moth**—night-flying insect with four wings related to the butterfly.
9. **wasp**—winged insect with a poisonous sting.
10. **cricket**—small leaping insect known for its chirping.

Bulletin Board

The purpose of this bulletin board is to develop visual discrimination skills. Construct several butterflies, each of a different shape, out of tagboard. Trace the butterfly figures onto black construction paper to create shadows. Cut out and laminate the butterfly figures and shadows. Staple shadow butterflies to bulletin board. Punch holes in colored butterflies for children to hang on the pushpin of the corresponding shadow butterfly.

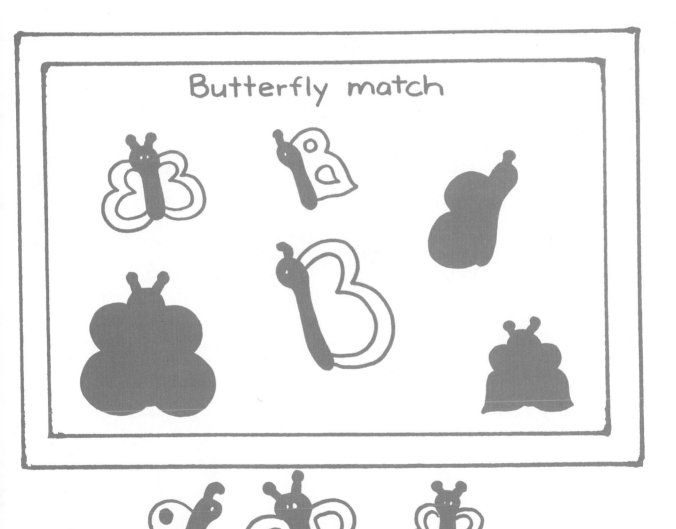

Parent Letter

Dear Parents,

We are continuing our study of animals. We are introducing a new category—insects and spiders. The children will become aware of the difference between insects and spiders and the ways that those creatures are helpful. Do you know the difference between insects and spiders? Most insects have three body parts and six legs. Spiders have two body parts and eight legs.

AT SCHOOL

Some of the learning experiences planned include:

- singing and acting out the song "One Elephant Went Out to Play." It's about an elephant that plays on a spider web!
- listening to a flannel board version of the story *The Very Hungry Caterpillar* by Eric Carle.
- watching and observing an ant farm set up in the science area.
- creating spiders and insects out of a variety of materials in the art area.

AT HOME

There are many ways to bring this unit into your home. Take a walk with your child and see how many spiders and insects you can find. Avoid touching unknown types of insects or spiders with your fingers. Instead, use a clear jar with a lid to observe the creature close up. Release the insect or spider after the observation.

We will be having a snack this week called ants on a log. Let your child make some for you! Spread peanut butter on pieces of celery. Top with raisins. Enjoy!

Enjoy your child!

404

Music

1. **"The Eensie Weensie Spider"**
   (traditional)

   The eensie weensie spider crawled up the
       water spout.
       (walk fingers of one hand up other hand)
   Down came the rain and washed the spider
       out.
       (lower hands to make rain, wash out
       spider by placing hands together in front
       and extending out to either side)
   Out came the sun and dried up all the rain,
       (form sun with arms in circle over head)
   And the eensie weensie spider went up the
       spout again.
       (walk fingers up other arm)

2. **"The Elephant Song"**
   (chant)

   One elephant went out to play
   On a spider's web one day.
   He had such enormous fun,
   That he called for another elephant to come.

   Elephant! Elephant! Come out to play!
   Elephant! Elephant! Come out to play!

   Two elephants . . .

3. **"The Insects and Spiders"**
   (Sing to the tune of "The Wheels on the Bus")

   The bugs in the air fly up and down,
   up and down, up and down.
   The bugs in the air fly up and down all
       through the day.

   The spiders on the bush spin a web.
   The crickets in the field hop up and down.
   The bees in their hive go buzz, buzz, buzz.

Fingerplays

ANTS

   Once I saw an anthill, with no ants about.
   ·So I said "Little ants, won't you please
       come out?"
   Then, as if they heard my call, one, two,
       three, four, five came out.
   And that was all!

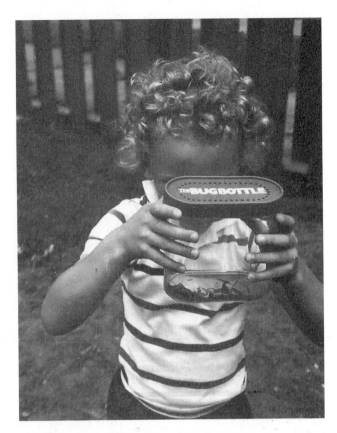

Children enjoy observing bugs.

BUMBLEBEE

   Brightly colored bumblebee
   Looking for some honey.
   Flap your wings and fly away
   While it still is sunny.

THE CATERPILLAR

   A caterpillar crawled to the top of a tree.
       (index finger of left hand moves up right
       arm)
   "I think I'll take a nap," said he.
   So under a leaf, he began to creep
       (wrap right hand over left fist)
   To spin his chrysalis and he fell asleep.
   All winter long he slept in his chrysalis bed,
       (keep right hand over left fist)
   Till spring came along one day, and said,
   "Wake up, wake up little sleepy head."
       (shake left fist with right hand).
   "Wake up, it's time to get out of bed!"
   So, he opened his eyes that sunshiny day
       (shake fingers and look into hand)
   Lo—he was a butterfly and flew away!
       (move hand into flying motion)

© 2000, Delmar

405

LITTLE MISS MUFFET

Little Miss Muffet
Sat on a tuffet
Eating her curds and whey.
Along came a spider
And sat down beside her
And frightened Miss Muffet away!

Spiders can be prepared in the art area.

Science

1. **Observe an ant farm.**

   The children can watch the ants dig tunnels, build roads and tunnels, build roads and rooms, eat and store food, etc. (Ant farms are available in some commercial play catalogs.)

2. Go outside and observe anthills in the playground area.

3. Observe deceased flies and ants under a microscope.

4. Observe insects and spiders in a caged bug keeper or plastic jars with holes in the lids.

5. Listen to a cricket during quiet time.

6. Capture a caterpillar and watch it spin a chrysalis and turn into a butterfly.

Dramatic Play

1. **Scientist**

   The children can dress up in white lab coats and observe spiders and insects with magnifying glasses.

2. **Spider Web**

   Tie together a big piece of rope to resemble a spider web. Have children pretend they are spiders playing on their web.

3. **Spider Sac**
   Tape together a 10-foot by 25-foot piece of plastic on the sides. Blow it up with a fan to make a big bubble. Make a slit in the plastic for the entrance. The children can pretend to be baby spiders coming out of the spider sac when they are hatching.

4. **The children can act out "Little Miss Muffet."**

Arts and Crafts

1. Cut easel paper in the shape of a butterfly.
2. Fingerpaint creepy crawly pictures.
3. Make insects and spiders out of clay. Use toothpicks, straws, and pipe cleaner segments for the appendages.
4. Make insects and spiders with thumbprints. Children can draw crayon legs to make prints look like insects and spiders.
5. Egg carton caterpillars. Cut egg cartons in half, lengthwise. Each child paints a carton half. When dry, children can make a face on the end of the carton and insert pipe cleaners or straws for feelers.
6. Have children make spiders from black construction paper—one large black circle for a body and eight strips for legs. Children can paste on two yellow circles for eyes. Hang by a string around the room.
7. Make ladybug shapes out of red and orange construction paper. Have children sponge paint dots and legs on the bugs.
8. Make butterfly templates.
9. Sprinkle crayon shavings between two pieces of waxed paper and iron. Put a butterfly template over the waxed paper and glue it on. A pretty butterfly will be the final product!
10. Tissue paper butterflies. Have children lightly paint white tissue paper or use colored tissue paper. Fasten a pipe cleaner around the middle. Add circles on the ends for antennae.

11. Balloon bugs. Blow up several long balloons. Cover them with strips of paper dipped in wallpaper paste. Put on three to four layers of this sticky paper. Let dry for two to three days. Then paint your own giant bug!

12. Have insect and spider stencils set out for the children to draw and trace.

Sensory

Add soil and plastic insects to the sensory table.

Large Muscle

Have children pretend to walk as different insects when in transition from one activity to another.

Field Trips/ Resource People

1. Go on a walk to a nearby park to find bugs. Look under rocks, in cracks, in sidewalks, in bushes, etc.

2. Have someone who has a butterfly collection come in.

3. Visit a pet store. Ask them to show you what kind of insects they feed to the animals in the store. Do they sell any insects?

4. Invite a zoologist to come in and talk about insects and how important they are.

5. Invite an individual who raises bees to talk to the children. Ask him to bring in a honeycomb for the children to taste.

Math

1. **Butterfly Match**

   Make several triangles of different colors. On one triangle put the numbers 1 to 10; on the other make dots to correspond to the numbers 1 to 10. Have the children match the dots to the numbers and clip them together with a clothespin to form a butterfly.

2. **Ladybug Houses**

   Paint several 1/2-pint milk cartons red. Write the numerals 1 to 10 on each. Make 50 small ladybugs dotting 5 sets of 1 to 10. Have children put ladybugs in their correct houses by matching dots to numerals.

3. **Numeral Caterpillar**

   Make a caterpillar with 10 body segments and a head. Have the children put the numbers in order to complete the caterpillar's body.

4. Sing the song "The Ants Go Marching One by One," and have the children act out the song using their fingers as numbers.

5. Make an insect and spider lotto or concentration game with stickers for children to play.

Social Studies

1. Take the children on an insect hunt near your school. When the children are finished, have everyone show the rest of the class what they found. Talk about where they found the insects (on a tree, under a log, etc.).

2. Have children make homes for all the insects they found. They can put dirt, grass, twigs, and small rocks in plastic jars and cans.

3. Discuss what it is like to be a member of a family. Ask the children if each

member of their family has a certain job. Then focus on ant colonies or families. Ants live together much like people do, except that ants live in a larger community. Each ant has a certain task within the community. Some of the jobs are:

- nurse: to look after the young
- soldier: defend colony and attack the enemies
- others: search for food; enlarge and clean the nest (house)

Group Time
(games, language)

1. **Matching Insects**

   Divide children into two groups. Hand out pictures of different spiders and insects, one to each group that matches one in the other group. Point to a child from one group and have that child act out the insect they have in some way (movement or noises). The child that has the same insect from the other group must go and meet the child in the middle and act out the insect also.

2. Have many pictures of insects and spiders on display. Talk about a different insect or spider every day. Include where it lives, how it walks, what it might eat, etc.

Cooking

1. **Honey Bees**

   1/2 cup peanut butter
   1 tablespoon honey
   1/3 cup nonfat dry milk
   2 tablespoons toasted wheat germ
   unsweetened cocoa powder
   sliced almonds

   In a mixing bowl, mix peanut butter and honey. Stir in dry milk and wheat germ until well mixed. Lay waxed paper on a baking sheet. Using 1 tablespoon at a time, shape peanut butter mixture into ovals to look like bees. Put on baking sheet. Dip a toothpick in cocoa powder and press lightly across the top of the bees to make stripes. Stick on almonds for wings. Chill for 30 minutes.

   Source: *Better Homes and Gardens Kids' Snacks*. (1979). Iowa: Meredith Corporation.

2. **Ants on a Log**
   (traditional)

   Cut celery pieces into 3-inch strips. Fill the cavity of the celery stick with peanut butter. Garnish with raisins. (As with all recipes calling for celery, this might be more appropriate for older children.)

Books

The following books can be used to complement this theme:

Arnosky, Jim. (1996). *Crinkleroot's Guide to Knowing Butterflies and Moths*. New York: Simon & Schuster.

Banks, Kate. (1997). *Spider, Spider*. Illus. by Georg Hallensleben. New York: Farrar, Straus & Giroux.

Carle, Eric. (1969). *The Very Hungry Caterpillar*. Harlow, NY: Longman.

Cassie, Brian and Jerry Pallotta. (1995).*The Butterfly Alphabet Book*. Illus. by Mark Astrella. Watertown, MA: Charlesbridge Publishers.

Cole, Joanna. (1996). *The Magic School Bus inside a Beehive*. Illus. by Bruce Degen. New York: Scholastic.

Cole, Joanna. (1997). *The Magic School Bus Spins a Web: A Book about Spiders*. Illus. by Bruce Degan. New York: Scholastic. (Pbk)

Cole, Joanna. (1995). *Spider's Lunch: All about Garden Spiders*. Illus. by Ron Broda. New York: Grosset & Dunlap. (Pbk)

Crewe, Sabrina. (1997). *The Bee*. Austin, TX: Raintree/Steck Vaughn.

Dallinger, Jane. (1989). *Grasshoppers*. Illus. by Yuko Sato. Minneapolis, MN: Lerner Publications.

Fowler, Allan. (1997). *It Could Still Be a Butterfly*. Chicago: Children's Press.

Fowler, Allan. (1996). *Spiders Are Not Insects*. Chicago: Children's Press.

Gerholdt, James E. (1996). *Black Widow Spiders*. Minneapolis: Abdo & Daughters.

Gerholdt, James E. (1996). *Jumping Spiders*. Austin, TX: Raintree/Steck Vaughn.

Gerholdt, James E. (1996). *Trapdoor Spiders*. Minneapolis: Abdo & Daughters.

Gerholdt, James E. (1996). *Wolf Spiders*. Minneapolis: Abdo & Daughters.

Gibbons, Gail. (1997). *The Honey Makers*. New York: William Morrow.

Gibbons, Gail. (1993). *Spiders*. New York: Holiday House.

Greenberg, David T. (1997). *Bugs!* Illus. by Lynn Munsinger. Boston: Little, Brown.

Hariton, Anca. (1995). *Butterfly Story*. New York: Dutton.

Heiligman, Deborah. (1996). *From Caterpillar to Butterfly*. Illus. by Bari Weissman. New York: HarperCollins.

Hillyard, P. D. (1993). *Insects and Spiders*. New York: Dorling Kindersley.

Jeunesse, Gallimard. (1997). *Bees*. New York: Scholastic.

Jeunesse, Gallimard. (1997). *Butterflies*. New York: Scholastic.

Krulik, Nancy E. and Joanna Cole. (1996). *The Magic School Bus: Butterfly and the Bog Beast: A Book about Butterfly Camouflage*. Illus. by Dana and Del Thompson. New York: Scholastic. (Pbk)

Laughlin, Robin Kittrell. (1996). *Backyard Bugs*. Illus. by Sue Hubbell. New York: Chronicle Books.

Ling, Mary. (1992). *Butterfly*. Photos by Kim Taylor. New York: Dorling Kindersley.

MacDonald, Amy. (1996). *The Spider Who Created the World*. Illus. by G. Brian Karas. New York: Orchard Books.

MacQuitty, Miranda. (1996). *Amazing Bugs*. New York: Dorling Kindersley.

McDonald, Megan. (1995). *Insects Are My Life*. Illus. by Paul Brett Johnson. New York: Orchard Books.

Oppenheim, Joanne. (1998). *Have You Seen Bugs?* Illus. by Ron Broda. New York: Scholastic.

Pallotta, Jerry. (1993). *The Icky Bug Alphabet Book*. Illus. by Ralph Masiello. Watertown, MA: Charlesbridge Books.

Pinczes, Elinor. (1995). *A Remainder of One*. Illus. by Bonnie MacKain. Boston: Houghton Mifflin.

Polacco, Patricia. (1993). *The Bee Tree.* New York: Philomel Books.

Porte, Barbara Ann. *"Leave That Cricket Be, Alan Lee."* Illus. by Donna Ruff. New York: Greenwillow.

Ring, Elizabeth. (1994). *Night Flier.* Photos by Dwight Kuhn. Brookfield, CT: Millbrook Press.

Ryden, Hope. (1996). *ABC of Crawlers and Flyers.* New York: Clarion Books.

Ryder, Joanne. (1994). *My Father's Hands.* Illus. by Mark Graham. New York: William Morrow.

Savage, Stephen. (1995). *Butterfly.* Cincinnati, OH: Thomson Learning.

Savage, Stephen. (1995). *Spider.* Illus. by Phil Weare. Cincinnati, OH: Thomson Learning.

Thompson, Mary. (1996). *Gran's Bees.* Illus. by Donna Peterson. Brookfield, CT: Millbrook Press.

Trapani, Iza. (1993). *The Itsy Bitsy Spider.* Dallas, TX: Whispering Coyote Press.

Wechsler, Doug. (1995). *Bizarre Bugs.* New York: Cobblehill.

Multimedia

The following multimedia products can be used to complement this theme:

Griffith, Joelene. (1993). *We Like Bugs* [cassette and book]. East Wenatchee, WA: Learning Workshop.

Insects and Spiders [video]. (©1993). New York: Sony Kids' Video.

The Multimedia Bug Book [CD-Rom]. (©1995). New York: Workman Publishing Co.

Murphy, Jane Lawliss. (1993). *Songs about Insects, Bugs and Squiggly Things* [cassette]. Long Branch, NJ: Kimbo Educational.

Tell Me Why: Insects [video]. (1987). Marina del Rey, CA: Tell Me Why.

Recordings and Song Titles

The following recordings can be used to complement this theme:

Songs about Insects, Bugs and Squiggly Things

Musical Play Fun—"Fuzzy Wuzzy Caterpillar"

It's Toddler Time—"Butterfly"

Singing, Moving and Fun (The Learning Station)—"I Got a Mosquito"

Nursery Rhymes for Little People—"Spider and the Fly"

Animal Walks—"Caterpillar–Cocoon–Butterfly"

THEME 42

Symbols

hat
mailbag
mail truck
badge

Delivers

letters
postcards
boxes
magazines
cards
books

Post Office

post office boxes
stamp machines
address books
scales
mailboxes
envelopes
shelves
rubber stamps

Mail Carrier

Duties of Mail Carrier

delivers mail
picks up mail
sorts mail
stamps mail

Mailing Address

name
house number
street name
city name
state name
zip code
stamp

Modes of Transportation

trucks, walking, bicycles, cars

Theme Goals

Through participating in the experiences provided by this theme, the children may learn:

1. Duties of a mail carrier.
2. Symbols identifying a mail carrier.
3. Objects found in a post office.
4. Parts of a mailing address.
5. Types of postal deliveries.

Concepts for the Children to Learn

1. A man or woman who delivers mail is a mail carrier.
2. The mail carrier usually wears a badge and a hat.
3. A mail carrier sometimes drives a truck or jeep.
4. Mail carriers deliver cards, letters, postcards, boxes, books, and magazines.
5. Stamps are used for mailing.
6. Names, house numbers, street names, city names, state names, and zip codes are on mailing labels.
7. A post office has stamp machines, address books, mailboxes, and envelopes.
8. Scales are used to weigh mail.

Vocabulary

1. **post office**—place where mail is sorted.
2. **letter**—a printed message.
3. **zip code**—the last numbers on a mailing address.
4. **address**—directions for the mail carrier.
5. **mail**—letters, cards, postcards, and packages.
6. **envelope**—a cover for a letter.
7. **stamp**—a sticker put on mail.
8. **mail carrier**—person who delivers mail.
9. **mail bag**—bag that holds letters and postcards.

Bulletin Board

The purpose of this bulletin board is to reinforce the mathematical skill of matching a set to its written numeral. Construct mailboxes out of tagboard. Each mailbox should include a red flag, and contain a numeral. The number will depend upon developmental appropriateness. A set of dots, corresponding to the numeral on the flag, should be placed on the mailbox. Hang the mailboxes on the bulletin board. Next, construct letters by using small cards with sets of dots on them. The children can match the dots on the cards to the dots and numerals on the mailboxes. If desired, magnet pieces can be attached to both the mailboxes and the cards.

Parent Letter

Dear Parents,

During the past several weeks, we have been busy discussing the roles of a variety of community helpers. Next we will focus the curriculum on the role of the mail carrier. The children will be learning about letters, stamps, and addresses, and will be able to identify objects found in a post office. They will also become aware of what needs to be included on a letter or package before it is delivered. Moreover, they will learn how mail is delivered.

AT SCHOOL

Some of the many learning activities scheduled include:

- listening to the story *Adventures of a Letter* by Warren G. Schloat.
- playing in a post office set up in the classroom.
- making mailboxes and postcards.
- weighing letters and packages.
- delivering mail to our friends in our room.

AT HOME

Let your children help or watch you open the mail. Give your child the "junk mail" to play with. Show your child where your address is on your house and mailbox. You may also enjoy having your children dictate a letter to a grandparent, favorite aunt, or cousin. As you write the letter, show your child the printed alphabet letters to develop an awareness of alphabet letters. After you finish the letter, address an envelope. Let your child lick the stamp and show the proper placement. Then it's off to the post office!

Enjoy your child!

414

Music

1. **"Mailing Letters"**
   (Sing to the tune of "The Mulberry Bush")

   This is the way we mail a letter,
   Mail a letter, mail a letter.
   This is the way we mail a letter,
   So early in the morning.

2. **"Let's Pretend"**
   *(Sing to the tune of "Here We Are Together"
   and "Did You Ever See a Lassie")*

   Let's pretend that we are mail carriers,
   Are mail carriers, are mail carriers.
   Let's pretend that we are mail carriers,
   We'll have so much fun.
   We'll carry the letters and put them in
      boxes.
   Let's pretend that we are mail carriers,
   We'll have so much fun.

Fingerplays

The mail used to be delivered by pony.

LITTLE MAIL CARRIER

I am a little mail carrier
   (point to self)
Who can do nothing better.
I walk.
   (walk in place)
I run.
   (run in place)
I hop to your house.
   (hop in place)
To deliver your letter.

FIVE LITTLE LETTERS

Five little letters lying on a tray.
   (extend fingers of right hand)
Mommy came and took the first one away.
   (bend down thumb)
Daddy said, "This one's for me!"
I counted them twice, now there are three.
   (bend down pointer finger)
Brother Bill asked, "Did I get any mail?"
He found one and cried, "A letter from
   Gail."
   (bend down middle finger)

My sister Jane took the next to the last
And ran upstairs to open it fast.
   (bend down ring finger)
As I can't read, I am not able to see,
Whom the last one is for, but I hope it's for
   me!
   (wiggle last finger, clap hands)

THE MAIL CARRIER

I come from the post office
   (walk from post office)
My mail sack on my back.
   (pretend to carry sack on back)
I go to all the houses
   (pretend to go up to a house)
Leaving letters from my pack.
   (pretend to drop letters into mailbox)
One, two, three, four
   (hold up fingers as you count)
What are these letters for?
   (pretend to hold letters as you count)

One for John. One for Lou.
　　(pretend to hand out letters)
One for Tom and one for you!
　　(pretend to hand out letters to others)

LETTER TO GRANDMA

Lick them, stamp them
　　(make licking and stamping motions)
Put them in a box.
　　(extend arms outward)
Hope that Grandma
Loves them alot!
　　(hug self)

Dramatic Play

1. **Post Office**

   Develop the dramatic play area into a post office. Provide a mailbox, mail carrier hats, mailbag, stamps, cash register, rubber date stamps, and a letter scale. The children may enjoy acting out the role of a mail carrier or a post office worker.

2. **Letters**

   Provide a variety of writing materials. Include different colors of paper, writing tools, and envelopes. The children can dictate a letter to a friend or a family member. After all interested children have completed dictation, apply stamps and walk to the nearest mailbox or post office. (Contact a local printer, office supply store, or card shop and ask for discontinued samples or misprinted envelopes.)

Science

1. **Dress the Mail Carrier**

   Place flannel board pieces representing seasonal clothing for a mail carrier. Let the children select the appropriate clothing for the weather. This may be an interesting activity to introduce daily during group time.

2. **Weighing Mail**

   A variety of letters, boxes, stamps, and a scale can be placed in the science area. The children can weigh letters and packages. This activity can be extended by placing materials in the boxes and weighing them, noting the difference.

3. **How Does the Mail Feel?**

   Place different types of envelopes and stationery on the sensory table for the children to explore. Include airmail paper, onionskin, bond paper, typing paper, and different kinds of stationery. Also, provide a magnifying glass.

Field Trips/ Resource People

1. **Post Office**

   Plan a field trip to the local post office. Observe the mailboxes, stamp machines, address books, scales, and rubber stamps with the children. Mail a postcard back to the center. Count the number of days it takes to arrive.

2. **Mail Carrier**

   Invite the mail carrier who delivers mail or the local postmaster to your center or school to visit in the classroom. Ask the mail carrier to share his mailbag, hat, etc., with the children.

Social Studies

Mailboxes

Plan a walk around the neighborhood. Observe the different types of mailboxes and addresses.

Math

The number of items and numerals used in these activities needs to be adjusted to reflect children's level of development.

1. **Dominoes**

   Create dominoes out of envelopes. Have the children match the numbers and dots.

2. **How Many Stamps?**

   Write an individual numeral on an envelope. Make or collect many stamps. The children can place the correct number of stamps in the envelope with the corresponding numeral. A variation of this activity is to make mailboxes from shoeboxes. Again, write a numeral on each box. Make or collect many different envelopes. The children can put the correct number of letters in the corresponding mailboxes.

3. **Package Seriation**

   Prepare several packages and letters of different sizes. The children can place the letters and packages in order from largest to smallest or smallest to largest.

Arts and Crafts

1. **Easel Ideas**

   Cut easel paper in the shape of envelopes, letters, stamps, or mailbags.

2. **Postcards**

   Have children make postcards at school to send to family and friends. Provide index cards. Let the children design the postcards.

3. **Mailboxes**

   Make mailboxes out of old shoeboxes. Each child can decorate his own box. Names can be added by the child or teacher. Include a home address for older children.

4. **Mail Truck**

   Construct a mail truck out of a large cardboard box. Provide paint for the children to decorate it. When dried, place chairs and, if available, a steering wheel inside for the children to drive.

5. **Stamps**

   Collect assorted stamps or stickers. Cancelled stamps can be reglued. The children can make a stamp collage.

Group Time
(games, language)

Thank You

Write a thank-you note to the postmaster or mail carrier after visiting.

Cooking

Zip Code Special

1 1/2 cups nonfat dry milk
2 cups fresh or frozen berries
1 teaspoon vanilla
1 cup water
1 tray ice cubes

Blend all ingredients in a blender. Serve and enjoy.

Books

The following books can be used to complement this theme:

Gibbons, Gail. (1987). *The Post Office Book: Mail and How It Moves.* New York: HarperCollins.

Henkes, Kevin. (1995). *Good-Bye, Curtis.* Illus. by Marisabina Russo. New York: Greenwillow.

Keats, Ezra Jack. (1998). *A Letter to Amy.* Reprint edition. New York: Viking.

Lakin, Pat. (1995). *Red-Letter Day.* Illus. by Doug Cushman. Austin, TX: Raintree/Steck Vaughn.

Landstrom, Olof, and Lena Landstrom. (1994). *Will Goes to the Post Office.* New York: Farrar, Straus & Giroux.

Levinson, Nancy Smiler. (1992). *Snowshoe Thompson.* Illus. by Joan Sandin. New York: HarperCollins.

Lillegard, Dee. (1997). *Tortoise Brings the Mail.* Illus. by Jillian Lund. New York: Dutton.

Miller, Robert H. (1994). *The Story of "Stagecoach" Mary Fields.* Illus. by Cheryl Hanna. Englewood Cliffs, NJ: Silver Press.

Rylant, Cynthia. (©1989, 1993). *Mr. Griggs' Work.* Illus. by Julie Downing. New York: Orchard Books.

Schloat, G. Warren. (©1949). *Adventures of a Letter.* New York: Scribner.

Scott, Ann Herbert. (1994). *Hi.* Illus. by Glo Coalson. New York: Philomel Books.

Skurzynksi, Gloria. (1992). *Here Comes the Mail.* New York: Macmillan.

Multimedia

The following multimedia products can be used to complement this theme:

At the Post Office [video]. (1995). Tallahassee, FL: Dogwood Video.

Post Office [video]. (1991). National Geographic.

Postal Station [video]. (1991). TV Ontario/distributed by Films for the Humanities.

There Goes the Mail [video]. (1997). NY: KidVision.

Recording and Song Title

The following recording can be used to complement this theme:

People in Our Neighborhood—"The Community Helper Hop"

THEME 43

Enemies
people, dogs, hawks, foxes, snakes, owls, rats, other mice, cats

Foods
insects, leaves, roots, seeds, leather, fruits, nuts, cheese

Homes
barns
attics
basements
fields
nests

Mice

Types
house
American harvest
grasshopper
deer

Noises
squeaking
scratching
chattering

Size
small

Colors
white
black
brown

Body Parts
head, body, tail, ears, eyes, mouth, whiskers

Needs
food
water
shelter

Theme Goals

Through participating in the experiences provided by this theme, the children may learn:

1. Body parts of mice.
2. Size of mice.
3. Care of mice.
4. Color of mice.
5. Sounds made by mice.
6. Foods mice eat.
7. Homes mice make.
8. Enemies of mice.
9. Use of mice.

Concepts for the Children to Learn

1. A mouse is a small animal.
2. Mice is the word to use when you refer to more than one mouse.
3. There are four main types of mice: house, American harvest, grasshopper, and deer.
4. The body of a mouse is 2 1/2 to 3 1/2 inches long. The tail is almost as long as the body.
5. The body of a mouse is covered with fur.
6. Mice may have white-, brown-, or black-colored fur.
7. Mice need water, food, and shelter to live.
8. Mice eat plants, insects, leaves, roots, seeds, leather, fruits, and nuts.
9. Barns, attics, basements, fields, and nests are homes for mice.
10. Mice live where they can find food and shelter.
11. Mice have good hearing but poor sight.
12. Mice have strong, sharp front teeth that keep growing.
13. Mice have a head, body, tail, ears, eyes, mouth, and whiskers.
14. A house mouse has a brown back and white belly.
15. People can sometimes hear mice squeak, scratch, and chatter.
16. House mice are good climbers. People sometimes hear them running inside the walls of their homes.
17. Mice are sometimes used for pets and for health-care discoveries.
18. People, cats, dogs, hawks, foxes, snakes, owls, rats, and other mice can be enemies of mice.

Vocabulary

1. **mouse**—a small furry animal that has a head, ears, eyes, a mouth, whiskers, four legs, body, and tail.
2. **squeaking**—a clear, sharp sound made by a mouse.
3. **scratching**—a noise a mouse makes by rubbing his nails against a surface.

Bulletin Board

The purpose of this bulletin board is to promote the identification of written numerals as well as matching a set to a written numeral. Construct cheese and mice shapes out of construction paper or tagboard. Draw a set of dots on each piece of cheese. The number of dots used should correspond to the developmental level of the children. Print a corresponding numeral on each mouse. Staple the cheese pieces to the bulletin board along the side edges and the bottom, creating a pocket. The children should be encouraged to match the written numeral of each mouse to the corresponding set of dots on the cheese pieces and place the mice in the pockets.

Parent Letter

Dear Parents,

Squeak! Squeak! Squeak! We will be enjoying a new theme that will provide us with discoveries about small animals called mice. The children will be learning about types and colors of mice, care of mice, and enemies of mice.

AT SCHOOL

Learning experiences planned for this unit include:

- Visiting the pet store to observe mice.
- Pretending to be mice in the dramatic play area.
- Listening to the stories titled *Mouse Paint* and *Mouse Count* by Lois Ehlert.

AT HOME

Go to the library and check out some children's books about mice. Some titles to look for include:

- *If You Give a Mouse a Cookie* by Laura Numeroff
- *Mouse Poems* by John Foster

Have a nice week!

Can you squeak like a mouse?

Music

1. **"Ten Little Mice"**
   (Sing to the tune of "Ten Little Indians")

   One little, two little, three little mice.
   Four little, five little, six little mice.
   Seven little, eight little, nine little mice.

2. **"Two Little Brown Mice"**
   *(Sing to the tune of "Two Little Blackbirds"
   or "Baa Baa Black Sheep")*

   Two little brown mice,
   Scampering through the hall.
   One named Sarah.
   One named Paul.

   Run away Sarah.
   Run away Paul.
   Come back, Sarah.
   Come back, Paul.

   Two little brown mice,
   Scampering through the hall.
   One named Sarah.
   One named Paul.

3. **"Find the Mouse"**
   (Sing to the tune of "The Muffin Man")

   Oh, can you find the little mouse,
   The little mouse, the little mouse.
   Can you find the little mouse,
   He's somewhere in the house.

4. **"One Little Mouse"**
   (Sing to the tune of "Six Little Ducks")

   One little brown and whiskery mouse
   Lived in a hole in a cozy house.
   When the cat came along to
   Take a little peek,
   The mouse ran away with a "Squeak,
     squeak, squeak."
   "Squeak, squeak, squeak."
   "Squeak, squeak, squeak."
   "The mouse ran away with a "Squeak,
     squeak, squeak."

5. **"Three Little Brown Mice"**
   (Sing to the tune of "Three Blind Mice")

   Three brown mice, three brown mice.
   See how they run. See how they run.
   They were chased through the house
     by the big black cat.
   Lucky for them, she was lazy and fat.
   Did you ever see such a sight as that?
   Three brown mice, three brown mice.

423

Fingerplays

WHERE ARE THE BABY MICE?

Where are the baby mice?
(hide fists behind back)
Squeak, squeak, squeak!
I cannot see them.
Peek, peek, peek.
(show fist)
Here they come out of their hole in the wall.
One, two, three, four, five, and that is all!
(show fingers one at a time)

FIVE LITTLE BABY MICE

Five little mice on the kitchen floor.
(hold up five fingers)
This little mouse peeked behind the door.
(point to thumb)
This little mouse nibbled at the cake.
(point to index finger)
This little mouse not a sound did he make.
(point to middle finger)
This little mouse took a bite of cheese.
(point to ring finger)
This little mouse heard the kitten sneeze.
(point to pinky)
"Ah-choo!" sneezed the kitten,
And "squeak" they cried.
As they found a hole and ran inside.
(move hand behind back)

LITTLE MOUSE

See the little mousie,
(place index and middle finger on
thumb to represent a mouse)
Creeping up the stair,
(creep mouse slowly up the forearm)
Looking for a warm rest.
There—Oh! There!
(spring mouse into an elbow corner)

HICKORY DICKORY DOCK

Hickory, dickory, dock.
(bend arm at elbow; hold up and open palm)
The mouse ran up the clock.
(run fingers up the arm)
The clock struck one,
(hold up index finger)
The mouse ran down,
(run fingers down arm)
Hickory, dickory, dock.

MOUSE

Here is a mouse with ears so funny,
(place index and middle finger on
thumb to represent a mouse)
And here is a hole in the ground.
(make a hole with the other fist)
When a noise he hears, he pricks up his ears.
And runs to his hole in the ground.
(jump mouse into hole in other fist)

Science

Mice

Purchase or borrow mice from a pet store to keep as classroom pets. Place the cage on the science table for the children to observe. Allow the children to assist in caring for the animals.

Dramatic Play

1. **Mouse House**

   The children can pretend to be mice! Construct mouse ears out of fabric or construction paper and attach to headbands. Provide large cardboard boxes to represent houses for the mice.

2. **Pet Store**

   Arrange the dramatic play area as a pet store. Provide props such as a cash register, play money, stuffed animals, animal cages, animal toys, and empty pet food boxes. Display posters of pets, including mice.

Arts and Crafts

1. **Mouse Sponge Painting**

   Cut sponges into mice shapes. Place on the art table with paper and a shallow pan of thick tempera paint. The children can make designs by pressing the sponge into the paint and then on a piece of paper.

424

2. Seed Collage

Place a variety of seeds, glue, and paper on a table in the art area. The children can create designs with the materials.

Sensory

Add to the sensory table:

- ⊚ grains with scoops, cups, and spoons.
- ⊚ seeds with pails and shovels.
- ⊚ clean cedar chips (animal bedding) with measuring cups, scoops, and pails.

Field Trips

1. Pet Store

Visit a pet store to observe the colors of pet mice and animal accessories. Photographs can be taken during the trip and later displayed in the classroom.

2. Mouse Walk

Take a walk around your school and look for places mice might live.

Group Time
(games, language)

1. "Mouse, Mouse, Where's Your Cheese?"

This game is played in a circle formation. Arrange the chairs and place one in the center of the circle. Place a block to represent the cheese under the chair. Select one child, the "mouse," to sit on the chair and close his eyes. Then point to another child. This child must try to remove the cheese without making a sound. After the child returns to his chair in the circle, instruct all of the children to place their hands behind their backs. Then in unison the children say, "Mouse, Mouse, where is your cheese?" The mouse then opens his eyes and tries to guess who is holding the cheese.

2. Language Chart

Across the top of a piece of tagboard, print the question, "Where would you like to live if you were a mouse?" During group time introduce the chart and record the children's responses. Display the chart in the classroom.

Cooking

1. Macaroni and Cheese

Purchase prepackaged macaroni and cheese. Prepare following the directions provided on the container. Compare the flavor to the recipe that follows:

3–3 1/2 cups of cooked macaroni
1/4 cup of butter or margarine
1/4 cup chopped onion (optional)
1/2 teaspoon salt
1/2 teaspoon pepper
1/4 cup flour
1 1/2 cups of milk
1/2 pound of Swiss or American cheese cut into small cubes

Combine butter, onion, salt, and pepper in a saucepan; cook over medium heat until onion is tender. Blend in the flour. Lower heat and stir constantly until the mixture is smooth and bubbly. Add milk and heat to boiling, stirring constantly. Stir and boil one minute. Remove from heat. Add cheese and stir until melted.

Place macaroni in ungreased 1 1/2 quart casserole. Stir cheese sauce into the macaroni. Bake in an oven heated to 375 degrees for 30 minutes. (Makes five servings.)

2. Mouse Cookies

With the children, prepare a batch of drop cookie dough according to the recipe. Demonstrate how to drop three spoonfuls of dough onto a cookie sheet so that it will resemble a mouse head with two ears when baked. The mouse cookies can be frosted or details can be added with raisins, chocolate chips, and string licorice.

Books

The following books can be used to complement this theme:

Brett, Jan. (1994). *Town Mouse, Country Mouse*. New York: G. P. Putnam.

Cowley, Joy. (1995). *Mouse Bride*. Illus. by David Christiana. New York: Scholastic.

Craig, Helen. (1993). *Angelina's Ice Skates*. Illus. by Katharine Holabird. New York: C. N. Potter Publishers.

Duke, Kate. (1992). *Isabelle Tells a Good One*. New York: Dutton.

Edwards, Pamela Duncan. (1996). *Livingstone Mouse*. Illus. by Henry Cole. New York: HarperCollins.

Farris, Pamela J. (1996). *Young Mouse and Elephant: An East African Folktale*. Illus. by Valeri Gorbachev. Boston: Houghton Mifflin.

Fleming, Denise. (1992). *Lunch*. New York: Holt.

Galvin, Laura Gates et al. (1998). *Deer Mouse at Old Farm Road*. Illus. Katy Bratun. Norwalk, CT: Soundprints.

Krensky, Stephen. (1995). *Three Blind Mice Mystery*. Illus. by Lynn Munsinger. New York: Delacorte.

McBratney, Sam. (1996). *The Dark at the Top of the Stairs*. Illus. by Ivan Bates. Cambridge, MA: Candlewick Press.

McMillan, Bruce. (1993). *Mouse Views: What the Class Pet Saw*. New York: Holiday House.

Monson, A. M. (1997). *Wanted: Best Friend*. Illus. by Lynn Munsinger. New York: Dial.

Palazzo-Craig, Janet. (1995). *Max and Maggie in Spring*. Illus. by Paul Meisel. Mahwah, NJ: Troll.

Patten, Brian. (1988). *Mouse Poems*. London: Scholastic.

Reiser, Lynn. (1995). *Two Mice in Three Fables*. New York: Greenwillow.

Riley, Linnea Asplind. (1997). *Mouse Mess*. Blue Sky Press.

Ring, Elizabeth. (1995). *Lucky Mouse*. Illus. by Dwight Kuhn. Brookfield, CT: Millbrook Press.

Roth, Susan. (1997). *My Love for You*. New York: Dial.

Sathre, Vivian. (1995). *Mouse Chase*. Illus. by Ward Schumaker. Orlando: Harcourt Brace.

Schindel, John. (1994). *What's for Lunch?* Illus. by Kevin O'Malley. New York: Lothrop, Lee & Shepard.

Summers, Kate. (1997). *Milly and Tilly: The Story of a Town Mouse and a Country Mouse*. Illus. by Maggie Kneen. New York: Dutton.

Waber, Bernard. (1995). *Do You See a Mouse?* Boston: Houghton Mifflin.

Walsh, Ellen Stoll. (1996). *Samantha*. Orlando: Harcourt Brace.

Young, Ed. (1992). *Seven Blind Mice*. New York: Philomel Books.

Multimedia

The following multimedia products can be used to complement this theme:

If You Give a Mouse a Cookie [CD-ROM]. (1995). New York: HarperCollins Interactive.

Lionni, Leo. "Frederick" on *Five Lionni Classics* [video]. (1987). New York: Random House Home Video.

Palmer, Hap. "The Mice Go Marching" on *Rhythms on Parade*. [compact disc]. (1995). Baldwin, NY: Educational Activities.

Sharon, Lois, and Bram Sharon. "Three Blind Mice" and "Hickory, Dickory, Dock" on *Mainly Mother Goose* [compact disc]. (1984). Toronto, Ont.: Elephant Records.

Recording and Song Title

The following recording can be used to complement this theme:

Singable Nursery Rhymes—"Three Blind Mice"

THEME 44

Body Sounds

stamping, clapping, whistling, marching, snapping, singing

Equipment

tape recorder
record player
compact disc player

Sounds

high
low
loud
soft

Music

Tempo

fast
slow

Kinds

holiday
ceremonial
rock and roll
classical
jazz
rhythm and blues
country
inspirational

Instruments

piano, autoharp, tambourine, drum, shaker, sandpaper blocks, bell, sticks, triangle, guitar

Language Concepts

numbers
colors
letters
shapes
animals
people

Theme Goals

Through participating in the experiences provided by this theme, the children may learn:

1. Music is a language.
2. Kinds of music.
3. Music tempos.
4. Language concepts.
5. Different sounds.
6. Names of many musical instruments.
7. Body sounds.
8. Equipment used for playing and recording music.

Concepts for the Children to Learn

1. There are many types of instruments.
2. Each instrument has its own sound.
3. Music sounds can be high, low, loud, and soft.
4. Music can express different moods.
5. Music can be played in different rhythms.
6. Songs can tell stories.
7. Our bodies are musical instruments.
8. Our hands can clap.
9. Our feet can stamp and march.
10. Our fingers can snap.
11. Our mouths can whistle and sing.
12. The piano, autoharp, and guitar are played with our fingers.
13. Sticks are used on the triangle, drum, xylophone, and bells.
14. We shake bells, shakers, and tambourines.
15. We rub sandpaper blocks.
16. There are many kinds of music.
17. We can tape music with a recorder.
18. A record, tape, or compact disc player can play music.

Vocabulary

1. **music**—a way of expressing ideas and feelings.
2. **instrument**—makes musical sounds.
3. **tempo**—the speed of music.
4. **body sounds**—sounds made by moving one or more body parts.
5. **mallets**—special sticks used to play the xylophone and bells.

Bulletin Board

The purpose of this bulletin board is to develop visual discrimination and visual memory skills. Create a musical bulletin board by drawing musical instruments on tagboard as illustrated. Color the instruments with markers, cut out, and laminate. Trace these pieces onto black construction paper. Cut out the pieces and attach to the bulletin board. A magnet strip should be attached to both the colored pieces and the black shadow pieces. The children can match the appropriately shaped instrument piece to its shadow on the bulletin board.

Parent Letter

Dear Parents,

We will be singing and playing instruments during our curriculum unit on music. Music is a universal language. It is a way of communicating and expressing oneself. For young children, singing is not that much different from talking—as I'm sure you've noticed from observing the children! Throughout the unit the children will be making interesting discoveries about the many sounds that we can make with our voices, body parts, and musical instruments.

AT SCHOOL

A few highlights of our scheduled musical learning activities include:

- making musical instruments.
- painting at the easel while listening to music with headphones.
- trying on band uniforms (courtesy of Mead School) in the dramatic play area.
- forming a rhythm band outside in the play yard.

AT HOME

To stimulate creativity and language, create verses with your child for this song to the tune of "Old McDonald Had a Farm:"

Mr. Roberts had a band,
E-I-E-I-O.
And in his band he had a drum
E-I-E-I-O.
With a boom, boom here, and a boom, boom, there,
Here a boom, there a boom,
Everywhere a boom, boom.
Mr. Roberts had a band,
E-I-E-I-O.

And in his band he had a horn . . .

Continue adding instruments that your child can think of.

Provide materials for your child to make simple musical instruments. A drum can be made using an empty oatmeal carton or coffee can. Your child can personalize the instrument by decorating the outside of the container with paper, crayons, and markers. A kazoo can also be made with a cardboard tube and a small piece of waxed paper attached to the end of the tube with a rubber band. Poke a small hole in the waxed paper and your child will be ready to blow up a storm! The sounds produced by the different instruments can be compared to develop auditory discrimination skills.

Keep a song in your heart!

430

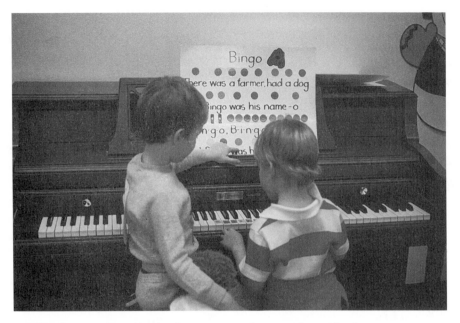

Children enjoy listening to and creating their own music.

Music

Music for this unit should consist of the children's favorite and well-known songs. The children will enjoy singing these songs, and you will be able to focus on the sound of the music. Here are some suggestions of traditional songs that most children enjoy:

1. **"Old MacDonald Had a Farm"**

2. **"Five Green Speckled Frogs"**

3. **"The Farmer in the Dell"**

4. **"Row, Row, Row Your Boat"**

5. **"Mary Had a Little Lamb"**

6. **"Hickory Dickory Dock"**

7. **"If You're Happy and You Know It"**

8. **"ABC Song"**

9. **"The Little White Duck"**

10. **"Six Little Ducks"**

Fingerplays

I WANT TO LEAD A BAND

I want to lead a band
With a baton in my hand.
   (wave baton in air)
I want to make sweet music high and low.
Now first I'll beat the drum
   (drum-beating motion)
With a rhythmic tum-tum-tum,
And then I'll play the bells
A-ting-a-ling-a-ling,
   (bell-playing motion)
And next I'll blow the flute
With a cheery toot-a-toot.
   (flute-playing motion)
Then I'll make the violin sweetly sing.
   (violin-playing motion)
Now I'm leading a band
With a baton in my hand.
   (wave baton in air again)

IF I COULD PLAY

If I could play the piano
This is the way I would play.
   (move fingers like playing a piano)

If I had a guitar
I would strum the strings this way.
   (hold guitar and strum)

If I had a trumpet
I'd toot to make a tune.
   (play trumpet)

But if I had a drum
I'd go boom, boom, boom.
   (pretend to play a drum)

MUSICAL INSTRUMENTS

This is how a horn sounds
Toot! Toot! Toot!
   (play imaginary horn)

This is how guitars sound
Vrrroom, Vrrroom, Vrrroom
   (strum imaginary guitar)

This is how the piano sounds
Tinkle, grumble, brring.
   (run fingers over imaginary keyboard)

This is how the drum sounds
Rat-a-tat, grumble, brring.
   (strike drum, include cymbal)

JACK-IN-THE-BOX

Jack-in-the-box all shut up tight
   (fingers wrapped around thumb)
Not a breath of air, not a ray of light.
   (other hand covers fist)
How tired he must be all down in a heap.
   (lift off)
I'll open the lid and up he will leap!
   (thumbs pop out)

Science

1. **Water Music**

   Fill four identically sized crystal glasses each with a different amount of water. The children can trace their wet finger around the rim of each glass. Each glass will have a different tune. Older children may enjoy reordering the glasses from the highest to the lowest tone.

2. **Pop Bottle Music**

   Fill six 12-ounce pop bottles, each with a different amount of water. For effect, in each bottle place a drop of food coloring, providing six different colors. Younger children can tap the bottles with a spoon as they listen for the sound. Older children may try blowing directly into the opening for sound production.

3. **Throats**

   Show the children how to place their hands across their throat. Then have them whisper, talk, shout, and sing while feeling the differences in vibration.

4. **Jumping Seeds**

   Set seeds or something small on top of a drum. Then beat the drum. What happens? Why? This activity can be extended by having the children jump to the drum beat.

5. **Identifying Instruments**

   Prepare a tape recording of classroom musical instruments. Play the tape, encouraging the children to identify the correct instrument related to each sound.

6. **Matching Sounds**

   Collect 12 containers, such as film canisters, milk cartons, or covered baby food jars, that would be safe to use with the children. Fill 2 containers with rice, 2 cans with beans, 2 cans with pebbles, 2 cans with water, and the remaining cans with dry pasta. Coins, such as pennies, could be substituted. Color code each pair of containers on the bottom. Let the children shake the containers, listening to the sounds, in an attempt to find the matching pairs.

Dramatic Play

1. Band

Collect materials for a band prop box, which may include band uniforms, a baton, music stand, cassette player, and tapes with marching music. The children can experiment with instruments.

2. Dramatizing

Add a cassette recorder and a small microphone to the dramatic play area. The children may enjoy using it for singing and recording their voices.

3. Disc Jockey

In the music area, provide a tape recorder and cassettes for the children.

Arts and Crafts

1. Drums

Create drums out of empty coffee cans with plastic lids, plastic ice cream pails, or oatmeal boxes. The children can decorate as desired with paper, paint, felt-tip markers, or crayons.

2. Shakers

Collect a variety of egg-shaped panty hose containers. Fill each egg with varying amounts of sand, peas, or rice, and securely tape or glue them shut. To compare sounds, empty film containers can also be filled.

3. Cymbals

Make cymbals out of old tinfoil pans. Attach a string for the handles.

4. Tambourines

Two paper plates can be made into a tambourine. Begin by placing pop bottle caps or small stones between the plates. Staple the paper plates together. Shake to produce sound.

5. Easel Ideas

Cut easel paper into the shape of different instruments such as a drum, guitar, or tambourine.

6. Musical Painting

On a table in the art area, place a tape recorder with headphones. The children can listen to music as they paint.

7. Kazoos

Kazoos can be made with empty paper towel rolls and waxed paper. The children can decorate the outside of the kazoos with colored felt-tip markers. After this, place a piece of waxed paper over one end of the roll and secure it with a rubber band. Poke two or three small holes into the waxed paper allowing sound to be produced.

8. Rhythm Sticks

Two wooden dowels should be given to each interested child. The sticks can be decorated with paint or colored felt-tip markers.

Large Muscle

1. Body Movement Rhythms

Introduce a simple body movement. Then have the children repeat it until they develop a rhythm. Examples include:

- stamp foot, clap hands, stamp foot, clap hands
- clap, clap, stamp, stamp
- clap, stamp, clap, stamp
- clap, clap, snap fingers
- clap, snap, stamp, clap, snap, stamp
- clap, clap, stamp, clap, clap, stamp

2. Body Percussion

Instruct the children to stand in a circle. Repeat the following rhythmic speech:

We walk and we walk and we stop (rest)
We walk and we walk and we stop (rest)
We walk and we walk and we walk and we walk
We walk and we walk and we stop. (stop)

3. March

Play different rhythm beats on a piano or another instrument. Examples include hopping, skipping, gliding, walking, running, tiptoeing, galloping, etc. The children can move to the rhythm.

Field Trips/ Resource People

1. **Band Director**

   Visit a school band director. Observe the different instruments available to students. Listen to their sounds.

2. **Who Can Play?**

   Invite parents, grandparents, brothers, sisters, relatives, friends, etc., to visit the classroom and demonstrate their talent.

3. **Radio Station**

   Visit a local radio station.

4. **Taping**

   Videotape the children singing and using rhythm instruments. Replay the video for the children. Save this for a future open house, parent meeting, or holiday celebration.

Math

1. **Colors, Shapes, and Numbers**

   Sing the song, "Colors, Shapes, and Numbers," mentioned in the shapes unit or make up a song about shapes. Hold up different colors, shapes, and numbers while you sing the song for the children to identify.

2. **Number Rhyme**

   Say the following song to reinforce numbers:

   One, two, three, four
   Come right in and shut the door.
   Five, six, seven, eight
   Come right in. It's getting late.
   Nine, ten, eleven, twelve
   Put your books upon the shelves.
   Will you count along with me?
   It's as easy as can be!

3. **Ten in the Bed**

   Chant the following words to reinforce numbers:

   There were 10 in the bed and the little one said,
   "Roll over, roll over."
   So they all rolled over and one fell out.

   There were 9 in the bed and the little one said,
   "Roll over, roll over."
   So they all rolled over and one fell out.

   Continue until there is only one left. The last line will be ". . . and the little one said, "Good night!"

4. **Music Calendar**

   Design a calendar for the month of your music unit. The different days of the week can be made out of musical notes and different instruments.

Social Studies

1. **Our Own Songs**

   Encourage the children to help you write a song about a common class experience. Substitute the words into a melody that everyone knows ("Twinkle, Twinkle, Little Star" or "The Mulberry Bush").

2. **Pictures**

   Put up pictures of instruments and band players in the room to add interest and stimulate discussion.

3. **Sound Tapes**

   Make a special tape of sounds heard in a home. Homes are full of different sounds. Included may be:

   ☙ people knocking on doors
   ☙ wind chimes
   ☙ telephone ringing
   ☙ teakettle whistling
   ☙ clock ticking

- toilet flushing
- popcorn popping
- vacuum cleaner
- doorbell
- running water
- car horn

Play the tape and have the children listen carefully to identify the sounds.

Group Time
(games, language)

1. Name Game

Say the following rhythmic chant as the whole class claps.

"Names, names, we all have names,
Play a game as we say our names.
Scott, (class echoes) Scott,
Melanie, (class echoes) Melanie,
Tommy, (class echoes) Tommy."

Repeat until all the children have had their name repeated.

Source: *The Kinder-Music House*. (1982). Fairfax County Public Schools.

2. Are You Here?
(Sing the following song to the tune of "Twinkle, Twinkle, Little Star")

Hello, children, here we are,
At our school from near and far.
Today we are going to play a game,
Please stand up when I call your name.

Source: Beckman, Simmons, & Thomas. (1982). *Channels to Children*. Colorado: Channels to Children Publishing Company.

Miscellaneous

Instrument of the Day

Focus on a different instrument each day. Talk about its construction and demonstrate the instrument's sound.

Cooking

Popcorn

Make popcorn and have the children listen to the sounds of the oil and corn popping. **Caution:** Supervise this activity closely because the corn popper will become hot. This activity is most appropriate for older children—younger children may choke on popcorn.

Books

The following books can be used to complement this theme:

Bartlett, T. C. (1997). *Tuba Lessons*. Illus. by Monique Felix. Orlando: Harcourt Brace.

Brett, Jan. (1991). *Berlioz the Bear*. New York: G. P. Putnam.

Buck, Nola. (1996). *Sid and Sam*. Illus. by G. Brian Karas. New York: Harper-Collins.

Davis, Wendy. (1997). *From Metal to Music: A Photo Essay*. Chicago: Children's Press.

Drew, Helen. (1993). *My First Music Book*. New York: Dorling Kindersley.

Eversole, Robyn. (1995). *Flute Player/La Flautista*. Illus. by G. Brian Karas. New York: Orchard Books.

Fleming, Candace. (1997). *Gabriella's Song*. Illus. by Giselle Potter. Colchester, CT: Atheneum.

Hayes, Ann. (1995). *Meet the Marching Smithereens*. Illus. by Karmen Thompson. Orlando: Harcourt Brace.

Hayes, Ann. (1995). *Meet the Orchestra*. Illus. by Karmen Thompson. Orlando: Harcourt Brace.

Hewitt, Sally. (1994). *Pluck and Scrape*. Illus. by Peter Millard. Chicago: Children's Press.

Imai, Miko. (1995). *Sebastian's Trumpet*. Cambridge, MA: Candlewick Press.

Kalman, Bobbie. (1997). *Musical Instruments from A to Z*. New York: Crabtree Publishing.

Livo, Norma J. (1996). *J. Troubadour's Storybag: Musical Folktales of the World*. Golden, CO: Fulcrum Pub.

Millman, Isaac. (1998). *Moses Goes to a Concert*. New York: Farrar, Straus & Giroux.

Moss, Lloyd. (1996). *Zin! Zin! Zin! A Violin*. Illus. by Marjorie Priceman. New York: Simon & Schuster.

Pinkney, J. Brian. (1994). *Max Found Two Sticks*. New York: Simon & Schuster.

Raschka, Chris. (1992). *Charlie Parker Played Bebop*. New York: Orchard Books.

Raschka, Chris. (1997). *Mysterious Thelonious*. New York: Orchard Books.

Rachlin, Ann. *Famous Children* series. Illus. by Susan Hellard. Hauppauge, NY: Barrons Educational Series. (Pbk) *Bach*. (1992); *Beethoven*. (1994); *Brahms*. (1993); *Chopin*. (1993); *Handel*. (1992); *Haydn*. (1992); *Mozart*. (1992); *Schubert*. (1994); *Schumann*. (1993); *Tchaikovsky*. (1993).

Multimedia

The following multimedia products can be used to complement this theme:

Child's Celebration of Showtunes [cassette]. (1992). Music for Little People.

Jenkins, Ella. *This is Rhythm* [compact disc]. (1994). Smithsonian/Folkways.

Jenkins, Ella. *Rhythm and Game Songs for the Little Ones* [cassette]. (1990). Smithsonian/Folkways.

Louchard, Ric. *Hey, Ludwig! Classical Piano Solos for Playful Times* [compact disc]. (1993). Music for Little People.

Meter [video]. (1994). Films for the Humanities & Sciences.

Pitch [video]. (1994). Films for the Humanities & Sciences.

Stanley, Leotha. *Be a Friend: The Story of African American Music in Song, Words and Pictures* [book and cassette]. (1994). Illus. by Henry Hawkins. Zino Press.

Stewart, Georgiana. *Multicultural Rhythm Stick Fun* [compact disc]. (1992). Kimbo Educational.

THEME 45

Names
symbol
name

Sources
clocks
rulers
telephones
calendars
games

Numbers

Uses
communication
identification
time
age
address
telephone number

Tools
calculator
abacus
pens
markers
pencils
typewriters
computers
cash registers

Theme Goals

Through participating in the experiences provided by this theme, the children may learn:

1. Uses of numbers.
2. Sources of numbers.
3. Number names.
4. Tools for recording numbers.

Concepts for the Children to Learn

1. A number is a symbol.
2. Each number symbol has a name.
3. Pencils, typewriters, and computers are tools used to make numbers.
4. Numbers can be found on clocks, rulers, telephones, and calendars.
5. Communication, identification, time, and age are uses for numbers.
6. Adding machines and cash registers have numerals.

Vocabulary

1. **numeral**—a symbol that represents a number.
2. **number**—a symbol used to represent an amount.

Bulletin Board

The objective of this bulletin board is for the children to match the numeral to the set by winding the string around the other pushpin next to the items. Construct the numerals out of tagboard. Construct objects familiar to the children and make one type of object correspond to each numeral. The number of objects and numerals should be developmentally appropriate for the group of children. Laminate. Staple the numbers down the left side of bulletin board. Staple the sets of objects in random order down the right side of the bulletin board as illustrated. Affix a pushpin with an attached string of sufficient length next to each numeral. Affix a pushpin in front of each set row.

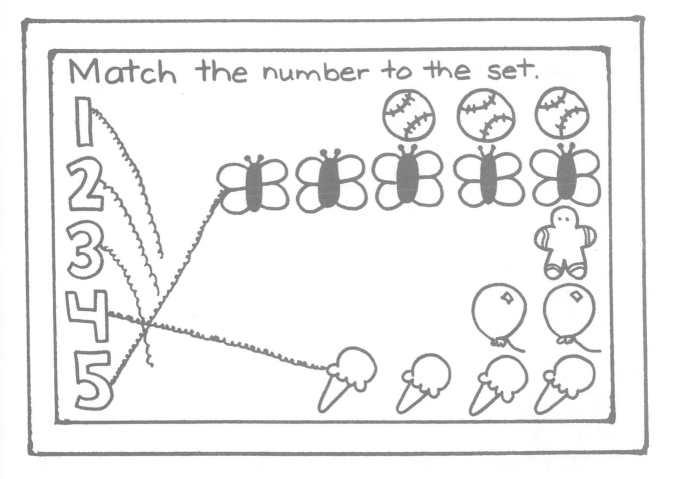

Parent Letter

Dear Parents,

Our next unit will be focusing on numbers. The children will be exposed to concepts of pairs, sets, and halves and wholes. They will also be participating in activities that include the language concepts of heavy/light, bigger/smaller, and more/less.

AT SCHOOL

Some of the play-related activities include:

- measuring with scales and rulers at the science table.
- charting our weight and height.
- listening to the book titled *I Can Count* by Lynn Grundy.
- using number cookie cutters with playdough.
- bowling with numbered pins.

Personnel from the telephone company will be visiting us Tuesday. They will show us a variety of phones. They will also stress the importance of knowing our telephone number. Feel free to join us for this activity.

AT HOME

Cooking provides a concrete foundation for mathematical concepts. It involves amounts, fractions, and measures. While you are cooking, have your child help. Count how many spoonfuls it takes to fill a one-cup measurer.

Your child can help you make this simple no-bake recipe for peanut butter treats.

Peanut Butter Treats

1/4 cup margarine
1/4 cup peanut butter
1 cup raisins
40 regular-size marshmallows
5 cups rice cereal

Melt margarine over low heat. Add marshmallows and melt. Add the peanut butter and stir. Add the rice cereal and raisins; stir until everything is mixed well. Spread the mixture into a buttered pan and press into a firm layer. Cool and cut into squares.

Enjoy counting with your child!

440

Developmentally appropriate software can be an effective way to teach children numbers.

Music

1. **"Hickory Dickory Dock"**
   (traditional)

   Hickory dickory dock.
   The mouse ran up the clock.
   The clock struck one,
   The mouse ran down.
   Hickory dickory dock.

2. **"Two Little Blackbirds"**
   (traditional)

   Two little blackbirds sitting on a hill
   One named Jack,
   One named Jill.
   Fly away, Jack,
   Fly away, Jill.
   Come back, Jack,
   Come back, Jill.
   Two little blackbirds sitting on a hill
   One named Jack,
   One named Jill.

Fingerplays

I CAN EVEN COUNT SOME MORE

One, two, three, four
I can even count some more.
Five, six, seven, eight
All my fingers stand up straight
Nine, ten are my thumb men.

FIVE LITTLE MONKEYS
SWINGING FROM A TREE

Five little monkeys swinging from the tree,
Teasing Mr. Alligator, "You can't catch me."
Along comes Mr. Alligator as sneaky as
   can be . . .
SNAP
4 little monkeys swinging from the tree.
3 little monkeys swinging from the tree.
2 little monkeys swinging from the tree.
1 little monkey swinging from the tree.
No more monkeys swinging from the tree!

ONE, TWO, THREE

1, 2, How do you do?
1, 2, 3, Clap with me.
1, 2, 3, 4, Jump on the floor.
1, 2, 3, 4, 5, Look bright and alive!
1, 2, 3, 4, 5, 6, Pick up your sticks.
1, 2, 3, 4, 5, 6, 7, We can count up to eleven.
1, 2, 3, 4, 5, 6, 7, 8, Draw a circle around your plate.
1, 2, 3, 4, 5, 6, 7, 8, 9, Get the trunks in the line.
1, 2, 3, 4, 5, 6, 7, 8, 9, 10, Let's do it over again.

Source: Wilmes, Liz & Dick. (1983). *Everyday Circle Times*. Elgin, IL: Building Blocks Publications.

FIVE LITTLE BIRDS

Five little birds without any home.
   (hold up five fingers)
Five little trees in a row.
   (raise hands high over head)
Come build your nests in our branches tall.
   (cup hands)
We'll rock them to and fro.

TEN LITTLE FINGERS

I have 10 little fingers and 10 little toes.
   (children point to portions of body as they repeat words)
Two little arms and one little nose.
One little mouth and two little ears.
Two little eyes for smiles and tears.
One little head and two little feet.
One little chin, that makes _____ complete.

Science

1. Height and Weight Chart

Design a height and weight chart for the classroom. The children can help by measuring each other. Record the numbers. Later in the year measure the children and record their progress. Note the differences.

2. Using a Scale

Collect a variety of small objects and place on the science table with a balancing scale. The children can measure with the scale, noting the differences.

3. Temperature

Place an outdoor thermometer on the playground. Encourage the children to examine the thermometer. Record the temperature. Mark the temperature on the thermometer with masking tape. Bring the thermometer into the classroom. Check the thermometer again in half an hour. Show the children the change in temperature.

Dramatic Play

1. Grocery Store

In the dramatic play area, arrange a grocery store. To do this, collect a variety of empty boxes, paper bags, sales receipts, etc. Removable stickers can be used to indicate the grocery prices. A cash register and play money can also be added to create interest.

2. Clock Shop

Collect a variety of clocks for the children to explore. Using discarded clocks, with the glass face removed, is an interesting way to let the children explore numerals and internal mechanisms.

3. Telephoning

Prepare a classroom telephone book with all the children's names and telephone numbers. Contact your local telephone company to borrow the training system. The children can practice dialing their own numbers as well as their classmates'.

Arts and Crafts

1. Marker Sets

Using rubber bands, bind two watercolor markers together. Repeat this procedure making several sets. Set the markers, including an unbound set, on the art table. The children can use the bound marker sets for creating designs on paper.

2. Clipping Coupons

Collect coupon flyers from the Sunday edition of the paper and magazines for this activity. Place the flyers with scissors on a table in the art area. If interested, the children can cut coupons from the paper.

3. Coupon Collage

Clipped coupons, paste, and paper can be placed on a table in the art area.

4. Ruler Design

Collect a variety of rulers that are of different colors, sizes, and types. Using paper and a marking tool, the children can create designs.

5. Numeral Cookie Cutter

Numeral cookie cutters should be provided with playdough.

Sensory

Add to the sensory table colored water and a variety of measuring tools.

Math

1. Number Chain

Cut enough strips of paper to make a number chain for the days of the month. During group time each day, add a link to represent the passage of time. Another option is to use the chain as a countdown by removing a link per day until a special day. This is an interesting approach to an upcoming holiday.

2. Silverware Set

Provide a silverware set. The children can sort the pieces according to sizes, shapes, and/or use.

3. Constructing Numerals

Provide each interested child with a ball of playdough. Instruct children to form some numerals randomly. It is important for the teacher to monitor work and correct reversals. Then children can add the proper corresponding number of dots for that numeral just formed.

Manipulatives for Math Activities

buttons	toothpicks	golf tees	bottle caps
beads	pennies	stickers	poker chips
bobbins	checkers	fishing bobbers	paper clips
craft pompoms	crayons	keys	clothespins
spools	plastic caps from	small toy cars	erasers
shells	markers, milk	plastic bread ties	
seeds (corn, soybeans)	containers,	marbles	
shelled peanuts	plastic bottles	cotton balls	

An extension of this activity would be to make cards with numerals. The children roll their playdough into long ropes that can be placed over the lines of the numerals.

Group Time
(games, language)

1. **Squirrels in the Park**

   Choose five children to be squirrels. The children should sit in a row while one child pretends to go for a walk in the park carrying a bag of peanuts. When the child who is walking approaches the squirrels, provide directions. These may include: feeding the first squirrel, the fifth, the third, etc.

2. **Block Form Board**

   On a large piece of cardboard trace around one of each of the shapes of the blocks in the block area. Let children match blocks to the shape on the board.

3. **Match Them**

   Show the child several sets of identical picture cards, squares, objects, or flannel board pictures. Mix the items. Then have the children find matching pairs. One method of doing this is to hold up one item and have the children find the matching one.

4. **Follow the Teacher**

   At group time, provide directions containing a number. For example, say: 1 jump, 2 hops, 3 leaps, 4 tiptoe steps, etc. The numbers used should be developmentally appropriate for the children.

Cooking

Peanut Butter Treats

1/4 cup margarine
1/4 cup peanut butter
1 cup raisins
40 regular-size marshmallows
5 cups rice cereal

Melt the margarine over low heat. Add marshmallows and melt. Add the peanut butter and stir. Add the rice cereal and raisins. Stir until all ingredients are well mixed. Spread the mixture onto a buttered pan and press into a firm layer. Let cool and cut into squares.

Books

The following books can be used to complement this theme:

Anno, Mitsumasa. (1995). *Anno's Magic Seeds.* New York: G. P. Putnam.

Big Fat Hen. (1994). Illus. by Keith Baker. Orlando: Harcourt Brace.

Blackstone, Stella. (1996). *Grandma Went to Market: A Round-the-World Counting Rhyme.* Illus. by Bernard Lodge. Boston: Houghton Mifflin.

Brusca, Maria Christina. (1995). *Three Friends: A Counting Book/Tres Amigos: Un Cuento Para Contar.* New York: Holt.

Carlstrom, Nancy White. (1996). *Let's Count It Out, Jesse Bear.* Illus. by Bruce Degen. New York: Simon & Schuster.

Challoner, Jack. (1992). *Science Book of Numbers.* Orlando: Harcourt Brace.

Cole, Norma. (1994). *Blast Off! A Space Counting Book.* Illus. by Marshall Peck III. Watertown, MA: Charlesbridge Publishers.

Dale, Penny. (1994). *Ten Out of Bed.* Cambridge, MA: Candlewick Press.

Five Little Ducks: An Old Rhyme. (1995). Illus. by Pamela Paparone. New York: North South Books.

Fleming, Denise. (1992). *Count!* New York: Holt.

Geisert, Arthur. (1992). *Pigs from 1 to 10.* Boston: Houghton Mifflin.

Geisert, Arthur. (1996). *Roman Numerals I to MM.* Boston: Houghton Mifflin.

Giganti, Paul. (1992). *Each Orange Had 8 Slices: A Counting Book.* Illus. by Donald Crews. New York: Greenwillow.

Goennel, Heidi. (1994). *Odds and Evens: A Numbers Book.* New York: Tambourine Books.

Harley, Bill. (1996). *Sitting Down to Eat.* Illus. by Kitty Harvill. Little Rock, AR: August House LittleFolk.

Jonas, Ann. (1995). *Splash!* New York: Greenwillow.

Mazzola, Frank. (1997). *Counting Is for the Birds.* Watertown, MA: Charlesbridge Publishers.

Noll, Sally. (1997). *Surprise!* New York: Greenwillow.

Ryan, Pam Munoz. (1996). *Crayon Counting Book.* Illus. by Frank Mazzola, Jr. Watertown, MA: Charlesbridge Publishers.

Schlein, Miriam. (1996). *More Than One.* Illus. by Donald Crews. New York: Greenwillow.

Sturges, Philemon. (1995). *Ten Flashing Fireflies.* Illus. by Anna Vojtech. New York: North South Books.

Wells, Robert E. (1993). *Is a Blue Whale the Biggest Thing There Is?* Niles, IL: Albert Whitman & Co.

Yektai, Niki. (1996). *Bears at the Beach: Counting 10–20.* Brookfield, CT: Millbrook Press.

Multimedia

The following multimedia products can be used to complement this theme:

Counting and Sorting [CD-ROM]. (1997). DK Multimedia.

How Much Is a Million? [video]. (1997). Hosted by LeVar Burton. GPN/WNED-TV 120.

Introduction to Letters and Numerals [video]. (1985). SRA/McGraw-Hill.

Jenkins, Ella. *Counting Games and Rhythms for the Little Ones*, Vol. 1 [cassette]. (1990). Smithsonian Folkways.

Millie's Math House [CD-ROM]. (1992). Edmark.

Palmer, Hap. *Learning Basic Skills* [video]. (1986). Educational Activities.

Palmer, Hap. *Math Readiness—Vocabulary and Concepts* [cassette]. Educational Activities.

Reader Rabbit's Preschool [CD-ROM]. (1997). Learning Company.

Recordings and Song Titles

The following recordings can be used to complement this theme:

Piggyback Songs—"Count to Three," "One Blue Square"

Nelson Gill—"Ten Little Ducks"

Songs about Me—"Count My Fingers"

A Rainbow of Songs—"Count Your Money"

Children Love to Sing and Dance (The Learning Station)—"Counting Together"

Tony Chestnut (The Learning Station)—"One, Two, Buckle My Shoe," "Five Little Monkeys"

Car Songs—"Five Little Monkeys," "Six Little Ducks"

Musical Playtime Fun—"Five Gray Sharks"

Toddlerific—"Let's Count the Animals"

Baby Games—"One Potato, Two Potato"

Singable Nursery Rhymes—"One, Two, Buckle My Shoe," "Three Little Kittens"

Toddlers on Parade—"Ten Little Goblins"

Diaper Gym—"Ten Little Indians"

Where Is Thumbkin?—"Roll Over," "Three Little Monkeys," "Five Little Ducks"

Put Your Finger in the Air—"We Are All Counting Today"

Six Little Ducks—"This Old Man," "Five Little Monkeys," "Six Little Ducks"

T H E M E 46

Uses

enjoyment
learning words
bedtime rituals

Forms

written
spoken
sung

Nursery Rhymes

Favorites

Little Bo Peep
Mary Had a Little
 Lamb
Old Mother
 Hubbard
Hey Diddle Diddle
Little Miss Muffet
Humpty Dumpty
Jack and Jill
Mary Mary Quite
 Contrary
Jack Be Nimble

Rub-a-Dub-Dub
The Muffin Man
Little Jack Horner
Old MacDonald
 Had a Farm
Two Little
 Blackbirds
Hickory Dickory
 Dock
Three Kittens'
 Mittens

Characters

animals
people
objects

Theme Goals

Through participating in the experiences provided by this theme, the children may learn:

1. Favorite nursery rhymes.
2. Uses of nursery rhymes.
3. Forms of nursery rhymes.
4. Characters portrayed in nursery rhymes.

Concepts for the Children to Learn

1. Nursery rhymes are fun to listen to and say.
2. Nursery rhymes can contain real or pretend words.
3. Some nursery rhymes are about animals.
4. Some nursery rhymes help us learn numbers and counting.
5. Some nursery rhymes teach us about different people.

Vocabulary

nursery rhyme—short, simple poem or rhyme.

Bulletin Board

The purpose of this bulletin board is to promote name recognition and call attention to the printed word. This can be used as an attendance bulletin board. Each child should be provided a bulletin board piece with his name printed on it. When the children arrive each morning at school, they should be encouraged to hang their name on the bulletin board. To create a "Find Your Mitten" bulletin board, cut a mitten out of tagboard for each child in the class. Use a paper punch to cut a hole in the top of each mitten. Three kittens can be constructed and attached to the bulletin board to represent the three little kittens who lost their mittens. Hang pushpins on the bulletin board for the children to hang their mittens.

Parent Letter

Dear Parents,

Nursery rhymes will be the focus of our next theme. These rhymes can serve as a bridge between the home and school. I'm sure many of you have shared favorite nursery rhymes with your child at home. Nursery rhymes are an easy introduction to poetry, as well as the concept of rhyming words.

AT SCHOOL

We have a fun-filled curriculum planned for our unit on nursery rhymes. A few highlights include:

- acting out various rhymes with puppets that represent different characters from familiar nursery rhymes.
- unraveling the riddle of the "Humpty Dumpty" nursery rhyme. (Why couldn't Humpty be put back together? Because Humpty was an egg!)
- creating "Little Miss Muffet" spiders in the art area.
- taking turns being nimble and quick as we jump over a candlestick to dramatize the rhyme of "Jack Be Nimble."

AT HOME

To foster concepts of the unit at home, try the following:

- Let your child help you crack eggs open to make scrambled eggs. Children like to feel that they have accomplished a grown-up task when they crack the eggs.
- Sing or recite some of the many rhymes your child already knows such as "Jack and Jill" and "Mary Had a Little Lamb." These also develop an enjoyment of music and singing.

Share a nursery rhyme with your child today!

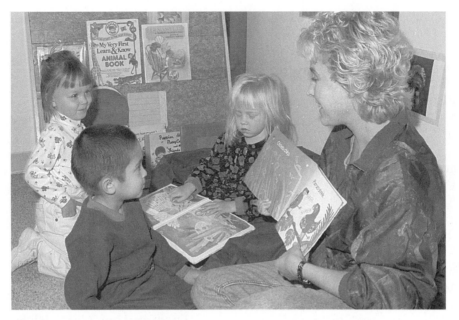

Reciting nursery rhymes can help relax a child.

Music

1. **"Hickory Dickory Dock"**
   (traditional)

   Hickory dickory dock
   The mouse ran up the clock.
   The clock struck one, the mouse ran down,
   Hickory dickory dock.

2. **"The Muffin Man"**
   (traditional)

   Oh, do you know the muffin man,
   The muffin man, the muffin man?
   Oh, do you know the muffin man
   Who lives on Dreary Lane?

   Yes, I know the muffin man . . .

3. **"Two Little Blackbirds"**
   (traditional)

   Two little blackbirds sitting on a hill
   One named Jack. One named Jill.
   Fly away, Jack. Fly away, Jill.
   Come back, Jack. Come back, Jill.
   Two little blackbirds sitting on a hill.
   One named Jack. One named Jill.

4. **"Jack and Jill"**
   (traditional)

   Jack and Jill went up a hill
   To fetch a pail of water.
   Jack fell down and broke his crown
   And Jill fell tumbling after.

Fingerplays

LITTLE JACK HORNER

   Little Jack Horner
   Sat in a corner
   Eating a Christmas pie.
      (pretend you're eating)
   He put in his thumb,
      (thumb down)
   And pulled out a plum
      (thumb up)
   And said, "What a good boy am I!"
      (say out loud)

PAT-A-CAKE

Pat-a-cake, pat-a-cake, baker's man.
Bake me a cake as fast as you can!
 (clap hands together lightly)
Roll it
 (roll hands)
And pat it
 (touch hands together lightly)
And mark it with a "B"
 (write "b" in the air)
And put it in the oven for baby and me.
 (point to baby and to yourself)

WEE WILLIE WINKLE

Wee Willie Winkle runs through the town
 (pretend to run)
Upstairs, downstairs in his nightgown,
 (point up, point down, then point to
 clothes)
Rapping at the window, crying through the
 lock
 (knock in the air, peek through a hole)
"Are the children all in bed, for now it's
 eight o'clock?"
 (shake finger)

OLD KING COLE

Old King Cole was a merry old soul
 (lift elbows up and down)
And a merry old soul was he.
 (nod head)
He called for his pipe.
 (clap two times)
He called for his bowl.
 (clap two times)
And he called for his fiddlers three.
 (clap two times then pretend to play
 violin)

HICKORY DICKORY DOCK

Hickory dickory dock
 (swing arms back and forth together,
 bent down low)
The mouse ran up the clock.
 (run fingers up your arm)
The clock struck one
 (clap, and then hold up one finger)
The mouse ran down.
 (run fingers down your arm)
Hickory dickory dock.
 (swing arms back and forth together,
 bent down low)

Science

1. **Mary's Garden**

   A styrofoam cup with the child's name
   printed on it and a scoop of soil should
   be provided. Then let everyone choose a
   flower seed. Be sure to save the seed packages. The children can plant their seed,
   water, and care for it. When the plant
   begins to grow, try to identify the names of
   the plants by comparing them to pictures
   on the seed packages.

2. **Hickory Dickory Dock Clock**

   Draw and cut a large Hickory Dickory Dock
   clock from cardboard. Move the hands of
   the clock and see if the children can
   identify the numeral.

3. **Wool**

   Pieces of wool fabric mounted on cardboard can be matched with samples.

4. **Pumpkin Tasters**

   Plan a Peter, Peter, Pumpkin Eater
   pumpkin-tasting party.

Dramatic Play

1. **Baker**

   Baking props such as: hats, aprons, cookie
   cutters, baking pans, rolling pins, mixers,
   spoons, and bowls can be placed in the
   dramatic play area.

2. **Puppets**

   A puppet theater can be placed in the dramatic play area for the duration of the unit.
   To add variety, each day a different set of
   puppets can be added for the children.

Arts and Crafts

1. Spiders

Add black tempera paint to a playdough mixture. In addition to the playdough, provide black pipe cleaners or yarn. Using these materials, spiders or other objects can be created.

2. Spider Webs

Cut circles of black paper to fit in the bottom of a pie tin. Mix thin silver or white tempera paint. Place a marble and two teaspoons of paint on the paper. Gently tilt the pie tin, allowing the marble to roll through the paint, creating a spider web design.

3. Twinkle, Twinkle Little Stars

The children can decorate stars with glitter and sequins. The stars can be hung from the ceiling. During group time sing "Twinkle, Twinkle, Little Star."

4. Little Boy Blue's Horn

Collect paper towel tubes. The tubes can be painted with tempera. When the tubes are dry, cover one end with tissue paper and secure with a rubber band. The children can use them as horns.

Sensory

Water and Pails

Add water, pails, and scoopers to the sensory table.

Large Muscle

1. Jack Be Nimble's Candlestick

Make a candlestick out of an old paper towel holder and tissue paper for the flame. Repeat the rhyme by substituting each child's name.

Jack be nimble. Jack be quick.
Jack jump over the candlestick.

2. Wall Building

Encourage the children to create a large wall out of blocks for Humpty Dumpty. Act out the rhyme.

Field Trips/ Resource People

1. Candlemaking

Invite a resource person to demonstrate candlemaking, or take a field trip to a craft center so that the children can view candles being made.

2. Greenhouse

Visit a florist or greenhouse to observe flowers and plants.

Math

1. Puzzles

Draw or cut out several pictures of different nursery rhymes ("Jack and Jill," "Jack Be Nimble," etc.) and mount on tagboard. Laminate and cut each picture into five to seven pieces. The children can match nursery rhyme puzzle pieces.

2. Rote Counting

Say or sing the following nursery rhyme to help the children with rote counting.

1, 2 buckle my shoe
3, 4 shut the door
5, 6 pick up sticks
7, 8 lay them straight
9, 10 a big fat hen.

3. Matching

Draw from one to ten simple figures from a nursery rhyme (mittens, candlesticks, pails, etc.) on the left side of a sheet of tagboard and the corresponding numeral on the right side. Laminate the pieces and cut each in half creating different-shaped puzzle pieces. The children can match the number of figures to the corresponding numeral.

4. **Mitten Match**

Collect several matching pairs of mittens. Mix them up and have children match the pairs.

Social Studies

Table Setting

On a sheet of tagboard, trace the outline of a plate, cup, knife, fork, spoon, and napkin. Laminate. The children can match the silverware and dishes to the outline on the placemat in preparation for snack or meals. This activity can be extended by having the children turn the placemat over, and arrange the place setting without the aid of an outline.

Group Time
(games, language)

Old Mother Hubbard's Doggie Bone Game

Save a bone or construct one from tagboard. Ask one child to volunteer to be the doggie. Seat the children in a circle with the doggie in the center and the bone in front of him. The doggie closes his eyes. A child from the circle quietly comes and steals the bone. When the child is reseated with the bone out of sight, the children will call,

"Doggie, doggie, where's your bone? Someone took it from your home!"

The doggie gets three chances to guess who has the bone. If he guesses correctly, the child who took the bone becomes the doggie.

Cooking

1. **Bran Muffins**
   (Use with the "Muffin Man" rhyme)

   3 cups whole wheat bran cereal
   1 cup boiling water
   1/2 cup shortening or oil
   2 eggs
   2 1/2 cups unbleached flour
   1 1/2 cups sugar
   2 1/2 teaspoons baking soda
   2 cups buttermilk

   Preheat the oven to 400 degrees. Line the muffin tins with paper baking cups. In a large bowl combine the cereal and boiling water. Stir in the shortening and eggs. Add the remaining ingredients. Blend well. Spoon the batter into cups about 3/4 full. Bake at 400 degrees for 18 to 22 minutes or until golden brown. Eat at snack and sing the "Muffin Man" song.

2. **Humpty Dumpty Pear Salad**

   For each serving provide 1/2 pear, 1 lifesaver, 1 tablespoon mayonnaise, 2 cherries, 1 raisin, and a lettuce leaf. The children can prepare their own salad. To do this each child puts a lettuce leaf on a plate and places a pear half on top of it, round side up. Then add the two cherries for eyes, a raisin for a nose, and the piece of lifesaver candy for a mouth. Add mayonnaise to taste.

   Source: Graham, Terry. (1982). *Let Loose on Mother Goose*. Terry Graham. Incentive Publishing Company.

3. **Cottage Cheese***

   2 quarts pasteurized skim milk (to make 1 to 3/4 pounds of cottage cheese)
   salt
   liquid rennet or a junket tablet

   Heat the water to 80 degrees Fahrenheit in the bottom part of a double boiler. Use a thermometer to determine the water temperature. Do not guess.

*This activity is time-consuming; it may be more appropriate for older children.

Pour the skim milk into the top of the double boiler. Dilute 1 or 2 drops of liquid rennet in a tablespoon of cold water and stir it into the milk. If rennet is not available, add 1/8 of a junket tablet to a tablespoon of water and add it to the milk. Allow the milk to remain at 80 degrees until it curdles, in about 12 to 18 hours. During this period no special attention is necessary. If desired, the milk may be placed in a warm oven overnight. Place the curd in a cheese cloth over a container to drain the whey. Occasionally, pour out the whey that collects in the container so that the draining will continue. In 15 to 20 minutes, the curd will become mushy and will drain more slowly. When it is almost firm and the whey has nearly ceased to flow, the cheese is ready for salting and eating. Salt the cheese to taste. The cottage cheese can be spread on crackers for a snack.

4. **Miss Muffet's Curds and Whey**

2 cups whole milk
1 teaspoon vinegar

Warm milk and add vinegar. Stir as curds separate from the whey. Curds are the milk solids and the whey is the liquid that is poured off. You can let your children taste the whey but they probably will not be thrilled by it. Strain the curds from the whey, then dump the curds onto a paper towel and gently press the curds with more towels to get out the liquid. Sprinkle with salt and refrigerate. Eat as cottage cheese. You can also serve the curds at room temperature. Stir them until they are smooth. Add different flavorings (such as cinnamon, orange flavoring, vanilla, etc.). Use as a spread on crackers. Curds mixed with peanut butter is great. Serves 12 (2 crackers each).

Books

The following books can be used to complement this theme:

Aylesworth, Jim. (1992). *The Cat and the Fiddle and More.* New York: Macmillan.

Aylesworth, Jim. (1994). *My Son John.* Illus. by David Frampton. New York: Holt.

Benjamin, Floella, ed. (1995). *Skip Across the Ocean: Nursery Rhymes from Around the World.* Illus. by Sheila Moxley. New York: Orchard Books.

Big Fat Hen. (1994). Illus. by Keith Baker. Orlando: Harcourt Brace.

Bornstein, Harry et al. (1992). *Nursery Rhymes from Mother Goose: Told in Signed English.* Washington, DC: Kendall Green Publications.

Chorao, Kay. (1994). *Mother Goose Magic.* New York: Dutton.

Christelow, Eileen. (1998). *Five Little Monkeys Jumping on the Bed.* Boston: Houghton Mifflin.

Dyer, Jane. (1996). *Animal Crackers: A Delectable Collection of Pictures, Poems, & Lullabies for the Very Young.* Boston: Little, Brown.

Eagle, Kin. (1994). *It's Raining, It's Pouring.* Illus. by Robert Gilbert. Dallas, TX: Whispering Coyote Press.

Five Little Ducks: An Old Rhyme. (1995). Illus. by Pamela Paparone. New York: North South Books.

Hale, Sara. (1995). *Mary Had a Little Lamb.* Illus. by Salley Mavor. New York: Orchard Books.

Heller, Nicholas. (1997). *This Little Piggy.* Illus. by Sonja Lamut. New York: Greenwillow.

Kroll, Virginia L. (1995). *Jaha and Jamil Go Down the Hill: An African Mother Goose.* Illus. by Katherine Roundtree. Watertown, MA: Charlesbridge Publishing.

Lansky, Bruce. (1993). *New Adventures of Mother Goose: Gentle Rhymes for Happy Times.* Illus. by Stephen Carpenter. New York: Simon & Schuster.

Little Robin Redbreast: A Mother Goose Rhyme. (1994). Illus. by Shari Halpern. New York: North South Books.

Lobel, Arnold. (1997). *Arnold Lobel Book of Mother Goose.* New York: Random House.

Manson, Christopher. (1993). *Tree in the Wood: An Old Nursery Song.* New York: North South Books.

Marks, Alan. (1993). *Over the Hills and Far Away: A Book of Nursery Rhymes.* New York: North South Books.

Marks, Alan. (1991). *Ring-A-Ling o' Roses and A Ding, Dong, Bell: A Book of Nursery Rhymes.* New York: North South Books.

Miranda, Anne. (1997). *To Market, to Market.* Illus. by Janet Stevens. Orlando: Harcourt Brace.

My Very First Mother Goose. (1996). Edited by Iona Opie. Illus. by Rosemary Wells. Cambridge, MA: Candlewick Press.

Old Mother Hubbard and Her Wonderful Dog. (1991). Illus. by James Marshall. New York: Farrar, Straus & Giroux.

Opie, Iona Archibald. Cambridge, MA: Candlewick Press. (1997). (Board books). *Humpty Dumpty and Other Rhymes; Pussycat Pussycat and Other Rhymes; Wee Willie Winkie and Other Rhymes.*

Polacco, Patricia. (1995). *Babushka's Mother Goose.* New York: Philomel.

Scieszka, Jon. (1994). *The Book That Jack Wrote.* Illus. by Daniel Adel. New York: Viking.

Slier, Debby. (1993). *Real Mother Goose Book of American Rhymes.* Illus. by Patty McCloskey-Padgett et al. New

York: Scholastic.

Sweet, Melissa. (1992). *Fiddle-i-ee: A Farmyard Song for the Very Young.* Boston: Little, Brown.

Van Rynbach, Iris. (1995). *Five Little Pumpkins.* Honesdale, PA: Boyds Mills Press.

Multimedia

The following multimedia products can be used to complement this theme:

Children's Treasury II Rhymes, Poems, Stories [CD-ROM]. (1994). Fairfield, CT: Queue Inc.

Mixed-Up Mother Goose [CD-ROM]. (1995). Bellevue, WA: Sierra On-Line.

Nursery Songs and Rhymes [video]. (1993). Sandy, UT: Waterford Institute.

Olde Mother Goose [paperback and cassette]. (1993). Performed by the Hubbards. Illus. by Blanche Fisher Wright. August House Audio.

Palmer, Hap. *Hap Palmer Sings Classic Nursery Rhymes* [cassette]. (1991). Freeport, NY: Educational Activities.

Rusty and Rosy Nursery Songs and Rhymes [video]. (1993). Sandy, UT: Waterford Institute.

Recordings and Song Titles

The following recordings can be used to complement this theme:

Rock 'n' Roll Songs That Teach (The Learning Station)—"Rock 'n' Roll Nursery Rhymes"

Singable Nursery Rhymes

Nursery Rhymes for Little People

THEME 47

Occupations

Transportation
taxi driver, bus driver, car salesperson, pilot, ambulance driver, truck driver, gas station attendant, astronaut

Other
homemaker
unemployed
seasonal
part-time
self-employed
shift
cottage
migrant

Health
doctor
nurse
dentist
hygienist
paramedic
child care

Production
farmer, cook/chef, baker, miner, factory worker

Sports
announcer, umpire, coach, athlete

Construction
carpenter, plumber, cabinetmaker, architect

Community Helpers
police officer
firefighter
mail carrier
judge

Communications
computer operator, television reporter, telephone operator, newspaper reporter, actor

Service Workers
teacher, librarian, waitress/waiter, banker, cashier, custodian, secretary, auto mechanic, butcher, clerk, sanitation engineer

Theme Goals

Through participating in the experiences provided by this theme, the children may learn:

1. Occupations of community helpers.
2. Sports figure occupations.
3. Health occupations.
4. Transportation occupations.
5. Communications occupations.
6. Construction occupations.
7. Production occupations.
8. Service occupations.

Concepts for the Children to Learn

1. An occupation is a job a person performs.
2. There are many different kinds of occupations.
3. Taxi drivers, pilots, and ambulance drivers are in transportation occupations.
4. Doctors, nurses, and dentists are in health occupations.
5. A community helper is someone who helps us.
6. Teachers, librarians, and custodians are in service occupations.
7. Cooks, factory workers, and farmers are in production occupations.
8. Football and baseball players are in sports occupations.
9. Television and newspaper reporters are in communications occupations.
10. Builders and architects are in construction occupations.

Vocabulary

1. **occupation**—the job a person performs to earn money.
2. **job**—type of work.
3. **service**—helping people.

Bulletin Board

The purpose of this bulletin board is to stress that men and women can be doctors, farmers, construction workers, teachers, judges, etc. To prepare the bulletin board, construct a boy and girl out of tagboard. Design several occupational outfits that may be worn by either sex. Color and laminate the pieces. Magnet pieces or pushpins and holes should be provided to affix clothing on children.

Parent Letter

Dear Parents,

Hello! We will be exploring a new unit on occupations. Through experiences provided by this theme the children will become aware of a great number of occupations and the way these workers help us today: policeman, farmer, hairstylist, librarian, pilot, postal worker, construction worker, etc.

AT SCHOOL

Some learning experiences include:

- listening to books and records about people in our neighborhoods.
- making occupation hats.
- visiting a police station on Wednesday at 2:00 p.m. Join us if you can!
- observing an ambulance and talking with a paramedic.
- designing a job chart for our classroom.

AT HOME

Page through magazines with your child. Discuss equipment and materials that are used in various occupations. Questions such as the following can be asked to stimulate thinking skills: Who might use a typewriter to perform a job? What occupations involve the use of a cash register? Your child might be interested in visiting your place of employment!

Enjoy your child!

460

Abduraham likes to dress up as a police officer.

Fingerplays

FARM CHORES

Five little farmers woke up with the sun.
  (hold up hand, palm forward)
It was early morning and the chores must
  be done.
The first little farmer went out to milk the
  cow.
  (hold up hand, point to thumb)
The second little farmer thought he'd
  better plow.
  (hold up hand, point to index finger)
The third little farmer cultivated weeds.
  (point to middle finger)
The fourth little farmer planted more seeds.
  (point to fourth finger)
The fifth little farmer drove his tractor
  round.
  (point to last finger)
Five little farmers, the best that can be
  found.
  (hold up hand)

TRAFFIC POLICEMAN

The traffic policeman holds up his hand.
  (hold up hand, palm forward)
He blows the whistle,
  (pretend to blow whistle)
He gives the command.
  (hold up hand again)
When the cars are stopped
  (hold up hand again)
He waves at me.
Then I may cross the street, you see.
  (wave hand as if indicating for someone
  to go)

THE CARPENTER

This is the way he saws the wood
  (right hand saws left palm)
Sawing, sawing, sawing.
This is the way he nails a nail
  (pound right fist on left palm)
Nailing, nailing, nailing.
This is the way he paints the house
  (right hand paints left palm)
Painting, painting, painting.

Dramatic Play

1. Hat Shop

Police officer hats, firefighter hats, construction worker hats, businessperson hats, and other occupation-related hats should be placed in the dramatic play area.

2. Classroom Cafe

Cover the table in the dramatic play area with a tablecloth. Provide menus, a tablet for the waitress to write on, a space for a cook, etc. A cash register and play money may also be added to encourage play.

3. Hairstylist

Collect empty shampoo bottles, combs, barrettes, ribbons, hair spray containers, and magazines. Cut the cord off a discarded hair dryer and curling iron and place in the dramatic play area.

4. Our Library

Books on a shelf, a desk for the librarian, stamper and ink pad to check out books should be placed in the dramatic play area. A small table for children to sit and read their books would also add interest.

5. Workbench

A hammer, nails, saws, vises, a carpenter's apron, etc., should be added to the workbench. Eye goggles for the children's safety should also be included. **Caution:** Constant supervision is needed for this activity.

6. An Airplane

Create an airplane out of a large cardboard refrigerator box. If desired, the children can paint the airplane.

7. Post Office

A mailbox, letters, envelopes, stamps, and mail carrier bags can be set up in the dramatic play or art area.

8. Fast-Food Restaurant

Collect bags, containers, and hats to set up a fast-food restaurant.

9. A Construction Site

Hard hats, nails, a hammer, large blocks, and scrap wood can be provided for outdoor play. Cardboard boxes and masking tape should also be made available.

10. Prop Boxes

The following prop boxes can be made by collecting the materials listed.

Police Officer
- badge
- hat
- uniform
- whistle
- walkie-talkie

Mail Carrier
- letter bag
- letter/stamps
- uniform
- mailbox
- wrapped cardboard boxes
- paper
- pencil
- rubber stamp
- ink pad
- envelopes

Firefighter
- boots
- helmet
- hose
- uniform
- gloves
- raincoat
- suspenders
- goggles

Doctor
- stethoscope
- medicine bottles
- adhesive tape
- cotton balls
- Red Cross armband
- chart holder

Arts and Crafts

1. Mail Truck

Pre-cut mail truck parts including: 1 rectangle, 1 square, and 2 circles. The children can paste the pieces together and decorate. This activity is most appropriate for older children.

462

2. Occupation Vests

Cut a circle out of the bottom of a large paper grocery bag. Then from the circle cut a slit down the center of the bag. Cut out arm holes. Provide felt-tip colored markers for the children to decorate the vests. They may elect to be a pilot, police officer, mail carrier, baker, flight attendant, doctor, firefighter, etc.

3. Mail Pouch

Cut the top half off a large grocery bag. Use the cutaway piece to make a shoulder strap. Staple it to the bag. The children can decorate the bag with crayons or markers.

Sensory

The following materials can be added to the sensory table:

- ☺ sponge hair rollers with water
- ☺ wood shavings with scoops and scales
- ☺ sand with toy cars, trucks, airplanes
- ☺ pipes with water

Large Muscle

Cut large cardboard boxes to make squad cars. Take the boxes and spray paint them either blue or white. Emblems can be constructed for the sides.

Field Trips/ Resource People

1. Take field trips to the following:

- ☺ bank
- ☺ library
- ☺ grocery store
- ☺ police station
- ☺ doctor/dentist office
- ☺ beauty salon/barber
- ☺ television/radio station
- ☺ courthouse
- ☺ airport
- ☺ farm
- ☺ restaurant

Excursions

Special excursions and events in an early childhood program give opportunities for widening the young child's horizons by providing exciting direct experiences. The following places or people are some suggestions:

train station	offices	hospital	shoe repair shop
dentist office	animal hospital	meat market	print shop
post office	fire station	library	artist's studio
grocery store	tree farm	apple orchard	bowling alley
zoo	car wash	farm	department store
dairy	children's houses	airport	windows
family garden	garage mechanic	riding stable	potter's studio
poultry house	television studio	barber shop	teacher's house
construction site	drugstore	college dormitory	street repair site
beauty shop	bakery		

2. **Invite the following resource people to school:**

- police officer with squad car
- firefighter with truck
- ambulance driver with ambulance
- truck driver with truck
- taxi driver with cab
- librarian with books

Social Studies

1. **Occupation Pictures**

    Pin occupation pictures on classroom bulletin boards and walls.

2. **A Job Chart**

    Make a chart containing classroom jobs. Include tasks such as feeding the class pet, watering plants, sweeping the floor, wiping tables, etc.

Group Time
(games, language)

1. **Brushes as Tools**

    Collect all types of brushes and place in a bag. The children can reach into the bag and feel one. Before removing it, the child describes the kind of brush. When using with younger children, limit the number of brushes. Also, before placing the brushes in the bag, show the children each brush and discuss its use.

2. **Machines as Helpers Chart**

    Machines and tools help people work and play. Ask the children to think of all of the machines they or their parents use around the house. As they name a machine, list it on a chart and discuss how it is used.

3. **Mail It**

    Play a variation of "Duck, Duck, Goose." The children can sit in a circle. One child holds an envelope and walks around the circle saying, "letter," and taps each child on the head. When he gets to the one he wants to chase him, have the child drop the letter and say, "Mail it!" Then both children run around the circle until they return to the letter. The chaser gets to "mail" the letter by walking around and repeating the game.

Cooking

Cheese Treats
cheese chunks
pretzel sticks

Cut cheese into small squares. Poke a pretzel into each cheese chunk.

Source: Wilmes, Liz & Dick. *Everyday Circle Times.*

Books

The following books can be used to complement this theme:

Brandenberg, Alexa. (1996). *I Am Me.* Orlando: Harcourt Brace.

Ready, Dee. *Community Helpers* series. San Francisco: Children's Book Press. *Astronauts.* (1998); *Bakers.* (1998); *Construction.* (1998); *Doctors.* (1997); *Farmers.* (1997); *Fire Fighters.* (1997); *Garbage Collectors.* (1998); *Nurses.* (1998); *Police Officers.* (1997); *Teacher.* (1998); *Veterinarians.* (1997); *Zoo Keeper.* (1998).

Gibbons, Gail. (1992). *Say Woof!: The Day of a Country Veterinarian.* New York: Macmillan.

Grossman, Patricia. (1991). *The Night Ones.* Illus. by Lydia Dabcovich. Orlando: Harcourt Brace.

Henkes, Kevin. (1995). *Good-Bye, Curtis.* Illus. by Marisabina Russo. New York: Greenwillow.

Florian, Douglas. *How We Work* series. New York: Greenwillow. *An Auto Mechanic.* (1994). (Pbk); *A Chef.* (1992); *A Fisher.* (1994); *A Painter.* (1993).

Kunhardt, Edith. *I'm Going to Be* series. (Pbk) New York: Scholastic. *A Fire Fighter.* (1995); *A Police Officer.* (1995); *A Vet.* (1996).

Isaacs, Gwynne. (1991). *While You Are Asleep.* Illus. by Cathi Hepworth. New York: Walker & Co.

Kalman, Maira. (1993). *Chicken Soup, Boots.* New York: Viking.

MacKinnon, Debbie. (1996). *What Am I?* Illus. by Anthea Sieveking. New York: Dial Books.

Maynard, Christopher. (1997). *Jobs People Do.* New York: DK Publishing.

Miller, Margaret. New York: Greenwillow. *Guess Who?* (1994); *Who Uses This?* (1990); *Whose Hat?* (1997). (Pbk reprint).

Moses, Amy. (1997). *Doctors Help People.* Mankato, MN: Child's World.

Our Neighborhood series. San Francisco: Children's Book Press.

Duvall, Jill D. (1997). *Chef Ki Is Serving Our Dinner.*

Duvall, Jill D. (1997). *Meet Rory Hohenstein, a Professional Dancer.*

Duvall, Jill D. (1997). *Mr. Duvall Reports the News.*

Duvall, Jill D. (1997). *Ms. Moja Makes Beautiful Clothes.*

Duvall, Jill D. (1997). *Who Keeps the Water Clean?: Ms. Schindler!*

Flanagan, Alice K. (1997). *Ask Nurse Pfaff, She'll Help You.*

Flanagan, Alice K. (1996). *A Busy Day at Mr. Kang's Grocery Store.*

Flanagan, Alice K. (1997). *A Day in Court With Mrs. Trinh.*

Flanagan, Alice K. (1997). *Mrs. Murphy Fights Fires.*

Flanagan, Alice K. (1996). *The Wilsons, a House-Painting Team.*

Paulsen, Gary. (1997). *Worksong.* Illus. by Ruth Wright Paulsen. Orlando: Harcourt Brace.

Radford, Derek. (1995). *Harry at the Garage.* Cambridge, MA: Candlewick Press.

Rylant, Cynthia. (1993). *Mr. Griggs' Work.* Illus. by Julie Downing. New York: Orchard Books.

Multimedia

The following multimedia products can be used to complement this theme:

Big Job [CD-ROM]. (1995). Discovery Channel Multimedia.

Harriet's Magic Hats IV series [video]. (1986). Edmonton, AB: Access Network, Alberta Educational Communication Corp. 25 videos. 15 min. Primary level.

Dog Trainer	*Rodeo Cowboy*
Hotel Manager	*Sheep Farmer*
Hat Maker	*Ski Instructor*
Librarian	*Telephone Installer*
Museum Curator	*Toy Tester*
Naturalist	*Vegetable Processor*
Newspaper Reporter	*Veterinarian*
Palaeontologist	*Water Treatment Engineer*
Pasta Maker	*Weather Forecaster*
Photographer	*Welder*
Potter	*Zookeeper*
Puppeteer	

THEME 48

Pets

Sounds
barking
meowing
squeaking
chirping

People
breeders
trainers
groomers
owners
veterinarians

Body Covering
fur
feathers
scales
shell

Care
food
water
attention
air
exercise
grooming
allergies

Kinds

HOUSE		FARM
dogs	rabbits	pig
cats	snakes	horse
hamsters	lizards	sheep
gerbils	spiders	goat
turtles	mice	cow
guinea pigs	ferrets	
fish	chinchillas	
birds		

Movement
swimming
walking
flying
hopping
running

Theme Goals

Through participating in the experiences provided by this theme, the children may learn:

1. Some animals are kept as pets.
2. Pet care.
3. Places pets live.
4. Body coverings of pets.
5. Sounds of pets.
6. Movements of pets.

Concepts for the Children to Learn

1. An animal kept for enjoyment is called a pet.
2. Dogs, cats, fish, hamsters, gerbils, and birds can all be house pets.
3. Pigs, ponies, horses, sheep, goats, and cows can be pets on a farm.
4. Pets need food, water, shelter, and loving care.
5. Barking, meowing, squeaking, and chirping are pet sounds.
6. To move, pets may swim, walk, fly, hop, or run.
7. The care of a pet depends on the type of animal.
8. Skin coverings on pets differ.
9. A veterinarian is an animal doctor.

Vocabulary

1. **pet**—animal that is kept for pleasure.
2. **fur**—hairy coating of some animals.
3. **feathers**—skin covering of birds.
4. **scales**—skin covering of fish and reptiles.
5. **veterinarian**—an animal doctor.
6. **collar**—a band worn around an animal's neck.
7. **leash**—a cord that attaches to a collar.
8. **whiskers**—stiff hair growing around the animal's nose, mouth, and eyes.

Bulletin Board

The purpose of this bulletin board is to encourage the development of mathematical skills. To prepare the bulletin board, construct fishbowls out of white tagboard or construction paper. Write a numeral beginning with one on each fishbowl and the corresponding number of dots. Hang the fishbowls on the bulletin board. Next, construct pieces as illustrated that will fit on top of the fishbowl to represent water in the bowl. Draw fish to match the numerals in each bowl. The pieces can be attached to each other to hang on the bulletin board by using magnet pieces, or pushpins and a paper punch. The children should count the fish in each water piece and match it to the corresponding numbered fishbowl.

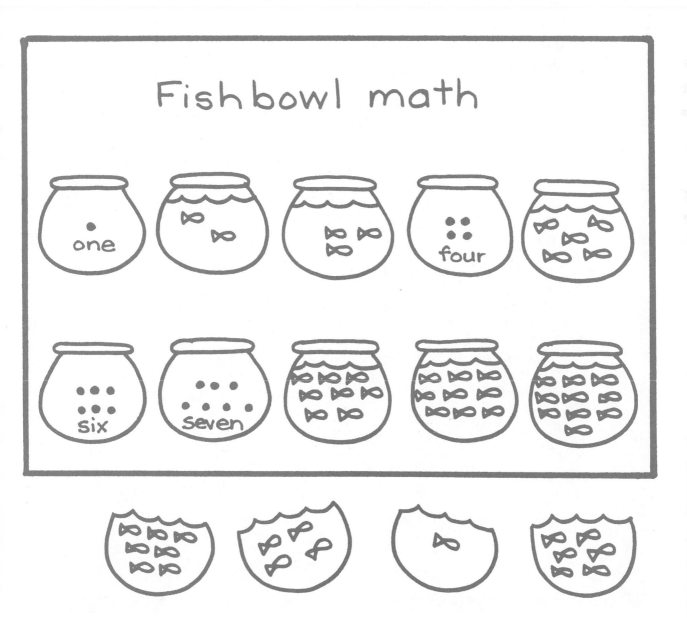

Parent Letter

Dear Parents,

Children are naturally curious about animals. To build on their interests, we will be starting a curriculum unit on pets, and I'm sure that we'll be busy! The children will discover the kinds of animals most people keep as pets. They will also learn the care that is involved in having a pet.

AT SCHOOL

The following are some of the learning experiences your child will participate in during our pet unit:

- making a special treat for Greta, our classroom gerbil.
- creating a large doghouse out of an appliance box for the dramatic play area.
- interacting with a variety of pets. Dani and Donny will bring their rabbit on Tuesday, and Cindy will bring her bird on Wednesday. If you are willing to bring your family pet to school to show the children, we welcome you. Contact me and we can arrange a time that would be convenient for you (and your pet).
- listening to the story *Clifford, the Big Red Dog*, by Norman Bridwell.

AT HOME

Is your family considering adding a pet to your household? If so, there are many variables to be taken into consideration because not all households are meant to include pets. Allergies, fears, and lifestyles are three things that need to be considered. Also, you will need to consider your child's readiness for a pet.

To develop fine motor skills, provide magazines and newspapers for your child to cut or tear out pictures of animals. These can be used to create an animal alphabet book or a collage to hang in your child's bedroom.

Enjoy your child!

470

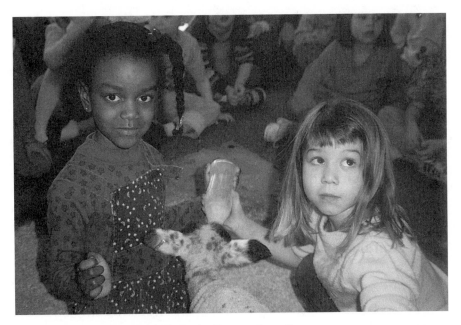
Children enjoy feeding baby animals.

Music

1. **"Rags"**
(*Sing this song to one of the children's favorite tunes*)

I have a dog and his name is Rags.
(point to self)
He eats so much that his tummy sags.
(hold tummy)
His ears flip-flop and his tail wig-wags.
(flip hands by ears and wag hands at back)
And when he walks he zigs and zags.
(put hands together and zig-zag them)

Flip-flop
Wiggle-waggle
Zig-zag   (Repeat the same actions)
Flip-flop
Wiggle-waggle
Zig-zag

2. **"Six Little Pets"**
(*Sing to the tune of "Six Little Ducks,"
a traditional early childhood song*)

Six little gerbils I once knew, fat ones,
skinny ones, fair ones too. But the one
little gerbil was so much fun. He would
play until the day was done.

Six little dogs that I once knew, fat ones,
skinny ones, fair ones too. But the one
little dog with the brown curly fur, he led
the others with a grr, grr, grr.

Six little fish that I once knew, fat ones,
skinny ones, fair ones too. But the one
little fish who was the leader of the crowd,
he led the others around and around.

Six little birds that I once knew, fat ones,
skinny ones, fair ones too. But the one
little bird with the pretty little beak, he
led the others with a tweet, tweet, tweet.

Six little cats that I once knew, fat ones,
skinny ones, fair ones too. But the one
little cat who was as fluffy as a ball, he
was the prettiest one of all.

3. **"Have You Ever Seen a Rabbit?"**
(*Sing to the tune of "Have You Ever Seen
a Lassie?"*)

Have you ever seen a rabbit, a rabbit,
    a rabbit?
Have you ever seen a rabbit go hopping
    around?
Go hopping, go hopping, go hopping, go
    hopping
Have you ever seen a rabbit go hopping
    around?

Fingerplays

MY PUPPY

I like to pet my puppy.
  (pet puppy)
He has such nice soft fur.
  (pet puppy)
And if I don't pull his tail
  (pull tail)
He won't say "Grr!"
  (make face)

IF I WERE

If I were a dog
I'd have four legs to run and play.
  (down on all four hands and feet)
If I were a fish
I'd have fins to swim all day.
  (hands at side fluttering like wings)
If I were a bird
I could spread my wings out wide.
And fly all over the countryside.
  (arms out from sides fluttering like
  wings)
But I'm just me.
I have two legs, don't you see?
And I'm just as happy as can be.

THE BUNNY

Once there was a bunny
  (fist with two fingers tall)
And a green, green cabbage head.
  (fist of other hand)
"I think I'll have some breakfast," this little
  bunny said.
So he nibbled and he cocked his ears to say,
"I think it's time that I be on my way."

SAMMY

Sammy is a super snake.
  (wave finger on opposite palm)
He sleeps on the shore of a silver lake.
  (curl finger to indicate sleep)
He squirms and squiggles to snatch a snack
  (wave finger and pounce)
And snoozes and snores till his hunger is
  back.
  (curl finger on palm)

NOT SAY A SINGLE WORD

We'll hop, hop, hop like a bunny
  (make hopping motion with hand)
And run, run, run like a dog.
  (make running motion with fingers)
We'll walk, walk, walk like an elephant
  (make walking motion with arms)
And jump, jump, jump like a frog.
  (make jumping motions with arms)
We'll swim, swim, swim like a goldfish
  (make swimming motion with hand)
And fly, fly, fly like a bird.
  (make flying motion with arms)
We'll sit right down and fold our hands
  (fold hands in lap)
And not say a single word!

Science

1. **Pet Foods**

   Cut pictures of pets and pet foods and place on the science table. Include different foods such as meat, fish, carrots, lettuce, nuts, and acorns. The children can match the food to a picture of the animal that would eat each type of food.

2. **Bird Feathers**

   Bird feathers with a magnifying glass can be placed on the science table for the children to examine.

3. **Hamster and Gerbil Pet Food**

   The children can assist in preparing the pet food for hamsters or gerbils. The recipe is as follows:

   1/2 cup cracked corn
   1/2 cup flour
   1/4 cup water
   1/2 teaspoon salt

   Mix the water with flour in a bowl. Add salt. Form into balls and roll into cracked corn. Cool to harden. Serve once a day.

Source: Reynolds, Michelle. (1979). *Critter's Kitchen*. New York: Atheneum Publishing Company.

Dramatic Play

1. Pet Store

The children can all bring in their stuffed animals to set up a pet store. A counter, a cash register, and several empty pet food containers should be provided to stimulate play.

2. Veterinarian Prop Box

Collect materials for a veterinarian prop box. Include a stethoscope, empty pill bottles, fabric cut as bandages, splints, and stuffed animals.

Arts and Crafts

1. Pet Sponge Painting

Cut sponges into a variety of pet shapes. Place on the art table with paper and a shallow pan of tempera paint.

2. Doghouse

Provide an old large cardboard box for the children to make a doghouse with adult supervision. They can cut holes, paint, and decorate it. When dry, the doghouse can be moved into the dramatic play area or to the outdoor play yard.

3. Cookie Cutters and Playdough

Pet-shaped cookie cutters and playdough can be placed on the art table.

Sensory

Minnows

Fill the sensory table with cold water. Place minnows purchased from a bait store into the water. The children will attempt to catch the minnows. Teachers should stress the importance of being gentle with the fish and follow through with limits set for the activity. After participating in this activity, the children should wash their hands.

Field Trips/ Resource People

1. Pet Show

Plan a pet show. Each child who wants to show a pet should sign up for a time and day. If children can all bring in a pet the same day, have a big pet show. Award prizes for longest tail, longest ears, biggest, smallest, best groomed, loudest barker, most obedient, etc. Children who do not have a pet or cannot arrange to bring it to school can bring a stuffed toy.

2. Veterinarian

Invite a veterinarian to talk to the children about how a veterinarian helps pets and animals. Pet care can also be addressed.

3. Pet Store

Visit a pet store to observe types of pets, their toys, and other accessories. Pictures can be taken on the trip and later placed on the bulletin board of the classroom.

4. Pet Groomer

Visit a pet groomer. Observe how the pet is bathed and groomed.

Social Studies

1. Animal Sounds

Tape several animal sounds and play them back for the children to identify.

2. Feeding Chart

Design and prepare a feeding chart for the classroom pets.

3. Weekend Visitor

Let children take turns bringing class pets home on weekends. Prepare a card for each animal's cage outlining feeding and behavioral expectations.

Cooking

Animal Cookies

1 1/2 cups powdered sugar
1 cup butter or margarine
1 egg
1 teaspoon vanilla extract
1/2 teaspoon almond extract
2 1/2 cups flour
1 teaspoon baking soda
1 teaspoon cream of tartar

Mix powdered sugar, margarine, egg, and vanilla and almond extracts. Mix in flour, baking soda, and cream of tartar. Cover and refrigerate for 2 hours. Preheat oven to 375 degrees. Divide dough into halves. Roll out 1/2-inch thick on a lightly floured, cloth-covered board. Cut the dough into animal shapes with cookie cutters or let children cut. Place on lightly greased cookie sheet. Bake 7 to 10 minutes. Serve for snack.

Books

The following books can be used to complement this theme:

Baker, Karen Lee. (1997). *Seneca*. New York: Greenwillow.

Birdwell, Norman. (1992). *Clifford, the Big Red Dog*. Torrence, CA: Frank Schafer Publications.

Caseley, Judith. (1995). *Mr. Green Peas*. New York: Greenwillow.

Evans, Mark. (1993). *Fish: A Practical Guide to Caring for Your Fish*. New York: Dorling Kindersley.

Evans, Mark. (1993). *Hamster: A Practical Guide to Caring for Your Hamster*. New York: Dorling Kindersley.

Flanagan, Alice K. (1996). *Talking Birds*. San Francisco: Children's Book Press.

Gibbons, Gail. (1992). *Say Woof: The Day of a Country Veterinarian*. New York: Macmillan.

Johnson, Angela. (1993). *The Girl Who Wore Snakes*. Illus. by James Ransome. New York: Orchard Books.

Greenwood, Pamela D. (1993). *What About My Goldfish?* Illus. by Jennifer Plecas. New York: Clarion Books.

Giffith, Helen V. (1992). *"Mine Will," Said John*. Newly illus. edition by Jos. A. Smith. New York: Greenwillow.

Johnson, Angela. (1993). *Julius*. Illus. by Dav Pilkey. New York: Orchard Books.

Joose, Barbara M. (1997). *Nugget and Darling*. Illus. by Sue Truesdell. New York: Clarion Books.

King-Smith, Dick. (1995). *I Love Guinea Pigs*. Illus. by Anita Jeram. Cambridge, MA: Candlewick Press.

Kristine, Spangard. (1997). *My Pet Rabbit*. Photos by Andy King. Minneapolis: Lerner Publishing.

Nichols, Grace. (1997). *Asana and the Animals: A Book of Pet Poems*. Illus. by Sarah Adams. Cambridge, MA: Candlewick Press.

Petersen-Fleming, Judy et al. (1996). *Kitten Training and Critters, Too!* New York: Tambourine Books.

Petersen-Fleming, Judy et al. (1996). *Puppy Training and Critters, Too!* New York: Tambourine Books.

Pfeffer, Wendy. (1996). *What's It Like to Be a Fish*. Illus. by Holly Keller. New York: HarperCollins.

Reiser, Lynn W. (1992). *Any Kind of Dog*. New York: Greenwillow.

Ross, Michael Elsohn et al. (1998). *Ladybugology*. Illus. by Brian Grogan. Minneapolis: Lerner Publishing.

Rylant, Cynthia. (1993). *Everyday Pets*. Little Simon. (Board book)

Rylant, Cynthia. (1997). *Mr. Putter and Tabby Row the Boat*. Illus. by Arthur Howard. Orlando: Harcourt Brace.

Smith, Lane. (1991). *The Big Pets*. New York: Viking.

Wolf, Jake. (1996). *Daddy, Could I Have an Elephant?* Illus. by Marylin Hafner. New York: Greenwillow.

Ziefert, Harriet. (1996). *Let's Get a Pet.* Illus. by Mavis Smith. New York: Puffin Books. (Pbk)

Zolotow, Charlotte. (1995). *The Old Dog.* Revised and newly illus. by James Ransome. New York: HarperCollins.

Multimedia

The following multimedia products can be used to complement this theme:

Bourgeois, Paulette. *Franklin Wants a Pet* [cassette and book]. (1995). New York: Scholastic.

Cats [video]. (1985). National Geographic.

Dogs [video]. (1985). National Geographic.

Fish [video]. (1985). National Geographic.

Keats, Ezra Jack. *Pet Show.* [video]. (1987). Weston Woods.

Pets: See How They Grow [video]. Sony Video.

Recording and Song Title

The following recording can be used to complement this theme:

Make the Right Choice—"Love Your Pet"

THEME 49

Parts

seed, stem,
leaves, bud,
flower/fruit

Types of Plants

medicinal, flowers,
shrubs, trees,
grasses, bushes,
poisonous

Plants

Growth Sites

rainforest, garden,
greenhouse/nursery,
house, field,
forest/wood,
pond/lake

Plants We Can Eat

carrot, radish,
bean, celery,
asparagus, rhubarb,
lettuce, cabbage,
spinach, corn,
apple, berries, grape

Growth Needs

sunshine
water
soil

Theme Goals

Through participating in the experiences provided by this theme, the children may learn:

1. Types of plants.
2. Growth of plants.
3. The parts of a plant.
4. Plant growth sites.
5. Plants that provide food.

Concepts for the Children to Learn

1. Plants are living things that grow.
2. There are many kinds of plants.
3. Some plants grow from seeds.
4. Some plants grow from another plant.
5. Plants need water, sunlight, and soil to grow.
6. People and animals eat some types of plants.
7. The parts of a plant are the stem, roots, leaves, flower/fruit, and seeds.
8. There are different sizes, colors, and shapes of seeds.

Vocabulary

1. **plant**—living thing, usually green, that grows and changes.
2. **stem**—part of the plant that supports the leaves and grows upward.
3. **leaf**—part of the plant that grows on the stem.
4. **root**—part of the plant that grows into the soil.
5. **seed**—part of plant that can grow into another plant.
6. **vegetable**—a plant grown for food.
7. **fruit**—edible plant product that has seeds.
8. **flower**—a colored plant part that contains seeds.
9. **garden**—ground for growing plants.
10. **sprout**—first sign of growth.

Bulletin Board

The purpose of this bulletin board is to promote visual discrimination and numeral recognition skills. To prepare the bulletin board, construct flowerpots out of construction paper. Color each pot and draw dots on it as illustrated. Hang the pots on the bulletin board. Next, construct the same number of flowers with stems as pots. In the center of each flower, write a numeral. The children can place each flower in the flowerpot with the corresponding number of dots.

Parent Letter

Dear Parents,

Plants will be the focus of our next unit. Through the unit the children will become aware of the parts of a plant as well as discover where plants can be grown and what plants can be eaten.

AT SCHOOL

Some of the learning experiences related to plants will include:

- listening to the story *The Plant Sitter* by Gene Zion.
- sprouting alfalfa seeds to add to a salad.
- walking around our play yard to collect plants.
- playing hopscotch in the shape of a flower.

AT HOME

There are many ways to foster the concepts of this unit at home. If you have plants, let your child help water them. If you are planning to start a garden, section off a small portion for your child to grow plants.

At mealtimes, identify various parts of plants that are eaten. For example, we eat the leaves of lettuce, the stems of celery, the root of a carrot, and so on.

Plant some flower seeds with your child!

Music

1. "The Seed Cycle"
(Sing to the tune of "The Farmer in the Dell")

The farmer sows his seeds.
The farmer sows his seeds.
Hi-ho the dairy-o
The farmer sows his seeds.

Other verses:

The wind begins to blow . . .
The rain begins to fall . . .
The sun begins to shine . . .
The seeds begin to grow . . .
The plants grow big and tall . . .
The farmer cuts his corn . . .
He puts it in his barns . . .
And now the harvest is in . . .

Children can dramatize the parts for
each verse.

2. "This Is the Way We Rake the Garden"
(Sing to the tune of "Here We Go Round the Mulberry Bush")

This is the way we rake the garden,
Rake the garden, rake the garden.
This is the way we rake the garden,
So early in the morning.

Other verses:

This is the way we plant the seeds . . .
This is the way the rain comes down . . .
This is the way we hoe the weeds . . .
This is the way the garden grows . . .
This is the way we pick the vegetables . . .
This is the way we eat the vegetables . . .

3. "The Farmer in the Dell"
(traditional)

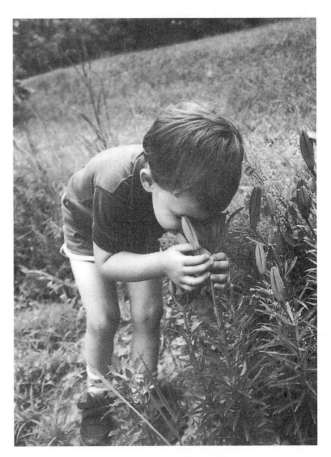

Which flower do you like best?

Fingerplays

MY GARDEN

This is my garden.
   (extend one hand forward, palm up)
I'll rake it with care
   (make raking motion on palm with other
   hand)
And then some flower seeds
   (make planting motion with thumb and
   index fingers)
I'll plant in there.
The sun will shine
   (make circle above head)
And the rain will fall
   (let fingers flutter down to lap)
And my garden will blossom
   (cup hands together, extend upward
   slowly until fingers stand straight)
And grow straight and tall.

PLANTS

Plants need care to help them grow
   (make fist with hand)
Just like boys and girls you know.
Good soil, water, sunshine bright.
Then watch them pop overnight.
   (extend fingers from fist)

Science

1. Watch Seeds Grow

Two identical plastic transparent plates and blotting paper are needed for this activity. Moisten the blotting paper. Then lay the wet paper on one of the plates. On the top of the paper plate place various seeds—corn, peas, squash, bean, etc. Place the other plate over the seeds to serve as a cover. Tie the plates together tightly. Stand the plate on its edge in a pan containing 1/2 inch water. Watch the seeds sprout and grow.

2. Colored Celery

In clear containers place several celery stalks with leaves. In each container add 3 inches of water and drop a different color of food coloring. The leaves of the celery should turn colors in a few hours. Try splitting a celery stalk in half, but do not split the stalk all the way up to the top. Put one half of the stalk in red water, and the other half in blue water. Watch what happens to the leaves.

3. Sunlight Experiment

Place seeds in two jars with a half-inch of soil. Place one jar in a dark place such as a closet or cupboard and avoid watering it. Keep the other jar in a sunny area and water it frequently. Which one grew? Why?

4. Growing Bean Plants

Each child can grow a bean plant.

5. Tasting Plants

Various fruits and vegetables grown from plants should be provided for the children to taste and smell.

6. Feely Box

In the feely box, place different parts of a plant such as root, stem, leaves, flowers, fruit, and buds. The children can feel and verbally identify the part of the plant before looking at it.

7. Root a Vegetable

Place a potato or carrot in a jar, root end down so that one-third is covered by water. A potato can be held upright by inserting toothpicks or nails at three points. This can be rested on the rim of the jar. The children can water as needed. Roots should grow out from the bottom and shoots from the top. Then plant the root in soil for an attractive plant.

8. Beans

Soak dry navy beans in a jar of water overnight. The next day compare soaked beans with dry beans. Note the difference in texture and color. Open some bean seeds that were soaked. A tiny plant should be inside the seed. These can be placed under a microscope for closer observation.

9. Budding Branches

Place a branch that has buds ready to bloom in a jar of water on the science table. Let the children observe the buds bloom. Notice that after all the stored food of the plant is used the plant will die.

Dramatic Play

1. Greenhouse

Provide materials for a greenhouse. Include window space, pots, soil, water, watering cans, seeds, plants, posters, work aprons, garden gloves, a terrarium, and seed packages to mount on sticks.

2. Jack and the Beanstalk

Act out the story *Jack and the Beanstalk*. The children can dramatize a beanstalk growing.

482

3. **Vegetable-Fruit Stand**

Display plastic fruits and vegetables. Set up a shopping area with carts, cash registers, and play money. Provide a balance scale for children to weigh the produce.

4. **Garden Planting**

Plant a small garden outdoors. Provide seeds, watering cans, garden tools, gloves, and garden hats.

Arts and Crafts

1. **Grass Hair**

Save 1/2-pint milk cartons. The children can decorate the outside of the carton like a face. Place soil in the cartons and add grass seeds. After approximately 7 days the grass will start to grow, and it will look like hair. If the grass becomes too long, have the child give it a haircut.

2. **Flower Collage**

Collect flowers and weeds. Press the flowers and weeds between paper and books. Old telephone directories can be used. Dry them for 7 to 10 days. The children can use the pressed foliage to create their own collages on paper plates or construction paper.

3. **Seed Pictures**

Supply the children with paper, paste or glue, and various kinds of seeds. Included may be grass, beans, and unpopped popcorn kernels. The children can express their own creativity through self-created designs.

4. **Nature Tree**

Cut a branch off a tree and place in a pail of plaster of paris. The children can decorate the tree with a ribbon and different forms of plant life that they have collected or made. Included may be flowers, plants, fruits, vegetables, and seeds.

5. **Leaf Rubbings**

Place a thin piece of paper over a leaf. Rub gently with the long side of a crayon.

6. **Easel Ideas**

Cut easel paper into different shapes such as:

- leaves
- flowers
- flowerpots
- fruits and vegetables

7. **Egg Carton Flowers**

Use egg cartons and pipe cleaners to make flowers. To make the flower stand up, place a pipe cleaner into the egg carton as well as a styrofoam block.

8. **Muffin Liner Flowers**

Use paper muffin tin liners to make flowers.

9. **Hand and Foot Flowers**

Create a flower by using the child's hands and feet. Trace and cut two left and right hands and one set of left and right feet. Put one set of hands together to form the top of the flower and the other set (facing down) to form the bottom side. Add a circle to the middle. Cut a stem from green paper and add the green feet, as leaves. This makes a cute Mother's Day idea. Mount on white paper.

Math

1. **Charting Growth**

The children can observe the growth of a small plant by keeping a chart of its growth. Record the date of the observation and the height. For convenience, place the chart near the plant table.

2. Flowerpot Match Game

Construct flowerpots. The number constructed will depend upon the developmental appropriateness. Write a numeral on each, beginning with the numeral one. Then make the same number of flowers, with the petals varying from one to the total number of flowerpots constructed. The children match the flowerpot to the flower with the same number of petals.

3. Counting and Classifying Seeds

Place a variety of seeds on a table. Encourage the children to count and classify them into groups. To assist in counting and classifying, an egg carton with each section given a number from 1 to 12 may be helpful. Encourage the children to observe the numeral and place a corresponding number of seeds in each section.

4. Plant Growth Seriation

Construct pictures of plants through stages of growth. Begin with a seed, followed by the seed sprouting. The third picture should be the stem erupting from the soil surface. Next a stem with leaves can be constructed. Finally, flowers can be added to the last picture. This could also be made into a bulletin board.

5. Seed Match

Collect a variety of seeds such as corn, pumpkin, orange, apple, lima bean, watermelon, pea, and peach. Cut several rectangles out of white tagboard. On the top half of each rectangle glue one of the seed types you have collected. Encourage the children to sort the seeds, matching them to those seeds glued on the individual cards.

Social Studies

1. Plant Walk

Walk around the neighborhood and try to identify as many plants as you can.

2. Play Yard Plants

Make a map of the play yard. The children can collect a part of each plant located in the playground. The plant samples can be mounted on the map.

3. Planting Trees

Plant a tree on your playground. Discuss the care needed for trees.

4. Family Tree

Make a Family Tree by mounting a bunch of branches in a pail of dirt. Each child can bring in a family picture to be placed on a leaf shape and hung on the tree branches.

Large Muscle

1. Leaf Jumping

Cut out eight large leaves from tagboard. Arrange the leaves in a pattern on the floor. Encourage the children to jump from one leaf to another. This game could also be played outdoors by drawing the leaves on the sidewalk with chalk.

2. Flower Hopscotch

Design a hopscotch in the form of a flower. Chalk can be used on a sidewalk outdoors or masking tape can be used indoors to make the form.

3. Vegetable, Vegetable, Plant

Play "Vegetable, Vegetable, Plant" as a variation of "Duck, Duck, Goose."

4. Raking and Hoeing

Provide the children with hoes and rakes to tend to the play yard.

Field Trips

1. Greenhouse

Visit a greenhouse or a tree nursery to observe the different plants and trees and inquire about their care.

2. Farm

Plan a visit to a farm. While there, observe the various forms of plant life.

3. Florist

Visit a florist. Observe the different colors, types, and sizes of flowering plants.

Group Time
(games, language)

Feltboard Fun

Construct felt pieces representing the stages of a flower's growth. Include a bulb, seed, cuttings, root, stem, leaves, and a flower. During group time, review the name and purpose of each part with the children. The children can take turns coming up to the flannel board and adding the pieces. After group time, the felt pieces should be left out so that the child can reconstruct the growth during self-selected activity period.

Cooking

1. Vegetable-Tasting Party

Prepare raw vegetables for a tasting party. Discuss the color, texture, and flavor of each vegetable.

2. Sprouts

Provide each interested child with a small jar. Fill the bottom with alfalfa seeds. Fill the jar with warm water and cover with cheesecloth and a rubberband. Each day rinse and fill the jar with fresh warm water. In three or four days the seeds will sprout. The sprouts may be used on sandwiches or salads at lunchtime.

3. Latkes (Potato Pancakes)

2 potatoes, peeled and grated
1 egg, slightly beaten
1/4 cup flour
1 teaspoon salt
cooking oil

Mix the ingredients in a bowl. Drop the mixture by tablespoons into hot oil in an electric skillet. Brown on both sides. Drain on paper towels.

4. Ground Nut Soup (Nigeria)

1 large tomato
1 large potato
1 onion
2 cups water
1 beef boullion cube
1 cup shelled, unsalted roasted peanuts
1/2 cup milk
2 tablespoons rice

Peel potato and onion. Dice potato, tomato, and onion. Place in saucepan with the water and boullion cube. Boil, covered, for 30 minutes. Chop and add the peanuts, milk, and rice to the boiling mixture. Stir. Lower heat and simmer 30 minutes. Serves 6 to 8.

Books

The following books can be used to complement this theme:

Ardley, Neil. (1991). *The Science Book of Things That Grow.* Orlando: Harcourt Brace.

Berger, Melvin. (1994). *All About Seeds.* Reprint edition. New York: Scholastic.

Charman, Andrew. (1997). *I Wonder Why Trees Have Leaves and Other Questions about Plants.* Stanwood, WA: Kingfisher.

Christensen, Bonnie. (1994). *An Edible Alphabet.* New York: Dial.

Dorros, Arthur. (1990). *Rain Forest Secrets.* New York: Scholastic.

Dunphy, Madeleine. (1994). *Here Is the Tropical Rain Forest.* Illus. by Michael Rothman. New York: Hyperion.

Fowler, Allan. (1998). *Good Mushrooms and Bad Toadstools.* Chicago: Children's Press.

Ganeri, Anita. (1995). *What's Inside Plants?* New York: Peter Bedrick Books.

Gibbons, Gail. (1991). *From Seed to Plant.* New York: Holiday House.

Guiberson, Brenda Z. (1991). *Cactus Hotel.* Illus. by Megan Lloyd. New York: Holt.

Jordan, Helene J. (1992). *How a Seed Grows.* Rev. ed. Illus. by Loretta Krupinski. New York: HarperCollins.

Luchts, Irmgard. (1995). *Red Poppy.* Translated by Frank Jacoby-Nelson. New York: Hyperion.

Maestro, Betsy. (1992). *How Do Apples Grow?* Illus. by Giulio Maestro. New York: HarperCollins.

Maestro, Betsy. (1994). *Why Do Leaves Change Color?* Illus. by Loretta Krupinski. New York: HarperCollins.

Marzollo, Jean. (1996). *It's a Seed.* Illus. by Judith Moffatt. New York: Scholastic.

Morgan, Sally. (1996). *Flowers, Trees and Fruits.* Stanwood, WA: Kingfisher.

Nielsen, Nancy J. (1992). *Carnivorous Plants.* New York: Franklin Watts.

Robbins, Ken. (1990). *A Flower Grows.* New York: Dial.

Sekido, Isamu. (1993). *Fruits, Roots, and Fungi: Plants We Eat.* Minneapolis: Lerner Publications.

Visual Dictionary of Plants. (1992). New York: Dorling Kindersley.

What's Inside? Plants. (1992). New York: Dorling Kindersley.

Yolen, Jane. (1993). *Welcome to the Green House.* Illus. by Laura Regan. New York: G. P. Putnam.

Zion, Gene. (1969). *The Plant Sitter.* Scholastic: New York.

Multimedia

The following multimedia products can be used to complement this theme:

Let's Explore the Jungle with Buzzy the Knowledge Bug [CD-ROM]. (1995). Woodinville, WA: Humongous Entertainment.

Tell Me Why Vol. 3: Flowers, Plants and Trees [video]. (1987). Marina Del Rey, CA: Tell Me Why.

Wonders of Growing Plants [video]. (1992). 3rd ed. Churchill Media/SVE.

Recordings and Song Titles

The following recordings can be used to complement this theme:

Save the Animals, Save the Earth

Science in a Nutshell—"I'm Going to Plant a Garden"

THEME 50

Puppets

Purposes
express feelings
entertainment
communication

Kinds
finger, hand,
stick, cloth,
rod, shadow,
marionette,
dummy

Stages
tables
bookcases
cardboard boxes
blankets
sheets

Types
animals
people
pretend creatures

Materials
paper/paper bags,
novelty sticks,
cloth, socks,
wooden spoons,
string, felt,
coat hangers,
pot holders,
mittens, gloves,
paper plates,
flyswatters

Movement
string
wire
rods
hands
fingers

Theme Goals

Through participating in the experiences provided by this theme, the children may learn:

1. The purpose of using puppets.
2. Kinds of puppets.
3. Types of puppets.
4. Materials used to make puppets.
5. Ways of moving puppets.
6. Types of puppet stages.

Concepts for the Children to Learn

1. Puppets can be fun.
2. Puppets can be used for communicating and entertainment.
3. We can use puppets to express feelings.
4. People talk for puppets.
5. Puppets can be made from paper, cloth, or even wood.
6. Puppets can be made to look like animals, people, or pretend creatures.
7. Puppets can be moved with hands or fingers.
8. Mittens, gloves, and paper plates can all be made into puppets.
9. Large boxes can be used for puppet stages.

Vocabulary

1. **puppet**—a toy that is moved by the hand or finger.
2. **marionette**—a puppet with strings for movement.
3. **puppet show**—a story told with puppets.
4. **puppeteer**—a person who makes a puppet move and speak.
5. **puppet stage**—a place for puppets to act.
6. **entertainment**—things we enjoy seeing and listening to.
7. **imaginary**—something that is not real.

Bulletin Board

The purpose of this bulletin board is to show a variety of puppets. The children's expressive language skills will be stimulated by interacting with the puppets. Design the bulletin board by constructing about five or six simple puppets for the children to take off the bulletin board to play with. Include a flyswatter puppet, a paper bag puppet, hand puppet, sock puppet, and a wooden spoon puppet. Hooks or pushpins can be used to attach the puppets to the bulletin board.

Parent Letter

Dear Parents,

Our new curriculum unit will focus on puppets. They are magical and motivating to young children. Sometimes a child will respond or talk to a puppet in a situation when he might not talk to an adult or another child. Through learning experiences involving puppets, the children will become aware of the different types of puppets and materials that can be used to make puppets. They will express themselves creatively and imaginatively.

AT SCHOOL

Some of the activities related to puppets include:

- creating our own puppets with a variety of materials.
- using the puppet stage throughout the week, putting on puppet shows for one and all.
- exploring various types of puppets, including finger, hand, stick, shadow, and marionette puppets.

AT HOME

The children enjoy retelling familiar stories and making up original stories for puppet characters. To stimulate this type of play, you and your child can make simple puppets at home with objects found around the house.

Paper Bag Puppets—Using small paper lunch bags, children can use crayons or markers to create a puppet. The fold in the bag can be used as the mouth. After the child's hand is in the bag, the puppet can talk. Yarn scraps can easily be glued on for hair and construction paper scraps can add a decorative touch.

Sock Puppets—I'm sure you have a couple of socks around the house that seem to have lost their mates. (Does your dryer eat socks, too?) Depending on your child's skills and how much supervision you can provide, you can sew or glue on the eyes, a nose, and hair made from a variety of materials (yarn, buttons, fabric). Insert your hand and your puppet is ready!

Stick Puppets—Make story characters' faces or bodies on heavy paper or on cardboard with crayons, markers, or paint. Cut the figures out and attach them with strong glue or tape to a ruler, popsicle stick, tongue depressor, or any stick that can be used to hold the puppet and move it. A large box or table can serve as the puppet stage.

Enjoy your child!

490

Young children become engrossed in puppet shows.

Music

"Eensy Weensy Spider"
(traditional)

Fingerplays

CATERPILLAR CRAWLING

One little caterpillar crawled on my shoe.
Another came along and then there were
    two.
Two little caterpillars crawled on my knee.
Another came along and then there were
    three.
Three little caterpillars crawled on the
    floor.
Another came along and then there were
    four.
Four little caterpillars, watch them crawl
    away.
They'll all turn into butterflies some fine
    day.

This fingerplay can be told using puppets
made from felt or tagboard.

Source: Indenbaum, Valerie, & Shapior, Marcia. (1983).
The Everything Book. Chicago: Partner Press.

SPECKLED FROGS

Five green-speckled frogs
Sitting on a speckled log
Eating the most delicious bugs,
Yum, yum!
    (rub tummy)

One jumped into the pool
Where it was nice and cool
Now there are four green-speckled frogs.

Repeat until there are no green-speckled
frogs.

This fingerplay can be told using puppets
made from felt or tagboard.

CHICKADEES

Five little chickadees sitting in a door
    (hold up hand)
One flew away and then there were four
    (put down one finger at a time)
Four little chickadees sitting in a tree
One flew away and then there were three.
Three little chickadees looking at you.
One flew away and then there were two.
Two little chickadees sitting in the sun.
One flew away and then there was one.
One little chickadee sitting all alone.
He flew away and then there were none.

This fingerplay can be told using puppets
made from felt or tagboard.

Science

1. Classify Puppets

During group time let the children classify the various puppets into special categories such as animals, people, insects, imaginary things, etc.

2. Button Box

A large box of buttons should be provided. The children can sort the buttons according to color, size, or shape into a muffin tin or egg carton.

Dramatic Play

1. Puppet Show

A puppet stage should be available throughout the entire unit in the dramatic play area. Change or add the puppets on a regular basis using as many different kinds of puppets as possible.

2. Puppet Shop

A variety of materials should be provided for the children to construct puppets. Include items such as buttons, bows, felt, paper bags, cloth pieces, socks, tongue depressors, etc.

Arts and Crafts

1. Making Puppets

Puppets can be made from almost any material. Some suggestions are listed here:

- cotton covered with cloth attached to a tongue depressor.
- paper sacks stuffed with newspaper.
- a cork for a head with a hole in it for a finger.
- socks.
- cardboard colored with crayon attached to a tongue depressor.

- flyswatter.
- oatmeal box attached to a dowel.
- nylon panty hose stretched over a hanger bent into an oval shape.
- empty toilet paper and paper towel rolls.

2. Puppet Stages

Puppet stages can be made from the following materials:

- boxes, including tempera paint and markers for decorating.
- large paper bags.
- half-gallon milk carton.
- towel draped over an arm.
- towel draped over the back of a chair.
- blanket covering a card table.

Sensory

Sensory Table

During this unit add to the sensory table all of the various materials that puppets are made of:

- string
- buttons
- felt
- toilet paper rolls
- cardboard
- paper
- sticks
- wood shavings

Large Muscle

1. Creative Movement

Demonstrate how to manipulate a marionette. Then have the children pretend that they are marionettes and that they have strings attached to their arms and legs. Say, "Someone is pulling up the string that is attached to your arm; what would

492

happen to your arm?" Allow the children to make that movement. Continue with other movements.

2. Large Puppets

Large puppets such as stick or rod puppets can provide the children with a lot of large muscle movement.

3. Pin the Nose on the Puppet

This game is a variation of the traditional "Pin the Tail on the Donkey." (This game would be more appropriate for five-, six-, seven-, and eight-year-old children.)

Field Trips/ Resource People

1. Puppet Show

Place puppets by the puppet stage to encourage the children to put on puppet shows.

2. Puppeteer

Invite a puppeteer to visit the classroom and show the children the many uses of puppets.

Math

1. Examine a Puppet

With the children, examine a puppet and count all of its various parts. Count its eyes, legs, arms, stripes on its shirt, etc. Discuss how it was constructed.

2. Puppet Dot-to-Dot

Draw a large puppet on a sheet of tagboard. Laminate or cover the tagboard sheet with clear adhesive paper. A grease pencil or felt-tip watercolor marker should be provided for the children to draw. Also, felt scraps should be available to remove grease markings. Otherwise, a damp cloth or paper towel should be available.

Social Studies

Occupation Puppets

Introduce various types of occupation puppets. Ask the children to describe each.

Group Time (games, language)

Puppet Show

Using your favorite classroom stories, put on a puppet show. The children can volunteer to be the various characters. Pre-tape the story so that the children can listen to it while they practice. This might be a good activity to invite parents to attend.

Cooking

1. Puppet Faces

Make open-faced sandwiches using peanut butter or cream cheese spread onto a slice of bread or a bun. Carrot curls can be used to represent hair. Raisins and green or purple grape halves can be used for the eyes, nose, and mouth.

2. Dog Puppet Salad

Place a pear half onto the plate. Two apple slices can be added to resemble a dog's ears hanging down. Then raisins or grape halves can be used to represent the eyes and nose of a dog.

Books

The following books can be used to complement this theme:

Babbitt, Natalie. (1989). *Nellie: A Cat on Her Own.* New York: Farrar, Straus & Giroux.

Bulloch, Ivan. (1997). *I Want to Be a Puppeteer.* Illus. by Diane James. Chicago, IL: World Book.

Collodi, Carlo. (1996). *Pinocchio.* Illus. by Ed Young. New York: Philomel Books.

Hoyt-Goldsmith, Diane. (1991). *Pueblo Storyteller.* Illus. by Lawrence Migdale. New York: Holiday House.

Jean Claverie's Fairy Tale Theater: Pop-Up Book with Puppets. (1996). Illus. by Jean Claverie. Hauppauge, NY: Barron's Educational series.

Keats, Ezra Jack. (1983). *Louie.* New York: William Morrow.

Little Red Riding Hood. (1997). Illus. by Peter Stevenson. St. Paul, MN: Cartwheel Books. (Finger Puppet Theater)

Wallis, Mary. (1994). *I Can Make Puppets.* Buffalo, NY: Firefly Books.

Weiss, George David and Bob Thiele. (1994). *What a Wonderful World.* Illus. by Ashley Bryan. New York: Simon & Schuster.

Multimedia

The following multimedia products can be used to complement this theme:

Adventures of Pinocchio [video]. (1994). Charlotte, NC: United American Video (UAV Corp.).

Introduction to Puppet Making [video]. (1996). Jim Gamble Puppet Productions. Available from Library Video.

Johnson, Laura. "Puppet Pals" on *Homemade Games and Activities: Make Your Own Rhythm Band!* [cassette]. (1987). Long Branch, NJ: Kimbo Educational.

T H E M E 51

Purple

Foods
grapes
eggplant
cabbage

Flowers
violet
iris
lilac

Shades
lavender (pale purple)
violet (bluish purple)

Color Mixing
red + blue = purple
purple + white = lavender

Theme Goals

Through participating in the experiences provided by this theme, the children may learn:

1. How the color purple is made.
2. Shades of purple.
3. Purple flowers.
4. Foods that are purple.

Concepts for the Children to Learn

1. Purple is the name of a color.
2. Mixing red with blue makes purple.
3. There are light and dark shades of purple.
4. Many objects are purple in color.
5. Grapes, eggplant, and cabbage are foods that are purple in color.
6. Some flowers are purple.
7. Purple is thought of as a royal color because many emperors and kings wore purple.

Vocabulary

1. **purple**—a color created by mixing red and blue together.
2. **tint**—variety of a color produced by mixing it with white.
3. **shade**—lightness or darkness of color.

Bulletin Board

The purpose of this bulletin board is to promote name recognition and call attention to the printed word. This bulletin board can also be used to check attendance. Trace and cut a crayon for each child in the class from purple tagboard. Then print each child's name on a crayon. Laminate and cut out the crayon pieces. Use a paper punch to cut a hole in the top of each crayon. Hang pushpins on the bulletin board for the children to hang their crayons.

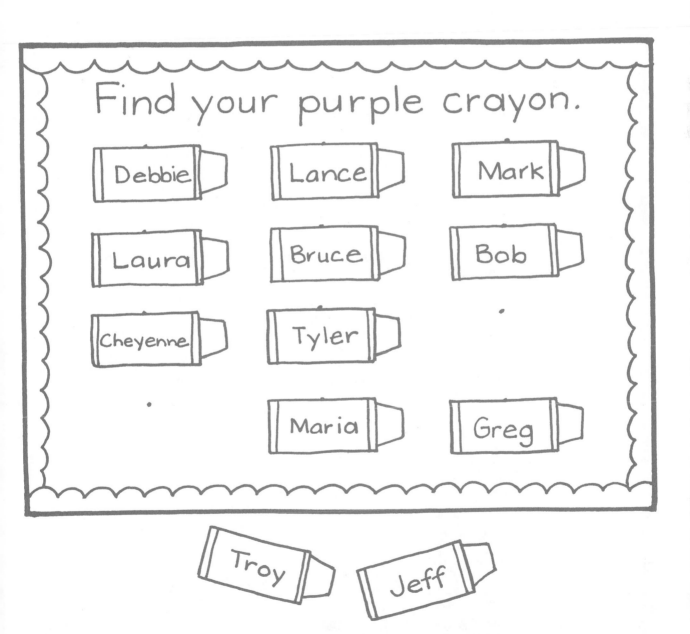

Parent Letter

Dear Parents,

What color is made when blue is mixed with red? The popular color PURPLE! This week at school we will explore aspects of the royal color purple. The children will learn how purple is made and find out about items that are purple in color.

AT SCHOOL

A few of this week's learning experiences include:

- creating designs and drawings in the art area with purple crayons, paints, markers, yarn, tissue paper, pom-poms, and glitter.
- listening to the story *Harold and the Purple Crayon* by Crockett Johnson. Afterwards, we will each make a page to create a classroom purple crayon book. Look for it in the book area by the end of the week!
- looking at various items that are purple. Could you help your child find an object that is purple and bring it to school on Wednesday? Thank you for your help!

AT HOME

The theme of purple can be explored at home as well. Feel free to try the following purple activities:

- preparing purple foods with your child for meals or snacks such as grapes, purple cabbage, gelatin, grape juice, or jelly.
- making grape popsicles by freezing grape juice or Kool-Aid.
- creating a purple collage by cutting out purple pictures and letters from magazines. Glue pictures on a purple sheet of construction paper.

Have a good week!

498

Music

1. **"A Lilac, a Lilac"**
   (Sing to the tune of "A Tisket, a Tasket")

   A lilac, a lilac, a pretty purple lilac.
   There's a lilac bush on the way to school.
   And on the way I picked some,
   I picked some, I picked some.
   And on the way I picked some.
   There's a lilac bush on the way to school.
   And on the way I picked some.

2. **"Purple Things"**
   (Sing to the tune of "Mary Had a Little Lamb")

   Many things are colored purple,
   Colored purple, colored purple.
   Many things are colored purple,
   Can you think of some?

3. **"Here's a Grape"**
   (Sing to the tune of "Hot Cross Buns")

   Here's a grape,
   A purple grape.
   What a yummy little fruit,
   A purple grape.

Children love painting with the color purple.

Fingerplays

PURPLE LOLLIPOP

Here is a purple, sweet lollipop.
   (make fist pretending to hold a stick
   of lollipop)
I bought it today at a candy shop.
One lick, mmm, it tastes so good.
   (pretend to lick)
Two licks, oh, I knew it would.
Three licks, yes, I like the taste.
Four licks, now I will not waste.
Five licks, keep on and on.
Six licks, oh! It's nearly gone!
Seven licks, it's getting small.
Eight licks and still not all.
Nine licks, my tongue goes fast.
Ten licks and that's the last!

ONE GRAPE AND ONE GRAPE

One grape and one grape, that makes two.
   (hold up two fingers)
But you have three friends, now what do
   you do?
   (shrug shoulders and hold hands up)
Go to the store and buy a few more.
Then you'll have a whole bunch.
   (hold out arms to create circle shapes)
They're great with your lunch!

Sensory

1. **Purple Water**

   Add red and blue food coloring to three
   inches of water in the sensory table. Add
   water toys (look for purple ones!) as tools
   to explore the properties of water.

2. **Purple Shaving Cream**

Spray the contents of one or two cans of shaving cream in a sensory table. Color the shaving cream purple by mixing in drops of red and blue food coloring.

3. **Purple Goop**

In a sensory table or dishpan, combine two cups of cornstarch, two cups of water, and red and blue food coloring.

Social Studies

Occupation: Painter

Invite a local wall painter to come to the classroom and talk about his or her job. If possible, perhaps painting tools and supplies could be shown and demonstrated.

Large Muscle

Purple Shape March

Using purple construction paper, cut large geometric shapes and tape them to the floor. Play music as the children walk, march, hop, etc., across the shapes.

Math

1. **Purple Chain**

Provide 8" × 1 1/2" strips of purple, lilac, and white construction paper. If necessary, demonstrate to children how to create a paper chain using tape or glue to fasten strips. Encourage children to create a pattern with the colored strips. Display chains in the classroom.

2. **Shades of Purple Sort**

Collect purple paint color strips from a hardware, paint, or building supply store. Have children assist in cutting the color strips apart. The paint chips can be used for sorting activities (light purple, dark purple, etc.) or for counting activities.

Science

1. **Purple Bubble Prints**

In a small plastic bowl or cup, mix one tablespoon purple liquid tempera paint with two tablespoons liquid dishwashing detergent and gently stir in a small amount of water. One child at a time can put a straw in the paint mixture and blow until bubbles rise above the rim of the bowl or cup. Remove straw and lay a piece of white paper on top of the bubbles. As the bubbles pop, they will leave prints on the paper. Supervise activity closely.

2. **Purple Carnation**

Insert a white carnation into a clear glass or vase of water. To the water, add drops of red and blue food coloring to create a dark purple. In a few days, the children should be able to observe the petals of the flower turning purple.

3. **Purple Glasses**

Help the children view the world through purple-tinted eyeglasses. For each child, cut frame shapes out of tagboard. Assist the children in gluing purple cellophane squares over the eye holes. Attach pipe cleaners to the sides of the frames and bend them to fit over the children's ears.

4. **Making Raisins**

Purchase one or two pounds of purple grapes. Wash them thoroughly. Spread grapes in a single layer on baking sheets. Dry by placing in a sunny windowsill for several days or bake in a slow oven.

Dramatic Play

Flower Shop

Collect artificial flowers, focusing on the color purple if possible, to create a flower shop in the dramatic play area. Additional props for the area could include vases,

500

flower pots, small garden tools, sheets of tissue paper, pictures and posters of flowers, and a cash register. Books on flowers and mail order catalogs or bulbs and flowers can also be displayed.

Arts and Crafts

1. **Marble Painting**

   For each child, place a 9" × 12" piece of white construction paper in a dishpan. Squeeze a few teaspoons of purple liquid tempera paint onto the paper. Place two or three marbles on the paper. Designs are created by holding the pan and tilting it back and forth, allowing the marbles to slide through the paint.

2. **Grape Prints**

   Wrap a piece of masking tape around three toilet paper tubes to create a stamp to make designs of grapes. The children can then dip the end of the stamp into a shallow tray of purple paint, then press it down on white construction paper to print bunches of grapes. After paint is dry, crayons or markers can be used to add stems or leaves.

3. **Purple Glitter Dough**

   Make purple playdough using your favorite recipe (or combine 1 cup flour, 1/2 cup of salt, 1 cup of water, 1 tablespoon of vegetable oil, 2 teaspoons cream of tartar, and red and blue food coloring). Cook for three minutes, stirring frequently until the mixture thickens and pulls away from the pan. Cool playdough. Give each child a lump of playdough and sprinkle a small amount of purple glitter on the tabletop. The children can work the glitter into the dough. **Caution:** Supervision is required with glitter activities.

4. **Wacky Watercolors**

   Combine 1 1/2 tablespoons corn syrup and 3 tablespoons cornstarch. Add 3 tablespoons baking soda and 3 tablespoons vinegar. Mix and watch it foam! Add food coloring of choice (red and blue to make purple). Pour mixture into shallow paint cups and allow to dry for two days. Use watercolors to create designs on paper.

5. **Purple Playdough Grapes**

   Make a batch of red playdough and a batch of blue playdough using your favorite playdough recipe. Give each child a small lump of the two playdough colors. The children can squeeze the lumps together to create purple. Then, small balls of playdough can be rolled to represent grapes. Allow to dry if desired.

Field Trips/ Resource People

1. **Art or Paint Store**

   Visit an art supply or paint store. Observe the many shades of purple paints and papers.

2. **Flower and Garden Shop**

   Make arrangements to tour a greenhouse or flower shop. Take note of the varieties of purple-colored flowers and plant leaves.

Group Time
(games, language)

1. **Game: "I Spy"**

   Have the children glance around the room. Begin game by saying, "I spy with my little eye something *purple*." Have the children try to guess what the object is. When a player guesses correctly, he or she has the next turn.

2. **Purple Color Bag or Box**

   Use purple fabric to make a drawstring bag for "Purple Day" or cover a box and lid with purple wrapping paper. Fill the bag or box with small purple items. At circle time, each child in turn can describe an item from the bag or box for others to identify. Repeat the activity throughout the week.

3. Purple Shapes "Hokey Pokey"

Cut a set of geometric shapes from purple construction paper for each child to use for this game. Game is played in circle formation.

"Purple Hokey Pokey"
(Sing to the tune of "Hokey Pokey")

Put your purple (shape name) in,
Put your purple (shape name) out,
Put your purple (shape name) in,
And shake it all about.

Do the hokey pokey,
And turn yourself around.
That's what it's all about.

Cooking

1. Purple Pops

    1 3-ounce package grape-flavored gelatin
    1 cup boiling water
    1 6-ounce can frozen grape juice concentrate
    3 cups water
    15 3-ounce paper cups
    15 wooden sticks

In a medium bowl, dissolve gelatin in boiling water. Add frozen juice concentrate and stir until melted. Add water and stir. Pour about 1/3 cup of juice mixture into each paper cup. Cover each cup with foil. Insert a stick through the foil into the juice mixture. Freeze overnight or until firm. To serve, peel paper cups off pops.

2. Purple Popcorn

    10 cups popped popcorn (remove all
        unpopped kernels)
    1 cup butter or margarine
    3/4 cups sugar
    1 3-ounce package grape-flavored gelatin
    3 tablespoons water
    1 tablespoon light corn syrup

Place the popcorn in a greased 17×12×2-inch baking dish. Keep popcorn warm in a 300-degree oven while making syrup mixture. In a heavy 2-quart saucepan, combine butter, sugar, gelatin, water, and corn syrup. Cook mixture over medium heat until it boils, stirring constantly. Clip a candy thermometer to the side of the pan. Continue cooking over medium heat, stirring constantly, until the thermometer reaches 255 degrees (hard-ball stage).

Pour syrup mixture over popcorn and stir gently to coat popcorn. Bake in a 300-degree oven for 5 minutes. Stir once and bake 5 minutes longer. Place popcorn mixture onto a large piece of foil. Cool completely. Break popcorn mixture into clusters. Store in an airtight container. Serves 14–16 children.

3. Purple Pudding

Spoon vanilla pudding into small paper cups. Add a few drops of red and blue food coloring to each cup. Children can stir their pudding with spoons to observe what happens.

4. Purple Cow

Pour one quart of milk into a blender. Add one six-ounce can of frozen grape juice concentrate. Blend until ingredients are well mixed. Pour into cups and serve. Serves six.

5. Purple Coleslaw

    6 cups shredded purple cabbage
    1 cup sliced purple grapes
    1 cup mayonnaise
    3 tablespoons lemon juice
    2 tablespoons sugar
    1 teaspoon salt

Combine mayonnaise, lemon juice, sugar, and salt. Stir in cabbage and grapes. Cover and chill until ready to eat.

Books

The following books can be used to complement this theme:

Atwood, Margaret. (1995). *Princess Prunella and the Purple Peanut.* Illus. by Maryann Kowalski. New York: Workman Publishing.

Henkes, Kevin. (1996). *Lilly's Purple Plastic Purse.* New York: Greenwillow.

Hest, Amy. (1986). *The Purple Coat.* Illus. by Amy Schwartz. New York: Four Winds Press.

Johnson, Crockett. (1987). *Harold and the Purple Crayon.* New York: Harper-Collins.

Mayer, Mercer. (1996). *Purple Pickle Juice.* New York: Random House.

Munsch, Robert N. (1992). *Purple, Green, and Yellow.* Illus. by Helene Desputeaux. Willowdale, ON: Annick Press.

Pearson, Tracey Campbell. (1997). *The Purple Hat.* New York: Farrar, Straus & Giroux.

Prelutsky, Jack. (1986). *Ride a Purple Pelican.* New York: William Morrow.

THEME 52

Rain

Measurement
gauge

Effects
rainbow
puddles
mud
floods
droughts
acid rain/pollution

Uses
WATERING
plants
crops
grass

FILLING
creeks
lakes
rivers
ocean

DRINKING
AND BATHING
people
animals

Clothing
rainhat
raincoat
rain shoes
umbrella

Forms
drizzle,
downpour,
shower,
sprinkle,
snow, dew, hail

Comes from
clouds

Theme Goals

Through participating in the experiences provided by this theme, the children may learn:

1. Uses of rain.
2. Effects of rain.
3. Clothing worn for protection from the rain.
4. Forms of rain.
5. Origin of rain.
6. The tool used for the measurement of rain.

Concepts for the Children to Learn

1. Rain falls as a liquid from the clouds.
2. Rain can fall in the form of drizzle, hail, snow, or a shower.
3. Rain can be used for watering lawns and filling lakes.
4. A rainbow sometimes appears when it rains while the sun is shining.
5. A rainbow is colorful.
6. An umbrella is used in the rain to keep us dry.
7. Raincoats, hats, and rubber shoes are rain clothing.
8. Puddles can form during a rainfall.
9. The amount of rain can be measured in a water gauge.
10. Farmers need rain to water the crops.

Vocabulary

1. **rain**—water that falls from the clouds.
2. **rainbow**—a colorful arc formed when the sun shines while it is raining.
3. **puddle**—rain collection on the ground.
4. **umbrella**—a shade for protection against rain.
5. **snow**—frozen rain.
6. **gauge**—a tool for measuring rain.

Bulletin Board

The purpose of this bulletin board is to develop an awareness of sets, as well as to identify written numerals. Construct clouds out of gray tagboard. Write a numeral on each cloud. Cut out and laminate. Next, trace and cut cloud shadows from construction paper. Attach the shadows to the bulletin board. A set of raindrops, from one to 10, should be attached underneath each cloud shadow. Magnet pieces or pushpins and holes in the cloud piece can be used for the children to match each cloud to a corresponding shadow, using the raindrops as a clue.

Parent Letter

Dear Parents,

"Rain, rain, go away. Come again some other day," is a familiar nursery rhyme. It is one that we may often hear as a unit on rain begins. Through the experiences provided, the children will become aware of the uses and forms of rain as well as how rainbows are created.

AT SCHOOL

The following activities are just a few that have been planned for the rain unit:

- a visit by TV 8's weatherman. Tom Hector will be coming at 2:00 p.m. on Tuesday to show us a video made for preschoolers that depicts various weather conditions.
- finding out about evaporation by setting out a shallow pan of water and marking the water level each day.
- creating a rainbow on a sunny day outdoors with a garden hose.

AT HOME

To develop language skills practice this rain poem with your child:

> Rain on the green grass
> And rain on trees.
> Rain on the rooftops,
> But not on me!!

Use an empty can or jar to make a rain gauge. Place the container outdoors to measure rainfall. Several gauges could be placed in various places in your yard.

Enjoy your child!

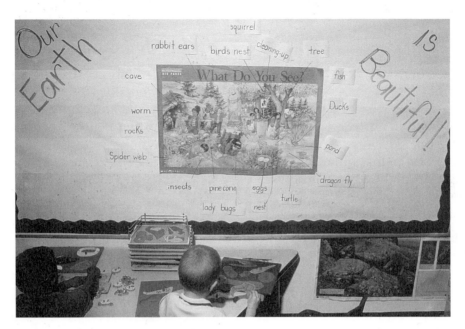

Rain serves many purposes.

Music

"Rainy"
(Sing to the tune of "Bingo")

There was a day when we got wet
and rainy was the weather
R-A-I-N-Y, R-A-I-N-Y, R-A-I-N-Y
and rainy was the weather.

Repeat each verse eliminating a letter and
substituting it with a clap until the last
chorus is all claps to the same beat.

Fingerplays

LITTLE RAINDROP

This is the sun, high up in the sky.
   (hold hands in circle above head)
A dark cloud suddenly comes sailing by.
   (slide hands to side)
These are the raindrops,
   (make raining motion with fingers)
Pitter patter down,
Watering the flowers,
   (pouring motion)
Growing on the ground.
   (hands pat the ground)

RAINY DAY FUN

Slip on your raincoat.
   (pretend to put coat on)
Pull up your galoshes.
   (pull up galoshes)
Wade in puddles,
Make splishes and sploshes.
   (make stomping motions)

THUNDERSTORM

Boom, bang, boom, bang!
   (clap hands)
Rumpety, lumpety, bump!
   (stomp feet)
Zoom, zam, zoom, zam!
   (swish hands together)
Rustles and bustles
   (pat thighs)
And swishes and zings!
   (pat thighs)
What wonderful noises
A thunderstorm brings.

RAIN

From big black clouds
    (hold up arms)
The raindrop fell.
    (pull finger down in air)
Drip, drip, drip one day,
    (hit one finger on palm of hand)
Until the bright sunlight changed them
Into a rainbow gay!
    (make a rainbow with hands)

Source of first four fingerplays: Wilmes, Dick & Liz. *Everyday Circle Times*. Building Block Publications.

THE RAIN

I sit before the window now
    (seat yourself, if possible)
And I look out at the rain.
    (shade your eyes and look around)
It means no play outside today
    (shake head, shrug)
So inside I remain.
    (rest chin on fist, look sorrowful)
I watch the water dribble down
    (follow up-to-down movements with eyes)
And turn the brown grass green.
    (sit up, take notice)
And after a while I start to smile
At Nature's washing machine.
    (smile, lean back, relax)

Source: Cromwell, Hibner, & Faitel. *Finger Frolics—Finger Plays for Young Children*.

Science

1. **Tasting Water**

   Collect tap water, soda water, mineral water, and distilled water. Pour the different types of water into paper cups and let children taste them. Discuss the differences.

2. **Evaporation**

   The children can pour water into a jar. Mark a line at the water level. Place the jar on a window ledge and check it every day. The disappearance is called evaporation.

3. **Catching Water**

   If it rains one day during your unit, place a bucket outside to catch the rain. Return the bucket to your science table. Place a bucket of tap water next to the rainwater and compare.

4. **Color Mixing**

   Using water and food coloring or tempera, mix the primary colors. Discuss the colors of the rainbow.

Dramatic Play

1. **Rainy Day Clothing**

   Umbrellas, raincoats, hats, rain shoes, and a tape containing rain sounds should be added to the dramatic play area. **Caution:** Be careful when selecting umbrellas for this activity. Some open quickly and can be dangerous.

2. **Weather Station**

   A map, pointer, adult clothing, and pretend microphone should be placed in the dramatic play area. The children can play weather person. Pictures depicting different weather conditions can be included.

Arts and Crafts

1. **Eyedropper Painting**

   Use eyedroppers filled with colored water as applicators.

2. **Waxed Paper Rainbows**

   Cut waxed paper in the shape of large rainbows. Then prepare red, yellow, green, and blue crayon shavings. After this, the children can sprinkle the crayon shavings on one sheet of waxed paper. Place another sheet of waxed paper on the top of the sheet with sprinkled crayon. Finally, the teacher should place a linen towel over the top of the waxed paper sheets. A warm iron should be applied to melt the two pieces together. Cool and attach a string. Hang from the window. **Caution:** This activity needs constant adult supervision.

3. **Rainbow Yarn Collage**

Using rainbow-shaped paper and rainbow-colored yarn, the children can make rainbow yarn collages.

4. **Thunder Painting**

Tape record a rain or thunderstorm. Leave this tape with a tape recorder and earphones at the easel. Grey, black, and white paint can be provided. Let the children listen to the rainstorm and paint to it. Ask the children how the music makes them feel.

5. **Rainbow Mobiles**

Pre-cut rainbow arcs. On these, the children can paste styrofoam packing pieces. After this, they can paint the pieces. Display the mobiles in the room.

Sensory

Add to the sensory table:

⊚ water with scoops, cups, and spoons.
⊚ sand and water (make puddles in the sand).
⊚ rainbow-colored sand, rice, and pasta.
⊚ rainwater

Large Muscle

Worm Wiggle

The purpose of this game is to imitate worm motions. Show the children how to lie on their stomachs, holding their arms in at their sides. The children should try to move forward without using their hands or elbows like a worm would wiggle.

Field Trips/ Resource People

1. **Reflection**

Take a walk after it rains. Enjoy the puddles, overflowing gutters, and swirls of water caught by sewers. Look in the puddles. Does anyone see a reflection? Look up in the sky. Do you see any clouds, the sun, or a rainbow? What colors are in a rainbow?

2. **The Weather Person**

Take a field trip to a television station and see what equipment a weather person uses.

Math

Rainbow Match

Fabrics of all the colors of the rainbow can be cut into pieces. The children can sort these and group them into different colors, textures, and sizes.

Group Time
(games, language)

1. **Creative Thinking**

Read this poem to your children and then ask them, "Why didn't I get wet?" You may have to read the poem again or you may have to encourage the children to use their imagination since the answer is not in the poem.

RAIN

Rain on green grass
and rain on the tree.
Rain on the rooftop,
But not on me!

Source: Wilmes, Liz & Dick. *Everyday Circle Times.* Building Block Publications.

2. Jump in Puddles

This game is played like "Musical Chairs." The puddles are made from circles on the floor with one child in each and one less circle than children so one child is out of the circles. On the signal, "Jump in the puddles," the children have to switch puddles. The child who was out has a chance to get in a puddle. The child who does not get into a puddle waits until the next round. This can be played indoors or outdoors. Hula hoops could also be used in small groups of four children using three hoops. (This activity is most appropriate for older children.)

Miscellaneous

1. Cut and Tell Story: "The Rainbow's End"

Source: Warren, Jean. *Cut and Tell Scissor Stories for Spring.* Everett, WA: Totline Press, Warren Publishing House.

2. Flannel Board Stories

Source: Stangl, Jean. *Flannel Graphs—Flannel Board Fun for Little Ones.* Belmont, CA: David S. Lake Publishers.

Cooking

Rainbow Fruits

Serve a different colored snack each day to correspond with the colors of the rainbow.

- strawberries
- oranges
- lemon finger gelatin (see a gelatin box for recipe)
- blueberries added to yogurt
- grape juice
- grapes or blackberries
- lettuce salad

Books

The following books can be used to complement this theme:

Baxter, Nicola. (1998). *Rain, Wind, and Storm.* Austin, TX: Raintree/Steck Vaughn.

Beecham, Caroline. (1996). *Rainbow.* New York: Random House.

Bogacki, Tomek. (1997). *Cat and Mouse in the Rain.* New York: Farrar, Straus & Giroux.

Branley, Franklyn M. (1997). *Down Comes the Rain.* New York: HarperCollins.

Buchanan, Ken and Debby Buchanan. (1994). *It Rained in the Desert Today.* Illus. by Libba Tracey. Flagstaff, AZ: Northland.

Calhoun, Mary. (1997). *Flood.* Illus. by Erick Ingraham. New York: William Morrow.

Canizares, Susan and Betsey Chessen. (1997). *Storms.* New York: Scholastic.

Carlstrom, Nancy White. (1993). *What Does the Rain Play?* New York: Macmillan.

Davies, Kay and Wendy Oldfield. (1995). *Rain.* Photos by Robert Pickett. Austin, TX: Raintree/Steck Vaughn.

Deming, Alhambra G. (1994). *Who Is Tapping at My Window?* Illus. by Monica Wellington. New York: Penguin.

Godfrey, Jan. (1994). *Why Is It Raining?* Illus. by D'Reen Neeves. Minneapolis: Augsburg Fortress Pub.

Hest, Amy. (1995). *In the Rain with Baby Duck.* Illus. by Jill Barton. Cambridge, MA: Candlewick Press.

Johnson, Angela. (1994). *Rain Feet.* Illus. by Rhonda Mitchell. New York: Orchard Books. (Board book)

Kuskin, Karla. (1995). *James and the Rain.* Illus. by Reg Cartwright. New York: Simon & Schuster.

Laser, Michael. (1997). *The Rain.* Illus. by Jeffrey Green. New York: Simon & Schuster.

Llewellyn, Claire and Anthony Lewis. (1995). *Wind and Rain.* Hauppauge, NY: Barron's Educational series.

London, Jonathan. (1997). *Puddles.* Illus. by G. Brian Karas. New York: Viking.

Lynn, Sara and Diane James. (1998). *Rain and Shine.* Illus. by Joe Wright. Chicago: World Book.

Markle, Sandra. (1993). *A Rainy Day.* Illus. by Cathy Johnson. New York: Orchard Books.

May, Garelick. (1997). *Where Does the Butterfly Go When It Rains?* Illus. by Nicholas Wilton. Greenvale, NY: Mondo Publications.

McPhail, David M. (1998). *The Puddle.* New York: Farrar, Straus & Giroux.

Merk, Ann and Jim Merk. (1994). *Rain, Snow and Ice.* Vero Beach, FL: Rourke Corp.

Nikola-Lisa, W. (1993). *Storm.* Illus. by Michael Hays. Colchester, CT: Atheneum.

Ray, Mary Lyn. (1996). *Mud.* Illus. by Lauren Stringer. New York: Harcourt Brace.

Reay, Joanne. (1995). *Bumpa Rumpus and the Rainy Day.* Illus. by Adriano Gon. Boston: Houghton Mifflin.

Shannon, George. (1995). *April Showers.* Illus. by Jose Aruego and Ariane Dewey. New York: Greenwillow.

Simon, Norma. (1995). *Wet World.* Illus. by Alexi Natchev. Cambridge, MA: Candlewick Press.

Stallone, Linda. (1992). *The Flood That Came to Grandma's House.* Illus. by Joan Schooley. Dallas, PA: Upshur Press.

Stevenson, James. (1997). *Heat Wave at Mud Flat.* New York: Greenwillow.

Multimedia

The following multimedia products can be used to complement this theme:

"Clean Rain" on *Evergreen Everblue* [compact disc]. (1990). Shoreline Records.

Cleaver, Mary. "Rain Is Falling Down" and "The Incey Wincey Spider" on *Songs and Fingerplays for Little Ones* [video]. (1993). Cleaver Productions.

"On a Rainy Day" on *A Rainbow of Songs* [cassette]. Kimbo Educational.

"Why Does It Rain" on *Our Earth* [CD-ROM]. (1992). Washington, DC: National Geographic.

Recordings and Song Titles

The following recordings can be used to complement this theme:

Authentic Indian Dances and Folklore—"Rain Dance"

Piggyback Songs—"Rain Song"

Where Is Thumbkin?—"Raindrop Song"

A Rainbow of Songs—"On a Rainy Day"

Songs about Native Americans—"Sun and Rain"

Rock 'n' Roll Songs That Teach (The Learning Station)—"Singing in the Rain"

THEME 53

Food

apples
strawberries
tomatoes
beets
radishes

Flowers

roses
tulips
carnations

Red

Signs

stop/danger
exit
traffic light
hot

Color Mixing

red + yellow = orange
red + blue = purple
red + white = pink

Theme Goals

Through participating in the experiences provided by this theme, the children may learn:

1. Red is a color.
2. Some foods are red.
3. Many objects are red.
4. Red can be mixed with other colors to make different colors.

Concepts for the Children to Learn

1. Red is a primary color.
2. Some foods, such as tomatoes and strawberries, are red.
3. Red and yellow mixed together make orange.
4. Red and blue mixed together make purple.
5. Red and white mixed together make pink.
6. Some fire trucks and fire hydrants are red.
7. A stop sign is colored red.
8. Some roses, tulips, and carnations are red.

Vocabulary

1. **red**—a primary color.
2. **primary colors**—red, yellow, and blue.

Bulletin Board

The purpose of this bulletin board is to reinforce the mathematical skills of matching sets of objects to a written numeral. Green produce baskets or other small baskets can be hung on the bulletin board for a strawberry-counting bulletin board. Attach baskets to the bulletin boards using staples or pushpins. Collect small plastic strawberries, or make strawberries out of tagboard. On each basket mark a numeral. The children can place the appropriate number of strawberries into each basket.

Parent Letter

Dear Parents,

Colors are everywhere and they make our world beautiful. That's why we'll focus on a specific color during our next curriculum theme: The color red! It's a popular color with young children and many objects in our world are red. The experiences provided will also help the children become aware of colors that are formed when mixed with red.

AT SCHOOL

A few of the curriculum experiences include:

- mixing the color red with yellow and blue to make orange and purple.
- setting up an art store in the dramatic play area where the children can act out the buying and selling of art supplies.
- exploring red-colored crayons, markers, pencils, chalk, paint, and paper.
- filling the sensory table with red goop.
- listening to stories related to the color red.

AT HOME

To reinforce the concepts in this unit, try the following activities at home with your child:

- To develop observation skills look around your house with your child for red items. How many red objects can you find in each room?
- Prepare red foods for meals such as apples, strawberries, tomatoes, and jam.
- Prepare red ice cubes to cool your drinks. To do this, just add a few drops of red food coloring to the water before freezing it.

Enjoy making colorful discoveries with your child.

Fingerplays

TULIPS

Five little tulips—red and bright
    (hold up hand)
Let us water them every day.
    (make sprinkle motion with other hand)
Watch them open in the bright sunlight.
    (cup hand, then open)
Watch them close when it is night.
    (close hand again).

MY APPLE

Look at my apple, it's red and round.
    (make ball shape with hands)
It fell from a tree down to the ground
    (make downward motion)
Come let me share my apple, please do!
    (beckoning motion)
My mother can cut it right in two—
    (make slicing motion)
One half for me and one half for you
    (hold out two hands, sharing halves)

FIVE RED APPLES

Five red apples in a grocery store.
    (hold up five fingers)
Bobby bought one, and then there were
    four.
    (bend down one finger)
Four red apples on an apple tree.
Susie ate one, and then there were three.
    (bend down one finger)
Three red apples. What did Alice do?
Why, she ate one, and then there were two.
    (bend down one finger)
Two red apples ripening in the sun.
Timmy ate one, and then there was one.
    (bend down one finger)
One red apple and now we are done.
I ate the last one, and now there are none.
    (bend down last finger)

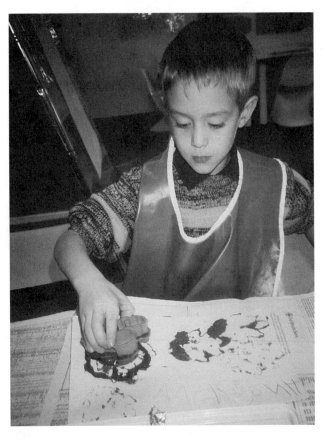

Sponges and red paint can make interesting designs.

Science

Mixing Colors

Place 2 or 3 ice cube trays and cups filled with red-, yellow-, and blue-colored water on the science table. Using an eyedropper, the children can experiment mixing colors in the ice cube trays. Smocks should be provided to prevent stained clothing.

Dramatic Play

1. **Art Store**

    Set up an art supply store. Include paints, crayons, markers, paper, chalk, brushes, money, and cash register.

2. **Fire Station**

   Firefighter hats can be added to the dramatic play area.

3. **Colored Hats**

   After reading *Caps for Sale* by Esphyr Slobodykina, set out colored hats for children to retell the story.

Arts and Crafts

1. **Red Paint**

   Red and white paint can be provided at the easels. By mixing these colors, children can discover shades of red.

2. **Red Crayons, Markers, etc.**

   Red markers, crayons, and chalk can be placed on a table in the art area. The children can observe the similarities and differences between these various items.

3. **Red Paper**

   Watercolors and red paper can be placed on a table in the art area.

4. **Red Crayon Rubbings**

   Red crayons, red paper, or both can be used to do this activity. Place an object such as a penny, button, or leaf under paper. Use the flat edge of a crayon to color over the item. An image of the object will appear on the paper.

5. **Paint Blots**

   Fold a piece of paper in half. Open up and place a spoonful of red paint on the inside of the paper. Refold paper and press flat. Reopen and observe the design. Add two colors such as blue and yellow and repeat process to show color mixing.

6. **Paint Over Design**

   Paint over a crayon picture with watery red paint. Observe how the paint will not cover the crayon marks.

7. **Glitter Pictures**

   The children make a design using glue on a piece of paper. Then shake red glitter onto glue. Shake the excess glitter into a pan.

8. **Red Fingerpaint**

   Red fingerpaint and foil should be placed on an art table. Yellow and blue paint can be added to explore color mixing.

Sensory

1. **Red Water**

   Fill the sensory table with water and red food coloring. The children can add coloring and observe the changes.

2. **Red Shaving Cream**

   Shaving cream with red food coloring added can be placed in the sensory table. During self-selected play the children can explore the shaving cream.

3. **Red Goop**

   Mix together red food coloring, 1 cup cornstarch, and 1 cup water in sensory table.

4. **Red Silly Putty**

   Mix together red food coloring, 1 cup liquid starch, and 2 cups white glue. This mixture usually needs to be stirred continuously for an extended period of time before it jells.

Large Muscle

1. **Ribbon Dance**

   Attach strips of red crepe paper to short wooden dowels or unsharpened pencils to make ribbons. The children can use the ribbons to move to their favorite songs.

2. Red Bird, Red Bird

The children should form a circle by holding hands. Then choose a child to be a bird and start the game. Children chant:

Red bird, red bird through my window
Red bird, red bird through my window
Red bird, red bird through my window
Oh!

The bird goes in and out, under the children's arms. The bird stops on the word "Oh" and bows to the child facing him. This child becomes the new bird. The color of the bird can be determined by the color of the clothing of each child picked to be the bird.

Field Trips/ Resource People

1. Art Store

Visit an art store. Observe all the red items for sale.

2. Take a Walk

Take a walk around the neighborhood and look for red objects.

3. Floral Shop

Visit a floral shop and specifically observe red flowers.

4. Fire Station

Visit a fire station. Note the color of the engine, hats, sirens, etc.

5. Resource People

Invite the following resource people to the classroom:

- artist
- gardener
- firefighter

Math

1. Color Cards

Construct color cards that start with white and gradually become cherry red. The children can sequence the cards from white to red or red to white. Discontinued sample color cards could be obtained from a paint store.

2. Bead Stringing

Yarn and a variety of colored beads should be available to the children. After initial exploration, the children can make patterns with beads, such as red, yellow, red, yellow, red.

3. Colored Bags

Place three bags labeled red, yellow, and blue and a variety of blocks on a table. The children can sort the blocks by placing them in the matching colored bag.

Social Studies

1. Discussion about Colors

During group time discuss colors and how they make us feel. Hold up a color card and ask a child how it makes him feel.

2. Color Chart

Construct a "My Favorite Color Is . . ." chart. Encourage each child to name his favorite color. After each child's name, print his favorite color with a colored marker. Display the chart in the classroom.

3. Colored Balloons

Each child should be provided with a balloon. The balloons should be the colors of the rainbow: red, orange, yellow, green, blue, and purple. Arrange the children in the formation of a rainbow. Children with red balloons should stand together, etc. Take a picture of the class. Place the picture on the bulletin board.

Group Time
(games, language)

1. Colored Jars

Collect five large clear jars. Fill 3 with red water, 1 with yellow water, and 1 with blue water. Show children the 3 red jars. Discuss the color red. Discuss that it can make other colors too. Show them the yellow jar. Add yellow to red. What happens? Add blue water to other red jar. What happens? Discuss color mixing.

2. Play "Red Light, Green Light"

Pick one child to be your traffic light. Place the "traffic light" about 30 feet away from the other children facing away from children who have formed a long line. With back to children, the traffic light says, "green light." Children try to creep toward the traffic light. Traffic light may then say, "red light," and turn toward the children. Children must freeze. The traffic light tries to see if any children are still at the starting line. The game continues with "green light." The first child to reach the traffic light becomes the new light.

Cooking

1. Raspberry Slush

Thaw and cook four 10-ounce packages of frozen raspberries for 10 minutes. Rub the cooked raspberries through strainer with wooden spoon. Cool. Add 1 can (6 ounces) of frozen lemonade concentrate, thawed. Just before serving, stir in 2 quarts of ginger ale, chilled. Makes 24 servings, about 1/2 cup each.

Books

The following books can be used to complement this theme:

Barton, Byron. (1993). *The Little Red Hen.* New York: HarperCollins.

Bazilian, Barbara. (1997). *The Red Shoes.* Dallas, TX: Whispering Coyote Press.

Carle, Eric. (1998). *Hello, Red Fox.* New York: Simon & Schuster.

Carroll, Kathleen S. (1994). *One Red Rooster.* Illus. by Suzette Barbier. Boston: Sandpiper.

Casey, Mike. (1996). *Red Lace, Yellow Lace: Learn to Tie Your Shoe!* Hauppauge, NY: Barron's Educational Series.

Hoban, Tana. (1978). *Is It Red? Is It Yellow? Is It Blue?* New York: Greenwillow.

Lucht, Irmgard. (1995). *The Red Poppy.* New York: Hyperion.

Peek, Merle. (1998). *Mary Wore Her Red Dress, and Henry Wore His Green Sneakers.* Boston: Houghton Mifflin.

Serfozo, Mary. (1992). *Who Said Red?* New York: Maxwell Macmillan.

Walsh, Ellen Stoll. (1989). *Mouse Paint.* Orlando: Harcourt Brace.

Whitman, Candace. (1998). *Ready for Red.* New York: Abbeville Publishing.

Woolfitt, Gabrielle. (1992). *Red.* Minneapolis: Carolrhoda Books.

Multimedia

The following multimedia products can be used to complement this theme:

Colors, Shapes and Size [CD-ROM]. (1995). StarPress Multimedia.

JumpStart Preschool [CD-ROM]. (1996). Glendale, CA: Knowledge Adventure.

"Little Red Caboose" on *Toddler Favorites* [cassette]. (1998). Redway, CA: Music for Little People.

Rock 'n' Learn Colors, Shapes, and Counting [video]. (1997). Conroe, TX: Rock 'n' Learn.

THEME 54

Safety

Indoors
walking
scissor care
fire drills
metal detectors
rules

Outdoors
rules
animals
street
bicycle
drugs
guns

Field Trips
rules

People
police officers
firefighters
doctors
nurses
ambulance drivers
strangers

Vehicles
traffic signs
seat belts
rules
airbags

Theme Goals

Through participating in the experiences provided by this theme, the children may learn:

1. Indoor safety precautions.
2. Play yard safety.
3. People who keep us safe.
4. Field trip safety.
5. Vehicle safety.

Concepts for the Children to Learn

1. We walk indoors.
2. Play yard rules help keep us safe.
3. We have special rules for field trips.
4. Fire drills prepare us for emergencies.
5. Scissors need to be handled carefully.
6. Wearing a seat belt is practicing car safety.
7. Traffic signs help prevent accidents.
8. Police officers, firefighters, doctors, nurses, and ambulance drivers help keep us safe.
9. Talk only to people you know.

Vocabulary

1. **safety**—freedom from danger.
2. **sign**—a lettered board.
3. **seat belt**—strap that holds a person in a vehicle.
4. **rule**—the way we are to act.
5. **fire drill**—practicing leaving the building in case of a fire.

524

Bulletin Board

The purpose of this bulletin board is to help the children recognize safety signs. To prepare this bulletin board, construct six safety signs out of tagboard, each a different shape. Color appropriately and laminate. Trace the outline of these signs onto black construction paper to create shadow signs as illustrated. Staple the shadow signs to the bulletin board. Punch holes in the safety signs using a hole punch. The children can match the shape of the safety signs to the shadow signs by hanging them on the appropriate pushpins.

Parent Letter

Dear Parents,

Safety will be the focus of our next unit. We will be learning about safety at school, at home, and outdoors. Through this unit the children will also become more aware of traffic signs and their importance.

AT SCHOOL

A few of the activities planned for this unit include:

- taking a safety walk to practice crossing streets.
- counting the number of traffic signs that are in our school neighborhood.
- visiting the fire station on Tuesday morning. We will be leaving at 9:30 and should return to school by 11:00.

AT HOME

One of the songs we will be learning follows. It will help your child become aware of the purpose and colors of a traffic light. You may enjoy singing the song at home with your child. The song is sung to the tune of "Twinkle, Twinkle, Little Star." The words are as follows:

> Twinkle, twinkle, traffic light,
> Standing on the corner bright.
> When it's green it's time to go.
> When it's red it's stop, you know.
> Twinkle, twinkle, traffic light,
> Standing on the corner bright.

During your daily routines, share safety tips with your child.

526

Music

1. **"Twinkle, Twinkle, Traffic Light"**
   (Sing to the tune of "Twinkle, Twinkle, Little Star")

   Twinkle, twinkle, traffic light,
   Standing on the corner bright.
   When it's green it's time to go.
   When it's red it's stop, you know.
   Twinkle, twinkle, traffic light,
   Standing on the corner bright.

2. **"Do You Know the Police Officer"**
   (Sing to the tune of "The Muffin Man")

   Oh, do you know the police officer,
   The police officer, the police officer?
   Oh, do you know the police officer
   Who helps me cross the street?

   This song can be extended. For example,
   the song can be continued substituting
   "who helps me when I'm lost" or "who
   helps one cross the street."

3. **"We Are Safe"**
   (Sing to the tune of "Mulberry Bush")

   This is the way that we are safe
   We are safe, we are safe.
   This is the way that we are safe,
   Every day of the year.

   This is the way we cross the street—
   Look left, then right, left then right.
   This is the way we cross the street—
   Look left, then right for safety.

   This is the way we ride in the car—
   Sit up straight, buckle your belt.
   This is the way we ride in the car—
   Buckle your belt for safety.

   Resource: Wilmes, Liz & Dick. (1983). *Everyday Circle
   Time.* IL: Building Blocks Publication.

**Safety in even the simplest activities
must be reinforced.**

Fingerplays

SILLY TEDDY BEAR

   Silly little teddy bear
   Stood up in a rocking chair.
      (make rocking movement)
   Now he has to stay in bed
      (lay head on hands)
   With a bandage round his head.
      (circular movement of hand around head)

CROSSING STREETS

   At the curb before I cross
   I stop my running feet
      (point to feet)
   And look both ways to left and right
      (look left and right)
   Before I cross the street.
   Lest autos running quietly
   Might come as a surprise.
   I don't just listen with my ears
      (point to ears)
   But look with both my eyes.
      (point to eyes)

RED LIGHT

Red light, red light, what do you say?
I say, "Stop and stop right away!"
   (hold palms of both hands up)
Yellow light, yellow light, what do you say?
I say, "Wait till the light turns green."
   (hold one palm of hand up)
Green light, green light, what do you say?
I say "Go, but look each way."
   (circle arm in forward motion and turn
   head to the right and left)
Thank you, thank you, red, yellow, green
Now I know what the traffic light means.

FIVE POLICE OFFICERS

Five strong police officers standing by a
  store.
   (hold up the one hand)
One became a traffic cop, then there were
  four.
   (hold up four fingers)
Four strong police officers watching over me.
One took a lost boy home, then there were
  three.
   (hold up three fingers)
Three strong police officers all dressed in
  blue.
One stopped a speeding car and then there
  were two.
   (hold up two fingers)
Two strong police officers, how fast they
  can run.
One caught a bad man and then there was
  one.
   (hold up one finger)
One strong police officer saw some smoke
  one day.
He called a firefighter who put it out right
  away.

THE CROSSING GUARD

The crossing guard keeps us safe
As he works from day to day.
He holds the stop sign high in the air.
   (hold palm of hand up)
For the traffic to obey.
And when the cars have completely stopped
And it's as safe as can be,
He signals us to walk across
   (make a beckoning motion)
The street very carefully.

Science

1. Sorting for Safety

Collect empty household product containers. Include safe and dangerous items such as cleaning supplies, orange juice containers, etc. Place all the items in one large box. The children can separate the containers into "safe" and "dangerous" categories. Younger children may be able to separate the containers into edible and nonedible categories.

2. All About Me

On a table place identification items. Prepare a separate card for each child. Record the following information on the cards:

- height
- weight
- color hair
- color eyes
- fingerprint
- signature (if child can or a teacher can help)

Dramatic Play

1. Fire Engine

A large cardboard box can be decorated by the children as a fire engine with yellow or red tempera paint. When the fire engine is dry, place it in the dramatic play area with short hoses and firefighter hats. This prop could also be placed outdoors, weather permitting.

2. Prop Boxes

Develop prop boxes such as:

Firefighter	Police Officer
bell	hat
jacket/uniform	badges
boots	handcuffs
whistle	stop sign (for holding)
hose	
oxygen mask	
hat	

528

3. **Firefighter Jackets**

Construct firefighter jackets out of large paper bags. Begin by cutting three holes. One hole is used for the child's head at the top of the bag. Then cut two large holes for arms. These props may encourage the children to dramatize the roles of the firefighters.

4. **Seat Belts**

Collect child-sized car seats. Place them around like chairs and let the children adjust them for themselves or their dolls.

Arts and Crafts

1. **Firefighter Hats**

Cut firefighter hats out of large sheets of red construction paper for the children to wear.

2. **Easel Painting**

On the easel, place cut-out shapes of fire hats or boots.

3. **Traffic Lights**

Construct stop and go lights out of shoeboxes. Tape the lid to the bottom of the box. Cover with black construction paper and have children place green, yellow, and red circles in correct order on the box. The red circle should be placed on the top, yellow in the middle, and green on the bottom.

4. **Officer Hats and Badges**

Police officer hats and badges can be constructed out of paper and colored with crayons or felt-tip watercolor markers.

Sensory

1. **Pumps and Hoses**

Water pumps, hoses, and water can be placed in the sensory table.

2. **Trucks**

Small toy fire trucks and police cars can be placed in the sensory table with sand.

Large Muscle

1. **Safety Walk**

Take a safety walk. Practice observing traffic lights when crossing the street. Point out special hazards to the children.

2. **Stop, Drop, and Roll**

Practice "Stop, Drop, and Roll" with the children. This will be valuable to them if they are ever involved in a fire and their clothes happen to catch on fire. Usually a firefighter will teach them this technique while they are visiting the fire station.

Field Trips/ Resource People

1. **Firefighter**

Invite a firefighter to the classroom. Ask him to bring firefighter clothing and equipment and to discuss each item.

2. **Police Car**

Invite a police officer to visit the classroom. Ask him to bring a police car to show the children.

Math

1. **Sequencing Hats**

Draw pictures of three police hats. Make each picture identical except design three different sizes. The children can sequence the objects from largest to smallest or smallest to largest. Discuss the sizes and ask which is largest, smallest, middle.

529

2. Safety Items

Walk around the school and observe the number of safety items. Included may be exit signs, fire drill posters, fire extinguishers, sprinkler systems, fire alarm/drill bells, etc.

Social Studies

1. Safety Pictures and Signs

Post safety pictures and signs around the room.

2. Stop and Go Light

Draw a large stop and go light on a piece of tagboard. Color with felt-tip markers. Print the following across from the corresponding colors:

Green means go we all know
Yellow means wait even if you're late,
Red means stop!

3. Safety Signs

Take a walk and watch for safety signs. Discuss the colors and letters on each sign.

Group Time
(games, language)

Toy Safety

Collect a variety of unsafe toys that may have sharp edges, such as a broken wagon, etc. During group time discuss the dangers of each toy.

Cooking

1. Banana Rounds

4 medium bananas
1/2 tablespoon honey
1/8 teaspoon nutmeg
1/8 teaspoon cinnamon
1/4 cup wheat germ

The children can peel the bananas and then slice them with a plastic knife. Measure the spices, wheat germ, and honey. Finally, mix them with the bananas. Chill. Serves 8.

2. Stop Signs

eight-sided crackers
peanut butter
jelly

Spread a thin layer of peanut butter and jelly on each cracker.

3. Yield Signs

triangle crackers
yellow cheese

Cut yellow cheese into triangles. Put the cheese on the crackers.

Books

The following books can be used to complement this theme:

Arnosky, Jim. (1990). *Crinkleroot's Guide to Walking in Wild Places*. New York: Simon & Schuster.

Boelts, Maribeth. (1997). *A Kid's Guide to Staying Safe around Water*. New York: Rosen Publishing.

Brown, Marc Tolon and Stephen Krensky. *Dinosaurs, Beware: A Safety Guide*. Boston: Little, Brown.

Butler, Daphne. (1996). *What Happens When Fire Burns?* Austin, TX: Raintree/Steck Vaughn.

Girard, L. W. (1985). *Who Is a Stranger and What Should I Do?* Illus. by Helen Cogancherry. Niles, IL: Albert Whitman.

Givon, Hannah Gelman. (1996). *We Shake in a Quake*. Illus. by David Uttal. Berkeley, CA: Tricycle Press.

Lakin, Patricia. (1995). *Aware and Alert*. Photos by Doub Cushman. Austin, TX: Raintree/Steck Vaughn.

Loewen, Nancy. (1996). *Bicycle Safety*. Illus. by Penny Danny. Mankato, MN: Child's World.

Loewen, Nancy. (1996). *Traffic Safety*. Illus. by Penny Danny. Mankato, MN: Child's World.

Marzollo, Jean. (1996). *I Am Fire*. Illus. by Judith Moffatt. New York: Scholastic.

Rand, Gloria. (1996). *Willie Takes a Hike*. Illus. by Ted Rand. Orlando: Harcourt Brace.

Rathmann, Peggy. (1995). *Officer Buckle and Gloria*. New York: G. P. Putnam.

Schulson, Rachel. (1997). *Guns—What You Should Know*. Illus. by Mary Jones. Niles, IL: Albert Whitman.

Spelman, Cornelia. (1997). *Your Body Belongs to You*. Illus. by Teri Weidner. Niles, IL: Albert Whitman.

Multimedia

The following multimedia products can be used to complement this theme:

Child Safety Outdoors [video]. (1994). Chino Hills, CA: KidSafety of America.

K.C.'s First Bus Ride. [video]. (1994). Chino Hills, CA: KidSafety of America.

Play It Safe [kit includes books, sound cassettes, video, etc.]. (1995). Bothell, WA: Wright Group.

Safety on Wheels [video]. (1994). Films for the Humanities & Sciences.

Seat Belts Are for Kids Too [video]. (1987). AIMS Media.

Recordings and Song Titles

The following recordings can be used to complement this theme:

Piggyback Songs—"Never Play with Matches"

Make the Right Choice—"Child Abuse Won't Do," "Don't Talk To Strangers," "Don't Drink and Drive," "Buckle Up"

Halloween Fun—"Are You Ready for Halloween?"

People in Our Neighborhood—"Safety Pros KNOW" (RONNO)

Singing, Moving, and Fun (The Learning Station)—"Say No (To Strangers)"

Pre-K Hooray—"Stop at the Red Light"

Cars, Trucks, and Trains—"Signs and Signals"

THEME 55

Scissors

Construction
plastic
metal

Care
cleaning
storing
handling
sharpening

Types
left-handed
paper
pinking
cloth
cuticle
shears
haircutting
electric
toenail
kitchen
children's

Parts
handle
blade

Materials to Cut
paper
cardboard
fabric
hair
fingernails
toenails
yarn/thread
pastry

Tool
cutting
trimming

Users
barber
hairstylist
tailor/dressmaker
sheep shearer
cook/chef
animal groomer
adult
child

Theme Goals

Through participating in the experiences provided by this theme, the children may learn:

1. Parts of scissors.
2. Uses of scissors.
3. Materials that can be cut with scissors.
4. Care of scissors.
5. People who use scissors.
6. Sizes and shapes of scissors.

Concepts for the Children to Learn

1. Scissors are tools.
2. Scissors help us do our work.
3. Scissors cut paper, fingernails, hair, and material.
4. There are many types of scissors.
5. Some people need scissors for their job.
6. Hand motions make scissors cut.
7. Scissors need to be handled carefully.

Vocabulary

1. **blade**—cutting edge of scissors.
2. **pinking shears**—sewing scissors.
3. **shears**—large scissors.

Bulletin Board

The purpose of this bulletin board is to have the children match the colored scissors to the corresponding colored skein of yarn. To prepare the bulletin board, construct six scissors out of tagboard. With felt-tip markers, color each scissor a different color and laminate. Fasten the scissors to the top of the bulletin board. Next, construct six skeins of yarn out of tagboard. Color each skein a different color to correspond with the scissors. Attach the skeins to the bottom part of the bulletin board. Fasten a string to each of the scissors and a pushpin to each of the skeins of yarn.

Parent Letter

Dear Parents,

Snip, snip, snip! This sound will be heard frequently in the classroom as we start a curriculum unit focusing on scissors. Through the experiences provided the children will be introduced to various kinds and uses of scissors. They will also learn the proper care and safety precautions to consider when handling and using scissors.

AT SCHOOL

Some activities related to scissors will include:

- discussing safety and proper uses of scissors.
- experimenting cutting with different kinds of scissors.
- cutting a variety of materials such as yarn, fabric, paper, wallpaper, and aluminum foil.
- visiting Tom's Barber Shop on Wednesday morning. We will be leaving at 10:00 a.m. and expect to watch a haircut demonstration. Also, we will observe the tools and equipment used by a barber.
- listening to the story "Michael's New Hair Cut"

AT HOME

Children need many experiences working with scissors before they are able to master cutting skills. Each child will learn this skill at his own rate. To assist your child, save scraps of paper and allow your child to practice cutting them using child-sized scissors. Once the cutting skills have been mastered, your child may enjoy cutting coupons out of newspaper sections or magazines.

Have fun with your child!

536

Fingerplay

OPEN SHUT THEM

Open, shut them, open, shut them.
   (use index and middle finger to make
   scissors motion)
Give a little snip, snip, snip.
   (three quick snips with fingers)
Open, shut them, open, shut them.
   (repeat scissors motion)
Make another clip.
   (make another scissors motion)

Science

1. **Scissor Show**

   Place a variety of scissors on an overhead
   projector. Encourage the children to describe
   each by naming it and explaining its use.

2. **Shadow Profiles**

   Tape a piece of paper on a wall or bulletin
   board. Stand a child in front of the paper.
   Shine a light source to create a shadow of
   the head. Trace the outline of each child's
   shadow. Provide scissors for the children to
   cut out their own shadows.

3. **Weighing Scissors**

   On the science table, place a variety of
   scissors and a scale. The children should
   be encouraged to note the differences in
   weight.

Dramatic Play

1. **Beauty Shop**

   Set up a beauty shop in the dramatic play
   area. Include items such as curling irons,
   hair dryers, combs, and wigs. Also, include
   a chair, plastic covering, and Beauty Shop
   sign. A cash register and money can be
   added to encourage play. **Caution:** For
   safety purposes, cut the cords off the hair
   dryer and curling irons.

Some children need left-handed scissors;
others can use right-handed scissors.

2. **Tailor/Dressmaking Shop**

   Materials that are easy to cut should be
   provided. Likewise, a variety of scissors
   should be placed next to the material.
   Older children may want to make doll
   clothes.

3. **Bake Shop**

   Playdough, scissors, and other cooking
   tools can be placed on a table. If desired,
   make paper baker hats and a sign.

4. **Dog Groomer**

   A dog grooming area can be set up in the
   dramatic play corner with stuffed animals,
   brushes, and combs. If available, cut off the
   cord of an electric dog shaver and provide
   for the children.

Arts and Crafts

1. **Scissor Snip**

   Strips of paper with scissors can be provided for snipping.

2. **Cutting**

   For experimentation, a wide variety of materials and types of scissors can be added to the art area for the children.

Sensory

Playdough

Scissors can be placed next to the play-dough in the sensory area.

Field Trips/ Resource People

1. **Hairstylist**

   Visit a hairstylist. While there, observe a person's hair being cut. Notice the different scissors that are used and how they are used.

2. **Pet Groomer**

   Invite a pet groomer to class. If possible, arrange for a dog to be groomed.

Math

Shape Sort

Cut out different-colored shapes. Place the shapes on a table for the children to sort by color, shape, and size.

Pastes

Bookmaker's Paste

1 teaspoon flour
2 teaspoons cornstarch
1/4 teaspoon powdered alum
3 ounces water

Mix dry ingredients. Add water slowly, stirring out all lumps. Cook over slow fire (preferably in a double boiler), stirring constantly. Remove when paste begins to thicken. It will thicken more as it cools. Keep in covered jars. Thin with water if necessary.

Cooked Flour Paste

1 cup boiling water
1 tablespoon powdered alum
1 pint cold water
1 pint flour
1 heaping teaspoon oil
   of cloves
oil of wintergreen
   (optional)

To 1 cup boiling water add powdered alum. Mix flour and fold in water until smooth; pour mixture gradually into boiling alum water. Cook until it has a bluish cast, stirring all the time. Remove from fire, add oil of cloves, and stir well. Keep in airtight jars. Thin when necessary by adding water. A drop or two of oil of wintergreen may be added to give the paste a pleasing aroma.

Colored Salt Paste

Mix 2 parts salt to 1 part flour. Add powdered paint and enough water to make a smooth heavy paste. Keep in airtight container.

Crepe Paper Paste

Cut or tear 2 tablespoons crepe paper of a single color. The finer the paper is cut, the smoother the paste will be. Add 1/2 tablespoon flour, 1/2 tablespoon salt, and enough water to make a paste. Stir and squash the mixture until it is as smooth as possible. Store in airtight container.

Group Time
(games, language)

Scissor Safety

Discuss safety while using scissors. The children can help make a list of "How we use our scissors safely." Display chart in room.

Cooking

Pretzels

1 1/2 cups warm water
1 envelope yeast
4 cups flour
1 teaspoon salt
1 tablespoon sugar
coarse salt
egg

Mix the warm water, yeast, and sugar together. Set this mixture aside for 5 minutes. Pour salt and flour into a bowl. Add the yeast mixture to make dough. Roll the dough into a long snake form. Cut the dough into smaller sections using scissors. The children can then form individual shapes with dough. Brush egg on the shapes with pastry brush and sprinkle with salt. Preheat the oven and bake pretzels at 425 degrees for 12 minutes.

Books

The following books can be used to complement this theme:

Birch, Barbara and Beverly Lewis. (1995). *Katie and the Haircut Mistake*. Illus. by Taia Morley. Minneapolis: Augsburg Fortress Publishers.

Klinting, Lars. (1996). *Bruno the Tailor*. New York: Holt.

Landstrom, Olof et al. (1993). *Will Gets a Haircut*. Stockholm, NY: R&S Book Co.

Moore, Eva. (1997). *The Day of the Bad Haircut*. Illus. by Meredith Johnson. St. Paul, MN: Cartwheel Books. (Pbk)

Robins, Joan. (1993). *Addie's Bad Day*. Illus. by Sue Truesdell. New York: HarperCollins.

Ruediger, Beth. (1997). *The Barber of Bingo*. Illus. by John McPherson. Kansas City: Andrews McMeel Pub.

Tusca, Tricia. (1991). *Camilla's New Hairdo*. New York: Farrar, Straus and Giroux.

THEME 56

Names

circle
triangle
rectangle
square
oval

Shapes

Construction

lines
round
four sides
three sides

Theme Goals

Through participating in the experiences provided by this theme, the children may learn:

1. The names of basic shapes.
2. Identification of basic shapes.
3. Objects have shapes.

Concepts for the Children to Learn

1. There are many shapes of different sizes and colors in our world.
2. Some shapes have names.
3. A circle is round.
4. Triangles have three sides.
5. Rectangles and squares have four sides.
6. All objects contain one or more shapes.
7. We can draw lines to make shapes.

Vocabulary

1. **circle**—a shape that is round.
2. **rectangle**—a shape with four sides.
3. **square**—a shape with four sides of equal length.
4. **triangle**—a shape with three sides.
5. **line**—a mark made with a pencil, crayon, etc., to make a shape.
6. **oval**—shaped like an egg.

Bulletin Board

The purpose of this bulletin board is to have the child make a shape train. To prepare the bulletin board use the model shown to construct a train using basic shapes. Color the shapes, cut them out, and laminate. Trace laminated shapes onto black construction paper to construct shadow shapes. Cut out the shadow shapes. Staple the shadow shapes onto the board in a train pattern. The children can affix the colored shape pieces to the shadows by using magnets.

Parent Letter

Dear Parents,

Hello again! Shapes will be the focus of our new curriculum unit. Our world consists of shapes. The children will become aware of this on an introductory walk around the block. They also will become familiar with the names of shapes and will classify objects according to their shapes. Consequently, the children will be more aware of all the shapes in our world. In addition, the children who are developmentally ready will practice drawing some of the basic shapes.

AT SCHOOL

Some of the fun-filled learning activities scheduled for this unit include:

- playing a game called "Shape Basket Upset."
- listening to the story *Shapes and Things*, by Tana Hoban.
- feeling and identifying objects by shape in a feely box.
- making and baking cookies of various shapes.

AT HOME

You can reinforce the activities included in this curriculum unit at home by observing shaped objects in your house. Each day at school we will have a special shape theme. Your child can bring in an object from home to fit the shape of the day. I will send home the shape the night before so you and your child will have time to look for an object. The following fingerplay can be recited to foster language and memory skills.

Circle and Square

Close my eyes, shut them tight.
    (close eyes)
Make a circle with my one hand.
    (make a circle with one hand)
Keep them shut; make it fair.
    (keep eyes shut)
With my other hand, make a square.
    (make a square with other hand)

Enjoy your child!

What can you make with these shapes?

Music

The following songs can be found in Butler, Talmadge, Kirkland, Terry, & Leach. (1975). *Music for Today's Young Children*. Broadman Press.

1. "Colors, Shapes, and Numbers"
2. "Different Shapes"

Fingerplays

RIGHT CIRCLE, LEFT SQUARE

Close my eyes, shut them tight.
  (close eyes)
Make a circle with my one hand.
  (make circle with one hand)
Keep them shut; make it fair.
  (keep eyes shut)
With my other hand, make a square.
  (make square with other hand)

LINES

One straight finger makes a line.
  (hold up one index finger)
Two straight lines make one "t" sign.
  (cross index fingers)
Three lines made a triangle there
  (form triangle with index fingers
  touching and thumbs touching)
And one more line will make a square.
  (form square with hands)

DRAW A SQUARE

Draw a square, draw a square
Shaped like a tile floor.
Draw a square, draw a square
All with corners four.

DRAW A TRIANGLE

Draw a triangle, draw a triangle
With corners three.
Draw a triangle, draw a triangle
Draw it just for me.

DRAW A CIRCLE

Draw a circle, draw a circle
Made very round.
Draw a circle, draw a circle
No corners can be found.

WHAT AM I MAKING?

This is a circle.
   (draw circle in the air)
This is a square.
   (draw square in the air)
Who can tell me
What I'm making there?
   (draw another shape in the air)

Science

1. **Feely Box**

   Cut many shapes out of different materials such as felt, cardboard, wallpaper, carpet, etc. Place the shapes into a feely box. The children can be encouraged to reach in and identify the shape by feeling it before removing it from the box.

2. **Evaporation**

   Pour equal amounts of water into a large round and a small square cake pan. Mark the water level with a grease pencil. Allow the water to stand for a week. Observe the amount of evaporation.

3. **Classifying Objects**

   Collect four small boxes. Mark a different shape on each box. Include a circle, triangle, square, and rectangle. Then cut shapes out of magazines. The children can sort the objects by placing them in the corresponding boxes.

4. **What Shape Is It?**

   Place objects with distinct shapes, such as marbles, dice, pyramid, deck of cards, book, ball, button, etc., in the feely box. Encourage the children to reach in and identify the shape of the object they are feeling before they pull it out.

Dramatic Play

1. **Baker**

   Provide playdough, cake pans, and cookie cutters.

2. **Puppets**

   A puppet prop box should be placed in the dramatic play area. A puppet stage should be added if available. Otherwise a puppet stage can be made from cardboard.

Arts and Crafts

1. **Sponge Painting**

   Cut sponges into the four basic shapes. The children can hold the sponges with a clothespin. The sponge can be dipped in paint and printed on the paper. Make several designs and shapes.

2. **Shape Mobiles**

   Trace shapes of various sizes on colored construction paper. If appropriate, encourage the children to cut the shapes from the paper and punch a hole at the top of each shape. Then, put a piece of string through the hole and tie onto a hanger. The mobiles can be hung in the classroom for decoration.

3. **Easel Ideas**

   Feature a different shape of easel paper each day at the easel.

4. **Shape Collage**

   Provide different-colored paper shapes and glue for the children to create collages from shapes.

5. **Stencils**

   Prepare individual stencils of the basic shapes. The children can use the stencils for tracing.

6. My Shape Book

Stickers, catalogs, and magazines should be placed on the art table. Also, prepare booklets cut into the basic shapes. Encourage the children to find, cut, and glue the objects in each shape book.

Sensory

Add the following items to the sensory table:

1. marbles and water
2. different-shaped sponges and water
3. colored water
4. scented water
5. soapy water

Large Muscle

1. Walk and Balance

Using masking tape, outline the four basic shapes on the floor. The children can walk and balance on the shapes. Older children may walk forwards, backwards, and sideways.

2. Hopscotch

Draw a hopscotch with chalk on the sidewalk outdoors. Masking tape can be used to form the grid on the floor indoors.

Field Trip

Shape Walk

Walk around the school neighborhood. During the walk, observe the shapes of the traffic signs and houses. After returning to the school, record the shapes observed on a chart.

Math

1. Wallpaper Shape Match

From scraps of old wallpaper, cut out two sets of basic shapes. Then mix all of the pieces. The children can match the sets by pattern and shape.

2. Shape Completion

On several pieces of white tagboard draw a shape, leaving one side, or part of a circle, unfinished or dotted. Laminate the tagboard. The children can complete the shape by drawing with watercolor markers or grease pencils. Erase with a damp cloth.

Group Time
(games, language)

1. Shape Hunt

Throughout the classroom hide colorful shapes. Each of the children can find a shape.

2. Twister

On a large old bed sheet, secure many shapes of different colors, or draw the shapes on with magic markers. Make a spinner. Have children place parts of their bodies on the different shapes.

3. Shape Day

Each day highlight a different shape. Collect related items that resemble the shape of the day and display throughout the classroom. During group time, have each child find an object in the classroom that is the same shape as the shape of the day.

Cooking

1. Shaped Bread and Peanut Butter

The children can cut bread with different-shaped cookie cutters. Spread peanut butter or other toppings on the bread.

2. Fruit Cut-outs

1/2 cup sugar
4 envelopes unflavored gelatin
2 1/2 cups pineapple juice, apple juice, orange juice, grape juice, or fruit drink

In a mixing bowl, stir the sugar and gelatin with rubber scraper until well mixed. Pour fruit juice into a 1-quart saucepan. Put the pan on the burner. Turn the burner to high heat. Cook until the juice boils. Turn burner off. Pour boiling fruit juice over sugar mixture. Stir with a rubber scraper until all the gelatin is dissolved. Pour into a 13-inch × 9-inch × 2-inch pan. Place in the refrigerator and chill until firm. Cookie cutters can be used to make shapes. Enjoy! This activity requires close supervision.

3. Shape Snacks

Spread cheese or peanut butter onto variously shaped crackers and serve.

Serve cheese cut into circles, triangles, squares, and rectangles.

Serve vegetable circles—cucumbers, carrots, zucchini.

Cut fruit snacks into circles—bananas, grapefruit wedges, apple slices, grapes—serve.

4. Nachos

4 flour tortillas
3/4 cup grated cheese
1/3 cup chopped green pepper (optional)

With clean kitchen scissors, cut each tortilla into 4 or 6 triangle wedges. Place on a cookie sheet and sprinkle the tortilla wedges with the cheese. Garnish with green pepper if desired. Bake in a 350-degree oven for 4 to 6 minutes or until the cheese melts. Makes 16 to 20 nachos.

To Teach Math Concepts

Before a child can learn the more abstract concepts of arithmetic, he must be visually, physically, and kinesthetically aware of basic quantitative concepts. Included could be:

Form Discrimination	Vocabulary			
circle	big	top	all	few
square	little	bottom	none	more
triangle	small	long	some	less
rectangle	smaller	short	first	through
	large	tall	last	around
	larger	high	middle	fast
	heavy	low	near	slow
	light	thick	far	up
	in	thin	above	down
	out	front	below	most
	over	back	many	least
	under	behind		

548

5. Swedish Pancakes

3 eggs
1 cup milk
1 1/2 cups flour
1 tablespoon sugar
1/2 teaspoon salt
4 tablespoons butter
1 cup heavy cream
2 tablespoons confectioner's sugar or a
   12-ounce jar of fruit jelly

Using a fork or whisk, beat the eggs lightly in a large mixing bowl. Add half the milk. Fold in the flour, sugar, and salt. Melt the butter and add it, the cream, and the remaining milk to the mixture. Stir well. Lightly grease a frying pan or griddle, and place it over medium-high heat on a hot plate or stove. Carefully pour small amounts of the mixture onto the frying pan or griddle. Cook until the pancakes are golden around the edges and bubbly on top. Turn the pancakes over with a spatula and cook until the other sides are golden around the edges. Remove to a covered plate. Repeat until all the mixture is used. Sprinkle pancakes lightly with confectioner's sugar, or spread fruit jelly over them. Makes 3 dozen pancakes.

Books

The following books can be used to complement this theme:

Dillon, Leo et al. (1994). *What Am I? Looking Through Shapes at Apples and Grapes.* New York: Scholastic.

Ehlert, Lois. (1990). *Color Farm.* New York: Lippincott.

Ehlert, Lois. (1989). *Color Zoo.* New York: Lippincott.

Grover, Max. (1996). *Circles and Squares Everywhere.* Orlando: Harcourt Brace.

Hoban, Tana. (1986). *Shapes, Shapes, Shapes.* New York: William Morrow.

Hoban, Tana. (1992). *Spirals, Curves, Fanshapes & Lines.* New York: Greenwillow.

MacDonald, Suse. (1994). *Sea Shapes.* Orlando: Harcourt Brace.

Morgan, Sally. *World of Shapes* series. Cincinnati, OH: Thomson Learning. *Circles and Spheres.* (1994); *Spirals.* (1995); *Squares and Cubes.* (1994); *Triangles and Pyramids.* (1995).

Serfozo, Mary. (1996). *There's a Square: A Book About Shapes.* Illus. by David A. Carter. New York: Scholastic.

Sharman, Lydia. (1994). *The Amazing Book of Shapes.* New York: Dorling Kindersley.

Multimedia

The following multimedia products can be used to complement this theme:

Colors, Shapes & Size [CD-ROM]. (1995). San Francisco, CA: Star Press Multimedia.

Jumpstart Preschool [CD-ROM]. (1996). Glendale, CA: Knowledge Adventure.

Let's Start Learning [CD-ROM]. (1996). Freemont, CA: The Learning Co.

Millie's Math House [computer disks]. (1992). Redmond, WA: Edmark.

Rock 'n' Learn Colors, Shapes & Counting [video]. (1997). Conroe, TX: Rock 'n' Learn.

Shape Up! [CD-ROM]. (1995). Cupertino, CA: Sunburst Communications.

Traugh, Steven et al. "Shapes" on *Music and Movement* [cassette]. (1993). Cypress, CA: Creative Teaching Press.

Recordings and Song Titles

The following recordings can be used to complement this theme:

There's Music in the Colors

I Like Myself—"Draw a Circle"

Where Is Thumbkin?—"The Color Song"

Pre-K Hooray—"Color Wheel Dance"

Homemade Games—"Color Square"

Piggyback Sons—"Colors"

Children Love to Sing and Dance (The Learning Station)—"Everything Has a Color"

Let's Visit Lullaby Land—"Colour My World"

Rainbow of Songs—"Primary Colors"

Shapes in Action

THEME 57

Participants

spectators, players, coaches, umpires, scorekeepers, announcers

Places

yards, fields, swimming pools, tennis courts, roads, gyms, golf courses, bowling alleys, ski slopes, lakes

Types

baseball, basketball, football, soccer, rugby, swimming, tennis, volleyball, skiing, biking, bowling, skating, track/running, fishing, golf, hockey

Sports

Clothing

uniforms, swimsuits, shorts, jerseys, sweatshirts, sweatpants, hats, ski clothing, jacket, gloves, pants, goggles

Equipment

balls, bats, shoulder pads, rackets, bikes, skis, boots, poles, gloves, helmets, golf clubs, skates

Theme Goals

Through participating in the experiences provided by this theme, the children may learn:

1. Places used for sports participation.
2. Types of sports people play.
3. Types of equipment used for sports.
4. Kinds of clothing worn for sports participation.
5. There are many people who participate in sports.

Concepts for the Children to Learn

1. Swimming pools, playing fields, tennis courts, roads, gyms, golf courses, backyards, bowling lanes, lakes, and ski slopes are all places that are used for sports.
2. Spectators, players, and coaches are all sports participants.
3. Baseball, biking, hockey, football, and golf are all types of sports.
4. Balls, bikes, and golf clubs are sports equipment.
5. Uniforms are worn when playing some sports.
6. Some sports are played indoors, others outdoors.
7. There are individual and team sports.

Vocabulary

1. **team**—a group of people who play together.
2. **uniform**—clothing worn for some sports.
3. **ball**—equipment used for sports.
4. **sport**—an activity played for fun.

Bulletin Board

The purpose of this bulletin board is to encourage the children to hang each ball with a numeral on the glove that has the corresponding number of dots. To prepare the bulletin board, construct baseball mitts out of brown tagboard. Cut out the mitts and attach dots starting with one on each of the gloves. The number of gloves prepared and dots will depend upon the developmental maturity of the children. Hang the gloves on the bulletin board. Next construct white baseballs. Write a numeral, starting with one, on each of the balls.

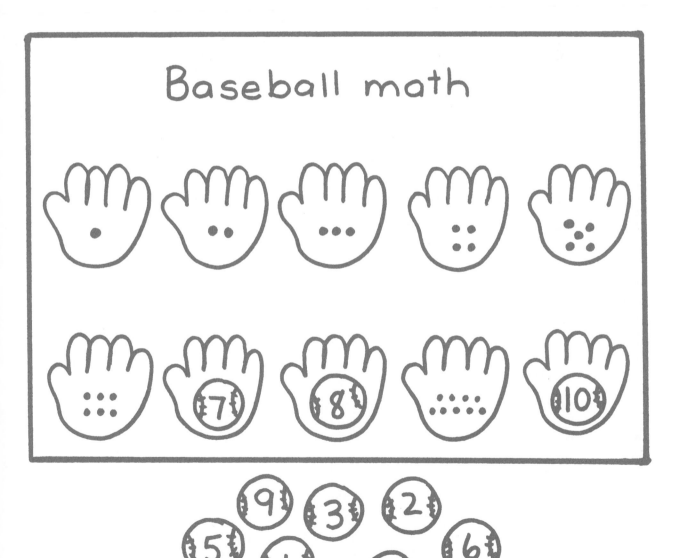

Parent Letter

Dear Parents,

Sports will be the focus of our next unit. Through the experiences provided, the children will become familiar with sports equipment and clothing. They will also recognize sports as a form of exercise.

AT SCHOOL

Activities planned to foster sports concepts include:

- exploring balls used in different sports and classifying them into groups by size, color, and ability to bounce and roll.
- trying on a variety of clothing used in different sports, including a swim cap, goggles, shoulder and leg/knee pads, helmets, gloves, and uniforms.
- skating in the room by wrapping squares of waxed paper around our feet and attaching them with rubber bands around our ankles. Our feet will then easily glide over the carpet!

AT HOME

You can incorporate sports concepts at home by:

- looking through sports magazines with your child and pointing out the equipment that is used or the clothing that is worn. This will develop your child's observation skills.
- observing a sporting event with your child, such as basketball, baseball, or football. Likewise, let your child watch you participate in a sport!
- participating in a sport together. Your child will enjoy spending special time with you!

Enjoy your child!

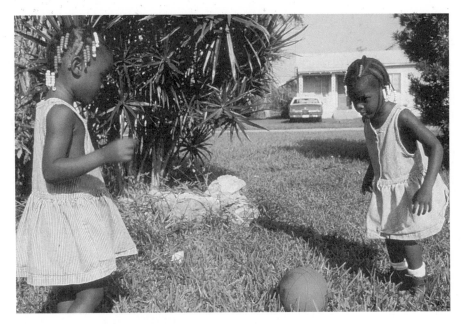

Soccer is a good physical activity.

Fingerplays

HERE IS A BALL

Here's a ball
   (make a circle with your thumb and
   pointer finger)
And here's a ball
   (make a bigger circle with two thumbs
   and pointers)
And a great big ball I see.
   (make a large circle with arms)
Now let's count the balls we've made,
One, two, three.
   (repeat)

FOOTBALL PLAYERS

Five big football players standing in the
   locker room door.
One had a sore knee
And then there were four.

Four big football players down on their
   knees.
One made a touchdown
And then there were three.

Three big football players looking up at you.
One made a tackle
And then there were two.

Two big football players running in the sun.
One was offsides
And then there was one.

One big football player standing all alone.
He decided to go home
And then there were none.

Science

1. **Feely Box**

   Place a softball, hardball, golf ball, and
   tennis ball in a feely box. The children
   can reach into the box, feel, and try to
   guess the type of ball.

2. **Ball Bounces**

   Observe the way different balls move.
   Check to see if footballs, basketballs, and
   soccer balls can be bounced. Observe to see
   if some go higher than others. Also repeat
   using smaller balls such as tennis balls,
   baseballs, and golf balls.

3. **Wheels**

   Observe the wheels on a bicycle. If possible
   bring a bike to the classroom and demonstrate how peddling makes the wheels move.

4. Examining Balls

Observe the composition of different balls. Ask the children to identify each. Then place the balls in water. Observe to see which ones float and which ones sink.

5. Types of Grass

Place real grass and artifical turf on the science table. The children can feel both types of grass and describe differences in texture.

Dramatic Play

1. Baseball

Baseball caps, plastic balls, uniforms, catcher's mask, and gloves can be placed in the dramatic play area.

2. Football

Balls, shoulder pads, uniforms, and helmets can be provided for the children to use outdoors.

3. Tennis

Tennis rackets, balls, visors, sunglasses, and shorts for the children can be placed outdoors. A variation would be to use balloons for balls and hangers with nylon pantyhose pulled around them for rackets.

4. Skiing

Ski boots and skis can be provided for the children to try on.

5. Skating

Waxed paper squares for children to wrap around their feet and ankles can be provided. The children can attach the waxed paper with rubber bands around their ankles. Encourage the children to slide across the carpeting.

Arts and Crafts

1. Easel Ideas

Cut easel paper in various sports shapes:

- baseball glove
- baseball diamond
- tennis racket
- bike
- tennis shoe
- football
- baseball cap
- football helmet
- all different sizes of balls

2. Baseball Glove Lacing

Prepare pre-cut baseball gloves out of brown construction paper. The older children might be able to cut them out themselves. Punch holes with a paper punch around the outer edge of the paper. Using yarn, let the children lace in and out of the holes of the gloves. Tie a knot at the end to secure the yarn.

3. Collages

Using sports-related magazines, encourage the children to cut out various pictures. These pictures can be pasted onto another piece of paper.

4. Ball Collages

Balls used in various sports come in all different sizes. Using construction paper or wallpaper, cut the paper in various round shapes, as well as football shapes. Encourage the children to paste them on a large piece of construction paper and decorate.

5. Golf Ball Painting

Place a piece of paper in a shallow tray or pie tin. Spoon two or three teaspoons of thin paint onto the paper. Then, put a golf ball or ping-pong ball in the tray and tilt the pan in a number of directions, allowing the ball to make designs in the paint.

Sensory

1. Swimming

Add water to the sensory table with dolls or small people figures.

2. Weighing Balls

Fill the sensory table with small balls, such as golf balls, styrofoam balls, wiffle balls, or tennis balls. Add a balance scale so that the children can weigh the balls.

3. Measuring Mud and Sand

Add a mud and sand mixture to the sensory table with scoops and spoons.

4. Feeling Turf

Line the bottom of the sensory table with artificial turf.

Large Muscle

1. Going Fishing

Use a large wooden rocking boat or a large box that two to three children can sit in. Make fish out of construction paper or tagboard, and attach paper clips to the top. Tie a magnet to a string and pole. The magnet will attract the fish.

2. Kickball

Many sports involve kicking a ball. Discuss these sports with the children. Then provide the children with a variety of balls to kick. Let the children discover which balls go the farthest and which are the easiest to kick.

3. Sports Charades

Dramatize various sports including swimming, golfing, tennis, and bike riding.

4. Golfing

Using a child-sized putter and regular golf balls, the children hit golf balls. This is an outdoor activity that requires a lot of teacher supervision.

5. Beach Volleyball

Use a large beach ball and a rope or net in a central spot outdoors. Let the children volley the beach ball to one another.

Field Trips

Suggested trips include:

1. a football field
2. a baseball field
3. tennis court
4. health (fitness) club
5. stadium
6. a swimming pool
7. the sports facilities of a local high school or college

Math

1. Ball Sort

Sort various balls by size, texture, and color.

2. Hat Sorting

Sort hats such as baseball cap, football helmet, biking helmet, visor, etc., by color, size, texture, and shape.

Group Time
(games, language)

"What's Missing?"

Provide the children in a large group with a tray of sports equipment such as a ball, baseball glove, golf ball, sunglasses, goggles, etc. Let the children examine the tray of items. Then have the children close their eyes and place their heads in their laps. Remove one item from the tray and see if the children can guess what is missing. This activity will be more successful if the numbers are related to the age of the child. For example, with two-year-old children, use only two items. Three-year-olds may be successful with an additional item. If not, remove one.

Cooking

Cheese Balls

8 ounces cream cheese, softened
1 stick of butter, softened
2 cups grated cheddar cheese
1/2 package of onion soup mix

Blend all of the ingredients together. Shape the mixture into small balls. Roll the balls in chopped nuts if desired.

Books

The following books can be used to complement this theme:

Adler, David A. (1997). *Lou Gehrig: The Luckiest Man.* Illus. by Terry Widener. Orlando: Harcourt Brace.

Blackstone, Margaret. (1993). *This Is Baseball.* Illus. by John O'Brien. New York: Holt.

Borden, Louise. (1993). *Albie the Lifeguard.* Illus. by Elizabeth Sayles. New York: Scholastic.

Brown, Mark Tolon. (1993). *D. W. Rides Again!* Boston: Little, Brown.

Carrier, Roch. (1993). *The Longest Home Run.* Illus. by Sheldon Cohen. Plattsburgh, NY: Tundra Books.

Dragonwagon, Crescent. (1993). *Annie Flies the Birthday Bike.* Illus. by Emily Arnold McCully. Colchester, CT: Atheneum.

Florian, Douglas. (1994). *A Fisher.* New York: Greenwillow.

Gibbons, Gail. (1995). *Bicycle Book.* New York: Holiday House.

Hest, Amy. (1994). *Rosie's Fishing Trip.* Illus. by Paul Howard. Cambridge, MA: Candlewick Press.

Jakob, Donna. (1994). *My Bike.* Illus. by Nelle Davis. New York: Hyperion.

Johnston, Tony. (1996). *Fishing Sunday.* Illus. by Barry Root. New York: William Morrow.

Kessler, Leonard. (1988). *Old Turtle's Soccer Team.* New York: Greenwillow.

Kessler, Leonard. (1996). *Kick, Pass, and Run.* Orlando: HarperCollins.

Loewen, Nancy. (1996). *Bicycle Safety.* Illus. by Penny Danny. Mankato, MN: Child's World.

London, Jonathan. (1995). *Froggy Learns to Swim.* Illus. by Frank Remkiewicz. New York: Viking.

London, Jonathan. (1994). *Let's Go Froggy!* Illus. by Frank Remkiewicz. New York: Viking.

Martin, Bill and Michael Sampson. (1997). *Swish.* Illus. by Michael Chesworth. New York: Holt.

McKissack, Patricia C. (1996). *A Million Fish . . . More or Less.* Illus. by Dena Schutzer. New York: Random House.

Moran, George. (1994). *Imagine Me on a Sit-Ski!* Illus. by Nadine Bernard Westcott. Beaver Dam, WI: Concept Books.

Norworth, Jack. *Take Me Out to the Ballgame.* Illus. by Alec Gillman. New York: Simon & Schuster.

Parish, Peggy. (1996). *Play Ball, Amelia Bedelia.* Illus. by Wallace Tripp. New York: HarperCollins.

Pulver, Robin. (1997). *Alicia's Tutu.* Illus. by Mark Graham. New York: Dial Books.

Rice, Eve. (1996). *Swim!* Illus. by Marisabina Russo. New York: Greenwillow.

Sampson, Michael. (1996). *The Football That Won . . .* Illus. by Ted Rand. New York: Holt.

Teague, Mark. (1992). *The Field Beyond the Outfield.* New York: Scholastic.

Tryon, Leslie. (1996). *Albert's Ball Game.* Colchester, CT: Atheneum.

Welch, Willy. (1995). *Playing Right Field.* Illus. by Marc Simont. New York: Scholastic.

Wells, Rosemary. (1995). *Edward in Deep Water.* New York: Dial Books.

Weston, Martha. (1995). *Tuck in the Pool.* New York: Clarion Books.

Wolff, Ashley. (1993). *Stella and Roy.* New York: Dutton.

Multimedia

The following multimedia products can be used to complement this theme:

Brown, Marc Tolon. *Arthur Makes the Team* [cassette and book]. (1998). Old Greenwich, CT: Listening Library.

"Take Me Out to the Ballgame" on *Six Little Ducks* [compact disc]. (1997). Long Branch, NJ: Kimbo Educational.

Recordings and Song Titles

The following recordings can be used to complement this theme:

People in Our Neighborhood—"There's a Game Today"

Six Little Ducks—"Take Me Out to the Ball Games"

THEME 58

Plants
flowers
dandelion
grass
tree buds

Activities
flying kites
gardening
fishing
baseball
picnics
golf
tennis
camping
walking
bicycling

Colors
green
white
yellow
pastels

Spring

Weather
rain
wind
warmer
thunderstorms

Holidays
St. Patrick's Day
Mother's Day
Arbor Day
May Day
Memorial Day
Easter

Animals
chicks
lambs
birds
calves
robins

Insects
caterpillars
butterflies
spiders
ants

Theme Goals

Through participating in the experiences provided by this theme, the children may learn:

1. Spring colors.
2. Spring weather.
3. Plants that grow in the spring.
4. Insects seen during the spring.
5. Springtime holidays.
6. Spring animals.
7. Spring activities.

Concepts for the Children to Learn

1. Spring is a season.
2. It rains in the spring.
3. Light colors are seen during the spring.
4. Caterpillars and butterflies are insects seen in the spring.
5. Some holidays are celebrated in the spring: Mother's Day, Easter, St. Patrick's Day, May Day, Arbor Day, and Memorial Day.
6. Chicks, lambs, and birds are springtime animals.
7. Some people go on picnics in the spring.
8. Many gardens are planted in the spring.
9. Flowers, dandelions, and grass are spring plants.
10. Gardens are often planted in the spring.

Vocabulary

1. **spring**—the season that comes after winter and before summer.
2. **garden**—a place where plants and flowers are grown.
3. **rain**—water from the clouds.

Bulletin Board

The purpose of this bulletin board is to have the children place the proper number of ribbons on each kite tail. To do this, they need to count the number of dots on the kite. Construct kites and print the numerals beginning with one and the corresponding number of dots on each. Construct ribbons for the tails of the kites as illustrated. Color the kites and tails and laminate. Staple kites to bulletin board. Affix magnetic strips to each kite as the string. Affix a magnetic piece in the middle of each ribbon.

Parent Letter

Dear Parents,

The temperature is slowly rising, and there are patches of green grass on the playground. In other words, spring is here! And spring is the subject we will be exploring at school. Throughout the week, the children will become more aware of the many changes that take place during this season, as well as common spring activities.

AT SCHOOL

Some of the learning experiences for this curriculum unit include:

- finding a suitable place on the playground to plant flowers.
- taking a walk around the neighborhood to observe signs of spring.
- planting grass seed in empty eggshells at the science table.
- creating pictures and designs with pastel watercolor markers in the art area.

AT HOME

To foster concepts of spring at home, save seeds from fruits such as oranges and apples. Assist your child in planting the seeds. Your child can also sort the seeds by color, size, or type to develop classification skills. The seeds could also be used for counting. Happy seed collecting!

Enjoy your child as you explore concepts related to spring.

564

Music

1. **"Catch One If You Can"**
   (Sing to the tune of "Skip to My Lou")

   Butterflies are flying. Won't you try and
   catch one?
   Butterflies are flying. Won't you try and
   catch one?
   Butterflies are flying. Won't you try and
   catch one?
   Catch one if you can.

   Raindrops are falling. Won't you try and
   catch one?
   Raindrops are falling. Won't you try and
   catch one?
   Raindrops are falling. Won't you try and
   catch one?
   Catch one if you can.

2. **"Signs of Spring"**
   (Sing to the tune of "Muffin Man")

   Do you see a sign of spring,
   A sign of spring, a sign of spring?
   Do you see a sign of spring?
   Tell us what you see.

3. **"Let's Be Windmills"**
   (Sing to the tune of "If I Were a Lassie")

   Oh I wish I were a windmill, a windmill, a
   windmill.
   Oh I wish I were a windmill. I know what
   I'd do.
   I'd swing this way and that way, and this
   way and that way.
   Oh I wish I were a windmill, when the
   wind blew.

Fingerplays

SEE, SEE, SEE

   See, see, see
      (shade eyes with hands)
   Three birds are in a tree.
      (hold up three fingers)

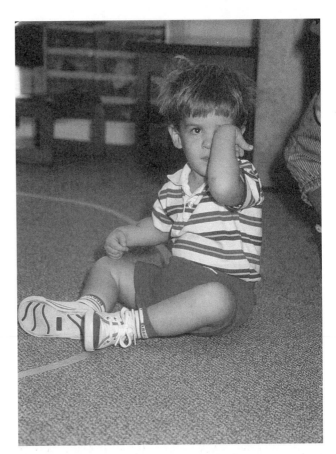

Bears wake up from long naps in the spring.

   One can chirp
      (point to thumb)
   And one can sing.
      (point to index finger)
   One is just a tiny thing.
      (point to middle finger, then rock baby
      bird in arms)
   See, see, see
   Three birds are in a tree
      (hold up three fingers)

   Look, look, look
      (shade eyes)
   Three ducks are in a brook.
      (hold up three fingers)
   One is white, and one is brown.
   One is swimming upside down.
      (point to a finger each time)
   Look, look, look
   Three ducks are in a brook.
      (hold up three fingers)

THIS LITTLE CALF

(extend fingers, push each down in succession)

This little calf eats grass.
This little calf eats hay.
This little calf drinks water.
This little calf runs away.
This little calf does nothing
But just lies down all day.
    (rest last finger in palm of hand)

RAINDROPS

Rain is falling down.
Rain is falling down.
    (raise arm, flutter fingers to ground,
    tapping the floor)
Pitter-patter
Pitter-patter
Rain is falling down.

CREEPY CRAWLY CATERPILLAR

A creepy crawly caterpiller that I see
    (shade eyes)
Makes a chrysalis in the big oak tree.
    (make body into a ball)
He stays there and I know why
    (slowly stand up)
Because soon he will be a butterfly.
    (flap arms)

MY GARDEN

This is my garden.
    (extend one hand forward, palm up)
I'll rake it with care
    (make raking motion on palm with three
    other fingers)
And then some flower seeds
I'll plant there.
    (planting motion)
The sun will shine
    (make circle with hands)
And the rain will fall.
    (let fingers flutter down to lap)
And my garden will blossom
And grow straight and tall.
    (cup hands together, extend upwards
    slowly)

CATERPILLAR

The caterpillar crawled from a plant, you see.
    (left hand crawls up and down right arm)
"I think I'll take a nap," said he.
So over the ground he began to creep
    (right hand crawls over left arm)
To spin a chrysalis, and he fell asleep.
    (cover right fist with left hand)
All winter he slept in his bed
Till spring came along and he said,
"Wake up, it's time to get out of bed!"
    (shake fist and pointer finger)
So he opened his eyes that sunny spring day.
    (spread fingers and look into hand)
"Look I'm a butterfly!" . . . and he flew away.
    (interlock thumbs and fly hands away)

Science

1. **Alfalfa Sprouts**

Each child who wishes to participate should be provided with a small paper cup, soil, and a few alfalfa seeds. The seeds and soil can be placed in the cup and watered. Place the cups in the sun and watch the sprouts grow. The sprouts can be eaten for snack. A variation is to plant the sprouts in eggshells as an Easter activity.

2. **Weather Chart**

A weather chart can be constructed that depicts weather conditions such as sunny, rainy, warm, cold, windy, etc. Attach at least two arrows to the center of the chart so that the children can point the arrow at the appropriate weather conditions.

3. **Thermometers**

On the science table place a variety of out-door thermometers. Also, post a thermometer outside of a window, at a low position, so the children can read it.

4. **Sprouting Carrots**

Cut the large end off a fresh carrot and place it in a small cup of water. In a few days, a green top will begin to sprout.

5. **Nesting Materials**

Place string, cotton, yarn, and other small items outside on the ground. Birds will collect these items to use in their nest building.

6. **Grass Growing**

Grass seeds can be sprinkled on a wet sponge. Within a few days the seeds will begin to sprout.

7. **Ant Farm**

An ant farm can by made by using a large jar with a cover. Fill the jar 2/3 full with sand and soil, and add ants. Punch a few air holes in the cover of the jar, and secure the cover to the top of the jar. The children can watch the ants build tunnels.

Dramatic Play

1. **Fishing**

Using short dowels prepare fishing poles with a string taped to one end. Attach a magnet piece to the loose end of the string. Construct fish from tagboard and attach a paper clip to each fish. The magnet will attract the paper clip, allowing the children to catch the fish. Add a tackle box, canteen, hats, and life jackets for interest.

2. **Garden**

A small plastic hoe, rake, and garden shovel can be placed outdoors to encourage gardening. A watering can, flower pots, seed packages, and sun hats will also stimulate interest.

3. **Flower Shop**

Collect plastic flowers, vases, wrapping paper, seed packages, and catalogs and place in the dramatic play area. A cash register and play money can be added.

4. **Spring Cleaning**

Small mops, brooms, feather dusters, and empty pails can be placed in the dramatic play area. A spray bottle filled with blue water, which can be used to wash designated windows, can also be provided.

Arts and Crafts

1. **Butterfly Wings**

Fold a sheet of light-colored paper in half. Show the children how to paint on only one side of the paper. The paper can be folded again and pressed. The result will be a symmetrical painting. Antennae can be added using crayons and markers to make butterflies.

2. **Pussy Willow Fingerprints**

Trace around a tongue depressor with a colored marker. Then, using ink pads or fingerpaint, the children can press a finger on the ink pad and transfer the fingerprint to the paper. This will produce pussy willow buds.

3. **Caterpillars**

Cut egg cartons in half lengthwise. Place the long rows on the art table with short pieces of pipe cleaners, markers, and crayons. From these materials, the children can make caterpillars.

4. **Kites**

Provide diamond-shaped construction paper, string, hole punch, crepe paper, glue, glitter, and markers. For older children, provide the paper with a diamond already traced. This provides them an opportunity to practice finger motor skills by cutting out the shapes. Using the triangle shapes, the children can create kites, and use them outdoors.

Science Activities

Twenty-five other interesting science activities include:

1. Observe **food forms** such as potatoes in the raw, shredded, or sliced form. Fruits can be juiced, sliced, or sectioned.

2. **Prepare tomatoes** in several ways, such as sliced, juiced, stewed, baked, and pureed.

3. **Show corn** in all forms including on the cob, popcorn, fresh cooked, and canned.

4. **Sort** picture cards into piles, living and non-living.

5. **Tape record voices.** Encourage the children to recognize each others' voices.

6. **Tape record familiar sounds** from their environment. Include a ticking clock, telephone ringing, doorbell, toilet flushing, horn beeping, etc.

7. Take the children on a **sensory walk**. Prepare by filling dishpan-sized containers with different items. Foam, sand, leaves, pebbles, mud, cold and warm water, and grains can be used. Have the children remove their shoes and socks to walk through.

8. **Enjoy a nature walk.** Provide each child with a grocery bag and instructions to collect leaves, rocks, soil, insects, etc.

9. Provide the children with **bubbles**. To make the solution, mix 2 quarts of water, 3/4 cup liquid soap, and 1/4 cup glycerine (available from a local druggist). Dip plastic berry baskets and plastic six-pack holders into the solution. Wave to produce bubbles.

10. Show the children how to feel their **heartbeat** after a vigorous activity.

11. Observe **popcorn** popping.

12. Record **body weights and heights**.

13. Prepare **hair and eye color charts**. This information can be made into bar graphs.

14. If climate permits, **freeze water outdoors**. Return it to the class and observe the effects of heat.

15. **Introduce water absorption** by providing containers with water. Allow the children to experiment with coffee filters, paper towels, newspaper, sponges, dishcloths, waxed paper, aluminum foil, and plastic wrap.

16. Explore **magnets**. Provide magnets of assorted sizes, shapes, and strengths. With the magnets, place paper clips, nuts, bolts, aluminum foil, copper pennies, metal spoons, jar lids, feathers, etc.

17. Plan a **seed party**. Provide the children with peanuts, walnuts, pecans, and coconuts. Observe the different sizes, shapes, textures, and flavors.

18. Make a **desk garden**. Cut carrots, turnips, and a pineapple 1 1/2 inches from the stem. Place the stem in a shallow pan of water.

19. Create a **worm farm**. Place gravel and soil in a clear, large-mouth jar. Add worms and keep soil moist. Place lettuce, corn, or cereal on top of the soil. Tape black construction paper around the outside of the jar. Remove the paper temporarily and see the tunnels.

20. Place a **celery stalk** with leaves in a clear container of water. Add blue or red food coloring. Observe the plant's absorption of the colored water. A similar experiment can be introduced with a white carnation.

21. Make a **rainbow** with a garden hose on a sunny day. Spray water across the sun rays. The rays of the sun contain all of the colors, but the water, acting as a prism, separates the colors.

22. Make **shadows**. In a darkened room, use a flashlight. Place a hand or object in front of the light source, making a shadow.

23. Produce **static electricity** by rubbing wool fabric over inflated balloons.

24. Install a **birdfeeder** outside the classroom window.

25. During large group, play the **What's Missing game**. Provide children with a variety of small familiar items. Tell them to cover their eyes or put their heads down. Remove one item. Then tell the children to uncover. Ask them what is missing. As children gain skill, remove a second and a third item.

Sensory

The following items can be added to the sensory table:

- string, hay, sticks, and yarn to make birds' nests
- tadpoles and water
- dirt with worms
- seeds
- water and boats
- ice cubes to watch them melt

Large Muscle

1. **Windmills**

   The children can stand up, swing their arms from side to side, and pretend to be windmills. A fan can be added to the classroom for added interest. Sing the song "Let's Be Windmills," which is listed under music.

2. **Puddles**

   Construct puddles out of tagboard and cover with aluminum foil. Place the puddles on the floor. The children can jump from puddle to puddle. A variation would be to do this activity outside, using chalk to mark puddles on the ground.

3. **Caterpillar Crawl**

   During a transition time, the children can imitate caterpillar movements.

Field Trips

1. **Nature Walk**

   Walk around your neighborhood, looking for signs of spring. Robins and other birds are often early signs of spring and can usually be observed in most areas of the country.

2. **Farm**

   Arrange a field trip to a farm. It is an interesting place to visit during the spring. Ask the farmer to show you the farm equipment, buildings, crops, and animals.

Math

1. Seed Counting

On an index card, mark a numeral. The number of cards prepared will depend upon the developmental appropriateness for the children. The children are to glue the appropriate number of seeds onto the card.

2. Insect Seriation

Construct flannel board pieces representing a ladybug, an ant, a caterpillar, a butterfly, etc. The children can arrange them on the flannel board from smallest to largest.

Social Studies

1. Animal Babies

Collect pictures of animals and their young. Place the adult animal pictures in one basket and the pictures of the baby animals in another basket. The children can match adult animals to their offspring.

2. Spring Cleanup

Each child should be provided with a paper bag to collect litter on a walk to a park, in your neighborhood, or even on your playground. The litter should be discarded when you return to the center. Also, the children should be instructed to wash their hands.

3. Dressing for Spring

Flannel board figures with clothing items should be provided. The children can dress the figures for different kinds of spring weather.

4. Spring Clothing

Collect several pieces of spring clothing such as a jacket, hat, galoshes, and short-sleeved shirts. Add these to the dramatic play area.

Group Time
(games, language)

1. What's Inside?

Inside a large box, place many spring items. Include a kite, an umbrella, a hat, a fishing pole, etc. Select an item without showing the children. Describe the object and give clues about how the item can be used. The children should try to identify the item.

2. Insect Movement

During transition time, ask the children to move like the following insects: worm, grasshopper, spider, caterpillar, butterfly, bumblebee, etc.

Cooking

1. Lemonade

1 lemon
2 to 3 tablespoons sugar
1 1/4 cups water
2 ice cubes

Squeeze lemon juice out of lemon. Add the sugar and water. Stir to dissolve the sugar. This makes one serving. Adjust the recipe to accommodate your class size.

2. Watermelon Popsicles

Remove the seeds and rind from a watermelon. Puree the melon in a blender or food processor. Pour into small paper cups. Insert popsicle sticks and freeze. These fruit popsicles can be served at snack time.

Books

The following books can be used to complement this theme:

Agell, Charlotte. (1994). *Mud Makes Me Dance in the Spring.* Gardner, ME: Tilbury House Publishers.

Baxter, Nicola. (1997). *Spring.* Illus. by Kim Woolley. Chicago: Children's Press.

Brown, Craig. (1994). *In the Spring.* New York: Greenwillow.

De Coteau Orie, Sandra. (1995). *Did You Hear Wind Sing Your Name?: An Oneida Song of Spring.* Illus. by Christopher Canyon. New York: Walker & Co.

Emberley, Michael. (1993). *Welcome Back, Sun.* Boston: Little, Brown.

Janovitz, Marilyn. (1996). *Can I Help?* New York: North South Books.

Kinsey-Warnock, Natalia. (1993). *When Spring Comes.* Illus. by Stacey Schuett. New York: Dutton.

Kroll, Virginia L. (1993). *Naomi Knows It's Springtime.* Illus. by Jill Kastner. Honesdale, PA: Boyds Mills Press.

Maass, Robert. (1996). *When Spring Comes.* Madison, WI: Demco Media. (Rebound)

Rau, Dana Meachen. (1995). *Robin at Hickory Street.* Illus. by Joel Snyder. Norwalk, CT: Soundprints Corp.

Ray, Mary Lyn. (1996). *Mud.* Illus. by Lauren Stringer. Orlando: Harcourt Brace.

Richardson, Judith Benet. (1996). *Old Winter.* Illus. by R. W. Alley. New York: Orchard Books.

Rockwell, Anne F. (1996). *My Spring Robin.* Madison, WI: Demco Media.

Shannon, George. (1996). *Spring: A Haiku Story.* Illus. By Malcah Zeldis. New York: Greenwillow.

Walters, Catherine. (1998). *When Will It Be Spring?* New York: Dutton.

Multimedia

The following multimedia products can be used to complement this theme:

Let's Find Out about Spring [video]. (1991). Hightstown, NJ: American School Publishers.

Through the Seasons with Birds: Spring [video]. (1994). Evanston, IL: Altschul Group Corp.

Recordings and Song Titles

The following recordings can be used to complement this theme:

Piggyback Songs—"Spring Morning," "Season Song"

Singing Calendar—"April"

THEME 59

Weather

warm
sunny
rainy
humid

Activities

vacationing
swimming
biking
water games
sunbathing
boating
water sports
baseball
camping
golfing
picnics

Summer

Holidays

Bastille Day
Memorial Day
Labor Day
Fourth of July
Father's Day
Grandparent's Day

Clothing

shorts
swimsuits
sunglasses
sundress
lightweight fabrics

Theme Goals

Through participating in the experiences provided by this theme, the children may learn:

1. Summer holidays.
2. Types of summer clothing.
3. Summer clothing needs.
4. Summer activities.

Concepts for the Children to Learn

1. Summer is usually the warmest season.
2. Summer months are usually warm and sunny.
3. Lightweight clothing is worn in the summer.
4. Shade trees protect us from the sun during the summer.
5. Memorial Day, Father's Day, Grandparent's Day, the Fourth of July, Bastille Day, and Labor Day are all summer holidays.
6. Swimming, biking, and camping are all summer activities.

Vocabulary

1. **shorts**—short pants worn in warm weather.
2. **swimming**—a water sport usually enjoyed by many people during the summer months.
3. **hot**—a warm temperature experienced during summer months.
4. **beach**—a sandy place used for sunbathing and playing.
5. **shade**—the shadow of something.

574

Bulletin Board

The purpose of this bulletin board is to promote the identification of written numerals as well as matching sets of objects to a written numeral. Pairs of pails are constructed out of various scraps of tagboard. Using a black marker print a different numeral on each pail. The number of pairs made and numerals used should depend upon the developmental level of the children. Cut seashells out of tagboard and decorate as desired. Laminate all pieces. Attach pails to the bulletin board by stapling them along the side and bottom edges, leaving the tops of the pails open. The children should place the corresponding sets of shells in each pail.

Parent Letter

Dear Parents,

Summer is the favorite season of most children. As summer approaches, we will be starting a unit on the season. Through this unit, the children will become more aware of summer weather, activities, food, and clothing.

AT SCHOOL

Learning experiences planned to highlight summer concepts include:

- exploring the outside and inside of a watermelon and then eating it!
- trying on shorts, sunglasses, and sandals in the dramatic play area.
- preparing fruit juice popsicles.
- eating a picnic lunch on Wednesday. We will be walking to Wilson Park at 11:45. Please feel free to pack a sack lunch and meet us there!

AT HOME

To reinforce summer concepts at home, try the following:

- Plan a family picnic and allow your child to help plan what food and items will be needed.
- Take part in or observe any summer activity such as boating, fishing, biking, camping, or taking a bike ride.

Have a good summer!

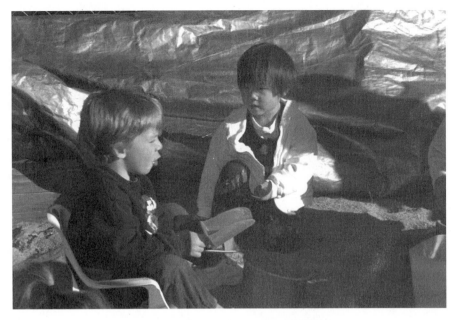

Summer means a lot of outdoor activities.

Music

1. **"Summer Clothing"**
   (Sing to the tune of "The Farmer in the Dell")

   Oh, if you are wearing shorts,
   If you are wearing shorts,
   You may walk right to the door,
   If you are wearing shorts.

   Also include: stripes, sandals, tennis shoes, flowers, a sundress, blue jeans, belt, barrettes, etc.

   This song can be used during transition times to point out children's summer clothing.

2. **"Summer Activities"**
   (Sing to the tune of "Skip to My Lou")

   Swim, swim, swim in a circle.
   Swim, swim, swim in a circle.
   Swim, swim, swim in a circle.
   Swim in a circle now.

   Also include: jump, hop, skip, run, walk, etc.

   Use this song as a transition song to introduce summer activities.

Fingerplays

HERE IS THE BEEHIVE

Here is the beehive. Where are the bees?
   (make a fist)
They're hiding away so nobody sees.
Soon they're coming creeping out of their hive,
1, 2, 3, 4, 5. Buzz-z-z-z-z.
   (draw fingers out of fist on each count)

GREEN LEAF

Here's a green leaf
   (show hand)
And here's a green leaf.
   (show other hand)
That you see, makes two.

Here's a bud
   (cup hands together)
That makes a flower.
Watch it bloom for you!
   (open cupped hands gradually)

A ROLY-POLY CATERPILLAR

Roly-poly caterpillar
Into a corner crept.
Spun around himself a blanket
   (spin around)
Then for a long time slept.
   (place head on folded hands)

Roly-poly caterpillar
Wakened by and by.
   (stretch)
Found himself with beautiful wings
Changed into a butterfly.
   (flutter arms like wings)

Science

1. Science Table

Add the following items to the science table:

- all kinds of sunglasses with different-colored shades
- plant grass seeds in small cups of dirt, water daily
- dirt and grass with magnifying glasses
- sand with scales and magnifying glasses
- pinwheels (children use their own wind to make them move)
- blow bubbles outdoors

2. Water and Air Make Bubbles

Bubble Solution Recipe

3/4 cup liquid soap
1/4 cup glycerine (obtain at a drugstore)
2 quarts water

Place mixed solution in a shallow pan and let children place the bubble makers in the solution. Bubble makers can be successfully made from the following:

- plastic six-pack holder
- straws
- bent wire with no sharp edges
- funnels

3. Flying Kites

On a windy day, make and fly kites.

4. Making Rainbows

If you have a hose available the children can spray the hose into the sun. The rays of the sun contain all the colors mixed together. The water acts as a prism and separates the water into colors creating a rainbow.

Dramatic Play

1. Juice Stand

Set up a lemonade or orange juice stand. Use real oranges and lemons to prepare and let the children squeeze them and make the juice. The juice can be served at snack time.

2. Ice Cream Stand

Trace and cut ice cream cones from brown construction paper. Cotton balls or small yarn pompoms can be used to represent ice cream. The addition of ice cream buckets and ice cream scoopers can make this activity more inviting during self-selected play periods.

3. Indoors or Outdoors Picnic

A blanket, picnic basket, plastic foods, purses, small cooler, paper plates, plastic silverware, napkins, etc., can be placed in the classroom to stimulate play.

4. The Beach

In the dramatic play area place beach blankets, lawn chairs, buckets, sunglasses, beach balls, magazines, and books. If the activity is used outdoors, a sun umbrella can be added to stimulate interest in play.

5. Camping Fun

A small freestanding tent can be set up indoors, if room permits, or outdoors. Sleeping bags can also be provided. Blocks or logs could represent a campfire.

6. Traveling by Air

Place a telephone, tickets, travel brochures, and suitcases in the dramatic play area.

Arts and Crafts

1. **Outdoor Painting**

   An easel can be placed outside. The children choose to use the easel during outdoor playtime. If the sun is shining, encourage the children to observe how quickly the paint dries.

2. **Chalk Drawings**

   Large pieces of chalk should be provided for the children to draw on the sidewalks outdoors. Small plastic berry baskets make handy chalk containers.

3. **Foot Painting**

   This may be used as an outdoor activity. The children can dip their feet in a thick tempera paint mixture and make prints by stepping on large sheets of paper. Sponges and pans of soapy water should be available for cleanup.

4. **Shake Painting**

   Tape a large piece of butcher paper on a fence or wall outdoors. Let the children dip their brushes in paint and stand two feet from the paper. Then show them how to shake the brush, allowing the paint to fly onto the paper.

5. **Sailboats**

   Color styrofoam meat trays with markers. Stick a pipe cleaner in the center of the tray and secure by bending the end underneath the carton. Prepare a sail and glue to the pipe cleaner.

Sensory

Sensory Table

The following items can be added to the sensory table:

- sand with toys
- colored sand
- sand and water
- water with toy boats
- shells
- small rocks and pebbles
- grass and hay

Large Muscle

1. **Barefoot Walk**

   Check the playground to ensure that it is free of debris. Then sprinkle part of the grass and sandbox with water. Go on a barefoot walk.

2. **Balls**

   In the outdoor play yard place a variety of large balls.

3. **Catching Balloons**

   Balloons can be used indoors and outdoors. Close supervision is required. **Caution:** If a balloon breaks it should be immediately removed.

4. **Parachute Play**

   Use a real parachute or a sheet to represent one. The children should hold onto the edges. Say a number and then have the children count and wave the parachute in the air that number of times.

5. **Balloon Racket Ball**

   Bend coat hangers into diamond shapes. Bend the handles closed and tape for safety. Then pull nylon stockings over the diamond shapes to form swatters. The children can use the swatters to keep the balloons up in the air by hitting them.

Field Trips/ Resource People

1. Picnic at the Park

A picnic lunch can be prepared and eaten at a park or in the play yard.

2. Resource People

The following resource people may be invited to the classroom:

- A lifeguard to talk about water safety.
- A camp counselor can talk to the children about camping and sing some camp songs with the children.

Math

Sand Numbers and Shapes

During outdoor play informally make shapes and numbers in the sand and let children identify the shape or number.

Social Studies

1. Making Floats

To celebrate the Fourth of July, decorate the trikes, wagons, and scooters with crepe paper, streamers, balloons, etc. Parade around the school or neighborhood.

2. Summer at School

Take pictures or slides of community summer activities. Construction workers, parades, children playing, sports activities, people swimming, library hours, picnics, band concerts, and people driving are examples. Show the slides and discuss them during group time.

3. Summer Fun Book

Magazines should be provided for the children to find pictures of summer activities. The pictures can be pasted on a sheet of paper. Bind the pages by stapling them together to make a book.

Group Time (games, language)

1. Exploring a Watermelon

Serve watermelon for snack. Talk about the color of the outside, which is called the rind. Next cut the watermelon into pieces. Give each child a piece to look at. Examine it carefully. "What color is the inside? Are there seeds? Do we eat the seeds? What can we do with them?" The children can remove all the seeds from their piece of watermelon. Then eat the watermelon. Collect all of the seeds. After circle time, wash the seeds. When dry, they can be used for a collage.

2. Puppet Show

Weather permitting, bring puppets and a puppet stage outdoors and have an outdoor puppet show.

Cooking

1. Popsicles

pineapple juice
grape juice
cranapple juice
popsicle sticks
small paper cups

If frozen juice is used, mix according to the directions on the can. Fill the paper cups 3/4 full of juice. Place the cups in the freezer. When the juice begins to freeze, insert a popsicle stick in the middle of each cup. When frozen, peel the cup away and serve.

2. Watermelon Popsicles

Remove the seeds and rind from watermelon. Puree the melon in a blender. Follow the recipe for popsicles.

3. Zippy Drink

2 ripe bananas
2 cups orange juice
2 cups orange sherbet
ice cubes
orange slices

Peel the bananas, place in a bowl and mash with a fork. Add orange juice and sherbet and beat with a rotary beater until smooth. Pour into pitcher. Add ice cubes and orange slices.

4. Kulfi (Indian Ice Cream)

1 quart milk
1/2 pint heavy cream
1/4 cup sugar
1/2 cup chopped pistachio nuts
1/2 cup chopped almonds
1 tablespoon vanilla
2 drops red food coloring

Combine milk and heavy cream in a saucepan. Simmer over medium heat for about 20 minutes until thick. Add sugar, pistachio nuts, almonds, vanilla, and food coloring. Mix thoroughly. Let cool. Fill small paper cups halfway with kulfi and place in a freezer for 1 hour until the kulfi has the consistency of soft sherbet. Makes 10 servings.

Source: *Wonderful World Macmillan Early Skills Program*. (1985). New York: Macmillan Educational Company.

Books

The following books can be used to complement this theme:

Agell, Charlotte. (1994). *I Wear Long Green Hair in Summer*. Gardner, ME: Tilbury House Publishers.

Aliki. (1996). *Those Summers*. New York: HarperCollins.

Appel, Karel. (1996). *Watermelon Day*. Illus. by Dale Gottlieb. New York: Holt.

Baxter, Nicola. (1997). *Summer*. Illus. by Kim Woolley. Chicago: Children's Press.

Crews, Nina. (1995). *One Hot Summer Day*. New York: Greenwillow.

George, Lindsay Barrett (1996). *Around the Pond: Who's Been Here?* New York: Greenwillow.

Giovanni, Nikki. (1994). *Knoxville, Tennessee*. Illus. by Larry Johnson. New York: Scholastic.

Maass, Robert. (1995). *When Summer Comes*. New York: Holt.

Rylant, Cynthia. *Mr. Putter & Tabby Row the Boat*. Illus. by Arthur Howard. Orlando: Harcourt Brace.

Van Leeuwen, Jean. (1997). *Touch the Sky Summer*. Illus. by Dan Andreasen. New York: Dial Books.

Yolen, Jane. (1995). *Before the Storm*. Illus. by Georgia Pugh. Honesdale, PA: Boyds Mills Press.

Yolen, Jane. (1993). *Jane Yolen's Songs of Summer*. Illus. by Cyd Moore. Honesdale, PA: Boyds Mills Press.

Multimedia

The following multimedia product can be used to complement this theme:

Let's Find Out About Summer [video]. Hightstown, NJ: American School Publishers.

Recording and Song Title

The following recording can be used to complement this theme:

Musical Playtime Fun—"Summer Fun"

THEME 66

Holiday

family celebration
giving thanks

Symbols

Native Americans,
harvest, turkey,
cornucopia,
fruits/vegetables,
Pilgrims

Thanksgiving

Foods

turkey
dressing
potatoes and gravy
corn
squash
cornbread
vegetables
cranberries
pumpkin pie

**Giving
Thanks**

our health
our friends
our families

Theme Goals

Through participating in the experiences provided by this theme, the children may learn:

1. The purpose of Thanksgiving.
2. Thanksgiving celebration.
3. Thanksgiving foods.
4. Thanksgiving symbols.

Concepts for the Children to Learn

1. Thanksgiving is a holiday.
2. Thanksgiving is a time for giving thanks.
3. Families celebrate together on Thanksgiving.
4. Turkey, dressing, potatoes, vegetables, cranberries, and pumpkin pie are eaten on Thanksgiving by many families.
5. A turkey, cornucopia, Pilgrims, and Native Americans are Thanksgiving symbols.

Vocabulary

1. **Thanksgiving**—a holiday in November.
2. **Pilgrims**—early settlers who sailed to America.
3. **thankful**—expressing thanks.
4. **turkey**—large bird that is cooked for Thanksgiving.
5. **Native Americans**—natives who lived in America when the Pilgrims first arrived.
6. **cornucopia**—a horn-shaped container with fruits, vegetables, and flowers.

Bulletin Board

The purpose of this bulletin board is to have the children hang the color-coded card with the printed word onto the corresponding colored feather. Construct a large turkey out of tagboard. Color each feather a different color. Hang the turkey on the bulletin board. Then hang a pushpin in each feather. On small index cards, make a circle of each color and write the color name above it as illustrated. Use a hole punch to make a hole in each card.

Parent Letter

Dear Parents,

During the month of November each year, we celebrate Thanksgiving. To coincide with this holiday at school, we will be focusing our curriculum on Thanksgiving. Through activities provided, the children will develop an understanding of the foods of Thanksgiving, as well as become more aware of the many people and things for which we are thankful.

AT SCHOOL

Planned learning experiences related to Thanksgiving include:

- popping corn.
- creating hand turkeys.
- visiting a turkey farm.
- exploring various types of corn with scales and magnifying glasses.

AT HOME

There are many ways for you to incorporate Thanksgiving concepts at home. Talk with your child about the special ways your family celebrates Thanksgiving. Involve your child in the preparation of a traditional Thanksgiving dish. Also, emphasize things and people for which you are thankful.

REMINDER

There will be no school on Thursday, November 27th.
For those of you who are traveling during the Thanksgiving weekend, drive safely!

Happy Thanksgiving from the staff!

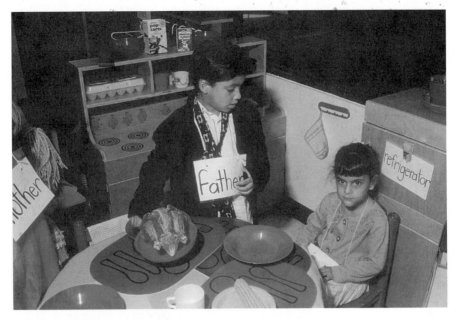

Families like to celebrate Thanksgiving.

Music

1. **"Popcorn Song"**
   (Sing to the tune of "I'm a Little Teapot")

   I'm a little popcorn in a pot.
   Heat me up and watch me pop.
   When I get all fat and white, then I'm
       done.
   Popping corn is lots of fun.

2. **"If You're Thankful"**
   (Sing to the tune of "If You're Happy")

   If you're thankful and you know it clap
       your hands.
   If you're thankful and you know it clap
       your hands.
   If you're thankful and you know it, then
       your face will surely show it,
   If you're thankful and you know it, clap
       your hands.

   Additional verses could include: stamp
   your feet; tap your head; turn around,
   shout hooray; etc.

Fingerplays

THANKSGIVING DINNER

Every day we eat our dinner.
Our table is very small.
    (palms of hands close together)
There's room for father, mother, sister,
    brother, and me—that's all.
    (point to each finger)
But when it's Thanksgiving Day and the
    company comes,
You'd scarcely believe your eyes.
    (rub eyes)
For that very same reason, the table
    stretches until it is just this size!
    (stretch arms wide)

THE BIG TURKEY

The big turkey on the farm is so very
    proud.
    (form fist)
He spreads his tail like a fan
    (spread fingers of other hand behind fist)
And struts through the animal crowd.
    (move two fingers of fist as walking)
If you talk to him as he wobbles along
He'll answer back with a gobbling song.
"Gobble, gobble, gobble."
    (open and close hand)

Science

1. Corn

Display several types of corn on the science table. Include field corn, popcorn, and popped popcorn.

2. Wishbone

Bring in a wishbone from a turkey and place it in a bottle. Pour some vinegar in the bottle to cover the wishbone. Leave the wishbone in the bottle for 24 hours. Remove it and feel it. It will feel and bend like rubber.

Sensory

The following items can be placed in the sensory area for the children to discover:

- unpopped or popped popcorn
- pine cones
- cornmeal and measuring cups

Dramatic Play

Shopping

Set up a grocery store in the dramatic play area. To stimulate play, provide a cash register, shopping bags, as well as empty food containers including boxes, packages, and plastic bottles.

Arts and Crafts

1. Thanksgiving Collage

Place magazines on the art table for the children to cut out things they are thankful for. After the pictures are cut, they can be pasted on paper to form a collage.

2. Thanksgiving Feast

Place food items cut from magazines and the newspaper on a table along with paste and paper plates. Let the children select the foods they would like to eat for their Thanksgiving feast.

3. Cornmeal Playdough

Make cornmeal playdough. Mix 2 1/2 cups flour with 1 cup cornmeal. Add 1 tablespoon oil and 1 cup water. Additional water can be added to make desired texture. The dough should have a grainy texture. Cooky cutters and rolling pins can extend this activity.

4. Popcorn Collage

Place popped popcorn and dried tempera paint into small sealable bags. Have children shake bags to color the popcorn. Then have them create designs and pictures by gluing the popcorn onto the paper. You can also use unpopped colored popcorn. **Caution:** Make sure the children do not eat any of the popcorn after it has been mixed with paint.

5. Hand Turkey

Paper, crayons, or pencils are needed. Begin by instructing the child to place a hand on a piece of paper. Then tell them to spread their fingers. If possible, have the child trace his own fingers. Otherwise, you need to trace them. The hand can be decorated to create a turkey. Eyes, a beak, and a wattle can be added to the outline of the thumb. The fingers can be colored to represent the turkey's feathers. Then legs can be added below the outline of the palm.

Large Muscle

Popping Corn

Pretend to be popping corn. Begin by demonstrating how to curl down on the floor, explaining that everyone is a kernel of corn. Then plug in the popcorn popper and listen to the sounds. Upon hearing popping sounds, jump up and down to the sounds.

Field Trip

Turkey Farm

Visit a turkey farm. The children can observe the behavior of the turkeys as well as the food they eat.

Math

1. Turkey Shapes

Give children several geometric shapes to create their own turkeys with circles, squares, and triangles. Have children identify the shapes and colors as they create their turkeys.

2. Colored Popcorn

Provide the children with colored popcorn seeds. Place corresponding colored circles in the bottom of muffin tins or egg cartons. Encourage the children to sort the seeds by color.

Group Time
(games, language)

1. Turkey Chase

Have the children sit in a circle formation. The game requires two balls of different colors. Vary the size, depending on the age of the children. Generally, the younger the child, the larger the ball size. Begin by explaining that the first ball passed is the "turkey." The second ball is the "turkey farmer." The first ball should be passed from child to child around the circle. Shortly after, pass the second ball in the same direction. The game ends when the turkey farmer, the second ball, catches up to the turkey, the first ball. This game is played like hot potato.

2. Feast

Place several kinds of food on a plate in the middle of the circle. Tell the children to cover their eyes. Choose one child to take something from the plate to eat. The child hides one item, and the others open their eyes and try to guess which food item the child has eaten! The number of items included in this activity should be determined by the children's developmental age. It may be advisable to begin with only two food items.

3. Turkey Keeper

To play this game, a turkey cut from cardboard or even a small plastic replica is needed. Instruct one child to cover his eyes. Then quietly hide the turkey in the classroom. After this, instruct the child to open his eyes and begin to look for the turkey. When the child begins walking in the direction of the turkey, the rest of the children quietly provide a clue by saying, "gobble gobble." As the child approaches the turkey, the children's voices serve as a clue by becoming louder. Once the turkey is located, another child becomes the turkey keeper.

4. Drop the Wishbone

Tell the children to sit in a circle formation. Choose one child to walk around the outside of the circle and drop a wishbone behind another child. (If a real wishbone is unavailable, a wishbone can be cut from cardboard.) The child who had the wishbone dropped behind him must pick it up and chase the first child. If the first child is tagged before he runs around the circle and sits in the second child's place, he is "it" again. If not, the second child is "it." This is a variation of "Drop the Handkerchief."

5. Turkey Waddle

Provide the children with verbal and visual clues to waddle like turkeys. The following terms may be used:

- ◎ fat turkey
- ◎ little turkey
- ◎ fast turkey
- ◎ slow turkey
- ◎ tired turkey
- ◎ happy turkey
- ◎ proud turkey
- ◎ sad turkey
- ◎ hungry turkey
- ◎ full turkey

Cooking

1. Fu Fu—West Africa

3 or 4 yams
water
1/2 teaspoon salt
1/8 teaspoon pepper
Optional: 3 tablespoons honey or sugar

Wash and peel yams and cut into 1/2-inch slices. Place slices in a large saucepan and add water to cover them. Bring to a boil over a hot plate or stove. Reduce heat, cover saucepan, and simmer for 20 to 25 minutes, until yams are soft enough to mash. Remove saucepan from stove and drain off liquid into a small bowl. Let yams cool for 15 minutes. Place yam slices in a medium-sized mixing bowl, mash with a fork, add salt and pepper, and mash again until smooth. Roll mixture into small, walnut-sized balls. If mixture is too dry, moisten it with a tablespoon of the reserved yam liquid. For sweeter Fu Fu, roll yam balls in a dish of honey or sugar. Makes 24 balls.

2. Muffins

1 egg
3/4 cup milk
1/2 cup vegetable oil
2 cups all-purpose flour
1/3 cup sugar
3 tablespoons baking powder
1 teaspoon salt

Heat oven to 400 degrees. Grease bottoms only of 12 medium muffin cups. Beat egg. Stir in milk and oil. Stir in remaining ingredients all at once, just until flour is moistened. Batter will be lumpy. Fill muffin cups about 3/4 full. Bake until golden brown about 20 minutes. For pumpkin muffins: stir in 1/2 cup pumpkin and 1/2 cup raisins with the milk and 2 teaspoons pumpkin pie spice with the flour.

For cranberry-orange muffins: stir in 1 cup cranberry halves and 1 tablespoon grated orange peel with milk.

3. Cranberry Freeze

16-ounce can (2 cups) whole cranberry sauce
8-ounce can (1 cup) crushed pineapple, drained
1 cup sour cream or yogurt

In a medium bowl, combine all the ingredients and mix well. Pour the mixture into an 8-inch square pan or an ice cube tray. Freeze 2 hours or until firm. To serve cut into squares or pop out of the ice cube tray.

Books

The following books can be used to complement this theme:

Accorsi, William. (1992). *Friendship's First Thanksgiving*. New York: Holiday House.

Alden, Laura. (1993). *Thanksgiving*. Illus. by Susan Lexa-Senning. Chicago: Children's Press.

Bauer, Caroline Feller. (1994). *Thanksgiving; Stories and Poems*. Illus. by Nadine B. Westcott. New York: HarperCollins.

Behrens, June. (1996). *Thanksgiving Feast: The First American Holiday*. Illus. by Joann Rounds. Newport Beach, CA: York House Publishers.

Boynton, Alice B. (1996). *Priscilla Alden and the First Thanksgiving*. Morristown, NJ: Silver Burdett Press. (Pbk)

Bruchac, Joseph. (1996). *Circle of Thanks: Native American Poems and Songs of Thanksgiving*. Illus. by Murv Jacob. Moraga, CA: Bridgewater Books.

Capote, Truman. (1996). *Thanksgiving Visitor*. Illus. by Beth Peck. New York: Knopf.

Cowley, Joy. (1996). *Gracias, the Thanksgiving Turkey*. Illus. by Joe Cepeda. New York: Scholastic.

DeRubertis, Barbara. (1996). *Thanksgiving Day: Let's Meet the Wampanoags and the Pilgrims*. Illus. by Thomas Sperling. New York: Kane Press. (Pbk)

Dubowski, Cathy E. (1997). *Squanto: First Friend to the Pilgrims*. Illus. by Steven Peruccio. Milwaukee: Gareth Stevens.

Hallinan, P. K. (1993). *Today Is Thanksgiving*. Lake Forest, IL: Forest House Publishing.

Hintz, Martin and Kate Hintz. (1998). *Thanksgiving*. Chicago: Children's Press.

Jackson, Alison et al. (1997). *I Know an Old Lady Who Swallowed a Pie*. Illus. by Byron Schachner. New York: Dutton.

MacMillan, Dianne M. (1997). *Thanksgiving Day*. Springfield, NJ: Enslow Publishers.

Ross, Katharine. (1995). *The Story of the Pilgrims*. Illus. by Carolyn Cross. New York: Random House.

Tryon, Leslie. (1994). *Albert's Thanksgiving*. New York: Simon & Schuster.

Woods, Andrew. (1996). *Young Squanto: The First Thanksgiving*. Illus. by Chris Powers. Mahwah, NJ: Troll.

Multimedia

The following multimedia products can be used to complement this theme:

Gallina, Jill. *Holiday Songs for All Occasions* [cassette]. Kimbo Records.

Holiday Action Sons [cassette]. Kimbo Records.

Squanto and the First Thanksgiving [video]. (1993). Rabbit Ears Productions.

Thanksgiving [video]. (1994). Schlessinger Video Productions.

Recordings and Song Titles

The following recordings can be used to complement this theme:

Holiday Songs for all Occasions—"The Turkey Wobble"

Holiday Piggyback Songs—"Hello Mr. Turkey," "We Are Thankful"

Where Is Thumbkin?—"Five Fat Turkeys Are We"

Holiday Action Songs—"The Pilgrims," "Come Let's All Pray Together," "The Indians," "The Strutting Turkey," "The Chick in the Yard"

Singing Calendar—"November"

THEME 61

Kinds

hardwoods
softwoods
evergreens
deciduous

Parts

leaves
branches
bark
trunk
roots

Trees

Care

soil
water
sunlight

Purposes

shade
wood
wood products
clean air
food
animal homes

Theme Goals

Through participating in the experiences provided by this theme, the children may learn:

1. Parts of a tree.
2. Kinds of trees.
3. Care of trees.
4. How trees help us.

Concepts for the Children to Learn

1. A tree is a large plant.
2. There are many kinds of trees including hardwoods and softwoods.
3. A tree has many parts: leaves, branches, bark, trunk, and roots.
4. The leaves of some trees are like needles.
5. The trunk is the stem of the tree and is covered with bark.
6. The roots of a tree are underground.
7. Roots help the tree stand; they also get water and nutrients from the soil.
8. Sap is a liquid that supplies food to the tree.
9. Trees need soil, water, and sunlight to grow.
10. Trees provide us with wood.
11. Many items are made from wood, such as houses, chairs, tables, some toys, doors, fences, paper, and paper products.
12. Some fruits grow on trees.
13. Apples, bananas, and oranges are examples of fruits that grow on trees.
14. Trees provide homes for many animals.
15. Trees provide us with shade to keep us cool and protect us from the sun.

Vocabulary

1. **tree**—a large plant.
2. **trunk**—the main stem and largest part of a tree.
3. **bark**—the tough, outer covering of a tree.
4. **sap**—the fluid part of a tree.
5. **root**—the underground part of a plant.

Bulletin Board

The purpose of this bulletin board is to provide numeral identification as well as matching sets of objects to numerals. To prepare the bulletin board construct tree trunks out of brown tagboard. Print a numeral on each trunk. Next, construct treetops out of green tagboard. Draw sets of leaves on each treetop. Trace and cut out treetop shadows from black construction paper. Using the illustration as a guide, attach the shadows and tree trunks to the bulletin board. Adhesive magnet pieces or map tacks can be used by the children to match each tree trunk to the corresponding treetop.

Parent Letter

Dear Parents,

Did you ever stop to think about what our world would be like without trees? Trees serve many purposes; consequently, we will be exploring a theme on trees beginning this week. Through the experiences provided in this curriculum unit, the children will become aware of the parts of a tree, kinds of trees, and, of course, the importance of trees.

AT SCHOOL

We will use wood to build houses, schools, chairs, tables, and all kinds of other objects. We will make paper. We will talk about foods that grow on trees. The foods served at snack time will be those foods that are grown on trees. Some of the week's activities will include:

- creating leaf and bark rubbings in the art area.
- going on a "tree walk" and recording the number and kinds of trees we see.
- cooking with foods we get from trees.
- creating our own books in the writing center.
- planting citrus fruit seeds and an avocado seed.
- listening to stories related to trees.

AT HOME

Walk around your home and find all the things that are made from wood. Which room contains the most wood items?

Polish your furniture with your child. Show him or her how to care for fine wood products.

Try preparing the following recipe with your child:

Apple Bake

Core an apple and place it in a dish with a tablespoon or two of water. Sprinkle with cinnamon and a dash of sugar, if desired. Cover and bake at 350 degrees for 20 minutes. If you prefer microwaving, cover with plastic wrap and cook on "high" for five minutes.

Enjoy your child!

Children enjoy a brush as a tool to apply paint.

Music

1. **"Little Leaves"**
   (Sing to the tune of "Ten Little Indians")

   One little, two little, three little leaves.
   Four little, five little, six little leaves.
   Seven little, eight little, nine little leaves.
   Ten little leaves fall down.

2. **"Foods That Grow on Trees"**
   (Sing to the tune of "The Farmer in the Dell")

   Foods that grow on trees.
   Foods that grow on trees.
   Let's sing a song about
   Foods that grow on trees.

   Apples grow on trees.
   Apples grow on trees.
   Pick them, red and sweet.
   Apples grow on trees.

   Bananas grow on trees.
   Bananas grow on trees.
   Pick them, yellow and long.
   Bananas grow on trees.

   Oranges grow on trees.
   Oranges grow on trees.
   Pick them, sweet and juicy.
   Oranges grow on trees.

   Walnuts grow on trees.
   Walnuts grow on trees.
   Pick them, brown and crunchy.
   Walnuts grow on trees.

Fingerplays

THE APPLE TREE

   Way up high in the apple tree
      (raise arms over head)
   Two little apples smiled at me.
      (make fists or circles with hands)
   I shook that tree as hard as I could
      (move hands as if shaking something)
   Down came the apples
      (falling motion with fists)
   Mmmmmmmmmm—were they good!
      (rub tummy)

ORANGE TREE

   This is the orange tree with leaves so green
      (raise arms over head, making a circle)
   Here are the oranges that hang in between.
      (make fists)
   When the wind blows the oranges will fall.
   Here is the basket to gather them all.
      (make circle with arms in front of body)

I AM A TALL TREE

I am a tall tree.
I reach toward the sky
   (reach upward with both hands)
Where the bright stars twinkle
And white clouds float by.
   (sway arms above head)
My branches toss high
As the wild winds blow.
   (wave arms rapidly)
Now they bend forward
Loaded with snow.
   (arms out front swaying)
I like it best
When I rock birds to sleep in their nest.
   (place hands at the side of head and
   close eyes)

THE WIND

Who has seen the wind?
Neither I nor you;
But where the leaves hang trembling,
   (hold hands downward and wiggle
   fingers)
The wind is passing through.

Who has seen the wind?
Neither you nor I;
But when the trees bow down their heads,
   (move head downward)
The wind is passing by.

Science

1. Weighing Nuts

Provide a balance scale and acorns, pinecones, or nuts at the science table.

2. Planting Seeds

Collect and plant seeds from fruits that grow on trees such as apples and citrus fruits. Make and record predictions about when the plants will sprout.

3. Grow an Avocado Tree

Remove a seed from an avocado. Peel off the brown outer covering of the seed. Poke three toothpicks into the avocado seed at equal distances from one another. Place the seeds in a glass of lukewarm water with the largest end submerged. Replace the water once a week. Sprouts will appear in about three weeks. When the stem and roots are several inches long, transplant the avocado into a pot that is about 1 inch wider than the avocado.

4. Leaf Book

Collect leaves from various trees. Mount each leaf on a piece of construction paper or tagboard. Then print the name of the tree the leaf represents. Gather the pages and bind with loose-leaf rings. Place the book in the science area for the children to review.

5. Shade Versus Sun

Place an outdoor thermometer in direct sunlight and another beneath the shade of a tree. Compare results. A chart could also be made for this activity and results could be compared for several days.

6. Pinecone Bird Feeders

Collect pinecones. Attach a piece of yarn or string to the stem. Use a plastic knife to spread peanut butter over the pinecone; then roll in birdseed. Hang the bird feeder outside.

7. Make Paper

Cut a piece of screen 7 inches × 11 inches and frame with wood. Tear construction paper or tissues into one-inch pieces. Place the shredded paper pieces in a blender. Add enough water to cover and blend the paper into pulp. Pour the pulp into a 9-inch × 13-inch tray. Use the framed screen to pan the pulp, moving it to get an even layer of pulp. Lift the screen out of the pan in a straight, upward direction. Place the screen on a stack of newspapers. Roll with a rolling pin to squeeze out water. Lift off the newspaper and gently peel the homemade paper from the screen; allow it to dry on paper towels or newspaper.

Dramatic Play

1. Construction Site

Design a construction site in the dramatic play area. Provide props such as hard hats, blueprints, floor plans, rulers, tape measures, lumber scraps, wooden blocks, and cardboard boxes.

2. Birds

Trace and cut bird masks and wings out of tagboard for the children to wear. Display pictures of trees and birds. Play a tape of bird songs. A variation would be to decorate a climber with green crepe paper to resemble a tree.

Arts and Crafts

1. Tree Rubbing

Use crayons or chalk to create rubbings of various tree parts. Place leaves under a single sheet of newsprint. Rub the crayon over the top of the paper until the imprint of the leaf appears. Try making additional rubbings using bark and maple seeds.

2. Twig Painting

Twigs from trees can be used as painting tools. Provide the children with trays of tempera paint of a thick consistency and construction paper to create designs. The children may also enjoy experimenting with the twig as a writing tool.

3. Pine Needle Brushes

Cut branches from a pine needle tree. Place the branches at the easel so that the children can use them as brushes to apply paint.

4. Decorating Pinecones

Collect pinecones of different sizes. Place them on the art table with trays of thick, colored tempera paints, glitter, glue, yarn, sequins, and strips of paper for the children to decorate the pinecones.

5. Sawdust Playdough

Combine two cups of sawdust, three cups of flour, and one cup of salt. Add water as needed to make a pliable dough. (Sawdust can be obtained, usually at no cost, from a local lumber company.)

6. Textured Paint

Add sawdust to prepared paints for use at the art table or easel.

7. Paper Product Sculptures

Collect magazines, newspapers, boxes, and paper towel rolls for the children to use to create designs and sculptures. Place all of the items on the art table along with glue, scissors, and paint.

8. Make a Tree

Collect paper towel and toilet paper rolls. The children can paint or cover them with construction paper to resemble tree trunks. Branches and leaves can be fabricated from pipe cleaners and construction paper. The branches and leaves can then be attached to the trunk.

Sensory

1. Wood Shavings

Obtain wood shavings from a local lumber company. Place them in the sensory table along with scoops and pails.

2. Pinecones

Collect pinecones of various sizes and place them in the sensory table. Small boxes, pails, and scoops can be added.

3. Acorns

Collect acorns and allow them to dry thoroughly before placing in the sensory table. Add accessories to encourage participation such as pails, small paper bags, scoops, and spoons.

Large Muscle

1. Wooden Climber

If available, set up a wooden climber on the playground or in the classroom for the children to practice their climbing skills.

2. Wooden Balance Beam

If available, set up a wooden balance beam in an open area of the classroom. Suggest ways for the children to cross the beam: Walking heel to toe, walking sideways, crawling, and walking holding an object. Older children may be able to walk backwards.

Field Trips/ Resource People

The following sources can be contacted for more information:

- area forest industries such as paper mills and logging companies.
- Department of National Resources.
- university or county extension offices.
- national, state, and local parks.
- nature centers.
- university departments of biology, botany, construction, and forestry.

Math

1. Trace Walk

Record the number of trees observed on a walk. If appropriate, the trees might also be classified as "broadleaf" or "evergreen" or by the type of tree, such as maple, oak, pine, etc.

2. Sorting and Counting Activities

The following items can be collected and used for various sorting and counting activities:

- acorns
- small pinecones
- walnuts
- pecans
- almonds
- apple seeds
- citrus fruit seeds

3. Items Made From Trees

Collect items from around the classroom for children to sort and classify those made from trees as "wooden items" and others as "nonwooden items." Label and provide boxes or similar containers for the children to place the items. If appropriate, the children can count the number of items in each category and record the results.

Social Studies

1. Family Tree

Cut a tree trunk out of brown tagboard. Cut a treetop out of green tagboard. Attach the trunk and treetop to a bulletin board and display on a wall. Ask the children to bring family photographs that can be displayed on the tree.

Group Time
(games, language)

1. Tree Chart

On a large piece of tagboard, print the title "Things Made from Trees." During group time, present the chart and record the children's responses. Display the completed chart and refer to it throughout the theme.

2. **Movement Activity—"Happy Leaves"**

Cut leaves out of various colors of construction paper. During group time give each child one leaf. When the children hear the color of their leaf in the following rhyme, they may stand up and move like leaves:

Little red leaves are glad today,
For the wind is blowing them off and away,
They are flying here, they are flying there.
Oh, little red leaves, you are everywhere.

Repeat the rhyme and insert additional color words.

Cooking

1. **Guacamole Dip**

   1 medium avocado
   2 tablespoons of chopped onion
   1/4 teaspoon chili powder
   1/4 teaspoon garlic salt
   2 tablespoons mayonnaise or salad dressing

   Peel and cut the avocado into pieces and process at medium speed in a blender. Add remaining ingredients and blend. Serve the dip with tortilla or corn chips.

2. **Orange Pecan Cookies**

   1 cup sugar
   3/4 cup softened butter or margarine
   1/4 cup milk
   1 teaspoon vanilla
   1 egg
   2 cups flour
   1/2 cup finely chopped pecans
   2 tablespoons grated orange peel
   1 teaspoon baking powder
   3/4 teaspoon salt

   Combine sugar, butter, milk, vanilla, and egg in a large mixing bowl. Add remaining ingredients and blend well. Drop by rounded teaspoonfuls onto ungreased cookie sheets. Bake for 9–12 minutes or until lightly browned in a 370-degree oven. Remove cookies from sheet and cool.

3. **Prepare recipes that include:**

almonds	dates	olives
apples	figs	oranges
apricots	grapefruit	peaches
avocados	lemons	pears
cashews	limes	pecans
cherries	mangoes	prunes
cinnamon	maple syrup	walnuts
cloves	nectarines	
coconuts	nutmeg	

Caution: Beware of the potential of children choking on nuts. Avoid using them or grind them finely in recipes for young children.

Books

The following books can be used to complement this theme:

Aldridge, Josephine Haskell. (1993). *A Possible Tree*. Illus. by Daniel San Souci. New York: Simon & Schuster.

Arnosky, Jim. (1992). *Crinkleroot's Guide to Knowing the Trees*. New York: Simon & Schuster.

Bunting, Eve. (1993). *Someday a Tree*. Illus. by Ronald Himler. New York: Houghton Mifflin.

Burns, Diane L. (1990). *Sugaring Season: Making Maple Syrup*. Illus. by Cheryl Walsh Bellville. Minneapolis: Carolrhoda Books.

Carrier, Lark. (1996). *A Tree's Tale*. New York: Dial Books.

Dorros, Arthur. (1997). *A Tree Is Growing*. Illus. by S. D. Schindler.

Drawson, Blair. (1996). *Mary Margaret's Tree*. New York: Orchard Books.

Edwards, Richard. (1993). *Ten Tall Oaktrees*. Illus. by Caroline Crossland. New York: William Morrow.

Ehlert, Lois. (1991). *Red Leaf, Yellow Leaf*. Orlando: Harcourt Brace.

Gackenbach, Dick. (1992). *Mighty Tree*. Orlando: Harcourt Brace.

Hall, Zoe. (1996). *The Apple Tree*. Illus. by Shari Halpern. New York: Scholastic.

Jaspersohn, William. (1996). *Timber*. Boston: Little, Brown.

Levine, Ellen. (1995). *The Tree That Would Not Die*. Illus. by Ted Rand. New York: Scholastic.

Manson, Christopher. (1993). *The Tree in the Wood: An Old Nursery Song*. New York: North South Books.

Maestro, Betsy. (1994). *Why Do Leaves Change Color?* Illus. by Loretta Krupinski. New York: HarperCollins.

Oppenheim, Joanne. (1995). *Have You Seen Trees?* Illus. by Jean and Mou-Sien Tseng. New York: Scholastic.

Pluckrose, Henry Arthur. (1990). *Trees*. Illus. by Joy Friedman. Chicago: Children's Press.

Reed-Jones, Carol. (1995). *The Tree in the Ancient Forest*. Illus. by Christopher Canyon. Nevada City, CA: Dawn Publications.

Sanders, Scott R. (1996). *Meeting Trees*. Illus. by Robert Hynes. Washington, DC: National Geographic Society.

Tresselt, Alvin. (1992). *The Gift of the Tree*. Illus. by Henri Sorenson. New York: Lothrop, Lee & Shepard.

Zalben, Jane Breskin. (1995). *Pearl Plants a Tree*. New York: Simon & Schuster.

Multimedia

The following multimedia products can be used to complement this theme:

Bean, Norman and Sandy Bean. *A First Look at Trees* [video]. (©1992). Van Nuys, CA: AIMS Media.

Cole, Joanna. *Goes the Seed* [video]. (1995). NY: KidVision. (*Magic School Bus* series)

Cutting, Michael. *The Little Crooked Christmas Tree* [video]. (1990). Stamford, CT: ABC Video.

Tell Me Why: Flowers, Plants and Trees [video]. (1987). Marina del Rey, CA: Tell Me Why.

What Is a Leaf? [video]. (1991). Washington, DC: National Geographic.

THEME 62

Symbols

hearts
Cupid
cards
candy
arrows
flowers

Colors

red
pink
white

Valentine's Day

Purpose

share feelings
show love

Activities

parties
card giving
flowers
gifts

Theme Goals

Through participating in the experiences provided by this theme, the children may learn:

1. Valentine's Day colors.
2. Valentine's Day activities.
3. Symbols of Valentine's Day.
4. Purpose of Valentine's Day.

Concepts for the Children to Learn

1. Red, pink, and white are Valentine's Day colors.
2. On Valentine's Day we share our love with others.
3. Hearts, Cupids, and flowers are symbols of Valentine's Day.
4. People send cards on Valentine's Day.

Vocabulary

1. **heart**—a symbol of love.
2. **Valentine**—a card designed for someone special.
3. **Cupid**—a symbol of Valentine's Day, usually a baby boy with a bow and arrows.
4. **card**—a decorative paper with a written message.

Bulletin Board

The purpose of this bulletin board is to have the children place the correct number of hearts into the corresponding numbered box. Using decorated boxes as illustrated, a Valentine's Day bulletin board can be created. The bottom of each box should be cut, so it can be taped shut while putting hearts in and easily opened to release the hearts. Mark each box with a numeral and a corresponding number of hearts as illustrated. The number of numerals will depend upon developmental appropriateness. Attach the boxes to the bulletin board using pushpins or staples. Next, construct many small hearts.

Parent Letter

Dear Parents,

Valentine's Day is a special day, so this unit celebrates Valentine's Day. It is a day when we share our positive feelings about special people. This day also provides an opportunity to talk about the importance of sharing, giving, loving, and friendship.

AT SCHOOL

Some of the activities related to Valentine's Day will include:

- having a post office in dramatic play to mail valentines to friends.
- constructing valentine mobiles to decorate our room.
- constructing a "What a Friend Is . . ." chart to hang in our room.
- sending and receiving valentines.
- watching the video *Valentine's Day.*
- inviting special people at school, including the custodian and secretary, to a party.
- listening to Valentine's stories and poems.

AT HOME

Try to set aside time to have a heart-to-heart chat with your child. To develop self-esteem talk to your child about feelings and why you are proud of him. Also, help your child make a valentine for a grandparent, aunt, uncle, or other person. A special note could be dictated by your child and written by you.

Have a Happy Valentine's Day!

Music

1. **"My Valentine"**
(Sing to the tune of "The Muffin Man")

   Oh, do you know my valentine,
   My valentine, my valentine?
   Oh, do you know my valentine?
   His name is _____.

   Chosen valentine then picks another child.

2. **"Ten Little Valentines"**
(Sing to the tune of "Ten Little Indians")

   One little, two little, three little valentines.
   Four little, five little, six little valentines.
   Seven little, eight little, nine little valentines.
   Ten little valentines here!

3. **"Two Little Cupids"**
(Sing to the tune of "Two Little Blackbirds")

   Two little cupids sitting on a heart.
      (hold hands behind back)
   One named _____. One named _____.
      (bring out one pointer for each name)
   Fly away, _____. Fly away, _____.
      (place one pointer behind back for each name)
   Come back, _____. Come back, _____.
      (bring out pointers one at a time again)
   Two little cupids sitting on a heart.
      (hold up two fingers)
   One named _____. One named _____.
      (wiggle each pointer separately)

   For each _____ insert a child's name.

Fingerplay

FIVE LITTLE VALENTINES

   Five little valentines were having a race.
   The first little valentine was frilly with lace.
      (hold up one finger)
   The second little valentine had a funny face.
      (hold up two fingers)
   The third little valentine said, "I love you."
      (hold up three fingers)

Be my Valentine.

   The fourth little valentine said, "I do too."
      (hold up four fingers)
   The fifth little valentine was sly as a fox.
   He ran the fastest to the valentine box.
      (make five fingers run behind back)

Science

1. **Valentine's Day Flowers**

   In the science area, place various flowers and magnifying glasses. The children can observe and explore the various parts of the flowers.

2. **Valentine's Day Colors**

   Mixing red and white tempera paint, the children can make various shades of red or pink.

Dramatic Play

1. **Mailboxes**

   Construct an individual mailbox for each child using shoeboxes, empty milk cartons, paper bags, or partitioned boxes. Print each child's name on the box or encourage the child to do so. The children can sort mail, letters, and small packages into the boxes.

2. **Florist**

   Plastic flowers, vases, styrofoam pieces, tissue paper, ribbons, candy boxes, a cash register, and play money can be used to make a flower shop.

3. **Card Shop**

   Stencils, paper, markers, scraps, stickers, etc., can be provided to make a card-making shop.

Arts and Crafts

1. **Easel Painting**

   Mix red, white, and pink paint and place at the easel.

2. **Chalk Drawings**

   White chalk and red and pink construction paper can be used to make chalk drawings.

3. **Classroom Valentine**

   Cut out one large paper heart. Encourage all children to decorate and sign it. The valentine can be hung in the classroom or be given to a classroom friend. The classroom friend may be the cook, custodian, center director, or principal.

4. **Heart Prints**

   On the art table place white paper and various heart-shaped cookie cutters. Mix pink and red tempera paint and pour into shallow pans. The children can print hearts on white construction paper using the cookie cutters as a tool and then paint them.

5. **Heart Materials**

   The children can cut hearts out of construction paper and decorate them with lace scraps, yarn, and glitter to make original Valentine's Day cards. Pre-cut hearts should be available for children who have not mastered the skill. For other children who have cutting skills, a heart shape can be traced on paper for them to cut.

Sensory

Soap

Mix dish soap, water, and red food coloring in the sensory table. Provide egg beaters for children to make bubbles.

Large Muscle

1. **Hug Tag**

   One child is "it" and tries to tag another child. Once tagged, the child is "frozen" until another child gently hugs him to "unfreeze" him.

2. **Balloon Ball**

   Blow up two or three red, pink, or white balloons. Using nylon paddles made by stretching nylon pantyhose over bent coat hangers, the children can hit the balloons to each other. The object is to try to keep the balloon up off the floor or ground. This activity needs to be carefully supervised. **Caution:** If a balloon breaks, it needs to be removed immediately.

Field Trips

1. **Visit a Post Office**

   Visit the local post office. Valentine's Day cards made in the classroom can be mailed.

608

2. Visit a Floral Shop

Visit a flower store. Observe the different valentine arrangements. Call attention to the beautiful color of the flowers, arrangements, and containers.

1. Broken Hearts

Cut heart shapes out of red and pink tagboard. Print a numeral on one side and a number set of heart stickers or drawings on the other side. Cut the hearts in half as a puzzle. The children can match the puzzle pieces.

Materials to Collect for the Art Center

aluminum foil	fabrics	paper napkins	spools
ball bearings	felt	paper newspaper	stockings
barrel hoops	felt hats	paper tissue	sweaters
beads	flannel	paper towels	tacks
belts	floor covering	paper tubes	tape
bottles	glass	paper wrapping	thread
bracelets	gourds	phonograph	tiles
braiding	hat boxes	records	tin cans
brass	hooks	photographs	tin foil
buckles	inner tubes	picture frames	tongue depressors
burlap	jars	pinecones	towels
buttons	jugs	pins	tubes
candles	lacing	pipe cleaners	twine
canvas	lampshades	plastic board	wallpaper
cartons	leather remnants	plastic paint	wax
cellophane	linoleum	pocket books	window shades
chains	marbles	reeds	wire
chalk	masonite	ribbon	wire eyelets
chamois	metal foil	rings	wire hairpins
clay	mirrors	rope	wire hooks
cloth	muslin	rubber bands	wire mesh
colored pictures	nails	rug yarn	wire paper clips
confetti	necklaces	safety pins	wire screen
containers	neckties	sand	wire staples
copper foil	oilcloth	sandpaper	wooden beads
cord	ornaments	seashells	wooden blocks
cornhusks	pans	seeds	wooden clothespins
cornstalks	paper bags	sheepskin	wooden sticks
costume jewelry	paper boxes	shoelaces	wool
crayon pieces	paper cardboard	shoe polish	yarn
crystals	paper corrugated	snaps	zippers
emery cloth	paper dishes	soap	
eyelets	paper doilies	sponges	

2. Heart Seriation

Cut various-sized hearts from pink, red, and white construction paper. The children can sequence the heart shapes from small to big or vice versa.

Social Studies

1. Sorting Feelings

Cut pictures of happy and sad people out of magazines. On the outside of two boxes, draw a smiling face on one and a sad face on the other. The children can sort the pictures into the corresponding boxes.

2. Sign Language

Show the children how to say, "I love you," in sign language. They can practice with each other. When the parents arrive, the children can share with them.

I	point to self
love	cross arms over chest
you	point outwards

Group Time
(games, language)

Valentine March

Place large material hearts with numerals on them on the floor. Include one valentine per child. Play a marching song and encourage children to march from heart to heart. When the music stops, so do the children. Each child then tells the numeral he is standing on. To make the activity developmentally appropriate for young children, use symbols. Examples might include a ball, car, truck, glass, cup, door, etc.

Cooking

1. Valentine Cookies

2/3 cup shortening
1 egg
3/4 cup sugar
1 teaspoon vanilla
1 1/2 cups flour
1 1/2 teaspoons baking powder
4 teaspoons milk
1/4 teaspoon salt

Mix all of the ingredients together. If time permits, refrigerate the dough. Roll out dough. Use heart-shaped cookie cutters. Bake at 375 degrees for 12 minutes. Frost. The children can make two cookies, one for themselves, and one to give to a friend.

2. Heart-shaped Sandwiches

1 loaf bread
heart-shaped cookie cutters
strawberry jam or jelly

Give each child 1 or 2 pieces of bread (depending on size of cutter). Cut out 2 heart shapes from bread. Spread on jam or jelly to make a sandwich. Eat at snack time.

610

Books

The following books can be used to complement this theme:

Bauer, Caroline Feller. (1993). *Valentine's Day: Stories and Poems*. Illus. by Blanche Sims. New York: HarperCollins.

Carrick, Carol. (1995). *Valentine*. Illus. by Paddy Bouma. Boston: Houghton Mifflin.

Devlin, Wende and Harry Devlin. (1991). *Cramberry Valentine*. New York: Simon & Schuster.

Hoban, Lillian. (1997). *Silly Tilly's Valentine*. New York: HarperCollins.

Hopkins, Lee Bennett. (1992). *Good Morning to You, Valentine*. Illus. by Tomie De Paola. Honesdale, PA: Boyds Mills Press.

Hurd, Thacher. (1990). *Little Mouse's Big Valentine*. New York: HarperCollins.

London, Jonathan. (1997). *Froggy's First Kiss*. Illus. by Frank Remkiewicz. New York: Viking.

Nerlove, Miriam. (1992). *Valentine's Day*. Niles, IL: Albert Whitman & Co.

Sabuda, Robert. (1992). *Saint Valentine*. New York: Simon & Schuster.

Sharmat, Marjorie Weinman. (1994). *Nate the Great and the Mushy Valentine*. Illus. by Marc Simont. New York: Dell Publishing.

Shannon, George. (1995). *Heart to Heart*. Boston: Houghton Mifflin.

Watson, Wendy. (1993). *A Valentine for You*. Boston: Houghton Mifflin. (Pbk)

Multimedia

The following multimedia products can be used to complement this theme:

Coleman, Warren. *Valentine's Day* [video]. (1993). United Learning.

Valentine's Day [video]. (1994). Schlessinger Video Productions.

Recordings and Song Titles

The following recordings can be used to complement this theme:

Holiday Songs for All Occasions—"On Valentine's Day"

Holiday Piggyback Songs—"Special Friend," "Lacey Hearts," "I'm a Valentine for You," "H-E-A-R-T"

Singing Calendar—"February"

THEME 63

Reaction

mix
absorb

Purposes

drinking
cleaning
energy
recreation

Water

Forms

liquid
solid
vapor

Uses

soak
dilute
spray
sprinkle
flood
moisten

Water Sports

swimming
fishing
skiing
boating
skating

Theme Goals

Through participating in the experiences provided by this theme, the children may learn:

1. Uses of water.
2. Forms of water.
3. Water sports.
4. Purposes of water.

Concepts for the Children to Learn

1. All living things need water.
2. Water takes three forms: liquid, vapor, and solid.
3. Ice is a solid form of water.
4. Steam is a vapor form of water.
5. Some things mix with water, others do not.
6. Some things absorb water, others do not.
7. Some things float when placed on water.
8. Some animals and plants live in bodies of water.
9. Water can be used to soak, dilute, spray, sprinkle, flood, and moisten.

Vocabulary

1. **water**—a clear, colorless, odorless, tasteless liquid.
2. **lake**—a large body of water surrounded by land.
3. **ocean**—body of salt water.
4. **swimming**—moving yourself through water with body movements.
5. **cloud**—water droplets formed in the sky.
6. **rain**—water that falls from clouds.
7. **snow**—water that freezes and falls from the sky.
8. **liquid**—substance that can be poured.
9. **freeze**—hardened liquid.
10. **melt**—to change from a solid to a liquid.
11. **ice**—water that has frozen.
12. **sink**—to drop to the bottom of a liquid.
13. **float**—to rest on top of a liquid.

Bulletin Board

The purpose of this bulletin board is to develop visual discrimination and matching skills. Construct and color four or five pictures of swimming and water-related items from tagboard. Laminate. Trace these pictures on black construction paper to make shadows. Staple the shadows on the bulletin board. Encourage the children to hang the colored picture over the correct shadow.

Parent Letter

Dear Parents,

Did you know all living things have something in common? They all need water to survive. Water will be the theme that we will be exploring with our next curriculum unit. The children will become familiar with the forms, uses, and bodies of water, as well as sports that require water to be played.

AT SCHOOL

Some of the learning experiences planned to include water concepts are:

- placing celery stalks in colored water to observe plants' use of water.
- experimenting with objects that sink or float when placed in water.
- washing doll clothes in the sensory table.
- observing ice with magnifying glasses and watching it change from a solid to a liquid.
- watching a video titled *Let's Explore Water.*
- looking at books about water.

AT HOME

There are many ways that you can reinforce water concepts at home. Try any of the following with your child.

- Allow your child to assist in washing dishes after a meal. This will give your child a sense of responsibility and will develop self-esteem.
- Provide water and large paintbrushes for your child to paint sidewalks and fences outdoors.
- Bubbles made with an eggbeater in a container of soapy water are fun for children of all ages!

Enjoy your child!

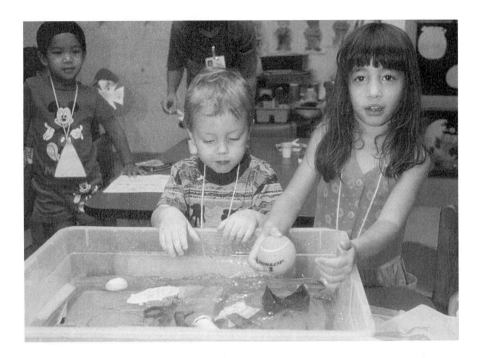

A water table can be used for science activities.

Music

"Raindrops"
(Sing to the tune of "London Bridges")

Raindrops falling from the sky,
From the sky, from the sky.
Raindrops falling from the sky
On my umbrella.

Fingerplays

FIVE LITTLE DUCKS

Five little ducks
   (hold up five fingers)
Swimming in the lake.
   (make swimming motions)
The first duck said,
   (hold up one finger)
"Watch the waves I make."
   (make waves motions)
The second duck said,
   (hold up two fingers)
"Swimming is such fun."
   (smile)

The third duck said,
   (hold up three fingers)
"I'd rather sit in the sun."
   (turn face to sun)
The fourth duck said,
   (hold up four fingers)
"Let's swim away."
   (swimming motions)
The fifth duck said,
   (hold up five fingers)
"Oh, let's stay."
Then along came a motorboat.
With a Pop! Pop! Pop!
   (clap three times)
And five little ducks
Swam away from the spot.
   (put five fingers behind back)

SWIMMING

I can dive.
   (make diving motion with hands)
I can swim.
   (swimming motion)
I can float.
   (hands outstretched with head back)
I can fetch.
But dog paddle
   (paddle like dog)
Is the stroke I do best.

FIVE LITTLE FISHES

Five little fishes swimming in a pond.
  (wiggle five fingers)
The first one said, "I'm tired," as he yawned.
  (yawn)
The second one said, "Well, let's take a nap."
  (put hands together on side of face)
The third one said, "Put on your sleeping cap."
  (pretend to pull on hat)
The fourth one said, "Wake up! Don't sleep."
  (shake finger)
The fifth one said, "Let's swim where it's deep."
  (point down and say with a low voice)
So, the five little fishes swam away.
  (wiggle fingers and put behind back)
But they came back the very next day.
  (wiggle fingers out front again)

THE RAIN

I sit before the window now
  (sit down)
And look out at the rain.
  (shade eyes and look around)
It means no play outside today,
  (shake head)
So inside I remain.
  (rest chin on fist; look sad)

I watch the water dribble down
  (look up and down)
As it turns the brown grass green.
And after a while I start to smile
At Nature's washing machine.
  (smile and lean back)

Science

1. **Painting Sidewalks**

   On a sunny day, allow children to paint sidewalks with water. To do this, provide various paintbrushes and buckets of water. Call attention to the water evaporation.

2. **Measuring Rainfall**

   During spring, place a bucket outside with a plastic ruler set vertically by securing to the bottom. Check the height of the water after each rainfall. With older children, make a chart to record rainfalls.

3. **Testing Volume**

   Containers that hold the same amounts of liquid are needed. Try to include containers that are tall, skinny, short, and flat. Ask the children, "Do they hold the same amount?" Encourage them to experiment by pouring liquids from one container to another.

4. **Freezing Water**

   Freeze a container of water. Periodically, observe the changes. In colder climates, the water can be frozen outdoors. The addition of food coloring may add interest.

5. **Musical Scale**

   Make unique musical tone jars by pouring various levels of water into glass soda bottles. Color each bottle of water differently. Provide the children with spoons, encouraging them to experiment with sounds by tapping each bottle.

6. **Plants Use Water**

   Place celery stalks in colored water. Observe how water is absorbed in their veins.

7. **Chase the Pepper**

   Collect the following materials: water, pepper, shallow pan, piece of soap, sugar. Fill the pan with water and shake the pepper on the water. Then take a piece of wet soap and dip it into the water. What happens? (The pepper moves away from the soapy water to the clear water.) The surface skin on water pulls, and on soapy water the pull is weak. On clear water it is strong and pulls the pepper along. Now take some sugar and shake it into the soapy water. What happens? Sugar gives the skin a stronger pull.

618

8. **Warm Water/Cold Water**

Collect the following materials: a small aquarium, a small bottle, food coloring, water. First fill the aquarium with very warm water. Fill the small bottle with colored cold water. Put your thumb on the mouth of the bottle. Hold the bottle sideways and lower it into the warm water. Take away your thumb. What happens? (The cold water will sink to the bottom of the tank. The cold water is heavier than the warm water.) Now fill the tank with cold water and fill the small bottle with colored warm water. What do you predict will happen when you repeat the procedure?

9. **Wave Machine**

Collect the following materials: mineral oil, water, food coloring, transparent jar. Fill the jar 1/2 to 2/3 full with water. Add a few drops of food coloring. Then add mineral oil to completely fill the jar. Secure the lid on the jar. Tilt the jar slowly from side to side to make waves. Notice that the oil and water have separate layers and do not stay mixed after the jar is shaken.

10. **Water and Vinegar Fun**

Collect the following materials: two small jars with lids, water, and white vinegar. Pour water into one jar and an equal amount of vinegar into the other jar. Replace caps. Then let the children explore the jars of liquids and discuss the similarities. Then let the children smell each jar.

Dramatic Play

1. **Firefighter**

Place hoses, hats, coats, and boots in the dramatic play area.

2. **Doll Baths**

Fill the dramatic play sink with water. Children can wash dishes or give dolls baths.

3. **The Beach**

Provide towels, sunglasses, umbrellas, pails, shovels, and beach toys for the children to use indoors or outdoors.

4. **Canoeing**

Bring a canoe into the classroom or onto the play yard. Provide paddles and life vests for the children to wear.

Arts and Crafts

1. **Liquid Painting**

Paper, straws, thin tempera, and spoons can be placed on the art table. Spoon a small amount of paint onto paper. Using a straw, blow paint on the paper to make a design.

2. **Bubble Prints**

Collect the following materials: 1/2 cup water, 1/2 cup liquid soap, food coloring, straws, and light-colored construction paper. Mix together the water, soap, and food coloring in a container. Place a straw in the solution and blow until the bubbles reach about one to two inches over the top of the container. Remove the straw and place a piece of paper over the jar. The bubbles will pop as they touch the paper, leaving a print.

3. **Wet Chalk Drawings**

Chalk, paper, and water in a shallow pan are needed for this activity. The children can dip chalk into water and then draw on paper. Encourage children to note the difference between wet and dry chalk.

Sensory

1. **Colored Ice**

   Fill the sensory table with colored ice cubes for the children to explore.

2. **Sink and Float**

   Fill sensory table with water. Provide the children with a variety of items that will sink and float. Let them experiment. A chart may be prepared listing items that sink and float.

3. **Boating**

   Fill the water table. Let the children add blue food coloring. Provide a variety of boats for them to play with.

4. **Moving Water**

   Provide the children with a variety of materials that move water. Include the following:

   - sponges
   - basters
   - eye droppers
   - squeeze bottles
   - empty film canisters
   - funnels
   - pitchers
   - plastic tubing
   - measuring cups

Large Muscle

Catch Me

Children form a circle with one child in the middle. While walking in a circle they chant:

_____ over the water.
_____ over the sea.
_____ caught a tunafish.
But he can't catch me!

(Insert child's name.)

On "me," all the children stoop quickly. If the child in the middle touches another child, the fish, before he stoops, that child is it. Likewise, he now goes into the middle. This game is for older children.

Math

Measuring

Assorted measuring cups in a variety of sizes can be added to the sensory table or sandbox.

Group Time
(games, language)

Water Fun

Discuss the various recreational uses of water. Included may be swimming, boating, ice fishing, ice skating, fishing, and canoeing. Encourage the children to name their favorite water activities. Prepare a chart using each child's name and favorite water activity along with a small picture of that activity. Display in the room.

Cooking

1. **Fruit Ice**

   Mix 1/2 can partially thawed juice concentrate with 2 cups of crushed ice in the blender. Liquify until the contents become snowy. Serve immediately.

2. **Floating Cake—Philippines**

   2 cups sweet rice flour
   1 cup water
   1/2 to 3/4 cup sugar
   1/2 cup toasted sesame seeds, hulled
   1 cup grated coconut

   Mix rice flour and water. Form into 10 to 20 small balls. Flatten each ball into a round or elongated shape and drop into 8 to 10 cups boiling water. As each cake floats to the surface, remove from water with a slotted spoon. Roll in grated coconut and coat with sugar and sesame seeds. Adult supervision is required. Makes 4 servings.

Water Play and Sensory Experiences

Sensory experiences are especially appealing to young children. They delight in feeling, listening, smelling, tasting, and seeing. They also love to manipulate objects by pulling, placing, pouring, tipping, shoving, as well as dipping. As they interact, they learn new concepts and solutions to old problems. When accompanied by other children, these experiences lead to cooperative, social interactions. As a result, the child's egocentricity is reduced, allowing him to become less self-centered.

Containers

Begin planning sensory experiences by choosing an appropriate container. Remember that it should be large enough so that several children may participate at any given time. If you select a dishpan, due to its size, you may want to use several. Other containers that may be used include a commercially made sensory/water table, baby bathtub, wash tub, pail, wading pool, sink, or bathtub.

Things to Add to Water

A variety of substances can be added to water to make it more inviting. Food coloring is one example. Start by individually choosing and adding one primary color. Later soaps can be added. These may be in liquid or flake form. Baking soda, cornstarch, and salt will affect the feel of the water. Baby and vegetable oil may leave a residue on the child's hand. Extracts add another dimension. Lemon, almond, pine oil, peppermint, anise, and orange all permit a variety for the child. On the other hand, ice cubes allow the child to experience an extreme touch.

Tools and Utensils

A wide variety of household tools can be used in the water play table. Measuring cups, small pitchers, small pots and pans, and film canisters can all be used for pouring. Scoops, spoons, turkey basters, small squeeze bottles, and funnels can be used for transferring the liquid from one container to another. Pipes, rubber hoses, sponges, wire whips, and eggbeaters all can be used for observing water in motion. Plastic toys, corks, spools, strainers, boots, etc., also encourage exploration.

(continued)

Water Play and Sensory Experiences (continued)

Other Sensory Experiences

There are wide varieties of other materials that can be used in the sensory table. Natural materials such as sand, gravel, rocks, grain, mud, wood chips, clay, corn, and birdseed can be used. Children also enjoy having minnows and worms in the table. They delight in visually tracking the minnow and worm movement. As they attempt to pick them up, eye-hand coordination skills are practiced. Styrofoam pieces and shavings are attractive materials that can lend variety.

A strange mixture called goop is a fun material to play with. To prepare goop empty 1 box of cornstarch into a dishpan or similar container. Sprinkle a few drops of food coloring on the cornstarch. Add small amounts of water (about 1/2 cup) at a time and mix with a spoon or with fingers. (This is a unique sensory experience!) The mixture feels hard when you touch it on the surface, yet melts in your hands when you pick some up! (This will keep for up to one week if kept covered when not in use. You will probably need to add water the next time you use it.)

Silly putty is just as easy to prepare as goop. This mixture is prepared by combining 1 part of liquid starch, 2 parts of white glue, and dry tempera paint for color. Begin by measuring the liquid starch first, as it will prevent the glue from sticking to the measuring cup. Mix with a spoon, adding single tablespoons of liquid starch to get the right consistency. Then knead with hands. Store in an airtight container (such as a ziplock bag) in the refrigerator. You will be thrilled to find that it will keep for several weeks.

Enjoy yourself with the children, but always change the sensory experiences on a daily basis. In doing so, you stimulate the child's curiosity as well as provide a meaningful curriculum.

For health purposes, children should be encouraged to wash their hands after sensory play.

Books

The following books can be used to complement this theme:

Arnold, Tedd. (1995). *No More Water in the Tub.* New York: Dial Books.

Asch, Frank. (1995). *Water.* San Diego, CA: Gulliver Books.

Baker, Sanna A. (1996). *Mississippi Going North.* Illus. by Bill Farnsworth. Niles, IL: Albert Whitman & Co.

Bittinger, Gayle. (1993). *Exploring Water and the Ocean.* Illus. by Gary Mohrmann. Alderwood Manor, WA: Warren Publishing House.

Calhoun, Mary. (1997). *Flood.* Illus. by Erick Ingraham. New York: William Morrow.

Carlstrom, Nancy W. (1997). *Raven and River.* Illus. Jon Van Zyle. Boston: Little, Brown.

Cast, C. Vance. (1992). *Where Does Water Come From?* Illus. by Sue Wilkinson. Hauppauge, NY: Barron's Educational Series.

Challoner, Jack. (1996). *Wet and Dry.* Austin, TX: Raintree/Steck Vaughn.

Dunphy, Madeline. (1998). *Here Is the Coral Reef.* Illus. by Tom Leonard. New York: Hyperion.

Fleming, Denise. (1993). *In the Small, Small Pond*. New York: Holt.

Fowler, Allan. (1997). *It Could Still Be a Lake*. Chicago: Children's Press.

Fowler, Allan. (1995). *The Earth Is Mostly Ocean*. Chicago: Children's Press.

Fowler, Allan. (1997). *Life in a Pond*. Chicago: Children's Press.

Gibbons, Gail. (1998). *Marshes and Swamps*. New York: Holiday House.

Gibson, Gary. (1995). *Making Things Float and Sink*. Illus. by Tony Kenyon. Brookfield, CT: Millbrook Press.

Gordon, Maria. (1995). *Float and Sink*. Illus. by Mike Gordon. Austin, TX: Raintree/Steck Vaughn.

Graham, Joan B. (1994). *Splish Splash*. Illus. By Steven M. Scott. New York: Ticknor and Fields.

Jackson, Shelley. (1998). *The Old Woman and the Wave*. New York: Dorling Kindersley.

Llewellyn, Claire. (1995). *Rivers and Seas (Why Do We Have . . .)*. Illus. by Anthony Lewis. Hauppauge, NY: Barron's Educational Series.

Locker, Thomas. (1997). *Water Dance*. Orlando: Harcourt Brace.

The Magic School Bus Wet All Over: A Book about the Water Cycle. (1996). New York: Scholastic.

Marzollo, Jean. (1996). *I Am Water*. Illus. by Judith Moffatt. New York: Scholastic. (Pbk)

Murata, Michinori. (1993). *Water and Light; Looking Through Lenses*. Minneapolis: Lerner Publications.

Nielsen, Shelly and Julie Berg. (1993). *I Love Water*. Minneapolis: Abda Daughters.

O'Mara, Anna. (1996). *Oceans*. Chicago: Children's Press.

Rauzon, Mark J. and Cynthia O. Bix. (1994). *Water, Water Everywhere*. Sierra Club.

Speed, Toby. (1998). *Water Voices*. Illus. by Julie Downing. New York: G. P. Putnam.

Multimedia

The following multimedia products can be used to complement this theme:

Circle of Water [video]. (1995). Washington, DC: National Geographic.

Deep Sea Dive [video]. Washington, DC: National Geographic. Available from Kimbo Educational.

Oceans (*Science for You* series) [video]. (1992). Agency for Instructional Technology.

Let's Explore Water (*Science is Elementary* series) [video]. (1993). Agency for Instructional Technology.

Wet & Wild: Under the Sea with OWL/TV [video]. (1994). Toronto: Children's Group, Inc.: BMG KIDZ.

What's in the Sea?: Songs About Marine Life and Ocean Ecology [cassette]. Kimbo Educational.

Recording and Song Title

The following recording can be used to complement this theme:

What's in the Sea?

THEME 64

Sizes

small
medium
large

Materials

rubber
plastic
wood
metal

Functions

movement
transportation

Wheels

Uses

bicycles
motorcycles
trikes
scooters
cars
trucks
buses
planes
unicycles
wagons
wheelbarrows

carts
chairs
trailers
rollerskates
rollerblades
pulleys
gears
trains
wheelchairs
pizza cutters

Theme Goals

Through participating in the experiences provided by this theme, the children may learn:

1. Sizes of wheels.
2. Purposes of wheels.
3. Materials used to make wheels.
4. Movement of wheels.

Concepts for the Children to Learn

1. Wheels are round.
2. Wheels can help us to do our work.
3. Wheels help move people and things.
4. Cars, buses, motorcycles, and bicycles have wheels.
5. Wheels can be different sizes.
6. A unicycle is a one-wheeled cycle.
7. Wheels can be made of rubber, plastic, metal, or wood.
8. Wheels can be connected by an axle.

Vocabulary

1. **wheel**—a form in the shape of a circle.
2. **unicycle**—a vehicle with one wheel.
3. **wheelbarrow**—a vehicle used for moving small loads.
4. **wheelchair**—a chair on wheels.
5. **bicycle**—a two-wheeled vehicle.
6. **pulley**—a wheel that can be connected to a rope to move things.

Bulletin Board

The purpose of this bulletin board is to encourage the development of mathematical concepts. To prepare the bulletin board, draw pictures of a unicycle, bicycle, and tricycle on tagboard. Color, cut out, and post on the bulletin board. Next, construct the numerals *1, 2,* and *3* out of tagboard. Hang the numerals on the top of the bulletin board. A corresponding set of dots can be placed below the numeral to assist children in counting. A string can be attached to each numeral by using a stapler. Have the children wind the string around a pushpin connected to the vehicle with the corresponding number of wheels.

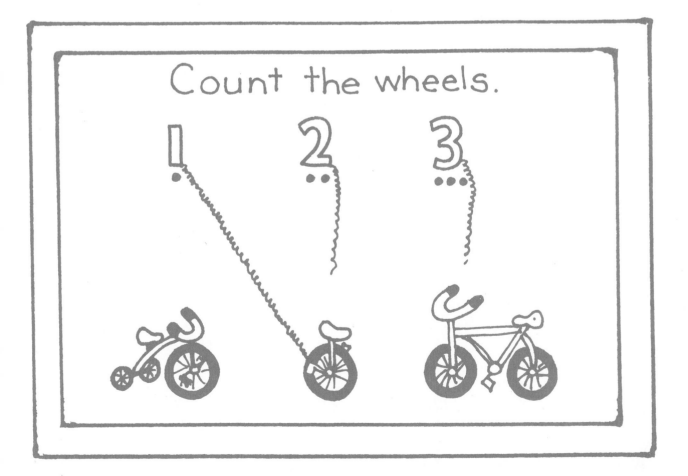

Parent Letter

Dear Parents,

Wheels! Wheelchairs, wheelbarrows, tricycle wheels, bicycle wheels, and car wheels! Children see wheels almost every day of their lives. We will be studying wheels. Through participating in the activities planned for this unit, the children will discover that wheels can be made from many different materials and that there are many different uses and sizes of wheels.

AT SCHOOL

We have many learning experiences planned for this unit, which include:

- examining tire rubber at the science table.
- painting with toy cars at the art table.
- singing a song called "The Wheels on the Bus."

AT HOME

There are many ways that you can incorporate this unit in your own home. Try any of these activities with your child.

- Walk around the neighborhood with your child. To develop observation skills look for different wheels.
- Count the wheels on the different types of transportation. Semi-trucks have several, while a unicycle has only one.
- Recite the following fingerplay with your child to foster language and memory skills. We will be learning it this week.

Wheels

Wheels big.
   (form big circles with fingers)
Wheels small.
   (form little circles with fingers)
Count them one by one.
Turning as they're pedaled
   (make pedaling motion with hands)
In the springtime sun!
1-2-3-4-5
   (count fingers)

Enjoy your child!

Music

"The Wheels on the Bus"

The wheels on the bus go round and
  round,
Round and round, round and round.
The wheels on the bus go round and round
All through the town.

Other verses:

The wipers on the bus go swish, swish,
  swish.
The doors on the bus go open and shut.
The horn on the bus goes beep, beep, beep.
The driver on the bus says, "Move on
  back."
The people on the bus go up and down.

Fingerplays

MY BICYCLE

One wheel, two wheels on the ground.
  (revolve hand in forward circle to form
  each wheel)
My feet make the pedals go round and
  round.
  (move feet in pedaling motion)
Handlebars help me steer so straight
  (pretend to steer bicycle)
Down the sidewalk, through the gate.

WHEELS

Wheels big.
  (form big circles with fingers)
Wheels small.
  (form little circles with fingers)
Count them one by one
Turning as they're pedaled
  (make pedaling motion with hands)
In the springtime sun.
1-2-3-4-5
  (count fingers)

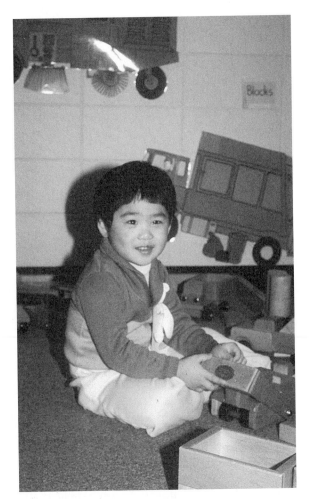

Cars and trucks need wheels to get
around.

Science

1. **Tire Rubber**

   Cut off several pieces of rubber from old
   tires. Provide magnifying glasses. Encourage the children to observe similarities and
   differences.

2. **Pulley**

   Set up a pulley. Provide the children with
   blocks so they may lift a heavy load with
   the help of a wheel. Supervision may be
   necessary for this activity.

629

3. Gears

Collect gears and place on the science table. The children can experiment, observing how the gears move. When appropriate, discuss their similar and different characteristics.

4. Wheels and Axles

Set out a few wheels and axles. Discuss how they work as a lever to help lift heavy loads. Encourage the children to think about where they might find wheels and axles.

Dramatic Play

1. Car Mechanic

Outdoors, place various wheels, tires, tools, overalls, and broken trikes. The children can experiment using tools.

2. Floats

Paper, tape, crepe paper, and balloons can be provided to decorate the wheels on the tricycles, wagons, and scooters.

Arts and Crafts

1. Circle Templates

Cut out various-sized circle templates from tagboard. Provide paper, pencils, and crayons for the children to trace the circles.

2. Car Painting

Provide small plastic cars, tempera paint, and paper. Place the tempera paint in a shallow pan. Car tracks can be created by dipping the car wheels in the tempera paint and rolling them across paper.

3. Wheel Collage

Provide magazines for the children to cut out pictures of wheels. The pictures can be pasted or glued onto sheets of paper.

4. Tracing Wheels

Provide sewing tracing wheels, pizza cutters, pastry wheels, carbon paper, and construction paper. The children can place the carbon paper on the construction paper and run one of the wheels over the carbon paper, making a design on the construction paper.

Sensory

Sensory Table

Add the following items to the sensory table:

- sand with wheel molds
- rubber from tires
- gravel and small toy cars and trucks

Large Muscle

1. Wheelbarrow

Place wheelbarrows in the play yard. Provide materials of varying weights for the children to move.

2. Wagons

Place wagons in the playground. Provide objects for the children to move.

Field Trips/ Resource People

1. Cycle Shop

Visit a cycle shop. Observe the different sizes of wheels that are in the shop. Talk about the different materials that wheels can be made of.

630

2. Machine Shop

Visit a machine parts shop. Look at the different gears, pulleys, and wheels. Discuss their sizes, shapes, and possible uses.

3. Resource People

- ⊚ cycle specialist
- ⊚ mechanic
- ⊚ machinist
- ⊚ person who uses a wheelchair

Math

1. Wheel Sequence

Cut out various-sized circles from tagboard to represent wheels. The children can sequence the wheels from largest to smallest.

2. How Many Wheels?

Pictures of a unicycle, bicycle, tricycle, cars, scooters, and trucks of all sizes can be cut from magazines and catalogs. Mount the pictures on tagboard. Laminate. Sort the pictures according to the number of wheels.

Social Studies

Wheelchair

Borrow wheelchair (child-sized if possible) from a local hospital or pharmacy. During group time discuss how wheelchairs help some people to move. Children can experience moving and pushing a wheelchair.

Group Time
(games, language)

Who Took the Wheel?
(Variation of "Who Took the Cookie from the Cookie Jar")

Who took the wheel off the car today?
_____ took the wheel off the car today.
   (fill _____ with a child's name)
Chosen child says, "Who me?"
Class responds, "Yes, you!"
Chosen child says, "Couldn't be!"
Class responds, "Well then, who?"

The chant continues as the chosen child picks another child. Continue repeating the chant using the children's names.

Cooking

1. Cheese Wheels

Using a cookie cutter, cut cheese slices into circle shapes to represent wheels. Top the pieces with raisins or serve with crackers.

2. Pizza Rounds

Provide each child with a half an English muffin. Demonstrate how to spread pizza sauce on a muffin. Then lay a few skinny strips of cheese across the top, making the cheese look like wheel spokes. Now let the children prepare their own. Bake in an oven at 350 degrees for 5 to 7 minutes or until the cheese melts. Cool slightly before serving.

Books

The following books can be used to complement this theme:

Butler, Daphne. (1995). *What Happens When Wheels Turn?* Austin, TX: Raintree/Steck Vaughn.

Cowen-Fletcher, Jane. (1993). *Mamma Zooms.* New York: Scholastic.

Dahl, Michael. (1996). *Wheels and Axles.* Chicago: Children's Press.

Hayward, Linda et al. (1996). *Wheels.* New York: Random House.

Healey, Tim. (1993). *The Story of the Wheel.* Illus. by Nicholas Hewetson. Mahwah, NJ: Troll.

Hindley, Judy. (1994). *The Wheeling and Whirling-Around Book.* Illus. by Margaret Chamberlain. Cambridge, MA: Candlewick Press.

Kalman, Bobbie and Petrina Gentile. (1997). *Big Truck, Big Wheels.* New York: Crabtree Publishing.

Kovalski, Maryann. (1990). *The Wheels on the Bus.* Boston: Little, Brown. (Pbk)

Mellentin, Kath. (1998). *The Wheels on the Bus.* Illus. by Jenny Tulip. Reistertown, MD: Flying Frog Publishing.

Miller, Margaret. (1997). *Wheels Go Round.* New York: Simon & Schuster.

Nikola-Lisa, W. (1994). *Wheels Go Round.* Illus. by Jane Conteh-Morgan. New York: Doubleday.

Raffi. (1998). *Wheels on the Bus.* New York: Crown Books.

Regan, Dana. (1996). *The Wheels on the Bus.* New York: Scholastic.

Rotner, Shelley. (1995). *Wheels Around.* Boston: Houghton Mifflin.

Rush, Caroline. (1997). *Wheels and Cogs.* Illus. by Mike Gordon. Austin, TX: Raintree/Steck Vaughn.

Scarry, Richard. (1997). *Richard Scarry's Pop-Up Wheels.* New York: Simon & Schuster.

Zelinsky, Paul O. (1990). *The Wheels on the Bus: With Pictures That Move.* New York: Dutton.

Multimedia

The following multimedia product can be used to complement this theme:

Fisher, Diana. *Wee Sing Wheels Sounds and Songs* [cassette]. (1996). New York: G. P. Putnam.

Recordings and Song Titles

The following recordings can be used to complement this theme:

Cars, Trucks and Trains
Six Little Ducks—"The Wheels on the Bus"

THEME 65

Winter

Characteristics
colder, may be icy,
may be snowy,
may be sleety,
may be shivery

Outdoor Clothing
hats, jackets, coats,
mittens/gloves,
boots, scarves,
earmuffs,
snowpants,
snowsuits

Cold Weather Sports
ice skating
sledding
snowmobiling
ice fishing
hockey
skiing
tobogganing

Holidays
Christmas
Hanukkah
Valentine's Day
New Year's Day

Animals That Hibernate
chipmunks
bears
snakes
turtles
frogs/toads

Theme Goals

Through participating in the experiences provided by this theme, the children may learn:

1. Winter holidays.
2. Characteristics of winter weather.
3. Winter sports.
4. Winter clothing.
5. Hibernating animals.

Concepts for the Children to Learn

1. Winter is one of the four seasons.
2. Winter is usually the coldest season.
3. It snows in the winter in some areas.
4. People wear warmer clothes in the winter.
5. Some animals hibernate in the winter.
6. Trees may lose their leaves in the winter.
7. Lakes, ponds, and water may freeze in the winter.
8. Sledding, skiing, toboganning, and ice skating are winter sports in colder areas.
9. To remove snow, people shovel and plow.
10. December, January, and February are winter months.

Vocabulary

1. **ice**—frozen water.
2. **cold**—not warm.
3. **frost**—very small ice pieces.
4. **snow**—frozen particles of water that fall to the ground.
5. **temperature**—how hot or cold something is.
6. **sleet**—mixture of rain and snow.
7. **hibernate**—to sleep during the winter.
8. **snowperson**—snow shaped in the form of a person.
9. **ski**—a runner that moves over snow and ice.
10. **icicle**—a hanging piece of frozen ice.
11. **sled**—transportation for moving over snow and ice.
12. **boots**—clothing worn on feet to keep them dry and warm.
13. **shiver**—to shake from cold or fear.

634

Bulletin Board

The purpose of this bulletin board is to provide the children with an opportunity to match patterns. Construct several pairs of mittens out of tagboard, each with a different pattern, as illustrated. Laminate the pieces. On the bulletin board, string one of each pair of the mittens through a rope or clothesline (one or two rows). Tie enough clothespins in place by putting the line through the wire spring of the clip clothespins to put up the matching mittens. (Tie the clothespins beside the first mitten.) Children can match the mittens by hanging the second next to the first with a clothespin. This is a good matching exercise for twos, who sometimes need help with the clothespins. It is mainly a small motor exercise for older children, unless you make the mittens with detailed patterns that are somewhat similar. This will increase the difficulty of the task.

Match the mittens.

Parent Letter

Dear Parents,

We are beginning a curriculum unit on winter. The children will be learning about the coldest season by taking a look at winter clothing, changes that occur during this season indoors and outdoors, and winter sports. Throughout the unit, the children will develop an awareness of winter activities.

AT SCHOOL

Some of our learning experiences related to winter include:

- creating cottonball snowpeople.
- sorting mittens by size, shape, and color.
- enjoying stories about winter.
- setting up an ice-skating rink in the dramatic play area.
- experiencing snow and ice in the sensory table.

AT HOME [DELETE THIS PARAGRAPH IF SNOW IS UNAVAILABLE.]

To experience winter at home, try this activity—snow in the bathtub! Bring in some snow from outside and place in your bathtub. Also place some measuring cups, spoons, and scoops in the bathtub and let your child use mittens to play in the snow. In addition, a spray bottle filled with colored water (made with food coloring) will allow your child to make colorful sculptures. This is sure to keep your children busy and will develop an awareness of the senses.

From all of us!

636

Some children live in areas where there is no snow in the winter.

Music

1. **"Snowperson"**
   (Sing to the tune of "Twinkle, Twinkle, Little Star")

   Snowperson, snowperson, where did
     you go?
   I built you yesterday out of snow.
   I built you high and I built you fat.
   I put on eyes and a nose and a hat.
   Now you're gone all melted away
   But it's sunny outside so I'll go and play.

2. **"Winter Clothes"**
   (Sing to the tune of "Did You Ever See a Lassie?")

   Children put your coats on, your coats on,
     your coats on.
   Children put your coats on, one, two, and
     three.

   (hats, boots, mittens, etc.)

3. **"Mitten Song"**
   (chant)

   Thumbs in the thumb place, fingers all
     together.
   This is the song we sing in mitten weather.

Fingerplays

FIVE LITTLE SNOWPEOPLE

Five little snowpeople standing in the door.
This one melted and then there were four.
   (hold up all five fingers, put down
   thumb)
Four little snowpeople underneath a tree.
This one melted and then there were three.
   (put down pointer finger)
Three little snowpeople with hats and
   mittens too.
This one melted and then there were two.
   (put down middle finger)
Two little snowpeople outside in the sun.
This one melted and then there was one.
   (put down ring finger)
One little snowperson trying hard to run.
He melted too, and then there were none.
   (put down pinky)

Variations:
- Make five little snowpeople finger
  puppets and remove them one by one.
- Make five stick puppets for children
  to hold and sit down one by one at
  appropriate times during fingerplay.

MAKING A SNOWPERSON

Roll it, roll it, get a pile of snow.
  (make rolling motions with hands)
Rolling, rolling, rolling, rolling, rolling
  here we go.
Pat it, pat it, face it to the south.
  (patting motion)
Now my little snowperson's done, eyes
  and nose and mouth.
  (point to eyes, nose and mouth)

ZIPPERS

Three little zippers on my snowsuit,
  (hold up three fingers)
Fasten up as snug as snug can be
It's a very easy thing as you can see
Just zip, zip, zip!
  (do three zipping motions)
I work the zippers on my snowsuit.
Zippers really do save time for me
I can fasten them myself with one, two,
  three.
Just zip, zip, zip!
  (do three zipping motions)

THE SNOWPERSON
AND THE BUNNY

A chubby little snowperson
  (make a fist)
Had a carrot nose.
  (poke thumb out)
Along came a bunny
And what do you suppose?
  (other hand, make rabbit ears)
That hungry little bunny
Looking for his lunch
  (bunny hops around)
Ate that snowperson's carrot nose.
  (bunny nibbles at thumb)
Crunch, crunch, crunch.

BUILD A SNOWPERSON

First you make a snowball,
  (rolling motion)
Big and fat and round.
  (extend arms in large circle)
Then you roll the snowball,
  (rolling motion)
All along the ground.
Then you build the snowperson

One-two-three!
  (place three pretend balls on top of each
  other)
Then you have a snowperson,
Don't you see?
  (point to eyes)
Then the sun shines all around and
Melts the snowperson to the ground.
  (drop to the ground in a melting motion)

Science

1. **Weather Doll**

Make a felt weather doll. Encourage the children to dress and undress the doll according to the weather.

2. **Make Frost**

Changes in temperature cause dew. When dew freezes it is called frost. Materials needed are a tin can with no lid, rock salt, and crushed ice. Measure and pour 2 cups of crushed ice and 1/2 cup rock salt in a can. Stir rapidly. Let the mixture sit for 30 minutes. After 30 minutes, the outside of the can will have dew on it. Wait longer and the dew will change to frost. To hasten the process, place in a freezer.

3. **Make Birdfeeders**

Roll pine cones in peanut butter and corn-meal mixture and then in birdseed. Attach a string to the pine cones and hang them outside. Encourage the children to check the birdfeeders frequently. **Caution:** Be sure to mix about 5 cups cornmeal to each cup of peanut butter. It is possible for birds to choke on peanut butter.

A birdfeeder can also be prepared from suet. To do this, wrap suet in a netting. Gather the edges up and tie together with a long string. Another method is to place suet in a net citrus fruit bag.

638

4. Snow

Bring a large container of snow into the classroom. After it is melted, add colored water and place the container outdoors. When frozen, bring a colored block of ice back into classroom and watch it melt.

5. Examine Snowflakes

Examine snowflakes with a magnifying glass. Each is unique. For classrooms located in warmer climates, make a snow-like substance by crushing ice.

6. Catching Snowflakes

Cover a piece of cardboard with dark felt. Place the cardboard piece in the freezer. Go outside and let snowflakes land on the board. Snowflakes will last longer for examination.

7. Coloring Snow

Provide children with spray bottles containing colored water, preferably red, yellow, and blue. Allow them to spray the snow and mix colors.

8. Thermometers

Experiment with a thermometer. Begin introducing the concept by observing and discussing what happens when the thermometer is placed in a bowl of warm water and a bowl of cold water. Demonstrate to the children and encourage them to experiment under supervision during the self-selected activity period.

9. Signs and Sounds of Winter

On a winter walk in colder climates have the children watch and listen for signs and sounds of winter. The signs of winter are weather: cold, ice, daylight is shorter, darkness is earlier; plants: all but evergreen trees are bare; and people: we wear warmer clothes, we play inside more, we shovel snow, we play in the snow. Some of the sounds of winter are: boots crunching, rain splashing, wind howling, etc. (Adapt this activity to the signs of winter in your climate.)

Dramatic Play

1. Ice-skating Palace

Make a masking tape border on a carpeted floor. Give child 2 pieces of waxed paper. Show children how to fasten waxed paper to their ankles with rubber bands. Play instrumental music and encourage the children to skate around on the carpeted floor.

2. Dress Up

If available, put outdoor winter clothing such as coats, boots, hats, mittens, scarves, and earmuffs in the dramatic play area of the classroom with a large mirror. The children may enjoy trying on a variety of clothing items.

Arts and Crafts

1. Whipped Soap Painting

Mix 1 cup Ivory Snow flakes with 1/2 cup warm water in bowl. The children can beat with a hand eggbeater until mixture is fluffy. Apply mixture to dark construction paper with various tools (toothbrushes, rollers, tongue depressors, brushes, etc.). To create variety, food coloring can be added to paint mixture.

2. Cottonball Snowman

Cut a snowperson figure from dark construction paper. Provide the children with cottonballs and glue. They can decorate the snowperson by gluing on cottonballs.

3. Snowflakes

Cut different-sized squares out of white construction paper. Fold the squares in half, and then in half again. Demonstrate and encourage the children to cut and open their own designs. The snowflakes can be hung in the entry or classroom for decoration.

4. Windowpane Frost

On a piece of construction paper, draw an outline of a window. Spread glue around and on the frame and sprinkle with glitter.

5. Winter Mobile

Cut out pictures of winter from magazines or have children create their own winter pictures. Attach several pictures with string or yarn to a branch, hanger (masking taped), or paper plate. Glitter can be added.

6. Ice Cube Art

Place a popsicle stick in each ice compartment of a tray and fill with water. Freeze. Sprinkle dry tempera paint on paper. Then to make their own design, the children can move an ice cube on the paper.

7. Frosted Pictures

Mix 1 part Epsom salts with 1 part boiling water. Let the mixture cool. Encourage the children to make a crayon design on paper. The mixture can be brushed over the picture. Observe how the crystals form as the mixture dries.

8. Winter Shape Printing

Cut sponges into various winter shapes such as boots, snowmen, mittens, snowflakes, fir trees, and stars. The children can use the sponges as a tool to print on different pieces of colored construction paper.

9. Easel Ideas

Feature white paint at the easel for snow pictures on colored paper. Or, cut easel paper into winter shapes: snowmen, hats, mittens, scarves, snowflakes, etc.

10. Snow Drawings

White chalk and dark construction paper can be placed in the art area.

11. Snow Painting

Using old spray bottles filled with colored water, let the children make pictures in the snow outside. This activity is limited to areas where snow is available.

Sensory

The following items can be placed in the sensory table.

- snow and ice (plain or colored with drops of food coloring)
- cottonballs with measuring/balancing scale
- pine cones
- ice cubes (colored or plain)
- snow and magnifying glasses

Large Muscle

1. Freeze

Play music and have the children walk around in a circle. When the music stops, the children freeze by standing still in a stooped position. Vary the activity by substituting other actions such as hopping, skipping, galloping, sliding, etc.

2. Snowperson

During outdoor play make a snowperson. Decorate with radish eyes, carrot nose, scarf, hat, and holding a stick. Other novel accessories can be substituted by using the children's ideas.

3. Snow People

After a snowfall, have the children lie down in the snow and move their arms and legs to make shapes.

4. Snowball Target

Since children love throwing snowballs, set up a target outside for children to throw at.

640

5. Shovel

Provide child-sized shovels for the children to help shovel a walk.

6. Balance

Make various tracks in the snow, such as a straight line, a zig-zag line, a circle, square, triangle, and rectangle.

Field Trips/ Resource People

1. Visit an ice-skating rink. Observe the ice and watch how it is cleaned.

2. Visit a sledding hill. Bring sleds along and go sledding.

3. Invite a snowplow operator to school to talk to the children. After a snowfall, the children can observe the plowing.

4. Take the children to a grocery store and view the freezer area. Also, observe a refrigerated delivery truck.

Math

1. Shape Sequence

Cut three different-sized white circles from construction paper for each child to make a snowperson. Which is the largest? Smallest? How many do you have? What shape? Then have children sequence the circles from largest to smallest and smallest to largest.

2. Winter Dominoes

Trace and cut 30 squares out of white tagboard. Section each square into four spaces diagonally. In each of the four spaces, draw different winter objects or stick winter stickers on. The children can match the pictures by playing dominoes.

3. Dot to Dot

Make a dot-to-dot snowperson. The children connect the dots in numerical order. You can also make dot-to-dot patterns of other winter objects such as hats, snowflakes, mittens, etc. This activity requires numeral recognition and order, so it is restricted to the school-aged child.

4. Puzzles

Mount winter pictures or posters on tagboard sheets. Cut into pieces. The number of pieces cut will be dependent upon the children's developmental age. Place in the small manipulative area of the classroom for use during self-selected activity periods.

Social Studies

1. Travel

Discuss ways people travel in winter such as sled, toboggan, snowmobile, snowshoes, skis, etc.

2. Winter Happenings

Display pictures of different winter happenings, sports, clothing, snow, etc., around the room at the children's eye level.

3. Winter Book

Encourage the children to make a book about winter. Do one page a day. The following titles could be used:

⊚ What I wear in winter.
⊚ What I like to do outside in winter.
⊚ What I like to do inside in winter.
⊚ My favorite food during winter.
⊚ My favorite thing about winter.

(This activity may be more appropriate for the school-aged child.)

4. Winter Clothing Match

Draw a large paper figure of a boy and of a girl. Design and cut winter clothing to fit each figure. The children can dress the figures for outdoor play.

Group Time
(games, language)

1. Who Has the Mitten?

Ask the children to sit in a circle. One child should sit in the middle. Make a very small mitten out of felt or construction paper. Tell the children to pass the mitten around the circle. All the children should imitate the passing actions even if they do not have the mitten in hand. When the verse starts, the child in the middle tries to guess who has the mitten. Chant the following verse while passing a mitten.

I pass the mitten from me to you to you,
I pass the mitten and that is what I do.

2. Hat Chart

Prepare a hat chart by listing all the types and colors of hats worn by the children in the classroom.

Cooking

1. Banana Snowpeople

2 cups raisins
2 bananas
shredded coconut

Chop the bananas and raisins in a blender. Then place them in a mixing bowl. Refrigerate until mixture is cool enough to be handled. Roll the mixture into balls and into shredded coconut. Stack three balls and fasten with toothpicks. **Caution:** Close supervision is needed when using toothpicks with young children.

2. Hot Chocolate

Add warm water or milk to instant hot chocolate and mix. Heat as needed.

3. Snow Cones

Crush ice and spoon into small paper cups. Pour a fruit juice over the ice. Serve.

4. Snowballs—China

1/4 cup walnuts, ground
1/4 cup almonds, ground
1/4 cup sesame seeds, toasted
1/2 cup sugar
1 tablespoon shortening
1 pound glutenous rice flour

In a bowl, mix nuts, sesame seeds, sugar, and shortening. Form mixture into 1/2-inch balls. Fill a big mixing bowl with 1/2-inch layer of rice flour. Moisten the nut balls by dipping them into water. Place balls individually in floured bowl and shake bowl back and forth, coating the balls with flour. Redip coated balls in water and coat three times. Slip balls into boiling water and gently boil for about 5 minutes until balls float to the surface. Add a cup of cold water and boil for about 3 to 4 minutes. Serve about 4 to each person along with the hot liquid. This activity requires supervision.

Books

The following books can be used to complement this theme:

Agell, Charlotte. (1994). *I Slide Into the White of Winter.* Gardner, ME: Tilbury House.

Bancroft, Henrietta and Richard G. Van Gelder. (1996). *Animals in Winter.* Newly illus. by Helen K. Davie. New York: HarperCollins.

Barasch, Lynne. (1993). *A Winter Walk.* New York: Tickor and Fields.

Berger, Melvin and Gilda Berger. (1995). *What Do Animals Do In Winter?* Illus. by Susan Harrison. Nashville, TN: Hambleton-Hill Publishing.

Capucilli, Alyssa Satin. (1995). *Peekaboo Bunny: Friend in the Snow.* Illus. by Mary Melcher. New York: Scholastic. (Peek-a-book)

Carlstrom, Nancy White. (1993). *How Does the Wind Walk?* New York: Macmillan.

Chapman, Cheryl. (1994). *Snow on Snow on Snow.* Illus. by Synthia Saint James. New York: Dial Books.

Dunphy, Madeleine. (1993). *Here Is the Arctic Winter.* Illus. by Alan James Robinson. New York: Hyperion.

Ehlert, Lois. (1996). *Snowballs.* Orlando: Harcourt Brace.

Evans, Lezlie. (1997). *Snow Dance.* Illus. by Cynthia Jabar. Boston: Houghton Mifflin.

Fain, Moria. (1996). *Snow Day.* New York: Walker & Co.

Fleming, Denise. (1996). *Time to Sleep.* New York: Holt.

Galbraith, Kathryn Osebold. (1992). *Look! Snow!* Illus. by Nina Montezinos. New York: Simon & Schuster.

Gammell, Stephen. (1997). *Is That You, Winter?* Orlando: Harcourt Brace.

George, Jean Craighead. (1993). *Dear Rebecca, Winter Is Here.* Illus. by Loretta Krupinski. New York: HarperCollins.

George, Lindsay Barrett. (1995). *In the Snow: Who's Been Here?* New York: Greenwillow.

Hiscock, Bruce. (1995). *When Will It Snow?* New York: Simon & Schuster.

Howard, Kim. (1994). *In Wintertime.* New York: Lothrop, Lee & Shepard.

Joosse, Barbara M. (1995). *Snow Day!* Illus. by Jennifer Plecas. Boston: Houghton Mifflin.

Lee, Huy-Voun. (1995). *In the Snow.* New York: Holt.

Lerner, Carol. (1994). *Backyard Birds of Winter.* New York: William Morrow.

London, Jonathan. (1992). *Froggy Gets Dressed.* Illus. by Frank Remkiewicz. New York: Viking.

Maass, Robert. (1993). *When Winter Comes.* New York: Holt.

Richardson, Judith Benet. (1996). *Old Winter.* Illus. by R. W. Alley. New York: Orchard Books.

Ryder, Joanne. (1997). *Winter White.* Illus. by Carol Lacey. New York: William Morrow.

Simon, Seymour. (1994). *Winter across America.* New York: Hyperion Books.

Stoeke, Janet Morgan. (1994). *A Hat for Minerva Louise.* New York: Dutton.

Willard, Nancy. (1996). *A Starlit Somersault Downhill.* Illus. by Jerry Pinkney. Boston: Little, Brown. (Pbk)

Multimedia

The following multimedia products can be used to complement this theme:

Keats, Ezra Jack. *The Snowy Day* [cassette, book]. Kimbo Records.

Let's Find Out about Winter [video]. (1991). American School Publishers.

Piggyback Songs: Singable Poems Set to Favorite Tunes [compact disc]. (1995). Includes 21 songs/poems for Fall/Winter. Kimbo Records.

Snowplows at Work [video]. (1994). Bill Aaron Productions.

Where Do Animals Go in Winter? [video]. (1995). Washinton, DC: National Geographic.

Recordings and Song Titles

The following recordings can be used to complement this theme:

Piggyback Songs—"Season Song," "Sing a Song of Winter," "Snowflakes Falling from the Sky"

Where Is Thumbkin?—"Jingle Bells"

Preschool Action Time—"Snow Fun"

THEME 66

Color Mixing

yellow + blue = green
yellow + red = orange

Yellow

Signs
traffic light
yield signs

Flowers
daisy
dandelion
rose
daffodil

Animals
chicks
canary
cats

Food
pineapple
banana
lemon
corn
grapefruit
cheese
egg yolk

Objects
sun
paint
cars
bikes
clothes

Theme Goals

Through participating in the experiences provided by this theme, the children may learn:

1. Yellow flowers.
2. Yellow traffic signs.
3. Yellow animals.
4. Yellow-colored foods.
5. Colors formed by adding yellow.
6. Yellow objects.

Concepts for the Children to Learn

1. Yellow is a primary color.
2. Yellow mixed with blue makes green.
3. Yellow mixed with red makes orange.
4. The sun is a yellow color.
5. The middle color on a traffic light is yellow.
6. Daisies, dandelions, and daffodils are yellow flowers.
7. A canary is a yellow bird.
8. Pineapples, bananas, and corn are yellow foods.
9. Bikes, cars, and cats can be yellow.

Vocabulary

1. **yellow**—a primary color.
2. **primary colors**—red, blue, and yellow.

Bulletin Board

The purpose of this bulletin board is to have the children match the shapes, providing practice in visual discrimination. To prepare the bulletin board, collect yellow tagboard, a black felt-tip marker, scissors, yellow string, and pushpins. Using yellow tagboard, draw sets of different-shaped balloons as illustrated. Outline with a black felt-tip marker and cut out. Take one balloon from each set and attach to the top of the bulletin board as illlustrated. Staple a yellow string to hang from each balloon. Next, attach the remaining balloons on the bottom of the bulletin board. A pushpin can be fastened next to each balloon, and the children can match the balloons by shape.

Parent Letter

Dear Parents,

Colors are such a big part of our world. Consequently, our new theme will focus on the color yellow. Throughout this week, the children will become aware of the color in their environment. It should be a bright time discovering the color yellow!

AT SCHOOL

Some learning experiences planned for the unit include:

- making scrambled eggs.
- visiting a paint store.
- learning the fingerplay "Six Yellow Chickadees."
- making yellow soap crayons.
- playing with corn kernels in the sensory table.

AT HOME

At school we will be making yellow playdough. The children enjoy helping prepare the playdough and, of course, playing with it! It would be great fun for them to make it at home and they will be exposed to the mathematical concepts of amounts, fractions, and measurements. Here is the recipe.

> 2 cups flour
> 1 cup of salt
> 1 cup of water
> 2 tablespoons cooking oil
> food coloring

Let your child assist in gathering and measuring the ingredients. Then mix all the ingredients together. To encourage play, provide some tools for your child to use: rolling pins, cookie cutters, spatulas, or potato mashers. Have fun!

Enjoy your child!

648

Fingerplays

SIX YELLOW CHICKADEES

(Suit the actions to the words)

Six yellow chickadees sitting by a hive.
One flew away and then there were five.
Five yellow chickadees sitting by the door.
One flew away and then there were four.
Four yellow chickadees sitting in a tree.
One flew away and then there were three.
Three yellow chickadees sitting by my shoe.
One flew away and then there were two.
Two yellow chickadees sitting by my
    thumb.
One flew away and then there was one.
One yellow chickadee flying around the sun.
She flew away and then there were none.

TEN FLUFFY CHICKENS

Five eggs and five eggs
    (hold up two hands)
That makes ten.
Sitting on top is the mother hen.
    (fold one hand over the other)
Crackle, crackle, crackle
    (clap hands three times)
What do I see?
Ten fluffy chickens
    (hold up ten fingers)
As yellow as can be!

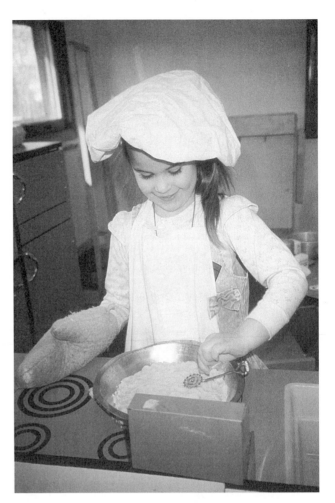

The yolk of an egg is yellow in color.

Science

1. Paper Towel Dip

Fold a paper towel in half several times. Dip the towel into red water and then into yellow water. Open the towel carefully and allow it to dry. Orange designs will appear on the paper towel.

2. Carnation Coloring

Put a carnation into a glass of water that has been dyed yellow with food coloring. Soon the carnation will show yellow streaks. During the summer other white garden flowers can be substituted.

3. Yellow Soap Crayons

Measure one cup of mild powdered laundry soap. Add one tablespoon of food coloring. Add water by the teaspoonful until the soap is in liquid form. Stir well. Pour the soap into ice cube trays. Set in a sunny, dry place until hard. Soap crayons are great for writing in the sink, tub, or sensory table.

Dramatic Play

Paint Store

Set up a paint store by including paint caps, paintbrushes, pans, rollers, drop cloths, paint clothes, a cash register, and play money.

Arts and Crafts

1. **Yellow Paint**

   Provide yellow fingerpaint and yellow tempera paint in the art area.

2. **Corncob Painting**

   Cover the bottom of a shallow pan with thick yellow tempera paint. Using a corncob as an applicator, apply paint to paper.

3. **Popsicle Stick Prints**

   Cover the bottom of a shallow pan with thick yellow tempera paint. Apply the paint to paper using a popsicle stick as an applicator.

4. **Yellow Playdough**

   Combine two parts flour, one part salt, one part water, and two tablespoons cooking oil. Add yellow food coloring. Mix well. If prepared dough becomes sticky, add more flour.

5. **Baker's Clay**

   Combine 4 cups flour, 1 cup salt, and 1 1/2 cups water. Mix the ingredients. The children can shape forms. Place the forms on a cookie sheet and bake at 350 degrees for about 1 hour. The next day the children can paint the objects yellow.

6. **Yarn and Glue Designs**

   Provide yellow yarn, glue, and paper for the children to make their own designs.

7. **Record Player Designs**

   Punch a hole in the middle of a paper plate and place on the turntable of a record player. Turn the record player on. As the turntable spins around, the children can apply color by holding a yellow felt-tip marker on the paper plate. Interesting designs can be made.

Sensory

1. **Shaving Cream Fun**

   Spray the contents of one can of shaving cream in the sensory table. Color the shaving cream by adding yellow food coloring.

2. **Corn Kernels**

   Place corn kernels in the sensory table.

3. **Yellow Goop**

   In the sensory table, mix one cup cornstarch, one cup water, and yellow food coloring. Mix together well.

4. **Water Toys**

   Add yellow food coloring to three inches of water in the sensory table. Provide water toys as accessories to encourage play during self-selected play activites.

Field Trips

1. **Paint Store**

   Visit a paint store and observe the different shades of yellow. Collect samples of paint for use in the art area. If possible, also observe the manager mixing yellow paint.

2. **Yellow in Our World**

   Take a walk and look for yellow objects. Prepare a language experience chart when you return to the classroom.

3. **Greenhouse**

   Visit a greenhouse and observe the different kinds of yellow flowers.

650

Math

Sorting Shapes

Cut circles, triangles, and rectangles out of yellow tagboard. Place on the math table. The children can sort the yellow shapes into groups. For younger children, the objects can be cut from different colors. Then the objects can be sorted by color.

Social Studies

Tasting Party

Cut a banana, a pineapple, a lemon, and a piece of yellow cheese into small pieces. Let the children sample each during snack time. The concept of color, texture, and taste can all be discussed.

Group Time
(games, language)

Guessing Game: What's Missing?

Use any yellow familiar objects or toys that can be easily handled. The number will depend upon developmental appropriateness. For two-year-olds choose only two objects. On the other hand several objects can be used for five-year-olds. Spread them out on the floor and ask children to name each item. Then ask the group to close their eyes. Remove one item. When the group opens their eyes, ask them to tell you which item is missing.

Cooking

1. Banana Bobs

Cut bananas into chunks and dip into honey. Next roll in wheat germ and use large toothpicks for serving. **Caution:** Close supervision is needed when using toothpicks with young children.

2. Carribean Banana Salad

3 green (unripe) bananas, peeled
2 cups water
1 teaspoon salt
2 medium carrots, shredded
1 small cucumber, sliced
1 medium tomato, chopped
1 avocado, cubed
1 stalk celery, sliced
vinaigrette dressing

Heat bananas, water, and salt to boiling; reduce heat. Cover and simmer until bananas are tender, about 5 minutes. Drain and cool. Cut bananas crosswise into 1/2-inch slices. Toss bananas and remaining ingredients with vinaigrette dressing.

Source: *Betty Crocker's International Cookbook*. (1980). New York: Random House.

3. Corn Bread

1 cup flour
1 cup cornmeal
2 tablespoons sugar
4 teaspoons baking powder
1 teaspoon salt
1 cup milk
1/4 cup cooking oil or melted shortening
1 egg, slightly beaten

Preheat oven to 425 degrees. Grease (not oil) an 8- or 9-inch square pan. In medium mixing bowl, combine the dry ingredients. Stir in the remaining ingredients, beating by hand until just smooth. Pour batter into prepared pan. Bake for 20 to 25 minutes or until toothpick inserted in center comes out clean.

Books

The following books can be used to complement this theme:

Bang, Molly. (1991). *Yellow Ball*. New York: William Morrow.

Cabrera, Jane. (1997). *Cat's Colors*. New York: Dial Books.

Carle, Eric. (1998). *Let's Paint a Rainbow*. New York: Scholastic.

Dodds, Dayle Ann. (1992). *The Color Box*. Illus. by Giles Laroche. Boston: Little, Brown.

Faulkner, Keith. (1995). *My Colors: Let's Learn about Colors*. New York: Simon & Schuster.

Heller, Ruth. (1995). *Color*. New York: G. P. Putnam.

Hoban, Tana. (1995). *Colors Everywhere*. New York: Greenwillow.

Hoban, Tana. (1987). *Is It Red? Is It Yellow? Is It Blue?* New York: Greenwillow.

Jackson, Ellen B. (1995). *Brown Cow, Green Grass, Yellow Mellow Sun*, Vol. 1. Illus. by Victoria Raymond. New York: Hyperion.

Lionni, Leo. (1994). *Little Blue and Little Yellow*. New York: William Morrow. (Pbk)

Munsch, Robert. (1992). *Purple, Green and Yellow*. Illus. by Helene Desputeaux. Willowdale, ON: Annick Press.

Rogers, Alan. (1997). *Yellow Hippo*. Chicago: World Book.

Rotner, Shelley. (1996). *Colors Around Us*. New York: Simon & Schuster. (Lift-the-flap book)

Seuss, Dr. (1996). *My Many Colored Days*. Illus. by Steve Johnston. New York: Knopf.

Walsh, Ellen Stoll. (1989). *Mouse Paint*. Orlando: Harcourt Brace.

Multimedia

The following multimedia products can be used to complement this theme:

Big Yellow School Bus [sound cassette]. (1991). Alfred Publishing.

Bingham, Bing. "Primary Colors" from *A Rainbow of Songs* [sound cassette]. Kimbo Records.

Color, Shapes and Size [computer file]. (1995). Star Press Multimedia.

Colors, Shapes & Counting [video]. Kimbo Records.

My Silly CD of Colors [CD-ROM]. (1995). Discis Knowledge Research.

Peter's Colors Adventure [CD-ROM]. (1994). Arborescence.

"A Yell for Yellow" on *There's Music in the Colors* [cassette]. Kimbo Records.

Recordings and Song Titles

The following recordings can be used to complement this theme:

There's Music in the Colors

I Like Myself—"Draw a Circle"

Where Is Thumbkin?—"The Color Song"

Pre-K Hooray—"Color Wheel Dance"

Homemade Games—"Color Square"

Piggyback Sons—"Colors"

Children Love to Sing and Dance (The Learning Station)—"Everything Has a Color"

Let's Visit Lullaby Land—"Colour My World"

Rainbow of Songs—"Primary Colors"

Kinds

elephants
giraffes
monkeys
snakes
lions
bears
zebras
camels

Homes

cages
fences
water
trees

Zoo
Animals

Needs

food
water
shelter
air

Caretakers

zookeeper
veterinarian

Theme Goals

Through participating in the experiences provided by this theme, the children may learn:

1. Names of zoo animals.
2. Needs of zoo animals.
3. Types of animal homes.
4. The caretaker's role.

Concepts for the Children to Learn

1. A zoo is a place for animals.
2. Zoo animals are kept in cages, fences, water, or in trees.
3. Elephants, giraffes, monkeys, snakes, lions, zebras, camels, and bears are zoo animals.
4. A zookeeper feeds and takes care of the animals.
5. Zoo animals need food, water, and shelter.
6. Veterinarians are animal doctors.

Vocabulary

1. **zoo**—a place to look at animals.
2. **cage**—a home for animals.
3. **zookeeper**—a person who feeds the zoo animals.
4. **veterinarian**—an animal doctor.

Bulletin Board

The purpose of this bulletin board is to encourage the children to place the correct number of balls above each seal corresponding to the numeral on the drum. To prepare the bulletin board, construct seals sitting on a drum as illustrated. Place a numeral on each drum with the corresponding number of dots. Construct colored balls from tagboard. Laminate and cut out the pieces. Staple the seal figures and drums to bulletin board. Place a magnetic strip above each seal. Also adhere a magnetic strip on the back of each ball.

Parent Letter

Dear Parents,

Our new theme is called zoo animals. This is an appropriate theme to introduce to the children because they are fascinated by the zoo and the animals that live there. Through our study of zoo animals, the children will become familiar with the names of many zoo animals. They will also be introduced to new occupations: the zookeeper and the veterinarian.

AT SCHOOL

Some of the experiences planned for the zoo animal unit include:

- looking at peek-a-boo pictures of zoo animals.
- using zoo animal-shaped cookie cutters with playdough at the art table.
- pretending to be caged zoo animals using boxes as cages in the dramatic play area.

FIELD TRIP

Our class will be taking a field trip to the Dunn County Reserve Park on Friday. There we can see some unusual animals. Please let me know by Wednesday if you are interested in accompanying the group. We will be leaving the center at 9:30 a.m. and be returning by 11:30 a.m.

AT HOME

To develop observation skills, you can show your child pictures of zoo animals from books or magazines. Plan a family trip to a zoo. Many opportunities for learning present themselves at the zoo. Children can actually see different kinds of animals and many times, such as at petting zoos, are able to touch and feed them. What a great way to develop an appreciation and respect for animal life!

Enjoy your child!

Can you roar like a leopard?

Music

1. **"Zoo Animals"**
   (Sing to the tune of "Muffin Man")

   Do you know the kangaroo
   The kangaroo, the kangaroo?
   Oh, do you know the kangaroo
   That lives in the zoo?

   (Adapt this song and use other zoo animals
   such as the monkey, elephant, giraffe, lion,
   turtle, bear, snake, etc.)

2. **"One Elephant"**

   One elephant went out to play
   On a spider web one day.
   He had such enormous fun
   That he called for another elephant to come.

   (Makes a nice flannel story or choose one
   child to be an "elephant." Add another
   "elephant" with each verse.)

3. **"Animals at the Zoo"**
   (Sing to the tune of "Frère Jacques")

   See the animals, see the animals
   At the zoo, at the zoo.
   Elephants and tigers, lions and seals
   Monkeys too, monkeys too.

Fingerplays

LION

I knew a little lion who went roar, roar, roar.
   (make sounds)
Who walked around on all fours.
   (walk on both hands and feet)
He had a tail we could see behind the bars
   (point to tail)
And when we visit we should stand back far.
   (move backwards)

ALLIGATOR

The alligator likes to swim.
   (two hands flat on top of the other)
Sometimes his mouth opens wide.
   (hands open and shut)
But when he sees me on the shore,
Down under the water he'll hide.

THE MONKEY

The monkey claps, claps, claps his hands.
   (clap hands)
The monkey claps, claps, claps his hands.
   (clap hands)
Monkey see, monkey do.
The monkey does the same as you.
   (use pointer finger)
   (change actions)

ZOO ANIMALS

This is the way the elephant goes.
    (clasp hands together, extend arms,
    move back and forth)
With a curly trunk instead of a nose.
The buffalo, all shaggy and fat.
Has two sharp horns in place of a hat.
    (point to forehead)
The hippo with his mouth so wide—
Let's see what's inside.
    (hands together and open wide and close
    them)
The wiggly snake upon the ground
Crawls along without a sound.
    (weave hands back and forth)
But monkey see and monkey do is the
    funniest animal in the zoo.
    (place thumbs in ears and wiggle fingers)

THE ZOO

The zoo holds many animals inside
    (make a circle with your hands and peer
    inside)
So unlatch the doors and open them wide.
    (open your hands wide)
Elephants, tigers, zebras, and bears
    (hold up one finger for each animal)
Are some of the animals you'll find there.

Science

1. **Animal Skins**

   Place a piece of snakeskin, a patch of animal hide, and animal fur out on the science table. The children can look and feel the differences. These skins can usually be borrowed from the Department of Natural Resources.

2. **Habitat**

   On the science table, place a bowl of water, a tray of dirt, and a pile of hay or grass. Also, include many small toy zoo animals. The children can place the animals in their correct habitat.

Dramatic Play

1. **The Zoo**

   Collect large appliance boxes. Cut slits to resemble cages. Old fur coats or blankets can be added. The children may use the fur pieces while pretending to be animals in the zoo.

2. **Pet Store**

   Cages and many small stuffed animals can be added to the dramatic play area.

3. **Block Play**

   Set out many blocks and rubber, plastic, or wooden models of zoo animals.

Arts and Crafts

1. **Paper Plate Lions**

   Collect paper plates, sandwich bags, and yellow cotton. Color the cottonballs by pouring powdered tempera paint into the sandwich bag and shaking. The children can trim the cut side of the paper plate with the yellow cotton to represent a mane. Facial features can also be added. This activity is for older children.

2. **Cookie Cutters**

   Playdough and zoo animal-shaped cookie cutters can be placed on a table in the art area.

Sensory

Additions to the sensory table include:

- sand and zoo animal models
- seeds and measuring scoops
- corn and scales
- hay
- water

658

Large Muscle

1. Walk Like the Animals

"Walk Like the Animals" is played like "Simon Says." Say, "The zookeeper says to walk like a giraffe." The children can walk as they believe that particular zoo animal would walk. Repeat using different animals such as monkeys, elephants, lions, tigers, bears, etc. This activity can also be used for transition.

2. Zookeeper, May I?

Designate one child to be the zookeeper. This child should stand about six feet in front of the remaining children. The zookeeper provides directions for the other children. To illustrate, they may say take three elephant steps, one kangaroo hop, two alligator glides, etc. Once the children reach the zookeeper, the zookeeper chooses a child to be his successor.

Field Trips

1. Zoo

Visit a local zoo if available. Observe the animals that are of particular interest to the children such as the elephants, giraffes, bears, and monkeys.

2. Reserve Park

If your community has a reserve park, or an area where wild animals are caged in a natural environment, take the children to visit. Plan a picnic snack to take along.

Math

1. Animal Sort

Collect pictures of elephants, lions, giraffes, monkeys, and other zoo animals from magazines, calendars, or coloring books. Encourage the children to sort the pictures into labeled baskets. For example, one basket may be for large animals and another for small animals.

2. Which Is Bigger?

Collect many toy models of zoo animals in various sizes. Encourage the children to order from smallest to biggest, etc.

3. Animal Sets

Cut and mount pictures of zoo animals. The children can classify the pictures by sorting. Examples might include birds, four-legged animals, furry animals, etc.

Social Studies

Helpful Zoo Animals

During large group discuss how some animals can be useful. Show the children pictures of various helping animals and discuss their uses. Examples include:

- camel (transportation in some countries).
- elephant (often used to pull things).
- dogs (seeing-eye dogs, sled dogs).
- goats (used for milk).

Group Time
(games, language)

What Am I?

Give the children verbal clues in which you describe an animal and the children guess which zoo animal you are talking about. An example is, "I am very large, gray-colored, and have a long nose that looks like a hose. What zoo animal am I?"

Cooking

1. Animals on Grass

Take a graham cracker and spread either peanut butter or green-tinted cream cheese on the top. Stand an animal cracker on the top of the graham cracker.

2. Peanut Butter Log

1/2 cup peanut butter
1/2 cup raisins
2 1/2 tablespoons dry milk
2 tablespoons honey

Mix together, roll into log 1 inch × 10 inches long. Chill and slice.

Books

The following books can be used to complement this theme:

Aliki. (1997). *My Visit to the Zoo.* New York: HarperCollins.

Ancona, George and Mary Beth Ancona. (1991). *Handtalk Zoo.* New York: Simon & Schuster.

Arnold, Caroline. (1992). *Camel.* New York: William Morrow.

Arnold, Caroline. (1993). *Elephant.* New York: William Morrow.

Arnold, Caroline. (1993). *Lion.* New York: William Morrow.

Arnold, Caroline. (1993). *Monkey.* New York: William Morrow.

Barton, Byron. (1996). *Zoo Animals.* New York: HarperCollins. (Board book)

Benjamin, Cynthia. (1995). *I Am a Zookeeper.* Illus. by Miriam Sagasti. Hauppauge, NY: Barron's Educational series. (Board book)

Buehner, Caralyn and Mark Buehner. (1992). *The Escape of Marvin the Ape.* New York: Dial Books.

Denim, Sue and Dave Pilkey. (1996). *The Dumb Bunnies Go to the Zoo.* New York: Scholastic.

Finnegan, Evelyn and Margaret Bruno. (1998). *My Little Friend Goes to the Zoo.* Scituate, MA: Little Friend Press.

Ford, Miela. (1995). *Bear Play.* New York: Greenwillow.

Ford, Miela. (1994). *Little Elephant.* Illus. by Tana Hoban. New York: Greenwillow.

Ford, Miela. (1998). *Watch Us Play.* New York: Greenwillow.

Fowler, Allan. (1996). *The Biggest Animal on Land.* Chicago: Children's Press.

Hazelaar, Cor. (1997). *Zoo Dreams.* New York: Farrar, Straus & Giroux.

Hendrick, Mary Jean. (1993). *If Anything Goes Wrong at the Zoo.* Illus. by Jane Dyer. Orlando: Harcourt Brace.

Hewett, Joan. (1993). *Tiger, Tiger Growing Up.* Illus. by Richard Hewett. New York: Clarion Books.

Hosea Hilker, Cathryn. (1992). *A Cheetah Named Angel.* New York: Franklin Watts.

Kalman, Bobbie and Hannelore Sotzek. (1997). *A Koala Is Not a Bear.* New York: Crabtree Publishing.

Kenny, David et al. (1995). *Klondike and Snow: The Denver Zoo's Remarkable Story of Raising Two Polar Bear Cubs.* Niwot, CO: Roberts Rinehart Publishers. (Pbk)

Koebner, Linda. (1997). *Zoo Book.* New York: Tor Boks.

Lee, Julie and Jackie Northard. (1995). *Animals A to Zoo.* Illus. by Kristine Kirkeby. Minnesota Zoo.

Lemmon, Tess. (1993). *Apes.* Illus. by John Butler. New York: Ticknor & Fields.

Maestro, Betsy. (1992). *Take a Look at Snakes.* New York: Scholastic.

Martin, Ann M. (1998). *Baby Animal Zoo.* Illus. by Charles Tang. New York: Scholastic. (Pbk)

Martin, Bill. (1991). *Polar Bear, Polar Bear, What Do You Hear?* Illus. by Eric Carle. New York: Holt.

McMillan, Bruce. (1995). *The Baby Zoo.* New York: Scholastic. (Pbk)

Morozumi, Atsuko. (1998). *My Friend Gorilla.* New York: Farrar, Straus & Giroux.

Noble, Kate. (1994). *The Blue Elephant.* Illus. by Rachel Bass. Chicago: Silver Seahorse Press.

Ormerod, Jan. (1991). *When We Went to the Zoo.* New York: Lothrop, Lee & Shepard.

Oxenbury, Helen. (1991). *Monkey See, Monkey Do.* 2nd ed. New York: Dial Books. (Board book)

Paxton, Tom. (1996). *Going to the Zoo.* Illus. by Karen Schmidt. New York: William Morrow.

Rathmann, Peggy. (1994). *Good Night, Gorilla.* New York: G. P. Putnam.

Robinson, Martha. (1995). *The Zoo at Night.* Illus. by Antonio Frasconi. New York: Simon & Schuster.

Rowan, James P. (1990). *I Can Be a Zoo Keeper.* Chicago: Children's Press. (Pbk)

Simon, Seymour. (1992). *Snakes.* New York: HarperCollins.

Smith, Roland. (1992). *Cats in the Zoo.* Illus. by William Munoz. Brookfield, CT: Millbrook Press.

Tibbitts, Alison and Alan Roocraft. (1992). *Polar Bears.* New York: Capstone Press.

Waber, Bernard. (1996). *A Lion Named Shirley Williamson.* Boston: Houghton Mifflin.

Multimedia

The following multimedia products can be used to complement this theme:

A Day at the Zoo [video]. Kimbo Records.

At Home with Zoo Animals [video]. (1992). Washington, DC: National Geographic Society.

At the Zoo [video]. Kimbo Records.

At the Zoo: 2 [video]. Kimbo Records.

Let's Go to the Zoo [video]. Kimbo Records.

National Zoo [videodisc]. (1989). Washington, DC: Smithsonian Institution.

Sharon, Lois, and Bram at the Zoo [video]. (1985). Golden Book Video.

Zoo Keeper [computer file]. (1992). Davidson & Associates.

Zoo opolis [CD-ROM]. (1994). Compton's New Media.

Recordings and Song Titles

The following recordings can be used to complement this theme:

A to Z, the Animals and Me

Save the Animals, Save the Earth

Animal Walks

What's in the Sea?

Do It Yourself Kids' Circus—"Animal Acts," "Prancing Ponies"

Alphabet in Action—"Let's All Be Giraffes"

Preschool Action Time—"Monkey Town"

Six Little Ducks—"Going to the Zoo," "Five Little Monkeys"

APPENDIX A

International Holidays

When planning the curriculum, it is important to note international holidays. The exact date of the holiday may vary from year to year; consequently, it is important to check with parents or a reference librarian at a local library. These international holidays for Buddhist, Christian, Eastern Orthodox, Hindu, Jewish, and Muslim people are as follows:

Buddhist

Nirvana Day (Mahayana Sect)—observes the passing of Sakyamuni into Nirvana. He obtained enlightment and became a Buddha.

Magna Puja (Theravada Sect)—one of the holiest Buddhist holidays; it marks the occasion when 1,250 of Buddha's disciples gathered spontaneously to hear him speak.

Buddha Day (Mahayana Sect)—this service commemorates the birth of Gautama in Lumbini Garden. Amida, the Buddha of Infinite Wisdom and Compassion, manifested himself among men in the person Gautama.

Versakha Piya (Theravada Sect)—the most sacred of the Buddhist days. It celebrates the birth, death, and enlightenment of Buddha.

Maharram—marks the beginning of Buddhist Lent, it is the anniversary of Buddha's sermon to the first five disciples.

Vassana (Theravada Sect)—the beginning of the three-month period when monks stay in their temple to study and meditate.

Bon (Mahayana Sect)—an occasion for rejoicing in the enlightenment offered by the Buddha; often referred to as a "Gathering of Joy." Buddha had saved the life of the mother Moggallana. The day is in remembrance of all those who have passed away.

Pavarana (Theravada Sect)—celebrates Buddha's return to earth after spending one Lent season preaching in heaven.

Bodhi Day (Mahayana Sect)—celebrates the enlightment of Buddha.

Christian

Ash Wednesday

Palm Sunday—the Sunday before Easter, which commemorates the triumphant entry of Jesus in Jerusalem.

Holy Thursday—also known as Maundy Thursday; it is the Thursday of Holy Week.

Good Friday—commemorates the crucifixion of Jesus.

Easter—celebrates the resurrection of Jesus.

Christmas Eve

Christmas Day—commemorates the birth of Jesus.

Eastern Orthodox

Christmas

First Day of Lent—begins a period of fasting and penitence in preparation for Easter.

Easter Sunday—celebrates the resurrection of Jesus.

Ascension Day—the 40th day after Easter, commemorates the ascension of Jesus to heaven.

Pentecost—commemorates the descent of the Holy Spirit upon the Apostles, 50 days after Easter Sunday. Marks the beginning of the Christian Church.

Hindu

Pongal Sankrandi—a three-day harvest festival.

Vasanta Pachami—celebrated in honor of Saraswati, the charming and sophisticated goddess of scholars.

Shivarari—a solemn festival devoted to the worship of Shiva, the most powerful of deities of the Hindu pantheon.

Holi—celebrates the advent of spring.

Ganguar—celebrated in honor of Parvari, the consort of Lord Shiva.

Ram Navami—birthday of the God Rama.

Hanuman Jayanti—birthday of Monkey God Humumanji.

Meenakshi Kalyanam—the annual commemoration of the marriage of Meenakshi to Lord Shiva.

Teej—celebrates the arrival of the monsoon; Parvari is the presiding deity.

Jewish

Yom Kippur—the most holy day of the Jewish year, it is marked by fasting and prayer as Jews seek forgiveness from God and man.

Sukkot—commemorates the 40-year wandering of Israelites in the desert on the way to the Promised Land; expresses thanksgiving for the fall harvest.

Simchat Torah—celebrates the conclusion of the public reading of the Pentateuch and its beginning anew, thus affirming that the study of God's word is an unending process. Concludes the Sukkot Festival.

Hanukkah—the eight-day festival that celebrates the rededication of the Temple to the service of God. Commemorates the Maccabean victory over Antiochus, who sought to suppress freedom of worship.

Purim—marks the salvation of the Jews of ancient Persia, through the intervention of Queen Esther, from Haman's plot to exterminate them.

Passover—an eight-day festival marking ancient Israel's deliverance from Egyptian bondage.

Yom Hashoah—day of remembrance for victims of Nazi Holocaust.

Sahvout—celebrates the covenant established at Sinai between God and Israel and the revelation of the Ten Commandments.

Rosh Hashanah—the first of the High Holy Days marking the beginning of a ten-day period of penitence and spiritual renewal.

Muslim

Isra and Miraj—commemorates the anniversary of the night journey of the Prophet and his ascension to heaven.

Ramadan—the beginning of the month of fasting from sunrise to sunset.

Id al-Fitr—end of the month of fasting from sunrise to sunset; first day of pilgrimage to Mecca.

Hajj—the first day of pilgrimage to Mecca.

Day of Amfat—gathering of the pilgrims.

Id al-adha—commemorates the Feast of the Sacrifice.

Muharram—the Muslim New Year; marks the beginning of the Hedjra Year 1412.

Id al-Mawlid—commemorates the nativity and death of Prophet Muhammad and his flight from Mecca to Medina.

APPENDIX B

Early Childhood Commercial Suppliers

ABC School Supply, Inc.
6500 Peachtree Industrial
   Boulevard
P.O. Box 4750
Norcross, Georgia 30091
(404) 447-5000

Beckley Cardy
One East First Street
Duluth, Minnesota 55802
1-800-227-1178

Childcraft Educational
   Corporation
20 Kilmer Road
P.O. Box 3081
Edison, New Jersey 08818-3081
1-800-631-5652

Children's Press
5440 North Cumberland
   Avenue
Chicago, Illinois 60656
1-800-621-1115

Constructive Playthings
1227 East 119th Street
Grandview, Missouri
   64030-1117
1-800-832-0224

Corporate Express
1233 West County Road E
St. Paul, Minnesota 55112
1-800-338-SPBS (7727)

Cuisenaire Company of
   America, Inc.
12 Church Street, Box D
New Rochelle, New York
   10802
1-800-237-3142

Delmar Publishers, Inc.
3 Columbia Circle
Box 15-015
Albany, New York
   12212-5015
1-800-477-3692

Environments, Inc.
P.O. Box 1348
Beaufort Industrial Park
Beaufort, South Carolina
   29901-1348
1-800-342-4453

Gryphon House, Inc.
3706 Otis Street
Mt. Rainier, Maryland
   20712
1-800-638-0928

The Highsmith Co., Inc.
W5527 Highway 106
P.O. Box 800
Fort Atkinson, Wisconsin
   53538-0800
1-800-558-2110

Kaplan School Supply
   Corporation
P.O. Box 609
Lewisville, North Carolina
   27023-0609
1-800-334-2014

Kimbo Educational
10 North Third Avenue
Long Branch, New Jersey
   07740
1-800-631-2187

Lakeshore Learning Materials
2695 E. Dominguez Street
Carson, California 90749
1-800-421-5354

School Specialty
9645 Gerwig Lane
Columbia, Maryland
   21046-1503
1-800-631-5652

School Specialty
1000 North Bluemound Drive
P.O. Box 1579
Appleton, Wisconsin 54913
1-800-242-3433

APPENDIX C

RAINY DAY ACTIVITIES*

1. Get Acquainted Game

The children sit in a circle formation. The teacher begins the game by saying, "My name is ———— and I'm going to roll the ball to ————." Continue playing the game until every child has a turn. A variation of the game is have the children stand in a circle and bounce the ball to each other. This game is a fun way for the children to learn each other's names.

2. Hide the Ball

Choose several children and ask them to cover their eyes. Then hide a small ball, or other object, in an observable place. Ask the children to uncover their eyes and try to find the ball. The first child to find the ball hides it again.

3. "Which Ball is Gone?"

In the center of the circle, place six colored balls, cubes, beads, shapes, etc., in a row. Ask a child to close his eyes. Then ask another child to remove one of the objects and hide it behind him. The first child uncovers his eyes and tells which colored object is missing from the row. The game continues until all the selections have been made. When using with older children, two objects may be removed at a time to further challenge their abilities.

4. "What Sound is That?"

The purpose of this game is to promote the development of listening skills. Begin by asking the children to close their eyes. Make a familiar sound. Then ask a child to identify it. Sources of sound may include:

tearing paper	blowing a pitch pipe	raising or lowering
sharpening a pencil	dropping an object	window shades
walking, running,	moving a desk or	leafing through
shuffling feet	chair	book pages
clapping hands	snapping fingers	cutting with
sneezing, coughing	blowing nose	scissors
tapping on glass,	opening or closing	snapping rubber
wood, or metal	drawer	bands
jingling money	stirring paint in	ringing a bell
opening a window	a jar	clicking the tongue
pouring water	clearing the throat	crumpling paper
shuffling cards	splashing water	opening a box
blowing a whistle	rubbing sandpaper	sighing
banging blocks	together	stamping feet
bouncing ball	chattering teeth	rubbing palms
shaking a rattle	sweeping sound,	together
turning the lights on	such as a brush or	rattling keys
knocking on a door	broom	

A variation of this game could be played by having a child make a sound. Then the other children and the teacher close their eyes and attempt to identify the sound. For older children this game can be varied with the production of two sounds. Begin by asking the children if the sounds are the same or different. Then have them identify the sounds.

*Carefully select games for young children. Most games are more appropriate for older four-, five-, six-, and seven-year-old children.

5. "Near or Far?"

The purpose of this game is to locate sound. First, tell the children to close their eyes. Then play a sound recorded on a cassette tape. Ask the children to identify the sound as being near or far away.

6. Descriptions

The purpose of this game is to encourage expressive language skills. Begin by asking each child to describe himself. Included with the description can be the color of his eyes, hair, and clothing. The teacher might prefer to use an imaginative introduction such as: "One by one, you may take turns sitting up here in Alfred's magic chair and describe yourself to Alfred." Another approach may be to say, "Pretend that you must meet somebody at a very crowded airport who has never seen you before. How would you describe yourself so that the person would be sure to know who you are?"

A variation for older children would be to have one of the children describe another child without revealing the name of the person he is describing. To illustrate, the teacher might say, "I'm thinking of someone with shiny red hair, blue eyes, many freckles, etc...." The child being described should stand up.

7. Mirrored Movements

The purpose of this game is to encourage awareness of body parts through mirrored movements. Begin the activity by making movements. Encourage the children to mirror your movements. After the children understand the game, they may individually take the leader role.

8. Little Red Wagon Painted Red

As a prop for the game, cut a red wagon with wheels out of construction paper. Then cut rectangles the same size as the box of the red wagon. Include purple, blue, yellow, green, orange, brown, black, and pink colors.

Sing the song to the tune of **"Skip to My Lou."**

*Little red wagon painted **red.***
*Little red wagon painted **red.***
*Little red wagon painted **red.***
What color would it be?

Give each child a turn to pick and name a color. As the song is sung, let the child change the wagon color.

9. Police Officer Game

Select one child to be the police officer. Ask him to find a lost child. Describe one of the children in the circle. The child who is the police officer will use the description as a clue to find the "missing child."

10. Mother Cat and Baby Kits

Choose one child to be the mother cat. Then ask the mother cat to go to sleep in the center of the circle, covering his eyes. Then choose several children to be kittens. The verse below is chanted as the baby kittens hide in different parts of the classroom. Following this, the mother cat hunts for them. When all of the kittens have been located, another mother cat may be selected. The number of times the game is repeated depends upon the children's interest and attention span.

Mother cat lies fast asleep.

To her side the kittens creep.

But the kittens like to play.

Softly now they creep away.

Mother cat wakes up to see.

No little kittens. Where can they be?

11. Memory Game

Collect common household items, a towel, and tray. Place the items on the tray. Show the tray containing the items. Cover with a towel. Then ask the children to recall the names of the items on the tray. To ensure success, begin the activity with only two or three objects for young children. Additional objects can be added depending upon the developmental maturity of the children.

12. Cobbler, Mend My Shoes

Sit the children in a circle formation. Then select one child to sit in the center. This child gives a shoe to a child in the circle, and then closes his eyes. The children in the circle pass the shoe around behind them while the rhyme is chanted. When the chant is finished, the shoe is no longer passed. The last child with the shoe in his hand holds the shoe behind his back. Then the child sitting in the center tries to guess who has the shoe.

Cobbler, cobbler, mend my shoe

Have it done by half past two

Stitch it up and stitch it down

Now see with whom the shoe is found.

13. Huckle Buckle Beanstalk

Ask the children to sit in a circle. Once seated, tell them to close their eyes. Then hide a small ball in an obvious place. Say, "Ready." Encourage all of the children to hunt for the object. Each child who spots it returns to a place in the circle and says, "Huckle buckle beanstalk." No one must tell where he has seen the ball until all the children have seen it.

14. What's Different?

Sit all of the children in a circle formation. Ask one child to sit in the center. The rest of the children are told to look closely at the child sitting in the center. Then the children are told to cover their eyes while you change some detail on the child in the center. For example, you may place a hat on the child, untie his shoe, remove a shoe, roll up one sleeve, etc. The children sitting in the circle act as detective to determine "what's different?"

15. Cookie Jar

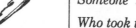

Sit the children in a circle formation on the floor with their legs crossed. Together they repeat a rhythmic chant while using alternating leg-hand clap to emphasize the rhythm. The chant is as follows.

Someone took the cookies from the cookie jar.

Who took the cookies from the cookie jar?

Mary took the cookies from the cookie jar.

Mary took the cookies from the cookie jar?

Who, me? (Mary)

Yes, you. (all children)

Couldn't be. (Mary)

Then who? (all children)

——————— took the cookies from the cookie jar. (Mary names another child.)

Use each child's name.

16. Hide and Seek Tonal Matching

Sit the children in a circle formation. Ask one child to hide in the room while the other children cover their eyes. The children in the circle sing, "Where is ——————— hiding?" The child who is hiding responds by singing back, "Here I am." With their eyes remaining closed, the children point in the direction of the hiding child. All open eyes and the child emerges from his hiding place.

17. Listening and Naming

This game is most successful with a small group of children. The children should take turns shutting their eyes and identifying sounds as you tap with a wooden dowel on an object such as glass, triangle, drum, wooden block, cardboard box, rubber ball, etc.

18. Funny Shapes

Ask each child to choose a partner. One partner must make a large shape with his body. The other partner must follow the directions of movement. Roles reverse for the second set of directions. Provide directions such as:

1. Make a big shape.

go *over*
go *under*
go *through*
go *around*

2. Make a small shape.

go *over*
go *under*
go *through*
go *around*

19. Drop the Handkerchief

Direct the children to stand in a circle formation. Ask one child to run around the outside of the circle, dropping a handkerchief behind another child. The child who has the handkerchief dropped behind him must pick it up and chase the child who dropped it. The first child tries to return to the vacated space by running before he is tagged.

20. "If You Please"

This game is a simple variation of "Simon Says." Ask the children to form a circle around a leader who gives directions, some of which are prefaced with "if you please." The children are to follow only the "if you please" directions, ignoring any that do not begin with "if you please." Directions to be used may include walking forward, hopping on one foot, bending forward, standing tall, etc. This game can be varied by having the children follow the directions when the leader says, "do this," and not when he says, "do that." Play only one version of this game on a single day. Too much variety will confuse the children.

21. Duck Duck Goose

Ask the children to squat in a circle formation. Then ask one child to walk around the outside of circle, lightly touching each child's head and saying "Duck, Duck." When he touches another child and says "Goose," that child chases him around the circle. If the child who was "it" returns to the "goose's" place without being tagged, he remains. When this happens, the tapped child is "it." This game is appropriate for older four-, five-, six-, and seven-year-old children.

22. Fruit Basket Upset

Ask the children to sit in a circle formation on chairs or on carpet squares. Then ask one child to sit in the middle of the circle as the chef. Hand pictures of various fruits to the rest of the children. Then to continue the game, ask the chef to call out the name of a fruit. The children holding that particular fruit exchange places. If the chef calls out, "fruit basket upset," all of the children must exchange places, including the chef. The child who doesn't find a place is the new chef. A variation of this game would be bread basket upset. For this game use pictures of breads, rolls, bagels, muffins, breadsticks, etc. This game is appropriate for older children.

23. Bear Hunt

This is a rhythmic chant which may easily be varied. Start by chanting each line, encouraging the children to repeat the line.

Teacher: *Let's go on a bear hunt.*
Children: *(Repeat. Imitate walk by slapping knees alternately.)*
Teacher: *I see a wheat field.*
Can't go over it;
Can't go under it.
Let's go through it.
(arms straight ahead like you're parting wheat)

I see a bridge.
Can't go over it;
Can't go under it.
Let's swim.
(arms in swimming motion)

I see a tree.
Can't go over it;
Can't go under it.
Let's go up it.
(climb and look)

I see a swamp.
Can't go over it;
Can't go under it.
Let's go through it.
(pull hands up and down slowly)

I see a cave.
Can't go over it;
Can't go under it.
Let's go in.
(walking motion)

I see two eyes. I see two ears.
I see a nose. I see a mouth.
It's a BEAR!!!
(Do all in reverse very fast)

24. "Guess Who?"

Individually tape the children's voices. Play the tape during group time, and let the children identify their classmates' voices.

25. Shadow Fun

Hang a bed sheet up in the classroom for use as a projection screen. Then place a light source such as a slide, filmstrip, or overhead projector a few feet behind the screen. Ask two of the children to stand behind the sheet. Then encourage one of the two children to walk in front of the projector light. When this happens, the children are to give the name of the person who is moving.

26. If This Is Red— Nod Your Head

Point to an object in the room and say, "If this is green, shake your hand. If this is yellow, touch your nose." If the object is not the color stated, children should not imitate the requested action.

27. Freeze

Encourage the children to imitate activities such as washing dishes, cleaning house, dancing, etc. Approximately every 10 to 20 seconds, call out "Freeze!" When this occurs, the children are to stop whatever they are doing and remain frozen until you say, "Thaw" or "Move." A variation of this activity would be to use music. When the music stops, the children freeze their movements.

28. Spy the Object

Designate a large area on the floor as home base. Then select an object and show it to the children. Ask the children to cover their eyes while you place the object in an observable place in the room. Then encourage the children to open their eyes and search for the object. As each child spies the object he quietly returns to the home base area without telling. The other children continue searching until all have found the object. After all the children are seated, they may share where the object is placed.

29. Who Is Gone?

This game is played in a circle format. Begin by asking a child to close his eyes. Then point to a child to leave the circle and go to a spot where he can't be seen. The child with his eyes closed opens them at your word, then looks around the circle and identifies the friend who is missing.

30. It's Me

Seat the children in a circle formation, and place a chair in the center. Choose one child to sit on a chair in the circle, closing his eyes. After this, ask another child to walk up softly behind the chair and tap the child on the shoulder. The seated child asks, "Who is tapping?" The other child replies, "It's me." By listening to the response, the seated child identifies the other child.

31. Feeling and Naming

Ask a child to stand with his back to you, placing his hands behind him. Then place an object in the child's hands for identification by feeling it. Nature materials can be used such as leaves, shells, fruit, etc. A ball, doll, block, Lego piece, puzzle piece, crayon, etc., may also be used.

32. Doggy, Doggy, Where's Your Bone?

Sit the children in a circle formation. Then place a chair in the center of the circle. Place a block under the chair. Select one child, the dog, to sit on the chair and close his eyes. Then point to another child. This child must try to get the dog's bone from under the chair without making a noise. After the child returns to his place in the circle, all the children place their hands behind them. Then in unison the children say, "Doggy, Doggy, where's your bone?" During the game, each dog has three guesses as to who has the bone.